ITEM

G000242267

355.69
SUTTON, D.J. (Ed)
The story of the R.A.S.C.
and the R.C.T. 1945-1982
0 436 50606 8

NW

HILLINGDON
BOROUGH
LIBRARIES

STORE

IF NOT IN DEMAND, THIS BOOK MAY BE RENEWED BY POST, TELEPHONE OR
PERSONAL CALL BY QUOTING THE ABOVE DETAILS, AND THE LAST DATE STAMPED.

NORTHWOOD HILLS
Tel. 24595

Please return this book on or before the last date
stamped below, otherwise a fine will be charged.

-3. DEC. 1984

08. APR 93

18. JUN 96

09. AUG 86

18. MAY 93

29. JUL 96

29. NOV 86.

28. JAN 94

08. JAN

10. OCT 89,

12. AUG 94

13 NOV

18. APR 92

15. DEC 94

WITHDRA

13. MAY 95

28. MAY 92

20. OCT 95

25 -

06.

READERS AR
AND RE

The Story of the
ROYAL ARMY SERVICE CORPS
and
ROYAL CORPS OF TRANSPORT
1945–1982

*To all ranks of the
Royal Army Service Corps
and
Royal Corps of Transport
who have served their Corps and Country
yesterday and today with distinction
and who have thus contributed
to this story.*

The Story of the
ROYAL
ARMY SERVICE CORPS
and
ROYAL
CORPS OF TRANSPORT
1945–1982

Editor in Chief
BRIGADIER DJ SUTTON OBE

LEO COOPER
in association with
SECKER AND WARBURG
London 1983

© 1983 THE INSTITUTION OF THE ROYAL CORPS OF TRANSPORT

First published 1984 by
Leo Cooper
in association with
Martin Secker and Warburg Ltd
54 Poland Street, London W1V 3DF

ISBN 0 436 50606 8

Designed by John Mitchell
Typeset by Tradespools Ltd at Frome
Printed in Great Britain by
Redwood Burn Ltd at Trowbridge

NORTHWOOD HILLS
Tel. 24595

[By courtesy of Brian and Jacynth Edwards]

Her Royal Highness Princess Alice, Duchess of Gloucester, GCB, CI, GCVO GBE, Colonel-in-Chief of the Royal Corps of Transport. From a painting by Richard Foster which hangs in the Headquarters Officers' Mess in Aldershot.

KENSINGTON PALACE
LONDON W8 4PU
TELEPHONE 01-937 6374

The predecessors of the Royal Corps of Transport have a proud record over 200 years, and their history has been well recorded up to the end of the Second World War. Since then, officers and soldiers of the Royal Army Service Corps, and their successors, the Royal Corps of Transport, have served with distinction in over forty countries, either helping to keep the peace, or in campaigns as diverse as those in Korea and the South Atlantic. This is the story of the part that they have played in their many roles over this period.

It tells of the good times and the bad, the amusing and the sad. It is hoped that it will remind those who have served in either or both Corps, of those times, and the part that they played. For those with little knowledge of the Corps, it is hoped that this story will illustrate to them the many skills involved in transportation and distribution in support of the present day Army.

Since the Second World War, 130 officers and soldiers of the Corps have been killed on active service, and many have been injured. We all have reason to be proud of their sacrifice and devotion to duty.

I commend this book to the old and new generations of readers. It is the story of those who followed the fine traditions of their predecessors and an example to those that follow on.

COLONEL-IN-CHIEF

PREFACE

THIS BOOK is the result of the work of many individuals, many retired, and rather fewer still serving. Some have produced much of the material for complete chapters, whilst others have told of an incident, confirmed important facts, or recalled an anecdote. To all we are tremendously grateful for their work, and certainly without the unstinted efforts of many, this story could not have been told. To those who do not find all their offerings used, we give our apologies. All contributions were invaluable, and provided background information for chapters, even when the detail could not be suitably used. In some cases, particularly in Part II, as much as we would have liked to have included more of the detail provided, such as in the TA Chapter, lack of space prevented it. However, all this material, whether used or not is now stored in the Corps archives, and will be available for any future research.

Although the information obtained from research and contributors enabled the book to be produced in its present format, it is a matter of some regret that much more information that should have been available proved to be exceedingly difficult or impossible to obtain from official sources. It suggests that the urge to record many of our activities, which was so carefully sustained during World War II, was lost in the post-war years. Amidst all the reorganizations that have taken place to produce the most effective structure of our Corps to meet the Army's requirements, the need to record in a suitably detailed form, what actually took place over the years, went unrecognized. Much important material, spread worldwide, was destroyed in the periodic process of 'weeding out', without thought to its historic value. It would be wrong not to admit to this shortcoming, as by doing so it is to be hoped that the future will be better recorded.

So it was that thirty five years after this story begins, the task of obtaining the information that we sought was immeasurably greater, and memories of those we turned to for help, more extended.

Happily some were prepared to tax their memories, and give their help to the limit, and we owe them much for their support.

As the book has no single author, readers will detect varying styles between the chapters, both in Part I and in Part II, and no attempt has been made to edit out these styles completely. For the same reason there is some duplication between activities recorded by countries and campaigns in Part I, and similar activities described in the specialist chapters in Part II, where the overall story of a particular element is given.

Many very deserving units and individuals have not received a mention in the pages that follow, but it is hoped that the overall size and scope of the book will itself make clear the reason for the omissions.

In addition to the written word, we have received many admirable photographs, for which we also are most grateful. We have tried to select the most suitable to represent our activities in all the major chapters. We hope that many readers will recognize both people and places, and if the picture that they themselves submitted is not in the book, that they will understand why.

All those that have contributed material of any sort are named in the List of Contributors. It is felt though that those who have made major contributions deserve special mention, and these are:– Brigadier G G Blakey, Brigadier D Cardle, Major C W P Coan, Lieutenant Colonel H N Cole, OBE TD DL, Major General P F Claxton CB OBE, Major A K Crisp Jones OBE TD, Major M F I Cubitt MBE, Lieutenant Colonel T A Danton-Rees, Lieutenant Colonel H M M Deighton, Colonel R F Discombe OBE, Colonel J M Grant OBE, Lieutenant Colonel P E Gray MM, Colonel A G Grevatt, Brigadier D W E Hancox, Lieutenant Colonel D M Ivison, Brigadier R E L Jenkins CBE, ADC, Lieutenant Colonel J A W Lerwill, Lieutenant Colonel J D McDonald OBE, G F K Mitchell Esq, Brigadier R A Nightingale MBE, Captain J D P Poyntz, Colonel J S Riggall MBE, Lieutenant Colonel E Robinson WRAC, Lieutenant Colonel W J Scoging OBE, Lieutenant Colonel T C Street, Brigadier D J Sutton OBE, Major D J Turner, Colonel J S M Walker, Major B V Wynn-Werninck MNI, 25 Transport & Movements Regiment RCT, 30 Regiment RCT.

Sadly, a prolific contributor to the book, Lieutenant Colonel Howard N Cole OBE TD DL, had to give up his work for the book because of illness and died a few months later when the last chapters were being written. He had been on the Committee from the very beginning, as the Historical Advisor. His considerable knowledge of military history, experience of the world of books, and generous advice were of tremendous value, and with his passing the Corps lost a good friend and staunch supporter.

Apart from those who have supplied the written word, many others have helped in a variety of ways in the production of this book, and we owe them our special thanks.

Publisher:	Leo Cooper.	*Consultant*:	John Mitchell.
Graphics:	Clive Antony.	*Artist*:	Major B V Wynn-Werninck MN
	George Prior.	*Reader*:	Colonel C G K Underhill.
Proof Reader:	Mrs Pat Elliott.	*Typists*:	Mrs C J Hall.
Annexes:	WO2 M V Moss.		Mrs Vera Bannister.
Indexing:	Officer Cadet P R Clarke.		Mrs Karin Whitecross.
Glossary:	Lieutenant J M Martin.		Mrs Hazel Reale.

Clerical Staff – RHQ.

Anthony Lewis – Assistant Editor, Mrs Berry Harrington.
  The Waggoner Mrs Hilary Waller.
Mrs Molly Stewart.

Research Assistance:

Army Historical Branch. War Office Library.
Public Record Office. RTR Museum Library.
HQ Training Group RCT. RHQ RCT.
School of Transportation. Army School of Mechanical Transport.
Depot Regiment RCT Army Department Railway Staff.

Sales Committee:

Colonel I R Jones OBE – Chairman, Warrant Officer Class 2 L V McRae,
Major W P B Moss, Staff Sergeant A Hutchison,
Major M D Isherwood, Miss Diana Willis,
Captain C J Plowright, Mrs Jo Watmore,
Lieutenant T C Tomlinson, Mrs Netta Romer.
Warrant Officer Class 2 D N Capper,

Our grateful thanks also to the Staff of Buller Officers' Mess for their cheerful and willing help in looking after us so well over the period of writing.

Finally on a personal note I should like to thank most sincerely all Members of the Editorial Committee for their help and support over the last few years. In particular I should like to single out Colonel J S M Walker, Lieutenant Colonel T A Danton-Rees, Brigadier D W E Hancox and Major C W P Coan. Without their faith, friendly encouragement and particular brands of expertise, I might have found staying the course much more difficult. As it is, with the help of everyone involved, I hope that we have produced a book that you will find interesting and enjoyable.

July 1983

D J S
EDITOR IN CHIEF

CONTENTS

PART THREE · APPENDICES

INTRODUCTION

THIS STORY of the Royal Army Service Corps and the Royal Corps of Transport starts in September 1945 at the end of World War II. The RASC became the RCT in July 1965 and divested some of the RASC responsibilities to the Royal Army Ordnance Corps and took on others from the Royal Engineers. This book illustrates the many roles and activities of the RASC until July 1965 and of the new Corps, the RCT from that date until December 1982.

It covers the overall period in two parts. Part I outlines the story of the units and those who served in them, both in peacetime and under operational conditions, in countries throughout the World. Events follow a chronological pattern within these countries and not overall. Part II – The Elements – provides some details of all those facets of the two Corps contributing to their roles, both outwardly in the tasks performed for the Army as a whole, and inwardly as a self-administering regimental organisation.

During the period covered, units and members of the two Corps have served wherever there was a British Army presence, in over forty countries. Some still serving might regret that today this number of countries is very greatly reduced, but the shedding of many of Britain's overseas responsibilities can only be indicative of the search for a more peaceful world. Our place in NATO now rightly offsets many of the responsibilities that Britain had in countries depicted in this book.

Of the representative number of countries covered, some remained peaceful until our Forces were withdrawn and a few still have garrisons remaining, but smaller than their immediate post-

World War II scale. In these places, the Corps' role has naturally been less eventful but nevertheless illustrative of the breadth of Corps activity. Most of the garrisons in this category have provided a pleasant routine existence, others, fortunately fewer, were climatically and socially trying and tested the patience and initiative of all concerned in overcoming the soldiers' other enemy; boredom. In a different, but still peaceful category, the British Army of the Rhine (BAOR) remains the largest commitment for the British Army outside the United Kingdom. Here the Corps still has much of its manpower. As with other stations that have remained peaceful throughout the period, BAOR exemplifies the 'keeping the peace' role of the British Army. The Corps has provided throughout the period, their element of the essential logistic backing in support of the army, and sometimes of the other two Services. In BAOR this has been on a major scale, not only for its day to day peacetime requirements, but in training for its vital operational role. The Berlin Air lift, the story of which, and the Corps' part in it, has its own chapter, provides an early example of BAOR's role in preserving the status quo in Europe. In the smaller countries, support has been more modest, but conditions have often provided the variety of problems on which initiative and improvisation have thrived.

Not all countries though have been so fortunate in maintaining peace within their borders. Many, from being peaceful garrisons, or protectorates, became the scenes of internal strife as a result of the post-World War II surge of anti-colonialism, or militant nationalism. This led the British Army into campaigns against various types of insurgency, some of several years duration, and all of which involved the Corps in its many roles. The war in Korea was in a different category, but our involvement as part of the United Nations Force was to be the forerunner of other United Nations peace keeping forces, in all of which the Corps was heavily committed.

In the period, the Corps, firstly as the RASC and later as the RCT has taken part in sixteen operations for which campaign medals have been awarded. The parts played by the Corps in each of these campaigns, which are described in Part I have differed greatly, and have depended on the aims, strengths and capabilities of the opposition and the terrain and climate of the country. These factors have produced different emphasis on the types of support given by the various transport elements of the Corps in maintaining our forces involved. In some campaigns for example, supply by air was of crucial importance, in others, water transport played a vital role. Prior to 1965, the responsibility for the provision and delivering of rations world-wide was a major part of Corps activity and, as is disclosed in Part I, the adjustments of rations and the method of delivering to meet conditions prevailing in different campaigns was of great consequence. In all though, road transport was always a key factor and the ubiquitous RASC or RCT driver, driving a wide range of vehicles, wherever the British Army was serving, took pride in getting through with his load under all conditions. Field Marshal Montgomery of Alamein when addressing a parade of RASC and RCASC in Germany on 26 November 1945 said:–

> 'I consider that the work done by the RASC in this war has been quite magnificent. I know well that without your exertions behind, and often in front, we should never have been able to advance as we did. No Corps in the Army has a higher sense of duty than you have. You have delivered supplies in all weathers and over all roads. You have driven your vehicles in rain, and snow and ice, and you have never once let us down. Without your supplies our battles could never have been won. It is a fine record, and I am glad to be here, publicly, to pay the RASC the tribute that it deserves.'

Since then the Corps has continued to play its part in maintaining the Army world-wide. Although equipment and methods may have changed, the men behind it, of many races, wearing the Corps badge have continued to enhance the reputation gained in World War II. This is their story.

Part I
THE STORY

CHAPTER ONE

Background

RESPONSIBILITIES OF THE ROYAL ARMY SERVICE CORPS (RASC)

AT THE START of this period in its history, the RASC's responsibilities in outline were:–

The provision, storage, inspection, distribution and accounting for food supplies, worldwide.

The provision, storage, inspection, distribution and accounting for petroleum, worldwide.

Distribution of ammunition to units in the field.

Operation of all road transport, other than unit transport, but including all transport of medical units.

Operation of animal transport.

Operation of amphibious transport.

Operation of water transport, except inland water transport.

Provision of air despatch crews and the operation of rear and forward airfield supply organisations.

Operation of the Barracks Services.

Provision of clerical services for the Staff.

All these responsibilities are described in greater detail in the appropriate chapters in Part II of this book.

The RASC also took over complete responsibility for the Army Fire Service on 1 July 1946 and all officers and soldiers at that time were RASC badged. The Army Catering Corps (ACC), although organized and badged as a separate Corps, with its own Director, was nevertheless sponsored by the Director of Supplies and Transport (DST) at the War Office, and at all RASC levels of Command, and was therefore not an independent Corps as such.

The administration of all RASC services and the policy affecting their operation was the responsibility of the Quarter Master General (QMG) at the War Office to whom the Director of Supplies and Transport was responsible for the efficient functioning of his Corps. For the training of the RASC, in particular for its wartime role, the DST was responsible in the first instance to the Chief of the Imperial General Staff (CIGS) who exercised control of all Military Training for the Army through the Director General of Military Training (DGMT) at the War Office. The Inspector RASC (at the beginning of the period, a major general) on the Headquarters of the DST was responsible for the supervision of all training and regimental matters on behalf of the DST and answered both to the DGMT and the QMG on matters affecting the Corps.

THE MCLEOD REORGANIZATION

During the period 1961 to 1963 there were discussions within the then War Office on the need to reorganize the Logistic Services. The proposition put forward was in general terms that there should be:–

> One Corps for supplying the Army.
> One Corps for moving the Army.
> One Corps for repairing the vehicles and equipment of the Army

Brigadier W J Potter (later Major General Sir John Potter KBE CB) was Director of Administrative Planning at the War Office, and with the then Quarter Master General, General Sir Gerald Lathbury developed the theme for the reorganization on the above lines. The QMG presented a paper to the Army Council (now Army Board) on the subject, and after a number of discussions by the Council, General Sir Roderick McLeod GBE KCB DL then GOC in C Eastern Command was appointed as

Head of the Committee to examine the proposals. The first meeting of General McLeod's Committee took place on 7 May 1963 and the Committee in a remarkably short time presented to the Army Council their proposals for the changes that would in fact produce an organization on the basis of the concept given above. These included the formation of a Transport Corps for the Army based on the RASC. A summary of the major proposals approved by the Army Council, as they affected the RASC, is as follows:–

> The RASC should become the Transport Corps of the Army (title later to be agreed as Royal Corps of Transport). It would hand over to the Royal Army Ordnance Corps (which would become the Supply Corps, retaining its present title) responsibility for Supplies, Petroleum, Barrack Services, RASC (GD) Staff Clerks, the Army Fire Service, RASC/EFI, and Boat Stores.

It was also agreed at the time that responsibility for the Army Catering Corps should pass to the RAOC. On a submission though, by Major General W J Potter (who by then had become Director of Supplies and Transport) to the QMG, the Army Council amended its decision and the ACC rightfully gained its full independence.

In addition, the Royal Engineers would hand over to the new Transport Corps, its transportation functions including Ports, Inland Water and Railways, (other than its civil engineering aspects and mechanical repair), and the Movement Control Service. The repair function remained the responsibility of the Royal Electrical and Mechanical Engineers, who retained their title, and the only effect of this on the new Transport Corps was that repair support of those RE Transportation Units being taken over, passed to REME.

So it was that as a result of the accepted recommendations of the McLeod Committee, a Royal Warrant dated 26 March 1965 changed the title of the Royal Army Service Corps to Royal Corps of Transport to be effective from 15 July 1965. Behind this simple statement lay a very great deal of work. It was not without its heart searching, frustrations, disappointments and indeed by some, recriminations. Suffice it to say that from its concept the new Corps was put on a sound footing by the painstaking efforts of all involved. Because of the interchange of personnel between Corps, RE to RCT, and RASC to RAOC the sensitive personal management of both officers and soldiers changing their corps badge was of the utmost importance for their morale, and for that of the Corps which they were joining. Selection to transfer between the Corps was very carefully made and balanced against both the needs of both Corps and the future prospects of the officers and soldiers concerned. It would be a travesty of the truth to say that all those selected for transfer were happy to change their cap badge. All in all though, time has proved that the system has worked well and has not detracted from the loyalty to their new corps or their future in it.

Apart from the paramount importance of the effect on officers and soldiers transferring in and out of the Corps, there were innumerable other decisions to be made. Such matters as the worldwide organization of units in their new roles, and the titles that everyone should have, from the Head of the Corps down to sub-units, might have been expected to be straightforward, but even these provided some controversy. Uniforms are always calculated to produce debate and those for the new Corps were to prove no exception. All these problems though and many others were to be solved by consultation and team work. As Inspector RASC, and deputy to Major General Potter, Brigadier E H G Lonsdale MBE (later Major General) played a leading part in guiding the new Corps through the many obstacles that only a major reorganization can produce. Very much involved with all the preparations for the establishment of the new Corps were the two Representative Colonel Commandants who provided the link to the Colonel in Chief HRH The Duke of Gloucester, who gave his full support to these changes, during the period covering the transition from RASC to RCT. These were Major General W H D Ritchie CB CBE and Major General A F J Elmslie CB CBE to whom the Corps is greatly indebted for their guidance and help.

Although in the transition from RASC to RCT, the Corps lost two important responsibilities, Supplies and Petroleum, the overall responsibility for replenishment in the field was to be little changed in the forward areas. The RCT was to remain responsible for the delivery of all combat supplies to Corps and Divisional Units. In Divisional RCT Regiments, as they were then to be named, the RAOC took over the RASC Composite Platoons and became responsible, in conjunction with the RCT Commander, for the planning of provision, holding, and supervision of issue of commodities to units.

From 15 July 1965, the RASC ceased to exist except in

history, and the RCT was formed. Its role is to provide transport and movement support to the Army in both peace and war. Transport support includes road, rail and maritime transport together with port operating and air despatch duties. Movements support comprises planning, policy, co-ordination and control of all non-tactical personnel and freight movement, by land, sea and air.

RESPONSIBILITIES OF THE RCT

The main responisibilities of the new Corps are:–

The operation of all forms of road, rail and inland water transport in support of the Army (other than transport organic to the unit). All aspects relating to movement affecting the Army by land, sea and air in peace and war, other than tactical movement.

All transport matters in connection with replenishment in the field including the distribution of all combat supplies forward of replenishment parks.

The operation of harbour and coastal craft and logistic seagoing ships of the Army Department Fleet.

The operation of military ports in the United Kingdom and overseas.

The management, tasking and control of the secure military lines of communication.

The operation of supply by air.

The formulation of doctrine and policy for the administration and operation of B Vehicle management and the control and use of non-operational road transport in the Army.

The management of the system of B vehicle and certain A vehicle driver training in the Army.

The co-ordination of road safety measures in the Army.

ORGANIZATIONAL INFLUENCES

It is inevitable that over the 37 years period covered by this book there should have been many changes in the overall organization of the Corps, from the Ministry down to units. Clearly, not all can be covered and not everyone will agree with those selected. The strength of the RASC at the beginning of the period was 350,000 officers and soldiers. In 1965 when the RCT was created, the strength was 13,500 and in 1982, 10,500, with an additional 10,000 in the Territorial Army. The first factor therefore affecting the organization of the Corps, and the changes which have taken place, is the reduction in the size of the Corps to match that of the Army as a whole. This was most dramatic immediately after the War, and then became more gradual, keeping pace with our withdrawal from overseas commitments. Intermingled with this withdrawal though were the various campaigns in which the Army was involved, these in turn affecting local organisation of the Corps to meet the varying tasks that had to be undertaken. Significant changes, particularly in BAOR, were brought about by modifications to military concepts, and the reorganization and relocation of formations to meet them. Of particular affect on the UK Army Organization were the changes brought about by the implementation of the recommendations of the Stainforth Committee (Chairman – Major General C H Stainforth CB, OBE late RASC) to abolish Home Commands and establish HQ United Kingdom Land Forces in the early seventies. Again, the Corps responded to all these changes. On these, and on many other occasions, changes were tempered by political economies involving manpower reductions, which left little or no room for manoeuvre and sadly decimated some worthy units.

In November 1949, the Executive Committee of the Army Council gave approval to what was to be known as Phase II REME. On the formation of the Royal Electrical and Mechanical Engineers in October 1942, responsibility for the heavy mechanical transport workshops of the RASC was transferred to REME and an appropriate number of officers and soldiers were re-badged. This left the Corps with its own RASC manned 2nd line workshops with each transport company and these were an integral part of the company. Phase II REME, in the case of the Corps, was to complete the transfer of the 1st and 2nd line repair function for RASC vehicles from the Corps to REME. Similar processes in varying degrees were to take place for the Royal Armoured Corps, Royal Artillery and Royal Engineers. An Army Council Instruction was published in 1950 (ACI 1961/50) for the implementation of Phase II REME, and in the case of the RASC this was to be spread over 18 months, with the operating date for the transfer being 1 July 1951. Some 95 officers from the RASC were transferred to REME, and 369 RASC artificer soldiers with the following trades:– Blacksmith, Carpenter and Joiner, Coach Painter, Coach Trimmer, Electrician, Sheet Metal Worker, Shipwright, Turner, Vehicle Mechanic and Welder. Although Phase II REME was inevitable and had been known about since the formation of REME, its implementation was nevertheless, somewhat naturally, not greeted with enthusiasm within units. Company commanders saw their intimate repair support being removed from their control, with visions of diminishing vehicle availability.

Such of course was not the case, and as with other sensible and logical reorganizations, Phase II REME was accepted and quickly assimilated into the system. No one can deny that there were problems, but these were within the scope of everyone to solve, and solved they were. The transition was helped by the fact that many officers and soldiers who had been re-badged, remained initially in their original workshops, and eased the transition through. The Corps is now totally dependent on REME for the effective and rapid repair of its vehicles and other equipment, to meet its many tasks. This dependency has been met with increasing skill and professionalism over the years and we have every reason to be grateful to our sister Corps, for their support.

The most sweeping changes took place when the RCT was formed in 1965 and there have been a considerable number of modifications to the original structure of the Corps since then, and some might say an indecent number of changes in nomenclature. It is perhaps both right and natural though, that any new organization should be subject to critical examination and the RCT has been no exception to this. Many of the changes have been brought about by outside influences, as logistic concepts have changed, and are designed to be beneficial to the Army as a whole. The formation of the Logistic Executive (Army) in April 1977 was a major influence on Corps organization and was to strengthen the position of the Director of the Corps in bringing together Transport and Movements under one head at Ministry of Defence level. The part played by the Corps in the vital Line of Communication (L of C) to BAOR was also greatly strengthened and this is brought out clearly elsewhere in this book.

Throughout the period also, the role of the Territorial Army in its various guises has always been of major importance to both the RASC and the RCT, affecting not only the organization of the two Corps but their joint role with the TA in wartime. This aspect is covered in detail in the TA chapter as well as under Germany and Movements.

Lastly, but by no means least in the influences on organisation, has been the development of equipment, the word used in its

Figure I
ORGANIZATION, SUPPLIES AND TRANSPORT
DIRECTORATE, WAR OFFICE and Links for
Technical Purposes to Subordinate Headquarters – 1960

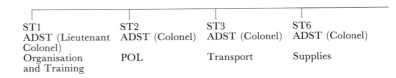

ST1	ST2	ST3	ST6
ADST (Lieutenant Colonel)	ADST (Colonel)	ADST (Colonel)	ADST (Colonel)
Organisation and Training	POL	Transport	Supplies

Note: Each Branch holds an appropriate number of
DADSTs (Major) and Staff Captains.

broadest sense to cover the total needs of the Corps to carry out its
tasks, ranging from vehicles to computers. In many ways, the items
which have revolutionized transportation have been the most
simple ones. The introduction of the NATO pallet in the late fifties,
with mechanical handling equipment of various sorts and vehicles
designed to carry maximum palletized loads, brought about
changes in RASC corps troops and divisional units. In the late
sixties the ISO container was to have a profound affect on the
distribution of stores worldwide but in particular to BAOR.
Radical changes in organizations were made to take advantage of
the tremendous opportunities offered by the ISO container in
improving logistic support for BAOR. The introduction of the
computer into transport management might have been expected to
bring greater changes in organization but although achieving
additional control and economy in transport operations, organizational changes as a result of ADP have so far been minimal.

The design of vehicles, particularly the High Mobility Load

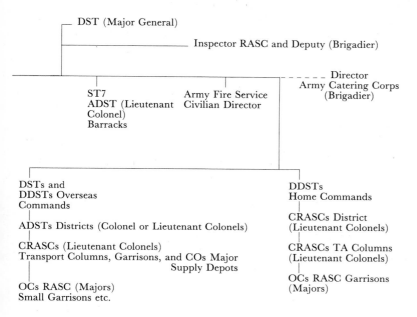

DST (Major General)

Inspector RASC and Deputy (Brigadier)

Director
Army Catering Corps
(Brigadier)

ST7
ADST (Lieutenant
Colonel)
Barracks

Army Fire Service
Civilian Director

DSTs and
DDSTs Overseas
Commands

ADSTs Districts (Colonel or Lieutenant Colonels)

CRASCs (Lieutenant Colonels)
Transport Columns, Garrisons, and COs Major
Supply Depots

OCs RASC (Majors)
Small Garrisons etc.

DDSTs
Home Commands

CRASCs District
(Lieutenant Colonels)

CRASCs TA Columns
(Lieutenant Colonels)

OCs RASC Garrisons
(Majors)

Carrier (HMLC), and the increased load capacity of the new wide range of vehicles which is covered in the Road Transport chapter have all influenced the organization of units from those responsible for the L of C forward to divisional units.

Organization of the RASC 1945–1965

As has been indicated above, it is only possible, because of the many changes that have taken place, to deal with the organizations at the various levels of command in general terms. In this period though, changes were not so radical as later, and the main titles and general structure remained throughout, but reducing in size.

The head of corps, the Director of Supplies and Transport (a Major General) at the War Office exercised technical and regimental control of the Corps through DSTs (Major Generals) at major commands abroad, BAOR, MELF and FARELF and to Deputy Directors Supplies and Transport (DDSTs) in other commands

Figure II

ORGANIZATION OF DIRECTORATE GENERAL OF TRANSPORT
AND MOVEMENTS LOGISTIC EXECUTIVE (ARMY) MINISTRY O
DEFENCE – 1982

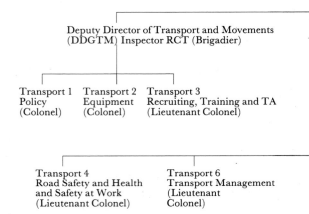

throughout the world, who were either Brigadiers or Colonels. All
Major Generals' posts other than the DST War Office were
downgraded to Brigadier by 1956. The DST's organization at the
War Office was mirrored in each command both at home and
abroad, with a lower rank structure. In the case of supplies and
POL for which the Corps was totally responsible, provisioning was
War Office controlled, and this control was exercised by the DST's
staff and is explained in the supply and POL chapters. In all other
matters the DDSTs had normal command autonomy, receiving
War Office directives on Supplies and Transport policy as necessary. As an example, the DST organization at the War Office in
1960 is given in outline at Figure I.

Figure I basically covers the static organization that provided the
RASC services, – supplies, transport, POL and barracks, and in
some cases, water and animal transport, in garrisons throughout
the world. In addition, not directly in this chain were the RASC
organizations with field formations who generally had no responsibility for static organizations, but drew on the facilities provided as

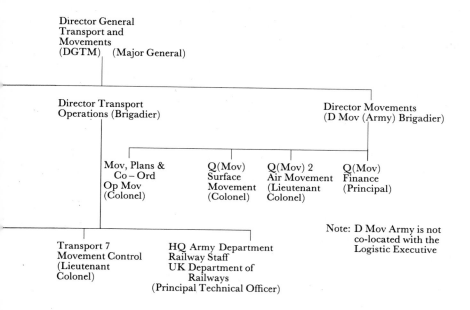

Director General
Transport and
Movements
(DGTM)   (Major General)

Director Transport
Operations (Brigadier)

Director Movements
(D Mov (Army) Brigadier)

Mov, Plans &
Co – Ord
Op Mov
(Colonel)

Q(Mov)
Surface
Movement
(Colonel)

Q(Mov) 2
Air Movement
(Lieutenant
Colonel)

Q(Mov)
Finance
(Principal)

Transport 7
Movement Control
(Lieutenant
Colonel)

HQ Army Department
Railway Staff
UK Department of
Railways
(Principal Technical Officer)

Note: D Mov Army is not
co-located with the
Logistic Executive

necessary in support of the formation. Examples are DDST 1 British Corps in BAOR and all CsRASC of divisional and corps troops columns. It should be noted that DDSTs and ADSTs did not command RASC units under their technical control, but were responsible to the local General Officer Commanding, on whose staff they were, for the provisioning of, and technical efficiency of their units.

ORGANIZATION OF THE RCT – 1965–1982

Of the four Corps most involved with the McLeod re-organization, RE, RASC, RAOC and REME, it was the RASC that was to undergo the most fundamental re-organisation. Whilst the initial concept of 'one corps for moving the Army' has not changed, responsibilities have been modified and organizations changed accordingly as new and improved systems have evolved. Also, major reorganizations carried out by the Ministry of Defence, over the past few years, for a variety of reasons, some of which have already been mentioned, have all led to corresponding changes in

RCT organization and responsibilities. It is not feasible to detail these many changes, but a selection of those with special significance, given below, is illustrative of the extent to which these have occurred. Before examining these however, it is interesting to note that in 1982 increasing emphasis was placed on the economies achieved by functional organization, to meet the Army's main task, the NATO defence role. Organizations were by then tailor-made to meet the operational task rather than on the standard 'brick system' which applied pre-McLeod, and in the early days of the RCT. Then, the organization was built up on a far more stereotyped system, since discarded in favour of a flexible response to the actual requirement. The disadvantage from a historical point of view is that a table to show these changes overall becomes too complicated to merit inclusion!

The establishment of the Logistic Executive (Army) and the organization of the Directorate General of Transport and Movement within it, (see Figure II for outline organization in 1982) was the first major step in bringing the transport and movements element of the Corps together at Ministry of Defence level, placing both under the direct control of the DGTM. Overall though, for the reasons already given, the technical control over the entire Corps by the DGTM became somewhat more complex, as standard titles and functions gave way to more flexible organizations.

After the UK commands had disappeared under the Stainforth re-organization, there were to be several re-organizations, and changes in title, at districts. The senior RCT officer in the HQ of District staffs by 1982 was the Commander Transport and Movements (Colonel or Lieutenant Colonel). In UKLF however the overall responsibility UK wide for transport and movements, previously that of the CTMO (Brigadier) UKLF was changed and the NATO titling of Deputy Assistant Chief of Staff (DACOS) G3 Transport and Movement, introduced with a downgrading of rank to Colonel. The importance of this appointment is illustrated in the Falklands chapter in Part I. Greater emphasis on the military L of C between UK and BAOR meant that Marchwood Military Port was built up to meet this requirement, and the Ports chapter in Part II gives details of this development. 3 Transport Group was formed to take over this task, and the Commander (Colonel) commands the port, and is responsible for the containerized maintenance of BAOR through the port. The Army School of

Mechanical Transport (ASMT) previously split between Longmoor and Bordon, moved to Leconfield in Humberside in 1977, and at the same time took on the driver training of all Corps drivers previously carried out at Aldershot. The DGTM is responsible to the Director General of Army Training (DGAT) for all Arms driver training, and apart from basic driver training by other Arms, advanced driver training for all arms is carried out at Leconfield.

In BAOR, since early in the period of this history, the principal representatives of the Corps were based with HQ BAOR (Brigadier) and HQ 1(BR) Corps (Brigadier). Each has had several changes of title but their relationship to each other changed little, the Brigadier at HQ BAOR having overall responsibility to the Commander-in-Chief for the efficiency of the RCT in BAOR as a whole, whilst the Brigadier in 1(BR) Corps was responsible to the Corps Commander for the operational efficiency of the RCT in 1(BR) Corps, and commanding the RCT Corps Troops units. In 1982 the titles were Commander Transport and Movements BAOR, and in 1(BR) Corps, Commander Transport. In Rhine Area BAOR, in 1982, 2 Transport Group (commander – Colonel) had responsibility for RCT transport units in the area west of 1(BR) Corps. The RCT organization in divisions in BAOR was particularly affected by the various changes in tactical concepts in BAOR from 1965 onwards, and from being standardized organizations were, by 1982, tailormade to meet the differing roles of each division. Their commanders' titles also changed from Commander RCT to Commander Transport.

Within other types of transport and movement units, functional changes also took place after the initial establishment of units in 1965. In the static chain, the advantages of combining transport units and movement cells were quickly realized, and combined transport and movement regiments were formed in BAOR. Elsewhere in the world such amalgamations took place within the overall CTMO organization.

At the end of this period of the History, the Corps organization is still evolving in the search for the most efficient and economical way to meet the transportation needs of the Army. The fact that these needs have changed so much over the short period that the RCT has been established has provided the challenge needed by a new Corps. This book sets out to show how this challenge has been met.

CHAPTER TWO
The United Kingdom

THE HOME BASE

THE SECURITY OF THE HOME BASE in the United Kingdom is of paramount importance in any defence policy of the Government of this Country. Northern Ireland has for some years posed special problems within the UK and is covered in the second section of this chapter. Units from both UK and BAOR on temporary duty have been involved there during the period covered in this history.

The Army in the UK contributes both to the security and to the reinforcement and logistic backup for our forces overseas, wherever they may be. This pattern of employment of our forces in the UK and overseas has changed radically since the end of

World War II. The very considerable reductions in our overseas commitments outside Europe and the development of a NATO orientated defence policy, gradually resulted in a much smaller manpower requirement overall, and a change in the structure of the UK Base to meet this situation. As a new structure evolved over the years, so the contribution made by the RASC, and later the RCT, changed to match the new requirements. These changes have been far reaching, and it is not proposed to attempt to cover them in any detail in this chapter, but rather to highlight briefly just some of the units, personalities and events that have played a significant part in the Corps activities in the UK. The units typify the several thousands which have formed part of the UK structure over the years since the end of World War II. Some of the many others not mentioned have their place more appropriately in Part II of this book, and the general structure of the Corps emanating from the UK has already been described in Chapter I. The large Corps representation in the Territorial Army, essentially part of the UK structure, again has its own chapter in Part II where this most important element of our Corps is described in some detail.

21

The activities of the Corps, not only in the UK, but worldwide have always been watched over with the greatest interest by our Colonel-in-Chief, who is appointed by the reigning sovereign. When this story opens our Colonel-in-Chief was His Royal Highness, Field Marshal The Duke of Gloucester, KG, KT, KP, GCB, GCVO ADC(P) who had been appointed by His Majesty King George VI on 20 February 1942. The death of His Royal Highness on 10 June 1974 was a great blow to the Corps. He had been a staunch supporter and most valued advisor to the Corps, not only during World War II, but in the post war era leading up to the formation of the RCT. Our sadness was tempered by the most enthusiastic support from his wife, Her Royal Highness the Duchess of Gloucester, who had stood in for her husband in the latter years of his life, when ill health prevented him attending Corps functions. We were indeed extremely fortunate in the time that she devoted to the Corps at that stage.

The last official function at which His Royal Highness was able to be present with the Corps was on 26 July 1967 when he unveiled a memorial plaque to mark the rebuilding of Buller Barracks at Aldershot. This was appropriately a major milestone in the Corps history – the start of the rebuild of the Corps home. Sadly he was not well enough to perform the subsequent opening ceremony for the new Buller Barracks on 11 July 1970 and the Duchess of Gloucester, again stood in for her husband. In so doing, she completed the task that he had initiated some three years previously.

The Corps was delighted that her Majesty appointed Princess Alice, Duchess of Gloucester GCB, CI, GCVO GBE as our Colonel-in-Chief on 8 February 1975. On the death of her husband, the Duchess had assumed the title Princess Alice and, with only a very small break in her official association with the Corps, took up the appointment with all the charm and enthusiasm that we had come to know. We look forward to her gracing the Corps activities for many years to come.

At the end of World War II, the RASC in the Home Base was involved in maintaining the large home defence forces spread throughout the country, with all the services that it provided. The supply organization, described in its own chapter in Part II, although running down from its wartime levels, was from its Reserve Supply Depots still dealing with the worldwide distribution of foodstuffs to the Army. In the Home Commands, the

Command Supply Depots which had existed at every large centre of military population, were gradually run down in line with the UK troop reductions, and eventually those remaining were handed over within the supply organization to the RAOC in 1965. Before this though, as explained in Part II, a number of major changes had taken place to rationalize the issue of supplies in the UK, including the involvement of the Royal Naval Supply Depot at Deptford in the supply chain. In the UK, POL was mainly an integral part of the supply organization, apart from the major Petroleum Depot at West Moors in Dorset, and followed the same pattern of rundown, which is described in Part II. The Barrack Services in each major garrison were heavily involved in the re-equipping of barracks designated for peacetime use, and the rebuilding programme for both barracks and married quarters, as the temporary wartime accommodation was released. Scales of accommodation and furnishing were gradually improved as the country came out of the austerity years, when shortage of fuel alone was a major problem. Many of the Barrack Officers were still from the pre-war era, and their experience was to be invaluable in the years of reconstruction of a sound peacetime barrack service in the UK. Their work is described in Part II.

The large RASC training organization, developed during the war for a conscript army, was coping with their own particular problems of demobilization, whilst at the same time playing their part in training an effective but smaller army. At that stage, whilst we still had widespread overseas commitments, trying to produce a balance of newly trained soldiers to replace some of those demobilized in every sort of Corps unit throughout the world, was no easy task. The introduction of National Service to replace wartime conscription was an additional problem facing the RASC training organization in this period of change. This was felt particularly in the driver training battalions. As with other Regiments and Corps, there was a constant turnover of instructors. Fortunately this situation was gradually improved with the intro-duction of civilian driver training instructors, starting with 15 Driver Training Battalion in 1949. These civilian instructors were to be the backbone of all future driver training, and many, who had been RASC drivers during the war, were to move, as the training organization contracted over the years, firstly to Aldershot, includ-ing a temporary move to Church Crookham, and ultimately to Leconfield, on the formation of the Army School of Mechanical

Transport. Their loyalty and hard work was a major contributory factor in the success of driver training within the Corps. The throughput of the various training battalions was high, with constant replacements required for service overseas. The RASC National Service officer and soldier quickly found themselves involved in the campaigns covered in later chapters – Malaya, Korea, Suez, and Kenya. Their training was to stand them in good stead and was quickly put to the test. Although there was undoubtedly a sigh of relief both from the Army, and those likely to be called up, when National Service ended in 1962, there is no doubt that those who served during the period benefited greatly from the training which they received, and the Regular Army certainly owed most a great debt of gratitude for their contribution to the units in which they served.

With the ending of National Service, and the introduction of the all Regular Army, the training commitment diminished considerably. 15 Driver Training Battalion at Blandford was disbanded, and although 6 Driver Training Battalion at Yeovil was to last into the time of the RCT, it too was disbanded on 31 March 1969, when its tasks were taken over by 12 Training Regiment in Aldershot. Until 1966, 12 Regiment, or 1 Battalion as it had been called, had been responsible for driver training only, but regimental training was then also taken over from 11 Regiment, which subsequently reverted to its old title of The Depot. Recruits therefore at this stage received all their training in one regiment. This was to change again in January 1971, when the Depot, then back in the rebuilt Buller Barracks with 12 Regiment, took back the responsibility for the regimental training of recruits from 12 Regiment. 12 Regiment were to concentrate on getting all recruits up to the standard of HGV III before they were posted to units. An open-ended system of driver training was introduced to meet this aim, and recruits stayed in 12 Regiment until they had passed their test. Previously, with the introduction of the Class III Heavy Goods Vehicle licence (HGV III), some recruits could not pass the test in the set time allowed, and units to which they were posted were responsible for the additional training to get them through their test. The new system obviated this, and conversely, drivers who passed the test earlier were posted to their units sooner. In 1977, all responsibility for RCT driver training passed to the Army School of Mechanical Transport (ASMT) at Leconfield and 12 Regiment was disbanded. A new era in driver training had started, and ASMT continues to meet all the driver training requirements of the Corps to the present day.

Whilst the Driver Training organization produced the trained driver for the Corps, and detail of all the training organization is given in Part II, responsibility for maintaining units at their proper strength with trained Warrant Officers, NCOs and soldiers, rested with the RASC and ACC Record Office, a War Office controlled unit. This unit is one of the very few which has existed throughout the period of this story, basically performing the same task as it did in World War II, and remaining at the same location – Hastings, – throughout. It changed its title on the formation of the RCT, (the Army Catering Corps had then become independent), and is now the RCT Manning and Record Office with similar responsibilities for the new Corps. Although controlled by the Vice-Adjutant General and the Director of Manning of the Adjutant General's department of the Ministry of Defence (Army) – (previously the War Office), which is responsibile for the distribution of the Army's manpower between regiments and corps, the position of the RCT Manning and Record Office is unique in relation to the Corps which it serves. Its responsibilities have always ensured that there is always the closest possible link with both the Head of the Corps and with all Corps units direct. These responsibilities cover those tasks in respect of the administration of soldiers, not carried out by units, and include enlistment, engagement, terms of service, posting, promotion and careers, also with their release from the Colours, recall to the Colours and discharge from the Army. To carry out these functions, it prepares and maintains every soldiers record of service. It is the manning of RASC/RCT units with the soldiers most appropriately qualified and suited for the job, that has brought it into closest contact with all Corps units over the years. The organization has always been commanded by a Colonel from the Corps, with only two or three other Corps officers – the number has varied over the years. The remainder of the staff, which numbered over one thousand at the end of the War, have always been civilians. The loyalty and hard work of this civilian staff over the years, in dealing with the whole range of problems brought about by rundowns, redundancies and reorganizations has ensured that the careers of our soldiers from private to Warrant Officer Class I, and the units in which they serve, have had the best possible help over the years.

One of the first major casualties of the changing defence policy after the war, was the disbandment of Anti-Aircraft Command in 1955. At this time the Command was divided into five AA Groups. The RASC representation in AA Command was high, though by 1955 predominantly Territorial Army. Each Group had one regular RASC MT company and two Territorial AA Group Transport Columns, except in the Group in Scotland where there was only one Column. At the Headquarters of the Command there was a DDST (Colonel) and a small S and T Staff. In addition to the normal maintenance responsibilities for the Groups, the RASC in 1948 also took on the responsibility for moving the static heavy AA guns of the Royal Artillery. The special transporters used to move these static guns were in a poor state of repair after much service in the war. Their design had weaknesses which led to frequent unserviceability and their performance was sometimes unpredictable. A driver of 6 Company RASC towing a 3.7 inch HAA gun on his newly acquired transporter was descending a steep mountainous road to a gunnery practice camp in Wales. He subsequently filled in a traffic accident report which stated: 'I looked out of my cab, and was surprised to see the gun which I was towing, passing me'. Fortunately, the gun met no vehicular opposition on its lone downward journey, only the mountainside at the next bend, where it became another accident statistic of AA Command! No doubt this story has had apocryphal successors, but we are assured of the authenticity of this one!

Whilst the regular Army units of AA Command were absorbed into the overall UK requirement, some 5,000 TA RASC were lost as a result of the disbandment of the Command, and this was a disheartening time for the TA. At this time those TA units not in AA Command were scaled down and earmarked for mobilization tasks in support of the Civil Defence Regions of the Country, and details are given in the TA Chapter in Part II. The last occasion when AA Command were brought to a state of readiness was at the time of the Berlin Airlift in 1948. Although the post-war period of AA Command was short and uneventful, after its wartime experience, it played its part in the overall defence plan for the UK, and those of the RASC, both Regular and Territorial who served in it did so with pride.

One of the best known of all the MT Units of the Corps is that now titled 20 Squadron RCT, which can trace its history back to 1885. Its responsibilities, initially as the War Office Car Company, and later as the Ministry of Defence Car Squadron have basically been the same since World War II, and indeed were throughout the War. Up until 1967 it provided only the staff cars and supporting vehicles for the Army Department of the Ministry of Defence (previously the War Office) and the staff cars, coaches and load carriers for HQ London District. In July of that year however it also took over responsibility for the MOD Car and Van Pools, and for all the transport requirements for the Central Staffs and the other two Service Departments. Within this overall responsibility is one special role. The unit has always provided the vehicles and drivers known as Her Majesty The Queen's Baggage Train for members of the Royal Family, visiting Royalty and Heads of State on official visits to the United Kingdom. In addition to HM The Queen's baggage vehicles the unit also provides the cars and drivers for members of the Royal Family, visiting Royalty and Heads of State attending functions sponsored by any of the three Services in the UK and BAOR. It maintains its special link with the Royal Household through the senior Corps officer at HQ London District at Horse Guards, now the CRCT. On 13 July 1971 (at a ceremony that was to be repeated eight years later) Her Majesty the Queen accompanied by His Royal Highness the Duke of Edinburgh, inspected informally the drivers and vehicles of The Queen's Baggage Train, at Buckingham Palace. The CRCT, Lieutenant Colonel A G Bell RCT presented the Officer Commanding 20 Squadron, Major C E Tanner RCT, and other officers and soldiers to Her Majesty. Her Majesty and Prince Phillip also spoke to the families of officers and soldiers who were invited to attend the parade.

The unit has a number of civilian drivers who are employed alongside their military colleagues. The Squadron moved to Regents Park Barracks in 1946, and has remained there ever since, providing continuity of service that has many unique features. Sadly, even in London there are now unfortunate hazards, and on 10 October 1981, Mr C W Liddiard, a civilian driver, was badly hurt when driving a squadron bus carrying the band of the Irish Guards, who were the target for an IRA bomb at Chelsea Barracks. In the attack, two innocent civilians were killed, and many of the bandsmen badly injured. The drivers of this unit, both military and civilian are constantly in the public eye with exacting individual responsibilities and their record of personal efficiency is one of which they are rightly proud.

With the high standards demanded, many of the NCOs and

HILLINGDON BOROUGH LIBRARIES

[By courtesy of PRO London District]

HM The Queen inspecting the Queens baggage vehicles of 20 Squadron RCT, accompanied by Lt Col A G Bell, CRCT London District.

drivers who have served in the unit over the years since the war, started their Army life in the Corps as Boy soldiers, later called Junior Leaders.

The Boys Company of 1 Training Battalion RASC, reformed after the war in 1947 at Aldershot, was to produce many of the potential Warrant Officers and NCOs of the Corps.

The development of the training of boys or Junior Leaders has throughout the period been an important part of the RASC/RCT training organization in the UK. The Boys' Company moved to Bordon in 1955 to occupy St Lucia Barracks. Here the term 'Boy' was dropped in favour of 'Junior Leader' which was considered a more accurate description of the young man joining the Corps. Until 1960 the unit was called Junior Leaders Company RASC, when with an increase in numbers the unit became a battalion. The increase in strength resulted in the Battalion having to move to

Norton Manor Camp at Taunton in Somerset. The unit settled down well there and built up its reputation with the surrounding community, and established many lasting friendships, in particular as a result of its support of local charities. In July 1965 the unit became the Junior Leaders Regiment RCT.

The task of this unit under each of its titles was the same. This was to train young school leavers to take their place in an RASC/RCT field force unit with developed qualities of leadership and character in order that they might earn early promotion. A high percentage have become non-commissioned officers and warrant officers, and many have achieved commissioned rank. Originally, boys were taken into the unit straight from school at the age of 15 years. They stayed in the unit for 2½ years or 7 terms, and were then posted to a field force unit overseas, normally BAOR, as a fully trained RASC/RCT soldier, and in later years becoming drivers with their HGV licence.

In 1971 the Government raised the school leaving age (known as ROSLA) to 16 years. Despite opposition by the Ministry of Defence who maintained that it was generally more advantageous to boys who wished to do so to go to Junior Leaders Regiments (most Arms and Corps had their own regiments) at 15 years rather than spend an extra year at school. However, despite this opposition the intake age for Junior Leaders was raised to 16. This is not the place to discuss the relative merits of the earlier or later entry from an educational point of view. Suffice it to say that those who in the earlier period entered at 15 achieved during their time at Junior Leaders Regiment remarkable success in attaining the higher educational standards which had eluded them at school. This was to the advantage of the individual and the Army as a whole. The immediate effect though of the public announcement of the proposed change was a flood of boys wishing to join Junior Leaders before they had to stay an extra year at school. The strength of the Regiment rose to over 1,000 Juniors and an extra squadron was formed. This situation continued for several years, until the intake at 16 years was fully introduced. At this stage the length of their stay with the Regiment was reduced to three terms totalling 15 months. Much of the time lost by this reduction was made up by intensifying the training, but the reduction nevertheless meant that the scope for the development of extramural activities was reduced. However, the range of activities undertaken is impressive, ranging from rock climbing to pot-

*Junior Leaders under
instruction.*

[By courtesy of Central Office of Information]

holing, skiing to sailing, tennis to treking, not forgetting the high
standard achieved in more conventional sports. The band (Corps
of Drums) has always been a flourishing feature of the Junior
Leaders Regiment, and they have been the UK Champions on
several occasions.

On 6 June 1972, the unit was proud to receive its first Royal
visit. This was made by Her Royal Highness The Princess Anne.
Her Royal Highness saw many of the activities of the unit, ranging
from education to demonstrations of abseiling on the training wall.
After lunch, Her Royal Highness inspected a full parade of the
Regiment, followed by a number of demonstrations. Adults and
children from a number of local charities supported by the
Regiment, were there to watch, and after the Parade, Princess
Anne spoke to many of those in wheelchairs. Equestrian activities
were not forgotten, and Her Royal Highness drove round the camp
and the Parade Ground in the Corps Coach. The Princess also met
the Regimental mascot, Bruneval, a Shetland pony, who was on his
best behaviour, and took his sugar lumps politely. His attitude to
VIPs in the past had not always been so respectful!

Boys and Junior Leaders have always had a very successful

and greatly needed role in the Corps, but like other organizations have suffered to a greater or lesser degree from change emanating from both direct political decisions (eg ROSLA) and those resulting from the general need to economize in Army manpower and the number of organizations sustainable in the Army. Those who have been Boys or Junior Leaders will know the value of the training that they received and the transformation which the unit is able to make to the young men which it receives. It is to be hoped that when the next history is written it will be able to record the continuing success that this unit has had with the young men who join it from school.

Not all units have seen such continuous service in the UK as 20 Squadron and the Junior Leaders Regiment but have nevertheless during the time that they were in existence made their mark on Corps history. 14 Air Despatch Regiment RCT was one such unit. The Regiment was formed on 15 July 1965 from 1 Army Air Supply Organization RASC which disbanded on that day on the formation of the RCT. Initially Regimental HQ was at RAF Odiham with HQ 38 Group RAF, for whom it provided air despatch support when their transport aircraft were employed in this role. On formation of the Regiment it had two air despatch squadrons who had been RASC air despatch squadrons of 1 AASO. These were 22 Air Despatch Squadron and 47 Air Despatch Squadron both of whom were very experienced. At this time the location of air despatch units was very much tied to the location and type of aircraft at RAF Transport Command Stations, rather than to a centralized location which had been the practice in the past. There were three types of transport aircraft then in service with the RAF, all ageing, but well proven – the Hastings, the Argosy and the Beverley. The two RCT Squadrons were therefore located by troops between the RAF airfields at which these aircraft were based. These were RAF Colerne, Benson and Abingdon, having Hastings, Argosy and Beverley aircraft respectively. RAF Tangmere was the nearest airfield at that time, where 22 Squadron could be located, in relation to RAF Thorney Island where the RAF trained with all three types of aircraft. The Air Despatch Training Wing was also located there. By 1967/1968 the Hastings and Beverley aircraft were being phased out and Andovers and Hercules introduced. This meant another change of location for the squadrons of the Regiment, and 47 Squadron was split between RAF Lyneham and Abingdon, whilst 22 Squadron was split between RAF Fairford, Tangmere and Thorney Island. Later, Regimental Headquarters moved with 38 Group RAF from RAF Odiham to RAF Benson in early 1972, and finally to RAF Upavon in 1973.

Although located in UK the Regiment was not lacking in overseas commitments. Operation Khana Cascade, a famine relief operation, was launched in 1973, and this is described in detail in the Nepal chapter of this story.

As a home based unit, the Regiment was called upon in 1973 for the distinction of being the first Royal Corps of Transport unit to provide an entire complement of guards for London Public Duties from 25 February to 10 March 1973. The Regiment which was then commanded by Lieutenant Colonel K C Davis MBE, (now Brigadier) provided the guards at Buckingham Palace, St James's Palace, the Tower and the Bank of England. It was one of the last units to mount guard at the Bank. The Guard was commanded by Major J M Riches RCT and the RSM was Warrant Officer class 1 D A Armitage RCT (now Major QM). Captains on the guard were Captain R Morgan (now Lieutenant Colonel) RCT, and Captain C J Upchurch RCT (now Major), Ensigns on the Guard were, Lieutenant T H Murray RCT, and Lieutenant G A Betts RCT (both now Majors).

By this time there had been further changes in the structure and locations of the Regiment, and these were to be the last before the Regiment disbanded in 1975. 55 Air Despatch Squadron, a very experienced squadron from the Far East whose activities there can be read about in the Malaya and Brunei Chapters, returned to UK and took over the commitments of 22 Squadron at RAF Thorney Island and Tangmere. 22 Squadron was then regrettably disbanded, but was reformed later as a Car Squadron at UKLF. A troop of 14 Regiment, 385 Air Despatch Troop, was located in teams split between Cyprus and the Arabian Gulf to meet the air despatch requirements with the RAF there.

Apart from its air despatch role the Regiment provided MT support in Northern Ireland, both with individuals and formed MT troops, and an interesting relief operation carried out by land in 1974. This was Operation Terminal I, when the Regiment delivered twenty 4 Ton vehicles to drought stricken Niger by ferry and overland route – Southampton, – Le Havre, Marseilles, Algiers and South across the Sahara to Niamy. The vehicles were provided under the auspices of the Overseas Development Ministry and the

Disasters Emergency Committee. Delivery involved a journey of three and a half thousand miles in twenty one days. The operation was commanded by Captain T H Murray RCT (now Major) with two other officers, Second Lieutenant Wetherall RCT and Lieutenant C White RAOC who was the procurement officer for the trip. The troop sergeant was Sergeant C Bracey RCT. The party was accompanied by a BBC camera crew and reporters, and a film of the journey entitled 'Desert Convoy South' was made by the team, and subsequently shown on BBC Television. Whilst crossing the Sahara, numerous explorers and adventurers crossing under their own arrangements were encountered. Some were well equipped, others totally unprepared for the hazards of the journey, and however venturesome, better suited for a day trip to Brighton. Some in the latter category were rescued by the convoy. On safe arrival in Niger the convoy was met with due ceremony by the Niger Transport Minister, and the vehicles duly handed over.

Also in its transport role, the Regiment provided a troop for a totally contrasting task. In 1973 it was decided by the Ministry of Defence that a UKLF Priority Freight Service should be established. This was to speed the delivery times for certain categories of defence material from Command Ordnance Depots to units. In May, a Priority Freight Troop RCT was established, to carry out this task. The inaugural troop from 14 Regiment was split between the Command Ordnance Depots at Bicester, Donnington and Chilwell. The troop delivered priority freight direct to airfields for transit overseas, and to certain major units. It also delivered freight to Ordnance Support Units for onward delivery to units within the given priority timings. The vehicles for this system which is now totally standard are now provided by 25 Freight Distribution Squadron RCT (L of C) (The Carmen's) under command 29 Transport and Movement Regiment RCT.

In 1975, it was decided that the air despatch commitment could be met within the capabilities of one air despatch squadron, and 14 (AD) Regiment was disbanded. The air despatch role was retained in 47 (AD) Squadron, which then became part of 29 Movement Control Regiment RCT. The second squadron in 14 Regiment, 55 Squadron, so long associated with air despatch in the Far East became 55 Movement Control Squadron. The story of 14 (AD) Regiment, although covering a short period in terms of Corps history is indicative of the versatility that can be provided by this type of unit in our Corps. Further details of Air Despatch are contained in that chapter in Part II, and that of 29 Regiment in the Combined/Joint Operations chapter.

Two important events affecting the Corps' relationship with the local people of our home in Aldershot took place during the period of this story. On 22 April 1970, the Freedom of the Borough of Aldershot, the home of the Corps, was conferred on the Corps by the Mayor, Aldermen and Burgesses of the Borough. A parade to mark the occasion, consisted of six squadrons of marching troops, (three squadrons from 12 Training Regiment, and one each from 2 Transport Group, 7 Squadron and 17 Squadron). The parade was commanded by Lieutenant Colonel R J Royle RCT. In addition to the troops on parade, a cavalcade of vehicles representing a cross section of the activities of the Corps provided by 3 Division Regiment RCT and 2 Transport Group drove past through the centre of Aldershot. Subsequently, as a result of Local Government reorganization, the Borough of Aldershot became the Borough of Rushmoor and on 29 May 1981 the freedom of the new Borough was granted to all Regiments and Corps who had previously held the Freedom of Aldershot. These were, the Royal Engineers, the Royal Hampshire Regiment, the Parachute Regiment, The Royal Corps of Transport, the Army Medical services, the Army Catering Corps and the Army Physical Training Corps. A representative parade of all the Regiments and Corps was held in Rushmoor arena attended by many who had been at their respective earlier Freedom Parades when granted by the Borough of Aldershot. The representative Colonel Commandant of the Royal Corps of Transport Major General Blunt CB MBE GM received the new scroll on behalf of the Corps.

The final unit in this summary of typical Corps units which have served in the Home Base is again one with a unique task over the years – 19 Tank Transporter Company RASC – later RCT. Sadly, it too has not survived the complete period of this story, but its task has continued, and the unit's number is now proudly borne within 4 Armoured Division Regiment RCT in BAOR.

This unit was the only Tank Transporter unit in the UK for most of the period after World War II until it was disbanded in 1977. As a General Transport Unit, it saw service in the War in France, Egypt, Greece, North Africa, Sicily, Italy, and finally North West Europe. However the unit was disbanded in BAOR in 1946 and was not reformed until 1 September 1950 at Ranby Camp, Retford in Nottinghamshire. Here it took over the United

Kingdom tank transporting role, when 336 Company was renumbered 19 Tank Transporter Company RASC.

The Company task was to move all tanks throughout the United Kingdom. This included the delivery of all new tanks from the manufacturers in the North of England to Ordnance Depots or units in the South and moves of unit tanks to training areas, including from the early 1960s the somewhat newsworthy moves, at first, of German Army Panzer Regiment tanks to training areas in Wales.

When the unit was formed in 1950 it was equipped with a mixture of types of tank transporters left over from the war. The merits and demerits of each type were the subject of much discussion. Those involved in the arguments ranged from the drivers, who were a very special breed of men, independent and proud of the fact that they were driving some of the heaviest loads in the country, to those possibly more erudite but less earthy in their assessments, who were trying to develop the right tank transporter for the future and agree the numbers required.

This is not the chapter to dwell on types of transporters in detail, as this is covered in the Road Transport chapter in Part II, but the introduction of the Thorneycroft Antar tractor in September 1951 followed by Antars with semi-trailers in 1953, was a milestone in tank transporter history.

The stories surrounding the activities of the drivers of 19 Company are legion, and fortunately most had happy endings. One illustrated the resourcefulness of the company when faced with a situation that was likely to prove somewhat disastrous. On a Friday afternoon in 1962, Drivers Lawson and Clayton, the two man crew, were carrying a Centurion tank on their Diamond T Tractor and Dyson trailer between Ashchurch in Gloucester and Woolwich. Routes were always very carefully selected in conjunction with the Police and strictly controlled, as 120 tons on the wrong route could prove difficult, as indeed it did in this case. The drivers lost their way on the route round London and were swept into the vortex of traffic heading for Central London. They soon found themselves on the Chiswick flyover, greatly to the consternation of the Police, the local road authorities, London Transport, and probably the drivers. In fact there was no way of turning the transporter round and it had to continue to Hyde Park Corner, where everyone was fearful that it would either damage the Underground, or descend into the excavations then taking place. The police eventually had it parked on the grass on the edge of the Park somewhat inconveniently near to the flat of the then CIGS, Field Marshal Sir Francis Festing and ordered that it should not be moved. By this time the telephone lines were getting hot and the Press and BBC were on the scene, but the Company Commander, Major P H Benson of the RASC (later Major General) was quick to take advantage of the possibility of good publicity being gained from an otherwise fraught situation. Clean overalls were rushed to the drivers, and overnight the vehicles were polished up, so that by the following morning they presented a shining face to the public, who found the transporter and tank parked where it was, an interesting spectacle. The CIGs had in the meantime seen the offending vehicle whilst going out to dinner on Friday night and stopped his car to question the drivers, who by now had been told not to talk to anyone or the Press. The CIGS, unrecognised, received something of a rebuff, but fortunately appreciated the situation. However, the DST on Saturday morning was requested to explain the situation to the CIGS, on Monday! Fortunately, in the event, he did not have to do so, for by Monday, Scotland Yard had planned a route out of London for the transporter, and it was duly extricated without further problems. The crew of the transporter had risen to the occasion admirably, and their dilemma was turned to the advantage of favourable publicity.

The DST at the time, Major General P G Turpin CB, OBE fought a hard battle within the Ministry of Defence to keep 19 Company at Ranby, which was well located, centrally to their tasks, but it was decreed that they should move to the purpose built Ward Barracks at Bulford, with its specially strengthened vehicle park. This they did in March 1969, amidst some gloom, as Ranby had become something of a legend in the tank transporter world. The Company became 19 Tank Transporter Squadron RCT in 1965, and continued with its tasks from Bulford, until it was decided that the requirement for tank transporters in the UK could be reduced to a one troop task. On 15 June 1977 a farewell parade for 19 Squadron was held at Ward Barracks. The parade was appropriately taken by Major General P H Benson CBE, the DGTM who had previously commanded the unit.

414 Tank Transporter Troop RCT took on the overall tank transporter responsibilities within UK as part of the Logistic support Battalion AMF (L). The unit sign of the Squadron, – XIX – and its number went to BAOR and the squadron in its new

role, was back, resuscitated, to where it had first been disbanded.

Although all the units described have had the sort of problems typical for all units in the Home Base, they were for the most part carried out under normal peacetime conditions. Such was not the case in the whole of the UK, and the following section, Northern Ireland, presents a totally different picture, which can only speak for itself.

NORTHERN IRELAND

SINCE THE PARTITION of Ireland in 1920 the Corps has had a continuous association with Northern Ireland. At the outbreak of World War II 26 and 53 Companies RASC were based in Belfast whilst 54 Company was stationed in Londonderry. Their task was to provide support to a four battalion brigade of infantry, three Irish regimental depots, the North Irish Coastal Defences and detachments of supporting arms. At the conclusion of the war Northern Ireland was re-established as a home station with the Corps commitment reflecting the scale of forces deployed therein. Therefore by 1969, the date at which this chapter begins its tale, much had changed, not least that the Corps had changed its name.

By mid-1969 the level of violence in the Province was becoming unacceptable. Between the 12 and 14 July the rioting in Londonderry and Belfast was so severe that garrison troops of the British Army were alerted in order to intervene if required. The escalation of violence had now taken a significant step. August saw a further deterioration in the situation with ten killings and over sixteen hundred injuries, half of whom had been policemen. Homes and factories were gutted by fire. The Government's reaction to this fast deteriorating situation was to dispatch, very hurriedly, troop reinforcements from 3 Infantry Division and other elements of the Strategic Reserve stationed in the South of England.

The state of emergency which now existed and had led to the move of reinforcements was formally declared on 16 August 1969. At that time it was presumed, certainly by the Protestant majority of the Province, that the events of the previous eighteen months had been inspired and masterminded by the IRA. This is now known not to have been entirely accurate. But although the IRA were not slow to help kindle the situation they had not as yet organized themselves for the long campaign ahead.

The Corps forces in Northern Ireland at this time comprised 26 Squadron and a small Transport and Movements Branch designed to support Northern Ireland District from Lisburn. The garrison by this stage, in the post-war force evolution, was composed of three major units. The squadron was equipped and organized to meet the peacetime military requirements of the Province. The establishment of a 4 ton task troop, a mixed WRAC/soldier car troop and a civilian troop looking after a miscellany of vehicles such as cars, vans and pantechnicons was totally inadequate to meet the sudden demands of a vastly increased garrison. Various temporary measures were taken to strengthen the Movements organization and 60 Squadron commanded by Major Peter Marzetti RCT from 24 Infantry Brigade based in Plymouth and 63 Parachute Squadron commanded by Major John Pitt RCT from 16 Parachute Brigade in Aldershot plus a Troop from 42 Squadron at Catterick were deployed as quickly as possible. Such was the haste to reinforce the distraught Province that elements of 60 Squadron moved direct from France, where they had been training, to Northern Ireland. The modus operandi was for these units to give direct and immediate transport support to infantry units to increase their mobility and flexibility in a very fluid, fraught situation. It is worth noting that a widely held view at the time was that the reinforcing elements would be home 'by Christmas'!

Emergency tours therefore took the form of an indefinite or indeterminate commitment. The stop gap, piecemeal assigning of units for weeks or months was a situation the effects of which plagued the Army for years to come. After the frenzied activities of the period up to the end of the year 1969 it seemed as if the situation was going to improve and stability return to the Province, because in 1970 only 7 Squadron commanded by Major David Fairs RCT from 5 Infantry Brigade in Tidworth and 42 Squadron were required to give additional support. Not only did the low level of violence contribute to this state of affairs but also the introduction of the policy that all Internal Security battalions should have their own integrated transport, sufficient for their needs, manned by their own drivers.

The immediate benefit of this policy was the creation of a totally self sufficient mobile force capable of operating within areas which could be cut off and isolated by temporary barricades. At the beginning of the campaign 4 ton 'soft skin' vehicles were adequate troop carrying vehicles (TCV). Sadly as hostilities dragged on and the conflagration spread and became more vicious, troops needed a safer mode of transport. To fill this requirement relics from previous campaigns in other parts of the world during the late '40s, '50s and early '60s were recovered and resurrected. The Humber one ton armoured troop carriers, last used in Malaya, and the Saracen armoured vehicle used in Aden were assigned the role. During this evolutionary phase in the campaign it was becoming evident that the duration of the army's commitment would have to be measured in terms of years rather than months; that the infantry unit's were very hard pressed and there was a need for more men to be made available for street patrolling and that infantry units were also having difficulty in providing sufficient drivers to man the unit's vehicles. The logical resolution of part of the infantry's problem was the employment of the Corps to drive the armoured vehicles. This however did not take place until 1972.

In the meantime in 1970 whilst the infantry were driving their own expanded fleets of 4 ton vehicles, 416 Troop was formed to provide non-operational transport support for troops in Londonderry. Subsequently this force, located in Shackleton Barracks Ballykelly, became an integral part of 26 Squadron, based in Lisburn. Until the second half of 1971, although the infantry units of the Army were very heavily committed, the Corps as yet had not experienced the demands of unit roulement tours of 4 months duration on anything like the same scale. The principal Corps task at this time was to maintain 26 Squadron and to cope with a considerable volume of movements traffic to and from the Province, although a troop each, both from 65 Squadron in Bulford were assigned to 8 Brigade in Londonderry and 39 Brigade in Belfast. To assist 26 Squadron, the HQ of 65 Squadron plus the remaining troop were assigned as Command Troops to be deployed under the orders of HQ NI. Likewise drivers from 14 Air Despatch Regiment and 18 Amphibious Squadron were allotted to 26 Squadron to bolster it. 'For the first time' since the campaign started 'the RCT had sufficient transport under command to provide proper support'. Thus Lieutenant Colonel Aubrey Evans MBE (now Brigadier) the CRCT HQ NI summed up the situation.

During 1971 there was a change of government, with Edward Heath replacing Harold Wilson. About this time there was also a dramatic deterioration in the situation within the Province. The IRA, which had not been well organized at the outset of the campaign in 1969 but had not been unduly harassed in the interim period, had by now established a sound framework for future effective operation.

During this crucial period in the campaign the impact on the

Corps was immediate. A second squadron was deployed to the Province in March. 65 Squadron was sent out initially to support units in 8 and 39 Brigades, whilst additional drivers from 14 Air Despatch Regiment and 18 Amphibious Squadron were attached to 26 Squadron and the unit renamed 18/26 Squadron. The agitation that resulted from the introduction of internment confirmed the need for this additional squadron for the foreseeable future and signalled the prospect of a continuing regulated commitment. In September 60 Squadron took over from 65 Squadron and significantly arrived with four troops, an increase of two over their predecessors. In November another highly significant development occurred, one that was to have a dramatic impact on the Corps. The TO in C(A) agreed with the GOC Northern Ireland that the RCT would take over the driving of the 1 ton Humber Pigs from the infantry if required.

The growing unrest throughout the Province and the intensity of ground operations undertaken by the infantry soon meant that the proposed role for the Corps became fact. In March 1972, 3 Tank Transporter Squadron from BAOR arrived to take over this new task. At a strength of 196 all ranks they were faced with a formidable task. They were in support of 39 Infantry Brigade which was, and still is, responsible for the Province's largest city, Belfast. They were required to support seven infantry battalions in such a manner that the drivers of the Pigs could react to demands for immediate support to section, platoon or company size operations. The task necessitated that the drivers had the ability to drive their vehicles with unerring judgement, through densely populated areas of Belfast, day or night, to precisely where the unit wished to be delivered, with everyone confident in the knowledge that the vehicle was so well tuned and serviced that it would deliver its load precisely as required. To achieve such support the drivers and NCOs, who controlled various sized fleets deployed around the city, had to become, very quickly, an integral part of the units they supported. Mutual confidence had to be established by proven performance, through a clear understanding of the infantry units task, plus real evidence of all the military skills necessary in urban warfare and an all embracing capacity on the part of each individual to assume in a chameleon like manner the character of the unit being supported.

Such was the nature of the task confronting the first unit to take on the role of Pig driving. Through their unstinting efforts and

[By courtesy of RCT Museum]

A Saracen APC driven by RCT units in Northern Ireland.

thoroughly professional approach there can be no doubt this
unique task for the Corps was impressively launched. This venture
was soon followed by another. In Londonderry a Saracen Support
Troop was formed in April. The nature of the aggression had
altered. The eruptions directed at the troops were becoming so
increasingly vicious and threatening that means had to be devised
to give the foot soldiers protection from their enraged stone and
bottle throwing adversaries and the armed terrorists. Hence the
inhabitants of such infamous enclaves in Londonderry as the
Bogside and the Creggan were soon to see and hear a 1950's-
designed Saracen armoured wheeled troop carrier whine its way
through their districts. Appropriately the first Corps unit to fill this
role was 1 Squadron from Colchester, commanded by Major
Freddie Selleck RCT.

Elsewhere much has been written about the operation and
handling of these vehicles, which were not normally on the Corps
inventory. But this dramatic shift in responsibility, which has had a
fundamental effect on the Corps image and responsibilities within
the Army, highlighted immediately a range of problems which have
beset subsequent units stationed in Northern Ireland. Firstly it was
found that driving and vehicle handling in the Province was a
unique experience. Apart from the mechanical and physical
limitations which characterized both vehicles, driving heavy armoured vehicles with limited visor vision on narrow roads, fringed
with rain soaked hedges and constructed with a pronounced
drainage assisting bevelled camber which seemed to divide and
ribbon their way around the irregularly shaped country holdings
and rise and fall over every ripple on the land, was unquestionably

a supreme test for an eighteen year old soldier who had just obtained his driving licence. In built up areas the scene was no less daunting. Under such circumstances the dangers from road accidents were and continue to be a considerable threat to operations. Despite the magnitude of the problem confronting each driver the vast majority of the accidents are non-attributable to the Army and statistically, by drawing on experience and adjusting training emphasis, the picture has improved over the years. In defence of all drivers it must be stated that whilst the Irish in the Province are generous in so many ways they are loath to fairly share their roads with other users! In addition to driving, weapon handling, shooting skill and confidence in urban warfare skills, drivers required lengthy and patient consideration and practice during training together with a thorough schooling in vehicle care and maintenance. From the outset it was appreciated that this task, if it were to be successfully executed, required a carefully thought out training package. Those who were instrumental in developing and directing the composition, of what was to become a fairly standard format, were wise to appreciate, that because of the likelihood of a changing situation and emphasis in the Province, there must be latitude and room for development and innovation in the training package.

The overriding aim was to ensure that mutual confidence was quickly established between the driver and the unit he was to support. The final principal problem that required attention by all units bound for the Province was a need to create a well organized rear party to look after the wives and alleviate any worries and if possible remove them from the members of the unit in Northern Ireland.

Before mentioning the significant role that Movements were playing, 1972 was far from over for the transport squadrons. The IRA had further developed their hold on the hearts and minds of Catholics north and south of the Border and appeared to have greatly expanded their 'army' and supporting echelons of sympathetic supporters. In a bold display of their increasing confidence 'no go' areas were created in Londonderry and Belfast over which they claimed sovereignty. Naturally this was unacceptable to the Government and Operation Motorman was mounted to regain control of and remove the 'no go' areas. 15 Squadron from Osnabruck under command of Major David Kinnear RCT, which had the task of supporting all the forces deployed in operations in the Border areas, arrived in the Province in July. Soon after arrival the unit was called upon to concentrate its Saracen resources with those of 1 Squadron, already in Londonderry, to support the operation. 110 Saracens were deployed. The operation was successful!

Increasingly, throughout 1972, vehicles were attacked by the IRA. Small arms fire, petrol bombs, high explosive bombs, stones and even paint to obliterate the vehicle visor, were used and continue to be. Inevitably, casualties resulted but generally by wise and discriminate action these were kept to a minimum. It is noteworthy that one of the outstanding features of the Corps operations at this stage was the remarkable tenacity and sense of duty the drivers displayed under increasing psychological and physical pressure. Despite the dangers, the loss of comrades and the demands of operating continuously for long periods, days and weeks with little rest and no break, their resilience was inspiring.

Whilst the transport squadrons became increasingly busy and more resources were being called upon, particularly infantrymen, the Movements staff and operators were exceptionally hard pressed. At this stage of the campaign reinforcements and deployments were being redirected at very short notice. Crisis management seemed to be the norm. All movement of troops in and out of the Province plus the resources to support them were handled by three staff officers at HQ Northern Ireland, a Port Movement Control detachment covering all relevant surface movement through Belfast, Larne and Dundrum Bay and an air transport liaison detachment covering RAF Aldergrove, Aldergrove Civil and Sydenham. The main tasks were:

a. Operational moves (either roulement or emergency) to and from UK or BAOR necessitating a permutation of civil ferry, LSL or RAF Air Support Command aircraft.

b. Routine movement, including container traffic.

c. Leave travel including the processing of the concessional air fare scheme involving 2400 applications per month.

d. All TAVR and cadet camp training (which of necessity had to be undertaken outside the Province).

The following statistics graphically and dramatically illustrate the volume of human traffic alone.

Period	Number of Unit Moves		
	Major	Minor	Others
Jan 69 – Mar 70	26	23	30
Apr 70 – Mar 71	64	40	40
Apr 71 – Mar 72	100	72	24

The total number of passengers for this last period topped the 100,000 mark.

In addition to the frenzied activities involving the APC Squadrons and the Movement Controllers, 18/26 Squadron's responsibilities had expanded to keep up with the increase in forces. It was necessary to provide a sizeable freight service covering the Province, which delivered ordnance stores, fresh meat and POL. Also mobile service teams to 3 and 8 Brigades operated out from the Squadron to help maintain a mixed fleet of multipurpose civilian vehicles which now numbered nearly 500.

During the period of Lieutenant Colonel Aubrey Evans' tour as CRCT Northern Ireland, from 1971 to 1973, the Irish problem exploded and by the beginning of 1973 a grim catalogue of events existed.

In August 1969 serious sectarian violence broke out in Londonderry and Belfast and the police, unable to cope, were assisted by the Army in the restoration of law and order. Stricter security policies were introduced in 1970 to cope with indiscriminate IRA action and their full scale terrorist campaign. In 1971, on 9 August, strongly urged on by local politicians and police the government introduced internment without trial. (An action that lasted until December 1975 and is now seen as having been an imprudent move.) Its real significance was to have an impact long after it ceased as since it by-passed normal legal procedures it conferred a 'political' status on those interned; this in turn stimulated both political and practical support for Republican terrorism and had the reverse effect on the quest for a cessation of violence. 30 January 1972 'Bloody Sunday' in Londonderry happened when 13 civilians were supposedly shot dead by the Army; 21 July 'Bloody Friday' saw the IRA explode 19 bombs in Belfast largely without warning, killing seven civilians, two soldiers and injuring over 130. Operation Motorman on 31 July followed and cleared the barricades around the no-go areas. 1972, with 467 killed and nearly 5,000 injured, had been an appalling year of violence.

| | | Dead | | | | Injured | | |
| | | Reg Army/ | | | | Reg Army/ | | |
Year	RUC	UDR	Civilians	Total	RUC	UDR	Civilians	Total
1969	1	–	12	13	711	22	–	733
1970	2	–	23	25	191	620	–	811
1971	11	48	155	174	315	390	1,887	2,592
1972	17	129	321	467	485	568	3,813	4,866

From this simple catalogue it is easy to register the results of the conflict, but impossible to anticipate what the future held. It seemed, nevertheless, indisputable that the Army were going to be committed indefinitely, unless a dramatic political solution could be found. It was not until the middle of the following year 1973 that the British White Paper on Northern Ireland proposing a new 80 seat Assembly with the power sharing executive was published.

After Operation Motorman and the withdrawal of the additional forces deployed for that operation a degree of pre-eminence seemed to emerge on the side of the Army and the Police. As this was perhaps not immediately apparent and the IRA still held the initiative, force levels continued to rise so that by the time Lieutenant Colonel John Riggall became CRCT in early 1973 there were 1,300 RCT all ranks at regimental and staff duty. Over twenty battalions were deployed.

The framework for Corps operations and procedures which had evolved through the earlier trials and tribulations was continued with the forces deployed capable of being modified, regrouped and redeployed as required. However, one of the major staff problems existing was the plotting of roulement unit tours from both BAOR and UKLF, in such a way that training and other operational commitments, such as UN Cyprus, could be met without exacerbating 'overstretch'. By 1973 the Army had become so heavily committed to Northern Ireland that there was a real danger that the strain on units and individuals or 'overstretch' would lead to a breakdown in morale and a reduction in unit strength from resignations of officers and men. It was this realisation by commanders that created the pressure for a concerted effort to be made to find ways of reducing force levels.

Such an anomaly as the newly acquired General Transport (GT) Squadrons from UKLF (sent to provide the additional general transport needed to assist an overworked 26 Squadron) doing six month tours when the APC Squadrons were doing four months was one of the first problems that had to be resolved. The 'patchwork' commitment of resources to tasks, where possible, also had to be rationalized. That these objectives were partially achieved is best illustrated by the fact that during the two years of Lieutenant Colonel John Riggall's tour as CRCT the Corps force level dropped from the all time high, of 1,300 to just over 1,000 personnel. This momentum for reducing, with occasional interruptions, has been maintained ever since with current levels just below

400. Gaps between unit tours, as little as eight months on average, was another serious problem taxing staff and commanders. The high frequency of tours, when roulement commitments became an established fact, totally disrupted the planned life of a unit. Units in BAOR had to sacrifice individual and collective training. Formation support and training was achievable in some cases only if by coincidence dates overlapped. Divisional regiments in BAOR never functioned as a complete unit, because of the piece-meal commitment to Northern Ireland of its squadrons, for almost five years. Yet rationalizing this situation was immensely difficult, if not impossible, because of the sheer scale of the commitment and the scarcity of resources. Such were the pressures that plagued the CRCT and commanders at all levels then and to a lesser degree now.

Numerically road transport accounted for almost all the RCT in the Province. The 'Movers' were a mere handful, less than twenty strong even when temporarily reinforced for particular operations yet their importance to the campaign was out of all proportion to the numbers. With most units on four month emergency tours the amount of routine movement in and out of the Province was very considerable. In 1973 169,000 personnel were moved – broadly the strength of the entire Army. The bulk of the passenger movement was by air through Aldergrove with a significant minority (38%) by sea. Most freight and vehicles were moved by sea, either by Landing Ship Logistic (LSL), one of which was permanently on station at Liverpool, or by the civilian ferries. The small Movement staff at HQ Northern Ireland under an SO2 (Mov) with two other officers and a mixed military and civilian staff, did all the planning and the booking with the civilian agencies. The Movement staff worked very closely with G (Operations) and G (Staff Duties) at the HQ and with all units in the Province. A daily three way telephone conference was held between the Ministry of Defence (Q (Movements) 2), HQ BAOR (Movements) and the Staff Captain (Air) during which air movement by RAF was arranged and late changes to the flying programme negotiated.

The CRCT found that Movement matters occupied far more of the attention of the Chief of Staff and Colonel AQ than those affecting transport. Transport support was taken for granted whereas Movement considerations affected every operation and the morale and well being of every soldier in the Province. The one precious long weekend at home during a four month tour hinged entirely around the travel arrangements and when they were interrupted by weather or mechanical problems it was a serious matter. Force levels were so sensitive that one leave party had to be back in the Province before the next could leave and the smooth flow of ships and aircraft was of daily interest to all concerned.

Similar considerations applied to battalion changeovers. It was tactically necessary to keep up the strength in company bases so every changeover of a unit was in effect, a relief in-the-line. Any hitch in the smooth flow of aircraft or ships therefore had a critical effect. Aldergrove was prone to fog although this was usually of limited duration. More difficult was the notorious weather in the Irish Sea. At sea a storm merely meant an uncomfortable voyage. It was at Liverpool however where the greatest difficulty lay. The locks, through which the LSL had to pass, were very tight and a strong wind from the wrong direction sometimes meant the LSL, with its high keel surface and flat bottom, was unable to lock in or out. With half a battalion and all their vehicles on board many a battalion changeover was put at risk.

As the campaign settled into a niche in British military history, with no immediate solution evident and the tempo of operations demanding at least 100 hours per week from everyone involved, cooperation and mutual support developed new bounds, with the Corps cast in the infantry role. During 1971 serious consideration had actually been given to the RCT taking their place on the Arms Group Roster in the infantry role. 10 Regiment RCT had been given a warning order and planning for the training was well advanced when it was decided that the Corps most valuable contribution would be to drive the APCs for all Arms. Nevertheless units actually in Ulster were frequently called upon to act as infantry for short periods. Drivers attached to battalions invariably joined foot patrols when not required to drive and the GT Squadron provided complete troops for up to a fortnight at a time. This need usually arose in 3 Infantry Brigade during a specific operation and the Troops were placed under command of the battalion concerned. They normally operated as a self contained unit and carried out a wide variety of tasks varying from the manning of static vehicle check points (VCPs) on the border crossings, through snap VCPs set up for a limited period, to active foot patrolling. While operating in the infantry role, task vehicles naturally had to be grounded and the decision to do this was invariably taken personally by the Commander Land Forces. The drivers enjoyed the change of role although they were usually pleased to return to driving, as much of the infantry work was monotonous and repetitive, once the novelty had worn off.

In Belfast, other than taking part as individuals in patrols, most of the non-driving work was in the docks searching incoming cargo containers for weapons and explosives, a task normally carried out by a special unit who called for assistance when they needed reinforcement. 1973 came to an end with the Sunningdale Conference in December affirming that the constitutional status of Northern Ireland could only be changed by the consent of the majority; and it also agreed to set up a Council of Ireland.

By 1973 the APCs were deployed as follows:

Unit	Size (Troops)	Formation	Location (SHQ)
Squadron	7	39 Brigade	Moscow Camp Belfast
Squadron	2	8 Brigade	Londonderry
Squadron	3	3 Brigade	Ballykinler

In 1973 despite a slight decrease in numbers, the average mileage (again excepting the December ceasefire) was still 116,000 miles. Hard pressed infantry company commanders with fewer vehicles and larger company areas merely used them harder in compensation.

The APCs were on the whole remarkably effective in their role. Only in the rural areas were they being used for the sort of task for which they were originally designed, but even in the narrow and crowded streets of Belfast and Londonderry they performed adequately. Their use without doubt reduced casualties from small arms fire and when mined they provided much better protection than Land Rovers and other soft skinned vehicles. Their major weakness was against anti-tank weapons, principally the Russian RPG 7. Fortunately few of these were in the hands of the IRA and when used were often captured soon after.

Many lessons were learnt or re-learnt about operating APCs – the RASC had an APC squadron in BAOR in the late 1940's – but without doubt the greatest benefit was to section commanders. The very large number of small detachments manned by a section or less meant that, once deployed, squadron and troop commanders could exert little immediate influence. The infantry company commander looked to the RCT section commander to produce the support he required and it was up to the junior NCO concerned to

[By courtesy of PR HQ Northern Ireland]

RCT 'Pigs' at an incident in Belfast.

respond. Young (and some not so young) Corporals, who in the confines of barracks or on heavily controlled exercises in BAOR had never really had the opportunity of being totally responsible for their command, found themselves completely on their own. In almost every case they reacted well, thrived on the responsibility and gained enormously in confidence, capability and pro-fessionalism from their tours. The few that failed were often the older junior NCOs who, knowing how to play the system, had avoided being found out in peace. The pressures of Ulster exposed their weaknesses very quickly. Squadron commanders also had the opportunity of getting to know their men in a way that was not possible in barracks and many young soldiers were quickly identified as outstanding potential leaders.

Workshop support was provided by the APC Workshops REME at Moscow Camp with detachments at Ballykinler and Londonderry in support of the other two squadrons. With over 400 Saracens and Humber 1 ton vehicles, many of which were fifteen or more years old, they had a major task in keeping the fleet serviceable. It was a large workshop, 100 strong, which worked continuous twelve hour shifts day and night throughout the year.

Availability was always high and invariably well exceeded the theoretical operational requirement of 70% on which both the manpower and spares scaling were based.

The whole APC organization was supported by a small staff at Moscow Camp of a technical QM, an SQMS and a Master Driver (APC's). Overall control was the responsibility of the SO2 (Tpt) on CRCT's staff who, with many other equally important tasks to be done, could only devote a very limited amount of his time to APC's. A case for the appointment of a Deputy to command the APC's with over 800 soldiers and the 450 APC's deployed in some 70 locations, was first rejected by the Ministry of Defence in 1973 but was to be accepted in 1974. The first Deputy CRCT, Commander APC's, was Lieutenant Colonel Philip Bulpin RCT who had already served as SO2 Movements HQ Northern Ireland. He assumed the appointment in January 1974 and the Corps APC strength peaked at 490 vehicles the next month. But there was now capacity and resources for proper long term planning and controlled use of the APC fleet. These vehicles, already elderly in 1974, are still in active use. That this is so owes much to the establishment of the post of Commander APC's and a proper support staff to monitor the equipment management.

The operational use of APC's continued to be dictated by local conditions and by tactical and political considerations, often their use was held to be 'provocative' and consequently from time to time useage was restricted.

By 1974 the casualty statistics were down and still going down:-

	DEATHS				INJURED			
	Reg Army				Reg Army			
Year	RUC	UDR	Civilians	Total	RUC	UDR	Civilians	Total
1972	17	129	321	467	485	568	3,813	4,866
1973	13	66	171	250	291	548	1,812	2,651
1974	15	35	166	216	235	483	1,680	2,398

Likewise the number of military personnel on the move to and from the Province was down by over 20,000 from the 1973 peak of 169,000.

So far no mention has been made of the activities of the RCT Troop that supported the Royal Engineers, Province wide. Like many of the tasks undertaken by the Corps it evolved out of a need to release drivers from the Arms units so their trade skills could be used to bolster up the Army's limited resources. The Troop headquarters and three sections were based at Antrim Bridging

Camp, collocated with a field squadron in support of 39 Brigade. One section comprised one 30 ton Scammell tractor and semi-trailer, four 20 ton Scammell Constructor tractors, three 20 ton Tasker trailers, two 10 ton tilt trailers and an AEC medium recovery vehicle. The second section at Antrim consisted of the Troop Commander's Land Rover, a Ferret scout car, three 4 ton Bedford RLs, one of which was fitted with a 2 ton HIAB crane, and a Leyland Comet pre-mix concrete truck. Antrim's third section, which until the end of July was attached to Belfast's Girdwood Park, consisted of six Aveling Barford dump trucks, and a 10 ton AEC tipper. In addition there were two detached sections, one at Castledillon with the field squadron in support of 3 Infantry Brigade, and one at Ballykelly with 8 Infantry Brigade. The composition of these two differed from each other and from the Antrim based sections. The section at Castledillon just north of Armagh comprised five 4 ton Bedford RLs, one fitted with a HIAB crane, an Aveling Barford and a 20 ton Scammell tractor and Tasker trailer. The section at Ballykelly, just east of Londonderry, had two Bedford RLs and two Aveling Barfords, one of which was on permanent standby at Ebrington Barracks, on the outskirts of Londonderry.

The RCT strength was gradually reduced from twelve troops to nine during the year and the number of APCs shrunk to around 320. This reduction was achieved by withdrawing detachments when battalions left the Province without being relieved. Significantly the mileage covered did not reduce in proportion. During 1974, with the exception of the 'Christmas truce' month of December the APCs averaged 127,000 miles per month.

The truce lasted until 19 January but was reintroduced on 9 February with 'Incident Centres' manned by Provisional IRA and Government officials. Their task was to monitor the very fragile ceasefire. This situation survived until 7 April when the IRA decided to abandon the ceasefire, as it was deemed by them to have served its purpose. On 24 July the Secretary of State Merlyn Rees announced the phasing out of internment which was completed by 5 December. The low level of activity resulting from the periods of ceasefire gave promise to the hope that there would be a sharp decline in death and injury from terrorist activities. This sadly was not to be, instead there were fifty more civilians killed, although fewer RUC and soldiers, than the previous year. Nevertheless the pressure to reduce force levels continued inexorably. To achieve any Corps reductions it was necessary to convince the infantry that they no longer needed their protective vehicle. Interestingly in some of the discussions at unit level it was clear that the vehicle could be removed but not the driver. It reflected great credit not only on the driver's ability to integrate so successfully, but on those responsible for his Northern Ireland training. Fortunately, the entire Army was suffering the ills of overstretch and repeated tours to the Province, and therefore workable readjustments and compromise solutions designed to ease the pressure on any element in Northern Ireland were normally quickly accepted and implemented.

To achieve these reductions it became necessary, as a matter of policy, for all the Corps elements and the APC force and GT units in particular to be interoperable when possible. It also meant that a Corps unit earmarked as an 'on call' reinforcement, known as 'Spearhead', and residing outside the Province had to be capable of very rapid induction and deployment. These reinforcements to the modus operandi of the Corps were very significant and admirable developments that were a feature during 1975 and 1976. That units were capable of being so flexible as to change roles, locations and theatres at very short notice highlighted not only that there existed a great depth of experience but that the finely tuned training package everyone was undergoing was correct.

Lieutenant Colonel Peter Evans RCT and Lieutenant Colonel Peter Shields RCT as the Commanding Officers of the APCs during this period were instrumental in achieving the harmonisation and flexibility necessary to convince everyone that reductions and changes were not only working well but were necessary. From the 490 APC that existed when Lieutenant Colonel Philip Bulpin RCT set up the APC Force Headquarters in 1972 the APC levels had more than halved to 225.

39 Brigade		8 Brigade		3 Brigade	
Saracens	Humber	Saracens	Humber	Saracens	Humber
22	107	16	20	60	—

As part of the reorganisation the country squadron, supporting 3 Brigade, moved its Headquarters from Ballykinler to St Angelo in mid 1975. Also that year the expansion of Moscow Camp continued and it began to acquire an air of respectability and

[By courtesy of PR HQ Northern Ireland]

An Explosives Ordnance Detachment RAOC driven by members of 21 Squadron RCT opposite City Hall Belfast.

permanence so that it could accommodate those who had previously lived on HMS *Maidstone* in Belfast Dock, such as Spearhead units and the RN contingent.

Major Alan Tapp, commanding 18/26 Squadron, found like his predecessors and successors his greatest challenge in command was to ensure that his officers and men survived the frantic pace and pressures of working within an operational theatre, at the same time as experiencing a satisfactory quotient of normality. Whilst roulement units from BAOR and Great Britain had to cope with separation and very long arduous work schedules, four and a half months of it can be handled by most. In contrast two years of operations, although accompanied by their families, is a long stint and the importance of creating some form or signs of normality were of incalculable value. When it became practical to make changes to the Corps operations, the resident unit thrived on any break to their heavy routine schedule. Although it was never an established squadron policy to search for trouble, drivers were shot at and confronted by the IRA. One instance of note involved Lance Corporal Frazer who was in plain clothes and about to collect someone from a local hotel. On arrival he was greeted by an IRA gang who were planting bombs. Immediately he was 'arrested' and searched. His survival was due to the, much argued and debated, squadron policy that no weapons would be carried on such routine duties. The topic never appeared on any agenda nor was it discussed again!

After a year which had promised so much beginning as it did with a truce, but ending with 247 people killed, it was hoped that the cessation of internment in December 1975 would have some success in the political arena. However the year that was beginning was to prove as busy as its predecessor and there was little scope for realignment or adjustment of resources. The commitment by resident and roulement troops was as unrelenting as before. 18/26 Squadron became more involved in IS Duties, in particular they were called upon to deploy vehicle and foot patrols in the Lisburn area. 3 Squadron returned from Sennelager for the fifth time since they had opened the batting as the first APC Squadron in March 1972. Major Bob Blackman was the squadron commander, who had also been in charge when the squadron had 'visited' the Province less than twelve months previously, in the same role. Typical tasks for the APC units at this stage in the campaign were:

> Post Office delivery escort throughout Belfast.
> Mobile patrols, Army and RUC.
> Vehicle check points – planned and snap.
> Movement of Court witnesses.
> Deployment of the Palace Barracks battalion into Belfast.
> Route closure during the marching season – June to September normally.
> Change over of guards on key points.
> Operation of all Ammunition Technical Officer's vehicles.
> When the APCs were not being used it was not unusual for RCT drivers to drive infantry unit Landrovers on mobile patrols.

In the country the squadron moved location from St Angelo Camp near Enniskillen to HM The Maze Prison near Lisburn and assumed the added responsibility of providing part of the prison defence force. Another change was the departure of Lieutenant Colonel Peter Shield and the arrival of Lieutenant Colonel Paul Fear in July. It turned out that he was to be the last Commander APC, as events in the following year were to dictate a further reorganization. In the meantime he became very involved in the vehicle management and development field as new equipment and replacement models for the present family of APCs were being considered. He also got caught up in the final development of Moscow Camp as the joint base for the RCT in Belfast and the RN in Northern Ireland, as well as being transit accommodation for roulement infantry and 'Spearhead' units.

Strenuous activity on the political front still produced little or no change on the ground. However the tragic murder of the British Ambassador to Ireland Christopher Ewart-Biggs on 21 July and the two quite unconnected responses north and south of the Border, firstly the birth of the Peace People movement the following month, then the Eire Government declaring a national state of emergency and introducing stricter security measures against terrorism in September, raised hope that sense was at last prevailing. But once again the casualty statistics gave lie to that:–

		DEATHS					INJURED		
		Reg Army					Reg Army		
Year	RUC	UDR	Civilians	Total		RUC	UDR	Civilians	Total
1974	15	35	166	216		235	483	1,680	2,398
1975	11	20	216	247		263	167	2,044	2,474
1976	23	29	245	297		303	264	2,162	2,729

The Movements staff and teams continued to be extremely busy particularly to meet the 'Spearhead' movements that took place on 'special' occasions. The number of personnel moved during 1976 exceeded 200,000. Another significant statistic was that by the end of 1976 only 160 APCs were being manned, a reduction of 65 over 1975.

In a policy study which became known as the 'Way Ahead' it was decided that the time was right to gradually transfer supremacy for the prosecution for acts of terrorism from the Army to the Royal Ulster Constabulary. This was a major political step and indicated to everyone that the Army, after so many years of sustaining the brunt of the burden of maintaining law and order in the Province, were now able to revert to their rightful original role of being in support of the police, when required.

As the new policy was beginning to manifest itself it seemed almost appropriate that Lieutenant Colonal Arnold Lewis, who had steered the Corps through the trauma of the last two very busy years, should hand over to a new CRCT. In May Lieutenant Colonel Ian Jones took over at a time of an undoubted shift in fortunes in the Province.

The effect of this 'Way Ahead' policy was to cause a sporadic reduction in military activity, an overall decrease in military manpower from the Regular Army on roulement tours and a closure of many of the well known and perhaps infamous bases in the rural as well as urban areas. At the beginning of the period the RCT numbered 1189 all ranks of which about 75% were on roulement tours, the rest on postings of any duration from 6 to 30 months. The organization was as follows:

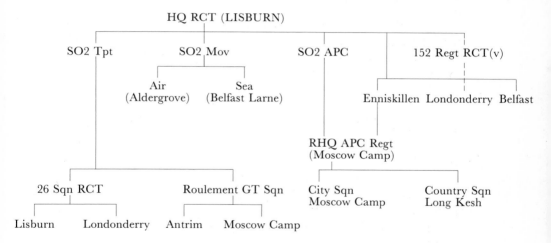

HQ RCT (LISBURN)

SO2 Tpt — SO2 Mov — SO2 APC — 152 Regt RCT(v)

Air (Aldergrove) — Sea (Belfast Larne)

Enniskillen Londonderry Belfast

RHQ APC Regt (Moscow Camp)

26 Sqn RCT — Roulement GT Sqn

City Sqn Moscow Camp — Country Sqn Long Kesh

Lisburn Londonderry Antrim Moscow Camp

It was to change quite significantly both in organization and numbers by 1979.

The opportunity for a reduction in commitment and thus a claw back of roulement personnel was quickly seized upon by both the Chief Transport and Movements Officer United Kingdom Land Forces (CTMO UKLF) and the Commander Corps Royal Corps of Transport 1 British Corps (CCRCT 1 (BR) Corps). The outcome of the negotiations, was, in brief, that UKLF lost its RCT general transport squadron roulement and Chief Transport and

Movements Officer British Army of the Rhine (CTMO BAOR) was to provide a much reduced GT troop.

This reorganization was accomplished by reducing the Corps tasks in parallel with that of the 'combat' areas. A complete reappraisal of the RCT support given in the province produced many surprising facts, which, when simplified showed once again the complete reluctance of both brigade and battalion commanders to offer up any RCT soldiers. They grudgingly admitted that in many areas of operations they rarely used the APCs but the Corps drivers were invaluable. Clearly then, with this attitude, commendable though it was, some compromise had to be agreed and thus the Commander Land Forces had to adjudicate and order that RCT drivers should only be used in their proper role. As a result the APC troop stationed at Ballykinler in support of the Province Reserve moved to join its Squadron HQ at Long Kesh and was reduced to 13 Saracens which were to be driven by Squadron HQ maintenance and servicing personnel. The GT roulement troop at Antrim Bridge Camp, in support of the Royal Engineers, driving a variety of Engineer owned vehicles, were withdrawn and replaced by a section of ten from 26 Squadron RCT. Further smaller but significant reductions were made throughout the Province producing a much more balanced troop to task ratio. In spite of this the APCs were only being used for 12% of their available time and in locations such as Forkhill only warmed up daily which caused occasional breakdown problems.

The introduction of the first roulement regiment RCT in March with Lieutenant Colonel David Whall and 4 Armoured Divisional Transport Regiment RCT with its RHQ in Moscow Camp, required a change in the camp organization. In Moscow Camp lived the roulement troop of the GT squadron, the city APC squadron and the REME Workshops supporting both units, as well as the shore based Royal Naval detachment Northern Ireland and the unique court witnesses section whose task was to administer the many thousands of servicemen – most of whom were now civilians – returning to give evidence in the civil courts. This placed a considerable administrative burden on the permanent camp staff whose task was not helped by having to live alongside a roulement commanding officer who naturally wished to exercise in full his command responsibilities. The latter problem was solved by appointing the CRCT Northern Ireland to be the Commanding Officer of the camp staff and responsible for the camp accounts. To complete the rationalization of the establishment of the camp a full tour (of two years) staff was authorised and the Camp Commandant and Staff Officer Grade 2 (SO2) APC, both RCT, were appointed. They both answered directly to the CRCT.

In addition to housing a variety of units and 'cap badges', Moscow Camp continued to be the Northern Ireland transit camp for many units, mainly those on emergency tours as reinforcements to the City of Belfast for a short period. To meet this commitment accommodation for a battalion was available at twelve hours' notice. The daily task of the RCT was to continue with little change, except that the emphasis was slowly changing from APC support to GT support as the intensity of operations reduced. In late April just as Lieutenant Colonel Lewis was handing over to Lieutenant Colonel Jones the duties of CRCT, The Ulster United Action Council, (UUAC) threatened a total loyalist strike starting on 2 May. This strike was to protest about the reduction in military activity and to try to force the Government to alter its policy on security. Reaction was swift; 3,200 reinforcements were moved into the Province. The airlift into RAF Aldergrove was longer than that for 'Op Motorman' with 125 sorties arriving during a forty eight hour period. The Movements organization consisted of twenty four RAF personnel and one Army sergeant. The latter was reinforced by the addition of the SO3 (Air). At the docks RFA *Sir Lancelot* discharged three times during that week and RFA *Sir Bedivere*, retasked from an amphibious exercise in the Hebrides anchored in Belfast Lough, in support, should the surface line of communications be disrupted by strike action.

The Corps involvement in the Military Aid to Civil Ministries (MACM) support, was, to be prepared to maintain the distribution of essential fuel supplies to roadside fuel stations, hospitals and essential industry. Clearly the organic GT support was stretched to the limit coping with the influx of reinforcements. RHQ 3 Armoured Divisional Transport Regiment RCT from Bulford was therefore ordered to the Province to direct the 'oil' operation under the command of the CRCT. This RHQ was on exercise in the North of England when the order to move came. To their credit they returned to Bulford, packed and were in Moscow Camp within 24 hours.

Lieutenant Colonel Peter Evans commanded 3 Armoured Division Transport Regiment RCT at that time, but he had also served in Ulster during the previous industrial strike. With his expertise, and those servicemen from all three services who had the technical skills to run an oil refinery, 120 RCT drivers with HGV 2 or 1 driving licences drawn from all over the Province, and an Infantry battalion to escort road tankers, the scene was set to take over the oil distribution system as directed by civil government. With so many RCT drivers committed to additional IS tasks and MACM, extra drivers had to be found to carry out the more routine GT tasks. The solution was simple, twenty four vehicles with their drivers were withdrawn from units all over the Province and amalgamated into a 4 ton GT troop working from Moscow Camp under the direction of the Officer Commanding 26 Squadron RCT. Fortunately the will to pursue industrial disruption was quickly sapped and the plans to take over the refinery were not tested. But procedures and tasks had again been thought through and refined – they were to be put to very effective use later.

One interesting problem that was solved during this period, was that of maintaining furnace oil stocks in the security force bases. The Corps took delivery of fifteen World War II 800 gallon Bedford OY tankers and five new Foden 22,000 litre Trucks Tanker Fuel (TTFs); the fuel being provided from the side tanks of the LSLs pumping direct into the road tankers. The troop of 60 Squadron RCT detailed to drive the tankers almost rebelled when they saw the aged machines. Their concern was such that they forgot to 'first parade' service them once off loaded from RFA *Sir Lancelot*, with the result that they all ran out of petrol within a mile from Belfast docks. 3am and the usual Belfast rain – a lesson not soon forgotten. The strike over, all reinforcements returned rather more slowly from whence they came, by LSL and civil shipping. But the road tankers remained, should they be required again. While they waited, they provided extra fuel storage in RAOC Kinnegar and were used to deliver fuel to those Security Force bases to which civilian drivers refused to go.

In August 1977 the Queen visited the Province as part of her Jubilee celebrations. The planning for the visit was done with utmost secrecy with the Army keeping an extremely low profile. The outline plan was that the Queen would live aboard Her Majesty's Yacht *Britannia* anchored off the North coast, and fly by Royal Flight Wessex helicopter to engagements at Hillsborough Castle, and to Coleraine University the following day. The Royal Land Rover was driven by Sergeant Hitchcock of 26 Squadron RCT. This was the only outward sign of Corps involvement in Her Majesty's visit.

On the IS front West Belfast was erupting yet again with rioting and street violence. 2 Armoured Divisional Transport Regiment RCT commanded by Lieutenant Colonel Mike Turner was the roulement regiment and his city squadron was truly blooded during this period.

One of the more routine operations undertaken by 26 Squadron RCT was the unloading of engineer stores for the rebuild of Crossmaglen and Forkhill Security Force bases. At two or three month intervals the Squadron would move over a 48 hour period some 3000 tons or more of building materials from the Engineer Park at Castledillon, into South Armagh. Timing was of great importance as it required two IS battalions to clear, hold and sweep the Lines of Communication (L of C) before the squadron moved down. A detailed through running plan utilizing fifty to sixty vehicles of all types including hired 20 ton capacity tippers was put into effect; the drivers resting only during the loading and offloading periods. It is a great compliment to 26 Squadron's skill and discipline that not one casualty occurred during the three years of this operation.

Even now vehicle movement in South Armagh is permitted only by APCs in the vicinity of the SF bases, the risk of culvert mines being assessed as too high. Thus day to day replenishment of the bases at Forkhill and Crossmaglen is carried out by support helicopters of the Royal Air Force. These helicopters lifting underslung loads and operating from Bessbrook Mill forward operating base fly over two hundred hours a month giving logistic support to the border bases.

The emphasis on GT support and the flexibility required by the RCT driver was again put to the test when the Government ordered the Army to counter the firemen's strike in December. 26 Squadron RCT collected twenty three Civil 'Green Goddess' fire engines from Scotland drove them to Lisburn and got down to the task of learning the fireman's trade. Joined by the Black Watch who were to crew the vehicles they deployed throughout Belfast and for six weeks provided an efficient fire service in the capital. Despite this extra commitment of a troop of fifty two fire fighters the squadron maintained its services to the rest of the Province. Christmas leave was cancelled and all but essential work cancelled or postponed.

Before moving on to describe the events of 1978 it should be noted that on 1 March 1977 18 Squadron RCT was disbanded. For five years Squadron HQ and one troop had been deployed in Northern Ireland to bolster up 26 Squadron. The acceptance of a redesigned establishment for 26 Squadron resulted in this small but vital element being written out of the Order of Battle. The Squadron which was originally formed in 1878 as 18 Commissariat Depot and had a number of different roles in its history, was reformed later in 1977 as 18 Maritime Squadron at Gosport as part of 17 Port and Maritime Regiment, an appropriate development as its post war service up until Northern Ireland had been in the amphibious role.

The APC Regiments who served in Ulster during 1978 were staffed by many who had previous experience in the Province. All agreed that to date it had been the quietest tour so far and there was optimism that perhaps the end of or certainly a marked decline in the IRA's fortunes was not too far away. Undoubtedly the tempo of operations was down, casualties were down and the Police were more and more assertive and more able to cope without the massive support of the Army. This apparent lull, because history indicated that trouble could be sparked off very quickly, was utilised to examine the Corps organization to see how further reductions might be achieved. Before any major alterations could be approved, positive proof was needed that the SF could react to a sudden conflagration and that they possessed sufficient in-theatre reserves and reaction capability. Everyone was very conscious of how disruptive 'Spearhead' deployments were. It became evident as the year progressed that not sufficient proof existed to make any changes yet.

Christmas 1978 brought the biggest test for the Corps in this period, when once again civil disruption of the oil and transport industry was threatened by a strike of drivers of the Transport and General Workers Union (TGWU) for higher pay, this time on a national basis. As little specialist reinforcement could be expected, the Corps was tasked to provide the maximum available skilled resources, although extra troops for escort duties and vehicles requiring HGV III qualified drivers could be brought in if absolutely necessary. Plans were made with the civil government initially, without consultation with CRCT staff, but it soon became clear that the point of contact between the government agencies and the oil industry had to be through HQ RCT. Many clandestine meetings were held to finalise the plan, and to determine the capacity of the Army to deliver fuels. This of course depended on so many imponderables that the only answer was to wait and see. The number of tankers that could be used was dictated by the number of escorts, Land Rovers and radios that could be made available for the escorts. The plan laid down that each tanker or convoy of tankers would require an escort vehicle with five guards both front and rear. As the threatened strike was from the drivers, the problem in planning was whether or not refinery personnel both management and workers would stay at work and provide the expertise to keep the fuel pipes open. Unlike the 1974 strike and that threatened in the UUAC debacle in 1977, there was no intention by Government of taking over and operating the refinery. There were not the personnel with the expertise to look after the intricate machinery in the refinery complex and not unnaturally the management were loth to have the Army meddling, or threatening to take over any part of their organization. By Christmas the plans were ready and reinforcement troops from Great Britain stood by. The national negotiations seemed to be successful but the Northern Irish TGWU were being very intransigent in their demands for higher pay rates.

The infantry reinforcements were two companies of the 1st Battalion Argyll and Sutherland Highlanders from Catterick and one company each from the Green Howards and 3 Royal Anglian Regiment, both 39 Brigade units, and the reinforcing RCT Squadron, 60 Squadron RCT also from Catterick garrison. Their advance parties had arrived in Moscow Camp before Christmas, the remainder on twelve hours notice to move by air or sea. Christmas and New Year were spent in barracks, but by 4 January with negotiations deadlocked, the movement order was given and they arrived in the Province and into Moscow Camp. The plan was now to be put into operation. This hybrid unit of a newly formed very trim HQ, four infantry companies and one RCT Squadron was commanded by Lieutenant Colonel John MacDonald, then the roulement APC Regiment (the Commanding Officer of 4 Armoured Divisional Transport Regiment RCT). The Headquarters was set up in the special office accommodation in Moscow Camp and a command and liaison team headed by Major Pat Carolan, then the SO2 APC, was ready to move a short distance from Moscow Camp into the refinery and control the allocation, filling up and movement of the requisitioned tanker fleet. The drivers were provided, in the main, by 16 Tank Transporter Squadron RCT who fortunately were on their roulement tour in the GT role.

Fortunately because here was a squadron of predominantly HGV 1 drivers, who had been trained during the preceding weeks on tanker operations. Demonstrating the Corps flexibility, 16 Tank Transporter Squadron RCT handed over their province wide GT tasks to 60 Squadron RCT whilst they concentrated on the 'fuel' problem. The actual requisitioning of the BP, Shell and Esso tanker fleets was the responsibility of the Department of Trade. This was done at 0300 hours on Friday 5 January. Regimental Sergeant Major Streeter of 4 Armoured Divisional Transport Regiment RCT with 16 Squadron RCT drivers took over the fleets and assembled then all on the main BP vehicle park adjacent to the refinery and conveniently opposite Moscow Camp. The entire plan was carried out without incident and by 0730 hours the first tankers were being filled and ready to move. However civil government officials were not quite so efficient and direction was not received until 1030 hours.

The distribution system operated so smoothly that by Sunday afternoon 240,000 gallons had been delivered with only one incident. This happened, as might be expected in the Bogside area of Londonderry, in which was situated the city's gas works. The production of gas required a highly volatile liquid Naphtha and this was rapidly running out. Despite a prior agreement that the Army would not handle dangerous products a request was accepted to move the Naphtha to Londonderry and 88,000 litres in two runs of two vehicles was delivered within twenty four hours. Both vehicles and their windscreens were stoned and smashed leaving the Bogside on the first run. The weather conditions could not have been worse, with ice on the roads and freezing fog for most of the time. In spite of this no accidents occurred at all, to the amazement of the oil industry road managers. A wonderful compliment to the skill and discipline of the RCT. The whole operation was so successful that the strikers agreed to return to work on the Monday. The tankers were cleaned and replaced in their respective parks by 0300 hours on 9 January and by the end of that week Moscow Camp returned to 'normal'.

Whilst the fuel delivery operation was underway in Belfast, 26 Squadron RCT were standing by for a similar one in Londonderry. However they were not required, for the drivers at the Shell Depot in Londonderry stayed at work, but the squadron had other problems. It had to operate a through trucking service from the UK RAOC depots into the Province to overcome the effects of the

TGWU hauliers strike. 40 ton tractors and trailers were hired in UK and a team of 26 Squadron RCT drivers operated round the clock using the Larne/Stranraer ferry for cross Irish Sea movement. They managed to keep the Army fully supplied with all essential items at a cost far lower than the normal civil delivery means. As well as this they operated a fuel delivery service using the service tankers remaining from the 1977 dispute and, as before, fuel was taken from the LSLs until the takeover of the refinery when fuels could than be drawn from there. Perhaps on reflection every operation went too smoothly, for the civil government began to believe that the Army had the ability and capacity to take over the entire fuel distribution system as well as that of the local hauliers when they threatened to strike. Clearly this could not be done, as it is not a task the Corps is qualified or trained to perform. Certainly the drivers who took part prided themselves on their ability but they did not enjoy it.

One of the most productive branches of the Army must be the HQ RCT Northern Ireland Movements cell. With a staff of 15 they are particularly busy. Their annual total throughput of passengers is just under half that of BAOR. During this period two distinct factors caused changes in emphasis for the Movements staff. The first was the change to total reliance on containers for civil freight movement. Secondly, there was a switch from civil surface movement to civil air for all troops and their dependants proceeding on leave or duty to the UK mainland. Container movement for the bulk of RAOC freight was of course a natural progression and little military managerial time was required to control the flow. The movement of passengers on the other hand required a total involvement in the processing of travel applications, booking of seats and monitoring eventual movement. As a result of discussions with the major airlines operating out of Aldergrove to UK, and particularly the major carrier British Airways, agreement was reached on a return fare which permitted all military passengers on duty or leave to travel by civil air. The major impact was that single soldiers who hitherto had not been able to travel home because of the time factor, were now able to take long weekends away from the Province. Travelling time to, say, Exeter by surface routes return is 36 hours – by air just four. The agreement initially with British Airways was signed in December 1978 and implemented in January 1979. British Airways increased their booking staff at HQ RCT Northern Ireland to three and installed a further Visual Display Unit (VDU) to their British Airways Booking computer at West Drayton. In addition to handle the problem of onward movement by rail, British Rail introduced a booking clerk who could issue tickets with those of the airlines. Thus any serviceman who applied for travel could receive all the tickets necessary to take him to his home and back.

Apart from the HQ Movements staff, those responsible for manning the ports of entry, the docks, airfield and beaches, should never be forgotten. Despite long hours often in adverse weather conditions and always with the threat of terrorist action the Movements staff working on their own never failed to perform their duty with total competence and cheerfulness.

MOVEMENT STATISTICS

	Freight			Passengers			
Year	Vehicles	Tons	Containers	RAF	Civil Air	LSL	Civil Sea
1975	7,325	10,839	NIL	41,111	49,797	18,199	26,017
1976	8,255	7,469	75	45,690	51,452	18,746	88,272
1977	8,944	2,087	428	48,210	48,196	18,428	93,781
1978	12,400	4,000	1,500	44,400	47,300	10,800	110,000
1979	13,220	600	8,084	36,839	110,167	11,137	54,587

A comparison of the responsibilities of the Northern Ireland HQ RCT Movement Branch with that of other areas shows that the Northern Ireland staff are answerable to the General Staff. The Movements Operations Centre was in times of crisis an extension of the G Ops centre.

The support given by 26 Squadron RCT and the roulement GT Squadrons was fairly consistent over the years. 26 Squadron RCT averaged 3½ million miles a year which is the highest mileage for any RCT squadron in peacetime. However 26 Squadron RCT was permanently on an operational footing. Its drivers always arrived on duty and despite never quite knowing where any hostile attack might come from, maintained high morale and the majority of them expressed a wish to stay on in Ulster for an extra tour. These requests were usually refused on the grounds that two years or more in such an environment was liable to have a debilitating effect.

The Squadron was tasked to improve its standards of VIP protection and to this end a course lasting one month was given to all the drivers who would be driving VIPs. The VIPs did of course have armoured staff cars – Ford Granadas – which could withstand small arms fire, grenades and to some extent culvert bombs. They were extensively equipped with radio and other security items and the drivers of them were rightly very proud of their work. Fifteen drivers were so trained and kept up to date with weekly practice in the specialized skills. In addition the Squadron kept twenty-four drivers trained in APC operating procedures should the roulement regiment become temporarily overwhelmed with APC tasking and require assistance.

The Warren Point massacre of 18 soldiers on route from Ballykinler to Newry highlighted the need for extreme caution when moving by road to the southern counties. On August Bank Holiday 1979 – the same day that Lord Louis Mountbatten was murdered by the IRA – a relief guard, from 2 Parachute Regiment was travelling towards their destination in Newry along the road parallel to the upper reaches of Carlingford Lough when the convoy was ambushed. In brief they were attacked by remote controlled mines and small arms fire from the southern bank in Eire.

The relieving rapid reaction group arrived on the scene very quickly and took up a command position along a derelict building which provided the only cover. The building too was mined and the subsequent detonation killed most of the group. The IRA were lucky as they had expected a police Land Rover; instead they murdered nearly an entire infantry platoon.

One area of operations with the APCs which developed rapidly was the introduction of a water firing gun mounted on a Saracen. This armament was developed to assist in riot control but proved extra ordinarily effective in dealing with blast incendiaries fixed to buildings. These vehicles were driven by RCT drivers for the Explosive Ordnance Disposal (EOD) team. The in service introduction with all the necessary consultations with the military engineering establishments was done by the SO2 (APCs). He and his staff of one REME Warrant Officer Class 1 and an RCT Warrant Officer Class 2 spent much of their time with EOD and engineering branch discussing and advising on the technical aspects of the Humber and Saracen variants and those vehicles which were being considered to replace them.

In addition to the Warren Point murders, 1979 witnessed the assassination of the British Ambassador to the Hague, Sir Richard Sykes and the murder by the Irish National Liberation Army (INLA) of the Conservative Northern Ireland spokesman Airey Neave at the House of Commons. The death and injury statistics nevertheless showed some improvement from earlier years.

| | | DEATHS | | | | | INJURED | | |
| | | Reg Army | | | | | Reg Army | | |
Year	RUC	UDR	Civilians	Total		RUC	UDR	Civilians	Total
1976	23	29	245	297		303	264	2,162	2,729
1977	14	29	69	112		183	183	1,081	1,449
1978	10	21	50	81		302	135	548	985
1979	14	48	51	113		155	135	557	847

'1980 could be regarded as a successful year for the Security Forces' recorded Lieutenant Colonel Bob Bullock who had succeeded Lieutenant Colonel Ian Jones in December 1979, as CRCT. The level of terrorist activity was down on the previous year as were the numbers of killed and injured, both security force and civilian. All the traditional marches and parades passed off without major incident. Against this background, the GOC (Lieutenant General Sir Richard Lawson) was able to reduce the roulement force levels and continue the move to 'restore normality'. By the middle of the year all roulement battalions had withdrawn from the 8 Brigade area, leaving two resident infantry battalions in Londonderry. During the course of the year a further roulement battalion was withdrawn from Armagh and two from Belfast. The latter included the City Centre battalion and the Grand Central Hotel was handed back to its original owners. On the other side of the coin the increased radio controlled independent explosive device (RCIED) threat in certain areas of the Province led to a reassessment of methods of movement and this had considerable impact on the general transport workload.

The end of the year saw the first Hunger Strike. Seven H Block inmates began their fast on 27 October. The strike collapsed on the 19th of December and the year ended on an optimistic note.

At the beginning of 1980 attempts were still being made to find a way of increasing the gaps between Northern Ireland tours for BAOR roulement regiments. With only five regiments on the roster the gap between tours was a mere sixteen months and this was still severely affecting training in BAOR. Fortunately the reduction in the teeth arm roulement units which took place during 1980 also made it possible to reduce the requirement for RCT APC drivers, particularly in the 8 Brigade area. It was agreed that in future resident battalions in 8 Brigade would drive their own APCs. In the light of the savings in APC drivers a review of the future shape and size of the RCT roulement support was undertaken. It was decided that with effect from November 1980 the roulement

RCT regiment would undertake both the APC and GT roulement task. This enabled BAOR to combine the APC and GT rosters and to insert a sixth regiment (7 Tank Transporter Regiment) into the roulement cycle. This, coupled with an increase in tour length from four to four and a half months, produced a twenty two month gap between tours, a significant improvement. To maintain a balance between the squadrons within the roulement regiment the decision was taken to allocate the GT task to the Country Squadron and to move that squadron headquarters from the Maze Prison to Moscow Camp, a decision that was anything but popular with past and future Country Squadron Commanders. It was a very reluctant 11 Squadron (Major Howard Moore) who left Long Kesh in early November to come under the watchful eye of the RHQ in Moscow Camp. The reorganization of the roulement regiment was undertaken by 4 Division Regiment RCT (Lieutenant Colonel John MacDonald) in the last week of their tour in preparation for the arrival of 2 Division Regiment RCT (Lieutenant Colonel George Vaughan). The reorganized roulement regiment, incorporating a GT troop which was APC trained was to provide greater flexibility. The value of this change was to be evident during the rioting in the early summer of the following year when additional APC drivers were required at short notice. With all the reduction and reorganization that took place during the year a number of bases which will hold memories (happy or otherwise!) for many were closed or the RCT withdrew from them.

APC operations followed their normal pattern throughout 1980. The APC mileage, and utilization, in the country locations with the exception, as always, of Crossmaglen, was low although the drivers were fully employed on a wide range of other duties. On 2 April Driver Maguire of 6 Squadron was badly burned when a car bomb was detonated in Crossmaglen as his Saracen was driving past. In Belfast the withdrawal of two roulement battalions increased the size of the tactical areas of responsibility (TAORs) and the demand for APCs. Mileages and utilization increased. It took the West Belfast Troop Commander the best part of a day to visit all his sections.

A major project in Belfast was the building of the new Whiterock base and ferrying of civilian contractors in and out of the base in Pigs became a regular part of the daily round. When the civilians baulked at moving in a quantity of aggregate the GT troop (16 Tank Transporter Squadron, Lieutenant John Kane) had an exciting two days running the gauntlet of stone throwing school children. They thoroughly enjoyed it as did the windscreen suppliers! November brought the threat of a firemans' strike and Northern Ireland's Green Goddesses were found lurking in a hangar in the middle of Aldergrove where they had lain forgotten and gathering dust since the last strike. Getting them ready was a challenge for the SO2 APCs (Major Alec Rennie). He and his team worked very long hours against the clock, changing, amongst other things, every single tyre; they had all perished. In the event it proved a false alarm but at least he and his team had the satisfaction of knowing that they had produced the number of runners required by the target date. Despite all the bustle and activity on the SF side the threat from the IRA was never far away. The major problem continuously posed by the terrorists was the threat from the RCIEDs. The prospect of unnecessary carnage and the IRAs ability to influence affairs suddenly without warning resulted in the restriction on the movement of Army or 'green vehicles' in large areas of the Province. In turn this produced an ever increasing demand on 26 Squadron's (Major Paul Holtam) civilianized fleet and a bill for self drive hired transport that made a mess of the financial estimates! Statistically the year had gone well. Injuries and deaths were down on the previous years and fewer troops were now involved in roulement tours. Yet the SF capacity to move large numbers quickly and efficiently was well demonstrated by the fact that once again over 200,000 troops had moved in and out of the Province.

On 27 October seven Republican prisoners in the H Blocks of the Maze Prison began a 'fast unto the death' in support of 'political status'. Three women prisoners at Armagh joined the movement on 1 December, twenty-three additional Republican prisoners joined on 15 December and finally seven more on the 16 December. On 18 December the original seven stopped and the others followed at intervals. These events proved to be the prelude to a traumatic experience for many Irish families.

Lieutenant Colonel George Vaughan, the Commanding Officer, was at the helm of the latest reorganized RCT roulement force at the dawning of yet another year in this interminable campaign. Happily the initiation of the 'slimmer APC and GT troops' was quiet and relatively peaceful. Anniversaries came and went with only token remembrance demonstrations but although the 'dirty campaign' in the Maze Prison continued it had long since ceased to be newsworthy, except for a very brief spell in January when ninety six inmates ended their dirty protest only to reverse this decision on 29 January, claiming the Government had not implemented promised improvements. On 9 February the Reverend Ian Paisley, the leader of the Democratic Unionist Party (DUP), began a series of 'Carson Trail' demonstrations. They were small affairs by Northern Ireland standards and were easily handled by the police. The following month on the first day an event began which was to achieve world wide notoriety, Bobby Sands started the 'Second Fast'. To focus attention on it the 'dirty protest' was called off on 2 March. At first it gained little publicity but gathered momentum in April when Bobby Sands was elected as the MP for Fermanagh/South Tyrone on 9 April. Before this momentous happening, 10 Regiment under Lieutenant Colonel Tony Stormer arrived aware that military involvement up to early April had been of a routine nature. The Regiment's secret hope was that circumstances would permit extensive driver training to be undertaken. Their hopes were dashed. The 'Second Fast' which was now being supported by others at regular intervals was gaining momentum and support and gradually publicity in local, then national and finally international media. To give the event its Northern Ireland flavour and dimension, violence and rioting broke out in the Republican areas and progressively intensified the longer the fast of Bobby Sands lasted.

To cope with the ugly scenes that were igniting across the Province the entire Regiment were soon deployed. There was a need to deploy the maximum number of Pigs possible at various interface points in Belfast, round the clock! When it became clear that the task might go on for weeks rather than days, APC trained elements of the GT Troop were redeployed together with twenty drivers from 26 Squadron. The situation continued to deteriorate to the point when the 'Spearhead' battalion was brought in on 6 May with an RCT Troop from BAOR, 7 Tank Transporter Regiment, soon to be followed by a second troop from 4 Armoured Division Regiment. They remained for a month and were busy. During this period petrol bombing became the norm and it was discovered 'that some of the Pigs leaked at the joints!' A substance was produced to solve the problem, but the trial at Moscow Camp became prolonged when the Commanding Officer of 10 Regiment and a high powered team of helpers found that they were not as adept at igniting petrol bombs as were some of the inhabitants of

West Belfast. Eventually, a thoroughly doused Pig was set on fire and the trial declared a success!

Sands died on 5 May, the 66th day of his fast. Predictably widespread rioting followed in Londonderry, Belfast and Dublin. Between 12 May and 20 August nine more hunger strikers died to an accompaniment of intense rioting mainly confined to the Republican areas. During this period there were two RPG7 attacks on APCs in Belfast. In the first on 22 May Lance Corporal Howe of 36 Squadron of 10 Regiment received a shrapnel wound in the left shoulder. In the second on 2 August the driver had a remarkable escape when the projectile came through his door and passed beneath his legs. Unfortunately it hit the vehicle commander, a Corporal of 3 Royal Fusiliers and he lost both his legs. On 19 May a Saracen was blown up by a culvert bomb near Newry and all five soldiers in the vehicle were killed including Driver Bulman of 17 Squadron. The 'Second Fast' came to an end on the 3rd October after a total of ten hunger strikers had died, but the level of associated rioting had already decreased and fizzled out before that date. Despite the upsurge in activity in the early summer, the process of returning to normality continued and on 15 September 3 Brigade closed down and boundaries were redrawn to divide the Province between 8 and 39 Brigade.

Few changes in Movement policy were implemented during either 1980 or 1981 but due to many industrial disputes their reserves of patience and flexibility were severely tested. Air traffic controllers and dockers saw fit to withold their skills and the P & O closed their ferry link between Belfast and Liverpool in February 1981 without notice. The security situation in the border areas led to a review of the procedures for the changeover of roulement battalions, and a very effective system was developed using all three elements, land, sea and air. Now the incoming units arriving by LSL, are collected and driven to an airhead and then inserted into locations by helicopters. The outgoing unit use the system in reverse. This concept was largely devised by the transport and movements staff and is now well tried and tested.

At the time of writing, the struggle for peace in the troubled Province still continues. The British Army and the Security Forces face a difficult task and the Corps as part of those forces will also continue to provide the essential support required to sustain the troops in Northern Ireland.

CHAPTER THREE
Western Europe

GERMANY

On VE Day in May 1945, the British forces on the continent of Europe, mainly under Field Marshal Montgomery in 21 Army Group, consisted of three corps (1,8 and 30 Corps) with more than a dozen divisions, plus a similar number of separate brigades. Here, in support of this vast army at the end of hostilities, lay the greatest workload the RASC had to undertake.

Today, maintaining BAOR remains Britain's major military commitment, within the framework of the NATO alliance, and the bulk of Britain's Army are there with the infrastructure to support it. Not surprisingly, there has been, over thirty-seven years, a very large RASC or RCT representation in BAOR. Few are the members of the Corps who, during their military careers, have not found themselves at some stage serving a tour of duty there. Today, the majority of the total RCT regular manpower is serving in BAOR, and in wartime the RCT Territorial Army elements will provide over half of the RCT order of battle. As will be discussed in this chapter, the size and scope of the RASC and RCT role in BAOR, has changed in many ways over the past thirty-seven years, and there has been a turnover of many hundreds of Corps units in the period. However, when considered objectively, the overall responsibility now of the RCT to support Britain's major field Army remains similar to that of the RASC immediately following the war. Although procurement of supplies and petroleum is no longer a Corps responsibility, that of delivery to units remains. There have also been many organizational and operational developments over the past years, to which the RASC and RCT have responded, but the role of supporting our forces in BAOR is still the Corps' primary task.

Because of the sheer magnitude both of the numbers involved and the complexity of the changes in types and nomenclature of units over the years in BAOR, it is not practical to cover the post-war story of the RASC and RCT in Germany in as much detail as other areas or sections in this book. This chapter will therefore only consist of highlights of policy and significant developments. Individual units will only be mentioned if they illustrate these situations. Two specific and important facets of BAOR – the Berlin Airlift, and the operation of the MSO/MCTG, are covered in more detail in other chapters.

Section of Antar tank transporters loaded with Centurion tanks moving out of Barracks

[By courtesy of British Army Magazine]

THE TRANSITION FROM WAR TO PEACE

The end of the war in Europe on 8 May 1945, found that continent in a dazed, chaotic and ruined state. Six years of violent conflict had left countries and individuals in a shattered and desperate condition. Whole nations and millions of individuals were on the brink of starvation, with the basic infrastructure vital to support a nation's existence largely destroyed during the hostilities. Not surprisingly, the nation to have suffered most damage was the aggressor, Nazi-led '1,000-year Reich' of Germany.

Under the terms of the 1944 Potsdam Conference, the major Allied powers agreed the post-war responsibilities and division of Germany into occupation zones to be controlled by the victors. In the case of Britain, her occupation zone covered the huge area roughly bounded in the west by Germany's normal international boundaries with Holland and Belgium, to the North Sea as far east as Hamburg and Bremen, following south the lines of the River Leine, the boundary with the Russian zone of occupation, to Hessen then west again to Cologne, adjoining the French zone.

As well as providing occupation forces for this vast area, under the same Potsdam agreement, the four major Allied nations were to share the responsibility for administering the enemy capital of Berlin. Occupational duties were not unfamiliar to the RASC but in the case of Germany as it was then, its cities in ruins, its people demoralized and apathetic, its economy shattered, new features and new problems were inevitably encountered.

In addition to controlling and re-establishing the population of Germany, there was at first, immediately after the capitulation, the added necessity of housing, feeding, clothing and transporting to their own countries hundreds of thousands of displaced persons.

The RASC driver often found himself exchanging his role of goods carrier for one of passenger carrier, and instead of delivering supplies to a supply point he delivered anxious men, women and children to the point where a new life began. Many an unhappy woman or child smiled again with real joy as they were fed with RASC fresh bread and food and helped by kindly hands into an RASC vehicle to begin the first stage of their journey home. The displaced persons thus set on their homeward path included many nationalities. French, Dutch, Polish, Yugoslav and Russian nationals, and others, first realized their new-found freedom as they sat in a RASC vehicle speeding them back to the countries from which they had been ruthlessly removed.

Having set the homeless on the right road, the RASC were then called upon to assist in ensuring that the Germans, subdued and eager to please, should not suffer the final catastrophe of starvation with its accompanying diseases which loomed over them. To this end, Operation Barleycorn, was devised. This scheme entailed the demobilization and return home of non-Nazi officers and men of the German armed forces, who were required to gather in the harvest and assist in the preparation of the fields for the crops on which the existence of their own people depended. The numbers to be moved were too great for the Corps to deal with unaided and so transport platoons officered and manned by 'other Arms' were formed. RASC NCO's were allotted to the platoons, and each platoon was generally attached to an RASC 'parent' company. These platoons picked up the German prisoners of war at the laagers and carried them to dispersal points near their own homes.

While these tasks and many others were proceeding, the release from wartime service of large numbers of our own officers and soldiers progressed with a rapidity which was sufficient to give the DST and his staff a fairly constant headache. A Reorganization and Disbandment Centre. RASC was set up at Herford and this proved invaluable in controlling the interchanges of personnel, equipment and vehicles and in easing the strain considerably. During the winter of 1945 the Corps was reorganized in BAOR and Divisional Occupational Transport Companies were established, each division being allotted two companies, one company consisting of four platoons of 3 tonners, while the other company comprised a platoon of 10 tonners, one of troop carrying vehicles (TCVs), one of 1,750 gallon petrol tankers and one of 800 gallon petrol tankers. There were also a number of tank transporter companies, and general transport (GT) companies and to maintain and repair vehicles independent station maintenance sections were also set up.

To support the large garrison, continually being added to by the influx of thousands of civilian and governmental members of the Control Commission Germany (CCG), static supply, petrol and solid fuel depots were established together with a large barrack and quartering organization. With the return to UK on demobilization of many experienced soldiers the demand for clerks, cooks, butchers, vehicle mechanics and other specialists became increasingly urgent and to meet these needs 4 Training Brigade RASC was established in Lippstadt in July 1945.

It was at 4 Training Brigade RASC on 26 November 1945 that Field Marshal Montgomery, for the first time addressed a large parade solely composed of RASC and RCASC soldiers, and his words are quoted in the Introduction to this book.

It is surprising how quickly the transition from war to peace time soldiering was made. It was only a few months after the end of the war when soldiers' families started arriving in BAOR, with as far as the RASC was concerned, the commitment to house, feed and provide transport support, again another task which has not eased today. Of passing interest was a Thomas Cook advertisement in the June 1946 RASC Review, advertising 14 days holiday in Switzerland, all-in including transport to and from London for £30!

As life returned to peace-time soldiering, troop strengths were dramatically reduced. 30 Corps and 8 Corps were disbanded during 1946, leaving only 1 (British) Corps. Even this formation disappeared in 1948 to be resurrected again in 1951. Over the years the command structure in BAOR changed with remarkable frequency and with it, the RASC organization required to support our forces in Germany. Basically, however, the RASC role continued to be divided between the support required for the static administrative organization, headquarters, and units, and that required to support the 'field force' units on training and exercises.

Brief mention should be made at this early stage of the BAOR story to the formation of transport, supply and labour units recruited from the mass of unemployed displaced persons from many nationalities and from the German populace. This vast reservoir of available manpower was drafted into use to ease the burden on heavily committed military units in restoring the continent of Europe to normality. Many thousands were recruited and their successors continue today in the Military Service Organization (MSO) and Military Civilian Transport Group (MCTG) units in BAOR. Their work is of so much significance and value, that a separate chapter is devoted to their story in Part II of this Book.

Despite the many organizational changes dictated on governmental, financial or military grounds the Corps' responsibilities to support our forces has changed in degree only. The dichotomy of responsibility between supporting our 'field force' units within the divisions and 1 (British) Corps on one hand, and the equally vital

[By courtesy of PR HQ BAOR]

An RCT Troop in BAOR moves out from the harbour area

role of providing support to the infrastructure necessary to sustain our forces and their families in Germany, led to the parallel and mutually dependent field force and static garrison units and organizations. Paramount in the RASC/RCT units directly supporting the division and Corps fighting formations, were and are the transport regiments (formerly transport columns) integral to that division or corps. These were responsible for the maintenance and resupply of the front line units, and covered the carriage and distribution of virtually all the formations requirements, including fuel, ammunition, rations, and the multitude of stores necessary to sustain a modern army in the field. Other specialist units established to support the front line formations included bridge-carrying units, tank transporter units and, today, units to transport nuclear delivery means. Prior to the McLeod reorganization resulting in the formation of the RCT, RASC field force units also ran supply and petroleum units in the field and today the RCT remains responsible for the distribution of combat supplies, and much time is spent on the exercising and perfecting of the procedures and techniques necessary to fulfil this role.

Also at this time, the Corps took over the Movements responsibility from the Royal Engineers and this was also absorbed into the static chain of CRCTs. With the increasing movement between UK and BAOR of both soldiers and their families by air there was a subsequent reorganization of Corps units to deal more effectively with both routine and reinforcement movement. This is dealt with in more detail later.

Quite apart from the requirement in peace to train for war, it must be recognized that there is another vital function which must be fulfilled – to maintain and supply an army in an overseas theatre in times of peace. Not only is there a requirement to provide the soldier with a certain level of twentieth century comfort and amenities, there is also the very substantial obligation to provide equivalent facilities for his wife and family. The provision of these facilities invariably involves transport in one mode or another. Visits to Medical Centres or hospitals, NAAFI shops or amenity centre, and transporting children to school, all involve road transport. As a result, a substantial proportion of RASC and later RCT support over the years since the war, has been devoted to more mundane but essential routine garrison tasks. To meet this commitment, a garrison, static RASC organization was developed immediately after the war, based on the major garrison towns. These organizations were under the command of a local CRASC eg CRASC Celle, CRASC Paderborn, CRASC Hamburg, etc. They commanded a variety of Corps units including Supply Depots, Barrack Services and a number of transport units. After 1965 CRCTs took over command of a larger number of transport units when the supply and barrack organizations were handed over to

Stalwarts moving into location on exercise in BAOR.

[By courtesy of MOD PR]

the RAOC. In certain instances Regular British manned transport units formed part of its static organization, so vital to the maintenance of morale. More frequently though, the task was from early on, and still is, undertaken by the locally recruited MSO/MCTG units. In all cases, however, in addition to their more prosaic role of operating administrative transport or providing a school bus service, all such units additionally, have a vital wartime role – buses can be quickly converted into ambulances, and the carriage of routine administrative stores speedily transformed into the outloading of ammunition depots.

The relatively distinct boundaries of responsibility between the 'field force' and 'static' transport units complement one another in peacetime, the one allowing the other to train for and perfect its wartime role.

BERLIN AIRLIFT

The transition from war to peace received a rude shock in May 1948, when the Russians – contrary to the Potsdam Agreement – closed the land-links from the Western half of Germany to Berlin. Road, rail and water links to Berlin were cut, effectively isolating not only the military garrisons of the Western Allies, but also over two million German citizens in the Western Allied-run sectors of the city. For over fifteen months, the British and American air forces supplied the complete needs of the western sectors of the encircled city. Naturally, in a major military operation such as this, the RASC was particularly heavily involved in running the airfield organizations and loading and unloading planes. More details of the Corps' role are contained in the Berlin Airlift chapter, which follows this chapter.

THE BERLIN TRAIN

Another element deserving individual mention, is the continuing existence of the British Military Train to Berlin. From 1945 a military train organization, commanded by the Royal Engineers, ran a daily train from the Hook of Holland, through the British Zone of Germany to Berlin. Many readers will recall their first posting to BAOR, travelling to Harwich, embarking on a cross-channel ferry to the Hook of Holland, and on arrival transferring to one of the smart military trains waiting to take them to their destinations in Germany and Austria. The daily service to Berlin continued, with a break during 1948–49 due to the blockade of Berlin, until 1960. The introduction of air trooping to BAOR in 1960 caused a reduction in frequency to two journeys a week on the Hook of Holland-Berlin route. The service still maintained a daily run, however, from Hanover to Berlin. Those trains not going directly from the Hook to Berlin were split four ways:–

    a. The Blue train from the Hook to Hanover via the Bentheim area.
    b. The Red train from the Hook to Hanover, via the Paderborn area.
    c. The through Berlin train covering the Ruhr area,
    d. The White train to Austria (until withdrawal of British forces).

In 1963 the full working of the air trooping system resulted in a further reduction of the Berlin train. The size of the train was reduced, the route now covered only Berlin to Braunschweig. The daily run from Berlin started at approximately 0845 hours from Charlottenburg station in the British Sector of West Berlin, covered the 145 miles to Braunschweig by 1230 hours, was then cleaned, and departed Braunschweig on its return journey to Berlin at 1600 hours, finally arriving back at Charlottenburg at 1945 hours. Responsibility for the running of the train passed from the Royal Engineers to the RCT on its formation in 1965 and now comes under the command of 62 Transport and Movements Squadron RCT (Berlin). This unique train service, commonly referred to now as the 'British Berliner', has completed well over 12,000 journeys since its inception, and it is interesting to note that the catering crew are still provided by the Compagnie Internationale des Wagon Lits (CIWL), some of whom were part of the crew when the train was on the former Hook to Berlin run.

POST-WAR DEVELOPMENTS.

Since the end of the war, Britain's major military contribution to world peace has been focused on the forces stationed in BAOR. Despite many external commitments (Korea, Malaya, Cyprus, Suez, Northern Ireland, South Atlantic), BAOR has been the theatre in which our continuing military development has been concentrated. The training of individuals, units and formations, and the development of tactics, techniques and new equipment, invariably stems from the requirements of BAOR. The support of the BAOR field army continues to be the RCT's number one priority and all organization, equipment and training is based on this priority.

To achieve this aim of supporting the front-line divisions, both the RASC and RCT have evolved their organization and operating methods since the end of the war. Thus, we have seen many developments affecting the Corps in BAOR over the past thirty-seven years, a few of which are briefly mentioned below.

ENDING OF NATIONAL SERVICE AND ROLE OF THE TERRITORIAL ARMY.

The decision to end National Service in the early sixties and to build up an all Regular Army, naturally had a dramatic effect on BAOR. Gone were the days of plentiful, relatively mature, intelligent and experienced manpower. Units were forced to cut back their organizations and at the same time rely upon the young Regular recruit to fulfil their role which had not diminished. Nevertheless, the changeover was completed smoothly and the benefits and stability of having long-term professional soldiers were gradually realized. The smaller number of Regular soldiers meant a greater reliance on the Territorial Army to fill the gaps in all arms and services, and to provide reinforcements in times of tension, leading to mobilization or war. The organization and movement of these Territorial Reservists to BAOR is a major RCT responsibility and is frequently practised. This role was most effectively tested during Operation Crusader/Spearpoint in 1980. Exercise Crusader 80 was the nickname used for a series of major inter-related exercises in September 1980; it included UK home defence, the reinforcement of BAOR by TA and Regular units and the American army's own 'Reforger' series of reinforcements. 1(BR) Corps exercise was Spearpoint 80, and its aims were to test the reinforcement and logistic plans for 1(BR) Corps as well as to fight the battle on the North German plain, in conjunction with American and German formations. The contribution of the RCT within 1(BR) Corps was considerable, and with its TA component and UK reinforcements, the RCT provided every form of support, including tank transporters, fuel tankers, ambulances, coaches, movement control, helicopter ground support, railhead operations,

[By courtesy of Central Office of Information]

RCT Troop Commander briefing an NCO on exercise in BAOR

port clearance, as well as the full range of outloading and combat replenishment tasks.

In general terms, the RCT component of 1(BR) Corps amounted to some 6,000 officers and men, operating over 2,000 task vehicles. Within the Corps area over 130 trains were handled covering 15,000 passengers, 500 tanks, 1,500 other vehicles, and 11,000 tons of freight. About 18,000 passengers were handled in over 100 sorties through RAF Gütersloh. Three million litres of fuel were lifted by bulk tankers together with 100,000 jerricans. Cargo and general freight totalled nearly 70,000 tons with a host of minor details. The tank transporter fleet proved outstandingly successful lifting British and American tanks over a total of a quarter of a million miles. As an example of the background detail needed to support the exercise, a coach pool was formed to cover all the passenger movement to and from the airfields as well as coping with the need for exercise ambulances and the movement of simulated casualties. In all the coaches covered nearly 67,000 miles and carried nearly 29,000 passengers. The exercise was important, also, as a means of validating new concepts, organizations and equipment, as well as highlighting some problem areas particularly the need to improve the peacetime driver/manning ratio in RCT units. It also indicated the long-felt need to provide a better and more coherent movement control organization within the Corps area to cope with the steady increase in railhead operations, and to ensure on the spot advice, planning and control over movements within the Corps.

This exercise was the largest reinforcement exercise held since the end of the war, and the transportation and movement aspects involved nearly every RCT unit and headquarters in BAOR, through the Benelux lines of communication and Channel ports, as well as the mounting and recovery of the exercise at the UK base. The exercise went a long way to demonstrating and validating the UK's commitment and ability to reinforce its units in BAOR during a period of tension, leading to mobilization over a short period. The major success of this exercise was in no small way due to the foresight and planning of the RCT staffs and long hours of work at all levels. The exercise also highlighted the vital function of the RCT TA soldiers and units who make up a significant proportion of the BAOR order of battle. It is fair to say that without the speedy and early arrival of the TA from UK to reinforce BAOR, it is doubtful whether the fighting formations would be able to present and sustain a credible deterrent to any potential aggressor.

EFFECTS OF MCLEOD REORGANIZATION

As in other areas of the world where British troops were deployed, the effects of the McLeod Report recommendations and the formation of the RCT caused considerable changes in BAOR. With RAOC taking over responsibility for supplies, POL, fire services, barrack services, etc., composite platoons in RCT squadrons in the divisions, became RAOC-manned. The largest field force unit to be handed over to the RAOC was 138 Supply Company, the supply company supporting 1(BR) Corps. Many other units also had to change their cap-badge and allegiance. On the credit side, however, the RCT took over considerable Movements responsibilities which later led to the evolution of the Transport and Movement Regiments BAOR. At HQ 1(BR) Corps level, one saw the redesignation of the DDST post to that of Commander Corps Royal Corps of Transport (CCRCT) (and later to Commander Transport).

DEVELOPMENT OF TRANSPORTATION SYSTEMS

In the constant search for economy and efficiency within the services, the peacetime method of supplying our forces in BAOR was critically examined. Since the war there have been significant changes in the methods of movement of passengers and freight in the civilian transportation field particularly in the years since the formation of the RCT, and these in turn have produced changes in systems directly affecting BAOR, and the organization of the RCT. The first and most important development in freight handling was the introduction of the International Standards Organization (ISO) container, and associated container ships, rail and road vehicles. By 1966, ISO commercial container traffic between the UK and Europe was gradually superseding the loose freight systems and specialized shipping. Both roll-on/roll-off vessels, to carry containers on trailers and specialized container ships to carry containers in bulk, were rapidly increasing in number. At the same time, British ports such as Felixstowe, Harwich and Tilbury, and their matching Continental ports of Rotterdam (Europort), Antwerp and Zeebrugge, were spending large capital sums on container and roll-on/roll-off port facilities with expensive handling equipment, and large stacking and marshalling areas.

The inherent advantages of ISO container movement – speed, economy, security, and reduced handling – were recognized by the Ministry of Defence at this relatively early stage of commercial development, and by mid-1966 container movement to BAOR using roll-on/roll-off ferries and specialized container ships, was under way. BAOR was not slow in utilizing the developing container system, and before the first one had reached Germany, the BAOR RCT Freight Service had been planned and introduced. The system was basically designed for the more speedy delivery of ordnance stores within BAOR, using long-haul MCTG RCT road transport to interlink a number of Central Distribution Points (CDP) based on ordnance depots where RCT Local Transport Control Centres (LTCC) were established. A system of movement from the CDPs to units was also developed, which was based on MCTG RCT units. A number of vehicles and trailers were introduced into the system to move ISO containers throughout BAOR.

In general terms, the introduction of the ISO container system cut down the average time for non-priority stores to reach

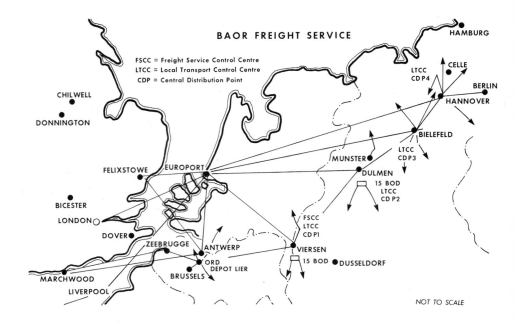

BAOR FREIGHT SERVICE

FSCC = Freight Service Control Centre
LTCC = Local Transport Control Centre
CDP = Central Distribution Point

CHILWELL
DONNINGTON
BICESTER
LONDON
DOVER
MARCHWOOD
LIVERPOOL
FELIXSTOWE
EUROPORT
ZEEBRUGGE
ANTWERP
ORD DEPOT LIER
BRUSSELS
VIERSEN
15 BOD DUSSELDORF
FSCC LTCC CD P1
MUNSTER
DULMEN
15 BOD LTCC CD P2
LTCC CD P3
BIELEFELD
HANNOVER
BERLIN
CELLE
LTCC CD P4
HAMBURG

NOT TO SCALE

BAOR from thirty days to four, and soon some 600 containers a month were carrying every sort of stores – except ammunition, large engineer stores and radioactive materials. Unaccompanied baggage was also included in the container system. The almost total dependence upon a commercial system for the movement of freight was rightly questioned, and greater use of Marchwood Military Port and military shipping and road transport was examined. The problem in BAOR lay in producing more man-power and vehicles to supplement the commercial system. These, at best, could only be produced by better utilization of the current transport resources; but these resources were very thinly spread for peacetime administration. An increase in military management also imposed a greater load on HQ BAOR and HQ British Forces Antwerp who control and handle, respectively, the movement of all freight into BAOR through the Continental ports. The changes in the movement of freight by container to and within BAOR have had a dramatic effect on the replenishment system for BAOR. Although not so dramatic, the availability of increasing numbers of roll-on/roll-off ships has made the movement of personnel and vehicles by sea much swifter, and this method is used extensively by TA units training in BAOR.

Changes in routine air-trooping have been less obvious. In

1969 trooping charter aircraft capacities doubled with the replacement of the BAC 1–11 by the Boeing 737, with a corresponding reduction in the number of sorties. The implications of the introduction of the short-range wide-bodied aircraft used on commercial routes carrying three times more than present trooping aircraft was studied. There had been long-range jumbo-jets in use for a number of years, but first experiences of the short range version which could be used for air-trooping to BAOR indicated the extent of the problems involved in their introduction. These basically were concerned with all aspects of passenger handling and reductions in frequency of service. Regrettably not all air movement to BAOR followed a standard charter pattern, and ad hoc charter, particularly for school children's visits, caused a disproportionate amount of effort to be expended to produce what was often a barely satisfactory service.

Although aircraft have changed little in the last few years, there have been considerable improvements to the facilities at the two civil airports, Hannover and Dusseldorf where two of the RCT Transport and Movements regiments operate the ground organization for the air trooping. These two airports, together with RAF Gütersloh, Wildenrath and Gatow, where similar improvements to facilities have been made, comprise the five service trooping terminals for Germany. The number of service passengers moving through these air terminals has increased considerably over the years. However changes in defence policy have, despite an increase in the number of school children carried, led to an overall reduction in the number of routine air trooping passengers, but this has been more than offset by increases in exercise and operational movement, notably movement to and from Northern Ireland and Suffield Training Area in Canada, which now accounts for over 8,000 passengers and 700,000 pounds of freight per month in the peak periods. The reduction in the Far East commitment released RAF aircraft to cover much of the balance of the air trooping requirement which was not met by the basic pattern of charter flights.

Although air movement for BAOR has produced no radical changes in recent years it has increased in volume, and improvements to the system are always being sought. The latest to be introduced is a joint service documentation system which standardizes the BAOR and UK systems and eases the burden on units. The future needs are for continuing improvements to commercial scheduling including the complex school children's visits, and the methods of employment of new ranges of aircraft as they are brought into service.

THE RCT BAOR CONTRIBUTION TO NORTHERN IRELAND

The continuing unrest in Northern Ireland has since 1972 had a significant effect on many units in BAOR, none more so than the RCT divisional and Corps transport regiments. Prior to the major outbreak of unrest and substantial military reinforcement to the Northern Ireland permanent garrison in 1972, a relatively small number of RCT officers and soldiers had been attached to units in Northern Ireland mainly to gain infantry experience. In 1972 however the RCT contribution from BAOR to the strengthening of the Northern Ireland garrison was one squadron of four reduced troops subsequently building up to two squadrons drawn from the Corps Troops regiments. Additionally small detachments were provided from the appropriate divisional regiment, with each infantry battalion, or Royal Artillery or Royal Engineer regiment in the infantry role. Details of the role of the Corps units are contained in the Northern Ireland chapter.

As Saracen APCs were introduced into Northern Ireland, they were taken over by the two squadrons, and it soon became clear that it was advantageous for the RCT to take over all the Saracens in the theatre. To do this it became necessary to reorganize the RCT support from BAOR completely, and this was achieved in March 1973. The new organization involved producing a third squadron in place of the detachments from the divisional regiments. Each of the three squadrons consisted of a headquarters and four transport troops giving a total number of personnel from BAOR RCT regiments in Northern Ireland at any one time of almost 800 all ranks, including RAOC, REME and ACC attached. The acceptance of the challenging and rewarding task of operating the Saracens naturally posed its problems. The expression 'operating the Saracens' is used purposely in the last sentence, since even more than with other types of vehicles the back-up for the driver and the vehicle is of paramount importance and it is the effectiveness of the total organization, culminating in the driving skill of the driver, which matters.

It is noteworthy that the RASC (specifically, 809 Armoured Transport Squadron and 105 Company RASC) up until 1957 had the task of operating tracked APC's in a divisional troop carrying role. In 1957 in one of the many re-organizations the RASC lost this task to save a well-known cavalry regiment from disbandment! So operating APC's was not new to the Corps.

With the first squadrons it is a regrettable fact that the high standard of specialized driving required to operate the unfamiliar Saracens and Pigs, particularly in the towns, was not possible to achieve before arrival in Northern Ireland. Too many traffic accidents marred the settling-in period of the earlier squadrons even though a very high standard was ultimately achieved. It would be wrong to gloss over this deficiency as it highlighted a major requirement in any training; that is the necessity to have the proper equipment to train with. This was sadly lacking in the early stages, and it was some time before the numbers of Saracens and Pigs for training in BAOR reached a minimum acceptable level. Squadrons now going to Northern Ireland receive the amount of training with these vehicles which is essential to achieve success from the outset of their operational tours.

As practical experience of Northern Ireland grew, everything of training value was fed back into the regimental training organizations and introduced into the squadron training syllabi. As

Armoured Personnel Carrier (APC) of 809 Armoured Transport Squadron RASC 1947.

[By courtesy of Mr A J Samson]

a result, techniques are continuously improving. Of the overall success of the RCT BAOR squadrons in Northern Ireland, there can be no doubt, and the experience of working in direct support of the infantry battalions not only in driving Saracens and Pigs but on foot patrols also, has been of the greatest value. Many facets of drivers' individual skills are enhanced by service in Northern Ireland, and this can only lead to increased operational effectiveness in their BAOR role. However the need to keep a considerable number of BAOR based RCT personnel in Northern Ireland or training to go there continues to be a severe strain on RCT manpower and effort. Nevertheless, the advantages are undisputed – good junior NCO's and experienced and mature soldiers return from the Province. The penalties, however, are mainly twofold. First, it is difficult to support or even train for, formation exercises which again affects the Corps primary role in BAOR of providing logistic support in case of war. Secondly, inroads are made into the quality of family and unit life which added to the problems of overstretch. These problems were gradually brought under control by a combination of reducing the commitment itself, lengthening the individual soldiers tour from four to four-and-a-half months and by bringing a further regiment into the roster of units providing reinforcements to Northern Ireland. The combined effects of these measures greatly eased overstretch and enabled formation training to be properly supported. At the same time, it brought greater stability to units and families.

OPERATIONAL AND EQUIPMENT DEVELOPMENTS

BAOR is the proving ground for the testing of the British Army's developments of operational concepts, organizations and equipment. With Britain's obligations to NATO since 1949 and the continued emphasis on Britain's primary defence commitment being the security of Europe, many developments have taken place in BAOR which have affected the RASC and RCT worldwide over the past years. In its role of providing support to the front-line fighting elements of the forces in BAOR, the RASC and RCT have continuously evolved their own organizations, procedures and equipment. Such evolution has often been spurred on by the introduction of new weapons or by frequent reductions in manpower and vehicles to meet periodic economy drives. Developments in military tactics since World War II have radically changed the

[By courtesy of MOD CS (REPS)]

FV 432 ambulance manned by RCT.

face of any potential European war. Today one is faced with the awesome prospect of a highly intensive conventional war possibly escalating to an all-out nuclear conflict. Such a conflict is likely to be of short duration but massive destruction and casualties are inevitable in this short time. The forces in BAOR are organized, equipped and have developed their plans to deter and, if required, to counter the threat of any potential aggressor. It follows that the RASC and RCT also had to develop their organization and procedures to support our forces.

The changes over the years have been many and varied but a few examples will suffice to illustrate the continuing developments since the end of World War II. The obvious example which springs to mind is the introduction of nuclear weapons into any future conflict. This had not only a dramatic effect on military tactics but has affected equipment, organizations and our own capabilities to deploy and use battlefield nuclear weapons. To provide the support for the deployment and use of our own nuclear weapons a dedicated RCT regiment was formed in BAOR. On the debit side, however, developments have dictated that the APC troop carrying role and the carriage of bridging equipment, previously the responsibility of the RASC and RCT, are now in the hands of the user units – the infantry run their own APC's and the Royal Engineers carry or drive their own bridging equipment.

The requirement for substantially larger quantities of artillery and tank ammunition has resulted in larger capacity and more mobile vehicles, palletization of loads, increased mechanical handling equipment, improved control and communications for logistic units and other developments to meet the greatly increased support requirements provided today by the RCT. Similarly, the vastly increased mechanization of our forces in BAOR has brought in its wake the requirement to improve on our former reliance on the jerrican to refuel vehicles. To support the fast moving battlefield of today the 4½ gallon jerrican is inadequate (but still indispensable). Today therefore we see RCT units equipped not only with petrol bowsers but with highly mobile fuel carrying vehicles capable of rapidly dispensing fuel to the most forward elements on the battlefield as well as the helicopters and the vertical take-off and landing (VTOL) Harrier aircraft.

The foregoing examples are only a few of the hundreds of military developments since the end of World War II. Such development is inevitable and essential as military tactics and philosophies continue to change and develop in response to countering any potential aggression.

This large and seemingly ever-increasing requirement to support the fighting units of 1(BR) Corps tends to further diminish the boundaries of transport responsibilities between those transport

Briefing RCT section commanders mounted on Canam motor cycles during an exercise in BAOR.

[By courtesy of Central Office of Information]

[By courtesy of PR HQ NORTHAG]

Officers and NCO's of NORTHAG/2 ATAF Transport Company commanded by Maj P A J H Benton RCT.

units integral to the Corps (ie, divisional transport regiments, Corps troops regiments, and other specialist regiments) and those transport units not integral to 1(BR) Corps, (the transport and movements regiments, the MSO/MCTG transport units, and others dedicated to units and headquarters). The ability to support the front-line units rests very largely on the support provided by third and fourth-line MSO/MCTG transport units and reinforcing TA units from UK. The less 'glamorous' transport units outside 1(BR) Corps are thus faced with the problems of preparing for a wartime role, whilst at the same time continuing to provide substantial, mundane but essential administrative support to the BAOR garrisons, in the form of schoolchildren's buses, movement of baggage and stores, provision of staff-cars, administrative transport, etc. Similarly, the RCT carries out a vital role in such non-RCT units as divisional field ambulances and the Headquarters and Signals regiments of division and corps headquarters. Significant numbers of RCT and WRAC drivers and NCOs form part of these units. In this context mention should also be made of an unusual unit commanded and partially-manned by RCT personnel – Northern Army Group (NORTHAG)/2nd Tactical Air Force (2 ATAF) Transport Company. This unit, with British, German, Belgian and Dutch staff, is an excellent example of NATO co-operation, providing transport support for the multinational NORTHAG and 2ATAF Headquarters in Rheindahlen.

Individuals and units may therefore often find themselves

participating in NATO or bilateral military exercises alongside troops of other nations, or sharing their exercise training facilities and areas. RCT units in BAOR frequently find themselves exercising with German, American, Danish, Dutch and Belgian forces. In the past also, RCT units were able to exercise in the French training area of Larzac in Southern France. Such joint training is essential in practising NATO plans and procedures and understanding the characteristics and capabilities of our allies in Europe. Many international friendships have thus been established and relationships founded. This friendship continues on the social side and many RCT units have built up close contacts with the local German community, both on an official and individual level. This happy relationship is particularly important to the wives and families of the British soldiers who might otherwise feel somewhat lost in the new foreign environment they find themselves in for the first time.

So far, no mention has been made of the social or sporting side of life in BAOR. As in other theatres, the Corps is naturally well-represented in the social and sporting life of the theatre. Fortunes vary over the years, but a glimpse at the chapter on sporting achievements will demonstrate the particular successes of the Corps on the rugby field, in the boxing ring, and on the ski-slopes.

Today, RCT units in BAOR continue to develop and evolve in step with the rest of the Army, and at the same time meet the task of providing peacetime administrative support for the British forces and their families in Germany. BAOR will continue for many years as the focal point for Corps operations, and as the practical training ground for all ranks of the Corps.

THE BERLIN AIRLIFT
1948–49

OPERATION PLAINFARE

BEFORE ENTERING into the details of the operation itself it is useful to understand the background to the decision to mount such a huge airlift in support of a major European city cut off from its normal sources of supply.

The British, United States and Russian European Advisory Commission, sitting in London during the war, agreed that there should be tripartite occupation of Berlin; a decision later modified to include the French, and confirmed at Yalta and at Potsdam. The western half of Berlin, after the end of the war, was occupied by the Western Powers whose occupying forces were thus placed well inside the Russian Zone of Germany. The Western Powers had the right of access to Berlin from their respective Zones. In May 1948, the Russians closed all road and rail links to Berlin from the Allied Zones.

Western Berlin contained a population of some 2,100,000 Germans plus a few thousand British, American and French troops and civil servants, together with a few semi-official persons such as welfare workers and Press correspondents. The city had been devastated by bombing, its public utilities largely wrecked, and its industry virtually stopped. Between 1945 and 1948 this ruined city had been brought back to a hard but tolerable standard of existence. The public utilities had been, to a degree, restored, an elected administration was functioning and industry was reviving. This rehabilitation was founded upon imports from other parts of Germany. The food came largely from the wide agricultural province of Lower Saxony (Niedersachsen) in the British Zone. This lay in an area, for the most part, of small farming and an almost peasant economy and it ranged from the sandy plains around Hamburg in the north to the more rolling countryside south of Hanover. The coal required for public utilities, industrial power

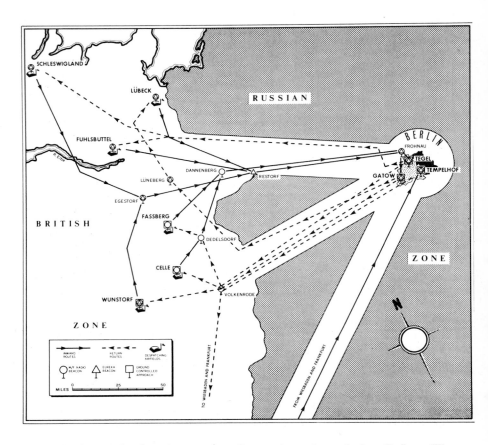

and domestic heating came from the pits of the Ruhr. The necessary electric current was imported chiefly from the Russian Sector of Berlin and from the Russian Zone outside Berlin, since the only modern power station in the Western Section, Berlin West, had been stripped by the Russians immediately after the war and the other power stations of the West were small and aged.

The raw material for the industry of West Berlin had been imported from several directions, much of it from eastwards of the city and many of the finished products had been exported also to East Germany and Eastern Europe, a traditional Berlin market. The total imports of all kinds upon which this restoration of West Berlin had been founded amounted to some 13,500 tons daily – food, coal, raw materials and so on. They came to Berlin by rail, road and water. There were also, by agreement of all the Powers concerned, three air routes into Berlin from the West. Each twenty miles wide, they converged upon Berlin in the shape of an arrowhead, with its point in the Western sectors. The northern corridor led from Hamburg in a south-easterly direction, the central corridor ran due east from Hanover, both from the British Zone. The southern and longest corridor stretched from the American Zone, opposite Frankfurt, proceeding north-east to Berlin. At the apex of the arrow, there were two airfields to handle the traffic. One was Tempelhof, the Berlin airport, in the American sector. The other was Gatow, a former training college of the Luftwaffe, almost equivalent to Royal Air Force Cranwell. It lay on the south-westerly edge of greater Berlin, near the Havel, Berlin's beloved lake. From Gatow to the city centre is a distance of some fifteen miles. While surface communications were still open, these air communications were ample for the needs of the Western Powers and West Berlin. They were traversed each day by a few passenger-carrying aircraft in the most leisurely fashion. Practically no freight was carried by air and very little mail.

When the surface communications were closed, apart from anything that could be smuggled past the Russian control posts around West Berlin and from what supplies the Russians allowed in for their own convenience, the only route by which freight and passengers could reach Berlin from the west was that slender arrow of air corridors; an insubstantial bridge of air. The problem could be simply stated, though it was of immense difficulty. The economy and the standard of existence of West Berlin had to be reduced to the lowest possible level consistent with the maintenance of public health and employment. The previous imports had to be reduced to the minimum for survival and that minimum had to be carried, at whatever cost in money and manpower, by air. The problem of reducing the daily tonnage of imports was not, in the beginning, quite as difficult as it sounds. There were already in West Berlin considerable stocks of commodities of one kind or another, particularly of industrial raw materials. These could be drawn upon at a carefully rationed pace and it was clear they would enable the weight of imports to be less than the minimum for survival for some months.

The main requirement of the airlift was that it should bring in food. There was no question of attempting to supply the whole 13,500 daily tons of pre-blockade imports. The original instruction given to the RAF was to carry to Berlin 440 tons a day so long as only twin-engined Dakota aircraft were operating and to increase this daily import to a weight of 840 tons as larger four-engined aircraft were added to the operation. This was 'Operation Carter-Paterson', a code-name that was very soon changed to 'Operation Plainfare'. The reason for the change is curious and indicative of the tension in Berlin at that time. The Russians, by means of their controlled Press and radio, seized upon the earlier name and made much play with the fact that it is the name of a well-known English removals firm. The object of the operation they proclaimed, was to remove as much as possible from Berlin preparatory to withdrawal. This propaganda had some effect, so the name was changed.

Originally, 'Operation Plainfare' was to bring to Berlin 840 tons of imports daily. The Americans, conducting a similar operation which they named 'Vittles' were to carry a considerably larger weight. Initially, the RAF was tasked only to supply food and fuel for the British occupying forces in the British Sector of Berlin. This was code-named 'Operation Knicker'. It was reported that certain drivers carried the necessary 'unmentionable' garment as a flag on their vehicles, which gave them right of way in the Berlin traffic.

Supplies for Berlin at Wunstorf, Aug 1948.

[By courtesy of Maj A K Crisp-Jones]

In addition to food, there would have to be an airlift of the raw materials of power – coal and liquid fuel. To keep West Berlin's industry running, even at reduced level, considerable quantities of raw material would have to be flown in and in order to maintain some sort of trade, the finished industrial products would have to be flown out. Fortunately, the industry of West Berlin produced, for the most part, articles of small bulk but high value, such as electrical equipment which was well suited to carriage by air. The lift would also have to handle a miscellany of articles necessary for the life of a city; some clothing, medical supplies, mail and an odd assortment of other objects. It was also necessary to meet the needs of the airlift itself.

In planning the commodity programme numerous intricate calculations had to be carried out. The weighing of a short-term burden against a long-term advantage were implicit in the organization and planning of what the airlift should carry.. For example, the Berlin Administration had to decide whether it would be more economical in airspace to import flour and the coal necessary to bake it into bread in the bakeries of Berlin, or to import loaves already baked (but containing 30 per cent of their weight in water) and thus save the necessity to bring in the coal. In this case it was found advantageous to bring in the flour and the coal; on the other hand it was found to be cheaper in airspace to import as much real coffee as possible, rather than the fuel required to manufacture ersatz coffee in Berlin itself. The example of coffee illustrates perfectly the topsy-turvy costing calculations that were imposed by the airlift. The import cost of a raw material was no longer reckoned against the selling-price of the finished article. That remained one of the considerations but only a minor one. The decision to import or to do without had to take into account all kinds of other factors such as the effect upon employment, the consumption of fuel and the reaction upon public morale. But the prime consideration was airspace. Thus, by a curious irony, Berliners who for so long had drunk ersatz coffee as a means of economy were now to drink a good deal of real coffee for the same reason. The calculation was no longer made in terms of export-import balances but in the amount that could be packed into the precious space inside the fuselage of an aircraft.

Considerations of this kind applied with particular force to the generation of electric power. If the existing power stations could be switched to the partial consumption of diesel oil, the weight of coal needed would be much reduced. If the biggest power station, the Berlin West, could be re-equipped and set to work again, it would be a great bonus. The reconstruction of a temporary bridge on the road between Gatow and the city centre would greatly reduce the road-haul of airlift freight once it had arrived and would thus reduce the quantity of petrol required to be flown in.

It was clear that the efficiency of the whole airlift could be greatly increased if the needs of West Berlin could be reduced by improving or adapting the equipment of the city. That meant the aircraft had to carry into Berlin an assortment of machinery and raw material with which to carry out this task, bulky and awkward things to carry by air.

It was a firm principle that all the planning concerning priorities of commodities which involved the decision as to what was needed should be done inside Berlin. This was on a tripartite basis. The British, American and French Commandants met regularly in Berlin and drew up the necessary schedules.

At the despatching end the Western Powers were well provided with airfields. There were German airfields available, though for the most part they were not in a high state of serviceability and a great deal of constructional work had to be done upon them by the RAF Airfield Construction Wings and the Royal Engineers. Eight airfields and one flying-boat base were chosen as the western supports for the airbridge. Six of them, and the flying-boat base, were in the British Zone. In the north were Schleswigland, Lubeck and Fuhlsbuttel (the airport for Hamburg). The flying-boats were based at Finkenwerde, near Hamburg, on the Elbe. To the south, in the Hanover area, were three more airfields, Wunstorf, Celle and Fassberg. The two others, at Frankfurt and Wiesbaden, were in the American Zone and were an exclusively American affair. These airfields were not all brought into the operation at once but were opened up one by one as the traffic over the airbridge increased in density. They were all in use before the end of 1948. In Berlin there were only the two, Gatow and Tempelhof.

It was obviously of immense importance that these Berlin airfields should be made capable of the maximum activity which depended upon the size of the airfield and facilities available. Gatow had been a grass airfield in German hands. Upon its surface the RAF had already laid a runway of pierced steel planking but that was far too weak to support for very long any intensive use of four-engined, heavy aircraft. Luckily, the construction of a modern concrete runway had been started in 1947 and when the blockade was imposed was nearing completion. Even so, Gatow and Tempelhof were insufficient to handle the traffic envisaged. A third airfield was therefore constructed during the operation at Tegal in the French sector of Berlin. It was built by the Americans and the French but it comes into the British side of the story because quite a proportion of the British aircraft on the lift were then diverted from Gatow to Tegal; the tonnage that could be carried was thereby much increased.

To make best use of the available runways at the Berlin end, it was necessary to land and despatch aircraft at an extremely high frequency. The target set for Gatow was to land one, and despatch another, during every three minutes, day and night. That is, an aircraft movement, in or out, every 90 seconds. In bad weather, the three-minute interval was stretched to five.

This remarkable intensity of traffic was achieved only by the aid of radio and radar. In this respect the RAF was well prepared. It possessed the finest possible equipment of this kind which was installed at Gatow with the most skilful men to work it. With two radio beacons and radio-telephone, the controller on the ground could bring in a stream of aircraft moving towards Gatow like beads slipping at regular intervals along several strings.

When the weather deteriorated, aircraft could be taken over one by one, for their close approaches, by a radar controller in a small caravan by the runway, using Ground Control Approach (GCA). The controller could watch the movement of each machine on his radar screen and give the pilot exact instructions, on how and where to fly second by second; he could 'talk him down' to a runway that until the last moment, the pilot could not see through the fog. Without these aids and the men to operate them, the whole airlift could have been carried out only in good weather.

Control of the operation was exercised by the Combined Airlift Task Force (CALTF) commanded by an American two star general with a British Deputy, an Air Commodore, who also commanded the Royal Air Force units engaged in the operation from his own HQ 46 Group RAF. CALTF was in Frankfurt in the UK Zone, 38 Group RAF initially at Wunstorf and then at Buckeberg in the British Zone. HQ CALTF worked under the joint direction of the Air Officer Commanding-in-Chief British Air Forces of occupation and the Commanding General of the United

States Army Air Force Europe. The British Army Headquarters tasked to operate alongside the air forces, the Army Air Transport Organization (AATO) was set up initially at Wunstorf alongside HQ 38 Group RAF and subsequently joining them on the move to Buckeberg. It was initially commanded by Brigadier G Lucas the DQMG BAOR who was soon succeeded by Brigadier J A Dawson.

The units responsible for handling the commodities at the despatching airfields including loading the aircraft and their receipt and disposal at the reception airfields in Berlin were Rear Airfield Supply Organizations (RASO) and at the receiving end, Forward Airfield Supply Organization (FASO). None of these units existed at the beginning of the operation and there was only one British unit in Europe at the time that had any experience in air supply matters. This was 749 Company RASC (Air Despatch) commanded by Major A K Crisp Jones TD, RASC stationed at Netheravon, Wiltshire. This unit had fortunately in May 1948 sent a detachment of two officers and fifty soldiers under the command of Captain (later Lieutenant Colonel) R J Royle to BAOR for air supply duties and they were located near Hanover which was fairly close to RAF Wunstorf, the first airfield to come into Plainfare use. The detachment was designated 68 Company RASC (Air Despatch).

On 24 May, 749 Company RASC was ordered to send 50% of its strength to join their BAOR detachment and arrangements were accordingly made for them to move in the RAF C47 (Dakota) aircraft with the RAF ground staff proceeding to Wunstorf on 26 May. This arrangement was cancelled and the Army party had to move by the surface route Netheravon–Salisbury–Waterloo–Liverpool Street–Harwich–Hook of Holland–Hanover–Wunstorf because the Treasury would not approve the cost of air travel! The first question to answer from the RAF Squadron commander was 'Where have you been?' or words to that effect, 'We've been waiting three days to get the aircraft loaded!' It is interesting to note that at no time during the operation lasting fifteen months was any RAF aircraft returning to the UK for technical inspections allowed to carry any Army personnel for a few days leave. This is not to say that, through the generosity and risk of disciplinary action by RAF aircrew, it did not sometimes happen!

The first supplies for British forces in Berlin ('Operation Knicker') were loaded into Dakotas by 68 Company RASC and left on 26 June. Obviously the arrival of the 749 Company RASC party under Major Crisp Jones RASC with Captain (later Lieutenant Colonel) J R Evans RASC, Captain (later Major) N O E Witt RASC and Lieutenants Ridler and Bright RASC and 60 soldiers considerably increased the sortie rate.

For the first few weeks in July it was very much an ad hoc affair. Wunstorf was bulging with every conceivable Army and RAF unit engaged in the air operation itself or providing and improving the airfield facilities to cope with the huge increase in activity. It was soon apparent that the combination of 749 Company RASC and 68 Company RASC was by no means sufficient to cope with the task. Consequently, more trained officers and men from 749 Company RASC were transferred from Nether-avon to Wunstorf. Further personnel were loaned from 62 Company RASC (MT), 5 Company RASC (MT) and 63 Company RASC (Parachute Brigade). This enabled OC 749 Company to form three platoons of two officers and 70 other ranks in each. These platoons worked shifts of twelve hours on and twenty-four hours off duty. They were given the task of loading and lashing freight into aircraft under the direction of the RAF Air Movements Staff. It soon became obvious that trained air despatch personnel were being wasted on this task which did not involve air despatch techniques. It was decided to combine the RAF Air Movements Staff and the trained air despatch personnel to form a supervisory staff with the German civil labour carrying out the manual work. Air despatch trained soldiers accompanied special and difficult loads in the aircraft to Berlin. This new shift system worked exceedingly well, giving the personnel the essential rest periods.

After the experience of one month of 'Operation Plainfare' it was obvious that certain standard procedures should be developed to ensure an efficient system for dealing with aircraft handling at the Base airfields. The system which evolved became fairly standard throughout the RASOs. Nissen huts were joined together on the perimeter track of the airfield, accommodating representatives of RAF Flying Control, RAF Maintenance and Refuelling Crews, RASC Air Despatch and RASC Transport. Alongside accommodation was provided for German labour. Returning aircraft from Berlin at twenty miles' distance called Wunstorf Flying Control which was also relayed to the Check Point. All concerned in the Check Point were able to hear this call by amplified loudspeaker. The captain of the aircraft stated whether the aircraft was serviceable and was, in his opinion, fit to return to

Berlin. He also declared any passengers or stores to be unloaded. This information was recorded on a large blackboard with the serial number of the aircraft and the various sections took appropriate action.

The refuelling, marshalling and servicing crews were detailed off to the aircraft in order to get ready to move out to it the moment it landed. The marshallers marked the position where the aircraft would be parked in the dispersal area on the Marshalling Plan Board. The Army representative, as soon as he knew that the aircraft was twenty miles away, would go to the air despatch table and inform a clerk that aircraft serial number 'X' was in the circuit. An air loading NCO detailed off the necessary crew to supervise the loading and lashing and handed them a manifest which had already been prepared. The manifest gave aircraft compartment weights and also the vehicle numbers containing the aircrafts' pre-planned compartment loads which had already been lined up by the NCO in charge of transport adjacent to the Control Point. The details of the load, aircraft to which allotted, crew number, vehicle numbers and times were noted on a master tally sheet for statistical purposes. The Supervisor would then go outside, collect vehicles and crew of ten German labourers for loading and wait for the aircraft to land. It will be seen that by this method all the arrangements for servicing, refuelling and loading were made before the aircraft landed, thereby cutting out any delay. Fuel bowsers, RAF fitters, loading crews and three supply vehicles converged on the aircraft as it taxied into the aircraft parking bay, controlled by RAF marshalling personnel. The next stage in the operation was to re-load the aircraft. After this was done and reported to the check-point, a new captain and aircrew were ferried out by truck to the aircraft for the next sortie. The 749 Company RASC contingent including Staff Sergeant Vick and Sergeants Barlow, Dandie and Bower contributed greatly to the initiation of this system of loading and control; it was used in various forms throughout the operation.

On 19 July 1948, the outline of the organization at Wunstorf was again changed. An appointment of CRASC was dispensed with and the new RASO Commander was Lieutenant-Colonel A Forward MC RASC.

The operation had a voracious appetite for absorbing officers and men as it expanded; Major H Fairley RASC, Captain (later Colonel) J S M Walker RASC and Major M Wilcox RASC were

[By courtesy of Maj A K Crisp-Jones]

Visit of Field Marshal Montgomery to Wunstorf, August 1948, accompanied by Lt Col A Forward MC RASC and Maj A K Crisp-Jones TD RASC

posted to the Air Lift from the Regular Officers' Course in Aldershot. They were soon filling appointments in various RASOs. Owing to the acute shortage of trained air despatch soldiers, it was necessary to defer the release of all men of National Service age and service groups 76 in 749 and 68 Companies RASC.

Towards the end of July 1948, the tempo of the operation was stepped up considerably. The new runway at Gatow in Berlin was completed, allowing greater payloads to be carried by all aircraft. At midnight on the 15 and 16 July 1948, alterations in the aircraft payloads were made, Dakota from 6,500 lbs to 7,500 lbs, York passenger aircraft from 10,000 lbs to 15,000 lbs and York freighter from 11,500 lbs to 16,500 lbs. These increases made it necessary to reinforce the existing companies with two extra platoons. This also needed extra German labour for loading. There were now two standard vehicle loads on a 3-tonner of 7,500 lbs and 1,500 lbs, a combination of these giving any three payloads required. The time taken to load an aircraft had naturally risen proportionately to the increase in the payload but the number of aircraft sorties per day was maintained at the same rate. On many of the aeroplanes returning from Berlin there were all kinds of stores and in consequence personnel of the RAOC had been attached to the Air

Despatch Organization in order to sort out the various stores being back-loaded.

On Monday 19 July 1948, all the original Dakota aircraft left for Fassburg, leaving 43 Yorks to carry out the remainder of the supply and coal lift to Berlin. The target had been set as 380 tons of food per day, 600 tons of coal and 20 tons of special lift with the British maintenance tonnages making a total target of a thousand tons. The target would be achieved when the serviceability of the aircraft improved but there were many difficulties and many aircraft were unserviceable owing to lack of spares, consequently a shuttle of aircraft was continually going from Wunstorf to Lyneham, Wiltshire to obtain the necessary repairs and to bring back stores.

One of the greatest problems of the whole operation was air traffic control. In the last week in August and the beginning of September 1948, various systems were tried for aircraft flow into and out of Berlin. Eventually the RAF together with the United States Army Air Force devised the 'Wave' System. York aircraft sorties were cut to allow more US Skymaster aircraft to be phased into Gatow from their base at Fassberg. The 'Wave' System – as it affected Wunstorf allowed 110 sorties per day:–

0755 to 0908	20 aircraft	
1155 to 1308	20	,,
1555 to 1708	20	,,
1955 to 2108	20	,,
2355 to 0108	20	,,
0355 to 0508	10	,,

Aircraft would be away from Wunstorf for approximately 2½ hours, requiring to be unloaded if necessary, re-loaded, re-fuelled and serviced in one hour. From a ground staff point of view, it would be a series of rush loading and servicing, a maximum effort every four hours. Special loads, which would take up to 3½ hours to load and lash, would be loaded on temporarily unserviceable aircraft needing only minimum service. The cutting down of York sorties had an adverse effect on all ranks as they were quite capable of flying up to 1,000 tons per day. However, the overall effect on the air lift had been improved by allowing American Skymaster aircraft, which carried a greater load, to land at Gatow, replacing the aircraft which carried a smaller load. Gatow either landed to took off one aircraft every one and a half-minutes.

Early in July it was decided that more UK aircraft should be committed and in the afternoon of 4 July, the first six Sunderland aircraft landed on the Elbe at Finkenwerde. Some of them had come from the Far East and had not stopped except for refuelling, such was the urgency of the task.

Headquarters Hamburg District together with the Burgomaster Hamburg were extremely efficient and overnight a suitable organization was set up which included the accommodation for the Coastal Command air crews, their maintenance and servicing personnel, and for the detachment of 749 Company RASC, under Lieutenant Blight RASC and his twenty NCOs and men. The RAF brought in their own equipment necessary for the maintenance of this advanced sea plane base.

The Sunderlands flew from the River Elbe to Lake Havel in the British Sector; each aircraft doing two sorties per day on an average but no night flying. Freight for the aircraft came by German transport to a control point and was stored in tents and some nearby warehouses. Other freight came by barge via the Elbe. Launches and DUKWs were loaded with complete aircraft loads and ferried to the Sunderlands which were moored in mid-stream. Petrol barges were used to re-fuel the Sunderlands and it was necessary to have fire floats in attendance. The system was operating within two days.

At this time the bakers in Berlin were short of salt. York, Dakota and Skymaster aircraft were not allowed to carry salt in bags as it seeped through into the controls underneath the floor boards and salt is a well known corrosive of aluminium. However, the Sunderlands had been anodised because they operated in salt water, so the problem of salt for the bakers was solved by the Sunderland aircraft. There was also a shortage of sanitary towels in Berlin. As these were so light there was a wastage of payload in standard aircraft and these were put into the holds of the Sunderlands. The rest of the space was filled with cigarettes.

Operating from Finkenwerde a short distance down the river from the centre of Hamburg was not easy. The aircraft were anchored in an exposed stretch of water, dotted along the edge with a number of wrecked ships, the result of RAF bombing during the war. After a time, some Hythe flying boats, the civilian version of the Sunderlands, joined the operation. At Havel in Berlin, moorings were improvised from those of a local British Yacht Club and unloading was done by launches. The flying boats kept up their work until mid-December, when there was danger of ice on the Havel, so they had to be withdrawn.

Looking now at the organization at the receiving end, a similar ad hoc organization was growing up. The situation at Tempelhof, the US forward airfield, is not discussed although a similar system existed there. Gatow, the British airfield in the British Zone of Berlin, was to receive all the RAF aircraft and it was building up accordingly. On the Army side a FASO was formed by Lieutenant Colonel Lord, Devonshire Regiment with Major Craig RASC as his second in command. The soldiers were found from BAOR including two sergeants from 68 Company RASC. There was plenty of German transport and labour available locally.

It was essential that the unloading and reloading was done as expeditiously as possible and after the load had been removed from the aircraft onto lorries it was sent direct to the various depots in Berlin. Petrol, oil and liquid fuels were pumped from the aircraft into underground tanks or piped direct into barges in the canal near Gatow. Two RASC soldiers supervised the unloading of each aircraft. The German civilian labour did most of the work and German civilian authorities accounted for all the food, fuel and industrial equipment, etc., that came in, whilst the Army accounted for and controlled all freight flown in under 'Operation Knicker', i.e. rations and freight for British troops in Berlin.

In July, Lieutenant Colonel (later Brigadier) R C Crowdy RASC was posted to Berlin to command the RASO. He had had considerable experience in Air Supply in the Burma Campaign, including despatching freight across the hump into China. He carried on initially with the original set up in Berlin. Shortly after the operation started a tailor-made unit was formed under the direct command of FASO. This was a Special Air Freight Company RASC commanded by Major C W P Coan RASC. The unit's task was a major one and perhaps one of the most demanding in the whole of the operation. Other RASC personalities in the FASO were Majors Batemen, Booth and Webb.

Fassberg was the next airfield to be put into operation. The RASO there was set up under the command of Lieutenant Colonel T H Downs RASC, later to be relieved by Lieutenant Colonel R C Crowdy RASC from Berlin. He had to assist him amongst others, Major M Wilcox RASC and Major (later Lieutenant Colonel) D S

[By courtesy of Maj A K Crisp-Jones]

Loading Yorks, Wunstorf

Barker-Simpson RASC. The aircraft operating out of Fassberg were C54 (Skymaster) of Troop Carrier Wing USAAF with a payload of 10 short tons, a significant increase in payload for those days.

Lubeck was the next airfield to open with the RASO commanded by Major (later Colonel) J Bell RA with Captain (later Lieutenant Colonel) M Wilcox RASC from Fassberg and Captain (later Colonel) J S M Walker RASC from Wunstorf and a party consisting of Second Lieutenants Rich and Bowden RASC and 16 air despatch soldiers reinforced by 55 drivers from 5 Company RASC (MT) at Nienburg. It started operations on 27 August only three days after the arrival of the staff at the airfield and the day after the arrival of a mixed bag of civil manned C47 (Dakota) aircraft sharing the dispersal areas with Meteors, Vampires and the odd Mosquito. The aircraft were owned by a various collection of operators, Westminster Airways, Trent Valley Air Corporation and, shades of London wartime nightlife, Ciros. On 25 September a further 20 RAF Dakotas arrived and the RASO was reinforced by more RASC drivers untrained in air supply.

These bases were followed by airfields at Fuhlsbuttel (Hamburg) on 6 October operating the bulk fuel tanker aircraft and Schleswigland in Schleswig Holstein on 12 November operating the new Hastings aircraft put into operational use before their planned date. The CRASO was Major Craig RASC. Celle followed on 16

OPERATION PLAINFARE
SUMMARY OF PERFORMANCE FOR NORTHERN AXIS BASES

RASO	OPENED	CLOSED	Services Account	Food
WUNSTORF	28 Jun 48	26 Aug 49	17,873	179,892
FINKENWERDE	5 Jul 48	15 Dec 48	4	6,201
FASSBERG	19 Jul 48	26 Aug 49	20	1,308
LUBECK	27 Aug 48	23 Sep 49	93	24,815
FUHLSBUTTEL	6 Oct 48	15 Aug 49	31	30,938
SCHLESWIGLAND	12 Nov 48	30 Sep 49	—	—
CELLE	16 Dec 48	31 Jul 49	—	22,718
TOTAL			18,021	265,872

The Southern Axis, Wiesbaden and Frankfurt, operated entirely by US.

December operating with a further wing of Skymasters of the USAAF with the RASO commanded by Lieutenant Colonel (later Colonel) J M Grant RASC. This brought the total number of RASOs to six in the British Zone (Finkenwerde closed on 15 December) and two in the American Zone at Frankfurt and Wiesbaden.

The forward airfields were becoming choked as these rear airfields came into operation and a new airfield was built from scratch at Tegel in the French sector of Berlin, much of the construction equipment being flown in from Lubeck.

The pace of the operation grew rapidly as a result of much trial and error in operating techniques, gathering experience at all levels and a tremendous spirit of cooperation between the Services, the Control Commission, the District Headquarters, the Allies and the German Civil Labour Organization (GCLO) transport units and labour units. Life on every station went on at the same rate, day and night, seven days a week including Christmas Day 1948. The only interruption to the flow of material into Berlin and exports back to the Zones was the weather. Diversions of aircraft into other than their home bases made life interesting to say the least for RASO and RAF staffs. It was a laid down requirement that not one pound of an aircraft's payload should be wasted and it was a challenge and a matter of some pride that visiting aircraft,

˙AGE LOADED					NUMBER OF AIRCRAFT LOADED	GREATEST TONNAGE LOADED ONE DAY
›nomic freight ˙c newsprint and mail)	Coal	Liquid Fuel	TOTAL			
4,320	54,490	54,175	310,750		38,656	1,252
—	—	—	6,205		2,120	111
—	537,752	—	539,080		59,413	3,127
14,691	33,539	—	73,138		20,936	412
—	—	14,233	45,202		7,327	425
4,001	51,809	23,985	79,795		9,852	704
2	261,578	—	284,298		28,661	2,626
23,014	939,168	92,393	1,338,468		166,965	

ed between these two airfields by Skymaster aircraft 712,140.2 tons.

mostly of differing payloads and layout, should be fully loaded and prepared for their next sortie and there could be twenty at a time, all this in addition to maintaining the home station activities.

The most successful days flying during the operation achieved a total tonnage into Berlin of 12,872 short tons; 8,657 tons came from the British Zone.

The Russians, realizing that Berlin was being maintained by air so successfully in fact a build-up of reserves was being achieved, decided to cease the blockade. Surface communications were restored on 11 May 1949. Perhaps as a matter of prudence and in order to continue building up the city's reserves it was decided to continue with the airlift. However, the rundown started soon after this date but with no particular urgency. Celle was the first station to cease Plainfare operations on 31 July 1949 followed by Fuhlsbuttel on 15 August, Fassberg and Wunstorf on 26 August, Lubeck on 23 September and lastly Schleswigland on 30 September. The RASO and FASO staffs dispersed to various new appointments and units such as the Special Air Freight Companies RASC were disbanded. Most of the air despatch specialists of 749 Company RASC (AD) had been withdrawn during the winter for tasks elsewhere, although a few did stay on until operations ceased.

During the period 28 June 1948 to 30 September 1949 a total of 2,050,608 short tons had been lifted.

A well-known anecdote that has survived the years concerns the over-loading of aircraft.

Fairly early on in the operation a Dakota at Wunstorf was loaded with freight intended for a York, more than double the payload. This was not discovered until the aircraft was airborne! When the pilot reported the fact to Traffic Control, he was told 'as you've got it up there you may as well take it to Berlin'. Descriptions of this herculean sortie are apt to vary with the teller but the pilots laconic comment is fortunately preserved. At Gatow he remarked mildly 'she landed a bit heavy you know'.

During the operation there were many well-known and distinguished visitors which RASC personnel had the opportunity to see and speak to. Amongst the visitors were the CIGS Field Marshal Viscount Montgomery, the Commander-in-Chief BAOR Lieutenant General Sir Charles Keightly, the Commander British Air Forces of Occupation Air Chief Marshal Slessor, the Chief of Air Staff Marshal of the Royal Air Force Lord Tedder, the Minister for Air Lord Halifax and finally the Prime Minister Mr. Clement (later Lord) Attlee accompanied by the Foreign Secretary Mr. Ernest Bevin.

When the rundown started the following signal was passed to RASO and FASO commanders:

'SPECIAL ORDER OF THE DAY(.) THE FOLLOWING SIGNAL DATED 8 AUG 49 HAS BEEN RECEIVED(.) FOR GOC-IN-C FROM SECRETARY OF STATE(.) PLEASE CONVEY TO THE TROOPS UNDER YOUR COMMAND THE SINCERE APPRECIATION OF THE ARMY COUNCIL FOR THE SUBSTANTIAL AND IMPORTANT PART WHICH THE ARMY PLAYED IN THE BERLIN AIRLIFT(.) PARTICULARLY I WOULD LIKE TO MENTION THE FOUR ORGANIZATIONS WHICH WERE PRINCIPALLY AND MOST DIRECTLY CONCERNED(.) FIRST(.) THE AIR FORMATION SIGNALS(.) SECOND(.) THE ARMY AIR TRANSPORT ORGANIZATION(.) THIRD(.) THE REAR AIRFIELD SUPPLY ORGANIZA-TION(.) FOURTH(.) THE FORWARD AIRFIELD SUPPLY ORGANIZATION(.) ONCE AGAIN THE ARMY HAS DEMONSTRATED ITS QUALITY BY ADAPTING ITSELF EFFICIENTLY TO NEW AND DIFFICULT PROBLEMS(.) FOR THIS THE NATION IS GRATEFUL(.)'

There were many other expressions of gratitude particularly by the people of Berlin and a commemorative book issued by the Magistraat was received by a number of personnel who had participated.

The Berlin Air Lift was not an operation of war, although sadly it caused the death of several gallant airmen but it was an operation carried out from start to finish, with the intensity of war. In fact it may have saved Europe from war. Many years after the operation, Lord Robens, who was in Clement Attlee's Cabinet at the time, said the whole Cabinet and Administration recognized that war had been averted because of the speedy and successful mounting of Plainfare.

The RASC, as the major contributor from the Army engaged in the operation can take pride in their part in the successful conclusion of this East/West Crisis; however, it was a joint operation with the Royal Air Force playing the dominant part, with the Army and civilian effort obviously playing an essential supporting role. The British and United States Army Air Force maintained the greatest sustained air supply operation that has ever been known in the history of flying.

AUSTRIA

TODAY IT SEEMS STRANGE to associate neutral, peace-loving Austria with 10 years of military occupation by British and other troops, but the RASC's work in Austria started with the arrival on 11 May 1945 of HQ 5 (British) Corps, spearhead of the famous 8th Army which had fought its way through North Africa and up the length of Italy. The Corps advance was some 250 miles in eight days, and inevitably this rapid advance outstripped its logistic base. The Corps 'tail' was over 150 miles behind its forward elements!

Thus arriving in Austria, the RASC had to start all over again, building up stocks at Klagenfurt – a five day turn round from their logistic bases in Italy. The Corps in these early days was issuing daily some 113,000 rations and 63,000 gallons of petrol.

Further problems – the feeding and transporting of vast hordes of surrendered German troops and of displaced persons – faced the RASC on arrival. All enemy supply dumps and transport had to be located, concentrated and recorded. Simultaneously, a ceaseless stream of Germans and displaced persons poured in from the mountains, until they totalled some 400,000, representing over 30 different nations.

78 Division was located in the Klagenfurt area with its Divisional Column initially, but on the disbandment of the division in 1946, the RASC element became a Transport Column, and the CRASC was Lieutenant Colonel Whittaker. Transport Companies in the Column included 57 and 328 Companies as well as several others, with higher numbers, indicating TA or only wartime origins. HQ British Troops Austria (BTA) was initially at Klagenfurt and for the early years the DDST was Colonel John Middleton. In the Graz area of Austria, 46 Division was the controlling formation, again with its CRASC and RASC Column, later downgraded to an OC RASC. 60 Company was one of the companies here, and continued in the area for most of the occupation.

[By courtesy of Brig N I B Speller]

Maj Gen C M Smith, Director of Supplies and Transport inspecting 69 Detail Issue Depot soldiers in Vienna, August 1948.

In Vienna was an Army Area Headquarters, as well as the Headquarters of the Allied Control Commission Austria (ACA), and the CRASC was responsible for support to both the Area and its troops and ACA, and the RASC units included for supplies, a supply depot, a POL depot and at least one car company and 14 Company, for general and station transport support. One of the early CRASC in Vienna was Lieutenant Colonel Maurice Smart who had transferred to the Corps in the later stages of the war. There were also other minor RASC units, and of chief interest was at least one independent station workshops RASC – REME Phase 2 being a thing of the future.

Elsewhere, notably in garrisons where there were training camps or military posts small RASC units or detachments were found, the largest probably being at Spital, North West of Villach. Austria, and Vienna were divided into zones occupied by the four major Allies, and the BTA zone was in the south west of Austria, and Vienna, although a four power city, was, as with Berlin, entirely surrounded by the Russian zone. The British zone had national frontiers with Yugoslavia and Italy, as well as a small part of the Hungarian border.

Within a week of arrival in Austria the RASC had opened slaughter houses, manned by German troops, to supplement their meagre rations with a daily issue of horse-flesh. One of these slaughter houses was capable of killing and butchering up to fifty horses a day and of producing as a by-product, 1,000 lb of horse sausage.

Animal lovers will be pleased to read, however, that only a small number of the 18,000 horses rounded up in Austria were destined for the slaughter-house. With the RASC in Austria at that time, was the headquarters of a Pack Transport Group. This Group had provided invaluable support to 5 (British) Corps during their advance through the mountains of Italy. Now they formed four horse-transport platoons manned by White Russian personnel.

On the MT side, a German Transport Column was formed from surrendered enemy personnel, under the general supervision of a small cadre of British officers and men drawn from various RASC units. A remarkable total of twenty four transport platoons organized into four companies and supported by its own vehicle workshops were formed – all manned entirely by German personnel. These transport companies were invaluable in distributing food, supporting engineer and municipal work throughout the British occupied areas of the war torn country.

This use of POWs applied particularly in the British Zone, but in Vienna there was much greater use of Austrian civilian drivers to save British military manpower. One feature of this was that the RASC platoon command structure was severely pruned and one subaltern might find himself commanding some 90 vehicles and civilian drivers, the equivalent of three platoons. Most of the load carrying transport was British Army current ranges, which included Dodges and Bedfords as well as Willys Jeeps. There was more variety in the lighter vehicles and staff cars often included captured enemy vehicles, BMW, Opels etc which were much sought after by senior officers! British vehicles were also sought after by other people, Europe being still a long way from prosperity and recovery. Thefts of wheels and whole vehicles were commonplace, and at one time, the company in Vienna had lost four

Bedford trucks in as many weeks – at least one of which was reported to have last been seen across the Yugoslav border – several hundred miles away.

One of the specialist transport tasks undertaken from Vienna was the monthly re-supply convoy, by road to the British Embassy in Prague – with its Military Mission headed by a two star general. This was of course long before the days of the Communist take over. The convoy, some dozen or so vehicles, in a strange relatively undeveloped country was a very worthwhile task for a young subaltern.

Border patrols, carried out by all units, were not all routine, and it is a reminder of the state of Europe in the post war years to recall that one RASC subaltern was shot dead by the Yugoslavs on their frontier.

There was an admirable tie-up between movements and transport as far as BTA was concerned. The main route for re-inforcements, and subsequently leave and release was via the Mediterranean Line of Communication (MEDLOC) route 'C'–'A' and 'B' serving other theatres – and this Route C was initially served by RASC Troop Carrying Vehicles (TCV) companies, driving from the English Channel ports overland to Austria, until such time as the European railway system was sufficiently repaired. Road gave way to rail, for the through run, still via the Channel ports, principally Calais, and MEDLOC 'C' trains ran through to Villach. At first the trains were day compartments only, and Continental stock, with meal halts en route – staffed by Army Pioneers and ACC Cooks. Later, surplus British (LNER) coaches were made available, providing some sleeping accommodation for the journey which exceeded a day due to speed restrictions. RASC transport units still provided the connecting links with the trains, including a nightly service to Vienna from Villach.

Service personnel in Vienna could not forget the four power control of the City, for the International Patrol, one military policeman each from USA, Russia, France and Britain patrolled the main areas of the city, especially the centre and corridors such as that leading to the British Zone, and to the airfield used by the British, Schewat.

Interesting aspects of life for members of the RASC in occupied Vienna, included the task of unloading at Schewat and bringing into the National Bank new Austrian currency, under great secrecy, as the Austrian schilling was to be devalued drastically, and old notes replaced by the new, to help stabilize the economy and defeat the black marketeers who were alleged to have huge bank balances – which would be reduced to a tenth at a stroke.

There was also the occasion when a RASC subaltern was arrested by the Russians for allegedly travelling on a road at the edge of the city, which they claimed to be in their zone. The British orderly officer eventually collected the unfortunate officer from a Russian Guard Room – otherwise the subaltern might have ended up in the salt mines!

During this period Carol Reed made the film, *The Third Man* – centred in Vienna, and most of the web equipment and other parts of the military wardrobe were borrowed from the quartermaster stores of 14 Company RASC.

Vienna was, as already mentioned, an island in a Russian sea, and recreation areas were at a premium. Sport could however be obtained in the Vienna Woods, including limited skiing in winter. Otherwise it involved a trip to the 'Zone' which involved motoring – in Army transport, no private cars in the immediate post war years – along a single road over the Semmering Pass, and then on to Graz or further South. There were Russian check points at either end of the road, and passage was allowed only on production of a properly completed 'Grey Pass' – in three languages – any inaccuracies or discrepancies often involved return to start point as Russian guards were not known for their flexibility.

Relationships between the Austrians and British forces were friendly and 'fraternization' with the local population, although initially forbidden was quickly relaxed and there is little doubt that Austria was regarded as a very good posting. Ski-ing in winter was popular and during the summer all normal sporting activities were enjoyed, with inter-allied matches and fixtures against the French and American forces. The Corps was always well-represented in these events.

By 1949 the 'occupation' role was modified and a defensive operational plan developed, based on using battalion groups to delay any Russian advance through the British Zone, aimed at the Italian frontier south of Villach. There was also the threat of a Yugoslav advance into Carinthia, which caused some anxiety.

The change of policy involved the Corps in many exercises in addition to routine station supply and transport duties. There is no doubt that these were enjoyed as well as providing valuable lessons.

In 1953 Graz was evacuated, Villach was run-down and BTA occupied Vienna and Klagenfurt only.

The DDST appointment had been downgraded in 1951 to that of ADST and in 1953 to CRASC. For political reasons the proposal that BTA should come under command of HQ BAOR was never implemented. Operationally the US and British Zones were under the more serious threat, the French being safely in the Tyrol and Western provinces. Fortunately the threat never became a reality. In 1955 the Russian Commission agreed to evacuate their forces from Austria in exchange for the country's strict neutrality. The agreement was finally ratified in July 1955. On ratification day the Middlesex Regiment mounted the Guard of Honour in Schönbrunn Barracks for the Chancellor of Austria and on the 17 September the Union Jack was lowered and the flag of Austria raised and saluted as the British forces withdrew and the small Austrian Army took over from the Allied forces.

TRIESTE

TRIESTE WAS INITIALLY OCCUPIED by 2 New Zealand Division on 2 May 1945, followed by 24 Guards Brigade. The city of Trieste is located in Venezia Giulia, the north eastern province of Italy – formerly within the boundaries of the old Austro-Hungarian Empire and transferred to Italy as part of the price demanded for its participation on the side of the Allies in the 1914–18 War. Following the collapse of Germany in May 1945 it was claimed by Jugoslavia, and Jugoslav guerrilla forces had actually entered Trieste before the arrival of the British Eighth Army. Immediate political pressure with the support of considerable superior air power, forced the Jugoslavian relinquishment of the City but they maintained their claim and the task of holding them back became a British commitment. At one time the situation was such that it almost led to active operations against the Jugoslav forces.

24 Brigade was soon called out in aid of the civil power to deal with the riots which stemmed from the activities of the adherents of the Jugoslavian claims but these disturbances were soon subdued and the 24 Guards Brigade settled down to the beginning of a period of nine years peaceful post-war garrison duties. HQ 13 Corps which had fought across the Western Desert and through Italy into Austria was disbanded as such early in 1946 and became HQ British Element Trieste Force (BETFOR). Together with United States Forces in the area, the role of the combined force was to support the Allied Military Government in the restoration of the normal life of the area and preserve the peace until the future of the territory could be determined.

The British force was at complete brigade group strength, but without artillery, this support being provided by the Royal Navy. The RASC was represented by a CRASC – Lieutenant Colonel J S Hassard-Thompson and his HQ, 65 Company RASC (GT) (of four platoons), a Supply Depot, which included a large Petrol Depot and an Army Fire Brigade. The original HQ was 26 General

Transport Column RASC subsequently redesignated HQ RASC BETFOR. Each RASC unit had a complement of locally employed civilians, employed as drivers, clerks or storemen.

The CRASC was also responsible for the administration of five hotels which were taken over for use as accommodation for married families due to the lack of suitable or available quarters in the City. The day-to-day running of these hotels was carried out by a small administrative headquarters, and a team of WVS (Womens Voluntary Service) acted as manageresses. In 1950, however, the accommodation position became such that a Barrack Service organization was formed and this replaced the administrative staff.

At the time that the British force moved into Trieste, the RASC/EFI (Expeditionary Forces Institutes) were still operating as such and Lieutenant E A Johnson RASC/EFI was attached to 24 Guards Brigade to set up the Naafi Services in the City. He was joined soon after by a subaltern of Auxiliary Territorial Services (ATS) EFI. The EFI immediately established a Bulk Issue Store and two large canteens. Later they opened an other ranks club, a families shop and a sports shop, all of which were located in the busy Via Carducci. The OC EFI was then Captain W Colthart, who when early in 1950 all Naafi staff serving overseas reverted to their civilian status, became the Naafi District Officer Trieste.

CRASC BETFOR was responsible direct to the DST, at the War Office for all departmental matters. Normal S & T Services were provided and local contracts were operated. Contracts for fresh fruit and vegetables were arranged with Italian suppliers and BETFOR also became the agency for the supply of fresh produce to British troops in Austria. Meat was shipped from the UK, the Supply Depot using refrigerated storage space in the Municipal Cold Store. Local contracts were made for the supply of petrol, the RASC Petrol Depot having its own bulk storage installation at San Sabba.

Throughout the occupation of the area it was always politically sensitive and in consequence a potential trouble spot. However, for the RASC, life settled down to a relatively peaceful pattern in which the claims for service were constant and a need arose to provide variety for the soldier and to give him a change of air from the stuffy heat of the city throughout the summer months. The climate in Trieste ranged from the hot and airless summers to winters characterized by onslaughts from the Bora – a wind which could reach 100 m.p.h. frequently causing damage, on one occasion wrecking the MT Company's garages and lifting the roof off the Workshops.

Consequently in 1949, the year in which there was a change of CRASC, and Lieutenant Colonel (later Major General) P F Claxton succeeded Lieutenant Colonel Hassard-Thompson, an RASC Training Camp was established, firstly at Prosecco, a thousand feet above Trieste and within sight of the Jugoslav frontier. Later the Camp was moved to Duino near the Italian border and within easy reach of the sea. The Camp operated from May until October and here a succession of two week courses were conducted for personnel of the Corps.

For the drivers of 65 Company, there were, during the summer months, regular fortnightly convoys to convey infantry to and from the Schmeltz Training Centre in Austria, the route passing through Udine and the border town of Tarvisio, and thence through the Karnischer Alps to Villach. In addition, there were regular convoys to army depots in Austria and to the leave centre at Cortina d'Ampezzo in the Dolomites.

65 Company had two hundred and fifty vehicles of varying types on its establishment ranging from staff cars to horse boxes and including a vintage Daimler Benz, believed to have been used at one time by Field Marshal Hermann Goering.

Incorporated into 65 Company was a civilian platoon – C Platoon – the drivers were all Italians engaged by the Allied Military Government but the transport control duties were carried out by Lance Corporals and Privates of the Corps from a tubular hut in the centre of the City facing the large building which housed the HQ of BETFOR. This 'taxi' service was based in the area of St Andrea, near the port, the vehicles were Personnel Utilities (PUs) and the service operated from 0900 to 2315 hours daily.

Field training was very restricted in a territory which was only 26 miles long and 6 miles wide at the most, which contained the city itself, the coastal road and some sensitive border areas in which troops did not exercise, 65 Company with the Supply Company provided support to 24 Guards Brigade when it took the field as a formation, and at least twice a year on exercises with the United States forces. The force was not called upon to operate outside the occupied territory but there was an exception late in 1951 when, following serious flooding in Northern Italy, British troops from Trieste were asked to help. Based on Rovigo, they worked on flood relief in the devastated area around the Po River delta.

In 1951, Lieutenant Colonel G MacLeod succeeded Lieutenant Colonel Claxton as CRASC, remaining so until 1954, the third and last CRASC in Trieste.

By 1953 the continued presence of British forces in Trieste began to arouse Italian suspicions of Britain's intentions and some politically inspired rioting occurred in October of that year.

Resulting from political pressure the decision was then made to evacuate the British Force, only twenty-one days being allowed for this to be carried out involving the disposal of all stores and equipment. By D+18 all the families had left Trieste, all quarters and non-essential accommodation had been vacated and the bulk of stores and equipment, if not disposed of locally, had been despatched to the UK, to Rhine Army or to British Troops in Austria.

Then, a matter of days before the date for final evacuation, the United Nations decided on a twelve months delay in the withdrawal. HQ 24 Guards Brigade and the three battalions under command had not been greatly affected by the movement and withdrawals to that date but the staff and services had been so efficiently and speedily rundown that there was an acute shortage of personnel and accommodation. Despite this sudden change of plan the support services continued to operate reasonably well.

The civil disturbances increased in frequency and severity and the Suffolk Regiment followed by the Loyal Regiment (North Lancashire) were called out in support of the civil power.

A year of uneasiness and tension followed and then, after the signing of a treaty in London by which Trieste was returned to Italy, units of the Italian Army took over the frontier posts from the Loyal Regiment on 25 October 1954 and the Lancashire Fusiliers handed over Rozetti Barracks in Trieste to the Italians the British battalions marching down to the docks to be embarked by the Royal Navy. On the following day the rear elements of HQ BETFOR and HQ 24 Guards Brigade embarked on the aircraft carrier HMS *Centaur* and a destroyer.

ALLIED COUNTRIES

THIS SECTION covers the activities of the RASC and to a lesser extent, the RCT, in a number of Allied countries post World War II. Although only a few countries are mentioned, it is recognized that there are many instances of quite sizeable numbers of individuals and national contingents serving after the war in the British Army. It is not possible to chronicle all such instances, but two will demonstrate the diversity of such examples. In Denmark, a former Resistance fighter, Mr Harry Henriksen, released from a German Concentration camp in 1945, was one of 2,500 Danes enlisted in the British Army. He was trained as a driver and served in the RASC in UK, Palestine and Egypt until his release in 1948. After enquiries at the British Embassy in Copenhagen in 1982, he was presented with his General Service Medal with a Palestine 1945–48 clasp, by the British Ambassador – some 37 years after he earned it! The second example is the case of Karl Traxler, former German Army, captured towards the end of the war and sent to UK. Discharged as a POW in 1948, he settled in UK and married an English girl. In 1954 at the age of 31 he joined the British Army, and became a Driving Instructor in 6 Battalion RASC at Yeovil. He subsequently served in Egypt, Benghazi, Aden, BAOR and in the UK. He was discharged in May 1976 as a substantive Corporal. To balance his German Army Iron Cross, Artillery Medal and a Rumanian Medal he is also the proud possessor of a British General Service Medal with an Arabian Peninsula clasp for his services in Aden and a Long Service and Good Conduct Medal. Such examples as the two quoted above could no doubt be extensively repeated and to such people we owe our gratitude for their service in the Corps.

BELGIUM

During the Allied invasion of Europe and advance into Germany in 1944–45, great reliance was placed on the supply route running

[By courtesy of MOD CS (REPS)]

Unloading 2 × 20 ft RCT Containers from LSL at Antwerp.

from UK through Belgium eastwards to the fighting units at the front. When peace came in 1945, this supply route, or Line of Communication, continued to provide essential support to the British forces stationed in Germany.

A number of British Army units were based in Belgium and their status was formalized with the establishment east of Antwerp of Advanced Base British Forces under a bi-lateral Anglo/Belgian agreement 'Gondola' on 12 November 1952. Under this agreement a base headquarters commanded by a Colonel was set up. Storage depots for:– Engineer stores, Survey (Maps), Medical stores, RASC (Petrol and Supplies) and Ordnance (General stores, vehicles, ammunition) were established, with the full range of administrative services to support such a large organization. From the RASC this involved the provision of transport, the detailed issue of rations and petrol and the running of a Barrack Stores and Fire Service.

In 1952 a HQ RASC was established in Grobbendonk, a small village east of Antwerp. Also in Grobbendonk was the large purpose built 1 Petroleum Reserve Depot (1 PRD) with a capability of loading or discharging from road or rail tankers or from barges on the Albert Canal. A jerrican reconditioning factory inspected, sold or repaired some 3 million World War II jerricans. Fuel for BAOR was received, held and issued in either bulk or packed form. There was a substantial jerrican filling capability with purpose built buildings. The depot, however, never reached its full capacity due to the development of the European and NATO pipeline systems.

On the supply side, 5 Supply Reserve Depot (5 SRD) was built at nearby Berlaar, with a rented cold store in Antwerp Docks. All food from UK destined for BAOR came by sea through Antwerp and massive reserve stocks were held at the depot – as an example, never less then 1 million pints of 'Carnation Milk' were held in store!

Transport support was provided by 601 Transport Unit RASC with, in 1953, a HQ in Herentals (15 miles east of Antwerp) with transport platoons in Geel, Tielen and Grobbendonk. The task of the unit was to provide domestic transport for the Advanced Base and to move stores into the Base from the Channel Ports and it was equipped with a range of cargo vehicles, fuel tankers, staff cars and later even tank transporters. In 1956 a fourth transport platoon was formed and the whole unit relocated in Grobbendonk. Over the years the size and title of the unit changed frequently. In 1958 it was redesignated as a Garrison Transport Unit (GTU); in 1965, on the formation of the RCT, it became '602 MT Unit' and in the same year '602 Transport Unit'. In 1970 one troop and the LAD were disbanded and the unit moved from Grobbendonk to nearby Emblem, to support 'British Forces Antwerp'. In 1975 its title changed again to 'Transport Support Unit (TSU) Antwerp' and back again to '602 Transport Unit RCT'. In 1978 the unit was reorganized into a HQ and two transport troops (one heavy, one light) which is basically the organization today. The manning of this very busy unit has always been by Belgian civilians with a uniformed British supervisory staff. Currently there is an RCT major commanding the unit, together with a staff sergeant quartermaster, but originally the British staff consisted of one sergeant per platoon/troop with up to 3 officers and 3 warrant officers or senior NCO's.

The Barrack Services and Army Fire Service deployed throughout the base became an RAOC responsibility, in 1965.

One further important task not mentioned so far, was the Movement Control function. Formerly the responsibility of the

Royal Engineers with a Movement Control Detachment in the Port of Antwerp, 487 Movement Control Troop RE became in 1965, 487 Movement Control Troop RCT. On 1 April 1970, this Troop and the Q(Mov) Staff of the HQ Advanced Base were integrated to form HQ RCT British Forces Antwerp. This was part of the Somerville reorganization which streamlined Advanced Base British Forces to form British Forces, Antwerp. This was completed in 1971 when 602 Transport Unit RCT was taken under command of the HQ RCT.

The importance of the Base and in particular the functions of the RASC were demonstrated during the 1956 Suez Emergency when massive quantities of vehicles, stores and equipment were moved to the Channel Ports. Again during the 1980 BAOR reinforcement 'Exercise Crusader' substantial support was provided in running a British Communication Zone. In normal peacetime operations some 95% of the maintenance requirements for BAOR comes through the Channel Ports and is controlled by British Forces Antwerp. The wartime role is similar but wider in scope and includes reinforcement in one direction and evacuation in the other and provides a vital link in the maintenance of British forces in BAOR.

NORWAY

The aftermath of the war in May 1945 demonstrated in Norway the huge task facing the Allies in re-establishing peacetime conditions, after years of enemy occupation.

Detailed planning for the liberation of Norway began in 1943 and plans were made for every contingency that could arise in this operation. This planning was carried out at Headquarters Scottish Command in Edinburgh, and in this the RASC was allocated its role in support of the Force whose task the liberation would be.

In the event, no invasion of Norway was launched to liberate that country, but the complete military defeat of the Wehrmacht resulted in the unconditional surrender of some 400,000 troops in the garrisons of German-occupied Norway. Immediately following the German surrender, troops of 1 British Airborne Division landed at Oslo and Stavanger on 9 May 1945. They were followed by many units of the Royal Navy and an SAS and two infantry brigades. HQ 50 Infantry Division on arrival became HQ British

Land Forces, Norway. The task of these British forces and the accompanying British-trained Norwegian forces was initially the demilitarization of the 400,000 Germans, which as far as the RASC was concerned meant the control of some one hundred and thirteen German Supply Depots scattered throughout the length of Norway. This, plus the feeding and training of the 50,000 strong, reconstituted Norwegian Army, the repatriation of some 75,000 Allied POW and the importation of vast quantities of Civil Affairs supplies vital to the speedy recovery of the country was a vast task to undertake. It was soon discovered that the original allocation of RASC units to Norway was completely inadequate and more units were rapidly brought in. It was only on account of the superhuman efforts made by all RASC personnel that the difficulties of the initial entry into Norway and of the first months thereafter were successfully overcome.

It is of interest to note the range of duties undertaken by the Corps:–

Supply by air	Guarding food dumps
,, ,, sea	Guarding 27 × 2 man
,, ,, road	submarines
,, ,, rail	Issuing confiscated wine
Troop Carrying	and spirits
Requisitioning transport	Local purchase
,, supplies	Assembly and repatriation
Refuelling aircraft	of Allied POW
Unditching aircraft	Assembly and repatriation
Vehicle repairs	of German POW
Marine repairs	Training of Norwegian Army
Water transport duties	in S & T duties.

To carry out these duties, some forty RASC units and sub-units were deployed the length of Norway. These duties were undertaken until it was adjudged that the Norwegian military or civil authorities were capable of taking over the tasks themselves. As Norway gradually got back to its feet again after five years of German occupation, the RASC responsibilities diminished, until by the end of December 1945 all British troops were withdrawn from Norway after a very busy and hectic eight months.

ITALY

Italy had, by joining the Allies in 1944, saved herself from the shame of punitive occupation after the war but, for over two years after VE Day, British troops continued to be stationed in different parts of the country which had been the lines of communication for Central Mediterranean Force and continued in that role in support of British Troops in Austria and the British Element Trieste Force.

The Peace Treaty with Italy was ratified in Paris on 15 September 1947 and under the terms of that treaty all British troops were to be out of Italy within ninety days from the date of ratification.

The plan for evacuation had been laid some months before, and at that time there were ten RASC units still in Italy all under command of CRASC 29 General Transport Column, a 'mixed bunch' of L of C units – 6 Base Supply Depot; HQ 13 Petrol Installation; 303 Petrol Base Sub Station; 7 Petrol Depot; 20 Detail Issue Depot; 134 Mobile Field Bakery, 19 Field Bakery and Cold Storage Depot; 29 Company (General Transport); 41 Company (General Transport); 45 Company (General Transport); 241 Company (Station Transport) and 247 Company (Water Transport).

The transport operated by these units covered almost the full range of Corps transport at that time. 247 Company provided the WD water transport in the Venice area, and comprised sixty eight launches, thirty eight barges – of different sizes – and six other craft including LCTs and schooners, most of the craft having been requisitioned from private owners through the Italian Naval Authority.

41 Company held the staff cars, and had a platoon of 10 ton 'Macks'; three platoons of 3 ton GS vehicles together with a domestic vehicle and two workshop lorries, 45 Company consisted of an ambulance platoon; one platoon of water tankers and three sections of tippers; a platoon of 3 ton GS lorries including one section of troop carrying vehicles. 241 Company comprised five platoons GS with Italian drivers and a small British cadre.

The evacuation date was fixed for 8 December 1947 and from October onwards there was a gradual run down of the RASC units. 241 Company was disbanded, 41 Company reorganized as a composite company and the water transport company was gradually reduced. By 2 December all personnel had left Italy by rail

[By courtesy of Brig B G E Courtis]

Field Marshal Montgomery inspecting RASC members of UNIFORCE 1951. Parade commanded by Capt B G E Courtis RASC.

except for the cadre of 29 GT Company, together with the CRASC. – Lieutenant Colonel C P Hurr, the last senior RASC Officer to serve in Italy – who finally left Venice by sea on 8 December – reaching Southampton on 16 December 1947. Thus ended the Corps association with this country after the war.

ALLIED HEADQUARTERS IN EUROPE

The Russian threat to the independence of Western Europe as manifested by the Berlin Blockade of 1948 led to closer political and military co-operation and the signing of the Brussels Treaty and the formation of Western European Union. The signatories were France, the Benelux countries and the United Kingdom who wished to establish some political and military cohesion between them. In September 1948 the Western Union Defence Organization was agreed and early in 1949 its Headquarters was established in Fontainbleau. This Headquarters, known as UNIFORCE, including its subsidaries UNIMER, UNITERRE and UNIAIR, had only 68 officers representing the three services of the five nations. The permanent Chairman of the Land, Naval and Air Commanders-in-Chief was Field Marshal Montgomery, his deputy was Marshal Juin of the French Army and the most junior hence the 68th Officer was Captain (later Brigadier) B G E Courtis RASC who had the responsibility for the running of the Headquarters transport, supplies and POL! There was one other RASC Officer on the staff namely Major K Lightfoot MBE, and some 40 drivers and clerks were members of the Corps.

Meanwhile on the other side of the Atlantic the USA and Canada appreciated that if the Atlantic Ocean was to be made secure in order to get help to Europe then a single mutual defence system, which would include and supersede the Brussels Treaty, was needed. On 4 April 1949 the North Atlantic Treaty was signed, by which twelve nations (later fifteen) joined together in a defence alliance to maintain international peace and security and to promote stability. NATO was born, and on 2 April 1951 General Eisenhower assumed operational command of the military alliance and set up his Supreme Headquarters of the Allied Powers Europe (SHAPE) at Versailles and UNITERRE and UNIAIR at Fontainbleau mushroomed into Allied Land Forces Central Europe (ALFCE) and Allied Air Forces Central Europe (AAFCE), whilst UNIMER crossed the Channel to Norfolk, Virginia.

To provide transport support to these large international Headquarters was a major task spread out amongst various nations. At SHAPE, France provided buses and cars; the Americans, buses, cars and trucks, and in 1956 the Germans, the buses, and the RASC, the cargo transport of 3 ton trucks. All this transport was controlled by an American run Motor Pool office. In addition to providing cargo transport support to the headquarters and to the British elements of the organization, the drivers could be used on a 'pool' basis to carry out any driving task. Thus it was that 19 year old RASC National Servicemen regularly drove US Army buses on the time-tabled services from the Arc de Triomphe in Paris to SHAPE and SHAPE village (a married quarters compound near St Germain en Laye. In addition to the 24 Bedford RL trucks operated by the RASC, there were also five unique staff cars. These being the personal transport of Field Marshal Montgomery and succeeding Deputy Supreme Commanders were definitely NOT for Motor Pool use no matter what anybody said!

Commanding the RASC element of the British Support Battalion at SHAPE was an RASC Major who in addition to his transport responsibilities also looked after the supply side of life. This involved the local purchase of fresh food for the British troops from the Paris central markets at Les Halles – a three times a week task at 5 o'clock in the morning inspecting, ordering and paying cash for meat, fish, vegetables and so on. He also had charge of a field bakery detachment established in a Napoleonic era bakery near Versailles!

Service in Paris with SHAPE and ALFCE came to an abrupt halt in 1966 when General de Gaulle requested the three NATO headquarters to move out of France. This move was spread over 18 months, with SHAPE moving to Mons in Belgium and ALFCE (now called Allied Forces Central Europe (AFCENT)) to a converted coal mine in Brunsum in Holland. The physical movement of this change of location was largely carried out by 10 Regiment RCT who were based in Bielefeld, West Germany. With many restrictions placed on them by the French Government, drivers from 9, 15, 17 and 36 Squadrons RCT quietly and efficiently carried out the 900 miles turn-round of stores, furniture and MFO for the two Headquarters over an 18 month period. Most of this was individual vehicle running placing a great responsibility on the young drivers, who had no administrative, workshop or breakdown back-up en route.

The RCT commitment continues to this day in both SHAPE and HQ AFCENT, with RCT drivers providing transport support both to the international NATO staffs and to the British support element of these headquarters.

CHAPTER FOUR
South East Asia

MALAYA

THE MALAY STATES had always presented a good and happy example of British Colonial rule. Over the years, as a result of the development in the growth of rubber and tin mining, Malaya became one of the richest areas of the Empire. In 1930 however, a Malayan Communist Party had come into existence – it was outlawed but, following the Japanese invasion in December 1941, it became a resistance movement, adopting the title of 'The Malayan People's Anti-Japanese Army'. The sudden collapse of Japan in 1945 served as an impetus to this so-called 'Army', which had by then acquired a vast quantity of Japanese weapons and was disbanded in December 1945 on the return of British administration; the communist element and its doctrines lingered on.

On 1 February 1948 the new Federation of Malaya came into existence. In the same month there was a revival of the Communist movement, the active element of which called itself 'The People's

Anti-British Army' which they later changed to 'Malayan Races Liberation Army', an organization which in April came out in the open with acts of sabotage, intimidation and murder of workers at the tin mines and on rubber estates. By June such attacks had been extended to Europeans.

The seriousness of the situation was such that a state of emergency was declared on 16 June 1948. The State of Emergency also covered Singapore Island, but here it only lasted until 31 January 1949.

At the start of the Emergency, the infantry component of the garrison in Malaya consisted of one British battalion, The King's Own Yorkshire Light Infantry, six Gurkha battalions and two battalions of the Malay Regiment. In addition, 26 Field Regiment Royal Artillery was quickly reorganized and used in an infantry role. All these units were re-deployed throughout Malaya in support of the Malayan Police Force, which was not equipped to combat rebellion, which indeed the situation rapidly became. At the outset, the Army lacked essential information about the enemy, soon to be referred to as 'terrorists' or 'bandits' and the task of meeting the considerable number of requests from the Civil Authorities and the Police for the protection of communities and communications presented major problems. The garrison was quickly reinforced by three more British battalions from Singapore and Hong Kong. Very large areas were assigned to each battalion in which their primary task was to instil confidence in the local population, and then to seek out and destroy the terrorists.

The RASC element in Malaya was established on a peacetime basis and spread throughout the Army Districts. At the time of the Japanese surrender in 1945, some 50% of the S&T responsibilities were being undertaken by the Royal Indian Army Service Corps (RIASC). The last RIASC transport unit did not leave Malaya until 11 December 1947, some four months after the granting of independence to India. The peacetime build-up of the RASC really started after the departure of the RIASC in 1947, and at the end of that year the RASC were coping with all the problems of a large garrison with only a proportion of the units that existed before. Such as remained, lost, in many cases, a considerable proportion of their strength as their RIASC personnel were withdrawn for return to India. The gap was filled by almost wholesale engagement of civilian clerks, storemen and other grades, and units were able to keep going. It was soon realized that with a shortage of British soldiers the RASC would have to rely on locally enlisted personnel to provide the bulk of unit strengths, and that British RASC officers and NCOs would have to command and administer the Malayan Other Rank (MOR) drawn from all races in Malaya, but largely Malays, in most units. Accordingly, the RASC School at Nee Soon, on Singapore Island was organized to undertake the training of MORs. The first intake of MOR passed through the RASC School in July 1947. Initially, preliminary training was carried out at an All Arms Primary Training Centre, but later the RASC School undertook both this preliminary training and trade training.

It was in this period of build-up and reorganization that the Emergency started in June 1948. Many of the RASC units were on a 'tailor-made' establishment at this time, with a mixed bag of British and Malay other ranks and locally employed civilians. The MOR were still semi-trained and largely an unknown factor. They were on the whole good, cheerful soldiers, but only partly understood by many of their British officers and NCOs; the language difficulty had not been fully overcome by either side. The supply units located in the centres of military population, though hard worked, were functioning well. In the transport units though, there was a shortage of vehicles and those that did exist were past their prime. This necessitated considerable hiring of vehicles from local contractors to carry out non-operational tasks. Even this was not easy as there were insufficient at this time on the civilian market. The problem was partly solved by transferring vehicles from disbanding units – other than RASC – to civilian contractors, who then operated them for the Army – spares and petrol being provided from military sources.

The immediate operational problems of the RASC on the outbreak of the Emergency, were firstly the maintenance and troop carrying requirements of the infantry units engaged in jungle operations and secondly, the provision of a suitable ration pack for the Gurkhas and Malays to carry with them on these operations.

Gradually as the tempo of operations increased, with more troops moving into the jungle, away from their land communications, so the requirement for supply by air became apparent. Air supply was to become the main operational function of the RASC throughout the campaign. Before dealing with this aspect of the Corp's activity in detail though, we must return to the initial problems of operational transport and the provision of ration packs.

The stepping up of the transport effort on the operational side was achieved by a careful review of routine details, which were largely met by the hiring method already outlined. RASC MT units then provided vehicles to bring the scale of transport available in infantry battalions up to a level sufficient for their operations, and small packets of vehicles for lifting patrols to the edge of the jungle. Fifteen cwt trucks were very popular for taking patrols along estate roads, but there was not a big demand for large scale troop movement. This was to change as the number of infantry battalions increased over the next two years and by 1950 there were six RASC companies providing transport in this role. Two of these companies (3 and 27) were manned by British drivers and four (24, 29, 52 and 69) were Malayanized, or going through the process of having their BOR drivers replaced by MOR drivers to this end. At this stage, all the officers were still British, as were all Warrant officers and some of the senior NCOs. The high standard of training of the MOR driver at the RASC School at Nee

Soon, and subsequently NCOs, was to prove its worth and Malays of officer, warrant officer and senior NCO quality developed rapidly and were to form a sound nucleus for the subsequent formation of the Malayan Army Service Corps in 1957. In the meantime, the MOR driver with his British counterpart were gaining experience rapidly in operating in a hostile jungle environment. There was the constant threat of ambush to small groups of vehicles on the roads outside towns and training in ambush drills was of major importance. In South Malaya, Lieutenant Colonel T W Atkinson, the CRASC, established a training camp at Batu Pahat to carry out such training. At this time though, fatal ambushes still occurred, and a British officer and four British RASC drivers were killed in an ambush on the road to the Cameron Highlands. In another ambush, Driver Ismail Bin Mura, although wounded, supported the RASC officer with him, who was mortally wounded, and drove his Jeep through the ambush. For his gallantry, he was awarded the Military Medal, the first MOR to receive this award.

In 1950 there was still a shortage of infantry and other Arms and Services were called upon to act in an infantry role. 3 Company RASC provided a jungle squad, which was trained by 1st Battalion the Suffolk Regiment. The squad was some thirty all ranks strong and after training was based at Bahrang, in an area made famous in 1942, when the Argylls and the Leicesters fought a gallant rearguard action against the Japanese. Sergeant Gordon Sampson was a member of this squad and recalls his experience in the jungle at the time. They were placed under command of a company of 2 Coldstream Guards which was commanded by Major Sir Ralph Anstruther MC, and were quickly given an operational task. They were sent out to locate and destroy a bandit camp and were soon aware of the difficulties of moving through the jungle. Leeches proved to be a considerable irritation, and they could reach the most awkward parts of the body, where the standard procedure for removing them, burning them with a lighted cigarette, could be somewhat hazardous. The patrol succeeded in finding a bandit camp, but no doubt their inexperience in jungle movement had given the occupants adequate warning of their arrival and they had fled. There was plenty of evidence of recent occupation of the camp incuding hollow bamboo ducts for catching their water supply, food and beds and bedding. After destroying the camp, the patrol commander, Lieutenant Johnson, decided that the patrol should be split, he taking a third and Sergeant Sampson the balance, with the aim of pursuing the bandits. Two further camps were discovered by Sampson's party, but these were disused and again were destroyed. Returning to the original camp they took the wrong track and eventually came upon another camp which had clearly only just been vacated and showed signs of being a rest camp for wounded. Although they heard movement nearby, Sergeant Sampson was not sure then of the whereabouts of Lieutenant Johnson's party and felt that any indiscriminate fire might endanger them. By now though, they were behind schedule and the network of tracks used by the bandits made the selection of the right one for their return to base a difficult decision. They were lost! A study of the map showed that if they marched west they would eventually reach the main road. This they did after making camp for the night. Eventually they reached the road as planned, having marched on a compass bearing, ignoring any tracks that did not go west. Although they had water, their food had finished the previous evening and they were glad of the coffee provided from a local coffee shop at mid-day the following day through the efforts of their Chinese interpreter who was accompanying them. He had up to then been regarded with some apprehension as he was on the bandits' wanted list and was no more at home in the jungle than those he accompanied!

Major Anstruther and Lieutenant Johnson, who had returned to the base camp with his party the previous night were concerned about the safety of the remainder of the patrol and were duly relieved at their return. Although late, the party had achieved much. The discovery of the camps confirmed information that the Police required and for the squad too had proved to be a significant experience. The lessons learned were to prove invaluable when they moved location to the Cameron Highlands where there had been considerable bandit activity, including the incident already mentioned when Second Lieutenant Richards, Sergeant Ritter, Corporal Hand, Lance Corporal Hoggett and Driver Jones had been killed when their vehicle was ambushed. Lance Corporal White and Driver Marsh survived the ambush. They were all members of 3 Company RASC.

The squad was to serve in the infantry role for some three months, during which time they were employed in a number of operations gaining confidence as they acquired jungle skills. Although they laid a number of ambushes, they were unable to claim any kills, but harassed the bandits and discovered a number of camps. When they returned to their driving duties with their new found skills and experience and certainly with a wealth of stories, they had the satisfaction of knowing that they had achieved in their temporary role a standard with which they had every reason to be pleased.

Attention has already been drawn to the problem at the start of the Emergency, of providing a suitable ration pack for Gurkhas and Malays on jungle patrols. HQ RASC Malaya District undertook the task of producing an equivalent to the British soldier's 24 hour and 'Compo' packs that would be suitable for the Gurkha and Malay soldier. The CRASC at the time was Lieutenant Colonel A P Campbell (later Brigadier), who considered himself lucky in having as his DADST (Supplies) an officer who was well suited to solve the particular problem. This was Major Harry Lukes RASC, who was a 'bit of a character', but whose energies and talents once harnessed to the task were to produce the complete answer. Once the GOC had been persuaded that the task should be undertaken locally, all the stops were pulled out and trial packs were produced. All the corners could not be cut though and consultation and agreement had to be part of the process. In designing the packs the Staff, the Medical and S&T Branches, the Army Catering Corps, the Civil Service financiers and last, but not least, the soldier in the field all had a special interest in the result. It is difficult to relate bulk, nutritive value, palatibility, speed of preparation and finance into a mutually acceptable ration. This however, was the achieved aim. When dealing with Gurkha and Malay rations all parties agreed that 50% of the pack should consist of rice. The remaining items were chiefly a question of proportion, i.e. need against weight. Only items which were already on the ration scale could be considered. The main problem in this respect was to provide a meat or fish element, meat particularly owing to the observance of religious customs. In the event, the selected canning firm was able to produce curried mutton or goat from animals especially slaughtered according to Muslim or Hindu custom.

There were no can-making firms in Malaya, and most of the fruit packing was done in Singapore by a well-known firm whose prices were expensive for the budget which had been wrung grudgingly from the Financial Adviser in Singapore for limited trial purposes. This did not deter S&T Branch in HQ Malaya and Major Lukes found a Chinese who had a backyard shop where he produced a small quantity of tins locally. On being shown some very nice samples of 'Singapore' tins, he agreed to produce two dozen free of charge. So it was from these first steps that a suitable pack for both Gurkhas and Malays was produced. Each had various types of curry and rice as the main meal and they were an immediate success. The next problem was to expand production and here there were problems. Private enterprise was not stifled as 'Tenders' and 'Contracts' had to be brought into the system. Increased pressure had to be applied to the Chinese entrepreneur who had taken on the task as he had doubts on his ability to cope despite the lure of more money. What was never in doubt was that he could submit the lowest tender and this he duly did. From then on all HQ RASC's efforts proved their worth. Extra sheds were added to the Supply Depot and a packing factory was set up where with a supply of tins, a sealing machine and female labour, the first operational packs were produced. They were rapidly in the supply pipeline, issued to the Air Despatch Detachment and dropped by RAF aircraft to the troops in the jungle. To speed the tempo of production in the packing sheds, 'music while you work' was introduced. Although the resulting sound was described as 'awful' by the CRASC, it nevertheless had the desired result and within six months the target of 10,000 packs had been achieved. Later in the time of Lieutenant Colonel Campbell, the 100,000 mark was reached and an improvement to the British 24 hour ration pack was also made. This local achievement which ran contrary to many accepted ideas at the time could not have been achieved without the support of the DST FARELF at the time, Brigadier Pat Eassie and his staff, and later as the tempo of the Emergency increased in 1950, this now fully established venture was transferred from Malaya. It was decided that the scale of production now necessary should more properly take place in Singapore and the operation was transferred to 4 Supply Reserve Depot (SRD). In the two years that HQ RASC Malaya pioneered this new side of RASC work in the Far East, almost one and a half million rations were produced and all the difficulties that naturally arose one after another in a job of this kind had been overcome, giving not only valuable experience to the initiators, but also to those that took over.

Having produced a suitable ration pack for jungle operations, the next step in the maintenance chain was its delivery to the soldier deep in the jungle, together with all his other requirements to enable him to live and fight. The RAF and the RASC Air

Despatch organization together provided this link with tactical air supply. The importance of tactical air supply in Malayan operations could be measured by the fact that without it the depth to which the security forces on the ground could penetrate the jungle would be limited by the amount of food, ammunition and other requirements they could carry on their backs. As it was, the man on the ground knew from experience that patrols that penetrated deep into the jungle could remain there as long as was necessary and, whatever the terrain, they could rely on air supply wherever and whenever it was requested.

As there was no opposition to our aircraft either from air or ground attack in Malaya, the main hazards of operational flying were absent. In their place were however the most powerful enemies of the security forces in the air and on the ground − the jungle, the terrain and the climatic conditions. The Malayan jungle covers both the flat and the mountainous regions of the country and is broken only by extensive swamps. The trees in deep jungle almost invariable reach a height of some 200 feet and have long bare trunks ending in a dense mass of leaves and branches which form an unbroken canopy above the ground. The weather conditions are normally fairly good in the early part of the day, but deteriorate rapidly, bringing a high degree of turbulence, while the thick cloud in the humid climate usually covers wide areas creating a very real hazard when operating in the mountainous terrain. Even when thick cloud was absent, small clouds and jungle mists lurking in the deep valleys made it dangerous for any aircraft to penetrate them, particularly the larger, less manoeuverable types. A forced landing was virtually impossible owing to the unbroken carpet of undergrowth, the tall trees and lack of clearings. Personal parachutes for aircrews and air despatchers were regarded as superfluous and were not carried, since flying on supply runs was done at approximately 300−400 feet altitude. Great skill and judgement on behalf of the pilot and close cooperation by RASC despatching crews was required for successful dropping under such conditions and much practice was needed to achieve this success. A thorough examination of the Dropping Zone (DZ) was always made from a safe height to determine the best run-in/run-out. If the pilot considered it essential, a dummy run would be made and if necessary the line of run-in/run-out could be changed. This obviated the need for changing whilst the actual dropping run was being made when the crews would be at their dropping stations in

[By courtesy of PR Far East Air Force]

Despatching 1 ton container over the Malayan jungle.

the aircraft and the loads unlashed and loose.

All AD crews wore overalls and jungle boots and carried a .38 revolver, ammunition and an emergency jungle pack. This pack contained insect repellent, first aid outfit, fishing line, sharpening stone, water sterilizing outfit, razor blades, waterproof matches, rabbit snares, burning glass, socks, mosquito-proof hat, survival compass, rubber water bottle, survival pack container, emergency flying rations, knife, sewing kit, aircrew first aid outfit (containing paludrine and morphine), fishing hooks and spinners, heliograph, gloves, a small Union Jack and USA flag (presumably a relic from the last war). While actual despatching was in progress a safety-harness was worn by the AD crew in the aircraft. The RASC crew commander carried a headset through which he communicated with the pilot. The pilot transmitted all dropping signals to the despatchers by bell: the headset was used as a means of communication between the pilot and crew commander only.

The heights from which supplies were dropped varied from some 300 to 1,000 feet in isolated cases, but the normal height was 300 to 400 feet above ground level to give greater accuracy in dropping. However, because of the height of the trees this represents only 100 feet to 200 feet above tree level.

Great accuracy in dropping was essential. Supplies falling short or over-shooting the DZ could result in many hours or even days of work for the soldier on the ground in retrieving them. The terrorists were quick to fasten on to supply drops lost to the security forces and were known to retrieve food and equipment with their ingenuity, born of necessity, put to many uses. The accuracy achieved in dropping was very high. The percentage of success was well over 90% and even then lack of success was more usually due to parachute failure than inaccuracy in dropping. Aircraft were almost always in wireless contact with the DZ and awaited assurance that packs were recoverable before leaving the area. The usual reason for an aircraft returning with undropped supplies was the refusal of the DZ to accept them because of a change of plan. The only other cause of failure was when particularly dense cloud precluded dropping and this happened only occasionally in the monsoon periods.

The selection of the DZ was entirely the responsibility of the patrol commander on the ground. The right to veto a DZ however, rested with the RAF but was rarely, if ever, exercised. The DZs varied in dimensions from the size of a tennis court to a jungle clearing of a few square feet or even in some cases no clearing at all. In the latter event, supplies were aimed at grenade or wood fire smoke visible above the trees or at marker balloons 50 feet above the trees and attached by line to the ground. These balloons were equipped with individual Hydride generators for inflation but because of the weight to be carried (7 to 9 lbs.) their use was restricted. Other marking aids used included smoke generators, ground flares and Verey signals. The normal DZ marking panels were used to form the DZ code letters which were allocated to units by Headquarters Malaya Command, and the number of bars to be used with these were allocated by the unit to its patrols.

When a unit had a number of patrols operating in the same area, the number of bars allocated to a DZ letter by the unit could be confusing to the pilot and identification of the DZ was most important. On one occasion, when a patrol of 1st Fiji Infantry Regiment was operating near a Gurkha patrol, the pilot confused the DZs and one pack was dropped on the wrong DZ. The Fijians were delighted to receive the Gurkhas' rum, and although only some few hundred yards separated the two patrols, the density of the jungle between them made it impracticable for the Gurkhas to retrieve the pack despite its contents. The pack was however re-supplied the following day to the correct DZ. Practically all units ensured that there was a wireless set on the DZ for ground to aircraft communications.

When drops were made where there was no DZ the main difficulty was in retrieving the packs when the parachutes had become entangled in the trees. Of the many methods which were tried, the best results were obtained by climbing the tree with the aid of climbing irons, blowing down the tree with explosives or burning the canopy of the parachute by setting fire to it with a Verey pistol cartridge.

On one occasion in August 1950 a patrol of 1st Battalion, The Devonshire Regiment, during a pursuit resulting from the abduction and subsequent murder of a planter's wife near Bentong, followed the terrorists so deeply into the jungle that it ran completely out of all supplies, including Verey cartridges and smoke grenades. No fire could be lit owing to the heavy rain which had been falling for several days, so no means of indicating their position was available. The platoon commander, a sergeant, was however in wireless contact with his battalion and the battalion in touch with the aircraft. The pilot was instructed to make several experimental runs over the area and the sergeant, correcting each run over the wireless, eventually guided the aircraft to a line over his position. The aircraft then made dropping runs along this line, despatching the supplies to the orders given by the sergeant on the ground. All the packs were retrieved and the majority fell within 25 yards of the position.

The main disadvantage of air supply was that the receipt of a drop could disclose the position of a patrol to the terrorists if they actually saw the drop in progress. Because of this, when troops were in pursuit or believed themselves to be in close contact, they would normally change their position immediately after the drop. They also requested dummy drops in the area. The number of times that a patrol was so compromised is, however, open to conjecture. Because of the dense jungle it was extremely difficult to see the actual drop even within yards of the DZ and the mere sound of aircraft in the vicinity did not indicate a drop or indeed the presence of a supply-dropping aircraft and could be more misleading than helpful. What is certain however is that without air supply, our troops could not have existed in deep jungle sufficiently long to achieve the success that they did.

Squadrons from the RAF, RAAF and RNZAF all provided aircraft and crews for air despatch during the Emergency, and the RASC Air Despatch Units provided the air despatch crews in each case. A variety of aircraft were used, but as a general purpose aircraft the Valetta proved to be the most suitable for operations in Malaya, the requirement being to carry out a large number of supply drops over a wide area during the short periods of favourable weather conditions. The RAF flew Dakota aircraft until 1952, and thereafter used Valettas. The RAAF also used Dakotas prior to 1952 when they returned to Australia. The RNZAF who flew Dakotas during their first tour, made a welcome return in 1955 with Bristol Freighters, which proved very suitable for the type of operations undertaken. Hastings aircraft, on trial in the Command, were flown by the RAF but in spite of their heavy payload were not considered suitable for Malayan operations because of their lack of manoeuvrability.

When the Emergency was declared in Malaya in June 1948 a platoon of 799 Company RASC (AD/GT) was located in Kuala Lumpur and this detachment was used to cope with the light air supply commitment, flying on an average two sorties a week in addition to the normal MT operations carried out by the remainder of the company which was based on Singapore. The first operation of any size occurred in August 1948 when a force of the 2/6th Gurkhas and police, sent to Gua Musang in Kelantan where bandits had captured the police station, were supplied by air. After this it was quickly realized that police outposts could be maintained by air and this constituted the main commitment for the rest of the year. 28 tons of stores were dropped during 1948. In December of that year the Kuala Lumpur detachment was relieved of its MT duties.

It was not until January 1949, when sufficient troops of the Guards Brigade and Gurkhas had been trained and deployed in the jungle, that air supply took the pattern which continued throughout the emergency, i.e. patrols remaining in the jungle for long periods entirely dependent on supply by air. The air supply commitment increased and 930 tons of stores were dropped in 1949.

During 1950, 1,885 tons of stores were dropped and in

September, 799 Company became 55 Company RASC (AD).

In 1951, 1,658 tons of stores were dropped. During these early years of the Emergency, RASC crews also despatched oil-bombs from Dakotas, bracketing areas known to contain Communists as a guide for Lincoln bombers following up.

It was not until 1952 that 55 Company was relieved of its other duties and became responsible solely for air supply in Malaya. On 9 February 1952 airborne forces were used for the first time in the Emergency in Malaya; some 54 parachutists of the SAS Regiment (Malayan Scouts) dropped into North Perak, near the Thailand border, during Operation Helsby. Air supply was not required on the first day of this operation although it had been prepared, but, as a diversion, fifteen dummy parachutists were dropped from 1,000 feet some six miles from the area in which the live drop had been completed. These dummy parachutists (Devices Tactical) have since been used in other airborne operations, the despatching again being carried out by RASC crews. 1,598 tons of supplies were dropped during this year.

In 1953, 2,580 tons were dropped and the detachment at Kuala Lumpur was increased to cope with this additional load. From 26 October to 9 December 1953 a force of some four battalions was entirely dependent on the air for supplies during Operation Valiant, simultaneous with other operations which were taking place in other parts of Malaya. This almost doubled the normal commitment and was further complicated by the locations of the DZs in the Valiant area. These were situated in the mountain range amidst 7,000 feet peaks, and were rarely sited below 4,000 feet. In spite of these conditions none of the troops on the ground went hungry.

Whilst 55 Company (AD) was building up both the volume of stores despatched by air, and its reputation, the MT companies were completing their reorganizations resulting from the introduction of the MOR into all the units with the exception of 3 and 27 Companies, which remained British manned. By 1952 there was a steady flow of MOR coming out of the RASC School at Nee Soon, and the senior British NCOs in Companies were being replaced by experienced MORs, a few of whom had seen service during World War II. 24 Company then commanded by Major D J Sutton (later Brigadier) had reached this stage by the end of 1952 and only the CSM and CQMS were still British. All the officers were however still posted into the unit from British manned units, some straight from UK. It was therefore very much a case of 'in job' training, the main problems being that of language, experience, or lack of it, and general background. The Company provided transport for 99 Gurkha Infantry Brigade in the Johore area, part of 17 Gurkha Division. In 1954, newly arrived in the Company now commanded by Major D Cuff MBE RCT, was Captain (later Lieutenant Colonel) J W Aggleton RCT direct from UK, who was sent to command two platoons of the Company located in an old pineapple factory between Johore Bahru and the new village at Scudai. The location was outside the wire perimeter protecting both these places, and was very much on its own. The factory was surrounded by its own perimeter fence, with the jungle on three sides and the main road on the fourth. Apart from Captain Aggleton, the entire detachment was Malay and he did not then speak a word of their language. His path was greatly smoothed however by the senior MOR, Warrant Officer Class 2 Attan bin Yattim BEM, who was one of those MOR who had served in the British Army before the Japanese invasion. (He subsequently commissioned into the Malaysian Army Service Corps.) Partly as a morale builder and partly to let any unfriendly listeners in the adjacent jungle know that the camp occupants were soldiers as well as lorry drivers, Aggleton gave his detachment elementary training in jungle patrolling and the emergency drills were well practised. The drills presupposed that any attack would have the armoury as its target. Aggleton though, with his then very limited experience with Malay soldiers, was still not certain how 'his friendly, gentle and indeed sometimes lethargic soldiers' would react in the event of a real emergency. However, any misgivings that he may have had were soon dispelled.

About 0300 hours on a very dark night, he was jolted out of his slumbers by a most infernal din. The noise arose from volleys being fired by terrorists on the road side of the compound at the corrugated iron pineapple factory! Fortunately the noise had the same effect on Aggleton's soldiers as it had on him and they had been right in assessing the enemy's tactics. The shots fired at the tin buildings from the front were a deliberate diversionary ploy and by concentrating their efforts on the rear – jungle-side of the location, they were able to foil the main body of the attackers in the act of cutting through the perimeter wire with the armoury – now empty! – as their objective. This was typical of one of the many sorts of incidents in which MOR soldiers of the RASC were involved during the campaign and proved their ability to cope with whatever situation came their way. For Captain Aggleton, it established his confidence in Malay soldiers and with his baptism of (jungle) fire behind him, was not long afterwards posted to HQ 99 Gurkha Infantry Brigade as the Brigade RASC Officer (BRASCO). The appointment of BRASCO which Captain Aggleton filled is one which serves to illustrate the overall responsibilities of the Corps in a brigade on operations, in an anti-terrorist role and we continue with his story with this in mind.

The responsibility of the BRASCO (as in other campaigns) was to ensure that units of the brigade received whatever transport and supplies that they required to enable them to operate under the prevailing conditions. In the case of 99 Brigade, there were ten infantry battalions under command at any one time, plus supporting units widely dispersed throughout Johore. In Malacca, where – owing to the nature of operations – HQ 63 Gurkha Infantry Brigade was for a time in the nature of a subordinate HQ to 99 Brigade, but they had no BRASCO and Aggleton doubled in that role for 63 Brigade.

The area covered by the two brigades was nearly 10,000 square miles, of which 80% was dense jungle, the remainder being rubber plantations (each with its own detachment of troops, as had the 'New Villages'), or swamp. Although 17 Division and its three Brigades – 26, 63 and 99 – included 'Gurkha' in their titles, a typical mix of battalions under command of 99 Brigade would be three Gurkha, two Malay (British Army Malay Regiments), one Fijian, one Northern Rhodesian, two British and one Police Field Force, making ten battalions in all. Each contingent had its own exacting ration scale and taboos and the problems of special ration packs have already been discussed. Even though by now a number of jungle forts and landing strips had been established, small patrol groups were often in the jungle for three weeks at a time and were dependent on air supply.

The BRASCO's job meant him living in the pockets of the Staff Officers of the two Brigade HQs and very close personal liaison with the battalions/companies/platoons or equivalent, was involved. It was essential that fast and accurate information should be transmitted to the RASC supporting units and that the requirements should be met completely effectively. The RASC units involved included the Supply Depots at Kluang and in Singapore for provisioning of rations and 55 Company (Air Despatch) and 24 Company, the Brigade Transport Company in

Kuala Lumpur and Kluang respectively for their delivery. There was also plentiful assistance obtained from across the causeway in Singapore for transport requirements particularly for the frequent battalion changeovers, whether on rotation to and from their home countries or to and from rest areas. The system worked extremely effectively and praise rather than any explanation for shortcomings was the order of things. Aggleton's travelling to visit units, both the providers and the recipients, involved air as well as ground transport and again the Corps were involved in the aircraft role. Hundreds of hours were spent 'jungle hopping' in Austers of 1911 Light Liaison Flight, often piloted by Captain Ben Bradbrook RASC (later Colonel).

Two events took place during this period which almost transcended all the operational problems and in which the Corps were to play their full part. Firstly, the Coronation of HM The Queen was celebrated throughout Malaya on 2 June 1953. In Kuala Lumpur, Taiping, Penang, the Cameron Highlands and Kluang, major parades involving all units in the areas were held. The Corps was represented by detachments on all these parades and No. 3 Dress was specially issued for the occasion. Following the ceremonial parades, suitable celebrations were held in units. As befitted Coronation Year, a very special effort was made over Corps Weeks held later in the month in all RASC units and some well earned relaxation was possible whilst still meeting all operational commitments.

The second event was more personal to Malaya and was the Diamond Jubilee of His Highness the Sultan of Johore, two years after the Coronation of HM the Queen. This was held on 12 July 1955 and HQ 99 Brigade was given the task of organizing the procession, the parade and other military events in Johore Bahru. The RASC was naturally much involved in the transportation that such an event requires but 24 Company's detachment on the parade were singled out for special praise for their immaculate turnout under their detachment commander Captain George Davenport RASC. There is no doubt that the Corps MOR were equally at home on the ceremonial parade ground as they were in their operational roles.

Continuing the story of the part played by the British manned 55 Air Despatch Company during this same period, we find that there was no respite for them from the intensity of their operations. In 1953 the Company HQ was located at Changi, Singapore and commanded by Major T A K Savage (later Brigadier) and the operations in Malaya were carried out by the detachment in Kuala Lumpur, then commanded by Captain P H Benson (later Major General). Mention has been made earlier of Operation Valiant which typifies the extent of the operations then taking place. This involved maintaining by air a large infantry brigade size force sent into the jungle in an effort to bottle up and capture Chin Peng, the Communist Terrorist (CT) leader. Sadly, he escaped, but the detachment worked round the clock for several weeks to meet all the demands made upon it and it never failed once. General Hugh Stockwell, then the GOC, made a special visit to the detachment to thank its members personally for their supreme effort. In one period of 24 hours, some 84,800 lbs of stores were dropped. These included millions of propaganda leaflets offering safe conduct to any terrorist giving himself up. To this splendid work by the air despatchers must be added the greatest possible praise for the pilots and crews of the RAF, RAAF and RNZAF, whose courage and determination made the support possible. There were many examples of their skills and fearlessness in the face of great difficulties. The detachment also worked during one period with the Royal Navy – 848 Helicopter Squadron RN, commanded then by Lieutenant Commander Jim Suthers. This fine Squadron worked in the closest cooperation with the 55 Company detachment and put in many flying hours in a great variety of tasks. One particularly useful chore carried out for the detachment was the recovery of parachutes from the jungle forts. If this had not been done, the supply of equipment would not have kept pace with the AD demands.

In 1954, the whole of 55 Company moved from Changi to Kuala Lumpur and Major L Barker-Simpson took over command. This year saw the Company reach the peak of air supply operations in Malaya, with monthly drops reaching a million pounds and as many as seventy-five DZs being served in one day. Regrettably, during the whole period of the Emergency, the Company paid a heavy price in casualties, and seven air crashes claimed the lives of thirty-five all ranks, in addition to the crews of the aircraft. This was the highest casualty rate of any army unit. Sixteen members of the Company won decorations, twenty-nine were mentioned in despatches and seven received C-in-C's Certificates. Subsequently a grateful Government of Malaya awarded a ceremonial Malayan kris to the Company for its services during the Emergency. Only three were awarded, the other two going to 15/19th Hussars and to

52 Squadron RAF, who had carried out so many missions carrying the air despatchers and their loads from 55 Company.

Before leaving 55 Company, a story of one of the air crashes serves to illustrate not only the appalling conditions which so often existed for the pilots and air crew (and despite their skills and courage sometimes defeated them), but also the high morale and resolution of the air despatchers who flew with them. On 10 December 1956, a Bristol Freighter of 41 Squadron RNZAF took off to drop supplies to units in the Cameron Highlands area. On board were the three RNZAF air crew, four air despatchers of 55 Company and two cameramen from the Malayan Film Unit. It was described as a 'day of terrible flying conditions', and the aircraft crashed about midday into the trees at the top of a steep ridge 4,200 feet high in the deepest primary jungle. The wreckage was seen in the late afternoon from a spotter plane and in the evening an effort was made to parachute from a helicopter a rescue patrol of the SAS, but the atrocious weather conditions which had persisted all day prevented such action. The bad flying conditions continued and it was not until the morning of the third day, that it was possible for an Auster aircraft to guide patrols to the scene of the crash. The obvious force of the impact and the fierceness of the fire which followed led the search parties and the Court of Inquiry to form the opinion that no-one could possibly have survived and next of kin were informed accordingly.

However, a detachment of 4 Malay Regiment with their native trackers remained for a while in the area, because in the vicinity of the tangled mass of burned wreckage, a patrol discovered what could possibly have been a shelter. This was nothing much on which to place any hope but as long as there was a chance that a survivor had somehow had a miraculous escape, it was decided to continue the search. The problem confronting the 4 Malay patrol was who made the shelter? Was it a survivor, considered an unlikely possibility, or a Communist terrorist? A few days later a faint track was found and the jungle trackers following it for some thousand yards found a rough but well constructed shelter. Following the trail, the patrol then found at the same distance, two more shelters and it became clear that the builder was going downhill away from the wreckage. A second patrol joined in the search and as the days went by evidence built up that they were on the trail of a survivor. On 21 December, the two patrols met up and their findings were such that they were confident that the man they sought was in the vicinity. On the morning of the twelfth day following the crash, a ragged figure was seen crossing a river by a bridge built by a 4 Malay patrol. It was Driver Lee of 55 Company. Apart from burned hands and arms and a very painful ankle, subsequently found to be broken, he was in good condition. A helicopter was flown in with a doctor and Driver Lee was taken to the British Military Hospital at Kinrara. 4 Malay patrol's persistence had paid off!

The remarkable determination and self discipline which sustained Driver Lee for the twelve days following the crash was an example to all. He had put into practice all the drills and used to the full the knowledge gained on a jungle survival course. In a direct line he had walked some six or seven miles through primary jungle, but the distance covered could well have been at least half as much again. He had taken from the wreck four Gurkha two-man ration packs, which he carried in a haversack which he made up from packing material. He rationed himself to one handful of rice each morning and evening. He had sufficient rice when found to have lasted him another ten days. He also ate jungle plants and fern tops. His efforts to trap the birds which came after his rice met with failure owing to the condition of his hands. Driver Lee's exploit proved that a well trained, mentally fit and alert man could overcome the physical hazards of the jungle under adverse conditions, and survive.

An important step towards the formation of the Federation Army which was to come into existence on Independence, was the creation of the Federal Division in 1954. 29 Company RASC had, by now, like 24 Company, with the exception of its British officers and a very few British senior NCOs, been completely 'Malayanized' and was the forerunner of RASC Companies to pass subsequently to the Federation Army as part of the Malayan Army Service Corps. The CRASC North Malaya at that time, Lieutenant Colonel E G H Lonsdale MBE RASC (later Major General) formed 1 Federal Division RASC from his original HQ and had under command 3 Company RASC which was British manned, but had a platoon of the Royal Australian Army Service Corps attached, 29 Company and 2 Supply Depot. The CRASC established the RASC in the Division on a regimental basis, separating his own HQ from the HQ of the Division. These were the first steps towards the formation of Regiments in the Corps which were to be established throughout the Corps a few years later.

Although the emergency was to continue until 31 July 1960, significant changes were to take place in the Corps organization before that date. The first was brought about on the creation of the Federation Army when the Malay States were granted Independence (Merdeka) within the Commonwealth on 31 August 1957. The Federation Army was formed prior to this date on 15 July 1957, and the Malayan (later Malaysian) Army Service Corps was born. Although it was not until 1965 that the Malaysian Service Corps was firmly established, having evolved from the Federation. Supplies and Transport Service of the Armed Forces Maintenance Corps, which had absorbed the MASC soon after its formation in 1957. A number of RASC Companies which had been previously converted to MOR manned companies passed to the MASC in toto, retaining their British officers. 29 Company commanded by Major (later Lieutenant Colonel) J A W Lerwill became 2 Transport Company and 52 Company which was in 17 Gurkha Division became 3 Transport Company. Other RASC Companies continued to have MOR until the units were finally disbanded on the withdrawal of British Forces from Malaya and Singapore from late 1967, though the Federation Army naturally attracted many of the Corps Malay and Chinese officers and senior MOR to their ranks from the outset. These were to become the well-trained leaders of the Malayan Army Service Corps.

British RASC officers were to play a major part in the successful establishment of the S&T element of the Federation Army, both as staff officers and in units. Lieutenant Colonel H I Charkham OBE RASC was loaned as the SO I S&T at the HQ of the Federation Army in 1957. His task was to implement the policy of the Malayan Government that the Federation Army S&T organization were to become totally independent of the British supply system. Initially the S&T Order of Battle was:

a. Regular Transport Companies   3
   (Nos. 2 & 3 already mentioned and No. 1
   formed from the Federation Transport Unit
   of the Malay Regiment.)
b. TA Transport Companies   3
   (Originally Federation of Malaya
   Volunteer Army Service Corps.)
c. Supply Depots   2
d. Reserve Supply Depot   1
e. Barrack Services

S & T became responsible for the provision and issue of Supplies, POL and Barrack Stores for all three Services of the Federation Forces. The task involved in assuming these overall responsibilities was considerable. New Ration Scales had to be produced, new contract procedures adopted, and specifications prepared for all items of supplies and POL. In addition, long term provision arrangements had to be made and new sources of supply found.

On the transport side, an Air Supply Platoon was formed and trained initially by 55 Air Despatch Company, using RAF aircraft from 52 Squadron RAF. This platoon subsequently had to adapt to the use of Twin Pioneer aircraft of which the Royal Malayan Air Force had six. There were many technical problems to be overcome before the aircraft could be used for efficient air despatch in the prevailing conditions, but with the combined experience of the seconded officers, RMAF and RASC, a viable payload was achieved. Not only was all unnecessary equipment removed from the aircraft (they were equipped for worldwide use), but lighter delivery equipment was designed. The result was that an extra 700 lbs of supplies could be carried.

In 1958, Lieutenant Colonel Charkham was joined by Major I Renwick (later Lieutenant Colonel) who was the DADST Supplies. At this stage it had become necessary to design a new 24-hour Ration Pack which until then had been provided by S&T FARELF from Singapore and this had also been designed locally, as related earlier in this chapter. Much of the same sort of process had to be gone through in the Federation Army, spurred on by their S&T Staff as had taken place some nine years earlier. The result was the highly successful CHARWICK Ration named after its originators, Lieutenant Colonel Charkham and Major Renwick. This pack was eventually used by the Gurkhas and Malays remaining in the British Army.

By this time, the strength of the multi-racial MASC in the Federation Army was over 1,500 all ranks. The aim of the seconded officers was to ensure that they passed on their knowledge to their Malay counterparts and that all officers received a general grounding in all aspects of Service training as well as technical training. Two Federation S&T officers passed and were selected for the Staff College Camberley, the first from the logistic service. The future leaders of the MASC were now coming to the fore all having served in the RASC and were experienced and ready to take over their responsibilities in their own Corps. The first Director of Supplies and Transport was to be Colonel (later Brigadier) Ungku Ahmed bin Abdul Rahman DK JSM SSIJ SPMJ JP, followed by Colonel Michael Peh Tek Foo Kmn. They were to set their new Corps on the path to success.

Colonel Ungku Ahmed took over as the first Director of Supplies & Transport in August 1962, when the post of SO 1 S&T was abolished on the departure of Lieutenant Colonel H I Charkham for UK. A senior seconded RASC/RCT officer was to remain on the S&T Headquarters for the next six years – Lieutenant Colonel R E Thomas OBE, and was to assist in the expansion of the MASC which was able to cope with all the tasks asked of it in support of the Malaysian Brigade in the subsequent Borneo Campaign. He was later to be decorated by the Malaysian Government with the award of the Kesatna Mangku Negara for his services. Other RASC/RCT officers continued to be seconded to what was by this time Malaysian Service Corps (MSC) and played an important part in establishing training organizations, now rapidly expanding to meet the needs of the growing army. Major J W Aggleton MBE, returning to Malaysia after earlier service with 24 Company, was tasked with establishing an MSC School, which was to provide all-arms driver training. This MSC School was to be sited near Taiping in the northern state of Perak and was to be the equivalent of the RCT Training Centre plus the Army MT School. The CO was Lieutenant Colonel (later Colonel) 'George' Gui Poh Chee, K, MVOMN, who had been commissioned into the British Army after a course at Mons Officer Cadet School as part of the progressive policy of General Sir Gerald Templer (later Field Marshal) in grooming local soldiers to take early responsibility in the Federation Army, then yet to be formed. The great benefits which the S&T branch of the Federation Army gained from this policy was readily apparent from the rapid progress which the new Corps made in all its activities.

The next stage in the development of the MSC School was the establishment of an Officers Training Wing. This was started by Major Aggleton, but taken over by the newly arrived Major (later Colonel) T K G S Barrett RCT when Major Aggleton departed for UK. Eventually there was within the Training Centre, an Officers' School, a Driver Training School, an NCO's Wing, an Air Despatch Wing and a Catering School. There was also an MSC Air Despatch Company in Taiping and air despatchers flew in the aircraft of RMAF to support the Malaysian Forces operating against the Communist terrorists on the Thai border. A small number of RCT officers, including Major Barrett were awarded the Pingant Perkhidmatan – the Malaysian General Service Medal for operations against the terrorists.

Whilst this considerable development of the MSC was taking place the Emergency continued beyond Independence, though waning, and the Corps maintained its operational support of the British forces that were still involved.

The second significant change to affect the overall organization of the Corps was the formation of the Gurkha Army Service Corps on 1 July 1958, in Singapore and Malaya. Full details of this new element of the Corps are given in Part II of this book. HQ Gurkha Army Service Corps was formed on 1 July 1960 at Kluang and remained there until 1970 when then as the Gurkha Transport Regiment, it moved to Hong Kong. From late 1967, at the start of the British Army rundown in the Far East, the CO had also been Commander RCT 17 Gurkha Division/ Malaya District located in Seremban and with his Regiment then spread between Malaysia, Singapore and Hong Kong, was certainly well occupied. The first company formed and located in Kluang, South Malaya, 30 Company, was able to provide support for 63 Gurkha Infantry Brigade towards the end of the Emergency, the remaining companies though were not at an operational state of readiness before the Emergency was declared over on 31 July 1960. Their time was to come however and two of the Companies, in addition to 30 Company, who by then had moved to Singapore, were to play an important role in the Brunei and Borneo Campaign. 31 Company were in Singapore at the start of the Brunei revolt and moved there in support of 99 Brigade. 34 Company remained in Kluang but sent detachments to Borneo as the campaign proceeded and was involved from Kluang in supporting operations against the Indonesian parachute landings on the west coast of Malaysia during 1964. 30 Company was to rotate with 31 Company throughout the Borneo campaign. Details of the Companies' role in the Brunei and Borneo campaign are given in that Chapter.

From the end of the Emergency, declared on 1 August 1960 until the start of the Brunei and Borneo Campaign in December 1962, the Corps had been able to concentrate on its own internal reorganizations which were affected by Independence and the formation of the Gurkha Army Service Corps. The senior Corps officer during this period in Malaya was the ADST at HQ 17 Gurkha Division/Overseas Commonwealth Land Forces, Colonel (later Brigadier) E V Molyneux OBE MC. 28 Commonwealth Brigade had now been formed at Malacca on the west coast and 3 Company RASC at Terendak Camp was the transport company of the brigade. It had now been in Malaya continuously since 1948. There were two Australian officers in the Company, both of the Royal Australian Army Service Corps, Captain V Smith and Lieutenant D Gough, commanding the Composite Platoon and C Platoon, an Australian platoon respectively. The OC was Major N O E Witt RASC serving for the second time in Malaya. The Company was subsequently to send detachments to serve in the Borneo Campaign.

In 1965, The Royal Corps of Transport was formed. This now only affected the British manned units of the Corps but all MORs in transport units were also rebadged Royal Corps of Transport. The Gurkha Army Service Corps became the Gurkha Transport Regiment as already mentioned. The post of ADST at HQ 17 Gurkha Division disappeared and was replaced by a CRCT dealing with transportation matters only. Lieutenant Colonel C Adwick OBE RCT was the first officer in this new appointment and was succeeded by Lieutenant Colonel A D Fitzgerald MBE in 1966. He was in fact to be the last 'one hatted' CRCT as the CO of the Gurkha Transport Regiment, as recounted earlier was to double up in the appointment by the end of 1967. In January 1966 when Lieutenant Colonel Fitzgerald became CRCT, the Borneo Campaign was showing signs of ending, though 'roulement' of units between Malaya and Borneo was still taking place. The Movements organization of HQ RCT had become a Corps responsibility the previous year on rebadging. Led by Major K French MBE RCT, who had been transferred from the Royal Engineers, they were an extremely busy part of the organization with the 'roulement' of all units being a particular responsibility in addition to the routine movement to UK and throughout the Far East by air from Kuala Lumpur airport. 28 Commonwealth Infantry Brigade Group in Malacca with 3 Company as its transport unit, had direct access to sea movement through a hard at Terendak Camp. LCTs with stores from Singapore were able to berth there and these operations too were controlled by Major French and his staff from HQ RCT very effectively.

During this period, 3 Company was commanded by Major J S Messervy (later Colonel) followed by Major K C Davis MBE (later Brigadier). 3 Company remained British and Australian manned, but the remaining transport units, now reduced in size to troop level, 402, 403 and 404 Troops, for Garrison duties in Penang, Seremban and Terendak, were all-Malay units. The troop in Seremban was commanded by a Chinese RCT officer, Lieutenant R N F Lee, but the remaining troops still had British officers. Malay potential officers were now tending to go direct into the Federal Army with whom close liaison was maintained. At this time the DST (they had not changed to a transport corps) Federal Army was Brigadier Doto Ungku Ahmed and the deputy, Colonel George Bui Poh Chui, both very well known to the Corps.

The popular Commander of the Division at that time was Major General A G Patterson, who saw a great deal of the Corps both in Malaya and Borneo. On meeting the British RSM of HQ RCT and being told that a few years earlier as a Corporal he had escaped from an ambush on the way to the Cameron Highlands, immediately said 'Good! I like to have men in my Division who have been ambushed – they teach the others.' The days of ambushes were almost past though, at least in Malaysia and Borneo as Confrontation drew to a close. The days remaining for the British Army in Malaysia were also limited as the British Government's policy for East of Suez took effect. The reduction in the size of the Corps in Malaysia ran parallel to that of the other units of the British Army over the next three years. The Gurkha Transport Regiment which had won its spurs in Borneo was, as already related, to move to Hong Kong. Our all-Malay units which had so successfully evolved over almost twenty-five years were disbanded. The Corps functions were left in the very good hands of the MSC whom we had helped to form and who had responded so well to the assistance that we provided. The many Corps officers who served with the MSC during the formative years will look back with pleasure and pride at their success.

BRUNEI, BORNEO AND SARAWAK

WHEN, ON 14 AUGUST 1945, Japan's unconditional surrender was accepted, 20 Indian Division was in Burma. In September the formation moved by sea and air to French Indo China, with the task of concentrating and disarming some 70,000 Japanese troops. The GOC had the additional role of commanding the Supreme Allied Commander South-East Asia (SACSEA) Control Commission.

On 28 December, 32 Indian Infantry Brigade was withdrawn from the Division embarked at Saigon and sailed for Labuan Island where, on 28 December 1945 it took over responsibility for Borneo, Sarawak and the North Borneo territory from 9 Australian Division.

With the Brigade were its attached RASC supply units commanded by Major P G Malins. These units comprised 4 Supply Company under Major W G Glahome; 363 Bulk Petrol Platoon commanded by Lieutenant I Fergusson; a Control Centre; Field Maintenance Area and 38 Indian Composite Platoon RIASC.

These units took over a Base Supply Depot on Labuan Island and Supply Depots at Kuching, Sarawak, and at Jesselton (now Kota Kinabalu, the capital of Sabah) and were responsible for rations and supplies for the Brigade, RAF and remaining Australian personnel together with the large number of Japanese Prisoners of War awaiting repatriation.

Large sections of the population were starving and the Brigade's RASC organization became involved in the distribution of food to these civilians including large quantities of Canadian and American wheat and flour and some 10,000 tons of ground nuts from Nigeria.

The bulk petrol installation was located on the dockside on Labuan Island and in addition to the responsibility for all petrol and lubricants for all military units in Borneo, the RASC Bulk Petrol Platoon provided aviation fuel for all aircraft using the Labuan airfield, which soon became the major staging post between Singapore and Australia, together with bulk kerosene – for civilian lighting and cooking, and diesel fuel for elements of the Pacific fleet. The installation proved far too small for the greatly increasing throughput and there was the constant problem of storage of each discharge from the two small tankers which brought in supplies from Singapore.

All POL supplies were shipped from Labuan to Kuching, Jesselton and other ports by small coastal craft operated by Indian Army personnel who had never been to sea before but who performed with great credit in the coral infested waters. Three RAF Sunderland flying boats were also made available to help with urgent supplies.

By June 1946 the duties of the force having been completed, all operations were closed down and the RASC units embarked for the UK.

The large island of Borneo, mainly part of Indonesia, has today along its Northern coastline two states of Malaysia, Sabah (formerly British North Borneo) comprising some 29,000 square miles, and Sarawak, some 48,000 square miles. Between them lies a former British Protectorate, the Sultanate of Brunei, comprising about 2,226 square miles.

By 1962, Indonesian ambitions to expand its sphere of influence and its territories were beginning to have repercussions both in Sarawak and Northern Borneo, but it was in December 1962 that open revolt broke out. The revolt in Brunei and the subsequent 'confrontation' with Indonesia had the common origin of opposition to the proposed creation of a Federation of Malaysia, conceived jointly by Britain and Malaya, and originally planned to incorporate Malaya, Singapore, Sarawak, Brunei and North Borneo (later Sabah). Although both Singapore and Brunei had reservations about the formation of Malaysia, the main opposition came from outside, from President Sukarno in Indonesia. He saw the formation of Malaysia with pro-Western affiliations as a frustration to his ambitions to incorporate the whole area into Maphilindo. He therefore organized opposition to the British and Malayan concept and offered to give direct help to anyone prepared to organize it. One Malay named Azahari was in this category and formed the secret North Kalimantan National Army with the aim of overthrowing the Sultan of Brunei and extending his own power to Sarawak and North Borneo (Sabah). His activities, initially in Brunei, were to start a campaign which was to last four years. At that time, apart from a small training camp which had been established near Kota Kinabalu in North Borneo, there was no other military station in the area.

A Far East Land Forces (FARELF) contingency plan existed for the sending at short notice of a small task force of infantry battalion strength in RAF transport aircraft to any part of its area. This would provide military assistance to meet an internal security threat to British territories requesting it. At the time of the outbreak of the revolt in Brunei, the nominated battalion for this small force was the 1st Battalion 2nd King Edward VII's Own Gurkha Rifles (The Sirmoor Rifles) who were located at Johore Bahru in Malaya within an hour's drive to the RAF Stations on Singapore Island. The DADST (Transport & Barracks) at 17 Gurkha Division Headquarters and Malaya Area, at Seremban, some 180 miles from Singapore, was the nominated administrative staff officer for this force, and at that time was Major W J B Seager RASC. His task with the force was to relieve the battalion commander of such matters as billeting, local purchase and/or requisitioning of transport, supplies and POL. His appointment with the force would last up to a month on operations, and he would be replaced should a large force become necessary, when the normal administrative elements of a brigade would take over. In the event this proved to be the situation on the first occasion that the force was called upon to act and thus it was that the RASC was represented on the ground from the very beginning of the subsequent operations in Brunei.

It was during the night of Friday/Saturday 7/8 December 1962 that, awakened in his quarter in Seremban by a telephone call from the Duty Officer of HQ 17 Gurkha Division, Major Seager was summoned to report immediately to Singapore, to take up his nominated appointment as administrative staff officer for an operation at that time in an un-named area. He was told that an Auster of the Divisional Air OP Flight would fly him to RAF Changi, Singapore, where he would be met and driven to the RAF Base at Seletar. After very hasty packing and departure from Seremban, he arrived at RAF Seletar early in the morning of 8th December, where he was soon to learn of his ultimate destination. The scene at Seletar, as he later recorded, was a hive of activity. Four Beverley freighter aircraft parked near the runway were being serviced and refuelled. Two companies of 1/2 GR, a small detachment of Royal Signals, and a ground party of RAF personnel, including an Air Transport Liaison Officer (ATLO)

Captain H Higgins RAOC, from 3 Army Air Supply Organization (AASO) RASC, were being marshalled into 'payloads'. Seager reported to the Force Commander, Major A Lloyd-Williams 2GR, who was second in command of 2GR. Soon after his arrival, in the early morning of 8th December, a party of officers from GHQ FARELF, led by the Brigadier General Staff, arrived at the airfield to brief the officers of 1/2 GR the now assembled Task Force.

It was disclosed that Brunei town (now Bandar Seri Begawan) was the 'trouble spot' although very few details were known, except that rioting and looting had taken place during the night, and several police stations had been attacked. The Commissioner of Police had asked for military assistance and it was thought at that time that the force assembled at Seletar would be adequate to deal with the situation. At this stage, under the contingency plan, the total RASC commitment was to provide seven days packed rations for this force.

Brunei airport was situated about four miles from the town and the departure of the Force from Singapore was so timed that it would arrive shortly after darkness had fallen, this being planned to give an element of surprise. The aircraft were scheduled to land at half hourly intervals in order that the off loading of each plane could be completed before the arrival of the next.

Seager with the Force Commander went in the first Beverley and as it neared Brunei the local air controller radioed that a party of armed rebels were assembled on the perimeter of the airport, on the far side of the runway, and had been firing at the control tower and airport building. Due to thick low cloud and no moonlight it was a pitch dark night. As the aircraft circled the airport the runway lights were suddenly switched on. The aircraft landed without delay and as it taxied towards the airport buildings, the landing lights were switched off again. As the party deplaned, a fusilade of shots were fired in their general direction but fortunately there was no casualties and stores were unloaded in 'double quick' time, followed by a rush for the cover of the airport building. The runway lights were switched on again just sufficiently long to enable the Beverley to take off.

The airport manager and his assistant, together with the Eurasian Traffic Controller, met the small force at the airport building. They were armed with 12 bore shotguns and had by then been on duty without a break since the trouble had flared up the previous evening; the number of shattered windows in the building were evidence of the precariousness of their situation. The Force Commander immediately took command of the situation and sent a platoon of his Gurkhas to deal with the rebels on the far side of the runway. They soon made contact and the rebels were rapidly dispersed after suffering a number of casualties and gave no further trouble that night.

Sentry posts were established round the building and LMG positions set up on the roof. The RAF personnel took over the general running of the airport and Major Seager assisted in establishing a temporary command post in the manager's office. The kitchens of the small restaurant were opened up and the RAF and Gurkha cooks set about producing tea and a hot meal from the compo rations brought with the Force.

The second aircraft was perforce slightly delayed in landing but the remaining two arrived on schedule. Brief contact was made by telephone with the Commissioner of Police at the Central Police Station in the centre of Brunei town and at about 2300 hours on the Saturday night, 8 December, the Force Commander with all his men except two platoons, set out for Brunei town. Two platoons were left to secure the airport and Major Seager remained at the Command Post.

On the approach march into the town several pockets of resistance were encountered resulting in casualties to both sides. Unfortunately five of the force were killed, including a British officer, Second Lieutenant Stevens; a Queens Gurkha Officer and five Gurkhas were wounded. The rebels as it was found later suffered many more casualties and some fifty prisoners were taken. At the airport, with the sound of firing nearby, the whole night was spent on the alert. Soon after dawn on Sunday morning, 9 December, two police Land Rovers and a 'Black Maria' with a Gurkha escort arrived to take Major Seager and the small HQ rear party to the Central Police Station, where the main body of the force were now established. Here it was learned that the small British Force were not up against the usual stone and bottle throwing hooligans who also had a few weapons, but well armed bands of rebels. Apart from arms and ammunition which must have been smuggled into the State prior to the revolt, on the Friday night, at a pre-arranged time, all the small police stations had been attacked and having overpowered the few policemen on duty, the weapons including LMGs had been stolen.

During the night, at the airport, a frustrating communication hitch had been discovered. The long range radio set installed in the Royal Signals Land Rover was inoperative. It seemed that when the vehicle was being unloaded it had slipped off the unloading ramps, landing very heavily, and causing damage to the set. As the last Beverley had left sometime before the extent of the damage was discovered, the Force had been unable to send a sitrep back to GHQ FARELF during the night. Although work went on all night to repair the set it was of no avail.

All the Force less the platoons left to protect the airport were now based on the Central Police Station. The rebels, as well as being in the adjacent Government buildings, had occupied the local radio station, the Cable and Wireless office, the transmitter station and the telephone exchange. The police expressed fears for the safety of the Sultan and his household as a gang of rebels had been seen near the Istana – the Sultan's Palace. Two platoons of Gurkhas were immediately dispatched to the Istana, and the sight of the Gurkhas must have proved too much for the rebels as, after a weak show of resistance, they fled in disorder. They left behind dead and wounded, together with a quantity of weapons. One platoon stayed to secure the Istana against further attacks, whilst the other returned with several prisoners.

It was now clear to the Force Commander and Major Seager that the force was up against more than a local incident, and that they were opposed by several hundred insurgents in gangs throughout Brunei. There was a pressing need to pass back information to GHQ Singapore as quickly as possible but, with the long range radio out of action, this presented some difficulty. However, eventually, a novel solution was hit upon. Instead of preparing a long situation report, a couple of short messages were prepared setting out the main problems. These were taken down to the airport, and the control tower managed to contact a passing BOAC airliner flying from Australia to Singapore, and passed the messages. The Captain of the aircraft was able to relay the messages to Singapore.

Late on Sunday afternoon a message was received reporting that gangs of rebels were known to be in the area of Seria town, some sixty miles along the coast. This was the centre of the local oil fields, so it was vital that it should not fall into rebel hands. The Police Commissioner asked for troops to be sent straight away, and in view of the size of the task, it was considered necessary to send a full company of Gurkhas. Because of the distance and the urgency it was essential to provide suitable transport to convey the Gurkha company to Seria. The local Public Works Department were able to produce a number of metal bodied tipper trucks, and as there was a stock of steel sheeting in the PWD workshops, with the help of some local fitters, these were speedily welded onto the sides of the trucks to produce an instant fleet of armoured personnel carriers. After a night of waiting, a report was received that the company had reached Seria and, despite skirmishes on the way, had achieved its objective.

Whilst this action was taking place on Sunday, an aircraft from Singapore flew into Brunei airport, bringing Brigadier J B A Glennie DSO from GHQ. Accompanying him was a Staff Officer, Major H Radice and a senior diplomat from the British High Commission, Mr Pumphrey. Brigadier Glennie had briefed the Force before it left Singapore. Their arrival was as a result of GHQ FARELF already appreciating that the situation in Brunei was far more serious and widespread than had been apparent when the initial Force was sent. The party's stay in Brunei was brief, but they quickly appreciated the situation, and confirmed the need for substantial reinforcement, which was already being rapidly organized by GHQ FARELF. They also visited the Sultan at the Istana, and persuaded him that as the Force currently there was becoming inadequate to safeguard him at the palace, he should move with his family temporarily into the Central Police Station with the Force HQ, and this he did.

Back in Singapore, as the reinforcement plan was put into operation, the RASC's contribution was by Sunday morning clearly beginning to be seen. 3 Army Air Supply Organization (AASO) RASC and 46 Squadron Landing Craft Tank (LCT) RASC were by this time on full alert. Later that day whilst the LCT's of 46 Squadron were being loaded, the advance party of 3 AASO together with major reinforcements from other arms took off from RAF Changi in Shackleton aircraft. The task of this party from 3 AASO, which consisted of the command elements of two air supply control sections (ASCS) was to form an air transport liaison organization to control activities at Labuan airfield. These were commanded by Major M D Isherwood RASC and Major R T S Daniell RASC.

Meanwhile the situation at the Main Police Station in Brunei town where the Force operations room was established in the Police Commissioner's office, was interesting to say the least. There was a severe problem of overcrowding with some extra one hundred and fifty troops and civilians occupying the building. The rebels took pot shots at the building from other Government buildings nearby, which they occupied at various times before being driven out by patrols of the Gurkhas. Prisoners taken were kept on the tennis court in front of the police station where their spirits were dampened by torrential rain; a large increase in their numbers necessitated their removal to the local cinema, taken over for the purpose.

During the first day at the police station, Major Seager reports that reinforcements for the operations room were two young Australian ladies who were on contract to the Brunei Government, and were employed as secretaries to senior officials. As they lived in a bungalow on the outskirts of the town, it was considered desirable to protect them in the police station, and a remarkable couple they proved to be. Apart from being a great asset in the operations room they turned their hand to any job given to them. They were both completely fearless and quickly won the respect of the troops, as they risked being shot as they calmly took tea to the Gurkhas in positions on the open verandahs. At this stage all in the operations room had been on continuous duty for thirty-six hours. The rest area consisted of two mattresses at the end of the operations room, Major Seager relates that on their first break at the end of this period, the mattresses were shared by the two Australian ladies, two burly policemen and himself! A surprising sight for any operations room, and one that provided some giggles from the ladies, relieving what was otherwise a fairly tense situation.

The airport at Brunei was still under pressure from the rebels, and the reinforcements now under way from Singapore were to be landed on the island of Labuan, some seventy miles off the North West coast of Brunei, which offered a secure base, and had a suitable airport. This island, which was part of the original Crown Colony of North Borneo, was to be the centre from which the complex logistic system for the ensuing operations was to be developed.

What had started as a supposedly local disturbance became a major insurrection. It was recognized as a campaign for which service from 8–23 December 1962 qualified for the award of the 1918–1962 General Service Medal with bar/clasp Brunei, and from 24 December 1962 until 11 August 1966, for the 1962 General

Service Medal bar/clasp Borneo.

Over the next few days, there was a continuous flow of infantry unit reinforcements and supporting administrative units, arriving by air and sea at Labuan. These included the balance of 1/2 GR, 1 Queens Own Highlanders, 1 Royal Greenjackets, who arrived by sea on HMS *Tiger*, 40 and 42 Royal Marine Commando, and the first elements of 31 Company Gurkha Army Service Corps. In this period the units were under command of the ad hoc Force Headquarters set up by Brigadier Glennie. However, shortly afterwards, as we shall see later, HQ 99 Brigade were to arrive to take over command of its units and to move to Brunei. The Queens Own Highlanders soon after arrival in Labuan, were flown by Beverley aircraft to assault the Anduki airstrip, then in rebel hands, and to link up with the Company of 1/2 GR in Seria Town. One of the Beverleys was hit by small arms fire but the operation was completely successful.

The transition of 99 Brigade, which had an Internal Security role in Singapore, to an air portable role for the Brunei/Borneo operation was very rapid indeed, and the RASC played no small part in this procedure, helped by the appointment of a DAQMG (Air) to the Headquarters from 3 AASO RASC. This post was filled by Major M D Isherwood RASC. In the event, two battalions of the Brigade preceded the Brigade Headquarters, which quickly followed them, and took over command in Brunei Town.

Simultaneously with the initial build-up of infantry through Labuan, eventually to six battalions, the maintenance backing for the rapidly growing force was being established there. In an area with few road communications, and large water gaps, RASC air despatch and water transport units were to play a vital role in the logistics of the operations now gathering momentum. Road transport though was still essential in those areas where land movement was possible, and in the maintenance area being established on Labuan. It fell to the Gurkha Army Service Corps to provide the bulk of the road transport, and in so doing to prove beyond doubt, if such proof were necessary, that the Gurkha soldier in the driving role on operations was as highly successful as in the infantry role. Initially the role of the Gurkha ASC was in the build-up of the maintenance area on Labuan, and their story starts where Major Seager's ends. With the arrival of HQ 99 Brigade in Brunei, Seager's task was finished and he flew to Labuan on his way back to Seremban. In Labuan he met Lieutenant Colonel (later Colonel)

B H J A O'Reilly MBE and Major Isherwood of 3 AASO RASC, and briefed them on the situation in Brunei. 3 AASO was subsequently to play an essential part in the maintenance of the Force now assembling. It was a task for which they had been established and trained. Before dealing with the air despatch element of the logistic system, we turn to the activities of 31 Company Gurkha ASC.

These initial activities cover the period from the carrying of the two companies of 1/2 GR who provided the original force for Brunei, to RAF Seletar on 8 December, to the time of its involvement in the actual operations of 99 Brigade. On 9 December, when it became clear to HQ FARELF that a larger force was required, the company continued to provide transport for the movement of troops and stores to the airfields and docks in Singapore, but then itself became involved as an element in the operation.

On Monday 10 December, the first intimation came that HQ 99 Brigade would become involved in the operation. That the Brigade Group was about to become air portable suddenly dawned on all concerned, and 31 Company were put on standby to proceed to Labuan.

On the same day, Major Allan Blackmore, the company commander, was called to General Headquarters (GHQ) to meet the Brigade DAA & QMG and to assist in writing the Brigade Order of Battle and Movement Table. After some four hours planning and with the allocation of GHQ resources, final movement bids were confirmed, and equipment tables for movement by both sea and air in order of priority were produced. A warning order was passed by telephone to Captain Jim Massey, the company second in command, indicating that there would be no move of the company before 1300 hours the following day. Major Blackmore eventually left GHQ at 1530 hours to brief his officers and await call forward on Tuesday 11 December.

However, this plan was not to be. The duty officer, Lieutenant David Turner, telephoned the company commander at 1700 hours to pass on orders that the first priorities were leaving in one hour ! The first aircraft chalk would consist of two officers, the company commander and Lieutenant Paul Honeyman, and eleven Gurkhas. They were to fly from RAF Changi on a Shackleton aircraft.

The rush was now on. Captain Massey excelled in organizing the parties and getting them to the airports and docks during the next seven days. There was no time to prepare advance lists by chalks, and drivers were added to the lists as they arrived back in unit lines from their transport details. Amazingly, the move went as smoothly as one could have wished. All this was the result of the competent work of the rear party and demonstrated the ease with which Gurkhas can be moved at short notice.

The Shackleton transporting the company advance party was diverted over the airfields of Seria, then in rebel hands, for Labuan. All aircraft taking units into the operation were purposely flown over the areas held by the rebels to give a show of force. Throughout the flight the officer commanding was sitting on the floor of the aircraft reading the Brigade Standing Operating Procedures trying to learn how a Brigade Maintenance Area (BMA) and Brigade Administrative Area (BAA) should operate in the Far East. Having recently completed No. 5 Long Transport Course he felt ready for any eventuality, but it was readily apparent that the current situation did not fit into a text book! The unit had not been rehearsed in the role that it had now assumed prior to the start of the operation, and procedures would have to be developed as events occurred. At Labuan, the only readily available shelter from the pouring rain on the airstrip was the now bulging Airport Hotel. Even the verandahs were crowded with recumbent bodies trying to snatch a few hours rest. Food was scarce as some units had failed to carry sufficient rations. Immediately, the District Officer's wife set up a stew point and provided a wonderful twenty-four hour service. It was going to be five days before the first re-supply ship arrived and composite rations could be issued in bulk. It was largely due to the efforts of Captain Freddy Wish RASC, the attached procurement officer, that the day was saved.

The first Land Rovers for the company arrived by air on Tuesday 11 December. However, it was to be a further week before the three ton cargo vehicles were to arrive. In the meantime, with the help of the District Officers, civilian transport was requisitioned.

On the evening of Wednesday 12 December, the first of the company main body arrived with Lieutenant Robin Marston RASC, Lieutenant David Turner RASC and Lieutenant Richard McAllister RASC. They, too, had travelled in a Shackleton aircraft, but were landed at Brunei by mistake.

The rebels took an instant dislike to them and machine gun fire assisted them to break all records in reaching the safety of the airport buildings. They joined the company later that night, but

Lieutenant Marston returned immediately to Brunei to set up the Brigade Administrative Area (BAA) in the cement works adjacent to the airport. Conditions were extremely difficult, and in the beginning rebels were still active in the area. At times, the detachment had to organize fighting patrols to assist in clearing the immediate area.

As the days went by, the Brigade Maintenance Area (BMA) began to build up on Labuan, at first out in the open ground around the airfield. Conditions improved when a Beverley load of tentage arrived. Stores and rations rapidly built up, with supplies being collected from both the docks and airfield and stored under tarpaulins. With the increase in holdings of fuel and ammunition, all of which had to be guarded, and with issues continuing around the clock, reinforcements from 3 Company RASC from Terendak Camp in Malaya were essential. The sheer quantity of stores arriving, preparation of issues, and variety of methods of supply called for long hours of work. Because of the distances involved and the water gap, few units were able to collect their supplies. 31 Company and its associated elements became responsible for the preparation of supplies for delivery by air drop, air landing, sea, rivers, and road. Daily deliveries by Landing Craft Tank (LCT) were made with perishable items being packed in ice boxes for the journey to the Forward Detachment. Accounting for all these supplies was made more difficult by the complete lack of any bills of lading for the first four weeks.

Good fortune resulted in the Company having four Massey Ferguson tractors on loan before leaving Singapore. The unit had built up a small number of experienced operators, and the forks and trailers with each machine proved invaluable throughout the whole operation. They were used for dockside clearance, loading and unloading aircraft, and moving stocks in both the BMA (Labuan) and BAA (Brunei). The tractors never stopped and never let the unit down.

The Composite Platoon and 3 Company element were able to sustain the high pressure of work for six weeks before being reinforced from UK. The most testing time was the lead up to Christmas when it was decided that everyone in the force, wherever they were, would receive traditional Christmas Fare.

So the turkeys, frozen vegetables and all the festive trimmings arrived in Labuan for issue to units. Fortunately, NAAFI sent the frozen items in a refrigerated vehicle, the first which was

available to the Army which obviated the need for large quantities
of ice previously used. Unfortunately, this most useful vehicle had
to be returned despite considerable efforts to retain it for military
use.

Eventually, in February 1963, a full Supply Platoon RASC
was despatched to assist in the now enormous task of resupply.
Accommodation was found in the docks, and large refrigerators
arrived with Royal Engineers assistance to maintain them; at this
stage the Composite Platoon was able to revert to its normal role
within the Brigade.

The operation of the BMA, presented three particular problems. The first concerns the intention of GHQ Singapore to operate
a floating Ordnance Field Park (OFP) off Victoria Harbour,
Labuan. After two days this proved impossible as it took hours to
find an urgent item, such as replacement jungle boots, which were
located in the bowels of the ship. A decision had to be made quickly
as to whether the OFP was to be:

a. Left on the boat.
b. Moved as close to Brunei as possible then the items cross loaded
   into other craft and taken up river to a suitable site found in
   Brunei Town. (As the majority of houses in Brunei Town were
   mounted on stilts, and at the time the town was under flood, it
   would have meant long delays and there were grave doubts if a
   suitable site could ever be found.)
c. Off-load onto Labuan Island and locate in the open until some
   form of covered accommodation could be found or even built.

It appeared that re-supply ships of the size sent from
Singapore would have to use the deep water harbour of Labuan,
unload into LCTs and everything moved to Brunei airfield. This
would mean items would have to be handled three times prior to
arriving at their final destination of storage.

It was decided to unload the OFP onto Labuan at a site
selected on the far side of the airfield. This was done in the most
appalling weather but time forbade any delays. The District Officer
provided a 24 hour service of coral hardcore so that the items could
be stored on the ground without sinking into a sea of mud. The
reaction from GHQ was immediate as they had not been consulted!
However, the brief from 99 Brigade Staff had been to make
decisions in the light of the prevailing circumstances. In spite of

this, the Brigade plan was criticized at the time, but was not countermanded as no other idea was forthcoming. The OFP remained in the location selected until the operation was completed some four years later. Fortunately, Labuan proved ideal.

The second problem was to find a method of daily re-supply to Brunei. The method adopted for the movement of all items needed by units on the mainland was the loading of 3 ton vehicles into an LCT and making a daily run. This method was strongly criticized initially, but it remained in being until the end of operations. Refrigeration was the third headache. Ice packed in containers had to be used for a long time until a Bedford RL, specially fitted with refrigeration designed by Major Russell-Pavier RASC, was sent some four months after the operation commenced. This vehicle was loaded in Labuan the same day. There was little spare room to store the vast quantities of cold items which arrived weekly from Singapore and so cold storage facilities used by local firms were also used for limited holding. For four months, movement of frozen items had to be carried out in cold containers which had a life of some ten hours before the items were spoilt.

Eventually, the number of units in the Force exceeded the capacity of the BMA and a larger organization, a Force Maintenance Area (FMA) was introduced.

Whilst all this was going on, 31 Company was involved elsewhere. With the restrictions on the number of roads the transport platoons were only partly used for second line replenishment. This meant fifteen three tonners per day moving onto the LCT at Labuan at 0500 hours, most vehicles having been loaded the night before. Items which required refrigeration were put on just before the vehicle moved onto the LCT. The vehicles travelled less driver, and when the LCT arrived in Brunei, there would be fifteen more drivers and vehicles waiting on the quayside. The vehicles were changed, one for one, and the drivers who met the boat then took the loaded vehicles to their respective destinations. The farthest journey was from Brunei to Miri, a 160 miles turn-around, which sometimes included driving along the beach as the road immediately became impassible after excessive rain. This then tied up 30 vehicles per day, of which half the time was spent on the eight hour Brunei/Labuan journey on the LCT.

The remainder of the vehicles were used on the airfields for unloading or loading aircraft, controlled by the ATLO, or when a supply ship arrived for dock clearance; plus local details on the island of Labuan and in Brunei Town itself.

A Land Rover Platoon was taken to Labuan, consisting of thirty-two Mark 3 Land Rovers and trailers. It was originally planned that this platoon would operate in Brunei supporting the five battalions along jungle tracks. This, however, did not prove to be feasible and all the resupply was carried out by air and river. The platoon did come into its own, when the numerous ad hoc units arrived in the theatre without their own vehicles, and were able to carry out all local details. In addition, Headquarters Combined British Forces Borneo (COMBRITBOR) was formed, later to become split into Director of Operations and Headquarters Combined Land Forces Borneo (COMLANDBOR), but had no organic transport. Part of the Land Rover Platoon became the domestic transport of the staff officers in their Headquarters. Later, a number of Land Rovers were transferred to various units and the remaining fifteen were shipped back to the Company Rear Party in Singapore, to be held as an airportable reserve. It is interesting to note that two years after the event, the Land Rovers and the tractors and trailers were still on excess issue to the Company and were fully employed in Kuching during the Confrontation phase of Borneo operations.

The system of transport operations remained constant until November 1963, when HQ 99 Brigade returned to Singapore for six weeks. 31 Company handed over the transport commitment to 61 Company RASC (MT) and followed its parent Brigade back to Nee Soon, and thus completed the first part of its story.

By 20 December 1962 the first phase of operations in the campaign was completed and, in the main centres of population, the rebellion was crushed and all the airfields were secured. The rebels then took to the jungle and the second phase began. This involved the redeployment of our troops into the jungle to cut off the hard core of rebels from their sources of aid via the Indonesian border and to destroy them. This continued until 21 January 1964 when the Indonesian 'confrontation' with Malaysia started, and continued until 11th August 1966.

Once our forces were deployed in the jungle 3 AASO became immediately involved in their supply since the water and road system already outlined was only suitable for the supply of the Force on the coastal fringes. At the time some delay occurred in the redeployment since the worst floods for thirty-six years hit Borneo, causing vast damage and hardship, and to support the

Civil Authorities, large quantities of food and clothing were air dropped or airlanded by helicopter. By the time our forces moved into the jungle, the Air Despatch organization consisting of elements of HQ 3 AASO, HQ 55 Company RASC (Air Despatch) with two Air Supply Platoons, and 22 Air Maintenance Platoon RAOC were fully operative on this task. From then on, air supply became the normal maintenance system for our troops in the jungle.

Back in the UK, the need for reinforcing the locally available air despatch organization was appreciated, and on 14th December 1962, 1 AASO RASC was given 72 hours notice to provide this reinforcement. Two Air Supply Control Sections (11 and 13 ASCS) with one Air Supply Platoon. A Platoon of 47 Company (Air Despatch) commanded by Major (later Brigadier) D Cardle was flown from Stanstead to Paya Leba, Singapore by British United Airways. 11 and 13 ASCS moved on to Brunei on 19th December, whilst A Platoon 47 Company (Air Despatch) remained in Singapore to help with air loading at RAF Changi. By mid-January 1963, 13 ASCS had returned to UK. A Platoon 47 Company had moved to Labuan and the HQ element and two air supply platoons of 55 Company had returned to Singapore, leaving small elements in Labuan with the advance HQ of 3 AASO.

The programme for air supply adopted during phase two of the operations, and subsequently used throughout the campaign was eventually the well tried three day cycle used in Malaya by 55 Company RASC (AD). On the first day of the cycle units listed their requirements and sent them to Brigade HQ by various means. These were checked and collated by the 'Q' staff and action taken to make bids for aircraft and to warn air supply platoons what to pack. On the second day items were delivered to packing sheds for packing by air supply platoons. By 1800 hours daily the total poundage to be dropped was notified to the aircraft allotment conference. Those units not in the jungle received their supplies by surface means as already outlined. The general routine for each day following a 7.30 a.m. parade was the departure of the sorties by the Beverley or Valetta aircraft. From 9 a.m. to midday stores for dropping the following day were assembled and packed. The packing was done in an open fronted shed, with troops, sleeping accommodation alongside; the aircraft were parked only five hundred yards from the packing bay and experience proved that the Fordson forklift with trailer was the ideal combination for this

[By courtesy of PR HQ FARELF]

Air despatchers of 3 AASO in action over Borneo.

type of loading operation.

Some indication of the volume of air supply during these operations can be taken from the records of A Platoon 47 Company (Air Despatch) which between late December 1962 and 11 April the following year despatched 529,208 lbs. of stores in 110 sorties.

By the end of January 1964, there was 'confrontation' between Indonesia and Malaysia and the campaign had entered its third phase. The operations now extended over Brunei, Sarawak and Sabah to cover the whole frontier with Indonesian Borneo to the south. The overall headquarters for the operation had been firmly established in Brunei Town and Major General Walter Walker had been appointed Director of Operations, taking over from Brigadier Glennie on 19 December 1963.

By now, 99 Brigade was responsible for the central area of operations and 3 Commando Brigade was established in the West, based on Kuching.

The build up of the Maintenance Area on Labuan continued and the supply systems by surface and air means were functioning well and coping with the extended operations.

In January 1964 as part of this process an element of the air despatch organization on Labuan had moved to Brunei airport and was employed on helicopter delivery of stores. This was still early in the campaign and we shall return later to the more extensive organizations that were developed as the scale of operations and size of the forces employed increased.

Turning now to the third element of the Corps involved in the campaign, we find that RASC Water Transport was involved from the very onset. At 1000 hours on 9 December 1962 when OC 3 Division (FE) of 46 Squadron RASC (Landing Craft Tank) in Singapore, was ordered by HQ FARELF to stand his unit to, his three Landing Craft Tank (LCT) were disposed as follows:

LCT 4086 RASCV *Arromanches* – at unit moorings in Singapore
LCT 4073 RASCV *Ardennes*   – returning from Port Swettenham
LCT 4085 RASCV *Ajedabia*   – within five days of completing her
                                      annual refit with Singapore Harbour
                                      Board

All these vessels were the LCT Mark VIII and were the only service manned landing craft capable of making the passage in safety from Singapore to Borneo in the weather conditions that existed in the NE monsoon in which period the initial operation took place. Loading of the *Arromanches* and the *Ardennes* started on 8 December and they both sailed on 10 December with a cargo of AFVs, cranes, forklifts and general cargo. The *Arromanches* was ten hours ahead of the *Ardennes* and had been ordered to proceed to Brunei Bay. As no more orders were received, on arrival off Brunei on 14 December, arrangements were made for a beach landing. However, the RN guard ship now on station was contacted at 0400 hours and expressed consternation at the LCT being right at the 'sharp end', and ordered the vessel to Labuan where the general cargo was discharged. The Captain was then briefed to attempt the Brunei river and discharge the AFVs as near to Brunei Town as possible.

En route to the river, the *Ardennes* was contacted and she followed the *Arromanches* through the approaches and entered the river. Some rifle fire was heard at this time and as it was low tide the river was navigated with caution. On arrival at the town, a small ramp was found, the doors opened, ramp lowered and the AFVs landed in copybook assault landing style. For the following three weeks both LCTs were kept extremely busy on a wide range of tasks. Troops and vehicles of 3 Commando Brigade were transhipped from HMS *Albion* anchored in Brunei Bay to Labuan and Brunei and vehicles and ammunition were discharged from Landing Ships Tank (LST) which had arrived and anchored off Labuan. Troops and vehicles were also moved from Labuan to Kuching, and during the whole period Brunei was maintained by the daily run from Labuan.

The third LCT, *Ajedabia* sailed from Singapore for Labuan on 18 December, and during the month the three vessels steamed 6,200 miles, carrying 1,300 passengers, 862 vehicles and 2,892 tons of ammunition and general stores. The daily maintenance run between Labuan and Brunei which was the system developed as soon as the Brigade Maintenance Area had been established at Labuan by 31 Company Gurkha ASC, was carried out by one of the LCTs up until April 1963. This entailed a round trip from Labuan of 14 hours during which the vessel beached and retracted twice. During the floods of February 1963, the LCT was the only means of communication for a four day period. Only on one occasion was a vessel unable to enter Brunei river despite the monsoon weather conditions.

From April 1963 onwards the maintenance of Brunei became a joint operation with a Ramped Cargo Lighter from 37 Company RASC (Water Transport) together with Ramp Powered Lighters and requisitioned Z craft of 10 Port Squadron RE. The discharge of troops and stores from HMS *Albion* and HMS *Bulwark* anchored off Labuan was also a task undertaken by these vessels, using pontoons, cranes and scrambling nets to assist.

Water Transport operations in Borneo were, inevitably, not without their lighter side. The relationship between the Royal Navy and the Army vessels, as always, resulted in some interesting situations.

On one particular occasion an RPL from 10 Port Squadron's Kuching Detachment, delivering defence stores to the forward areas, rounded a bend in the river to find an RN Inshore Minesweeper moored at the RPL's usual berth. The Minesweeper responded to the RPL's hoot of protest by making a crisp signal of which the clear inference was that the RPL should come alongside to await further instructions. As time was short due to the intense pressure on the Water Transport facilities and a rapid turnround essential, the skipper of the RPL replied that he was rather too busy; he then dropped his ramp on the bank a short way downstream from the Minesweeper and began to offload.

Within moments, a patently irate figure, dressed in impeccable tropical whites on which two gold rings were clearly visible, emerged from the Minesweeper and swept on board the RPL and up to the wheelhouse where the skipper, Sergeant Barker, dressed in his usual working rig of jungle boots, shorts OG and a particularly shapeless bush hat, was holding the RPL onto the bank at slow ahead. The Lieutenant demanded imperiously as to the whereabouts of the Captain of the RPL, to which Sergeant Barker replied: 'Sir, I am the Captain of this vessel – kindly leave the bridge!' For a moment the Naval Officer hesitated, balancing relative seniorities, service and rank against the tradition of the sea, but recognizing a Master Under God, he gracefully withdrew.

The subsequent impasse was eventually resolved by the Detachment Commander with the help of a considerable amount of pink gin.

A number of launches from 37 Company played an important role in communication duties and in operational tasks carrying troops. RASC Vessel *Forsa*, a 44 foot fast launch was particularly successful in this latter role, operating with the Royal Navy from Kuching and covered some 2,586 nautical miles in two months. This was a hazardous area for small craft owing to the large number of submerged logs which were swept along at high speed in the strong currents. There were other hazards, fortunately rare, to trap the unwary.

It was a well-proven strategy of General Walker, the Director of Operations Borneo (DOBOPS, often distorted GODOPS) that the cooperation of the local population was essential to the success of a campaign: commanders at all levels were carefully briefed on this 'Hearts and Minds' policy.

It was therefore with some concern that the commanding officer of 10 Port Squadron's Brunei Detachment, Major (now Brigadier) G G Blakey, learned that one of his RPLs had inadvertently run down a Dyak Long-Boat, which had shot out of a tributary of the main river at some 25 knots right under the RPL's bows. Although the owner had been rescued without injury, his boat and its outboard engine had sunk without trace. Rather than embark on the prolonged and locally incomprehensible compensation procedure, the OC arranged for the survivor of this regrettable shipwreck to be given another boat and a new outboard. He departed rejoicing and it was clear that both his heart and his mind had been won. The OC felt confident that the DOBOPSs policy had been effectively implemented. His confidence was, however, short lived. The following day, the first RPL to leave its moorings was assailed by literally dozens of long boats in various states of advanced deterioration which, with their crews leaping overboard with dramatic cries, hurled themselves against and under the Army vessel. The word had obviously got about that the generous Queen would replace old for new. It had to be explained, quickly and formally, that this was not the case and that there would be no compensation for self-inflicted damage!

During the whole period of the campaign the RE (Tn) and RASC Water Transport services worked closely together and their separate charters were disregarded to a large extent, enabling the closest possible cooperation, and the development of highly successful joint systems.

This augured well for the successful amalgamation of the Water Transport responsibilities of both Corps when the Royal Corps of Transport was formed on 15 July 1965 a year before the end of operations in Borneo.

On 16 September 1963, the new Federation of Malaysia, excluding Brunei, came into existence. Sarawak and North Borneo, now Sabah, became part of Malaysia, but Brunei elected to remain a British Protectorate. Outside Brunei therefore Britain ceased to be defending what had been their own possession, and immediately assumed the role of ally. The change in political control of the operation is not a necessary part of this story, but an infantry brigade from Malaysia subsequently became part of the Force operating in Sabah.

When 31 Company Gurkha ASC returned to Singapore with 99 Brigade in November 1963, as already related, 61 Company (MT) RASC detachment which took over from them moved into a well established maintenance area, with 50 Supply Depot RASC and an Ordnance Field Park RAOC. The maintenance systems continued as before by surface or air as appropriate. In January 1964, 99 Brigade were ordered to take over from 3 Commando Brigade in Kuching, and a detachment of two MT platoons from

31 Company accompanied the Brigade. From the Company detachment point of view, this was going to be far more interesting, than that in Labuan, as there were more road communications in the area. One particular road, running from Kuching to Engkilil, was a 250 mile turn around, of which 80 miles ran parallel to the Indonesian border, and in parts only a quarter of a mile distant. There was a constant threat of vehicles being ambushed, and armed soldier escorts had to be carried from Company resources plus armoured cars acting as escorts driven by Company drivers. The road conditions were appalling, consisting of a sharp flint surface, which never allowed a vehicle more than 1000 miles to a set of tyres. The detachment, which consisted of thirty 3 tonners, fifteen Land Rovers and four tractors and trailers, was considered sufficient to meet the Brigade requirements. It later required a further platoon of 3 tonners.

Back in Singapore, on 5 January 1964, an urgent signal was received from Major General Walker, Director of Operations ordering the Company to send a small Administrative Headquarters, the Composite Platoon, and a section of vehicles to move to Tawau immediately. Tawau was on the north coast of Sabah, lying close to the Indonesian border which meant that the Company then had detachments separated by virtually the length of East Malaysia. The move was undertaken with the 1st Battalion 10th (Princess Mary's Own) Gurkha Rifles in record time and they achieved eight enemy killed within four hours of arrival. The Composite Platoon had to set up a supply system from local resources.

The platoon commander, Lieutenant Frank Falle, was forced to use his considerable initiative in tapping these resources, and ensuring that a fair charge was levied against the taxpayer. In addition, the platoon held reserve rations which were shipped from 50 Supply Depot RASC in Labuan. The other commodities for which the platoon was responsible included all ordnance stores, defence stores and ammunition.

The detachment vehicles were shipped from the OFP Labuan and were required to use the only ten miles of metalled roads to be found in the area. The Detachment Headquarters, commanded by Captain Tony Meier, was responsible for administering and defending Naval, Army and RAF personnel, a slightly difficult task when you are a Gurkha unit as the language problem presents a barrier. But due to the initiative of the Gurkha soldier, and his powers to adapt himself to almost any conditions, the system functioned admirably.

It is interesting to record, that later on in this particular area, the Royal Navy (846 Naval Air Squadron) were responsible for the operating of aeroplanes, the Army (37 Company RASC) (WT) for the operation of boats, and the RAF for the operation of road transport; unique inter-service cooperation, which was enjoyed by all who originally served in this outpost. However, as operations expanded, more staff appeared, and later a Malaysian brigade moved in. The rest of the Company, consisting of an element of the headquarters and a transport platoon were left in Nee Soon to cope with any details for Singapore Base Area, and to stand by for possible Internal Security duties, for unrest was beginning to give rise for concern.

Thus, the Company was deployed in Kuching, Sarawak, Tawau, Sabah and Nee Soon until June 1964, when 30 Company Gurkha ASC relieved the detachment and deployed to cover additional commitments in Brunei, Labuan and Seria, where the arrival of 51 Gurkha Infantry Brigade Group had increased the second line transport requirement in this area. One transport troop was deployed to Seria to handle the huge quantity of furniture and accommodation stores brought in by LCT to set up the permanent camp for the Gurkha battalion now to be located in the Shell complex as a long term measure. This was dealt with by a newly established Barrack Service RASC.

The setting up of a Barrack Services RASC in Borneo whilst operations were still in progress was an interesting departure from normal. The newly appointed Officer in charge of barracks was Major Gardiner RASC followed by Major Monahan RASC.

The Assistant OI/c Barracks was Staff Sergeant E Faughnam and there was a staff of five RASC soldiers. They had a formidable task covering the whole of North Borneo – Sabah and Sarawak – and initially worked from requisitioned buildings in Kuching. Their first task was the establishment of the permanent camp at Seria, but as more barrack stores arrived from Singapore they were distributed to all units now in semi-permanent camps, and helped to improve living conditions for the troops. Ultimately, the Barrack Officer and stores moved into purpose built attap accommodation on the outskirts of Kuching, where they were later joined by a supply platoon RASC.

After the move of the barrack stores into the permanent camp at Seria, a detachment of 30 Company provided vehicles for the routine tasks of maintaining the Gurkha Battalion with its families which moved into the barracks. The task of 30 Company was further complicated by the increased need for transport in the Brunei area and of REME support from their workshops to be deployed to Labuan. However, by the time that they were due to be relieved again by 31 Company in November, the situation was well under control.

In the meantime, back in Singapore, 31 Company, hoping for rest and retraining was sadly disillusioned when two very vicious and frightening riots took place there. Indonesian parachutists had also landed in Malaya, and this necessitated a general commitment of a full platoon every day, as part of local defences. It was not a case though of going back to Borneo for a well earned rest, as the change over of companies had just been completed and everyone was looking forward to Christmas celebrations, when intelligence sources gave warning of a major build-up of Indonesian forces along the Sarawak border. Christmas was spent in a series of planning conferences and in early January 1965, HQ 3 Commando Brigade arrived in Sibu to take over command of part of the sector previously under HQ 99 Brigade. Two additional infantry battalions were also deployed, and in consequence the tonnage of stores through Kuching port and airfield increased sharply. To meet this task, the Commando Brigade transport platoon was sent to Kuching. OC 31 Company was ordered to move elements of his Company HQ from Singapore to take over command of his detachment and the Commando platoon.

In March 1965, HQ 3 Commando Brigade was relieved by HQ 19 Infantry Brigade from the United Kingdom. A platoon of 1 Company RASC accompanied this Brigade and took over from the Commando transport platoon, coming under command of HQ 31 Company Gurkha ASC.

In June 1965, 30 Company took over the first of the six monthly roulement tours. This was going to be the form for the future; equal tours of six months at a time between 30 and 31 Companies. The company on active service, directly supporting both 51 and 99 Gurkha Brigades, had under command the support elements of whichever UK brigade was in East Malaysia. In Singapore the Companies took over the commitments in support of Singapore Base Area, and carried out as much retraining as possible. For the period 1 January to 30 April 1965 the company in

Brunei and Kuching covered 363,984 miles for seven accidents in an area where roads were by no means ideal as the main line of communications.

Mention has been made of a detachment of 61 Company taking over from 31 Company in Labuan in November 1963. This detachment was formed on a local establishment and was organized to meet the requirements of the Maintenance Area. Its primary function was dock and airfield clearance and ferrying stores by LCT or RPL to Brunei. The Land Rovers provided a pool of passenger carrying vehicles for minor units, staff officers and the many visitors. In addition to their work in Labuan this independent platoon carried out other less humdrum tasks.

In January 1965, the Kota Belud training area 50 miles north east of Jesselton was reactivated and a British battalion arrived to acclimatize and carry out jungle training. It was decided to resupply this battalion every two weeks by ferrying loaded trucks by LCT from Labuan. The trucks disembarked at Jesselton, drove 50 miles to Kota Belud, unloaded and returned to the ship. This system operated well and was only held up by floods on two occasions.

Another unusual 61 Company task resulted from a RE requirement to build an airstrip at Meligan, deep in the jungle 80 miles east of Brunei. RE plant was airdropped into the DZ by medium stressed platform and the plan for the recovery of the platforms and parachutes involved the use of Belvedere helicopters to carry them to Tomani which was the nearest road head 25 miles north of Meligan. The transport problem was firstly moving sufficient drums of fuel to Tomani to allow the helicopters to do their task and secondly to return with the platforms and parachutes. Three 3 ton trucks loaded with 20 drums of fuel were carried by RPL from Labuan to Weston where they disembarked and moved by road to Beaufort. There they were loaded onto railway flats and taken by rail to Tenom and finally by road to Tomani. Incessant rain made the journey hazardous and the River Padas at Tenom had risen eight feet above normal so the party was delayed until the level dropped sufficiently for the ferry to operate.

The task was completed without mishap and the trucks returned by rail to Jesselton and thence to Labuan by LCT. The drivers welcomed this task as a change from normal routine and drove very well in difficult conditions. In particular, disembarking at Weston onto an unprepared landing site, and negotiating ramshackle ramps on and off railway flats called for both nerve and judgement.

On 15 July 1965, as a result of the reorganization of the 'Q' Services, and when the number of RASC units involved in the confrontation was at its highest, the Royal Corps of Transport was born. With the single exception of mules, every mode of transport including hovercraft, and even some local canoes, was employed to sustain the four brigades holding a thousand miles of frontier. The effect on MT and Air Despatch units was basically that they changed their cap badges and titles of units, but their tasks remained the same. In the case of supply units, these were handed over to the RAOC and most RASC supply personnel were rebadged RAOC. This also applied to the Barrack Services which had by then been established, based on Kuching. In the case of Water Transport Units, the effect was that the RE(Tn) units with whom they had been working closely since the beginning of the campaign, were also rebadged RCT, and the whole Water Transport operation thereafter was under single command.

The limited road system frequently became unusable in the monsoon periods, and normally accessible and navigable rivers were also generally affected at times. The nature of the terrain, the paucity of tactical airfields, and the distances of those airfields from our own forward locations were such that ground forces were almost entirely dependent on supply by air by one method or another. RAF and Air Despatch backing for this task was provided from Labuan and Kuching. Over fifty DZs were regularly supplied. This entailed aircraft flying up to three sorties daily but it was found advisable to restrict air despatchers to two sorties per day, such was the effort required to eject 17,000 lbs of small packs manually in a single sortie. The DZs in Borneo in no way approached ideal requirements. They ranged from small jungle clearings, levelled areas on the tops of hills, slopes of hills and low lying areas near the bends of rivers. The violent weather patterns particularly in the mountains, at times made missions particularly hazardous.

By 1965 also, the Air Despatch element in Borneo was at its busiest with the Force now at a strength of 14,000 including eighteen infantry battalions.

The troops were taken in by helicopter and thereafter everything from gun ammunition to toothpaste was dropped to them. When positions became rat-infested, cats were air-dropped. To satisfy the ration requirements of the Gurkhas, livestock was parachuted in. It was known for a crate of live chickens to disintegrate in the air leaving a flock of very surprised domestic birds planing over the jungle in their first, and probably their last, high level solo. Awkward loads were numerous. Many ad hoc dropping methods were conjured up by soldiers of all ranks to enable the units on the ground to receive such items as corrugated roof sheeting, defence pickets, coils of dannert wire, and even young rubber trees dropped to local tribesmen at the request of the civil authorities. Recovery of parachutes and containers was a major problem, and elaborate arrangements had to be made to recover these by helicopter, or light aircraft, where strips existed. When there was a danger of containers running out, ingenious methods were devised to replace them. Many examples of the air dispatchers' ingenuity were to be seen in Borneo, which have now been adopted as official practice.

There were now four infantry brigades in the force, which were designated by the areas in which they were located. East Brigade at Tawau was a Malaysian Brigade, covering the Eastern and Northern half of Sabah. Central Brigade was based on Brunei and covered the Western half of Sabah, Mid-West Brigade, the Fourth and Fifth Divisions of Sarawak, and West Brigade the First Division of Sarawak.

On the formation of the RCT on 15 July 1965, 3 AASO became 15 Air Despatch Regiment RCT, and its companies became squadrons. Two of these, 55 Squadron, commanded by Major R L Wallis, and a newly formed 69 Squadron, commanded by Major D H Garner, rotated between Singapore and Borneo every three months. The squadron in Borneo was split between the RAF airfields at Labuan and Kuching, with sections of the RAOC Air Maintenance Platoons.

Between January 1965 and October 1966, the following quantities of stores were dropped to units:

> From Labuan – 23,120,000 lbs.
> From Kuching – 19,950,000 lbs.

As a result of distinguished service in the field in Borneo by Lance Corporal A M Meiklejohn of 69 Squadron 15 Air Despatch Regiment, the Army Board approved his promotion to substantive Corporal and this was promulgated in the supplement to the

London Gazette dated 12 July 1966. As far as can be ascertained he was the first RASC/RCT soldier to receive promotion of this kind and the first soldier of any arm to receive promotion of this kind in peacetime. He was subsequently promoted Sergeant and in over 100 operational sorties over Borneo he displayed outstanding qualities in a task which makes rigorous demands on NCOs whose work is often dangerous, exacting and strenuous and calls for coolness, calmness and decision.

Throughout his duties Meiklejohn maintained the highest standards of discipline and his efficient and cheerful example earned him the admiration of officers and men of both the Army and the Royal Air Force. Whilst on detachment in Labuan in December 1965, and January 1966, his Troop at one stage, was without a Troop Commander or Troop Sergeant and no replacements were available. His Detachment Commander unhesitatingly nominated Meiklejohn to assume the combined duties of Troop Commander and operations Sergeant, despite the fact that he was the most junior NCO of his Troop. He carried out these duties in an exemplary fashion and succeeded, in addition, in earning high praise for his unit.

In July 1966 Sergeant Meiklejohn was awarded Commander Far East Air Force's certificate of good service following an incident over a Borneo dropping zone when his quick thinking and prompt reaction in making an emergency jettison of an aircraft load were largely responsible for saving the aircraft and its crew. His example and achievements add yet another proud chapter to the high reputation earned over the years by the air despatcher.

Also part of 15 Air Despatch Regiment was 130 Flight RCT (until 15 July 1965 – 30 Flight RASC), commanded by Major (later Colonel) J Riggall RCT, and based on RAF Seletar in Singapore. The Flight was formed from the two Beaver aircraft flights of the Army Air Corps, and operated six, subsequently ten, Beaver aircraft piloted by RASC, later RCT, Personnel in Borneo from April 1964. The Flight had aircraft based with Central, East and Mid-West Brigades, and were used for a wide range of tasks. These included carriage of VIPs, Commanders, and staff officers between Headquarters, units and outposts; reconnaissance, and operational troop lifts – five fully equipped troops could be carried. Further tasks were logistic support, casualty evacuation, and lastly directing the fire of the Artillery Batteries, and ships of the Royal and Commonwealth Navies.

[By courtesy of Col J S Riggall]

Fly past of 130 Flight RCT over Brunei Town 2 Apr 1966 in celebration of 2 years operations in support of 51 Gurkha Brigade.

187

Flying areas in Borneo were vast and the Brigade areas huge. Five hours of flying over one brigade area could cover a considerable portion of it, but would not reach either of the brigade boundaries. In the three brigade areas served by the Flight there were virtually no roads other than along parts of the coast, and air provided the sole means of communication, both for maintenance and troop movement. Operating conditions, with mountains of 5,000–7,000 feet, and high ambient temperatures, meant that aircraft were operating on their limits, and airstrips varying from the frightening to the very good, gave our Corps pilots all the excitement and experience that they needed, even with aircraft as excellent as Beavers. These same conditions of course applied to the Twin Pioneer aircraft, operated by the RAF, with whom 130 Flight worked very closely. The statistics of 130 Flight in their first year of operation, with six aircraft show the extent of their participation in the campaign.

Total hours flown:	3,600	hours
Total sorties flown:	5,954	sorties
which include:		
Visual, photo and passenger reconnaisance	330	sorties
Air observed shoots (Artillery & Naval):	66	sorties
Casualty evacuation:	100	sorties
numbers:	120	patients
Passengers carried:	11,694	passengers
Freight airlanded:	229,321	pounds
Average availability:	77%	

Further details of aircraft are given in the Aviation Chapter in Part II of this book.

The Borneo campaign was to see the introduction of a new element in the field of transportation in operations. The Joint Services Hovercraft Unit (Far East) was formed in July 1964. Included in the unit were Major R N Harris RASC, and Captain P A Beacon RASC. The two other officers in the unit belonged to the RN and RM, Lieutenant Christopher Stafford RN and Captain S L Syrad MC RM. There were also two RASC soldier crew members. There were two craft, both SRN Mk. 5. The unit moved to Tawau in Sabah to start operational trials in March 1965, and then moved to Sibu in Sarawak in August 1965. In both areas, the craft were used in the logistic support system of the operations and proved a marked success. They were not affected by the heavy river spates, rapids, sandbanks, or surface debris. The maintenance run up the Kalibakan river at Tawau took hovercraft about 3–4 hours for the round trip to the forward base, compared to the two whole days taken by a launch. The unit left Borneo before the end of the campaign in 1966, and completed its trials in Siam before disbanding in April 1966. The success of the hovercraft but its ultimate rejection for permanent use in the Army is related in the Hovercraft chapter in Part II of this book.

On the formation of the RCT, there was evidence of a need for

Hovercraft off the coast of Borneo.

[By courtesy of PR HQ FARELF]

improvement to be made in the transport organization and amongst the recommendations implemented was the CRCT at Labuan – Lieutenant Colonel H P Brown RCT to co-ordinate all transport matters and SO2's Transport at each of the four brigades. The CRCT, DAD (Mov). and the Joint Booking Centre were co-located at Force Headquarters.

All the elements of the Corps, less the hovercraft, continued operating until August 1966, when in Jakarta, the Foreign Ministers of Malaysia and Indonesia signed the formal agreement which ended hostilities. As soon as the agreement to the cessation of hostilities had been signed, the British Government undertook to withdraw their troops from Malaysian Borneo by the end of September 1966, and this was done. This brought forth from the then Minister of Defence the observation that 'In the history books it will be recorded as one of the most efficient uses of military force in the history of the World.'

The Campaign started with all elements of the Corps being RASC. It ended with the newly formed RCT having 'won its spurs' under Far East operational conditions. Some forty officers and 450 soldiers of the RASC/RCT plus even larger numbers from the Gurkha ASC/GTR were ultimately serving at any one time in the area, with the Royal Armoured Corps, Royal Artillery, Infantry units and other Services who they successfully maintained throughout the Campaign.

SINGAPORE

EVEN AS THE ATOMIC BOMBS fell on Hiroshima and Nagasaki a British amphibious force was at sea on Operation Zipper for the invasion and re-occupation of Malaya and Singapore.

Landing in Singapore in August 1945 the British forces were immediately faced with the task of disarming and repatriating the Japanese forces. Then followed the daunting period of re-establishment and reorganization of the British colony after three years of Japanese occupation.

One of the first units established in Singapore was 56 Water Transport Unit RASC, commanded by Lieutenant Colonel Gregory. Situated on the small island of Pulau Brani with detachments in Batavia and Hong Kong, this small island offered an excellent base for the RASC fleet in South East Asia, and continued to be used as such until the British withdrawal in the 1970s.

The local Chinese and Malayan population was extremely friendly and large numbers were soon employed by the RASC, as there was much work to be done in the rehabilitation of the island, for the Japanese had neglected everything and in some instances, wantonly destroyed facilities, services and buildings. Within a short space of time recreational facilities were introduced, an EFI detachment opened a NAAFI canteen and an Army film unit provided a weekly cinema show.

The RASC organization on Singapore Island was formed from 61, 75, 799 and 986 Companies with Lieutenant Colonel J H Jeffers as CRASC, the companies coming together as British forces reassembled in the colony following the Japanese capitulation. In many cases British troops disembarked with Japanese prisoners of war carrying their baggage. Internal security was a primary task of the infantry and it was emphasized that all ranks were to smile and wave when driving around the rubber estates in order to regain confidence among the local population.

All the former British barracks in Singapore and at Changi were reoccupied and the Japanese prisoners of war, still on the island in considerable numbers, were then concentrated in POW cages at Kluang in Malaya.

Late in 1946 it was decided to establish, mainly for the locally enlisted soldiers, a Far East RASC school in Singapore and this was opened in accommodation at the Chinese High School in Bukit Timah Road. Lieutenant Colonel E E G Lucas, OBE, was the first commanding officer, with Major H M J Jenson, OBE, as his second-in-command; RSM Forder and Warrant Officer Class 2 Attan bin Yatim, BEM (later Major, commanding 61 Company RASC) were the first two warrant officers.

At the outset the school was organized into an RHQ and HQ company; a driver training wing, a domestic transport platoon and a small RASC workshop element. Initial emphasis was placed on driver training, and MT maintenance, and the role of the school was soon expanded to include recruit training as well as drivers from other units. To overcome language difficulties, instructional classes in English were commenced for all Malayan other ranks. The first students at the school were twenty men from the 1st Singapore Regiment Royal Artillery from Blakang Mati island. The HQ company commanded by Captain Webb, dealt with specialist training, covering the work of clerks, artificers and firemen, as well as general regimental training.

The following year saw the formation of a driver training company, to replace the wing which preceded it. This company was located at Simpson Camp, Jurong Road, which took its name after the then DST FARELF. The accommodation was a former Japanese camp located on the hillside of a rubber estate. As the wooden camp buildings provided insufficient accommodation for all the personnel, marquees and tents were erected. Major Jenson took command.

Much hard work was necessary to convert the camp into a training establishment. The driver training company was then organized into a HQ platoon (for administration) and three platoons for driver training. All platoons were commanded by British officers, the remaining personnel being Malayan other ranks. By August 1947 and in consequence of the considerable increase in strength, the company was expanded to include a holding platoon to receive and cater for British, Malayan, Indian, Chinese, and Eurasian trainees.

Early in 1948, on the return of Lieutenant Colonel Lucas to the UK, Lieutenant Colonel Jensen became commandant. Major H I Salt, and later, Major R H Gilliatt, taking over the driver training company, an appointment he held until June 1949, when on being appointed Chief Instructor, his place was taken by Major E J Poole. During 1949 a regimental training company, commanded by Major A D Moyle, was formed to cope with the growing commitments of basic recruit training.

In February 1949, the driver training company rejoined the RASC school in Nee Soon, forming part of a large and well organized Far East Training Centre, which continued for many years, and even today forms part of the training organization for the Singapore Armed Forces.

Towards the end of June 1948, the routine of the Singapore garrison had been shattered by events in Malaya. It was on 23 June that an historic 'O' group was held at GHQ, Far East Land Forces at which the start of the Malayan Emergency was announced. One of the infantry battalions in Singapore was immediately moved to Malaya, followed by another within a matter of weeks; this was the start of the state of emergency which existed in Malaya for the next twelve years. In the case of service in the colony of Singapore the period of emergency lasted only from June 1948 until 31 January 1949, although the military life of the island was closely linked with the operations in Malaya for over a decade.

During the immediate post-war period following the reoccupation of Singapore, and particularly, following the start of the Malayan emergency, the pre-war barracks were found to be totally inadequate for all units and installations required to maintain the army of the day. In consequence extensive requisitioning was of necessity resorted to. A large area of land, known as the Pasir Panjang Estate, was therefore purchased by the War Department, and here extensive married quarters and installations to meet post-war requirements were built in 1950–51.

This was a large-scale project, and was conceived at a time when the Major-General in charge of administration was a former officer of the Corps, Major General Sir Reginald Kerr, with Brigadier D H V Buckle, then DQMG, on his staff. The success of this large undertaking was, it has been recorded, 'due in no small measure to the foresight and untiring efforts of these two Corps officers'.

A new, large RASC officers' mess, situated on the west coast on the high ridge overlooking Buona Vista village, was occupied in April 1951. From the mess, there was a magnificent all-round view of Singapore city and the adjacent islands, including Northern Sumatra.

The remainder of the RASC barracks were occupied during August and September 1951. The well appointed sergeants' mess 'affords', it was recorded in the RASC journal at the time, 'every comfort for its members'. The barrack rooms of modern design all had spacious verandas, ceiling fans with adjoining baths and showers. Married quarters adjacent to the barracks comprised five large blocks, each of six self-contained flats and six semi-detached houses. A large recreation ground was taken into use in 1953.

Corps units in Singapore at that time were two locally enlisted general transport companies, the supply depot at Alexander Barracks, No. 4 Supply Reserve Depot at Pasir Panjang, and 1 Water Transport Company on Pulau Brani, where the water transport units had been established in 1946.

At the RASC School, Lieutenant Colonel G P W Finzell had succeeded to command with Captain G F Duckworth as his adjutant. The regimental training company was disbanded in 1952 after which all recruits received their basic training at the Malayan Basic Training Centre; the Driver Training Company became the Driver Training Wing, and the Administrative Wing was formed. In 1953 three Malayan other-ranks, all of whom had passed through the school were commissioned. They were Warrant Officer Class 2 Low Poh Wat and Peh Teck Foo, and Sergeant Haron bin Ismail (all later becoming captains in the RASC).

Over the years, the RASC School in Nee Soon ran courses for a wide spectrum of RASC trades for soldiers from Australia, New Zealand, Fiji, East Africa, Burma, Nepal, Siam and Britain, but the majority of students were from Malaya or Singapore itself. In 1958, the training of the initial cadres of the newly raised Gurkha Army Service Corps (now the Gurkha Transport Regiment) were trained in MT and supply duties at the RASC School.

HQ 3 Army Air Supply Organization was formed in 1960 with, under command, 5, 6 and 7 Air Supply Control Sections, 55 Company RASC and 21 Air Maintenance Platoon RAOC. The organization also had the task of providing the Army representation at the Far East Land/Air Warfare Training Centre.

'Seldom', it was recorded in the Corps journal in 1963, 'can any Corps in peacetime have had to contend with such important operational tasks, in support of ground troops engaged in fighting insurgents, communists, rebels, and malcontents in general.'

The organization was immediately and heavily involved in December 1962, in what at the outset, was referred to as the Brunei

Rebellion, which rapidly became the Borneo Operation. A year later detachments of the Air Supply Organization were operating throughout Malaysia, Sarawak, Labuan and Brunei, with one composite detachment at Changi, in Singapore.

On the formation of the Royal Corps of Transport in 1965, the HQ RASC Singapore District commanding three MT companies (24, 25 and 6), 37 Water Transport Company and 47 LCT Squadron handed over responsibility for supplies, POL, barrack and fire services to the RAOC. The RASC School was divided into RCT and RAOC wings and later re-designated MT and Clerical Wing, of the Far East Training Centre.

The span of command of the newly organized Transport and Movements Branch, HQ FARELF, commanded as Chief Transport Officer by Brigadier W M E White, continued to cover a vast area, encompassing Nepal and India in the West to Hong Kong and Australia in the East. The organization of the new Corps in Singapore was rationalized and consisted basically of:—

15 Air Despatch Regiment RCT
    55 Squadron,   387 Troop   388 Troop   389 Troop
    69 Squadron,   386 Troop   390 Troop
    130 Flight (Beavers)
32 Regiment RCT
    24 Squadron (staff cars)   25 Squadron (Station transport)
    46 Squadron (coaches)   61 Squadron (General transport)
33 Maritime Regiment RCT
    10 Port Squadron   37 Maritime Squadron   74/75 LCT Squadron

On the Movements side, the span of control was equally large as shown by the diagram below:—

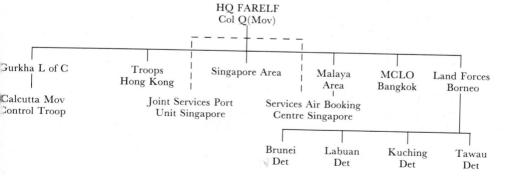

[By courtesy of Brigadier R A Nightingale]

The Duke of Gloucester in Singapore 1966

It will be apparent from the above that the Corps representation in Singapore was extremely large and was probably second in size only to BAOR as an overseas station as far as the RCT was concerned.

During the period 1963–66, many, if not all, the above units were involved to a greater or lesser degree, in East Malaysia during the Borneo Confrontation with Indonesia. The maritime, air despatch and movements units were very closely involved and fully deployed in Borneo, with the largely Malay-manned road transport units providing detachments in Borneo, where the bulk of the land transport support was provided by the squadrons of the Gurkha Transport Regiment. Nevertheless, all units in Singapore were kept busy in providing base support for the units deployed in Borneo.

Following the end of hostilities in Borneo in 1966, a substantial run-down and eventual withdrawal of British forces in Malaysia and Singapore took place. 15 Air Despatch Regiment disbanded in early 1968, leaving only 55 Squadron in the air despatch role; the Beavers of 130 Flight were flown back to UK on probably the longest ever ferrying flight for these small aircraft; 200 Hovercraft

[By courtesy of PR HQ FARELF]

Soldiers of 33 Maritime Regiment RCT on parade at the flag lowering ceremony in Pulau Brani 18 Jan 1971.

Squadron which put in a brief but valuable appearance in the theatre in support of the operations in Borneo, also returned to UK in December 1969. During 1970 and 1971 the pace of withdrawal from the Far East speeded up. 32 Regiment was disbanded on 2 July 1971, having given twelve years of excellent service in Singapore. HQ Transport Branch at HQ FARELF closed on 31 October 1971, leaving small Movements and Maritime detachments behind to represent the Corps. The formation of the small Australian/New Zealand/UK (ANZUK) force in Singapore with some 55 soldiers in the Base Transport Unit, briefly kept our MT presence alive until the final withdrawal of the British element of this force in 1974.

Thus, in 1974 we saw the final disappearance of the RCT presence on this very pleasant and friendly island. The period from 1945 had seen the recruiting, training and employment of many thousands of Malay and Singapore Chinese soldiers in the ranks of the RASC and RCT. Those British officers, NCOs and soldiers who were privileged to serve alongside them will remember them with affection.

HONG KONG

THE RASC WERE AMONG THE FIRST to return to Hong Kong
following the Japanese surrender in September 1945 and among
the relieving force was 781 Company – Civil Affairs GT Company –
which arrived early in October – and, at the same time a
detachment of the RASC/EFI landed from Singapore to repossess
the former NAAFI installations and set up a service for the
returning garrison. In the same month, an advance party – a
platoon of 387 GT Company arrived from Burma, moving into
accommodation on the Racecourse in Happy Valley – to be
followed by three more platoons which were, on arrival in January
and February 1946, stationed in Kowloon. The first post war
CRASC was Lieutenant Colonel S P Perry who held the appointment from 1945 to 1947.

781 Company was, on arrival, immediately involved in
clearing up the debris caused by the withdrawing Japanese and the
looting by infiltrating Chinese. The Company was eventually
disbanded in August 1946 when its vehicles and functions were
taken over by the re-established and reorganized Civil Government.

The GT Companies commanded by Lieutenant Colonel Perry
played an important role in the rehabilitation of the Colony. The
drivers worked very long hours engaged in tasks which varied from
moving large quantities of Japanese ammunition from numerous
tunnels where it had been stored to dump it in the sea; moving
loads of rubble; transporting Japanese prisoners of war to and from
different parts of the Colony; and dock clearance as well as carrying
out general transport duties for the Army and RAF.

The moving of the ammunition was difficult and extremely
hazardous work and on 21 March 1946, Driver Joseph Hughes
RASC was driving a 3-ton vehicle carrying ammunition and
explosives into the magazine in Lyemun Barracks. What then took
place is best described in the words of the following account
published in the *London Gazette* of 26th June 1947:

'As his vehicle was entering the magazine area, it started to
smoulder and then caught fire. Knowing full well that his vehicle

[By courtesy of RCT Museum]

The grave of Dvr Joseph Hughes GC.

was likely to blow up at any moment, Driver Hughes, instead of running for safety, did everything in his power to put out the fire. Notwithstanding small explosions, he first tried to remove the burning camouflage net. He then tried fire extinguishers which failed. A few minutes later his lorry blew up fatally injuring him. By his action the explosion was delayed and warning was given to troops in the locality who were able to take cover. Accordingly casualties which might have been heavy, were negligible, except for Driver Hughes' fatal injury.

Driver Hughes' courage in remaining at his task, thereby attempting to minimize the danger to others when he could have run to safety, was an outstanding example of devotion to duty.'

and he was subsequently awarded a posthumous George Cross.

387 Company became the GT Company for the garrison and after several moves was finally located in Argyle Street Camp, which had been used by the Japanese to accommodate prisoners-of-war, but considerable work was carried out on the camp by the Royal Engineers building excellent dining rooms and a cookhouse

and constructing a well equipped NAAFI canteen.

425 and 426 Supply Platoons with attached Indian Army Units operated all RASC Supply activities in the Colony until all the Indian Army units returned to India in December 1946. The departure of the RIASC led to a reorganization of the Supply Services. The Shamshuipo area which had been used by the Japanese as a Prisoner-of-War Camp was rehabilitated to form a large administrative area and here the Corps established a Field Supply Depot (FSD) and a Detail Issue Depot (DID).

During this post war reorganization of Hong Kong's garrison a considerable amount of work was thrown on the S&T Services 'The stretch of water between the mainland and the Island' it was recorded in the Corps Journal, 'certainly adds beauty and charm to the general setting of the Colony, and the ever changing shipping in the harbour adds gaiety to the scene', but the loading and off loading of troopships and freighters and the movement of whole units from the island to the mainland and vice versa, threw a heavy burden on the transport services and a number of problems at times for the Senior Supply Officer. During these moves the water transport unit, 79 Company, was very much in evidence and their craft were in constant demand for the carrying of personnel, vehicles and stores.

Hong Kong returned to normal conditions within a comparatively short space of time and soon, as the wartime soldiers after a brief stay in this far distant Empire garrison, gave place to the flow of National Servicemen whose fortune it was to perform their service on the island and in the New Territories of mainland China, Hong Kong garrison settled down to a routine way of life against a scenic background familiar to generations of their predecessors and successors.

By 1947 the Hong Kong garrison comprised an Infantry Brigade – two British and a Gurkha Battalion – and 25 Field Regiment RA. In July the following year, one battalion – 1 Royal Inniskilling Fusiliers – was hurriedly withdrawn and sent as reinforcements to Malaya, but it soon had to be replaced and the whole garrison reinforced for, at that time, Civil War was raging in China. By December 1948 the Red Army of Mao Tse-Tung had captured Peking, was spreading out east and south east and presenting such a threat to Shanghai that 1st Battalion the Buffs – the only British Battalion then in Hong Kong were embarked to sail to protect the evacuation of British subjects from that port.

This operation, though, did not take place. However, in May 1949, Shanghai fell to the Chinese Red Army, but there was no British intervention although losses were sustained by the Royal Navy in what was subsequently described as the 'Yangtse Incident'. A detachment of 799 Company (Air Despatch), later in the year becoming 55 Company (Air Despatch) from Singapore was at that time located in Hong Kong and in May two air despatchers from the detachment took part in the 'Yangtse Incident'. They were crew members of the Sunderland flying boat which landed alongside HMS *Amethyst* in the Yangtse river to deliver a doctor and medical supplies to the vessel. The drivers were awarded the Naval GSM for their part in the operation.

By then plans were made for the despatch of substantial reinforcements to Hong Kong, despite heavy commitments in Europe and in Malaya on an increasing scale. This was considered to be the best way of deterring Red China from an attempt to add Hong Kong to their conquests.

The Gurkha Brigade was brought up to full strength, 1 Royal Leicesters arrived in June, followed by 1 Middlesex and 1 Argyll and Sutherland Highlanders. Tanks were also sent – 3 Royal Tank Regiment – together with sufficient artillery and all supporting arms for a division. This force was joined by 3 Commando Brigade from Malta. Finally, from the UK, 28 Infantry Brigade consisting of 1 King's Own Scottish Borderers, 1 South Staffordshire Regiment and 1 King's Shropshire Light Infantry, arrived in October moving straight up into the rugged country on the British side of the frontier with China in the New Territories.

However, it was not to be on the borders of the New Territories that men of these battalions finally saw action against the Chinese; it was to be in Korea a year later.

The Corps' garrison duties were many and varied during this period, with the increased strengths and distribution of units throughout the Island and the New Territories providing an interesting work load. Tasks were not restricted to the normal and an example of the unusual was the task of moving the entire population of a small village of Kao Sai – just over a hundred men, women and children, together with all their goods and chattels and an equal number of pigs. The move, by sea, to a new site in Sai Kung Peninsula, was carried out in three LCMs under the command of Lieutenant Lawson RASC – the people were welcomed to their new homes complete with pigsties and virgin land for cultivation by the Director of Public Works and the OC 79 Company RASC.

It was during the last year of active operations in Korea in 1953 that Lieutenant Colonel (later Brigadier) J C C Shapland OBE, was appointed CRASC 40 Division and ADST Hong Kong. At that time the Garrison was made up of a British Brigade, a Gurkha Brigade, an Armoured Regiment and more than the usual complement of Divisional Artillery. The RASC element of the Formation was composed of 8 (Infantry Brigade) Transport Company, 56 (Hong Kong) Company and 79 Water Transport Company, 81 Pack Troop, a Base Supply Depot, a Supply Depot and a large Barrack Services Organization.

At this time, Captain (later Major General) Peter Blunt was Adjutant, Major Eric Dickens the DADST (Supplies) and Warrant Officer Class 1 John Martin (later Major Martin) RSM.

The mules of 81 Pack Transport Troop, then commanded by Captain Julian Hallum, had local Chinese drivers and were employed in transporting rations and ammunition to the forward troops on the New Territories defence lines, as well as providing transport for infantry engaged in patrolling and searching the off shore islands.

The Water Transport Company commanded by Captain R Wilson, operated harbour launches, LCMs and Motor Fishing Vessels (MFVs) and was used to clear seaward target shooting areas; move troops along the coastlines and as a general reserve of shipping for movement between Kowloon and Hong Kong Island. In the typhoon season – August to October – 79 Company had to run their harbour launches into safe naval berths. However, typhoons frequently burst without much warning when some boats were out on duty, particularly those on range clearance duties during artillery practice – there were occasions when radio communication broke down and craft at sea would make a run for shelter in some coastal inlet.

Towards the end of 1954, Lieutenant Colonel Victor Moly-neux MC (later Brigadier) succeeded Lieutenant Colonel Shapland as CRASC, an appointment he held until 1957. In the following year a Colony Defence Exercise was held. Rations for the Brigades participating issued from the Base Supply Depot were shipped up the coast to a beachhead by 79 Water Transport Company, taken over by 8 Company and distributed to supply points from where they were delivered to the infantry on the mules of 81 Pack Troop.

The Corps organization in these years remained as it had for the past six years, although there was a regular turnround of personnel.

A unique event in the history of the Corps took place on 24 March 1955 when a ceremonial parade was held at Tan Mei Camp for the presentation by the RASC officers of Far East Land Forces of a silver bugle to the 2/7th Duke of Edinburgh's Own Gurkha Rifles.

When, on 1 January 1948, the Gurkha Regiments of the old Indian Army were distributed between the British Army and the Army of India following the granting of independence, 7 Gurkhas, on becoming part of the British Army, were required to register their Regimental bugle call with the War Office. On making their application it was found that their call was identical with that of the RASC and this necessitated application being made to the Director Supplies and Transport for permission to use the call. Permission was immediately granted and officers of the Corps, serving in the Far East, subscribed towards a silver bugle which was presented to the Regiment on behalf of the Corps by the Inspector RASC – Major General G A Bond CBE, who afterwards received, on behalf of the RASC Hong Kong, a silver Kukri from the Commanding Officer of the Gurkhas.

It was in February 1958 that a Joint Naval and RASC Working Party was set up in Hong Kong to decide whether the RASC could victual the Ships and RN Shore Establishments if and when the Naval Victualling Yard closed down. As a result, in January 1959 the RASC in Hong Kong planned and carried out the victualling of the Royal Navy. This overseas base thereby achieved a coordination of food supply to all three Services which resulted, recorded Major S Mitton, 'in a considerable overall saving in manpower and a reduction of Naval administrative backing'. This task was taken over by the RAOC in 1965.

The early discussions had covered a wide area arising from the contrasting differences between Army rationing and Naval victualling. The Army method of provisioning on a fixed basis varied fundamentally from that of the Navy's drawing on a large range of commodities on an 'as required' basis. A comparison of Army and Navy food showed that in certain instances the sizes of the RASC packs were unacceptable due to the difficulties of stowage in small ships. Added to which there were some items such as 'boneless beef' which the RASC could not supply and tinned and dried fruits and jams which the Navy ordered by variety and the RASC supplied as available. It was soon decided that food would have to be divided into two main groups – common user items procured as normal by the RASC and the others which were only obtainable from naval sources to be obtained that way, possibly from Singapore. There were other problems to be overcome relating to powers of local purchase, reconcilliation and re-writing of food supply specifications, conditions of contract and tender schedules amended, and so on. . . .

No 3 Supply and Petroleum Depot was conveniently located to meet the Royal Navy's requirements – the main installation being at Kowloon with a subsidiary depot on Hong Kong Island close to HMS *Tamar* – the main Naval shore establishment. Any ship at moorings in the harbour would have to be supplied at sea by utilizing craft of 79 (Water Transport) Company.

All the problems had been discussed and partially resolved by the end of February 1958. Formal approval was given by the Admiralty and the War Office in September and the new coordinated system was put into operation on 11th January 1959.

In 1962 81 Company had 120 mules for lifting ammunition, equipment and food for units operating and training in the hill country and on the many islands surrounding the Island and off the mainland coast which they reached in Landing Craft Mechanized (LCMs) operated by 79 Company (Water Transport). Mules were replaced from either India or Australia.

In addition to their mules, 81 Company had six horses on their establishment – all ex-race horses presented to the Corps by the Royal Hong Kong Jockey Club. In consequence, mounted sports were very popular in the unit – these included mule racing and paper chases.

The geographical situation of Hong Kong – an island with a very indented southern coastline, numerous offshore islands and with its quite extensive leased territories on mainland China, reached through Kowloon across Victoria Bay, has always made it a station reliant on water transport and with all forms of aquatic sports among the garrison's pastimes. An active RASC Sailing Club flourished using Redwings and picturesque motorized Chinese sailing junks.

In 1962, 79 Company (Water Transport) was commanded by Major B G E Courtis (later Brigadier) and one of the well-known 'characters' who had served a number of years with the unit, Staff

Sergeant 'Pop' Tye, BEM, the Coxswain of one of the Company's VIP launches. It was said that he never trimmed his moustache and 'used it to feel his way around Victoria naval harbour on dark nights', his personality was such that no-one drew his attention to that paragraph of 'Queen's Regulations' which deals with 'hair, growth of'. He still lives in retirement in Hong Kong and 'decorates' many a Sergeants' Mess function.

As a result of reorganization of the Garrison in the early 1960s, 81 Company (Pack Transport) became 29 Company (Pack Transport) and 79 Company (Water Transport) was absorbed into 56 Company RASC.

In March 1967, Lieutenant Colonel Douglas Neighbour took over command as CRCT, and shortly after was confronted with the difficulties and problems arising from the Communist inspired riots which he later described as 'a very unpleasant experience with indiscriminate bombing and large scale crowd disturbances'. These activities were encouraged from mainland China and, at one point, part of the Colony's water supply was cut-off from that source. As a result, border manning was strengthened and additional observation posts established. These events had the effect of prolonging the life of 29 Pack Transport Squadron, albeit at troop strength. It had been scheduled for disbandment in 1968 but, as 414 Pack Transport Troop, remained in existence for another nine years.

During the years 1967–70, all the Corps units in Hong Kong were reorganized into a newly formed 31 Regiment which, in its time, was a microcosm of all Corps activities apart from Railways and Air Despatch. This Regiment existed side by side with units of the Gurkha Transport Regiment.

Early in April 1970, Lieutenant Colonel PC Bowser (later Brigadier) arrived in Hong Kong and took command of 31 Regiment RCT and also the appointment of CRCT Hong Kong. He then learned that he would also take over the Gurkha Transport Regiment from Lieutenant Colonel Arthur Bell RCT when that regiment moved from Malaya to Hong Kong two months later.

It was on 17 July that the Gurkhas arrived – The RHQ and 34 Squadron, then redesignated 'Gurkha All Arms MT Wing' moved into Sek Kong South Camp. The HQ of the Gurkha Transport Regiment was located alongside 28 Squadron GTR in Shamshuipo Camp. At this stage, Lieutenant Colonel Bell handed over his Gurkha Command to Lieutenant Colonel Bowser who later recorded that his 'days were never long enough and living in

[By courtesy of JSPRS Hong Kong]

A GTR Saracen moving through the streets of Kowloon.

Stanley was no advantage. On a typical day, I would travel into my office in Victoria, deal with routine matters of 31 Regiment and CRCT, take a fast launch across to Shamshuipo, deal with both RCT and GTR matters there and then the normal round of the Hong Kong social life!'

The new CO, who had not previously been involved with Gurkhas, quickly became assimilated in the Regimental 'family' – 'one could not help', he recorded 'but warm to the ready smile and courtesy of the Gurkha soldiers and the hospitality of the Gurkha officers and senior ranks' and recalls his first meeting with Gurkha Major Jarnabahadur Rai, MVO GTR who became a 'tower of strength' during his tour in command. It soon became clear that it was vital to produce a role for the Regiment in Hong Kong that was both economically sound and would give satisfaction to the Gurkha soldiers. There was, at that time, clearly no justification for two transport regiments to remain in Hong Kong.

Lieutenant Colonel Bowser, however, saw justification for one transport squadron with a full field force role to support internal security duties, with another squadron organized to meet routine administrative tasks on Hong Kong Island, in Kowloon and the New Territories. The Gurkha Transport Regiment could not meet all these tasks alone but there was no justification to retain two RHQs. Until the arrival of 31 Squadron, the full RCT commitment had been met by 31 Regiment RCT and 28 Squadron GTR. It was clear that the replacement of this Squadron by a British Squadron within 31 Regiment would solve the problem and this is what the MOD plan had been. The CRCT's alternative plan produced a combined RHQ with 31 Squadron GTR taking over the routine administrative tasks in the New Territories, 28 Squadron GTR continuing with its field force task with the balance of transport duties being carried out by the Chinese-manned RCT element in Kowloon and on Hong Kong Island. At the same time, the CRCT set up a Transport and Movements branch at HQ Land Forces to undertake the staff duties of Transport and Movements for the Colony and other stations such as Brunei, Korea, the British Gurkha Lines of Communication and such elements remaining in Singapore.

The CRCT had appreciated that the alternative to this plan was the possible disbandment of the Gurkha Transport Regiment and had to convince HQ Land Forces that his was a viable plan, even if it did mean giving up some Gurkha infantry posts to keep the Regiment alive. The support of the Commander British Forces, Major General D G T Horsford, was forthcoming. Major General Horsford later became Colonel of the Gurkha Transport Regiment. The Regiment was subsequently reorganized on this plan and Lieutenant Colonel Bowser handed over command of the Regiment in September 1971 to Lieutenant Colonel (later Brigadier) Bryan Colley. He remained however as Chief Transport and Movements Officer Hong Kong.

Lieutenant Colonel (later Colonel) R J Boyles took over from Lieutenant Colonel (later Colonel) R N Harris MBE as CTMO in January 1976. On arrival, Lieutenant Colonel Boyles was told that he was to be the last CTMO as one of the Defence Cost Agreement Savings and he later recorded, 'Economy was a major preoccupation during my period of tenure. We were successful in meeting most of the savings required of us and the quality of life suffered in consequence'. Arising from the savings being generally made, the Corps was required to take over the MT of the Royal Navy, absorbing it into 29 Squadron RCT.

Air transport at this time covered a twice weekly scheduled flight to the UK by VC10 with a fortnightly route extension to Brunei and a quarterly route extension to Korea. In addition, there was the regular Gurkha trooping, some sixty flights a year to Kathmandu and three or four a year to and from Brunei for the Gurkha battalion stationed there. In addition, Movements handled all the unscheduled flights for exercises outside Hong Kong to Australia, New Zealand, Fiji, Brunei and elsewhere and dealt with movement on civil aircraft at contract rates.

Movements were also involved in sea transport both military and civil; the annual arrival of a Landing Ship Logistic (LSL) which was the important ammunition carrier, sailings mainly by Royal Fleet Auxiliaries engaged in the clearance of stores ex-Singapore, dealing with containers and vehicles from the UK to Hong Kong by civil shipping and breaking bulk arriving from the UK for onward transit to Brunei and for Calcutta by civil shipping. The latter stores when landed at Kiddapore docks were sent for onward transit to Nepal by rail, being cross-loaded halfway from one railway gauge to another – a process that averaged three months from reaching Calcutta.

In 1976 the transport for the Garrison was still provided by two Regiments – 31 Regiment RCT comprising 29 and 56 Squadrons (including 415 Maritime Troop) and the Gurkha Transport Regiment, with 28 and 31 Squadrons, and a Gurkha MT School. The command of the two Regiments was in the hands of Lieutenant Colonel Bryan Colley, with the staff function and responsibility for Movements being under a CTMO, Lieutenant Colonel Boyles. In 1976 29 and 56 Squadrons combined as 29 Squadron and 31 Regiment was disbanded. During 1977 it was established that the CTMO's responsibilities extended not only throughout Hong Kong but as far afield as Nepal, Korea and Brunei. This, of course, gave scope for extensive visits not only by CTMOs but also by visiting senior officers. Also during 1977, Lieutenant Colonel Boyles handed over his post of CTMO to Lieutenant Colonel Terry Barrett and Lieutenant Colonel Tony Mitchell passed command of the Gurkha Transport Regiment to Lieutenant Colonel David Ivison – no stranger to the Regiment after five tours, serving from the Regiment's formation in 1958 on subsequent tours in all the units in the Regiment until taking over command.

Towards the end of 1979, the HQ RCT moved from the old Victoria Barracks to a gleaming new 26 storey headquarters building in HMS *Tamar*. The Project Officer for this magnificent building being a Corps officer – Major P I French. The Transport and Movements staff in the Headquarters consisted of a CTMO, an SO2 (Transport), a DAQMG (Movements) an EO Finance, with a small clerical staff. A Joint Services Movement Centre with responsibility for sea and air movement was based at Shamshuipo and at the civil airport, Kai Tak.

Far from being a tropical backwater, the Transport and Movements units were kept extremely busy operating in the most congested traffic environment in the world.

The Movements staff with their far-flung responsibilities for personnel and stores movement throughout South East Asia, Nepal, India, Korea, Brunei et al, have detachments in Nepal and under command of the Gurkha Transport Regiment, in Brunei – exciting and responsible jobs for small detachments.

On the transport side, apart from the routine exercise and administrative transport support to the large garrison, life has been made much busier providing transport to counter two 'invasions', the first from Vietnamese boat people fleeing their country with many thousands making the hazardous voyage to Hong Kong. The boats of 415 Maritime Troop, based on Stonecutters Island, were on constant patrol, intercepting vessels and moving refugees, after Government processing, to camps on outlying islands. Many thousands were moved.

The second 'invasion' was both a land and sea based one, from Communist China tens of thousands of Chinese attempting, over the period 1979–82, to reach the bright lights of Hong Kong. Again, 415 Maritime Troop were particularly busy, intercepting 'snake boats' smuggling refugees, or acting as 'mother ships' for Gemini and Rigid Raider type craft searching the approaches to Hong Kong. During 1979, our connections with hovercraft were again revived when two RN hovercraft were based with 415 Troop to assist in stemming the influx of illegal immigrants. To counter the land 'invasion', Chinese speaking soldiers of 29 Squadron RCT were attached as interpreters to British infantry units to assist in the interrogation of detained immigrants. The drivers of the Gurkha squadrons, were also used in an infantry role providing search and ambush parties on the border area.

To tidy up the organization of transport in Hong Kong

following the disbandment of 31 Regiment RCT, all the transport, RCT and GTR, in the Colony came in 1979 under the establishment and command of the Gurkha Transport Regiment. Thus one has, uniquely, Chinese, British and Gurkha soldiers serving harmoniously side-by-side in a Regiment which is probably the largest transport unit in the British Army.

In late 1979, Lieutenant Colonel Ivison handed over command to Lieutenant Colonel P E B Daniel, who had also served previously with the Regiment many years before in Malaya. He, in turn, in 1982 handed over to Lieutenant Colonel J White.

Hong Kong, as one of our few remaining overseas postings, continues to offer a pleasant but busy life in the field of transport and movements.

KOREA

FOR MANY YEARS Korea, a peninsula of just over 85,000 square miles with a population in 1950 of approximately 20 million, was the cockpit of the Far East. Some fighting took place during the Sino-Japanese war of 1894–95 and in 1910 it was annexed by the Japanese.

After the capitulation of the Japanese in Korea at the end of World War II in 1945, and their subsequent repatriation to Japan, the states of North and South Korea were eventually established. South Korea which was allied to the West became the Republic of Korea, whilst North Korea remained Communist dominated and influenced by China, the Russians having left in 1948. The division between the states was the 38th parallel of latitude, which had been agreed at Potsdam. This demarcation line which had initially been selected as a convenient line to the north of which Russia would supervise the withdrawal of the Japanese, and south of which the United States would do the same, quickly became a political and ideological division, and has remained so to this day.

On 25 June 1950 the North Koreans invaded the Republic of Korea across the demarcation line; the 38th Parallel, and started what came to be known as the Korean War. At that time, Korea was to the Western world an obscure and almost unknown country, and the full significance of the invasion was not then realized. At a meeting of the United Nations though, a resolution was passed which condemned the North Koreans as aggressors, and a call was made to all member nations to give every assistance to the South Koreans. The United Nations thus became allied to the Republic of Korea in its struggle against the communist aggression of North Korea.

The part played by the RASC in this campaign in the support of the British and Commonwealth forces of the United Nations, subsequently deployed against the North Koreans, was a remarkable one, not so much for the numbers involved, but as a tribute to the fortitude and resourcefulness of all those taking part, and in particular to the individual MT drivers of our Corps.

KOREA

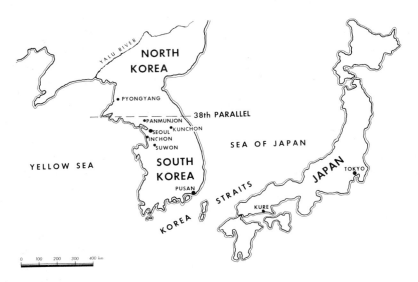

OUTLINE OF THE CAMPAIGN

25 June 1950–15 September 1950

The initial thrust of the North Koreans from 25 June 1950 was made in overwhelming strength, and three days later they captured Seoul, the South Korean capital. Within days, United States forces from Japan, including naval and air forces, were in action in support of the hard pressed South Koreans. During September the British 27 Brigade was despatched from Hong Kong, and was quickly in action as part of 24 US Division, and the United Nations force continued to build up. By mid-September some two thirds of South Korea was in Communist hands.

15 September 1950–24 November 1950

The United Nations forces now counter attacked, and by the end of November had driven the North Koreans back as far as the Manchurian border. During October, 78 Company RASC arrived from UK and were quickly operating in support of the British 27 Brigade. In early November, 57 Company RASC arrived with 29 Brigade Group from UK. Commonwealth Lines of Communication were by this time beginning to take shape in Korea, with Japan as the main base.

25 November 1950–24 January 1951

China, now intervened in earnest, and with great effect. Several South Korean formations were overrun, and it was not long before the UN force which had so successfully driven North to the Manchurian border was forced to withdraw. The withdrawal was conducted in the increasing severity of a Korean winter. By 4th January, Seoul had been evacuated for the second time, and the UN forces withdrew south of the Han River. Here, the Chinese advance was stemmed, and UN lines were finally established a few miles to the south of Seoul.

25 January 1951–31 March 1951

During this period the UN forces carried out successful counter attacks across the whole front, but with limited objectives only. Seoul was retaken and by the end of March the UN forces were established a little south of the 38th Parallel.

1 April 1951–31 May 1951

The Chinese now began a spring offensive and gained some initial success against South Korean formations. During April there occurred the famous Battle of the Imjin River in which the 1st Battalion the Gloucestershire Regiment so distinguished themselves. In this battle our RASC units were heavily involved in close support. The main UN defences held out, and the Chinese advance was halted after they had suffered heavy casualties.

1 June 1951–July 1953

There now ensued a long period of stalemate, during which the UN forces actively patrolled from defence lines which gradually became semi-permanent rather in the style of World War I trenchworks. Against these the Chinese, using 'human sea' tactics, battered their heads frequently, but in vain. In the process they suffered very heavy casualties, although the UN forces did not go unscathed.

On 25 July 1951, the three Commonwealth Brigade Groups now in the theatre, 29 British Brigade, 28 British Commonwealth and 25 Canadian Brigade, were gathered into one formation and given the title of 1st Commonwealth Division. 27 Brigade had returned to Hong Kong soon after the arrival of 29 Brigade. This, the first ever Commonwealth Division, comprised of units from Britain, Canada, Australia, New Zealand and India. All the infantry battalions, and many of the supporting Arms and Services had attached Korean porters, who, with their 'A' frames were invaluable for lifts into positions inaccessible to wheels. The

Divisional RASC Column consisted of three companies, one each from Britain, Canada and New Zealand. The Commonwealth Division was now part of a UN force some 300,000 strong, of which 60% were South Korean. Facing it was a North Korean force of about 800,000 including 75% of Chinese regular formations and units. The strengths of the opposing armies in this remote and little-known Theatre are perhaps surprising. Late in November 1951, a demarcation zone between the two opposing forces was agreed, with a view to the signing of an Armistice within thirty days. In fact, it was twenty months later before major fighting ceased, and during that time minor clashes – and some not so minor – were frequent. Eventually, in January 1953, the Commonwealth Division was withdrawn into reserve, after eighteen months continuous contact with the enemy. In July 1953 it reoccupied its former positions in the line. The Armistice was finally agreed and formally signed on 27 July 1953, three years and one month after the North Korean invasion.

1953–1956

During the final three years, the Commonwealth Division was gradually run down to a Brigade Group, and its final disbandment took place at a ceremonial parade held on 10 March 1956, fittingly, in Gloucester Valley. The RASC units of the Divisional Column of course ran down concurrently with the rest of the Division. Last of all to go was 10 Company RNZASC, which, having joined the Column in November 1951, was proudly on parade at the final ceremony in 1956.

THE RASC PARTICIPATION

78 Company RASC

As has been mentioned the first RASC Company to arrive in Korea was 78 Company, a unit originally raised in Aldershot in 1903 as an MT Company. It served in France throughout World War 1, at the end of which the Company was disbanded, and not raised again until 1950. It then mobilized for Korea as a Motor Ambulance Company, its personnel consisting of 80% Class A Reservists, 10% Regulars and 10% Volunteers for Korea. The role assigned to the Company, under the command of Major F H Potter, was a mixed one. It was to provide medical evacuation cover for 29 Brigade Group, then also mobilizing in England, and to send a detachment to Japan for duty in the expanding British Commonwealth Forces Korea base at Kure. However, when the Company disembarked at Zong-Song, Pusan at the beginning of October 1950, they were to be faced with a radical change of role, in a general transport capacity.

78 Company RASC was originally based in Pusan which had become the main entry port on the south east coast of Korea. The Company was mixed, with platoons of transport manned by British drivers and others manned by local Koreans. Though everyone was kept busy ensuring a continuous flow of supplies from and through the docks, there was time for some social liaison especially with the mixed staff of the Danish hospital ship moored in Pusan harbour. They quickly took to our habit of regular Sunday lunchtime curry sessions and managed to avoid any 'over heating' through acquiring a taste for Guinness. Friendly relations were maintained with the US forces who controlled the Pusan area and particularly appreciated was the invitation to use their very superior coffee, doughnuts and shower facilities.

Speed regulations were strictly enforced in the Pusan area by the American military police to the extent that one day, when overtaken by a US police jeep at well over the speed limit, the temptation could not be resisted by a British senior rank to pursue it through to its police base in the dock area and then to wheel the two somewhat shaken military policemen in front of their captain, who turned out to be a much larger than life US sheriff character and totally sympathetic to the Allied cause.

Pusan was also a major transit centre and as such the locals had developed a number of entertainment centres for the many visitors. One of these was in the form of the 'hubba-hubba' laundry located near 78 Company's main entrance. Many of the laundresses lived on the premises and took the opportunity of providing surreptitious 'off limit' relaxation facilities in the evening. One notable evening a Company town patrol raided the premises and surprised a number of the occupants. One male partner whose sole article of clothing was a Sergeant Major's badge of rank on a wrist band sprang to attention. The only decision to be made was 'was he correctly dressed for the sport in which he was engaged?'. History does not record the answer other than to say that the Sergeant Major was not from the Corps!

The Company's first task was to redeploy as general transport in the newly formed British Maintenance Area at Zong-Song on the shores of Pusan's enormous natural harbour. Some observers state that their first sight of this port was quite breathtaking and reminded them vividly of the shipping off Arromanches just seven years earlier. Most of the ships were carrying American supplies and war material, but a few were for the British. They carried ammunition for the RAOC Base Ammunition Depot and supplies for 1 Main Supply Depot RASC, both of which were in the process of establishing themselves in the British Maintenance Area. It was here that 78 Company (with locally employed drivers) was to furnish transport between the beaches, the depots, and the railway which provided the link to the 'sharp end'. Whilst the ammunition came direct from Hong Kong, UK and elsewhere, RASC supplies for Korea came from the BRITCOM Base Supply Depot at Kure in Japan.

Two ambulance platoons changed their ambulances for three tonners, and, together with Company HQ and the Workshop Platoon, proceeded rapidly north to the front to act in support of 27 Brigade. The Brigade was heavily involved in the fighting on the Eastern front, as part of the 24 United States Division. One platoon of TCVs and motor ambulances were to provide casualty evacuation facilities for 29 Brigade on its arrival. Finally, a small HQ detachment was to proceed to the base in Japan, where it was later to raise and operate two platoons of locally enlisted Japanese.

78 Company was now 'far-flung'; indeed, its platoons in Korea were, to begin with, far apart, and the Japanese detachment was some twenty hours away by sea. Nevertheless, the Company HQ remained responsible for the pay and documentation of all its detachments. Later, it also acquired operational command of a platoon of Royal Canadian Army Service Corps, and one of Royal New Zealand Army Service Corps. One can appreciate the remark of its OC that 78 Company was now a 'Transport Organization' rather than a normal unit. 'Life', he adds, 'was more than hectic, but it was enjoyable!' Let us now follow the fortunes of the main detachment of the Company which was providing support for 27 Brigade. The Brigade, hurriedly despatched from Hong Kong with only two Battalions (Argylls and Middlesex) had already seen much hard fighting, and had now acquired an Australian infantry battalion in addition. When 78 Company joined it, the Brigade was in the throes of the long withdrawal of November–January 1951, and throughout this period remained in close contact with the enemy. The Company was at once plunged into troop carrying in

216

[By courtesy of RCT Records]

RASC troop carrying Bedford QL vehicles transporting Australian troops in Korea.

increasingly severe winter conditions. During this early period the winter clothing essential in sub-Arctic conditions was still in extremely short supply. This was a period during which genuine hardship was suffered by drivers, and in which great resolution was required of them. It was perhaps fortunate that the Company contained such a high proportion of Reservists. These old campaigners had long since learned the hard way to look after their vehicles, their weapons and themselves. When their 18 month call-up later came to an end and they were gradually relieved by young Regulars and National Servicemen the wisdom and lore which they passed on was invaluable. Engaged mostly on troop carrying for the infantry battalions, the Company soon formed close and friendly relations with the fighting troops. A mutual respect quickly grew up between them, which continued as long as the campaign lasted. During February 1951, the Company acquired its first Commonwealth increment in the form of a 2½ ton GMC platoon of the RCASC. The arrival of the Canadian vehicles provided an interesting comparison with our own Bedfords. It was quickly noted that while the GMCs suffered greatly from spring breakages, the Bedfords gave little trouble in this respect. A further point was that the Bedford with its cab-over-engine arrangement was an infinitely warmer vehicle to drive. This was an important matter at that time of year. The Canadian drivers were quickly assimilated into 78 Company, and although they remained under their own national HQ for discipline, this was never any problem. Integration was rapid and complete. This applied equally on the arrival of a 3 ton platoon of the RNZASC about a month later, and this time there was the additional interest that they consisted largely of Maoris. They too remained under their national HQ for discipline, but once again no problems arose. The platoons of both countries quickly became just another part of 78 Company, and produced in the Company the tremendous spirit which was to prevail throughout the whole Commonwealth Division. The New Zealand platoon was employed entirely on ammunition duties for 27 Brigade. It really formed a large mobile Ammunition Point for all three battalions, and it later expanded its duties to include 25 pounder ammunition for the RNZA field regiment which was shortly to join the Brigade Group.

The withdrawal south was finally halted in the region of Kunchon, and it was not long before the Company was supporting the counter-attack by the UN forces, and then the slow advance north. By now it had a Brigade Group to maintain, and had had a very full experience of rough campaigning. As the company was now in all respects a Brigade Group Company, it needed some form of Composite Platoon, and this was provided by a detachment from 76 Supply Company RASC in Pusan. With this detachment the company formed a Supply Point at Tokchon, some 25 miles north of Seoul. This location gradually built up into a railhead for 1st US Corps including the Commonwealth Division. Between March and June 1951, the Company continued to act as a Brigade Group Company for what had now become 28 Commonwealth Brigade Group, re-titled because of the arrival of the Australian battalion and the New Zealand field regiment.

On 25 July 1951, 78 Company RASC became, for some three months, a unit of the newly formed 1st Commonwealth Divisional Column, until relieved by 10 Company RNZASC on 15 October. This much-travelled, highly-experienced, and, one might say, genuinely 'United Nations' unit now reverted to Lines of Communication duties in the Forward Maintenance Area, at the Advanced Base in Pusan and at the Base in Japan. With regret it left behind in the Divisional Column its Canadian and New Zealand platoons, which had joined their own national companies in the Column.

In August 1951, an event took place which set tongues wagging throughout the Division – and indeed throughout a considerable part of the English speaking world. A batman driver of the Company popularly known as 'Ginger' was rumoured among other things to be an old Harrovian and heir to an earldom – a circumstance which he did not deny. 'Ginger' was quite a popular soldier but he could not be described as a good driver and he was far from being the darling of the CSM. He was a passable batman. The Press camp, containing representatives of most of the world's press was twenty miles to the rear just north of Seoul in those days of early autumn 1951. Most of the British correspondents were known to the Company and called in search of human interest stories quite regularly. One evening the Company Duty Officer was asked over the phone by one of the British Press if he could speak to the newly inherited Earl. 'You've got the wrong number', he said 'try the 8th Hussars, down the road'. 'No' said the voice, 'A driver of your unit was heir to an earldom and has succeeded to the title today on the death of the 6th Earl.' Consternation. So 'Ginger' had not been indulging in a great leg-pull after all. He was summoned to the office truck and gave what in the circumstances was a quite composed telephone interview to the Press.

The next day pandemonium reigned at the Company location. In fact the war seemed to stop for a day. Every pressman within miles was drinking the Company booze ration in the canvas covered hole called the Mess. There were television cameras, a team from the Stars and Stripes, the US Army newspaper, which incidentally included the first Western woman the soldiers had seen in months. 'Ginger' was sent for but while waiting for him, the Americans became rather worried on a point of protocol. 'How' they said, 'do we have to address him? As "Your Grace" or perhaps "Earl, Sir"?.' In the middle of this learned discourse the voice of Sergeant Major Dennison was heard ringing across the location. 'Where's his effing Lordship? Come here you idle b...... There's a lot of Yankee reporters here to talk to you and if I hear you say one word out of turn I'll kick your arse all round this location'. To our American allies, an object lesson in democracy.

57 Company RASC

In late October and early November 1950, 29 Brigade Group arrived in Pusan by sea. With the Brigade came 57 Company RASC, as the Brigade Group Transport Company. The Company had a long and colourful history. After campaigning in North Africa, Sicily and Italy, it ended World War II in Austria, where it remained until its disbandment in 1948. It was immediately reformed in cadre form with 29 Brigade in England and mobilized with the Brigade for Korea in August 1950. Mobilization was based very largely on Reservists which made up a small Regular cadre to a strength of some 450 all ranks, with four MT Platoons, a Workshop Platoon and a Composite Platoon. Under command of Major M G M Crosby MC RASC, it sailed for Korea and disembarked at Pusan on 2 November 1950.

The Company at once moved by rail some 200 miles north to Suwon, a journey which took 2¼ days. Here it encountered its first taste of the Korean winter. The Company Commander remembers it vividly, even after thirty years. 'We were working in shirt sleeves on a warm afternoon when the wind suddenly changed. The blast from Siberia brought the temperature down to 10 degrees F.; about 22 degrees of frost.' There was worse to come. With every unit in the Korean War, the winter was a dominant factor in any type of operation. At the end of November 29 Brigade, under orders to join 1st US Corps, began to move further north towards Sinanju on the Yalu River ... up near to the Manchurian Border. OC 57 Company RASC, with the DAA and QMG of the Brigade, was ordered forward in advance of the Brigade to contact the Staff at 1st US Corps, to make arrangements for the Brigade's maintenance on arrival. With them went one platoon of the Company carrying ammunition, since British natures were not available from American ammunition points. Cordially received by their American colleagues, their stay was brief, scarcely had the platoon settled down when news came that the Chinese had broken through to the East. This, as we have seen, was the beginning of the full-scale Chinese intervention. It was also the beginning of the withdrawal of the whole of the UN forces from North Korea. 57 Company, like everyone else, had its hardships not the least of which was the maintenance of vehicles in anything up to 60 degrees of frost.

There was occasionally a lighter side to it of course. An officer of the Company recalls how, on one great occasion, about Christmas 1950, the first supplies of British beer arrived at Brigade Headquarters. The first case was opened with some ceremony, but, alas, 'inside the case were twelve beer lollipops standing in a bed of broken glass. It was the first really cruel lesson of the Korean winter.'

And so the long withdrawal continued, over appalling roads. On 4th January 1951 Seoul was evacuated for the second time and the UN forces withdrew to positions south of the Han River. All withdrawals are difficult and usually demoralizing, and this had been no exception. The endless crawl with frequent halts, averaged little more than 5 mph. Lack of sleep and the sub-Arctic conditions placed a great strain on drivers. The dreary pattern became established. Basically, it was, for both 57 and 78 Companies, a continuous round; offload stores and load troops ... take them back to the next layback position ... return to pick up the offloaded stores ... themselves withdraw to behind the layback positions ... wait about 48 hours and repeat the mixture as before. It became an unpleasant medicine to take, nor did it seem to do the patient much good! And yet, anyone who served in those days recalls one thing above all others ... the amazing morale and resilience of the soldier, when he might well have been expected to be despondent.

In an unofficial account recorded at the time by Headquarters 29 Brigade it was stated:

'During the whole of this period the help given by supporting arms and services was continuous and magnificent. In the case of the Services it is not possible to mention specific instances, but without them the Brigade could not have lived, moved, or fought in the manner expected of a British formation.'

By the end of January the withdrawal had at last ceased, and the United Nations line had been established. The next phase was to be the counter-attack, in which 57 Company would again play an essential part.

In February 1951, Major Crosby left on promotion to ADST of the base in Japan, with the task of building up the Supply and Transport links of the Lines of Communication. Major Crosby was succeeded by Major G W Moncur, who had been DADST at the Base, and who was already familiar with conditions in Korea. The advance north now began, with the limited objective of clearing South Korea but halting short of the 38th Parallel. This was achieved by the end of March 1951. In the course of this advance the UN Forces took some 170,000 prisoners of war, of whom 20,000 were Chinese. With the advent of Spring the Chinese now carried out a series of heavy counter-attacks in the general area of 29 Brigade. The withdrawal of some South Korean units left the

Brigade out on a limb, and during the third week of April, its biggest action of the war took place. This was the Imjin River battle. 57 Company RASC was heavily involved in support of the Glosters, Northumberland Fusiliers and the Royal Ulster Rifles, and there were enormous demands for 25 pounder and 4.2 inch mortar ammunition. Driver Comrie RASC was captured by the Chinese during this battle, but turned up again 48 hours later, having escaped in the confusion of a heavy American air attack; a good illustration of the resourcefulness and self-reliance of our drivers.

In August 1951, on the formation of 1 Commonwealth Division, 57 Company ended its successful career as a Brigade Company and became part of the Divisional Column.

In July 1952, the Company celebrated the 4,000,000 miles driven by their vehicles, members of the unit and visitors assembled in the unit lines heard the clanging of a bell and four red signal lights shot into the air. Around the corner, two files of men, led by one carrying a tattered red flag, hove into sight hauling an ancient and decrepit old three ton truck driven by Sergeant Ray Sayers bearing the sign 'Can do, have done, 4,000,000 miles'. The heaving men, pulling manfully, dragged the coughing and spluttering truck past signs announcing '3,999,999 and 8/10 miles,' '3,999,999 and 9/10 miles' and finally across a white tape which proudly bore the words 'Completed 4,000,000 combat miles.' As the crowd cheered and waved, the engine gave a final cough, green smoke poured out of the engine, black oily smoke from the exhaust and anchors were thrown out of the rear to bring the truck to a stop. The Company's REME team, led by Captain Buddy Wakely REME, then rushed to the scene and with much banging of sledge hammers soon covered the area with broken springs, shock absorbers, differentials and such like.

To complete the ceremony, an illuminated BLR (beyond local repair) certificate was presented to CREME who signed his name certifying that the truck had well and truly earned an honourable rest. Afterwards, Major Guy Newberry-Cobbett, the Company Commander, entertained visitors in the Officers' Mess. The occasion was also appropriately celebrated in the Sergeants' Mess and mens' centres.

Late in 1952, when the front line had stabilized just north of the Imjin River, the Chief Clerk of the composite platoon was sent on the rough and difficult journey to the American pipehead during foul weather to sort out some query over D – (denatured) alcohol which was used for flame thrower fuel (FTF). The Americans used D-alcohol mainly for ice cream machines and were reluctant to issue it to the Commonwealth Division, who they suspected, wanted it for ice cream machines in those units who had been enterprising enough to acquire them from the Americans by barter or other means. It was a difference of opinion which could have become serious had it not been for the good relations which generally existed between them. The Staff Sergeant went off in his 3 tonner – never to be seen again in the Commonwealth Division. During the journey, and while in an American section of the UN front, he had tumbled, complete with truck, driver and the section of road which had collapsed, halfway down a mountain. By the time this was known, he had been treated at the American MASH serving that sector of the line and was well along the evacuation chain. He was seriously ill and there were fears for his recovery. There was no question of visiting him but his platoon commander wrote to him and also wrote to his wife.

Years passed and that Staff Sergeant Bert Hallows – retired as a Lieutenant Colonel in 1978 having achieved the status of elder statesman among Corps Directors' staff officers. He served five Directors, Major Generals Errol Lonsdale, Pat Claxton, John Carpenter, Peter Blunt and Peter Benson. In 1954, one of the casualties from the prevalent haemorrhagic fever, which in 1952 had a mortality rate of 90 per cent, was a Platoon Commander in 57 Company RASC who had been evacuated to an American Field Hospital and was visited by an American General who was distributing the US Purple Heart medal. He pinned one on the hospital shirt of the subaltern, but, on being told later he was a British officer who had been wounded, took it off. It is not recorded what he said at the time but it is one medal that we still do not have in our Corps medal collection!

This was a vintage period in the life of 57 Company RASC, as the role of officers serving in it at the time will confirm. The administrative officer was Lieutenant Ron Jenkins who became Brigadier D(Mov)A, Platoon Commanders were Lieutenant Freddy Plaskett, a future Major General DGTM, Lieutenants Rupert Wallis who became a Colonel, Arthur Danton-Rees who became a Lieutenant Colonel and John Riggall who also became a Colonel.

Lieutenant Keith Davis, later to be Brigadier, Commander of

The Training Group was the MTO of the British 26 Field Ambulance, Lieutenant Derick Braggins, who later relieved Arthur Danton-Rees who went to HQ 29 Brigade as BRASCO, was to become a Major General Director General of Transport and Movements. Also in the Theatre was our present DGTM Lieutenant (now Major General) Bill Allen. Major (later Brigadier) Boris Eastwood, Major (later Colonel) Roden Parry and Lieutenant (now Colonel) Derick Turner.

57 Company RASC remained with the Division until 1955 when it moved to Japan on Base transport duties until its disbandment in 1956. It reappeared in 1977 as 57 (Junior Leaders) Squadron RCT, but that is another story.

THE COMMONWEALTH DIVISIONAL COLUMN RASC

The formation of the 1st Commonwealth Division on 25 July 1951 was an event of international military interest. It became part of 1 US Corps of the Eighth US Army throughout the remainder of the war although neighbouring divisions changed periodically. With the exception of a short period in 1952, when the Division went out of the line for its first and only time in two years, it was stationed two and a half hours drive north of Seoul and four hours from the West Coast.

The Divisional Column RASC had responsibility for maintaining three brigades; 25 Canadian, 28 Commonwealth and 29 British Infantry Brigades. The Tank Regiment in the brigade had 64 Centurions with 20 pounder guns and a Forward Delivery Squadron in 'B' echelon. In support of the Canadians was a squadron of Lord Strathcona's Horse with 20 Shermans armed with 75 mm guns. The Artillery consisted of three regiments of 25 pounders; a total of 72 guns and a light regiment of 24×4.2 inch mortars. This regiment also had an anti-aircraft and light locating battery with six 40 mm Bofors. There was an air observation post flight of 6 Austers and in the latter days of the conflict the Division was joined by a medium battery of 5.5 inch guns.

In the Divisional HQ all appointments were allocated by nationalities. The GOC, the AQ and heads of arms and services were always British. The GSO1 and 2 IC of arms and services and a few GSO3s were Canadian, Australian and New Zealanders with British sharing other appointments, excluding the staff captain who was always a South African. The DAQMG in the Divisional

Headquarters was always a RCASC Officer and the appointment of DAA and QMG Canadian Brigade was usually the outgoing 2 IC from CRASC. At one time the Corps filled the appointments of the DAQMG in the Divisional HQ, and the two brigade DAA and QMGs, and the Staff Captain AQ. The OC Divisional Rest Camp was also wholly staffed by the Corps Column. In Japan the DAAG, the GSO3 and OC Detention Wing were also RASC.

The Column was formed initially from 57 and 78 Companies RASC, with the addition of 54 (later 23) Company RCASC. This composition remained until 15 October 1951, when 78 Company was relieved by the newly formed 10 Company RNZASC. The following were the main types of task vehicles:

57 Company RASC	Four platoons of Bedford QLs
78 Company RASC	Two platoons of Bedford QLs
	One platoon of Chevrolets (RNZASC)
54 Company RCASC	Three platoons of 2½ ton 6×6 GMC

Under technical control of the CRASC were also the various Motor Ambulance detachments of the British, Canadian and Indian Field Ambulances, and the Divisional HQ Transport Platoon RNZASC.

The first CRASC of the Division was Lieutenant Colonel M G M Crosby, OBE, MC, RASC, who for the previous four months had been ADST of the Base in Japan. He had originally mobilized 57 Company in England, brought it to Korea and commanded it up to the end of January 1951. He was then relieved by Lieutenant Colonel J M Grant OBE who commanded until November 1952 when relieved by Lieutenant Colonel R R G G G Noyes OBE.

The life of the Column was of unrelenting toil and not inconsiderable hardship until January 1953 when the Division moved into reserve for the first time since 1951. It then spent four weeks resting and refitting before moving back into the line.

On 3 June 1953, an impressive ceremonial parade was held to mark the Coronation of HM The Queen and on 27 July 1953 at 10.00 hours came the long awaited signing of an Armistice. The shooting and the noise of battle finally died away. Naturally enough, demands on the Column continued. This was probably just as well, as there now ensued the always difficult period at the end of an overseas campaign, with all concerned restive for home. The old cry of 'Roll on' was indeed heard in the land, but the Column with its full daily routine to carry out was more happily placed than some of the other units. It was perhaps now that the advantage inherent in having an integrated Commonwealth Column was really appreciated. The comradeship forged in hard campaigning stood the test of peace and healthy rivalry between the National contingents went on unabated.

Command of the Column changed hands once again in December 1953 when Lieutenant Colonel Noyes was relieved by Lieutenant Colonel E H G Lonsdale, (later to become Major General Transport Officer in Chief). With the coming of peace, albeit an uneasy one, we now hear of the Column engaging in the various activities of a field formation which is 'resting'. Permanent and semi-permanent quarters were being organized and constructed. Brigade and Divisional exercises were being held periodically. For the first time, it was possible to celebrate Corps Week which was observed from 21 to 27 June 1954. A small-arms match, a boxing tournament, a jeep rally and an athletics meeting were held with great success, and the week concluded with a church service and ceremonial parade, at which the Divisional Commander took the salute. The events had the additional interest of each being, as it were, 'international'. New Zealand were the victors, with Britain and Canada coming in a close, and equal, second.

The CRASC, Lieutenant Colonel Lonsdale, was relieved on 19 September 1954 by Lieutenant Colonel K W McQueen, who thus became the fifth, and last, Commander of the Column. In August 1954 the Commonwealth Division was reduced to about one third of the strength at which it had remained since the signing of the Armistice. In effect although reduced to brigade group strength it retained the title of Division. The result on the Corps was that only one company would remain with the Division. This was 10 Company RNZASC which, it will be remembered, had joined the Column in November 1951. 23 Company RCASC left the Division on 27 November 1954, and was lucky enough to reach home in time for Christmas leave to be given to all ranks. On 4 December 1954, it was the turn of HQ RASC to disband, and the CRASC, Lieutenant Colonel K W McQueen, left to take up the appointment of Commander British Commonwealth Sub Area (South). He was succeeded by Major A Thorp RASC, who thus became the first DADST of the Division. 57 Company remained in Korea over Christmas, but early in 1955 most of its personnel embarked for various other theatres, while the Company itself reappeared in cadre form in the Commonwealth Base at Kure in Japan. This in effect concludes the story of the Commonwealth Divisional Column. 10 Company RNZASC remained with the reduced Division until its final disbandment on 10 March 1956. One likes to think that the Column will be neither forgotten nor unsung. Certainly, those who served in it, be they from Britain, Canada or New Zealand, will always honour its memory.

HONOURS AND AWARDS

The following Honours and Awards were gained by personnel of the Corps during the period mid-July 1951 to mid 1953. They include awards made to members of the RCASC and RNZASC while serving as members of the Commonwealth Divisional Column.

4 OBEs: 9 MBEs: 4 BEMs:

37 Mentions in Despatches

8 CinCs Commendations: 1 United States Bronze Star

In addition, Second Lieutenant Hugh Paterson MC RASC was awarded the Military Cross for gallantry at the Battle of the Imjin River whilst serving as an infantry officer attached to the 1st Bn King's Own Scottish Borderers.

THE MAINTENANCE SYSTEM

A commodity maintenance system was employed in Korea. Each company was responsible for the carriage and issue of either supplies, POL or ammunition. Companies changed responsibility occasionally, with the exception of ammunition which remained Canadian throughout due to the geographical site and the quantities held. The British and New Zealand Companies also ran an ammunition point each.

RATIONS

There were a multitude of complications coupled with rations mainly because of finance, religious food preferences and the fact that we had only a relatively small say in administrative matters. Having no normal HQ backing, we did as the US bade us. Fresh rations, including those for the Koreans, and ice in the hot weather, for all troops were obtained from the Americans then processed through a British Forward Maintenance Area to the railhead. The exception was the Canadian Brigade for which we dealt direct with the US Supply Points, as the Canadian Government paid the USA a fixed daily sum on a per capita basis, about five dollars a head for all commodities. This necessitated two Supply Depots including one for Canadians only. Bread and dry items were British supplied. The Indians were issued with rations on demand and had their dry items provided every six months from India. The composite platoons broke bulk into commodity stocks and issued directly to units. It was thought that there was nothing to be gained by setting up supply points as the possession of complete air superiority did not demand such time consuming dispersal.

A small amount of extra fresh rations was flown in every three days to augment the monotonous vegetables on issue. Compo rations were issued on average three times a month. The new five man pack recently introduced became very popular because it could be broken up very easily to share amongst individuals. Also available were the US K rations (equivalent to our Compo) for issue to units in exposed posts who were unable to use a cookhouse. These rations were ready mixed, beautifully packed in individual boxes and included a number of attractive extras. They cost £4 18s 7d, contained 4,700 calories a day, and weighed only 3.8 lbs. There was also an individual assault pack for special duties and patrols. The US ration was very attractive and some units attempted to live on them but soon grew tired of the lack of variety and high flavour content.

The fresh ration scale and quality was excellent. The British soldier had never fed like it before. However, this applied equally to the Americans; for instance – they had meat – 16 ozs (boneless) per day – which included beef, steaks, pork, ham, chicken, turkey, and mutton – potatoes and 1 lb bread and two eggs a day. The average British and Commonwealth feeding strength was 21,000. Over-drawals against unit strengths were brought down to 1.5% which in view of the mixed nature of the units was considered reasonable. Despite splendid rations however, the averge British soldier at the time still showed a preference for stew, bread and potatoes and often complained about 'this 'ere food!'

A supply problem not normally encountered was the need for candles. The scale of ½ lb per man was found to be inadequate. The reason was in the nature of the country itself, an utter wilderness, not a building existing in the battle area. The Division lived in dug out communities of three or four, the line battalions in bunkers all requiring some artificial light by day and night; a scale of 2 lb of candles per man had to be provided. Indeed the county of Durham presented their Regiment, the DLI, with a presentation crate of candles.

In 1951–52 it was thought that straw was required for the winter months to prevent wheels freezing to the ground, to provide flooring for trenches, sentry posts and to build wind breaks. Straw was therefore provided but despite the most strenuous sales drives, nobody wanted it. It was even announced that it would be rationed; and in the Division this was normally a sure way to succeed! The question was put to Canadian officers experienced in winter conditions in the Northlands of Canada where temperatures fall to 50° below zero – they all agreed that straw was unnecessary and so it was discontinued. A colourless lipstick per month, to save lips sticking together with frost, and hydrous lanoline for the hands were part of the cold weather issue. To witness a great burly Aussie lipsticking his lips was a sight for sore eyes but how those little tubes were blessed when the freezing and howling winds swept down from the Mongolian Hinterland.

SUPPLY BY AIR

There wasn't a great deal of supply by air. The available aircraft and helicopters were few and much needed for other tasks. But in September 1951, a helicopter lift of 6,500 lbs of rations and ammunition was made to two battalions cut off north of the river for some 48 hours by sudden flooding. This was controlled by HQ RASC and carried out by United States helicopters. In June 1953 an interesting exercise took place to test the feasibility of maintaining the Division by helicopter. Twelve Sikorsky H-MCs were used each carrying 1000 lbs inside the fuselage plus 800 lbs underslung. It was concluded that a throughput of 228 tons per day could be maintained by this method over a considerable period. Shades of things to come!

AMMUNITION

From stocks held in Kure, Japan, shipment was by sea to the main ammunition base just to the west of Pusan where lighters and DUKWs were used for off loading. Movement was then by rail to

[By courtesy of Lt Col RRGGG Noyes]

An early RASC involvement with resupply by helicopter, Injim River 1951.

the divisional railhead some 40 miles to the rear of the Division. The Royal Canadian Army Service Corps Company was designated to provide main transport and personnel for ammunition supply and control forward of the railhead. Ammunition was complicated by the inclusion of US type weapons in the Canadian Brigade, such as 81/60 mm Mor, 75 mm and 76 mm. Ammunition for all these weapons was collected from the US ammunition supply point and held in a British ammunition point. On every occasion that the Canadian Brigade was involved in a relief, there was almost a complete changeover of ammunition. This was a very considerable commitment, firstly for the infantry battalions, which had to assemble all their ground stocks from scattered weapon pits, and concentrate them into central and approachable dumps; and secondly for the RASC which had the task of collecting them and issuing the equivalent in British or American natures. When it is realized that something not far short of half a platoon of transport was required for this purpose for each of the three battalions involved, and that this commitment always had to be met at the same time as the heavy trooping commitment which a brigade relief involved, in addition to normal ammunition replenishment and daily maintenance, some idea of the strain on the RASC transport resources from time to time can be appreciated.

The selection of sites for the ammunition points was not always easy. Because of the mountainous nature of the country and the extensive paddy, suitable sites for administrative supporting units were few, and always under heavy competition. During one particular period, an ammunition point was established possibly further forward than had ever been established in Korea. It was admittedly reasonably well dug in, and at the foot of a steep reverse slope, nevertheless everyone was a little nervous about it as the shelling in the area was liable to be heavy. It was never hit though frequently near-missed. The near-misses usually landed round the brigade RAOC bath unit or the local RE water point two hundred yards away.

During the mobile phase at the beginning of this campaign, the RASC effort for the movement of ammunition alone was great but during the comparative quiet from the middle of 1951 HQ RASC was able to concentrate on the organization and training of the new Column without adversely affecting the routine maintenance of the Division. But towards the end of September things became much busier. A plan had been made for an attack across the whole front of the 1st US Corps, which of course included the Commonwealth Division. This was to carry the UN lines forward some five miles, and involved breaking into the main Chinese positions. A requirement of 2,000 tons of artillery ammunition in addition to normal maintenance gave the Column as much as it could do. Throughout the attack, which began on 5 October and ended successfully on 8th, the Column was heavily involved. A typical detail is recalled by the CRASC: 'Expenditure of 4.2 inch mortar ammunition was particularly heavy during the first days of the operation on the 28 Brigade sector. A considerable proportion of it was delivered direct to mortar troop positions over an extremely bad road which at one point ran along a river bed and was frequently under shell and mortar fire'.

In late 1951 and early 1952, the pattern for future operations was now emerging. The Division was rapidly strengthening its newly won positions. Very active patrolling was being carried out, and the whole programme was punctuated by a regular series of heavy Chinese counter-attacks, invariably at night. It was apparent that the one commodity the Chinese had in plenty was manpower, and they seemed to advance, quite literally, regardless of losses. The tactics in the face of these attacks were to sit tight in heavily mined and wired positions, while artillery, mortar and machine gun fire caused such losses among the attackers that even the Chinese had finally had enough. Such actions entailed heavy lifts of ammunition of all natures, and the Column was constantly busy on such details. This would not have been particularly troublesome in an otherwise static situation had it not been for constant and increasing demands for other transport. For example, vehicles were needed to support the Sappers in their three main tasks of fortifying the forward defence locations, improving the roads to them, and making new roads as necessary.

The six month period at the end of 1952 was operationally, until near the end, a quiet one, and the occasional infantry engagements were of no more than about company strength. Part of the period is referred to in official records as the 'Static Period'. From the RASC point of view this was something of a misnomer, since no divisional column is ever really static. It might therefore be appropriate at this point to present a short statistical table in support of this statement. The period covered is from February to October 1952, the greater part of which was the 'Static Period' referred to above.

Item	Amount	Number of 3 ton loads
POL issued	12,900,000 gallons	13,300
SAA	32,000,000 rounds	350
4.2 inch mortar	380,000 rounds	1,300
25 pounder	700,000 rounds	3,900

Total mileage in the period was 3,900,000 miles approximately. The table takes no account of the number of vehicles used for troop-carrying, rations, RE support, and miscellaneous details.

From 1952 onwards the major front line activity was patrolling and repelling Chinese attacks varying in strength from a company to a full brigade. Also in neutralizing, through artillery bombardment, the build up of enemy concentrations of men and supplies and last, but perhaps not least, in anticipating, preparing for and overcoming the climatic changes which varied from temperatures of minus 27°F to plus 103°F; from baked hard ground to rainfall capable of causing the River Imjin to rise at the Pintall Bridge point, some 38 feet in 24 hours and causing very difficult road conditions.

Throughout, the United Nations preserved air superiority and maintained constant daylight air surveillance over enemy territory.

The ammunition roadhead maintained ten days supply, approximately 1,000 tons, and catered for both rear based troops and for replenishing forward ammunition points (FAP), serving the daily drawing requirements of divisional troops. Initially, there was one FAP but from early 1953 the Q Branch agreed to a proposal to open two FAPs. These were opened on 24 April 1953, the left flank FAP (Teal) serving the left brigade and the supporting arms and the right flank FAP (Piccadilly) serving the centre and right brigades, supporting arms and the medium battery RA. To broaden the Divisional Column's knowledge of ammunition supply, the Teal FAP was manned by men of 10 Company RNZASC. Divisional Artillery was largely supplied with direct deliveries from the ammunition roadhead. Following the reorganization, actual tonnages of ammunition within the divisional area excluding 'First Line' amounted to:

Line reserves (mainly held with FAP)	1,135 tons
Teal and Piccadilly APs	480 ,,
Ammunition roadhead	1,000 ,,
Amazon reserve (to meet the possibility of bridges going 'out' in the rainy season)	285 ,,
	2,900 tons

Serving a very full and comprehensively equipped division with additional support for such specialist units as the attached US battery of 5.5 inch Howitzers via an extremely long supply line from Pusan to the ammunition roadhead, and being very conscious that the Division's requirements and equipment were unique within the United Nations forces, involved a stockholding by the Corps of some 96 varieties. In addition, there were some fifty items for Royal Engineers support plus materials and equipment required for the mixing and supply of flame thrower fuel (FTF).

Daily usage of all types during relatively quiet and static periods of activity amounted to approximately 100 tons per day with forty two 3 ton vehicles being on permanent ammunition duty.

An amusing incident (to some) was when the relieving division erected a large sign outside their HQ with the legend '2 US Infantry Division, Second to None'!.' The day following the NZ Signals Platoon responsible for maintaining the communications link and adjoining Divisional HQ was soon to have a new sign bearing the legend 'NONE'. It was not allowed to remain for long.

To illustrate the Corp's ability to respond to demand, there were in May 1953 three periods of heavy enemy activity which called for urgent ammunition replenishment during the following nights:

2/3 May   – 156 × 3 ton loads
20/21 May – 250 × 3 ton loads
28/29 May – 600 × 3 ton loads

This latter period was, when every available vehicle was being pressed into service, to bring up 25 pounder and 5.5 inch shells. The ammunition roadhead and FAPs had been operating flat out for some 18 hours when at 1500 hours on 29 May, a storage vehicle arrived at the Piccadilly FAP with a very cheerful but somewhat bewildered driver asking if he had come to the right place. The vehicle was a 5 tonner, apparently adapted and engaged for its specialist role with the Canadian Laundry and Bath Unit based in Seoul but on this occasion loaded (or rather overloaded) with 5.5 inch shells specially sent up from the ammunition roadhead at Tokchong. Finally, no discussion of ammunition would be complete without mentioning that the Commonwealth Division had a fairly rare appointment – that of Divisional Ammunition Officer on HQ CRASC, which underlines the critical nature of this commodity. This appointment was filled by Captain Neil Townsend RASC.

PETROL OIL AND LUBRICANTS (POL)

The provision of POL gave many a headache. In winter the normal daily consumption of gasoline was trebled. Indeed, consumption reached the staggering figure of four gallons per man per day as opposed to a little over one gallon per man per day during the summer months. This was all due to the heating appliances, issued and home made, which were used during the cold weather. It was the heating appliances, in fact, which provided the main Q problem. It is doubtful whether there was a unit in the division which did not have a destructive fire outbreak sometime during the winter.

Somehow, it was always the equipment and stores which were in anyway difficult to obtain, which were destroyed. Replacements, therefore, became increasingly hard to come by. It was over this period, too, that the general transfer of responsibility for a large number of grades of oil from the RAOC to the RASC had to be implemented in Korea. Learning the names and uses for these at the same time as trying to get accustomed to the names, uses and part numbers of all the petroleum items which were obtained from US Army supply points, was an additional worry. Forward petrol points and a main petrol point were operating holding some 100 tons plus oils and greases. All products came through the forward maintenance area and were a US supply. Products were packed in 53 US gal drums, mogas being brought by pipeline to within five miles of the front, from the port of Inchon. Three days stocks were maintained on the ground in the Division on orders of 1 Corps. This unusual practice in a divisional area was ordered as the tactical situation did not often demand mobile petrol points and because the 'roads' often became impassable for long periods due to snow, mud or just total collapse. Holdings of mogas and diesel had to be greatly stepped up in Autumn in anticipation of heavy demands to meet consumption for heating. Mogas was mainly used for heating in trenches, bunkers and in forward positions where the smoke from diesel was unacceptable. An analysis of fuel issued showed that an equal amount of mogas was issued for heating as for vehicle running, but diesel increased.

An item of special interest was denatured alcohol (refined methylated spirits) which was mixed with mogas for absorption of water in the petrol to avoid freezing up of the petrol system, to a proportion of one pint to fifteen gallons. Naturally another item of importance was antifreeze. A 60% total content of antifreeze was planned which gave adequate protection to −50°C. Infantry battalions had to be reminded not to overlook their water cooled Vickers machine guns. Containers 53 US gal were in short supply but were extremely useful for ramps, shelving and ovens. The Corps Commander was very hot on such malpractices. Indeed, one day a helicopter flew over 57 Company's petrol point which had such a ramp and had at the time taken off its camouflage netting. 'What are those drums doing there?' says he 'US' says the POL man. The next day down comes the Corps Commander again and says 'Soldier do you means US or U/S (unserviceable)?' The same General practiced speed controls from the air and one day landed on the road in front of a 57 Company driver and administered a rebuke to him for speeding.

THE LINES OF COMMUNICATION

At the onset of the Commonwealth's involvement in the war in Korea no provision was made following the arrival of the 27 Brigade from Hong Kong for a field force lines of communication organization. The Brigade was supported from United States sources, but later, with the impending arrival of 29 Brigade Group, to be followed by reinforcements from the Commonwealth, it became clear that a proper Commonwealth line of communication would be necessary. The decision was therefore taken that during the time the 29 Brigade Group was being mobilized in the United Kingdom, a staff and services would be raised at the same time. Originally designated British Element Korean Base, this was subsequently changed to British Commonwealth Forces Korea. At the outset the supplies and transport element was made up of only four officers and twenty soldiers trained in supply duties.

This Line of Communication organization reached Korea by air on the 15 October 1950 and was divided between the base at Pusan and that in Japan. The first task of the staff was the planning and organization for future maintenance. The S & T advice to the War Office at that time was that British troops should be maintained on United States Army rations with the addition of tea, sugar, milk, rum and cigarettes from Commonwealth sources. POL would be drawn entirely from US sources, but ammunition, was, with the addition of certain US types, to be met from the UK or stocks available in the Far East. In making these decisions it appears probable, in retrospect, that none of the UN planners envisaged a war of long duration.

Two obstacles soon arose over the plan for rations. American rations were not suited to the taste of the British soldier, and Government policy was that dollar expenditure should be kept to an absolute minimum. In consequence, plans were made at the Commonwealth Base in Japan for the provisioning of an acceptable British ration scale with a system for demanding, holding and distribution of rations within the theatre of operations. Satisfactory arrangements were finally achieved by a combination of ingenuity, expediency and compromise.

As the strength of Commonwealth troops increased, leading to the formation of the divisions, full RASC support was clearly essential. In consequence HQ 76 Supply Group RASC, with two platoons was mobilized at home and reached Korea in January

1951. The group's arrival coincided with the War Office decision that certain fresh goods from the US Army ration scales should be issued to the British Forces in addition to 'Compo' items.

By this time, the staff organization responsible for the maintenance of all Commonwealth Forces in Korea (HQ BCFK) had been established at Kure in Japan to control and operate the lines of communication. An Advance Base was located in Pusan, and it had become necessary to form a Forward Maintenance Area (FMA) on the outskirts of Seoul. All three establishments were operated by HQ 76 Supply Group which also provided a detachment to act as a Composite Platoon with 78 MT Company. In March 1951, two platoons of locally enlisted Japanese drivers were raised by the detachment of 78 MT Company RASC which had at this time no trained supply personnel on changing its role to a brigade group company from a motor ambulance company. June 1951 saw the arrival in Korea of 37 Field Bakery Platoon, soon to be followed by a headquarters and another platoon. They concentrated in the ruins of a biscuit factory to the north of Seoul and were soon producing some 20,000 lbs of excellent bread each day. This was welcomed by the troops. The American bread with which they had hitherto been issued was rapidly losing its initial popularity mainly because it lacked the bulk of the traditional British loaf. By August 1951, the British Commonwealth organization was firmly established, and, it had become apparent that to continue having two separate supply organizations, one British, one Canadian, was unnecessary. In consequence, on 15 December, they were amalgamated under Supplies and Transport at HQ British Commonwealth Forces Korea. All supplies for the theatre, from whatever source, were from then on received by 33 Supply Platoon RASC. From here they were despatched either to 252 Platoon RAASC for use in Japan or to 38 Platoon RASC at Pusan if destined for distribution in Korea. During the preceding six months a Base Supply Depot at Kure, and a Main Supply Depot at Pusan had been organized and stocked. In early 1952, HQ 76 Supply Company and 38 Supply Platoon were designated Main Supply Depot Pusan. Similarly 33 Supply Platoon in Japan operated a Base Supply Depot involving the responsibilities of local purchase of fresh food and solid fuel, sausage making, ice-production and the running of a large cold store. One comment on this organization was that 'the platoon was not underemployed'.

At HQ 'Britcom' Sub area at Seoul from 1952 was a Staff

Captain Supplies and Transport and a Staff Captain A/Q who was also an RASC officer. The work at this HQ was mainly concerned with the smooth running of the supply and reinforcement 'pipeline' from Japan via Pusan to the Tokchong railhead behind the rear boundary of the division. Under the administration of this sub area was a large number of lines of communication units, not the least of which was the leave camp at Inchon, established and efficiently operated by Captain 'Pop' Jenkins RASC.

The 'Britcom' Base Supply Depot at Kure, Japan was located on the shores of the Inland Sea in a former Japanese Naval Barracks, (renamed, after the Commonwealth Divisional Commander 'Cassels Camp') with very good accommodation in purpose built warehouses. The first CO of the depot was Major Stephen Hudson RASC who was later succeeded by Major Brian Garrard. The officer strength of the depot included a number of Australian officers. Apart from a few senior ranks of both the RASC and RAASC the depot, it has been recorded, was 'very efficiently' manned by locally employed Japanese.

The functions of the depot were to indent for and receive ex-ship all RASC – and equivalent – supplies for all Commonwealth troops throughout Japan and Korea. Supplies for the leave centre at Ebisu and for other small units in Tokyo were sent by rail; those for units in the Kure Base Area and the RAF flying boat station at Iwakuni went by road; and the Royal Navy were supplied via the RFA *Green Ranger*.

Local transport in the Kure area was provided by 58 Company RCASC. However, by far the greatest amount of supplies was shipped to the main supply depot at Zong-Song, in vessels on permanent charter from the British-owned China Navigation Company. These were called the *Esang* and *Wosang*.

Such was the RASC organization in Korea and Japan until 1956, reducing gradually as the Army in Korea slowly withdrew until in November 1956 all British Forces withdrew from Korea and from the bases in Japan.

CLIMATE AND OTHER HAZARDS

No discussion of this campaign would be complete without further mention of some of the difficulties, problems and hazards of life and work in Korea.

The Divisional Column, of ten platoons of general cargo carrying vehicles, was required to meet all general transport commitments virtually without prospect of supplement from other sources. There were no nice tidy supporting echelons to call upon as in a 'normal' campaign. The division had to live within itself, all of the time, and whatever the circumstances. Roads varied from good for the main routes, the result of brilliant Royal Engineer planning and vast effort, to appalling for the side roads and undeveloped tracks. Distances were long and ammunition consumption was heavy. The troop lifting commitment was always large and the wear and tear of vehicle engines was alarming. Before the campaign, very few roads of any kind existed in Korea outside the main towns. There were the main truck routes south to north through the country, Japanese built, and seldom of more than one vehicle width. Side roads were merely earth tracks winding alongside and sometimes across the paddy fields which fill every valley. These were mostly walking width only, as even bullock carts were rare. Such were the communications which had to be adapted for use by a mechanized army.

Road construction, therefore, became a major operational issue right from the start. The only road building materials available were stone from local outcrops of rock suitable for quarrying, and earth or sand from the river beds. Even suitable places for quarrying were difficult to find, and were often far from the scene of construction. Few tipper trucks were available to the division and therefore vehicles from the Divisional Column were in constant demand in large numbers. The ordinary 3 ton cargo truck was by no means an economical vehicle for use on this sort of work because of the time it takes to unload manually but there was no alternative. Even in the rare periods when there was no new road construction in hand, vehicles were still required from the Divisional Column for road maintenance work. The commitment by the Column was, therefore, never ending and the wear on vehicles ploughing in low gear over unmade roads and through stretches of axle-deep bog was immense. The troop lifting commitment was also higher than a divisional column would normally have to cope with. Apart from normal reliefs in the line there was a constant turnover of whole units in the theatre and an almost continuous commitment for lifting troops for work in rear areas. As much as possible was carried out by units themselves in first line transport, but the greater part of these tasks fell to the RASC.

All these tasks over inferior roads and long distances, with road surfaces always covered thickly in dust, or ice or mud, shortened the average vehicle engine life to 5,000 miles. The availability of replacement engines or replacement vehicles was never satisfactory, so all units, including units of the divisional transport column, were normally 10% below established vehicle strength. The transport supply and demand equation, a problem all the year round, became much intensified in the two months of the monsoon season when even a number of the good roads were unusable. Heavy rains were liable to occur, in fact, any time from 1 July to 30 September, though they were most prevalent from about the middle of July until the middle of September. Rainfalls over this period were always heavy though for the most part intermittent, but it is certain that every now and then over the period rain would fall without ceasing for anything up to 48 hours. When the ground was already thoroughly saturated by previous rainfalls a storm of this duration had an almost immediate effect on the rivers, which rose extremely rapidly and caused widespread flooding. Riverbeds, normally dry, became fast flowing torrents, and the River Imjin would rise between forty and fifty feet in a few hours and roar along at ten knots. Miles of roads were quickly inundated, most low lying ground flooded to a depth of many feet, bridges were swept away, and many unit locations isolated. The result, with four-fifths of the division north of the Imjin, was a major administrative problem. The bridges over the River Imjin were essential to our road communications. Teal bridge, an American floating treadway, took single line traffic only. A sign at both ends declared 'North bound traffic only'. An amusing incident involved the BRASCO of 29 Brigade who, heading North, encountered an American jeep half way across the bridge. 'What the hell are you doing' yelled the officer, 'can't you read'. An American private soldier stood up and said quietly 'Don't you realize that you are talking to a Marine!'. There was no answer to that.

In the circumstances where reliance could not be placed upon bridges, administrative planning had to be based on the assumption that road communications across the Imjin were non-existent and other means of maintenance had to be evolved. Amongst these was preparation for a resort to air supply. Dropping zones had to be prepared, the relevant administrative organization trained and stood by, and selected supplies and stores prepacked for air dropping. In addition cable-ways across rivers might have had to be constructed and the organizations for manning cable-way terminals and their incorporation into the maintenance system was prepared. Much of this work necessarily fell upon the Divisional Column. All these provisions were made for the first time against the 1952 monsoon. In the previous year, although on one occasion 28 and 29 Infantry Brigades were presented with a major problem of this nature, nothing approaching the same number of troops were involved as in general the Commonwealth units at that time were south of the river. In fact, not all the bridges over the Imjin succumbed so air supply did not have to be put into effect. Likewise, other diverse – and diverting – methods of maintenance did not have to be implemented in full. This was perhaps just as well, from the point of view of air supply because at one period, though only for 24 hours, even the prepared dropping zones were cut off by floods.

In writing of operations in Korea it is difficult to stay off the subject of the weather. Temperatures regularly fell to minus 20 degrees Fahrenheit and any form of movement in the bitter winds called for the warmest available clothing. It needed a certain amount of resolution to crawl out of a warm sleeping bag, especially at night. Such conditions were of course favourable to road movement with everything frozen hard. In fact, it was perfectly possible to drive tanks across the frozen Imjin River, and small rivers everywhere ceased to become an obstacle. Another advantage was that drafts of National Service drivers could be trained in cross-country movement when this was at its easiest. These drafts were the replacements for the reservists completing their 18 month tour, and the young arrivals quickly showed their adaptability. it was not long before many units, including some of the infantry battalions, consisted of as much as 50% of National Servicemen. Some of the old hands had wondered how these men would cope with the conditions which awaited them, but there need have been no such fear. No one who was there could forget how well these youngsters buckled down to their task. With very few exceptions, they were quick to learn from and to emulate the regulars and the experienced reservists. They were glad to be doing a job which was so evidently important. Indeed, it is difficult to imagine how the British units of the division could have been manned without National Service. From about the middle of March the thaw generally set in, and the good driving conditions became only a pleasant memory. Several platoons and company locations quickly became untenable because of mud, and some hurried moves had to be made to enable the maintenance of the division to continue.

These unpleasant conditions lasted until about mid-April, when a very marked improvement set in. With brilliantly sunny days and cool, dry nights, the mud and flash floods were soon forgotten. However, no soldier can ever be really happy without something to complain about, and this was soon provided by the dried-up mud. It quickly turned into a thick, very fine dust which was in its way equally tiresome.

In the early days the winter clothing was barely adequate but later issues were excellent, consisting of special rubberized boots, very warm, light and waterproof with a nylon sock, two pairs of socks heavy wool, long meridan pants, pyjamas, jersey under trousers, puttees, wind and waterproof combat trousers, string vest, heavy jersey, combat wind proof lined parka, wristlets, mittens and white rubber outer gloves. Two bags were used to sleep in and silk gloves worn under the mittens were a bonus and snow glasses a positive boon.

Fire was a frightening hazard of life in the cold conditions prevalent most of the time. The 57 Company RASC Officers' Mess tent was burnt down one night and the regularity of the incidence of fires generally was depressing and dangerous.

A further memorable experience suffered by some was a terrifying hurricane which kept everyone literally pinned to the ground until it blew itself out 48 hours later. It was impossible to stand up or walk and activities such as cooking were out of the question.

The campaign in Korea highlighted, not for the first time, the inherent ability of the British soldier, whether Regular, National Service or Reservist to adapt to his environment; to live and fight in extremes of climate, and to cooperate alongside other nationalities. Although the British, Canadian, Australian and New Zealand soldiers have a natural affinity towards each other, the success of the Commonwealth Division was not won without a good deal of tolerance and compromise by everyone. Our combined relationships with the American Army, with whom we worked, was excellent. Throughout the campaign, to a greater or lesser extent, we all shared the lines of communication and quickly learned to adapt to each other's working methods. Those items of each Army's stores and equipment not normally available to the other were soon exchanged on a more personal level to everyone's mutual advantage.

In the extremes of climate in which the Corps had to operate, the maintenance of morale was of paramount importance. The confidence that food, fuel and ammunition were all available in the right place at the right time was an essential ingredient in the maintenance of morale. In this, the RASC, RCASC, RAASC and RNZASC could all be proud of their achievements.

JAPAN

ALTHOUGH THE JAPANESE, following the dropping by the American Air Force of the Atom bombs on Hiroshima and Nagasaki, surrendered unconditionally on 15 August 1945, the defeated country was first occupied by United States Forces and it was not until March the following year that the first units of BCOF (British Commonwealth Occupation Force) landed in Japan. The force comprised 5 British Infantry Brigade (2nd Battalion the Dorset Regiment, 1st Battalion Queen's Own Cameron Highlanders and 2nd Battalion Royal Welsh Fusiliers), 268 Indian Infantry Brigade and 9 New Zealand Brigade, the leading elements arriving in HMT *Dorsetshire* on 8 March 1946.

The RASC element of the Force was composed of a RASC Headquarters, the CRASC being Lieutenant Colonel Williams RIASC and 8 Company RASC commanded by Major (later Lieutenant Colonel) H Lincoln Jones MBE, which had been stationed near Bombay for most of the preceding year. The RASC supported the three British Infantry battalions located on Kochi in the south of Shikoku and these were mainly supplied by rail. The Company was located on the island of Shikoku at the former Japanese sea-plane base of Tokushima where the access roads between paddy fields were narrow and only wide enough for Jeeps to pass. HQ RASC together with the RAASC and RIASC Companies were on the mainland.

Later, one platoon and a supply section moved four hundred miles to Tokyo where they were fully occupied dealing with the requirements of the Allied occupation visitors and officials for whom a visit to Tokyo was a 'must'.

It was necessary at this time for strict security precautions to be taken to safeguard both 'Q' and 'MT' Stores, particularly on the supply trains and although fraternization was discouraged it was necessary for personnel to work in close contact with the Japanese police and security guards.

Soon after the arrival of the British brigade a number of Japanese small vessels and launches were taken over and a Water Transport Company formed. Later, a number of larger sea-going craft were requisitioned to ply between Japan and Hong Kong for the transportation of supplies and stores. The crews of all these craft were entirely Japanese ex-sailors with RASC officers, WOs and NCOs in command.

The British Commonwealth Occupation Force was, however, of short duration and in January 1947 5 Infantry Brigade was withdrawn, the main occupation force being provided by the US Army. Only a token element of BCOF remained and with it, for a further three years, a small detachment of the Corps.

Corps units returned to Japan at the outbreak of the Korean war in October 1950. Their activities are covered in the chapter on Korea. All British forces were withdrawn from Japan in November 1956.

NETHERLANDS EAST INDIES

AS WAS THE CASE in many other parts of the world, the Japanese surrender did not bring peace to the population of the Netherlands East Indies and once again British troops found themselves engaged along with their Indian comrades in the bitter fighting that took place in Java and Sumatra, now Indonesia. Such was the scale of activity that the official history of the 1939–45 war includes the campaign here and in French Indo-China although it went on well into 1946.

Instead of surrendering to the Allies, the Japanese forces in Java and Sumatra handed their arms over to the Indonesian rebels who were determined to prevent the return of the Dutch and were busy setting up an Indonesian government and administration. There being no Dutch forces available at the time, troops from Burma and Malaya were despatched to restore legal government and to complete the release of many Allied prisoners of war and internees still in the area. 15 Indian Corps was tasked to undertake the operation. Three divisions (5, 23 and 26) together with elements of a parachute brigade and other supporting units, including air despatch units, were deployed along with considerable naval and air support.

Supply and transport units were almost entirely RIASC. There were a few individual RASC officers deployed. However, 69 and 70 Air Despatch Companies, who were stationed at Chittagong and Ramree Island, found themselves detailed to move to Keramon, the main airfield for Batavia (now Djakarta), to assist in the evacuation of the Allied POW and civilian internees. The HQ was established in the KLM building in the Königsplein, Batavia. It came as a great surprise to find that much of the support was provided by the Japanese forces and a Japanese liaison officer was attached to the unit. Captain (later Lieutenant Colonel) I Renwick OBE RASC later recorded his surprise at the appearance of well-being amongst the JSP (Japanese Surrendered Personnel) as they were referred to and the effort put into the tasks allotted to them.

Considerable difficulty was found in moving about the

country because of the rebel hold and therefore the majority of movement was by air, keeping the air despatch units fully employed. There was little chance to see the country or socialize as for most of the time there was a night curfew in the towns including Batavia. Dutch forces began arriving early in 1946 and a gradual transfer of responsibility took place. British forces were withdrawn as soon as the Dutch forces were in significant strength, the last British units leaving Sumatra on 28 November 1946 and Java on 29 November 1946.

One of the few bright memories of this campaign was the financial bonus of a free ration of money! When our forces arrived with the new Dutch guilders they found that the local economy was so geared to the Japanese occupation currency that they would not accept the new legal tender. Field Cashiers RAPC therefore had packing cases full of the old currency to be dished out at the rate of 300 per month for officers and 100 per month for soldiers!

CELEBES

The Celebes Islands to the south-east of Borneo and now part of Indonesia, were in 1945 one of the group of large islands which formed the Netherlands East Indies and had been occupied by the Japanese since 1942. As the British and Indian troops of 20 Indian Division were being withdrawn from French Indo-China following the arrival of French forces in sufficient strength to re-occupy their Colony, 80 Indian Independent Infantry Brigade Group was despatched to Celebes disembarking at the capital Macassar to take over from troops of 9 Australian Division which had arrived soon after 'VJ' Day. 80 Brigade was accompanied by 412 Supply Platoon RASC, a sub-unit of 4 Supply Company RASC. 102 Company RIASC took over from the Australian MT Company. The OC, Major Campbell Steward was then appointed OC RASC Celebes and was succeeded as OC by Major (later Lieutenant Colonel) J R Evans RASC.

On arrival at Macassar, the company which had left its vehicles behind with the French in Saigon, took over those of the Australians – described by Major Evans as a 'motley collection of Ford and other heavy vehicles'. Soon after his arrival, Major Evans was detailed to accompany a Dutch Admiral and his staff on a mission, travelling in Catalina aircraft, to visit all the surrounding islands where surrendered Japanese troops were concentrated, to tell them about the arrangements for their repatriation. They had been provided with a basic ration of 1200 calories per day and with seeds, picks and shovels and told to grow their own vegetables. 'It was surprising' he recorded, 'how well they had concentrated themselves into self-sufficient camps, each with vegetable gardens'.

The Celebes had been used by the Japanese as a camp for Dutch women and children and, in consequence, the difficulties encountered elsewhere in the Netherlands East Indies did not reach to the Island to any great extent. In due course, the Dutch reassumed control and the British and Indian troops were withdrawn, final withdrawal being on 14 July 1946.

FRENCH INDO-CHINA

IN SEPTEMBER 1945, following the surrender of Japan, 20 Indian Division moved from Burma by air and sea into French Indo-China, composed of the former French Protectorates of the Empire of Annam, the Kingdom of Cambodia and Lower Cochin China, South of latitude 16° North, with the tasks of concentrating and disarming some 70,000 Japanese troops, repatriating allied prisoners of war, and maintaining law and order pending the arrival of French forces.

The supply and transport organization of the division was made up entirely of Royal Indian Army Service Corps General Transport Companies, Composite Platoons and the Field Ambulance Transport. The CRIASC of the division was Lieutenant Colonel D C Macleod, RIASC and many of the British officers, WOs and NCOs were UK based and subsequently transferred to the RASC.

Within days of the advance units arrival civil war had broken out. This was the beginning of the war in Viet Nam as French Indo China later became. The capital Saigon and other main towns were blockaded by the Annamites – later to become known as the Viet Minh. In the North of the country, in and around Tonkin, there was widespread famine.

An ad hoc Civil Food Control Organization (CFCO) was established under the direction of Major P G Malins MC, RASC who had just transferred from the RIASC with responsibility for ensuring the collection and distribution of food and other essential supplies for the civil population. British and French Naval, Army and Airforce officers were attached to this organization which worked closely with the appropriate civil authorities. The CFCO had to take immediate relief measures for all communities be they French, Annamite, Chinese or Indian without distinction despite the Annamite action, and to make arrangements for the protection and continued working of all essential and ancillary food and supply services.

At the outset Japanese naval and army units were able to move supplies of food without being molested, but they were soon involved in a number of incidents caused by the Annamites, who arrested and opened fire on the Japanese on a number of occasions. It was for gallantry during one attack by Annamites that Major P G Malins was awarded the Military Cross. Due to the limited number of British and Indian troops available it became necessary for extensive use to be made of rearmed Japanese troops, motor transport, shipping and aircraft operating with their own officers acting under the orders of the CFCO.

Armed guards had to be mounted at all key installations – cold storage and pasturization plants, abattoirs and flour mills. Cattle and their owners were moved into defended areas to ensure the milk supplies, whilst guarded central markets and storage depots were established and all dumps of food and other supplies were moved into them.

Fresh produce was brought into Saigon from the Delta area, and from Dalat, north of the City, using road and water transport all with armed escorts. Maintenance convoys operated at ten day intervals between Phnom Penh, the capital of Cambodia using the Duperre Canal and the Mekong River. The convoys usually comprised three river steamers, seven tugs, twenty barges and a gun boat under command of a Royal Naval officer with a CFCO officer and 250 armed Japanese troops as escort.

Special measures were necessary to relieve besieged European communities in other centres, many of whom were short of food. In one instance a Lieutenant Commander RN sailed a landing craft with thirty tons of food from Saigon to Nha Trang for some 1,300 French civilians who had been without food for a week. Food and other much needed supplies for the beleagured community in Hue were flown to Tourane in Japanese aircraft and passed on to Japanese troops to take them on by road to Hue.

The British and Indian Forces were in a much stronger position to give and enforce orders to all communities until such time as the French could take over. The important Chinese community, while refusing to be seen with the French, were generally willing to work for British officers and they could act without partisanship to all communities and were therefore in a much stronger position than an equivalent French organization. 102 Company RIASC – a Divisional Troops Company – commanded by Major Campbell Steward RIASC (later RASC) arrived in Saigon in October and marched out from the docks to Cholan Racecourse to await the arrival of its vehicles. The racecourse, described as an 'ideal location but very isolated' was located in the Chinese quarter of the city. The French residents, only recently freed from the Japanese, were extremely friendly, but anxious to regain control of the city.

The company had only just settled in when the Annamite Independence Movement commenced guerilla operations against the French in this area. The Annamite were no respecters of the British flag and the racecourse came under attack on several occasions. It was a large perimeter to defend, and a re-armed Japanese infantry battalion was placed under command of 102 Company to deal with the Annamite threat.

4 Supply Company RASC which had been operating supply depots in Rangoon since June 1945 was dispatched to join 20 Indian Division arriving under the command of Major W Henderson RASC in Saigon on the 21 November and was immediately engaged in base supply duties.

By early 1946 sufficient French troops had arrived to repossess the country and it was possible for 20 Indian Division to be withdrawn, the last elements leaving on 30 March.

CHRISTMAS ISLAND

OPERATION GRAPPLE, the testing of British thermo-nuclear weapons, was planned to take place on Malden Island some four hundred miles south of Christmas Island in the South Pacific Ocean. The latter was selected as the main base for the operation and, although only about thirty-five miles in length and twenty-four miles at its greatest width, is the largest coral atoll in the Pacific.

The shape of the island has been described as resembling a lobster claw, the jaws of which contain a spacious and almost semi-circular lagoon, the island being surrounded by a reef several hundred yards wide. Day temperatures varied between 70° and 100°F but the easterly trade winds exerted a cooling influence; despite the high humidity, the heat is not oppressive.

The advance party whose task it was to prepare the camp and airstrip for the main force on the island contained a small RASC detachment of men and vehicles including DUKWs to provide the ship to shore movement. The unit formed at Depot Battalion RASC Bordon on 7 May 1956 and sailed in HMT *Devonshire* the following month. The ship with four hundred troops altogether arrived at Christmas Island on 25 June. Their vehicles including four DUKWs arrived the following day in the Landing Ship Tank (LST) *Reginald Kerr* from Singapore.

On 2 July another cargo ship arrived bringing landing craft, pontoons and another six DUKWs. This marked the beginning of a port; a crane was brought ashore and jetties were constructed by the Sappers who, three weeks later, moved on to start work on the construction of the main camp and airfield.

Between July and September more troops and cargo ships arrived together with HMS *Messina*. A steady flow of craft from ship to shore brought cargo into port, until the initial rush became regular routine and the use of DUKWs was less urgent; the RASC contingent was then able to concentrate on other matters. Firstly supplies and POL. The POL Depot, at this stage, with Staff Sergeant Major Silk in charge, his 2IC being Sergeant Cook (now Captain G T Cook RCT) was located along a mile of a narrow peninsular between the Pacific and a lagoon. A bakery with

Sergeant Smith in charge, was established later, followed by a butchery with Sergeant (later Warrant Officer Class 1) Sutcliffe as the Master Butcher. Fresh salad items were flown in weekly from Honolulu. By December 1956 a bulk POL tank and packed depot was in operation; the Corps contribution to the Task Force was thus well established. This Supplies and POL detachment was commanded firstly by Captain Robin Atkinson followed by Major Peter Twiss.

The amphibian problems at Christmas Island resulted from the distances between the shore and the ships; it was a round trip of almost five miles to the more distant berths. This long haul, in low gear, and the hot climate, caused excessive overheating of the engines and eventually the original DUKWs became beyond economic repair. One of them, filled with supplies, had sunk two hundred yards off shore and Sergeant Crampton braved the shark infested waters to fix wire ropes under the vehicle so that it could be recovered by the Royal Navy.

'By December', recalled Lieutenant (now Brigadier) A F R Evans, 'life was reasonable. The NAAFI sold beer, the AKC showed films, we had infrequent but welcome visits from the USAF band of the Pacific...' but, attention was then focused on Malden Island, a flat coral mass some twenty-five miles square, fringed with a coral reef and desolate except for a few palm trees and the derelict buildings around the deserted guano workings.

On this island too an RASC contingent served from December 1958 to March 1959, part of the small force of two officers and seventy soldiers (RE, RASC, REME and ACC) engaged in the task of erecting a camp with basic facilities, constructing an airfield and building installations required by the Atomic Weapons Research Establishment. The amphibians brought all the stores and equipment ashore. The task of the Corps was therefore basically the same as was carried out on Christmas Island but here it was even more important that the DUKWs maintained 100% availability. They had to carry everything from two ton steel plates to delicate electronic equipment through many vagaries of the sea and on the beach which varied from soft sand to coral shingle, the sand being so fine that DUKW tyres, even at minimum pressure, were unable to grip and the beach gradient varied from shallow to very steep according to the surf conditions.

By the end of February 1959, all stores were ashore and the airfield built. In mid March the scientists arrived as did HMS

Narvik acting as permanent support ship. An island water supply problem which arose was solved by putting a four hundred gallon tank into a DUKW which brought ashore ten tons of water per day from the *Narvik*. Another DUKW operated a 'bus service' between the ship and shore.

On the day before the test explosion of the atomic device, all tents were struck, all camp structures dismantled and everything buried in shelters. The DUKWs returned to meet the last aircraft carrying 'VIPs' and other official observers to take them out to HMS *Alert*. DUKWs then swam across to *Narvik* leaving on the Island only a small rear guard to complete certain last minute arrangements before being picked up by helicopter. 'It was strange' wrote Lieutenant A F R Evans later, 'driving across the deserted island, now much as we had found it; a few buildings; terns and boobies flying above, some shelters, silver in the evening sun, the last Dakota receding into the distance and only HMS *Narvik* and HMS *Alert* on the sea. The day after the explosion,' he continued, 'we returned to the island. One had a feeling of surprise. The boobies and terns still flew overhead, a few fires burned but little seemed to have changed, even the pigs still lived. By evening the camp was re-erected...'

In the subsequently produced Task Force Handbook it recorded 'All in all, the work of the DUKW Detachment has been of inestimable value to the operation as a whole'.

In 1958 two more nuclear tests were planned but before they could take place a considerable amount of construction work was necessary mainly by the Corps Engineer Regiment of the Army element of Tast Force 'Grapple'. The winter of 1957/58 was very wet and in consequence construction work was delayed. To free Sappers for engineering tasks a request was made for RASC drivers. Twenty were sent out and attached to the Engineers in February, but later, when a hundred more were asked for it was decided to provide an MT Company. On 14 April, the order was issued for the formation on 1 June of 94 Company RASC (MT) at Bordon. It was raised on a restricted establishment of six officers and 133 soldiers commanded by Major M D Gallagher RASC. Some of the personnel were sent to 6 Training Battalion at Yeovil for a special course, whilst back at Aldershot G.1098 stores were assembled. The Company left England between 3 and 17 June, flying by RAF chartered BOAC aircraft and American air lines via Iceland and Labrador or direct to New York, thence to San

Francisco and Honolulu before the final 1200 miles flight south to Christmas Island.

The transport offered to Major Gallagher on arrival was some 160 vehicles, some were new but others had been in service for many years – one had even been declared 'beyond economical repair' but had been resurrected in order to continue an essential task. Only two RE officers, four sergeants and some 130 Sappers had been available to control, drive and repair them and they had been used on arduous work in adverse conditions. It was clear that the shortage of drivers and trained supervisory personnel, coupled with the nature and pressure of the work was contributing to a deterioration of the mechanical condition of the vehicles. It was obvious that the unit would have problems in correcting and reversing the decline in availability but Major Gallagher was confident that it would be done and so it was. There was no vehicle inspection ramp and little cover for repair work during the unpredictable and very heavy rainstorms. There was a great shortage of spare tyres.

Taking these facts and conditions into consideration and having watched the vehicles at work, Major Gallagher recommended his taking over some 80 vehicles by 1 July, a number to be increased to nearly a hundred later. This was agreed and the takeover completed within a week. The platoon commanders then started what was to be a tough but successful task to improve the vehicles and their availability, REME assisting with a junior NCO, three vehicle mechanics and an electrician. The REME inspection confirmed that some vehicles were unsafe and irreparable and many others needed immediate attention to brakes, clutches and steering. The platoon commanders embarked on an exacting but successful programme to improve the availability of sound vehicles. A central servicing team, a Sergeant, Corporal and four Drivers operated a Tecalemit Servicing Unit and within a month the unit had built a ramp capable of taking a loaded ten-tonner, lights being installed to enable work to be carried out after dark. The general climatic and working conditions on the island produced a wide range of maintenance problems ranging from the contamination of fuel systems by water and coral dust, the shattering of windscreens by distortion and by flying lumps of coral on rough tracks to rust from the salt in the atmosphere and surface water which took a heavy toll of body work.

Among the many and varied tasks of the Company were the

carrying of coral aggregate from quarries to work sites, hot asphalt from the production machine to laying sites, collecting and delivering all stores and POL from port to delivery points around the island, carrying water supplies and troop carrying.

The work of the Corps was very exacting and despite the constant demands on transport in support of the RE construction work every effort was made to ensure that drivers were not required to drive more than eight or nine hours a day. That, in itself, was an exacting task and quite sufficient with the temperature around 90°F in the shade and much hotter in the cab of a vehicle. The tempo of the work was continuous, in consequence changes were occasionally made in men's duties in order to avoid staleness. The provision of liquid refreshment for the men working in such hot and dusty conditions was vital. Dry rations for tea making were a regular issue and tea was made and issued mid-morning and mid-afternoon at 'base'. Fresh, frozen, homogenized milk, flown in from Honolulu, was issued to all engaged on very dusty work.

At the end of the day everyone was still ready for a game of football and the Company made its own pitch where they were able to play, work permitting, several times a week. Transport was made available to take all ranks to swim in the lagoons, sea bathing being prohibited and other sports and hobbies were encouraged. The nearest town was Honolulu and that was 1200 miles away, six hours flying time, and most enjoyed four days' leave there during their year on Christmas Island.

During the year 1958–59 the Company witnessed the explosion of several 'devices'. On 12 June 1959 the Company was disbanded. They boarded a chartered Britannia aircraft and two days later were back in England.

94 Company RASC was relieved on Christmas Island by 146 Independent MT Platoon RASC which had been formed on 25 May on the island. The life of the unit however, was short. It was disbanded on 3 December 1959, there being no further requirement.

THE NEW HEBRIDES (VANUATU)

OPERATION TITAN

THE NEW HEBRIDES situated in the Pacific Islands was due to achieve independence on 30 July 1980. The government up to this time was the responsibility of a joint British and French arrangement.

Trouble started in February when Jimmy Stevens, an ex-bulldozer driver and leader of a Francophile secessionist party, closed down the Government Agent's office in Luganville, the capital of the island of Espiritu Santo. Although plans existed for the deployment of a joint Anglo-French force for internal security duties, it was hoped that the situation could be resolved locally without recourse to military intervention. But on 28 May, Stevens' supporters, who included armed French nationals, took over the police station, airport and other key points in Luganville and set up a provisional government, claiming that the November 1979 elections were rigged.

The British Resident Commissioner asked for military advice and a colonel and a squadron leader were duly sent to Vila, the capital of the New Hebrides, on 3 June to be followed later by an AQ adviser, a Military Intelligence Liaison Officer and an officer to help the local Police Mobile Unit. In the meantime, MOD, HQ UKLF and HQ 38 Group RAF were studying their contingency plans. On the advice received from Vila that, if joint Anglo-French action was taken, a battalion headquarters and one company would be sufficient. the decision was made to stand-by the leading elements of the current SPEARHEAD battalion, 42 Commando Royal Marines based at Plymouth, together with the necessary support, communications and logistic elements from UKLF. These attachments also gave the force a limited parachute capability if needed. Other deployment options considered were troops stationed in or on exercise in Hong Kong, Brunei and Australia, but they were ruled out mainly because RAF aircraft and heavy signals equipment would still be needed from the UK and also because of the disruption that would occur in their planned activities.

At first, the French were against military intervention. However, following trouble on the southern island of Tanna which threatened some of their nationals, they decided to deploy to Vila two platoons of their para-military gendarmerie from nearby New Caledonia on 12 June. The Prime Minister decided that a joint presence was vital and ordered the SPEARHEAD leading element to deploy immediately. The Commanding Officer – who incidentally had taken over command only two days previously – took off in the first VC10 on 13 June and the force of approximately 260 men was complete in Vila five days later, together with two in-theatre C130 Hercules aircraft for inter-island transport. By the time the first VC10 had landed in Vila, the first time an aircraft of that size had landed there, the French had withdrawn their gendarmes back to New Caledonia.

It is interesting to note that it required three VC10s and seven C130s (not including the route-activating aircraft), to deploy 260 men and their vehicles and equipment to Vila, in order to put one company group into the field. It also involved 10,700 nautical miles flying 'westabout' in six legs, with 24 hours in the air for the majority of the force in the VC10s and 38 hours for the few unfortunate enough to have to go with the vehicles and equipment in the C130s.

Whilst the force settled in, started jungle and internal security training and undertook some community relations work, negotiations continued in Vila to try to bring Jimmy Stevens to heel. However, following his failure to accept the New Hebridean Government's authority, it was decided that further pressure should be brought to bear before independence took place on 30 July. A joint Anglo-French force, under French command, flew by French Puma helicopters and RAF C130s from Vila to Pekoa Airport, Luganville on 24 July, with a company of French paratroops (flown in that day from New Caledonia) and the Royal Marines company on board, with the aim of regaining the key points and establishing the Government's presence. There were strict operational limitations imposed on the force but it met no violent opposition and it successfully achieved its limited objectives.

Independence took place on 30 July as planned, with HRH The Duke of Gloucester representing HM The Queen and a Royal Marines' guard of honour and band on parade.

At the request of the Vanuatu Government, the withdrawal of

Movements staff at Port Vila

[By courtesy of RCT Records]

the joint force after Independence was delayed until 19 August to allow time for a Pacific policing force to be constituted. A force from Papua New Guinea which had been present for the Independence celebrations was reinforced in early August and on 18 August, 150 members of this force flew to Luganville to take over from the Anglo-French force. On 19 August, the French returned to New Caledonia and the first VC10 left for UK. The withdrawal of the British force was completed by 28 August.

The Corps played a small but nevertheless vital part in this operation not only in the deployment and recovery of the force but also in providing as part of the UK logistic element deployed to support the Commando Group, a Force Movements Officer (FMO) Captain G A Betts RCT and a small Central Detachment from 29 Transport and Movements Regiment RCT, who remained with the force for the duration of the operation. The FMO deployed to Vila arriving on 12 June in time to witness the withdrawal of the French para-military gendarmerie to New Caledonia and to make the necessary arrangements for the reception and dispersal of the Commando Group on their arrival in the theatre. The Movement Detachment arrived on the first aircraft with the lead elements of the force.

Throughout the period of the operation the Detachment, in addition to providing daily executive movement support, were employed on such mundane tasks as planning for a proposed 'stand-off' of the group in Fiji. This requirement was based on Anglo-French political discussions regarding the question of the UK physical presence on the island but the plan was not implemented. In addition, the movement of the joint Anglo-French force on the occupation of Espiritu Santo involved considerable movement support and a sub-element of the Detachment moved with the force remaining with them until their recovery to Vila. Concurrent with this activity the FMO was required to complete the movement planning required to effect the total recovery of the Commando Group to the UK. The Detachment departed from Vila on 28 August 1980 in the last aircraft of the Force.

COCOS (KEELING) ISLANDS

THE COCOS (KEELING) ISLANDS lie roughly midway between Ceylon and Australia; they were declared a British possession in 1857. In 1878 they were placed under the control of the Governor of Ceylon and later annexed to the Straits Settlements. The administration of the Islands was transferred to Australia in 1955.

There are five main islands: Direction Island is the site of the cable and wireless station, West Island, the centre of all service activities, Home Island, the centre of the small civil population and South and Horsburg Islands which are uninhabited except for a special detachment on the latter.

An immediate post-war task was the clearing of the Direction Island airstrip and the roadway running the full length of the island. All materials and stores were brought ashore in landing craft, the supply ships lying at anchor offshore.

At times, both supplies and POL ran short because of the transport priority for Engineer and Royal Air Force stores, but nobody went short of a meal and POL was always ready when a bulldozer stopped to fill up; at that time even the RAF 2,500 gallon bowsers were filled from drums by hand. At the outset the force was supplied with water brought from India and wells had to be dug before the imported water was exhausted.

No clay was available so 73 Field Bakery Section RIASC covered their 'Beehive' ovens with a mixture of cement and coconut husks. Heavy rains before tents and tarpaulins could be erected added to everyone's difficulties. The bakery then moved into some batalee huts with improvised ovens and the Field Supply Platoon of the RIASC also moved into very large batalee huts were they installed five 16-ton cold storage chambers. 353 Petroleum Platoon RASC set up an installation of five bulk storage tanks with a sea line stretching some 1,500 yards into a lagoon.

The drivers of all the army transport had come from the 26/14th Punjabis until relieved by those of 'E' platoon of 898 General Transport Company RASC manned by Ceylonese personnel.

The climate of the Island is sub-tropical. Major FWH Deebank, writing in the Corps Journal in 1946 recorded that 'the trade winds kept everyone delightfully cool except those engaged in violent exercise in the perpetual sunshine. An even greater blessing to anyone who knows the East being the virtually complete absence of flies, mosquitoes and bugs, thanks to the liberal use of DDT sprays. The natural beauty of the islands', he added, 'is slight by tropical standards, but the infinite blues of the waters and the kaleidoscopic cloud-patterned skies at dawn and sunset are superb.'

Occupation of the islands and this pleasant way of life ended only too soon for some people and the British Forces withdrew in May 1946.

CHAPTER FIVE

India, Burma, Ceylon, Nepal

INDIA

At the start of the period covered by this history (1945) until India achieved its independence in 1947, the story of supplies and transport in that country is largely the story of that large and respected sister Corps, the Royal Indian Army Service Corps. As an integral part of the Indian Army, the history of the RIASC is not covered in this history. Suffice to say that it was largely organized and trained along RASC lines and many RASC officers and NCOs look back with pride at the privilege they had serving in the Royal Indian Army Service Corps.

Those British Army RASC units, and headquarters that were

in India up until 1947, naturally assisted in the hectic and hasty British withdrawal from that country.

One small organization remained however in India – a Movements office situated for many years in a British cantonment of Barrackpore, a few miles outside Calcutta.

This seemingly anomalous organization provided, in the days before airtrooping, a vital link on the Lines of Communication between Nepal and Gurkha troops stationed in SE Asia or Hong Kong. A single RASC, later RCT, officer with his civilian staff coordinated the movement of newly enlisted Gurkha recruits from the hills of Nepal arriving in Barrackpore after a lengthy rail journey, on to the troopships destined to take them to Penang and their recruit training depot in North Malaya. Similarly, all returning Gurkha leave parties, plus all the supplies necessary to maintain our recruiting depots in Nepal were phased through Barrackpore and on to the unreliable rail link to Nepal.

With the introduction of direct air trooping into Nepal from Hong Kong and Brunei in the 1970s, the Depot at Barrackpore was closed. The requirement to move supplies into Nepal by rail is now limited to cater only for major, bulky or heavy equipments not capable of being airlifted into Nepal and the Movements task in Calcutta is now contracted out to civilian firms.

BURMA

Following the surrender of the Japanese and their defeat in Burma by the XIV Army, the country achieved its independence on 4th January 1948 after which all British and Indian units were withdrawn. However, at the request of the friendly Burmese government, a Joint Services Mission was set up, under Major-General Bourne, to advise the Burma Defence Ministry at all levels. In this Mission were several RASC officers, Lieutenant Colonel F J B Kerr as ADST, Major David Hughes as DADST, Major Clifford Berridge as S&T Adviser on Animal Transport and Major Campbell Steward as S&T Adviser on all aspects of MT. Also on the S&T Staff were Majors Norman Price and George Stubbs.

All British personnel of the Mission were presumed to have had previous service in Burma but this condition was never communicated to AG8; its contravention seemingly did not affect the work of those concerned, all of whom spoke fluent Urdu and quickly mastered the essentials of Burmese.

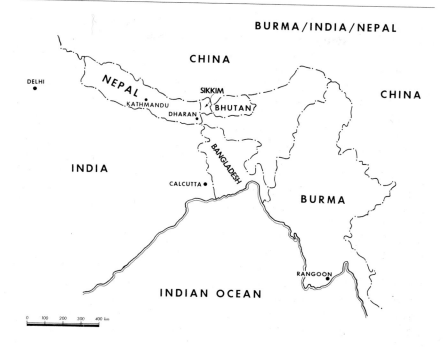

The S&T Advisory staff were stationed in the North of the country, whilst Major Steward stayed in the South, some fifteen miles north of Rangoon with 3 (Burma) GT Company, very nearly the same location where he was stationed when the war ended whilst serving at HQ IV Corps. Personnel of the GT Company were Delta Burmese and in addition to the normal chain of command, the unit had its own political 'boss' – a Corporal! Intrigue was rife, with discontent rising amongst the pre-war soldiers of the old Burma Army. An insurrection occurred in opposition to the Government and vehicles of 3 (Burma) GT Company carrying an infantry battalion were attacked from the air and the drivers and their passengers had to take to the jungle. The insurrection quickly fizzled out.

Major Sam Jay, a Karen, took over command of 3 Company and the training of the unit and drivers proceeded.

A second insurrection, involving Karen battalions, then occurred and was much more serious. The aim of this and the earlier revolt had been to get control of the main roads leading to and from Rangoon and the Karen insurrection nearly succeeded.

The main pipeline carrying Rangoon's water supply was blown up and 3 Company was issued with a number of water bowsers, which in conjunction with the Royal Engineers, supplied the area immediately north of Rangoon with clean water. All the European families in the area had been evacuated but their pet animals had been placed in the care of Campbell Steward and his small staff of British soldiers whilst their owners were away. None of these pets fortunately was lost!

Eventually the revolt was quelled after heavy fighting and the GT company reverted to a less strenuous role.

Politically Burma was in turmoil and following a coup by the militant Communists, a change of government took place and the British Military Mission was withdrawn.

CEYLON

Ceylon, a British Crown Colony since 1802, absorbed in 1815 the Kingdom of Kandy thereby bringing all Ceylon under British rule. It played an important part in World War II, following Japan's invasion of Hong Kong and Malaya in 1941. In 1943, Trincomalee became the main base of the Far East Fleet. Supreme Allied Commander South East Asia, Lord Louis Mountbatten with his staff and Headquarters Allied Land Forces South East Asia were established at Kandy. During this period, as many as three divisions, Indian, East African and Australian and a British Brigade, later to join the Chindits, were on the Island at one time, as well as large contingents of AA gunners, both RM and RA, to protect the Naval bases at Trincomalee and Colombo. RAF Stations were also spread throughout the Island and a number of battalions of the Ceylon Light Infantry, which together with the Ceylon Army Service Corps formed part of the Ceylon Defence Force, which was a pre-war volunteer force largely mobilized at the outbreak of hostilities. These local units subsequently developed into what was to be Ceylon's, later Sri Lanka's, post-war army.

During the War, the RASC and the RIASC split the responsibilities for S&T duties between them, whilst there was a number of Ceylon Army Service Corps (CASC) units in support throughout the Island. The RASC element was mainly in Colombo, where DDST Ceylon Army Command and his Staff controlled all S&T activities on the Island. The Base Supply Depot was located in Colombo, together with local transport companies and Barrack Services and all were eventually RASC or CASC manned. The RIASC generally manned the supply Depots located outside Colombo, whilst transport was provided from both the RIASC and EAASC of the divisions in their areas as well as from RIASC GT Companies. The British Brigade RASC MT Company during the Brigade's period on the Island was located at Kandy and there were a number of RASC Artillery MT Platoons in support of the RM and RA AA Regiments.

From the extensive S&T organization towards the end of the war the rundown was swift. SACSEA and HQ ALFSEA and the formations had left to reoccupy Singapore, Malaya and Hong Kong. Ceylon, as a military base, rapidly reverted to its pre-war situation. Because of the rundown of commitments, unlike Malaya, the RASC was able to absorb the tasks that had been previously undertaken by the departed RIASC and by 1947 the Corps was at Colombo, Kandy, Diyatalawa and Trincomalee on a greatly reduced scale. The large Supply Organization in Colombo was reduced to one unit known as the Ceylon Supply Depot and a parallel transport organization, MT Company Ceylon.

With the coming of independence in 1947, the Ceylon Army Service Corps began to emerge as a fully fledged Regular Corps and the two Corps worked together, the CASC gradually taking over responsibility, until the time came for the last RASC elements to leave the Island in 1950. By this time, the strength was such that there was now only an OC RASC, Major M B Hardwick, commanding the remaining elements of the Corps.

So ended a long association of the Corps with Ceylon and it is of great satisfaction that our sister Corps, now the Sri Lanka Army Service Corps, which had grown up beside us as the CASC, was able to assume its rightful role so smoothly and efficiently.

NEPAL

The responsibility for the despatch and return of Gurkha soldiers to and from Nepal has for many years been the responsibility of a small RCT staff (usually a Major and a Warrant Officer plus local civilian staff) based in either Katmandu, the capital of Nepal, or in Dharan, in the East of the country where a large British recruiting depot is situated.

Until recent years the workload of the RCT staff in Nepal was largely seasonal, in the spring and autumn of each year out of the monsoon season. During the monsoon season it was virtually impossible to travel in Nepal due to torrential rain, swollen rivers and frequent landslides. All movement in and out of Nepal for the Gurkha soldiers, their MFO baggage and other supplies had to be crammed into two short periods during the year. As the road system improved in Nepal, due to substantial foreign aid, and the facilities at the international airport of Katmandu were brought up to an acceptable standard, so the seasonal nature of movement in Nepal has diminished and the workload of the RCT staff spread more evenly throughout the year.

Wherever possible the RCT officers stationed in Nepal have a previous knowledge of the country, the Gurkha soldiers and their language through earlier service with the Gurkha Transport Regiment. It is also logical that a large number of the civilian staff are ex-soldiers who have served with the Gurkha Transport Regiment (or its predecessor the Gurkha Army Service Corps). The administrative motor transport supporting the British Gurkha depots in Nepal is likewise mainly manned by Gurkha Transport Regiment soldiers (or retired soldiers).

In 1973 there was significant RCT assistance, with the Royal Air Force, to help alleviate impending starvation in Nepal, due largely to a failure of crops and Government inability to move relief supplies to parts of the country due to heavy monsoon damage to the few roads in the country. Operation Khana Cascade was first envisaged when a formal approach was made to Mr Anthony Royle MP during his visit to Nepal between 17–21 November 1972. This was a request for help from the British Government to mount an airlift to the remote and inaccessible areas of Nepal which were suffering famine due to bad grain harvests during 1971 and 1972. A feasibility study was carried out during the early part of December 1972 and agreement made that a small force of four RAF Hercules and two Air Despatch Troops RCT would be deployed to Nepal to tackle the task of airdropping 1850 metric tons of rice and grain.

At about the same time as this decision was taken, 14 Air Despatch Regiment RCT had the honour to be called upon to produce the Royal Palace Guards for Public Duties in London and Windsor. The different roles of Warrant Officer Class 2 (SSM) and Warrant Officer Class 2 (Master Air Despatcher) became immediately apparent! Needless to say those selected to go to Nepal claimed their size would save weight in the aircraft. However the basis for selection may have had a different emphasis! The advance party commanded by Major Peter Evans (later Colonel) left on 14 February 1973 and after some frustrations and delays were followed by the main party leaving RAF Lyneham in the early hours of Sunday 25 February. The RAF had positioned slip crews along the route, not a normal practice for Hercules, and as a result the journey was a continuous thirty hours marathon interspersed with ninety minute intervals on the ground in Cyprus, Masirah and Bombay for crew changes and refuelling.

The detachment from 55 Air Despatch Squadron RCT which was commanded by Captain A V Case RCT was due to be based at Bhairawa, the western of the two small 3,000 ft airstrips on the Terai close to the Indian border. As luck would have it somehow during the flight from Lyneham the 'chalks' had got rearranged and neither of the first two aircraft to land had any mechanical handling equipment on board. After completing the onerous task of unloading these aircraft by hand, the detachment was rewarded with the spectacle of the third aircraft, the one loaded with the Eager Beaver fork lift trucks, overrunning the short strip and

14 Air Despatch Regiment RCT preparing loads for air drop in Operation Khana Cascade famine relief Nepal 1973

[By courtesy of PR HQ UKLF]

'bogging' itself in the thinly asphalted overshoot area. A shaking white-knuckled pilot was taken away for a cup of tea whilst his aircraft was unloaded. Recovery was effected by the two Eager Beavers and a local Land Rover straining on tow-chains and the Hercules in coarse-pitch high reverse!

There was more excitement yet to come on the first day when the RAF contingent discovered to their horror that the cookers that they had brought with them would not work. Fortunately the well prepared Air Despatch organization had sufficient stand-by 24-hour rations to enable everyone to have at least one meal that day. However the sight of a Hercules co-pilot trying to light a complete packet of Hexamine blocks with his cigarette lighter will not easily be forgotten.

The second day saw the start of the detailed briefings and recces of the dropping zones. The recces were to be done initially in a Pilatius Porter single engined turboprop aircraft. Its pilot, a Swiss-German working for the United Nations, had come to Nepal for a six week attachment and had stayed seven years! His local knowledge was invaluable to the RAF pilots and after three days of briefings and recce flights the aircrews and despatchers were ready to start the operation in earnest. On Friday 2 March, the first drop was made at Surket. The three Hercules at Bhairawa were kept busy making at least two flights a day each. During the first few days all drops were done at Surket with the aircraft sometimes only taking a partial load and extra fuel so that trial runs could be made over dropping zones further out and higher up in the Himalayas. It was on an initial Hercules recce trip into the Jumla Valley that the superb flying skills of the RAF aircrews showed themselves. In order to save fuel and time over the dropping zone the pilot decided that he would turn the aircraft in the valley, which resembled a Norwegian fiord, so that he would not have to climb out and circuit around a large peak to approach for his second run over the dropping zone. The effect of racing towards sheer rock walls as the pilot executed very tight turns was to say the least memorable. Other dropping zone approaches were equally 'hairy' especially the one at Silgari Doti where the approach had to be made by skimming over a crest and then diving down a re-entrant valley with 100% flap and the aircraft only maintaining about 50 feet above the valley floor as it flew down to the dropping zone.

The air despatch crews were in their element. Morale was extremely high, hours were long and at the end of each day, muscles were weary and throats dry. In order to maintain a high rate of dropping, work went on well into the night preparing loads for the next day's drop.

Such was the pace that after about two weeks the runway at Bhairawa began to crack up and the local engineers worked 23 hours non-stop to make it serviceable again. Further delays were caused by the non-arrival of locally produced baseboards on which all loads had to be despatched. This was overcome to a great extent by doubling up the despatch crew on the aircraft, loading loose sacks of grain and despatching them over the ramp in a big heap. It was on one of these sorties that the pilot was given a fire warning in one of the engines. Having feathered it he discovered fortunately that the warning had been a false alarm, however, having discharged the fire extinguisher he could not restart the engine. A landing back at Bhairawa was now impossible due to the need for all four engines to be put in reverse pitch on the short runway. Katmandu was cloud bound and so a diversion had to be made to Lucknow in India. An overnight stay was required and unfortunately nearly all the crew were taken ill with stomach trouble. When they arrived back at Bhairawa the aircraft engineer was on a stretcher and Sergeant Cummings and his two AD crews were all looking very weak at the knees.

To give everyone a break, two day R and R periods were organized in Katmandu. This gave everybody a chance to buy souvenirs and have a look around at the temples. During one of these R and R periods, there was a terrific storm at Bhairawa and everything was soaked and covered in mud. Most of the tents had been securely lashed to large fence poles but the Mobile Air Movements Section tent unfortunately had not and took off for India. It no doubt now provides shelter for some deserving Indian family!

With the average daily dropping rate around the 65 ton mark the end was beginning to come into sight. However, complacency was checked one day when the Hercules operating out of Birat-nagar, the other airfield, was involved in an incident. Despite being triple-sacked some bags were still splitting open when free dropped onto the dropping zone from 50 feet. One particular pilot had developed a cunning technique of putting down his undercarriage and actually running along the dropping zone with full power on whilst the despatchers frantically shoved the grain sacks out of the back. There had been one such sortie that morning and the

[By courtesy of MOD OS 12]

Air dropping supplies during Operation Khana Cascade.

Nepalese Army who were clearing all the dropping zones had piled up the sacks at the end of the small grass strip. It was whilst making the last run along the strip that the pilot left pulling back on the stick just a fraction too late and the underneath of the ramp caught the top of the pile of sacks! Fortunately the aircraft hardly felt it but on returning to Bhairawa to refuel, it was very apparent that a large section of fuselage skin was flapping merrily in the breeze as it came into land.

The signal sent back to MOD (Air) was hopefully not too frivolous but went something like ... 'whilst flying at 50 ft AGL, a set of 4 baseboards with 4 tons of sacks was despatched over the sill in accordance with SOPs. On contact with the ground one of the locally manufactured baseboards propelled a sack back up in the air hitting the aircraft on the underside of the ramp'. Fortunately the only reply we received was 'Your ...... ACK'!

By the end of the operation the target figure for grain and rice was exceeded by over 100 tons, the final figure being 1,957 tons, of which 1,750 had been flown from Bhairawa. Ten different dropping zones throughout the length of Nepal had been served by 153 aircraft sorties. Although the operation had been carried out under no conventional threat, the environment and the purpose of it made it an exacting and very rewarding task.

Despite the remoteness of Nepal, the British Army and the RCT continue to maintain close links with the friendly and loyal citizens of this independent kingdom. The strongest link is obviously through the Brigade of Gurkhas, an integral part of the British Army. The close RCT connection with the Brigade of Gurkhas is maintained through the Gurkha Transport Regiment to whom a chapter in this book is devoted.

CHAPTER SIX
Middle East

PALESTINE

As soon as the war was over the Palestinian Jewish community immediately re-opened the question of the clauses of the British Government's White Paper of May 1939, which had limited Jewish immigration into the country to a given maximum over a period of five years, after which no further immigrants would be permitted without the consent of the Arabs. In 1944 the British Government decided to extend the time limit of five years in consequence of delays resulting from the war, but no increase in the total number of immigrants was allowed and by the end of 1945 the total number of permitted immigrants – 75,000 – had nearly been reached.

Tension began to rise when the Jewish community realized the position and it was openly said among them that the British were continuing the Nazi policy of anti-Semitism. To the Jews the all important matter was the throwing open of Palestine as a home for displaced Jews from all over Europe and that for the immigration quota to be adhered to was regarded as inhuman. The Palestine Jews began to say that if the immigrants could not be legally admitted they must be brought in by any other means. The British Government was, of course, bound by the terms of the White Paper of May 1939 and could not agree to increasing the number of Jewish immigrants unless the Arabs agreed; such agreement was not forthcoming. The country was simmering with a growing political tension, for both Arabs and Jews were alert to the immediate post-war political problems of Palestine.

The political situation in Palestine at this time was such that it was soon apparent that the matter of internal security was of growing importance and although 1 British Infantry Division with a number of independent units and ancillary troops were already in the country, it was obvious that the then recently arrived 6 Airborne Division as part of the Strategic Reserve in the Middle East would also be called upon for internal security duties and such duties had to be understood and learned by the formation.

The position also called for re-deployment of the British forces in Palestine. At the end of October 1945 HQ 6 Airborne Division moved to Bir Salim; 3 Parachute Brigade to the Lydda District (which included Jaffa and Tel-Aviv); 6 Air Landing Brigade to the Samaria Area and the 2 Parachute Brigade to the Gaza District. 6 Airborne Division was soon involved in a difficult situation for there was widespread railway sabotage in the Divisional area on the night of 31 October and the following day a nightly road curfew was imposed. On 14 November large-scale riots developed in Tel-Aviv and the 3 Parachute Brigade was moved in to restore order, Tel-Aviv being placed under martial law for six days. This operation set the pattern of the Division's internal security work and henceforth 'Cordon and Search' was the order for maintenance of law and order and the rounding-up of terrorists, suspects and illegal immigrants.

This was the political climate in which the Corps had to operate throughout Palestine in the first post-war year – and continued so to do right up to June 1948.

It was in 1946 that the political situation in Palestine began to deteriorate, and there were increasing clashes between the British Army and the Jews, but, at that time it was the intention that the

British should remain for some years to come. Base Supply and Petrol Depots were planned as well as churches and general amenities in the new Brigade group areas.

Then, suddenly, the British Government's policy changed. It was decided to evacuate Palestine, Rafa only remaining as a base/garrison as part of 'British Troops in Egypt'. The order of evacuation was to be firstly the Gaza area, then Jerusalem and Sarafand and finally Haifa. The dates originally planned were subsequently advanced and, in consequence, the stocks to be moved at each stage became progressively larger.

HQ Palestine was located in the King David Hotel in Jerusalem, with the Supplies and Transport Headquarters in the Annex but they were moved to Haifa in the latter stages of the withdrawal. In 1946 Palestine was divided into three districts – North, Central and South with a sub-area in Jerusalem. There was a CRASC in each district at Haifa, Sarafand and Gaza with an OC RASC, at Jerusalem, and for a time at Mafraq in Transjordan.

GHQ had set up a base supply depot with its headquarters and one sub-depot in Haifa and a second sub-depot in Sarafand. This depot issued to supply platoons situated in Haifa, Hedera, Sarafand, Majdal, Rafa, Jerusalem and Mafraq, which in turn issued to formations. There was a cold storage section in Haifa which was used for meat and a similar store fifteen miles to the south which was used for potatoes. The meat arrived by sea at Haifa and was sent in rail refrigerator trucks which had one or more ten-ton storage chambers each. Potatoes were a source of worry as they did not keep well under warm climatic conditions and were liable to attack by the tuber moth. It was also found that shipments which had been loaded in damp and rainy conditions in the UK deteriorated rapidly.

Local resources were exploited as far as possible and in particular, potatoes were obtained by local contract, the seed being provided from the UK.

Towards the end of 1946 the S&T Staff at HQ Palestine were faced with the sudden arrival from home via Egypt – Moascar and the Sinai Desert – of HQ 48 Company (Air Despatch) and 800 Company RASC (Air Despatch). Both were stationed in Gaza and following visits and inspection by the DDST and CRASC, it was rightly decided that in the absence of any operation necessitating re-supply by air, the units would be best employed in a normal General Transport Company role.

It was soon after this that among the reinforcements sent to Palestine from Egypt was 223 Company which after movement by road, completed the journey with only one brief night stop, and with no Movement Control Order, reached their destination, the former RAF airfield at Gaza. The Company Commander recorded that 'Life at Gaza was spartan though not at all unusual for those days and the unit soon settled down to a GT role with some air despatch training at RAF Aquir'. The camp was described as 'somewhat open' and the men slept with 'weapons attached to their bodies' as was laid down in the Company Standing Orders. A serious problem at this time arose from the theft of spare wheels. and tyres and sometimes vehicle loads.

Not far away from 223 Company at Gaza Ridge was 6 Airborne Divisional RASC, serving the formation in its operational role and generally free from Garrison duties whereas 223 Company together with a Ceylonese Company served as the RASC workforce for HQ RASC South Palestine.

Following the departure from Palestine of the 1st Division, HQ 6 Airborne Division moved into their vacated quarters on Mount Carmel, Haifa, the Divisional RASC occupying Camp 80 at Hadera which in many ways was an ideal arrangement as the CRASC had his own HQ and units – 398 and 716 Companies – within one perimeter.

It was at this time that the worsening situation arising in the Israeli-Arab conflict became a major preoccupation of all units and the RASC took its full share of Internal Security duties. Simply protecting men and vehicles from the Jewish terrorists – the Irgun Zvei Leumi – was most demanding in manpower.

Camp 80 was surrounded by orange groves and perimeter security was particularly difficult. Clearing the groves to permit an open field of fire outside the wire fence surrounding the camp was not permitted, resulting in nightly attacks and 'stand to's'. A night of guard duty, followed by a day's driving was quite normal three nights a week. A solution to reduce the numbers engaged on security patrols was to saturate the perimeter wire with bursts of Bren gun fire at irregular intervals. This proved most successful but it enraged the local Jewish population who might have been strolling in the orange groves. Complaints were made by the local population to the GOC of 6 Airborne Division and resulted in an embargo being placed on what was thought to be a most effective form of camp defence.

Throughout the overall period, the RASC transport companies of a number of divisions, including 6 Airborne Division, were deployed for various times in Palestine, and were involved in the operations carried out by their Divisions. However, it was in the main the garrison RASC units, and in particular the transport companies, which bore the brunt of the task of maintaining continuously all the forces located in Palestine and Trans-Jordan.

At the beginning of 1947, there were thirteen MT Companies in Palestine in addition to the divisional companies. These MT Companies included some specialist units. There were motor ambulance companies; amphibian, bulk petroleum transport and air despatch companies, whilst in each district there was a station transport company. These were formed with a British Cadre and composed of half Arab and half Jewish personnel as drivers and civilian artificers. These companies were situated at intervals along the Sarafand–Gaza Road and with one Company in Jerusalem.

The motor ambulance and bulk petroleum companies had detachments everywhere and it was difficult for the officers commanding to maintain control of their units. Although the names of these units remained unchanged, they were issued with three ton lorries in place of their specialist vehicles which in turn were given to other companies in whose locality they worked.

As the situation worsened between the Jews and Arabs and resulting from the limited scope of single line railways, MT was employed to a much greater extent than in many other areas of British occupation or where British troops were deployed. The railways were always a target for sabotage by both Arabs and Jews particularly between the main port of Haifa and Sarafand and Sarafand to Jerusalem. Road timings and routing of convoys was carried out under the authority of Q (Movements).

The increasing tension in Palestine as 1947 progressed made it necessary for vehicles to move in pairs and to carry one armed man beside the driver, and a bren gun crew in the back of the vehicle. This meant that there was a requirement for eight men for a two vehicle task, and all had to be found from the unit providing the transport. At this time there was an overall deficiency of some 1600 drivers, which resulted, by the end of the year in each company being only effectively operating about a quarter of its vehicles at any one time. In consequence release from service was deferred for six months and reinforcements became available from units disbanding locally.

The theft of stores from vehicles, already mentioned, was only a short step from the theft of complete vehicles, and in Sarafand there were more elaborate though not totally successful precautions to prevent the illicit removal of vehicles from the lines by the locally employed Jewish or Arab drivers. All vehicle work tickets (i.e. authority for vehicle's journey) were required to be signed by an officer. Because of cases of forging of officers' signatures, officers were detailed for this task at irregular intervals, often being changed every hour. Vehicles were checked out of the camp at the guardroom by comparing the signature on the work ticket against specimen signatures for the particular time that the authorizing officer was on duty. Despite these precautions there were cases of the proper signature being forged on a work ticket within an hour of that authorizing officer coming on duty. Both Jews and Arabs had their official forgers close to hand! Some of the vehicles which then disappeared were used by the Jews in particular for later raids on depots and units.

Workshops also had their problems arising from an increasing deficiency of trained and experienced supervisory personnel and the shortage of spares. Provision of batteries and tyres was a constant problem and a considerable number of convoys of ten tonners were despatched at short notice to Egypt to collect a wide range of spares, the journey by road eliminating long delays in waiting for deliveries by rail.

Infantry division RASC columns were at this time organized on the basis of two four-platoon companies but just prior to the final evacuation in June 1948, 1 Infantry Division RASC reverted to the four company organization due to its brigades ceasing to be concentrated as a Division and moving to different localities. 3 Infantry Division was disbanded in Palestine and the RASC personnel of the formation who were, by virtue of their 'Age and Service Groups', ineligible for return to the UK, were absorbed as reinforcements in other RASC units.

6 Armoured Division, after service in North Africa and CMF, was redesignated 1 Armoured Division and readopting the original charging rhinoceros formation sign, arrived in Palestine from Austria. After a somewhat lengthy period for recovery from the journey and in order to reorganize, the formation was able to relieve some of the General Transport Companies north of Gaza as well as carrying out their normal divisional maintenance and training duties. The Division's stay in Palestine was shorter than

had been anticipated for within the year it moved to Egypt from where the Divisional RASC was despatched to East Africa for duty as a General Transport Column.

The Jewish organization – Haganah (The 'Peoples' Army') and their rival terrorist groups – the Stern Gang and the Irgun Zvei Leumi – opened up their offensive during the night of 31 October/1 November 1945 – explosion after explosion shattered the night from one end of Palestine to the other – one hundred and fifty-three breaches were blown in the railway system; three police launches were sunk; damage was done in Haifa to the oil refinery; the railway station and goods yard at Lydda were considerably damaged. From then on the British soldier in Palestine was on active service and the peace-keeping role he filled made him a target for both Jew and Arab, particularly the former to whom he became the 'enemy' along with the Arab population.

As 1946 and 1947 went by the Divisional RASC units always had part of their available transport ready for operational purposes which included transporting troops at short notice to the scene of disturbances and inter-racial strife; to areas subject to 'cordon and search' operations and for the transporting of illegal immigrants from their arrival points or temporary camp to re-embarkation points at Haifa. 'The carriage of illegals' recorded Colonel (later Brigadier) C F Neve, 'always meant extensive work for the coach-trimmers as the smallest hole in a tarpaulin soon became a slit for the occupants to gaze on their future land'.

The constant calls on transport at short notice for operational purposes increased in the last year of the British presence in Palestine as troops were concentrated in and around Haifa and Sarafand.

It was at this time, at the end of 1947, that the last remaining Cypriot pack transport company was disbanded, the mules being sold and the personnel being returned to Cyprus. This unit, 621 Company RASC (Cypriot Pack Transport) had been located at Saffuriya, near Nazareth, where it was available to perform an operational role in inaccessible country where mechanical transport could not operate. As this need did not materialize the Company was used to patrol the pipeline, carrying wireless communication sets to report on subversive activity.

During the period leading up to the evacuation of Palestine all units and depots were called upon to move stores, as and when facilities existed for their reception into depots at Rafa, just over the border in Egypt or at Haifa for shipment. In the Haifa docks area any available space was utilized to hold these stores until they could be loaded aboard ships. To avoid congestion transport in the docks area was kept to a minimum.

Stores such as steel sheets and rods, rails and bulky cases were moved on tank transporters. Royal Engineer pontoons were towed across Haifa Bay from RE Stores Depots to be shipped as deck cargo. This was a task for the RASC water transport detachment.

CRASCs of Districts were responsible for making local contracts for the supply of fresh fruit and vegetables; eggs and yeast were also obtained locally. Each supply platoon held reserves for fourteen days and considerable reserve stocks of all items were held in Jerusalem due to the uncertainty of road and rail communications remaining open. Before the final evacuation, the railway was out of action for several months and these reserve stocks were drawn upon until those remaining reached a level to be taken out by the last road convoys.

As the ration strength of the British force decreased, the depots at Mafraq, near the Jordan border, and Majdalon on the main line between Sarafand and Gaza were closed and that at Rafa was transferred to command of British Troops in Egypt. It was during this time that Jewish subversive activities took a new turn. It was during 1948 that a group of men wearing British uniforms drove up to the Supply Platoon at Hedera, held up the local guard and the platoon staff and emptied the depot of all its stocks – except the bacon! On another occasion, some of the buildings facing the supply platoon in Haifa were blown up, the blast damaging the store sheds and the bakery.

The petrol organization in Palestine was based on the civilian refinery and depot at Haifa. It was supplied by a branch of the Iraq crude oil pipeline and produced all MT spirits, up to 79 octane, diesel oil, kerosene and furnace fuel oil. No oils or aviation spirit were produced at this refinery and in consequence, they had to be imported and stored with the main army bulk reserve on a hillside a few miles from the town. A petrol platoon supervised the storage tanks and the filling operations. Large reserve stocks were held in containers near Haifa and north of Gaza. Near Sarafand was a large Royal Engineer Depot where jerricans were produced. Wastage of these items in Palestine was made good from this production and the balance was sent to Egypt. The pilfering of jerricans was always especially heavy when local drivers were employed and, recorded Colonel (later Brigadier) C F Neve, 'whole vehicle loads were known to disappear or to be exchanged for cans filled with water'.

Following the withdrawal of most of the remaining troops into the Haifa enclave, it was decided not to rely upon petrol stocks in the storage tanks but to hold a reserve in the barracks and to fill cans from rail tank cars held in the supply depot siding. Meanwhile, the petrol stocks stored in the hillside zones were pumped out and shipped out of Haifa to Beirut, Benghazi and the Canal Zone, whilst surplus canned stocks were sent to Cyprus in the four ammunition dumping craft, which on the return trip brought back fresh vegetables. At the end, as the evacuation date approached, the petroleum units embarked leaving an RASC Brigade Company holding a canned petrol reserve in the barracks.

RASC Fire Brigades were located in the port of Haifa and at two other locations, one to the East, the other near Hedera in the South; at Sarafand; the Royal Engineer Stores Depot; in Gaza and Jerusalem. Between 1946–48 the largest fire this service had to compete with was at the civilian petrol installation at Haifa, which lasted for several days. At that time, before the days of the use of foam for smothering fires, both the RASC and civilian fire fighters had to deal with the situation by their traditional methods. Another serious fire led. to the loss of a section of the Supply Depot at Sarafand and in Haifa the barrack ammunition store caught fire during the changeover of an incoming and outgoing battalion. The Fire Brigades departed in step with the general run-down but one remained in Haifa docks up to the final withdrawal.

The work of the Corps in Palestine during 1947–48, particularly during the last few months became more hazardous and of an operational character. As the weeks went by British troops, particularly convoys of vehicles, were vulnerable and subject to attack at all times by both Jews and Arabs seeking to plunder supplies of arms, ammunition and all forms of supplies. Surprise attacks were constantly being made by Jews upon Arabs and vice versa and British troops were caught in the crossfire when called upon to intervene to save life and property. The Jews always had superiority and, by possessing themselves of British Army vehicles and uniforms, not only set the Arabs against the British who were blamed for the crimes committed by the disguised Jews but were often able to enter our camps and installations before being detected. It was on the day of final redeployment before the withdrawal – 6 April 1948 – that the last of many such raids was carried out by the Irgun on the camp of a Gunner Regiment near Latrun. Three British Army lorries drove up to the camp guard-room, the sentry, as he examined the documents held out of the driving cab by a man in the uniform of a British officer, was shot dead from the lorry as was also the Bren gunner covering him from a sandbagged post. Immediately, an armoured car came out from behind the lorry with its machine gun spraying bullets all around the camp centre. A raiding party ran from the other vehicles straight to the battery's armoury, they shot or tied up the storemen and rushed back to their vehicles with loads of weapons. Other raiders lined up and shot the guard in their tent. The Commanding Officer, armed with a revolver, ran to the scene and tried to shoot the crew of the armoured car through the slits but he fell mortally wounded. There followed a concerted rush towards the lorries and, with a roar of the engines the Irgun were gone, but with their task only half done; sten gun bullets were pumped into their vehicles as they fled. It was significant that one Jewish civilian employee at the camp was never seen again.

The withdrawal from Palestine began on the morning of the 14 May when the British High Commissioner left Government House in Jerusalem where a guard of honour was mounted; he left with an escort of Life Guards. Another Guard of Honour received him at Haifa where he was piped aboard HMS *Euryalus* which remained in harbour until midnight. The main body of troops in Jerusalem, the 2 Infantry Brigade Group, moved southwards through Beersheba whilst troops attached to the Brigade withdrew into the Haifa enclave. On the same day, all 3 Brigade troops withdrew into a defensive 'box' around Latrun, Lydda and Sarafand, moving the next day southwards around Gaza into Egypt.

The final withdrawal, from the Haifa enclave, took place on 30 June. By midday the General Officer Commanding was the only one of the British Army left ashore. Saluting as the Union Jack was lowered, the General turned to say farewell to the British Consul General, and then strode up the gangway of HMS *Phoebe*, the ship's guns firing a salute and sailing out of the harbour.

Thus ended the British military associations with Palestine which dated back to 1917. In Palestine during the period 1945–48, the RASC in common with all branches of the Service, carried out their increasingly difficult and exacting task with cheerfulness and willingness and not without their share of problems, hardships and casualties.

As Brigadier C F Neve OBE wrote in the *Royal Army Service Corps Review*– 'The recollections of the months spent in the country while violence increased all around us bring back bitter memories, but many recall the comradeship and good humour of the British force which did so much to render conditions tolerable'.

EGYPT

ALTHOUGH BRITISH MILITARY ASSOCIATIONS with Egypt go back to the first year of the Nineteenth Century, when an Expedition was mounted in 1801 against the French Army in Egypt which Napoleon had deserted, it was not until 1882 that British troops were again stationed in that country, remaining there 74 years until the final withdrawal of the small rear party in June 1956. Between 1882 and 1914 and again from 1920 to 1940 – Egypt having been the British base for operations against the Turks, including the major Palestine Campaign during World War I – the British Army's presence consisted of a Brigade of Infantry in Cairo – including a battalion of Foot Guards at the Ksar-el-Nil Barracks – another Brigade (less one Company in Cyprus) in the Alexandria Area; a Cavalry Brigade and a Royal Horse Artillery Brigade at Abbassia (on the road today from the Centre of Cairo to the City's International Airport). The British troops in Egypt had, between 1920 and 1940, been supported in 1925 by four RASC Companies rising to eight Companies by 1938.

Again, during World War II, Egypt was a vital British base of operations against the Italians in Abyssinia and Eritrea, and in the Western Desert where they served with their German allies of the Afrika Korps.

Egypt had gained full independence in 1936 under a Treaty with Great Britain but it had allowed for the retention of a British military force in the 'Canal Zone' to cooperate 'with the Egyptian forces in the defence of the Canal'. The Egyptian Government had, under the terms of the treaty, agreed to build the necessary new barracks and access roads in the 'Canal Zone' but as no such action was speedily undertaken, British troops remained in the City barracks that they had occupied for over fifty years and there they still were at the start of World War II.

By the end of the World War II, Egypt had developed into a vast staging point and a huge base stores area. GHQ Middle East Land Forces and HQ British Troops in Egypt were still located in Cairo in the requisitioned buildings they had expanded into during the war years and the permanently hired flats for accommodation.

From Cairo, the staff controlled the many and varied depots and installations dotted about all over the country.

In 1945, four Base Supply Depots (Nos. 8, 18, 26 and 70) were operating at El Kirsh. Soon after VE Day these units were disbanded and formed into No. 4 CRASC operating as an SRD Just over a year later its designation was changed to 33 SRD Following the changes from war to peacetime organization, establishments and roles – all BSDs in the Middle East were disbanded, and personnel sailed for home for release from service or on 'Python'. In consequence 33 SRD became responsible for the replenishment of supplies for the whole Middle East Command which at that time (1946–47) included Egypt, Eritrea, Sudan, Aden, Cyprus, Palestine, Greece and the Dodecanese, whilst shipments were also made to Cyrenaica and East Africa. At this time an average of over a thousand tons of stores were being handled every day – the peak day was 12 May 1947 when 3,232 gross tons of stores were handled.

In July 1946, Brigadier Deverell, DDST for almost three years, returned to the UK. He was relieved by Colonel E Clarke who held the appointment until the arrival of Brigadier Bright Holmes. It was in this year that the practice of holding the King's Birthday Parade in June was resumed, both in Cairo – at Abbassia – in which the Corps participated, marching past for the first time to the then newly introduced Corps March. On the same day a similar parade was held in Alexandria with the RASC contingent commanded by Lieutenant Colonel Dunlop who had just taken over from Lieutenant Colonel Winsloe.

1946 saw the move of the DDST HQ British troops in Egypt from the Semiramis Hotel in Cairo to Moascar, and in the same year there were a number of changes in RASC commands – Lieutenant Colonel A H Houchin took over as CRASC Canal North District from Lieutenant Colonel J Thompson and Lieutenant Colonel J E Griffiths relieved Lieutenant Colonel C H Brown in the Canal South District, Lieutenant Colonel Summers became CRASC Cairo District and Lieutenant Colonel Freeman-Cowan CRASC Alexandria returning to the UK on retirement was succeeded by Lieutenant Colonel R A E Dunlop as CRASC 92 Corps Troops with, under command, 697 Company (Water Transport), 698 Company (Ammunition Dumping Craft) and 3 Boat Stores Depot.

The Ammunition Dumping Craft had the special role of

transporting the considerable stocks of obsolete and unserviceable ammunition from a depot on the Great Bitter Lake in loads of some 150 tons at a time, to dump it in the Mediterranean some thirty miles out.

Colonel Dunlop, with these units under command, took over the duties of the Port Said Services Sailing Club and it soon became a flourishing attraction with six Dorys and a number of sailing dinghies from ten to sixteen-footers. Eighty per cent of the Club members at this time came from the Corps; every Saturday a Club race was held and boats soon had to be booked well ahead.

The War over, the Egyptians had, at the end of 1945, requested a revision of the 1936 Treaty which amounted to a request for a British withdrawal. A considerable time elapsed before the Labour Government of the day announced on 7 May 1946 a plan for the complete evacuation of Egypt, but meanwhile rioting had broken out and, in February, there had been attacks on British Military property and Clubs and even the Kasr-el-Nil Barracks, Cairo were besieged by hostile mobs. Finally British troops withdrew from Alexandria in February 1947 and in the early morning of 28 March, the last British unit – a squadron of the Life Guards – drove out of the Ksar-el-Nil Barracks to complete the British withdrawal from Cairo.

The British forces in Egypt moved into their new accommodation in the Canal Zone which was divided into two Brigade districts, 3 Infantry Brigade being in the north and 17 Brigade in the south with a battalion at Suez. Spread between the two Districts were two armoured regiments and an artillery group.

Brigadier H C de la Bere, OBE, arrived in Egypt in April 1947 to take up his appointment as DDST, taking over from Lieutenant Colonel F Newmarsh who had been acting in that post since Brigadier G Bright Holmes had been invalided home in the preceding December. The S&T Staff at that time was made up of the ADST – Lieutenant Colonel W H Summers, and the ADST (Barracks) Lieutenant Colonel J R Coles; his DADST (Barracks) was Major R B A Rapson. The DADST (Transport) was Major G S Furtado with Captain A R Dickson as his Staff Captain; Major J C Smith was DADST (Supplies) with Captain L G Gichard as Staff Captain and Captain P J J White as Staff Captain (Local Resources). Major S R Auty was DADST (POL) and Captain A E Walker Staff Captain (Fire) with Regimental Sergeant Major Cunningham as Fire Adviser. The Chief Clerk at the DDST's HQ was Warrant Officer Class I J E Pender.

It was also in April 1947 that one of the last remaining amphibian companies – 101 Company (GT – Amphibian) – moved from Palestine to be stationed on the shores of the Bitter Lakes when the unit operated tracked amphibians and engaged in training of its newly posted all British personnel in driving and maintenance of the amphibians and the operation of No. 19 Wireless sets used for all control and communications. The Company's amphibian tracked 4-ton GS Freight carriers, generally referred to as 'Neptunes', were propelled both on land and in the water by their tracks which, having specially designed track plates, enabled them to be propelled when waterborne 'on the paddle-steamer principle' – they were powered by a horizontally opposed 12-cylinder petrol engine which was located beneath the floor-boards of the cargo area. The operational role of the 'Neptunes' was that of freight carriers and as troop carriers from LSTs at sea to beach heads.

In 1948, 697 and 698 Companies – then both designated Water Transport Companies, were based at Port Fouad from where they operated on routes extending westwards to Malta, eastwards to Cyprus, as far north as Salonika and south to Mombassa. Their craft at this time ranged from 4,000-ton LSTs to 400-ton MLs all flying the Blue Ensign with the Army's crossed swords in gold on the dark blue 'field'. The cargoes carried were numerous and varied – bulldozers and excavating machinery to Mombassa with timber on the return journey and, at the same time, drinking water – 800 tons at a time – going to Tobruk.

At this time there was a small Port Detachment – with a strength of eight other ranks – a Corporal, Lance Corporal and six Privates at Ataba, South of Suez town where Edward Faugham recalls the sinking of the *Empire Chubb* in the harbour after it caught fire during the dangerous operation of unloading empty 'jerricans' from the forward holds in step with loading of ammunition and supplies into aft holds. Despite every available man in the port, irrespective of rank, being engaged in an attempt to save the ship, which was eventually totally destroyed, it sank in the harbour; three men died in the attempt to salvage the vessel. On another occasion the detachment was called out one night to unload an urgent consignment in seven railway waggons – the waggons were all sealed but when opened up, all that remained of the scheduled delivery of 280 tons of supplies were five bottles of Yorkshire Relish in the centre of the middle waggon!

At the Cold Storage Depot at Suez which was commanded by Major R Bradford with Capt S Gater as second-in-command – who had both been Prisoners of War in the Far East – and Staff Quartermaster Sergeant Fred Goman as the Senior Warrant Officer – a hundred and fifty locally engaged Egyptian civilians were employed; they lived in a tented camp behind the Depot. 'Our efforts did not pass unnoticed' recorded Corporal Faugham 'and resulted in a visit from the Commander-in-Chief, who praised our work.' He presented the unit with a radio (then a rare and treasured gift) and £15 to be spent on cigarettes and 'Stella' beer.

Throughout this period a regular flow of drafts arrived in Egypt. Among those who disembarked from the liner *Georgic* at Suez in May 1948 was Driver S H Jones who had enlisted in 1946 on a 5 years engagement and, after initial training at Retford and Yeovil and several UK postings went on a draft to the Middle East. From the transit camp at Suez he was posted for duty at the British Military Hospital at Tel-el-Kebir where he served for two years as an ambulance driver. At the BMH, the RASC personnel – all drivers – came under the RAMC Commanding Officer for discipline, pay and postings as they had no parent RASC unit.

The British Military Hospital was located a mile or so outside the Tel-el-Kebir garrison boundaries on the Zag-a-Zig – Cairo road just inside the Canal Zone military boundary. Being thus isolated from the garrison, walking outside the hospital camp area was prohibited, transport was essential for all purposes – to and from 5 BOD for all supplies, the frequent twenty mile runs to Ismalia and the regular picking up of patients and other personnel from Tel-el-Kebir railway station. As the tensions grew and the situation worsened between the British Forces and the Egyptians, armoured scout cars from the garrison accompanied all vehicles going to and from the BMH. On other occasions however, RASC drivers 'rode shotgun', armed with rifles and pick-helves on their own vehicles. The RASC soon got to know the regular local lads who engaged in the anti-British activities concentrating on the movement between Tel-el-Kebir and the Hospital, and devised varying tactics and procedures to counter their activities to hold up and rob the small convoys and individual vehicles. The RASC plan was to get to the station well before the arrival or departure times and, in the case of the latter, to remain with departing personnel until their train had pulled out.

When, after two years, it was Jones' turn to leave the Hospital for Ismalia by this same route, he had to wait longer than usual for the train. In consequence his companions, much against their wishes, and due to other duties, had to leave him. Hardly had they driven out of sight when two of the known 'enemies' – regular members of the gang that for months had threatened the hospital vehicles – approached Jones. But instead of displaying their usual aggressiveness, they were quite friendly in their greeting and they talked for some time about each other's familities, where he lived in England and other casual matters. They parted with hand-shakes and admits Jones today 'I even left them my haversack rations!'

Jones was en route to the BMH at El Ballah, about a quarter of a mile from the Suez Canal near El Kantara, where he served until the completion of his three year tour of overseas service, where initially his main duty was meeting the trains from Port Said to convey RAMC Staff and patients to the hospital using one of the first 'Standard Vanguard' staff cars issued to the Corps for trials. At the end of his service in Egypt, Jones returned to Liverpool aboard the troopship *Empire Pride* which was on its way home from the Far East carrying the entire crew of HMS *Mauritius* which had 'paid off' in the Far East.

When the training establishments in Egypt were all concen-trated in the Canal Zone, the Middle East Training School of the Royal Army Service Corps was established on the banks of the Canal on the ground below the war memorial at Gebal Maryath.

Commanded in 1948 by Lieutenant Colonel B L Perceval with a staff of five officers and six NCO instructors, the School ran daily classes for upwards of a hundred and fifty students. Although drawn mainly from the Corps, courses were attended by officers and men from all arms of the Army. In a report in the Corps Journal by a 'military observer in Egypt' 'The subjects taught' he wrote, 'are legion. In its lecture rooms – in the school's immaculate hutted camp – one can learn anything from changing a wheel on a ten ton lorry to changing the ribbon on a typewriter; from rationing a division in the field to running an Army bakery...'

The 6 Airborne Division had arrived in Palestine between mid-September and early November 1945 and among the support-ing arms were 73 Air Despatch Company which was subsequently moved to the Canal Zone. Here the Company, except for exercises, was not called upon to fulfil its primary role in support of air landing operations. However, in January 1949, the Company was called upon to deliver grain to the starving villagers in the Hadhramaut in the south east corner of the Arabian peninsula. Working with the RAF, the Company flew 242 sorties between 4 February and 2 March, during which time 751 tons of grain was delivered. The average drop was of 3 tons 220 lbs. The work was difficult due to the nature of the Hadhramaut terrain with the country cut into deep wadis – almost ravines – which made suitable dropping zones difficult to find and frequently precluded the flying of aircraft sufficiently low to drop loads satisfactorily.

Eighteen months later, in August 1950, the Company was called upon to carry out a similar mission but this time, it was to drop food, petrol and cigarettes to a leave party of sailors who, landing at Akaba, had gone on to visit the ruined city of Petra, seventy miles to the north where they were snowed up in the mountains. Everything reached them safely except for the one jar of rum which broke on landing and the precious content was lost.

Port Said played a particularly important part in the life of Middle East Land Forces in the decade following the end of the war in 1945, when initially British Forces were still stationed in Iraq, Persia, Aden, the Sudan, Greece, Palestine, Eritrea and Egypt itself, calling for an extensive and complicated programme of shipping to maintain these forces, together with the constant flow of transports en route to and from India and the Far East. At one time, the handling of two troopships a day was the rule rather than the exception. The passengers on these frequently crowded troopships were destined for Australia, South and East Africa, Mauritius and Ceylon as well as the United Kingdom. The feeding of these troops presented the Corps with a variety of problems arising from the different ration scales with which each nationality had to be provisioned.

'During these days of intense activity in the port', recorded Major R J A Hockenhull, writing in the Corps Journal, 'RASC Water Transport based on Port Said was actively engaged.' Two Companies, one composed of ocean-going landing ship craft with refrigerated and water carrying vessels, the other made up of fast launches, harbour launches and motor fishing vessels. Both units worked both day and night with the port movement staff to keep up the flow of traffic and to maintain the flow of provisions to the Middle East garrisons.

The Water Transport Companies were often far from their

[By courtesy of Mag Gen C M Smith]

Major General C M Smith inspecting RASC soldiers in Egypt.

Port Said base and were responsible for maintaining troops all along the North African coast, down the Canal and up to Aquaba and across the Mediterranean to Famagusta and Haifa and also a weekly run to Rhodes, the main base in Dodecanese waters.

By 1954, the RASC in Port Said was no less actively engaged in the maintenance of forces stationed locally and along the North African coast. By then the LSTs had been handed over to a private shipping firm which operated the vessels on behalf of the Ministry of Transport, although operational control was retained by the Army. The garrisons in Tripoli, Benghazi and Tobruk were still maintained by the Corps from Port Said where small craft facilities in these and other ports in Middle East Command were provided by the RASC Water Transport Company.

The Corps operated the Cold Storage Depot at Port Said, imported and stored fresh beef, mutton and pork, butter, yeast, fish, bacon and cheese, all of which required careful handling and storage at correct temperatures and the Port Detachment RASC dealt with the import and export of almost everything. Due to the conditions resulting from strained relationships with the Egyptians, it became impossible to rely on local sources for the provision of fresh items and, in consequence, the Port Detachment had to import vast quantities of fresh fruit and vegetables, eggs and animal fodder which called for reliance on the MT Companies throughout the Zone for distribution and frequent use was made of refrigerated railway waggons to distribute frozen commodities throughout the Zone.

Although the RASC was always addressed as being in Port Said, the majority of the personnel lived in Port Fouad on the east bank of the Canal in the old established 'Waterman's Camp' which, over the years, had been continuously improved. The Camp was within easy reach of the bathing beaches, good messes existed and the Naafi facilities were of a high standard. Ample opportunities existed for recreation and amusement, there was great rivalry on both the cricket and football grounds – in fact in all fields of sport. There were three cinemas in Port Fouad – two operated by the AKC and within easy reach was the very popular and well organized NAAFI Seaview Holiday Camp. There is no doubt that in the later years of the British Army's presence in Egypt, the RASC at Port Said were much more fortunate than other members of the Corps in the less attractive locations in the Zone.

The nine years following the British withdrawal into the Canal Zone had been uneasy, relationships with Egypt deteriorated and, arising from the fluctuating political situations in that country following military defeat in what had been Palestine, the abrogating of the 1936 Treaty and the general upsurge of nationalism, these were difficult times for the British Army in dealing with serious riots in Port Said. At one time, in October-November 1951, the situation became so serious that the British Forces were increased by the despatch of some six thousand men, together with 330 vehicles and a very large tonnage of stores, bringing the troops in the Canal Zone to sixteen battalions of infantry, seven regiments of gunners and two and a half armoured regiments.

The difficult situation arising with the Egyptian government as a result of this action led to their Minister of the Interior enforcing an exodus of the greater proportion of the Egyptians employed by the British Army in the Canal Zone. The tradesmen, domestic barrack and mess staffs, the drivers, clerks and storemen – away they went, their worldly possessions loaded on handcarts or carried in huge bundles. However what was to be but a temporary crisis was soon overcome by the arrival of several thousand Pioneer troops from Mauritius, a civilian labour force of over three thousand enlisted in Cyprus and Malta and the arrival of some five thousand RAF tradesmen and technicians from home.

The Anglo-Egyptian relationships in the Canal Zone area reached a most difficult phase with the appearance of the 'Bulak Nizam', a new force of armed auxiliary Police, given battle training by the Egyptian Army, which engaged in shooting at service families accommodation and at individual servicemen, several of whom were killed in the Ismalia area and later at Suez there were numerous similar incidents. A small detachment of the Buffs guarding the Suez filtration plant was attacked, a military train was ambushed at Tel-el-Kebir and later the Grenadier Guards and a field regiment fought a successful engagement in the same area and so life went on. Over forty British soldiers lost their lives during this period which was not designated as being 'on active service'.

In July 1952, King Farouk of Egypt was deposed and the country was then ruled by a junta of 'free officers' with Major General Mohammed Neguib as Prime Minister.

The Canal Zone was dependent on Cairo for many of its vital local purchase contracts and on hearing the news of Farouk's downfall on the radio at breakfast, Colonel John Mullington, then Colonel ST (Supplies) GHQ MELF, signalled to a contact at the War Office (S&T) at Chessington to cancel the loading of a certain ship in Liverpool and substitute as much 'Compo' as could be taken aboard. This action saved by about a week everyone in the Canal Zone being put on 'half rations'.

A year later negotiations were again opened for the British evacuation of the Canal Zone – at which time there were some 70,000 British troops in the Zone. The Egyptian delegation at the discussions in Cairo was led by one Colonel Nasser. The negotiations broke down and in March 1954, fire was again opened up on British troops and over fifty attacks were made on them between early April and mid-May when the Egyptians brought an end to the campaign of violence and shortly after, negotiations leading to the evacuation began. In October, agreement was reached that British forces would be gradually withdrawn over a period of twenty months. By the end of the year, the 3 Division and the 14 Parachute Brigade had returned to England. The 3 Division Column RASC, commanded since early 1954 by Lieutenant

Colonel WJ Cockerill, comprising 14, 74 and 101 Companies, returned home aboard HMT *Cheshire*, and being the major unit on the ship, the CO became OC Troops for the voyage.

1 Division left Egypt for the UK a year later. Only 1 Guards Brigade remained located at Moascar and Port Said, with the RAF's last station, Abu Sueir.

Finally, the last fighting troops to leave, the 2 Grenadier Guards at Golfcourse Camp, Port Said, left by ship on the night of the 24/25 March 1956 leaving one Company as a rear party which followed by air from Abu Sueir. Two days later the last GOC British Troops in Egypt also left. Only a small administrative rear party remained to wind up British affairs, operating from Navy House in Port Said. Finally, the Brigadier in command, together with the last seventy-eight all ranks, which had composed the last staff unit of the Army in Egypt, embarked on a chartered tank transporter ship and sailed away in the early morning of 13th June. They were the last British troops to be in Egypt after seventy-four years, although it was not long before British Forces were back again, and in action...

Soon after seven o'clock on the morning of 5 November 1956, eighteen transport planes flew down from a blue, bright sunlit sky above Gamil airport at Port Said. The spearhead of a British Force made up of men of the 3 Battalion, the Parachute Regiment, together with their supporting arms including men of the 63 Company RASC who dropped onto their objective by parachute.

Among the force which dropped by parachute on Gamil airfield were ten members of the Corps, Sergeant Henderson, Lance Corporals Hallis and Davis, with Drivers Carter, Clarke, Melver, Mead, Miller, Murray and Palmer, all of 63 Company's Parachute Platoon. Their task was the operation of the re-supply DZ and DZ clearance. The Detachment suffered one casualty from a shrapnel wound.

The main body of 63 Company landed a few hours after the Commando assault on the beaches. The first party of forty, led by Major (Later Lieutenant Colonel) P de L Bainbrigge, was given the task of securing both civilian and Egyptian miliary transport to make the Brigade mobile until their own transport could be landed. This task was well carried out, with a fleet of civilian buses coming under RASC control.

Egyptian troops were firing at them as they floated down but within half an hour of landing, the Parachute battalion had cleared the airfield, was grouped in tactical order and was digging in; at the same time, a Sergeant and nine men of 63 Company were assembling supplies and preparing to receive more as they were flown in over the dropping zone.

This operation arose from the action of the Egyptian Government which, just over six weeks following the final evacuation of Egypt, had seized control of the Suez Canal and had nationalized the Canal Company.

Britain and France immediately sought the reinternationalization of the Suez Canal and the downfall of Nasser who had so openly flouted international agreements. The endeavours of these two Allies were, however, fraught by what has been described as the 'assiduous sabotage by the United States of every successive British and French endeavour to settle the crisis in a way beneficial to Western interests' for 'Among officials in the US State Department concerned with the Middle East, there had long existed a determination to destroy British and French influence in the region and replace it with American power'. These views and factors, which subsequently led to the sudden cessation of our successful joint operations in liaison with the French, were not immediately obvious and it has been recorded that Foster Dulles, the then American Secretary of State 'shamefully deceived the British and French over American intentions'. Our Secretary of State, Selwyn Lloyd, did not anticipate the duplicity of Dulles or of the indecisiveness of the then President Eisenhower for whom, at that time, it is recorded, the only thing that mattered was the result of the impending presidential election.

In seeking the reinternationalization of the Suez Canal, Britain and France united in their diplomatic efforts and made joint plans, as a last resort, for retaking the Canal by force should peaceful negotiation fail.

To this end the machinery was put into action for a selective recall of Regular Army Reservists and call-up of members and units of the Army Emergency Reserve. This brought in some 23,000 officers and men to bring units up to strength and others for the formation of specialized units. Lieutenant General (later General Sir Hugh) Stockwell was appointed to command the force with Brigadier (later General Sir Kenneth) Darling as his BGS. 3 Infantry Division mobilized early in August and entered upon a concentrated training period. 3 Infantry Brigade of the 1st Division was flown out to Malta and 16 Parachute and 3 Commando

Brigades, destined to be the assault troops, were despatched to Cyprus. An armoured formation and units were also maintained to complete the force. The French quickly responded to the needs of the moment and immediately made available the well equipped and powerful airborne and amphibious 10th Aeroportee Division and an Armoured formation, the 7th Mecanique Rapide equipped with tanks capable of a speed of 50 mph.

General Stockwell became the Allied Land Forces Commander with the French General Beaufre as his Deputy in the planning and execution of what was subsequently designated 'Operation Musketeer'. General Keightley was appointed Supreme Commander.

It was late in the afternoon of Friday 3 August that 3 Infantry Divisional Column RASC received orders to mobilize and was placed on seven days notice to move. The CO, Lieutenant Colonel W J Cockerill, was nearing the end of his tenure of command, his successor, Lieutenant Colonel L A Cardy, who had been nominated, arrived seven days later and their handover was completed in two days. BRASCOs were found for three infantry brigades and Transport officers for three field Ambulances. They were replaced in the Column by reservist officers.

All the old Bedford three-tonners were withdrawn and replaced by Bedford RL 4×4 vehicles, whilst every vehicle, not only of the Divisional Column but those of every mobilizing unit of the whole force, were repainted with the 'Desert Sand' colour, the front, back, sides and top also being painted with a white 'H' – for force recognition sign. This involved the organizing, on a 24 hour per day basis, of all painting resources and, with the help of REME teams drawn from Command Workshops, a regular continuous flow of yellow painted vehicles rolled out of the painting sheds.

Stores of all description to complete G 1098 Scales were received. Every man was issued with Khaki Drill uniforms and the regimental tailors were kept busy making necessary alterations and sewing on new formation badges. Every unit spent much time packing stores into crates and packing cases ready for shipment. Conferences were held at which priorities of embarkation and tactical loading of stores were decided upon. The Divisional Column being essential for the formation's maintenance, was almost completely allocated in the early stages, only a very few vehicles being left to follow up.

Second line loads of ammunition, POL and all supplies down to blankets, stretchers and water, were calculated in great detail.

The requirements for the Tank Brigade were communicated to 54 Company in Germany – which quickly brought a message from HQ BAOR to the effect that civil authorities on the continent would not permit the passage of ammunition through the inland waterways and the docks – a quick decision was made, 54 Company would return with the required POL whilst 3 Divisional Column would transport all the ammunition. Vehicles already loaded with POL standing by at Lingfield, Surrey – HQ CRASC and 14 and 101 Companies, commanded by Major R A Nightingale and Major J MacPherson respectively – and Hargrave Park, Stanstead in Essex – 74 Company commanded by Major (later Brigadier) D J Sutton – were offloaded and despatched to collect ammunition from a number of CADs. Whilst this changeover was in process, preliminary orders for embarkation were received. The plan was for vehicles to be embarked with only their drivers, all other personnel travelling on troopships, sailings being planned so that vehicles and personnel should reach the overseas destination at the same time.

The bulk of 3 Divisional Column's vehicles – some 120, including all of 14 Company under Major R A Nightingale – were taken aboard the *Marshall*; 74 Company's vehicles were split between the *Huntsland* and the *Kingsbury*, 22 on the former, 15 on the latter, which loaded at Southampton whilst all the other ships sailed from Cardiff or Barry. One platoon of 101 Company was allocated to an LST which loaded at Liverpool.

During the time of preparation for embarkation, retraining of the recalled Reservists was carried out, the emphasis being laid on proficiency with personal weapons, ambush drill and physical fitness. Every man fired his rifle or Sten gun, parties were on the ranges every day, there were battle drills, route marches and 3-ton vehicle driving. The Reservists, it was recorded, worked with a will and many undoubtedly were happy to be back in uniform.

Then followed a period of waiting which lasted throughout October until the weekend of 27/28, when several units in the Division were placed at immediate notice and quickly departed. Tac HQ of the Division prepared to follow. The CO received orders to accompany Tac HQ on 31 October and embarked in HMT *Asturias* on 2 November, having handed over command of the Column to his second-in-command who saw his vehicles and vehicle parties being 'called forward' to embark, some in organized convoys, others in single ships. The bulk of the personnel remained behind, alerted to embark at short notice.

At the same time as preparations for the launching the force from the United Kingdom was being organized, there was considerable activity in both Malta and Cyprus where advanced elements of the force were waiting, nearer to their objective.

Cyprus lies only some two hundred miles from Port Said, a day's sail by sea and under an hour's flying time by air, a position which made it an ideal 'stepping off' point for 'Operation Musketeer'. The only real Cypriot port, although of limited capacity, was Famagusta, but with the impending commitments of 'Musketeer', the smaller port had only facilities for small craft and large craft had to be worked in the roadstead. During the build up period, it was planned that the port could deal with some 300 tons of military stores per day. No rail facilities exist in Cyprus and in consequence, dock clearance depended on road movement and became mainly an RASC commitment.

Two 3-ton MT Companies, each of two transport platoons, were made available for duties in the Limassol area where a wired-in convoy assembly area was established adjacent to an MT Company location. At this time, the Transport organization comprised three RASC officers (Transport, Convoy Control and Docks Transport Officers) with small staffs.

The success of the British and French airborne landings at Port Said on the morning of 5 November followed by the beach landings by the Royal Marine Commandos, led to a day of fighting, sometimes on a major scale, to clear an area; at others dealing with pockets of resistance.

The helicopter operations during the Port Said landing demonstrated the outstanding value of these aircraft to the armed forces. On 6 November 1956, twenty-two helicopters took off from fleet carriers nine miles from the Egyptian coast and landed 415 men of 45 Royal Marine Commando, together with twenty-three tons of stores within the space of an hour and seventeen minutes.

The helicopters, both 'Whirlwinds' and 'Sycamores', came from the Joint Experimental Helicopter Unit and 845 Squadron Fleet Air Arm and it was the first operation of its kind. It was also the first time that a helicopter unit flown by both Army and RAF pilots, supported by RAF maintenance personnel and RASC drivers and clerks had been embarked in one of HM's Aircraft Carriers as part of the Ship's Company

In November, the first British helicopter group composed of

personnel of all three Services, sailed in two carriers from Malta. 45 Commando Royal Marines was divided between the two ships. The original plan for the employment of helicopters had been confined solely to casualty evacuation but this was subsequently changed to the landing of the Commandos by helicopter. To ensure full serviceability they had to be stowed below decks in the passage to Suez. On the night of 4/5 November, complete blackout conditions were imposed, with watertight doors closed and all operational and damage control stations manned.

The first wave of six 'Whirlwinds' took off at 12 minutes past six in the morning of 5 November, five minutes later six 'Sycamores' which had been rushed into position by the deck crews, started up and were airborne and away and this became a continual process until the whole airborne assault force was away. At Port Said, the operational landings were controlled by an RASC Major 'who found himself', recorded Major D S Wooles RASC (in *The RASC Review*) 'controlling the aircraft landing, organizing and assisting in the evacuation of wounded and adding his share to nearby street fighting which threatened his "parish"'.

Some casualties were immediately cleared from the landing zone by aircraft returning to bring in more troops, but the main casualty evacuation did not start until the trooplift had been completed. However, it is on record that the first wounded man was relanded aboard a carrier at 06.39 – he had left his ship nearly nine miles from the beachhead, played his part in the assault landing, was wounded, picked up by helicopter and was back in a hospital bed in his own ship all within the space of twenty minutes! 'The speed' recorded Major Wooles 'with which both sitting and lying cases arrived by air was most striking. In comparison, the transfer of cases between boats by sea took over an hour'.

Towards dusk, the two carriers steamed into Port Said and anchored in the basin. Two days later the Joint Helicopter Unit which had then made 160 deck landings and landed tons of stores and men and evacuated casualties under the shore based command of the Adjutant, an RASC officer, heard of the 'Cease Fire' order.

Soon after dark a meeting took place between the Commander of the Parachute Brigade and the Colonel commanding the French Parachutists and the local Egyptian Commander but no conclusion could be reached other than agreement to a provisional ceasefire. The Egyptians still had a line through to Cairo and late in the evening they received orders from Nasser for the garrison to fight to the last, adding that Russia had intervened on Egypt's behalf. At dawn, reinforcements came ashore in amphibians driven by the 7 Royal Tank Regiment packed with Royal Marine Commandos, followed during the morning by more men and vehicles which drove on into Port Said, through the town as far as the Water Works, south of the Raswa Bridge from where an advance was made towards El Tina, ten miles to the south.

Throughout the next day, seaborne reinforcements continued to arrive, landing at the fishing harbour, for the Egyptians, although cornered in Navy House, were still holding out as they did until following an air strike, after which 40 Commando moved in. Early in the evening, orders were given out for the following day's operations – the task of the Parachute battalions being to break out from the causeway and take the aerodromes at Abu Sueir whilst the French were to launch a combined airborne and waterborne attack on Ismalia. Returning to HMS *Tyne*, General Stockwell was told by the Admiral that he had received a message stating that he could expect the Russians to intervene in force. Shortly after, the Commander of the Parachute Brigade received a signal which ordered a ceasefire at midnight. These messages came both as a surprise and a shock and perhaps even more so to the Commander of the 3 Battalion the Parachute Regiment who, when he received them, was engaged in the issue of orders for an advance which would result in the final success of the operation. It was agreed however, that he should press ahead to the railway halt at El Cap, just five miles from the southern end of the causeway, which it was assessed to be as far as the advance could be made by midnight and this was achieved without resistance.

Despite the ceasefire, explosions and small arms fire continued in Port Said throughout the following day. At dawn, men of the Parachute Regiment were in action in the Arab quarter in making a link-up with the Royal Marine Commandos. Throughout the day and those that immediately followed, all activities were focused on making a return to a normal way of life. Civil Affairs Officers arrived from Cyprus, the Royal Military Police undertook work in addition to their normal duties, they concentrated prisoners of war and formed them into parties for the collection and identification of the dead, as well as arresting looters and holding them in custody. The Royal Engineers set to work in restoring public services and utilities, the RAMC moved into the overcrowded hospitals to bring succour to military and civilian wounded and sick. The RASC did all possible to speed up the unloading of ships and the distribution of supplies.

On 10 November, 3 Division – less the Guards Brigade – arrived off Port Said and commenced disembarkation. The Infantry, intended originally as reinforcements, came ashore and relieved the Parachute and Commando Brigades, which duly returned to Cyprus.

Among the ships in the convoy was HMT *Asturias*, among those aboard being the CO – Lieutenant Colonel L A Cardy – of 3 Division Column RASC who came ashore soon after midday and made contact with the ADST at 40 Sub-Area, the RASC element of which were responsible for the operation of the Base ammunition, Supply and POL Depots, small dumps of which were being formed near the Cassino Quay from which the Divisional units were drawing direct pending the establishment ashore of the Divisional Column. The following day, the Sub-Area began the establishment of larger dumps at the Abbas Hiimi Quay.

Early on 12th November, the first vehicles of the Column were disembarked from SS *Huntsland* – thirteen 3 tonners with eleven drivers. Only six of the vehicles could be put on the road, the REME Port Detachment taking over the balance to repair, mainly electrical faults. During the day, the vehicles went on to Abbas Hiimi, dropped their loads of POL and were immediately sent on to join the Royal Fusiliers and York and Lancaster Regiment who were completely without any first line transport.

The next day, five more vehicles with drivers, led by Sergeant White of 74 Company, were landed and the remaining two – making 22 three tonners and twenty other ranks – arrived four days after.

As a result of the political uncertainties of the situation, it was extremely difficult to make any firm plans. The ceasefire had to be most strictly observed, but troops were faced with considerable Internal Security Duties and had to be ready for any eventuality. There was still uncertainty as to what units, vehicles and stores would be arriving on which ships and when.

On Sunday 18 November, a scheme for a skeleton Column HQ and HQ 74 Company was prepared in the hope that some key personnel such as the Senior Supply Officer and Adjutant would be flown in. Meanwhile the vehicles ashore, still without an officer, were attached to 63 Company with the Parachute Brigade. By this time, there were in Port Said several small RASC units – a Port

Platoon, Supply Platoon, Petrol Platoon and a Petrol Laboratory together with a Field Bakery – they lacked and needed an RHQ. To meet this, the DDST 2 Corps, Brigadier Saunders, placed the Commander 3 Divisional Column in command until the arrival on 21 November of the CRASC Port Said.

Plans were made for the reception and accommodation of the Column on its arrival and also for meeting varying operational possibilities, for at this time it was generally thought they would be there for a longish stay. Then, on 21 November, the advance parties of a hastily assembled United Nations force arrived – a party of Norwegians wearing American style helmets painted a bright light blue. A vast crowd of the civilian population gave them an overwhelming, hysterical reception and the West Yorks had to be rushed up to rescue Egypt's new saviours to save them and their small RMP escort from being submerged in the mob.

The Column was however still expected, right up to 24 November, for the *Marshall* and the *Kingsbury* were still anchored in the outer roads, but on that same day the first moves in the withdrawal of 3 Division were taken. By the evening of 1st December, all men and remaining vehicles had been re-embarked on the LST *Salerno*; four days later the Tac HQ of the Division embarked on HMT *Dilwara* sailing for Southampton the following day.

During the last week of November and in early December, contingents of UN troops continued to arrive, relieving British troops until finally only 19 Brigade remained which was subjected to a number of attacks by guerrillas right up to the last.

Finally, the last troops embarked on the evening of 22 December – among them the RASC/EFI detachment which had been retained up to the last day to operate a canteen in the dock area – the last tank of the 4 Royal Tank Regiment reversed up into a landing ship and the rearguard of the 1 Battalion the West Yorkshire Regiment marched up the quay to embark on a landing craft straight from their last patrol in the streets adjacent to the dock area.

There remained a naval supply ship, then ordered to fly the flag of the UN Organization, which stayed to service the salvage fleet, and from her decks the following day, the ship's company had a ringside view of the attempts of a mob to blow up the famous de Lesseps statue. The first two charges were too small and failed to bring it down. The third charge was too big. The statue crashed down but the explosion killed at least two of the demolition team and injured a number of the excited shouting crowd. On the same day, a gang of Egyptians did their best to dislodge a large Union Jack flying from the masthead of a flagstaff on the jetty which had been run up by a party of British sailors just before they embarked. They had nailed it to the staff before cutting away the hoist rope and had then completely greased the pole. The infuriated Egyptians could not understand why their desperate attempts to shin the pole ended in failure. Finally, they chopped it down.

SUDAN

AT THE END OF WORLD WAR II nearly 100 British RASC officers and over 500 RASC soldiers were on the strength of the Sudan Service Corps. This Corps was the equivalent of the RASC to the Sudan Defence Force (SDF). As the Sudan was a Condominium with Egypt, all the British officers posted to the Sudan Defence Force were required to swear allegiance to the Governor General of the Sudan. They were granted brevet commissions and wore SDF badges of rank. It is of passing interest to note the difference with the British Army:–

British Rank	SDF Rank	SDF Badges of Rank
Captain	Bimbashi	One star, one crown
Major	Kaimakam	Two stars, one crown
Lieutenant Colonel	Miralai	Three stars, one crown (in line)

In 1946 the Sudan Service Corps had over 5,000 native troops, manning the following units:–

Eight General Transport Companies
Animal Transport Company
  (mules and camels)
A Training School

Two Petroleum Depots
Several Supply Depots
A Station Company
Ambulance Company

These units were spread over 1,000,000 square miles of the largest country in Africa, ranging from the comparatively civilized Khartoum to primitive Equatoria. The distances were vast and one company in Equatoria had outstations to its East and West, each over 300 miles from its headquarters! In West Central Sudan the farthest unit was some 500 miles from the nearest railhead, of which 200 miles was really bad going over very soft sand!

Since it was envisaged that the Sudan would achieve independence from both Britain and Egypt at a fairly early date, 'Sudanisation' of the SDF, including SSC was steadily carried out; all British Officers and other ranks had been replaced by Sudanese long before independence actually arrived in 1956.

The first Sudanese Kaid (Commander SDF,) was Lieutenant

[By courtesy of Lt Col Creighton]

66 Supply Depot RASC Khartoum

General Ahmad Mohed Pasha, previously an officer of the Sudan Service Corps. British relationships with the Sudanese, both military and civilian were, on the whole, excellent, but with our Condominium partners, the Egyptians, they tended to be more distant, mainly as a result of General Neguib's and Colonel Nasser's rise to power and Egypt's apparent desire to retain suzerainty after the British withdrawal. The appearance of General Neguib at the scheduled opening on 1 March 1954 of the first Sudan Parliament sparked off a violent demonstration by Mahdists against union with Egypt which caused some bloodshed, both Sudanese and British, in Khartoum. So it was with wariness towards Egyptian intentions that preparation for the British evacuation proceeded.

By 1955 the British military presence in the Sudan had been reduced to a small force comprising a headquarters, an infantry battalion, an RAF detachment (with a few aircraft) and some supporting arms and services (Royal Corps of Signals, RAMC, RASC, RAOC, RAPC and REME). The Commander British Troops Sudan, Major General Gifford, with a small staff (GSO II, DAQMG etc.) answered to British Headquarters in Egypt. His knowledge of Arabic proved of great value as arrangements for withdrawal progressed.

In the final year (1954–55) OC RASC Sudan (Major J A A R Frost) had under his command a Supply Depot, a Petrol Depot, a

Bakery, a Slaughterhouse, a Barrack Office and a Fire Service Section, all at Khartoum; also, a Detail Issue Depot and Bakery at Gebeit (500 miles NE of Khartoum and 60 miles SW of Port Sudan). There was no RASC Transport Company – RASC and other units had, of course, their own vehicles, and OC RASC sometimes procured supplementary transport by hiring.

RASC supplies and POL were obtained as follows:–

Dry rations: by sea and rail from the Canal Zone of Egypt (via Port Sudan.) Most fresh items, fuelwood and coal: by local contracts.
Fruit and vegetables: by local contracts (Jan–May) and by air from East Africa (Jun–Dec, when they were not available locally.)
Bacon and fresh butter by air from East Africa.
Gasoline was procured from the Shell Co of the Sudan, and oils, greases, miscellaneous items and disinfectants from the Canal Zone of Egypt.

The rations were of a much more luxurious standard than those prescribed in the austere scale for the Gordon Relief Expedition (1884–85) which the OC RASC came across in Omdurman museum! They included fruit juices for the hottest period. The climate is very dry and one of the hottest in the world. So during the most oppressive months (May–July), British wives and children were evacuated by air to the UK, and there were arrangements for military personnel to go for short leave periods, by air, to Cyprus. Because of the heat, work ceased from midday until early evening (when it resumed.) Occasional sandstorms (Haboobs) or swarms of locusts added to operating problems. The Moslem faith of almost all civilian employees necessitated their absence on Fridays to attend the Mosque – in addition to their taking the 'British Weekend'. They were often too weak to work well during the annual fasting month of Ramadan.

Civilian staff were, almost without exception, reliable and trustworthy. But time marches on. In 1955 they were persuaded by some union leaders that they had only to follow the example of British workers in the UK to obtain higher wages through striking. However, before they 'withdrew their labour' they appointed individuals to maintain what they considered 'key' services – for example, duty batmen in officers' messes! British soldiers (mainly from the infantry battalion) then took over such tasks as driving vehicles, baking bread and handling supplies. The strike collapsed

SUDAN/ETHIOPIA/ERITREA

in a short time and there was no increase in pay.

The incident tends to illustrate the basic qualities of most Sudanese who came into contact with the Army. They were found to be considerate, dignified, polite, and honest, with a well developed sense of humour. Many had quite an extensive working knowledge of English.

The population of the Sudan (some 17 m) is about 66% Arab and Moslem (mainly in the North and centre.) But in the South the negro Nilotic Peoples – Nuer, Dinka, Shilluk – largely Christian or pagan, have no particular regard for the more sophisticated Arabs to the north.

In August 1955 some 'Southern' units of the Sudan Defence Force at Juba (Equatoria) mutinied, and HQ British Troops Sudan at Khartoum (750 miles away) were surprised to receive signals from them seeking military assistance! By that time the SDF was completely 'Sudanized' and the country was on the eve of independence. The British therefore followed a policy of strict non-intervention. The Sudanese authorities quelled the mutiny quite quickly and a number of Courts Martial dealt with the ringleaders. The problem of the 'Southern Tribes' remained, however.

The evacuation of the Sudan, under the terms of the Cairo Agreement of 1953, took place in the period 16 August-14 November 1955. Military families left gradually by air, and troops by rail, sea and air. Large quantities of military equipment and stores (such as vehicles, foodstuffs, lubricants and furniture) were held by units and depots and it was not until quite late in the evacuation period that GHQ Middle East Forces issued definite orders on their disposal. Some were sold to the local population by auction. Eventually, however, the majority were handed over to the Sudan Defence Force who were amazed – and grateful – at their good fortune! OC RASC (Major J A A R Frost) having thus dealt with 'his' share, joined the last evacuation aircraft (which flew to Cyprus.)

On 1st January 1956 the Sudan formally celebrated its independence. The last British Governor-General, HE Sir Knox Helm, ceded his authority, and the Prime Minister, Ismail El Azhari (National Unionist Party) led the country towards a future free from control by both Britain and Egypt. That it has remained a friend of the West and a major trading partner of the United Kingdom surely reflects great credit on the 57 short years of British rule. In the military sphere this friendship continued in many areas, one of the more evident examples being the establishment of a Sudanese Army Staff College on British (Camberley) lines and staffed with a sizeable number of British officer instructors.

ERITREA

ERITREA ON THE WESTERN BANK of the Red Sea was a former Italian colony occupied and administered by the end of the war by a British Military Administration who in turn were responsible to the Kaid el 'Amm (or GOC Sudan). The fact that there were no telephone communications from Eritrea to the outside world made it somewhat of an independent command!

The capital city, Asmara, was a small but very modern city built in the heyday of Italian rule. It was in Asmara that the small RASC contingent were stationed. The major RASC presence was in the Supply Depot – which functioned as a Base Stores Depot, a Direct Issue Depot, a Field Butchery and a Petrol Depot, supporting the small British garrison. The sole transport organization in the country was a General Transport Company also based in Asmara. Apart from the few British officers and senior NCOs the Company was largely manned by Italian civilians.

A contemporary (1947) report in the *Waggoner* by the 'Eritrean correspondent' states:

'A climate which is never really too hot, with cool evenings and sometimes a mountain mist, makes it difficult to believe that we are only a short distance away from the Red Sea. Climate, together with the "usual amenities" of clubs, cinemas and games, makes Eritrea a pleasant spot. If your lot is to be in Eritrea we think you will enjoy it!'

As with many such pleasant places, the British withdrawal from the region in the early 1950s meant the end to another desirable posting.

ETHIOPIA

ETHIOPIA, SOMETIMES CALLED ABYSSINIA, covers more territory than the UK, France and Italy combined. In 1935 the country was invaded and subjugated by Italy with its Emperor Haile Selassie fleeing to England.

In January 1941, the Emperor re-entered his country escorted by a small British force under Brigadier Orde Wingate. By May 1941 the Italian forces had been routed and the dynasty was restored. The Emperor asked the British for a Military Mission to help him raise, organize and train an Ethiopian Army of two divisions with supporting arms and services. It was not easy to spare many British personnel for this task during the war years and it was only in late 1944 that a charter was drawn up for an Imperial Army Service Corps, to be organized in accordance with RASC principles and procedures.

In May 1945, sufficient RASC officers and soldiers were provided from East Africa Command to implement the proposal. A Lieutenant Colonel as CRASC, assisted by one major, six captains, three warrant officers and ten sergeants had the task of forming a HQ Imperial Army Service Corps, expanding the existing Supply and Transport framework into a General Transport Company of four platoons and a workshop platoon, establishing a regular supply system with a main depot in Addis Ababa and three subsidiary platoons in Harar, Dessie and Gondar and opening a school in Addis Ababa for training drivers and clerks. A formidable task!

On the supply side, problems were easily solved as Ethiopia is a land of vast agricultural resources. Soon 30 days maintenance and 30 days reserve for the whole Army were stocked in the main Supply Depot and a further 30 days maintenance stocks were held by the three supply platoons for those units supported by them. In the transport company there was one platoon of Dodge 3 ton, 4×2 trucks, with the remaining platoons under-implemented and containing a mixture of former British Army Fords and captured Italian vehicles of all shapes and sizes, including some 10 ton diesels and trailers. One of the regular monthly tasks of this unit was the running of a resupply convoy of 10–12 vehicles to Asmara in Eritrea. This was possibly the longest routine resupply convoy there ever was – a round trip of some 1,500 miles, taking on average 22 days – and this over torturous terrain in country infested by 'Shifta' (bandits).

The training school for drivers and clerks proved a most successful venture. It attracted the interest and attention of the Emperor and was recognized as one of the show pieces of the Army. Commanded in turn by two competent and conscientious Emergency Commissioned RASC officers, it turned out over 400 drivers between October 1945 – December 1947 and taught English and basic clerical duties to a large number of young Ethiopians.

By December 1947, the original RASC commitment had been largely fulfilled and authority was handed over to an Ethiopian ADST and staff who had been understudying all the key appointments. A very small number of RASC personnel remained in an advisory capacity until the final withdrawal of the British Military Mission.

Lower approaches to Tasseli Pass between Addis Ababa and Asmara.

[By courtesy of Maj J Perrins]

CHAPTER SEVEN

Mediterranean

GIBRALTAR

For a number of years after the war, the military population of the two square mile colony of Gibraltar consisted of two to three regiments of artillery, one to two battalions of infantry, substantial numbers of engineers, a large Air Force contingent and a sizeable Naval presence in the large Government Dockyard. To support these forces, a wide variety of RASC units was also deployed, ranging through conventional road transport, water transport and supply units, to fire and barrack services.

33 Company RASC was the major provider of road transport, with four platoons of vehicles – one of Jeeps – the other platoons being mainly tipper vehicles used to support the Royal Engineers who never tired of honey-combing the Rock with their tunnels.

82 Water Transport Company with their harbour launches, VIP launch and LCA (Landing Craft Assault) were kept busy

ferrying stores and personnel around the harbour, clearing the seaward artillery ranges, towing targets for the artillery and perhaps as important as all these, organizing pleasure cruises to the North African towns of Ceuta, Tangier or Tarifa.

65 Supply Depot, a large organization, was responsible for feeding the garrison and uniquely, supplying the complete civilian population with its meat. A very large cold storage facility housing the Butchery was ideally situated in a deep tunnel in the Rock. This cold store held sufficient meat and other frozen commodities to supply the garrison for nine months and resupply was by direct shipment from Australia and New Zealand.

6 Bakery, as part of the Supply Depot, always boasted that it produced the best bread in the Colony!

As was generally the case in the immediate post-war years, considerable civilianization of posts took place. This was not unusual in Gibraltar where traditionally the local population and the military garrison were closely integrated. It was not uncommon for units to have civilians on their strength with 20–30 years service.

Service life in Gibraltar was always pleasant, even more so in the days before the Spanish closed their border gates. Notes from units in Gibraltar are full of references to visits to the sherry bodegas of Messrs Sandeman or Williams and Humbert and trips to the Costa del Sol and holiday resorts on the North African coast.

Gradually, however, all this came to an end as far as the RASC was concerned. The garrison was substantially reduced in size and by 1963, no RASC units remained in Gibraltar. Before leaving, however, the Corps presented the Gibraltar Museum with a collection of crests, badges and buttons to act as a permanent reminder of their presence.

Today the RCT is represented in Gibraltar only by a small number of drivers and Movements personnel and no RCT unit as such exists in the Colony.

MALTA GC

FOLLOWING THE WAR YEARS of siege and deprivation the island of Malta GC looked forward in 1945 to settling down to a tranquil peace. War damage was rapidly repaired and conditions quickly improved on this most pleasant of Mediterranean islands.

Military service on Malta prior to the war had always been attractive with the tranquil climate and friendly local population and post-war conditions rapidly reverted to this state. The role of the RASC on the island being the routine support of the relatively large RN and RAF forces of the peacetime garrison. During this initial period of retrenchment, 689 Horse Transport Company RASC was disbanded in January 1946, leaving the garrison with basically the same RASC organization it had prior to the war.

HQ RASC, 67 Supply Depot and its associated Bakery, were situated in Sa Maison Pieta. 32 General Transport Company remained in their old location of Notre Dame Revelin and 80 Water Transport Company split between Hay Wharf and their main anchorage at Pieta Creek. Barrack Services were based at Mtarfa and St George's Barracks.

The MT unit, 32 Company, had a long history, having been formed in November 1889. It operated horse and mule transport successively in Dublin, Aldershot, Woolwich, Natal and Shorncliffe. They served in France and Belgium throughout the first war after which it was reformed in Malta in 1923, as a garrison transport company. 32 Company carried out garrison duties throughout the siege of Malta in World War II and in recognition of its civilian component's contribution to the maintenance of Malta during that war, the company was represented at the 1945 VE parades and celebrations in London by two of the Maltese civilian staff, Foreman Zammit and Storeman Borg.

In 1956 RASC Malta became heavily involved in the preparation for the British Suez intervention. 32 Company's duties included troop lifts for ships and aircraft, stores collection to and from the docks, the loading of Landing Craft Tank and the evacuation of casualties from the aircraft carriers HMS *Theseus* and HMS *Ocean* to the hospitals, BMH Imtarfa and RNH Bighi.

RCT Fast Launch preparing to cast off in Valetta.

[By courtesy of Central Office of Information]

In 1959 32 Company established a Central Servicing Station which incorporated responsibilities for the servicing and inspection of a large part of the island's first line transport. By 1969, although the unit strength had diminished to a figure of around 150 all ranks, the servicing and inspection dependency had grown to the point where the unit, by then 32 Squadron RCT, was responsible for well over 75% of the Army transport including that of the Royal Malta Artillery. By this time also, the squadron had embraced the first line transport of the majority of the Army's minor units and was applying the principles later to become developed as the Transport Support Unit concept. The unit was almost completely civilianized with the exception of the officers, Squadron Sergeant Major and key NCOs.

In 1969 also, the squadron assumed command of the water transport element. This had reduced over the years from a company, 80 Company RASC, a Captain's command, to a maritime troop comprising in 1969 of three permanent vessels, the 50 ft General Service Launch *Scrooge* (RCT crewed), 44 ft River Class fast launch *Eden* and the 48 ft Derby Winners Class target towing launch *Callboy*, the latter two craft having civilian crews. Additionally, the Ramped Powered Lighter 06 *Forth* was held on strength in 1968–69 and crewed on an occasional basis by the RCT GSL crew, prior to its return to Cyprus in the winter of 1969/70. (This 900 mile voyage conducted safely by dumb tow from a Royal

Fleet Auxiliary buoy maintenance vessel, probably constitutes a record for an unmanned voyage by any RCT vessel!)

The launches, which were familiar sights to Service visitors to Malta throughout the post-war years, were based at Hay Wharf having moved earlier from moorings in Pieta Creek and were employed on a variety of off-shore training tasks including range clearance, target towing, Joint Service exercises and the provision of adventurous training and recreational transport for the garrison. In addition RCTVs *Eden* and *Callboy* acted as the official 'barges' for the Governor-General and the UK High Commissioner respectively, for which service an annual charge was raised. Additionally RCTV *Eden* was used on at least two visits by the Royal Family, the most recent being the visit of the Prince of Wales and Princess Anne in July 1969.

In 1970, the first evidence of the forthcoming withdrawal of British forces was the loss of the posts of Commander Royal Corps of Transport and the Staff Officer Grade 3 (Movements), the last CRCT, Lieutenant Colonel A C James MC RCT, handing over to Major H Prescott RCT in the new post of Staff Officer Grade 2 (Transport). The RCT officer complement then stood at three majors and four captains.

70 Movements Squadron, which had formed in 1965, operated for a period of several years jointly with the RN and RAF as a Joint Services Port Unit based at Marina Pinto, an organization which continued to the final withdrawal from Malta.

In 1970, as a first phase of the British departure and greatly to the regret of all concerned, 32 Squadron was withdrawn from Floriana and moved into the former Royal Engineer lines at St George's Barracks which were hastily adapted to the needs of a transport squadron. The move coincided with a reduction in the strength of the squadron workshop REME which had, up to that point, held an enviable reputation for rapid repairs based on excellent cooperation at all levels between parent squadron and workshop; control and assessment of repair priorities being in the hands of the squadron commander.

From the time of the move from Floriana the process of implementing redundancy procedures for the civilian staff gathered pace. The reality of the situation started to be evident to the Maltese staff who were nevertheless still reluctant to accept that the Services would leave Malta and found it difficult to reconcile their record of service and loyalty, of which they were very proud, with

[By courtesy of Central Office of Information]

RCT Movement control staff checking vehicles for shipment in Malta.

impending redundancy. It says much for their maintained loyalty that they continued to work well to the eventual point of unit disbandment.

In January 1972 the withdrawal of British forces commenced and 32 Squadron and 70 Movements Squadron amalgamated to form 32 Transport and Movements Squadron, operating from Marina Pinto and the area of Parlatoria Wharf in Grand Harbour. As a rationalization measure a Joint Services Transport Organization was established at Lascaria which coordinated all Service road transport in Malta including that of the Property Services Agency. The withdrawal was completed and 32 Transport and Movements Squadron disbanded, by March 1972. With the limited return of British forces to Malta in the form of a RM Commando in April 1972, the Joint Service Port Unit was re-established under command of a Lieutenant Commander RN, the RCT staff including one captain, one warrant officer and two sergeants. This force too, was withdrawn on 31 March 1979 leaving no British forces on this historic and pleasant island after an association which had lasted 178 years.

LIBYA

THE SCENE OF THE 8th Army major campaigns in North Africa remained part of the British presence in the Mediterranean area for a number of years, after the end of World War II.

In Tripoli under HQ Libya and Tripolitania Area, HQ RASC Tripoli initially commanded two garrison transport companies (7 and 40), 123 Supply Depot, an Army Fire Brigade and a Barrack Services organization. 38 Company RASC took over the transport duties in 1957.

500 miles east of Tripoli in Cyrenaica, the Benghazi, Barce and El Adem garrisons were supported by three General Transport Companies (1, 13 and 806), 26 and 477 Supply Platoons and 112 Command Petroleum Depot. Later this garrison was substantially reduced leaving only a transport platoon and 33 Supply Depot RASC.

In Tobruk, 193 GT Company (manned by Mauritian soldiers) and 805 GT Company (manned by Germans) provided a cosmopolitan touch to transport support to the garrison. 115 Command Petrol Depot and 489 Supply Platoons plus Barrack Services and a few RASC Fleet harbour launches and Motor Fishing Vessels (MFVs) completed the RASC establishment in the area.

In 1953, in Tobruk, the OC RASC/OC Troops/OC 805 GT Company was Major (later Lieutenant Colonel) Ivor Renwick RASC who recalls:

'In 1953 HM The Queen visited RAF El Adem and Tobruk Garrison during a State visit to King Idris. The Queen was to fly into El Adem and depart from Tobruk on the Royal Yacht Britannia, on which young Prince Charles was waiting. Although the visit lasted only three hours or so, the preparations took more than that in months. As it was decided that British Servicemen (and their families) stationed as far afield as Tripoli (Tripolitania) should not be denied the chance of seeing Her Majesty, the problems of accommodating and feeding some 500 families, 500 Servicemen, 600 members of the Cyrenaica Defence Force, 300 police, 400 members

319

MEDITERRANEAN

'of the Guards of Honour of the Foresters and Greys to name but a few, were considerable. Suffice it to say that all the problems were solved with a little ingenuity and a lot of hard work, and the visit was a great success.'

A major task of the Garrison was the support of training by units and formations from both UK and BAOR. Two major exercises at brigade group strength, using RAF El Adem as the main airhead, took place in the early sixties. Both involved major participation by 3 Divisional Column RASC units, which flew in with light scales of transport and their Massey Ferguson tractors and trailers to operate forward airheads. The provision of rations and POL for these exercises was the responsibility of the local RASC organization.

The formation of the RCT in 1965 and the loss of all the supply, barracks and fire responsibilities to the RAOC meant that HQ RASC Tripoli was disbanded in January 1965 and indeed the British presence in the area virtually ended in 1966. 38 Squadron RCT was disbanded in April 1966 leaving only 401 Troop RCT in

[By courtesy of Brig A J Simmons]

Exercise Starlight near El Adem 1960.

Benghazi. An RCT transport troop finally withdrew from El Adem in early 1970 following the overthrow of King Idris by a coup in 1969. The evacuation of all British troops from Libya was effected between January to March 1970. A Movement Control staff, 52 Port Squadron RCT, a freight handling troop with lighterage detachment, traffic operators and tank transporter drivers were all sent out from UK to assist in the withdrawal from Libya. Using a combination of civilian and service shipping and aircraft, some 6,500 tons of cargo, over 1,000 vehicles and 3,500 servicemen and their families were safely evacuated to UK or Cyprus, finally ending our links with a region so significant in British military history.

Cpl Weedon RASC briefing Arab drivers of 28 Coy RASC, Tripoli, Libya

[By courtesy of PR HQ NEARELF]

GREECE

THE BRITISH INVOLVEMENT in Greece for the second time during World War II dated from 28 September 1944 when, at a conference at Allied Forces Headquarters in Italy, the two chief Greek guerilla leaders of internal resistance placed all their forces under British Command to co-operate in the liberation of Greece. German forces were by then beginning to withdraw northwards.

British action was swift. On 3 October men of the 2 Parachute Brigade landed in the Peloponneses and nine days later the rest of the Brigade made an airborne landing north of Athens, their task being to aid the Greeks in the liberation of their country. The British Force marched into Athens which was being cleared of the remaining enemy by Greek partisans.

The Parachute Brigade was soon reinforced by other troops from Italy, 23 Armoured Brigade; 139 Infantry Brigade, later the whole of the 4 Division and finally HQ 3 Corps which on arrival was designated HQ Land Forces Greece.

The liberation of Greece had been swiftly accomplished, involving little fighting, the strength of the available British Forces being such that action was limited to the harassing of the retreating Germans up to the Yugoslav borders. By 8 November 1944, Greece was entirely free from invaders.

However, a more serious position had arisen internally in Greece. The landing of the Parachute Brigade had been a signal for an armed uprising against the Government by the Greek Peoples Liberation Army leading, when opposed by the Greek National Liberation Front, to civil war and it fell to the lot of the first British troops to subdue the rising and restore order. Subsequently it became necessary to maintain a comparatively substantial force to exercise control, a situation which obtained up to the end of the war. Soon the Greek government was faced with civil war brought about by the Communists. The British Army took no part in this internal strife, but did much to preserve calm by their presence and, through a Military Mission, helped to train and equip the reformed Greek Army.

At this time and until Christmas 1945, the Corps had the task of supplying the British forces and providing a training element for the Greek national army particularly in the formation of an efficient Supply and Transport Corps. This was very much due to the efforts of the RASC personnel whose task it was to reform that element of the Greek Army.

Throughout this time there were sufficient British troops 'on the ground' to ensure an uneasy peace and the left wing guerrillas, in the main, refrained from taking any offensive action.

One of the problems which faced the Corps in particular was that land communications were far from any reasonable standard. During the German occupation, road repair and maintenance had virtually ceased. There had been severe damage to communications generally resulting from some guerrilla action, but much more by the withdrawing German rearguards who systematically destroyed roads, bridges and culverts as they went northwards. As a result, starting a few miles north of Athens, the roads which still existed were in such a state that the average speed of a 3 ton lorry was restricted to between ten to fifteen miles per hour as the vehicle negotiated pot-holes and diversions around demolitions, bridges and culverts; and even lower speeds were sometimes necessary when 'dirt tracks' were the only access to small towns and villages. The whole country had been ravaged by the Germans and starvation and disease were rife.

As a result of the breakdown in the whole Government and social order, the British troops had to be completely self-sufficient for feeding and in taking preventive medical measures to avoid heavy casualties from disease. So, during the period 1945–46, the Corps, under the direction of the DDST Land Forces Greece, performed its normal duties of supply and transport, much of which were carried out by the formation transport concerned; in addition to which, particularly up to the beginning of 1946, the Corps was responsible for the distribution of UNRRA relief supplies drawn from base ports to towns and villages in the interior. In practice, this resulted, for example, in a section corporal being responsible for the transportation of supplies from a port such as Volos to several isolated villages up to seventy miles inland, the final approach to which would be along dusty tracks.

All the transport companies in Greece were so fully committed that all leave was deferred.

Many of the men eligible had been overseas for three to four years and this restriction on leave caused morale problems.

The situation was rectified by the arrival of Lieutenant Colonel W G Roe as CRASC 4 British Infantry Division who authorized the 'laying-up' of a limited number of vehicles to enable drivers, who, in many cases had served with the British Expeditionary Force in France in 1939–40 and subsequently in the Middle East, North Africa and Italy, to go on a well earned leave.

1946 saw the first effects of demobilization under the Age and Service Group Scheme, as experienced officers and NCOs left for home. This caused a considerable amount of strain upon the Corps, as it did also on the Royal Engineers, both Corps being engaged in vital tasks, as opposed to other arms committed only to internal security, guard duties and their own training and 'housekeeping'. Various expedients were adopted to relieve the situation, for example a number of subalterns of the 17/21 Lancers who had but a few months to serve before release were loaned to the RASC to carry out duties with transport and in the maintenance areas.

Some indication of the difficulties under which the Corps operated at this time can be appreciated from the following account recorded by the Military Liaison Staff at Salonika:

'After the Civil War was over, the convoys started in earnest. All over northern Greece they went, over mountain tracks covered in ice, through deep, swift-running rivers. Thousands of tons of all kinds of supplies were taken out to towns and villages and all kinds of country produce such as vegetables and tobacco brought back to Salonika. A great deal of wood was also brought back as coal was too scarce to be used except in hospitals. There was practically no wood of any description within seventy miles radius of Salonika as the Greeks from the city had walked out from there during the German occupation to gather fuel to keep themselves warm – a good illustration of the straits to which they were reduced.

Convoys would be held up by flooded rivers or snowstorms but they always got through. A typical instance of a flooded river crossing was when the jeep, which normally carried the convoy commander, could not cross because the water was too deep. He would pull to one side and allow the tank portees loaded with food to cross the river and he would wait until the portee breakdown arrived. The two H-bar channels would be let down from the rear of the portee and the jeep would run up them on to the vehicle. The portee would then pull up the H-bars, cross the river, let down the H-bars, down would come the jeep and away would go the whole convoy again. If the river was too flooded for the portees then the convoy would wait until the water subsided sufficiently.

Another problem arose when climbing steep and narrow mountain roads. The roads generally sloped and were particularly dangerous during the winter, covered as they were with ice and snow. Frequently, there was a sheer drop of several hundred feet on one side and with no wall or kerb to stop a skid; drivers always went up or down these roads with their driving side doors tied open so that they could jump out if necessary. Only on one occasion did a driver have to jump; he was unscathed but the remains of the vehicle that went over the precipice did not even have one useful spare on it when it was found!

Convoys were attacked in the mountains on quite a number of occasions by brigands; fortunately no drivers were killed although vehicles were frequently 'peppered'. Subsequently platoons of infantry rode in the convoys as guards and such attacks ceased.'

The operation of such convoys continued until May 1945 when all vehicles, stores and equipment were handed over to the Greek government.

Covering the same period, from October 1944 to May 1945, a record was kept by 44 Company RASC during the period they were maintaining a brigade group in the Western Epirus district:

The Company location was near the small fishing village of Amfilokhia at the base of the Gulf of Arta. Here, between two mountain ridges on a level piece of ground, a brigade maintenance area was established from which the brigade drew its rations and petrol. With one vital exception, all rations and petrol were brought to the maintenance area by Caique, the traditional Greek sailing vessel, from Preveza, a crossing of some sixty miles. Owing, however, to the absence of a cold store at Preveza, fresh meat came from Patras by lorry which also carried the mail. As can well be imagined with troops in such an inaccessible mountain region, having none of the amenities beloved by the British soldier, the daily arrival of the company meat and mail lorry was a vital matter to everyone.

This meat and mail lorry had an involved journey each day. Patras, the starting point, a medium-sized seaport relatively undamaged by the war, lay on the South side of the Gulf of Patras, at this point nine miles wide. The vehicle crossed the gulf on a landing craft and the route to Amfilokhia then traversed a very bad mountainous road to its destination, a distance of sixty miles. Across the route flowed the River Akheloos, in summer a stony river bed 200 yards wide with a stream in the centre. The Germans in their retreat had not forgotten to blow the original bridge and across the centre stream a pontoon bridge had been built by the Royal Engineers. This was to last until the winter rains and in preparation for these the largest Bailey bridge in Greece, 600 feet long, was being built spanning the river bed at a height of some 30 feet.

The winter rains broke much earlier than expected and on one wet day in October the pontoon bridge broke its moorings and the whole 200 yards of the Akheloos was a swirling, muddy mass of water resembling a Severn bore.

A hurried reconnaissance of the river was made and Brigade HQ offer of a small boat to reach the lorry on the opposite bank was hastily refused, especially by the composite platoon, who anticipated manning it. The Bailey bridge was by then completely spanning the river, but not bolted or decked in position. Sufficient chesses existed to lay a single track of planks across and this was done. By this time, it was dark and to avoid any undue risk to life it was decided to do no more that night. At first light the following morning, a volunteer party carried the meat and mail across and it was rushed to the maintenance area in time for the morning issue.

This system of sea, road and porterage lines of communication continued for fourteen days until the bridge was finally opened for jeep traffic and resulted in the following item appearing in the 4 Division newspaper, *The Quadrant*:

> 'When the pontoon bridge on the Akheloos was swept away in a recent storm this set the RASC a knotty problem by cutting the supply route to 28 Brigade. 44 Company RASC solved it by manhandling all supplies on stretchers across the unfinished Bailey bridge.

During 1946 the pressures of demobilization and the general economic condition of the country caused a steady withdrawal of forces from Greece. The 4 Indian Division was repatriated to India and the 4 British Infantry Division moved up to the north of the country. This left most of the interior without any British presence. The withdrawal of British troops continued until Britain finally relinquished her role in 1947 as the chief ally of the Greek

Government, with the USA taking her place. The Communists were not slow to take advantage of the withdrawal of British troops despite the peace treaty signed at Varkiza in February 1945. The King had returned to Greece on 28 September 1946. Up to this date, there had been an increase in nuisance attacks mainly on Greek police and government offices, and roads were mined and movement was liable to ambush. After the return of the King, the Communists who had re-organized their forces under the title of the 'Democratic Army' commanded by General Markos, proceeded to move in strength into different parts of the country. This was the start of a long drawn out civil war. After prolonged fighting the war finally ended with the victory of the Greek Government Forces late in 1949. During all this period there was a Corps representation in Greece but it was against a background of savage civil war and once outside Athens, still a sophisticated European capital, conditions were not very dissimilar to those of the early Balkan wars. To give some indication of the savagery of the fighting, the head of one particularly unpleasant Communist guerrilla leader was displayed publicly – minus his body!

Many atrocities were committed during the civil war including those perpetrated by the Communists on British servicemen during the Christmas 1944 fighting. During one of the major engagements during 'Operation Grammos' the Greek National Army lost 801 killed and some 5,000 wounded and the Democratic Army 3,128 killed with over 6,000 wounded. It was as a result of abandoning guerrilla operations and entering into 'set-piece' battles, together with the final closing of the Yugoslav frontier (as a result of a dispute between Tito and the Kremlin) that the Communists under General Markos made their error in strategy that enabled the Greek National Army to become victorious.

Ray Mullard, an RASC artificer, recalls that he landed at Piraeus from the *Empire Trooper* on the morning of Christmas Day 1946 and was among those taken from the docks to the Transit Camp in Rouft Barracks in Athens on railway flat wagons, their stay there was brief, for they were soon driven off in a 15 cwt truck to join the Independent Workshops attached to 770 Company RASC at Edam. On arrival they were taken straight into the dining hall where Christmas Dinner was in progress, with, Ray Mullard recalls, 'empty bottles everywhere.' The draft was given a very warm welcome.

The duties of this workshop included the maintenance of 770 Company vehicles together with Dodge and Chevrolet and other staff cars, Bedford trucks, jeeps, captured Opels, together with staff cars, the Bedford tankers of a petrol company, Austin K2 ambulances from 97 General Hospital RAMC at Kiffissa, fire appliances and other types of special to arm vehicles. The workshops area was composed of corrugated iron sheds and the whole area paved with granite, 'most uncomfortable on the back', Mullard recalls 'When working under vehicles – leather jerkins became prized possessions as they did prevent bruising'.

Early in 1947, 770 Company moved nearer to Athens and were accommodated in the pre-war Ford assembly plant with much improved working conditions. The men slept in the car showrooms on a polished marble floor!

By this time, the spares situation was becoming acute for some vehicles and it became commonplace for new silencers to be made out of corrugated iron sheets rolled flat by driving a truck over them, backwards and forwards on a smooth concrete surface. Such reconditioned engines that were obtained, came from the REME Workshops in Egypt at Tel-el-Kebir, but the RASC often had to rebuild them with what resources and skills were available.

Towards the end of 1947, 34 Company RASC moved South from Salonika to Alexandra Camp at Glyfada but was soon to leave Greece. Within a few months the RASC presence had devolved upon 331 Company, then back in Rouft Barracks.

Corps units left Greece as the formations were withdrawn, but one company remained: this was 331 Company (General Transport), which was the first RASC unit to land in Southern Greece from Italy in November 1944 as the 23 Armoured Brigade Company RASC. The Brigade was disbanded in 1946 but the Company remained in Southern Greece. On the disbandment of the brigade, application was made by the company to the GOC Land Forces Greece for the unit to retain the Brigade's 'Liver Bird' formation sign – this was granted and retained until the final withdrawal of the company and all British Forces from Greece in February 1950.

No account of the part the Corps played in the 'rebuilding' of postwar Greece would be complete without reference to the formation of the Greek Supply and Transport Corps. Prior to the Second World War the Greek Army was basically organized on the French model, with a Motor Transport Corps and Supply corps. When the Greek National Guard was raised in November 1944, a form of Greek Army Service Corps was started as a result of a meeting between the DDST, then Colonel Gahill, and some half-a-dozen officers of the pre-war Greek Army. The supervision of its formation was vested in an advisory staff and when the Greek National Army was formed to replace the Greek National Guard, the liaison staff of the British Military Mission was considerably increased and, at one time, had an S&T establishment of 39 officers and 158 other ranks. On 15 May 1946 a new Corps, the Supply and Transport Corps, was formed and this played a normal logistical part in the heavy fighting which was soon to be undertaken by the Greek National Army. To give some idea of the size of the new corps, it was created from a training and reinforcement depot, two base supply depots, two general transport companies, seven detail distribution depots, three composite companies for the National Guard, three divisional companies, three petrol depots and two bakeries. Although, after 1947 the United States took the major part, the British Military Mission continued its work. The RASC gave particular emphasis to pack transport and a well known Corps officer, Major (later Colonel) Jock Degnan arrived to advise on this subject. By February 1951, the Corps element of the Mission was reduced to some seventeen officers and other ranks under the command of Colonel (later Brigadier) W O Phillips, this British element being withdrawn when the Americans assumed complete responsibility early in 1950.

In November 1949, HM King Paul of the Hellenes officially opened the demonstration rooms of the Greek Army's S&T Training Centre: these represented a great step forward in their teaching methods. At the time it was recorded that 'there was a distinct flavour of Aldershot about many of the exhibits owing to the fact that many Greek officers had received training in British schools' and also the fact that the Chief Instructor at this Training Centre was Major D Norman, formerly an instructor at the RASC School at Aldershot. Among those present on this occasion was the DDST Greece, Colonel W O Phillips.

By the end of 1949, only one British battalion remained in Greece, the 1st Battalion Bedfordshire and Hertfordshire Regiment stationed at Salonika. On 22 January 1950 a farewell parade was held in Aristotle Square. On 4 February they were driven to the dock in Greek Army transport and sailed the next day.

So ended the associations of the British Army with Greece and with it those of the Royal Army Service Corps, whose members had played a major part in that country's post World War II recovery.

CYPRUS

THE TURBULENT HISTORY OF Cyprus stretches back over the centuries. It belonged to Turkey for three hundred years from 1571 until they surrendered its administration to Britain in 1878. Britain annexed it in 1914 and made it a colony in 1925.

After World War II the Corps was represented in the garrison on a small scale. The largest unit being 471 (Cyprus Volunteer Force) Company RASC (GT). Together with 695 Company RASC (Station Transport), they were busily engaged up to 1948 in supporting the garrison and moving illegal Jewish immigrants to and from the docks and camps on the Island.

As part of the reorganisation in 1949 these two units were disbanded and replaced by 17 Company RASC. By 1950 CRASC Cyprus District commanded 17 Company, 74 Supply Depot, 539 Field Bakery, 252 Command Petroleum Depot and the Barrack Stores. In 1954 consequent on the impending move of GHQ Middle East Land Forces from Egypt, the Corps presence began to grow. A detachment from 58 Company arrived from Egypt. New accommodation was built at Dhekelia for a MT company, a supply company, a supply depot, static bakery and the petroleum depot was rebuilt. Captain (now Colonel) A D Crabtree RASC recalls that when he took over command of 136 Supply Platoon RASC at Wolsey Barracks, Nicosia in March 1955 he rationed 1,100 including RAF. Only a few months later the figure had risen to 25,000–30,000. There were three reasons, the Cyprus Emergency which started on 1 April and the build up of reinforcements, the arrival of GHQ Middle East Land Forces and the Suez Operation.

This build up required a complete reorganisation of S and T Services. New HQs and units were formed and others arrived complete from Egypt and the UK. CRASC Cyprus District became DDST Cyprus District. 1 Transport Column RASC was formed at Famagusta, CRASC Cyprus (West) at Limassol. 40 Company RASC (MT) was at Dhekelia, 42 Company RASC (MT) under canvas on the airstrip at Limassol, 65 Company RASC (GT) in Golden Sands Camp at Famagusta. At Episkopi, where the new accommodation for GHQ was under construction, three new units appeared, 45 Independent Transport Platoon RASC, Field Supply Platoon RASC Episkopi and Field Bakery Platoon RASC Episkopi. Other units who served in Cyprus during this hectic year included 138 Air Supply Platoon, 63 Company RASC (Parachute Brigade) and a much increased Barrack organisation.

The Corps sustained a number of casualties as a result of terrorist activity during 1955 and 1956. Staff Sergeant Cripps was killed by a time bomb in Kykko Camp Sergeants' Mess on 18 November 1955 and three days later Sergeant Steel was killed by a gun shot. A further six RASC soldiers were wounded in the closing stage of 1955. Lance Corporal Saville and Driver Evans of 42 Company, Drivers Bell and Murray of 65 Company and Drivers Potts and Brag of 45 Independent Transport Platoon. On 14 January 1956 Driver Boatman of 65 Company was shot in Famagusta. In November of that year Warrant Officer Class 1 Middleton was wounded outside his married quarters and Private Coulter was killed in Limassol. These were the casualties to the Corps. Considering the numbers involved and the many incidents of ambush and bombings that occurred, our casualties were light. It says a great deal for the high standard of performance and discipline of our soldiers, many of whom were young National Servicemen.

The Corps activities during this time were not confined to the logistic support of the garrison and RASC units regularly acted in an infantry role. In June 1956, Second Lieutenant Warren commanding a party of 25 men in the Troodos mountains during Operation Foxhunter and 63 Parachute Company were particularly commended for their hard work.

Operation Foxhunter was, however, cut short as a result of the sudden change of events in the Middle East and the subsequent Suez operation. On 29 October, 63 Company were packing their kit and unit equipment preparatory to moving to Egypt. By the following weekend the Company was ready to move and on Sunday 4 November sailed from Cyprus in convoy for Port Said. The Company returned to Cyprus towards the end of December when the British Forces handed over to United Nations forces and withdrew. The Corps part in the operation is recorded in the chapter on Egypt.

It was during Summer 1957 that 3 Division was deployed from UK to Cyprus, bringing with it 1 Company RASC, commanded by Major RC Thorpe RASC (later Brigadier). He recalls:–

'1 Company was encamped in unserviceable tents on the Kermia Plain. The time was approximately 0200 hrs. when a burst of automatic fire alerted the assembled brethren and I was called. On investigation we found that Driver Rose had dropped his Sten gun – the kind that fire by themselves. As Rose said "if we had proper weapons, instead of antiques" – he got no further as a shout from the dark interrupted with the statement "If we had proper ... soldiers we could all get some ... sleep. Give 'im a spear, Sir'.

On the 3 August 1958, during a period of sporadic outbursts of violence, Lieutenant Colonel Collier, then CRASC, was murdered whilst watering his garden at his hiring in Limassol and in the Autumn, the seventeen year old son of Sergeant L A Preece of 65 Company was killed by terrorists. This brutal murder was felt throughout the unit following on, as it did, the shooting of two women in Famagusta. The mood of the men at that time was difficult to contain; however, discipline prevailed.

In mid 1958 proposals for a workable constitution were put forward together with a plan for the government of Cyprus in association with both Greece and Turkey. This was however rejected by both the Greek Government and the Greek Cypriots. Finally, following a meeting in Zurich and a conference held in London an agreement was signed on 19 February 1959 by the United Kingdom, Greece, Turkey and the Greek and Turkish Cypriots whereby Cyprus would become a Republic. As a result, under the Cyprus Act of 1960 the Island became, on 16 August 1960, an independent sovereign republic.

Following the announcement of the date for independence the army commenced its withdrawal into the Sovereign Base Areas, for the United Kingdom retained full sovereignty and jurisdiction over two areas – Akrotiri and Dkhekelia and the use of roads and other facilities.

The run-down of the military presence in Cyprus had continued throughout 1959, and 42 Company was heavily committed to troop carrying operations and clearance of ordnance stores – part of the run-down operation. On 1 May 1960 40 Company was reformed under the title of 40 (Infantry Brigade Support Transport) Company.

As the military presence was reduced a major reorganization became essential. In March HQ RASC Cyprus (West) was redesignated HQ RASC Cyprus and assumed responsibility for all RASC matters, the HQ was established in Dhekelia as this was destined to be the future principal logistic base.

17 Company and 136 Supply Company were disbanded in May 1960 and the designation and role of 58 Company changed from the GHQ Company to a General Transport Company.

To give an increased heavy lift capability 94 Independent Transport Platoon (Heavy) was formed. Equipped with 10 ton vehicles, driven by civilians, the platoon was employed principally on dock clearance work.

58 Company, though still based in Episkopi, was largely civilianized with Cypriot drivers. The only military drivers that were retained were for C in C Near East and GOC in C Near East Land Forces.

In 1962 a major reorganization of British Forces in Cyprus was started. A result of this was that 40 company in Dhekelia was disbanded. Cyprus was sad to see 40 Company go, as it had over many years achieved a reputation for being 'second to none' in the sporting scene.

On 1 October, 58 Company started to move from its ragged accommodation in Episkopi, staging at 'Half Way House' to the richer accommodation in Dhekelia previously occupied by 40 Company. Two military platoons of 40 Company were taken over by 58 Company.

The two military platoons retained their roles, which was as field force units in support of the infantry battalions in Cyprus. The platoons frequently visited North Africa with the battalions, crossing the Mediterranean by LST, complete with all platoon vehicles.

The rest of the Company at Dhekelia consisted of a transport pool of 57 various vehicles which were, in the main, driven by civilian drivers. In addition, 58 Company also took over 94 Independent Platoon which became a detachment, based at Ayios Nikalaos. At Episkopi a small detachment, under command of a Staff Sergeant looked after the remaining Army elements.

A few days before Christmas 1963, there was a shooting incident between Greek and Turkish Cypriots in Nicosia. This put a match to the fuse, and by Christmas Day fighting between the two communities had spread all over Cyprus.

The offer of help from the British Forces was accepted by the Cyprus Government, and on Boxing Day a Truce Force was

[By courtesy of Central Office of Information]

A Troop Commander of 30 Regiment RCT briefing his section commanders on exercise in Cyprus in 1967.

established in Nicosia. The Force was commanded by GOC Cyprus District, Major General P C F Young CBE. As a result of this 58 Company's military strength was working round the clock, mostly on maintenance convoys. A report written at the time describes the efforts of the Company:

> '58 Company are on detail in all parts of the Island, unloading, off-loading, going-up, coming back and receiving innumerable compliments all the while'.

Two drivers, Drivers Keeler and Cassidy in particular were commended for their efforts whilst on ambulance duty. In addition to their normal transport duties 58 Company manned infantry type patrols and visited RASC units in Dhekelia. The Company was also required to provide a daily standby platoon. The crises continued for almost four months, however the rapid deployment of reinforcements from UK greatly eased the load taken by 58 Company. The Commanding Officer, Lieutenant Colonel B Edridge

RASC, was responsible for relief operations. Much credit for the success of the operation was given to the RASC.

During the period of the emergency, 7 Company RASC on emergency tour from UK commanded by Major T A Danton-Rees (later Lieutenant Colonel) with a platoon of 1 Company RASC under command and assisted by vehicles from the resident 58 Company, worked night and day alongside the Cyprus Field Park Squadron RE (commanded by Major Mike King RE) to complete King's Field Airstrip at Dhekelia. This airstrip was designed to allow RAF Beverley aircraft to land and resupply the garrison in the event of other airfields outside the Sovereign Base Area being out of use. The construction of this airstrip involved the moving of some 65,000 tons of earth.

1965 was the year of the implementation of the McCleod Report. In this period of major rationalization the role and commitment of the Corps changed dramatically. The principal change was the take over of the Port units from the Royal Engineers and the handover of supply units to the Royal Army Ordnance Corps. The units that were affected in this way were:

2 Petroleum Depot
4 Supply Depot
Barrack Services   }Handed over to RAOC
Army Fire Brigade
Royal Engineers Movement Control Troop
Cyprus Port Unit, Royal Engineers   }Taken over by RCT
71 Lighterage Troop Royal Engineers

On its formation in 1965 the role of the RCT in NEARELF was given as:

a. To control the executive function of movement for the Army and to advise the Staff on all Transport matters.
b. To control the operation, administration, training and discipline of the RCT units in Cyprus, and to be responsible for all Army Driver training and civilian transport contracts.
c. To provide first line transport support for those non-field force Army units which do not possess their own transport.
d. To provide second and third line transport support for the Services in Cyprus, including the RAF.
e. To direct the movement of military cargo through the port of

Famagusta and to provide military personnel for Air Movement duties with RAF Akrotiri.

f. To operate and maintain all military marine craft in Cyprus and also maintain those on loan to the RAF in the port of Tobruk.

With some modification this remains the basis of the charter of the Royal Corps of Transport in Cyprus (the commitment in Tobruk obviously lapsed with the British withdrawal from that area).

The establishment of the RCT in Cyprus after reorganization was to have been for a Regimental Headquarters, with two transport squadrons, a Port Squadron, and an Air Despatch Troop (to be detached from a UK Air Despatch Squadron). However, further political change resulted in greater troop reductions and the loss of one MT squadron.

In December 1965, 471 Lighterage Troop, which had been taken over from the Royal Engineers, was disbanded. Some of the troops were absorbed into 59 Port Squadron whilst others returned to UK. To complete the reorganization of the port, the Joint Services Port Unit was formed from 484 Movement Control Troop RCT and 20 Movement Unit RAF and placed under command of the OC 59 Port Squadron. At this time the 'Mole Project' at RAF Akrotiri was completed. The mole gave the Port Squadron the ability to deliver stores direct to Akrotiri should the need arise.

September 1967 saw a further run-down of 58 Squadron with the two military troops being reduced to one. The resurgence of ENOSIS (union with Greece) groups on the Island emphasized the need for greater efficiency in the internal security responsibilities of the Regiment. To this end operational procedures were constantly reviewed and revised.

By early 1969 it was clear that HQ RCT was not able to perform its staff function to the full from Dhekelia. It was therefore moved to be collocated with Headquarters Near East Land Forces (NELF) at Episkopi.

The advent of containerization was an important milestone for the RCT in Cyprus. Throughout 1970 trials were conducted to investigate how the Army could utilize this revolutionary method of transportation and indeed it was the Army who introduced containers into Cyprus for the first time. Initially there were many restrictions which needed to be overcome as the specialist handling equipment which is so much part of 'the system' was not available in Cyprus. The ingenuity of the military port operators managed to overcome the many and varied problems with which they were faced.

On 10 June 1971, 59 Port Squadron was renumbered as 10 Port Squadron thereby keeping alive the older traditions of the more senior squadron. At this time the squadron was commanded by Major Richard Moore RCT.

During the period 1971 to 1974 life for the RCT in Cyprus was fairly busy without any great military or political tension. In early July 1974, President Makarios made a request to the Government of Greece for the permanent repatriation of 650 Greek mainland officers serving with the Cypriot National Guard. An immediate result of this was the coup d'etat on 15 July and the Turkish invasion on the morning of 20 July. 7 Squadron RCT, who were again in Cyprus on a 6 month tour supporting the United Nations forces, were closely affected by the subsequent unrest.

Their camp was situated only 100 metres from Nicosia airport, and consequently, they had a grandstand view of the take over by the Greek National Guard and National Contingent. Their operations were disrupted by road blocks throughout the city and they found themselves rescuing RAF families and transferring them to Akrotiri. Life began to return to normal routine until 0430 hours on 20 July when it was announced that invasion by the Turkish forces was imminent. By 0500 hours the airport was under attack by Turkish aircraft and this continued until 23 July. Only one bomb actually landed in the company lines fortunately causing no damage. On 23 July the Garrison Sergeant Major on his way to the Sergeants' Mess from SHQ found his way blocked by a section of Turkish soldiers. However when they realised that they were on 'UN Territory' they soon withdrew.

Soon the battle between the Greek and Turkish forces began in earnest. The camp was caught in heavy crossfire with Greek positions firing between the camp buildings from the fourth floor of the Airport Terminal building. The four-man guard from B Troop, put on a newly-made gate, found itself under extremely heavy fire and later shared its building with two Greek tanks! A cease-fire was arranged after an hour. The OC, Major John Herbert RCT, and other officers and men of the squadron, played a very important part in the long and successful negotiations over the occupation of Nicosia Airport that involved very delicate political and tactical problems.

[By courtesy of PR HQ NEARELF]

Empire Gull *on the mole at Akrotiri.*

That afternoon A Troop sent out a convoy to get the UN second line ammunition from Dhekelia. It passed many Greek road blocks and Greek soldiers short of ammunition. That day also saw a small detachment sent to Kyrenia as part of the force, known as Gillforce, that assisted with the evacuation of British families and holidaymakers to HMS *Hermes*. The squadron later took over the Dome Hotel in Kyrenia and there protected about 700 Greeks and British from the Turks deployed in the area.

The following three weeks saw a general easing of the situation, although throughout the Island there were many localized violations of the cease-fire. During this time the squadron was employed full-time on resupply and humanitarian work and was also committed to Gillforce. The peace talks in Geneva broke down on the evening of 13 August 1974 and once again the United Nations forces prepared for a possible outbreak of violence. At 0500 hours on the morning of 14 August the air attacks began again. On this occasion the targets were further from 7 Squadron's camp.

Throughout the three days of this phase of the war, A Troop

Lcpl Stewart with his UNFICYP refrigerated vehicle.

[By courtesy of HQ UNFICYP]

continued to make its daily ration run to Dhekelia, escorted by the 16th/5th Lancers, and assisted in the evacuation of RAF and UN families who had returned to Nicosia after the initial cease-fire. Among their many experiences they watched a Turkish battalion, with armour and air support, attack a Greek fortified position only a mile away. This battle lasted for two days with the Greeks putting up stiff resistance before withdrawing. The Turks now established their forward positions in the vacated area along the UN boundaries.

The second cease-fire was arranged for 16 August and once more the Squadron resumed its normal role of resupply and humanitarian work. All members of the squadron gained invaluable experience of battle conditions over the six weeks and worked exceptionally hard with little rest. It was a tour they will never forget and quite different in character from the gentle and congenial work they had expected in the Mediterranean sun!

Brief mention was made at the beginning of 7 Squadron's account of the 1974 Cyprus Emergency that they were on a 6 month tour supporting the United Nations forces on the island. This United Nations force (UNFICYP – United Nations Forces in

Cyprus) was established in 1974 and was deployed in a buffer zone between the Greek and Turkish factions. Military contingents from Denmark, Britain, Canada, Sweden, Austria, Ireland and Finland together with police contingents from Australia and Sweden make up the UN force. Britain provides the logistic support and this includes a RCT transport squadron. To meet this commitment a squadron is deployed from UK (and on occasions from BAOR) on a 6 month tour to drive the white painted UN vehicles and wear the pale blue UN beret and badge. The list of RCT squadrons who have periodically carried out this UN task is long and, for fear of omitting a unit, is not listed here. Basically the squadron deploys to Cyprus with two transport troops and a small REME Workshop detachment. It has two major roles and to carry out the task divides into an X Troop (Heavy Troop), providing transport support for all the UN troops in the buffer zone and Y Troop (Light Troop) giving support of HQ UNFICYP with staff cars, Land Rovers, minibuses, coaches and ambulances. This UN commitment continues today and provides a very welcome six month overseas tour away from the bleaker climate of UK or BAOR.

To return to the chronological sequence of the Corps story in Cyprus, the Turkish invasion in 1974 resulted in the island being partitioned into the Turkish Federated State in the north east of the Island (some 36% of the total) and the Federal Republic of Cyprus (Greek-Cypriot) in the south west. Inevitably in between were the UNFICYP forces manning the so called 'Green Line' which now divides the Cypriot communities.

The Joint Services Port Unit (JSPU) and 10 Port Squadron both had to evacuate their locations during the hostilities and were sadly unable to return to their 'historical homes' after partition. 10 Port Squadron therefore moved to the harbour at RAF Akrotiri and the JSPU, after a brief stay at Dhekelia, moved into Limassol New Port when this opened in 1975.

58 Squadron had been heavily involved during the 1974 hostilities both with the evacuation of British nationals from the north and subsequently in assisting local authorities in providing basic amenities and provisions for the thousands of Greek-Cypriot refugees who fled to the south during the war. In January 1976 the Squadron moved to RAF Akrotiri as part of the contraction into the Western Sovereign Base Area leading, as was then planned, to ultimate withdrawal from the island. They left behind them one civilian transport troop and a Central Servicing Station which

formed the Transport Support Unit (TSU) for Dhekelia Garrison whilst the detachment at the other end of the island also changed its name to a Transport Support Unit to support Episkopi Garrison.

The withdrawal from Cyprus did not take place as planned and, with the exception of the RHQ, the basic Regimental organization has remained unchanged since 1976. RHQ, apart from being the HQ of 30 Regiment RCT was and is also Transport and Movement Branch in HQ Land Forces Cyprus and this created difficulties over location. In April 1978 the Headquarters of 30 Regiment was divided into two elements with RHQ in Akrotiri and Transport and Movement at Episkopi. Since this created serious manpower difficulties Transport and Movement Branch was subsequently moved to RAF Akrotiri to join the RHQ only for both of them to return, on the appointment of a new CO, to Episkopi on 1 April 1981. The current organization of the Regiment is RHQ/Tpt & Mov Branch at HQ Land Forces Cyprus in Episkopi except for the SO3 Mov and ATLO Staff at RAF Akrotiri, 10 Port Squadron at Akrotiri with the JSPU at Limassol under command and 58 Squadron also at Akrotiri with under command the two Transport Support Units at Episkopi and Dhekelia respectively.

The establishment of the Regiment has also changed considerably over the years. There are now less than 100 British officers and soldiers in 30 Regiment whilst the remainder of the establishment is made up of approximately 250 locally employed civilians. However no history of the Corps in Cyprus would be complete without particular reference to the civilian staff. Many have served with the British Forces since the end of World War II and some, particularly the seamen in 10 Port Squadron who came from Famagusta, are refugees from the north. Others have continued to serve the Regiment despite numerous changes of location and it is not uncommon for some of them to live in places like Nicosia and have to travel up to 3 hours daily in each direction to and from their places of work. The civilian staff undoubtedly form one of the most loyal and long serving workforces in any RCT unit world-wide.

Whilst there have been no major operations on the island since 1974, the Regiment has frequently been involved in other operations using Cyprus as a staging post. These include the evacuation of European nationals from Iran in February 79, Op

Agila (Southern Rhodesia monitoring force) from December 79 to March 80, the evacuation of refugees from Lebanon in June 82 and Op Hyperion, the mounting of the Multi-National Force in the Lebanon, in February 83. Additionally UK based units have continued to provide roulement squadrons on 6 month tours to provide transport support to UNFICYP based in Nicosia.

Apart from the support it provides for Cyprus based units of both the Army and RAF, the Regiment has continued to provide assistance to visiting units and ships. 58 Squadron provides MT support for UKLF units who continuously exercise on the island and 10 Port Squadron has, on numerous occasions, provided berthing, lighterage and ferry facilities to RN, Army and Royal Fleet Auxiliary vessels ranging from 55 foot yachts from the Joint Services Adventure Training Centre at Gosport to *HMS Bulwark*. There have also been various instances when the Regiment has provided support to local civilian authorities the most notable of which was the rescue of a seriously ill sailor from a visiting cruise liner in April 79. This was carried out by RPL 05 captained by Staff Sergeant M J Williams in severe weather conditions when no local sailor would put to sea and resulted in the crew of five receiving the Commander British Forces Cyprus Commendation for outstanding seamanship.

Whether serving with the resident 30 Regiment RCT or with the UN forces, the RCT soldier in Cyprus has one of the few remaining opportunities to serve in generally pleasant Mediterranean climatic conditions. It is to be hoped that this opportunity will continue for many years to come.

CHAPTER EIGHT
East Africa

KENYA

AMONG THE DRAFT OF TWENTY RASC Officers and a hundred other ranks which disembarked at Mombasa from the Union Castle liner 'Caernarvon Castle' in September 1945 was the officer destined to take command of 39 Company East African Army Service Corps and he summed up his first impressions as 'after the conditions prevailing in the UK and NW Europe at the end of the war, life in East Africa seemed like paradise'.

On disembarking, the draft travelled to Nairobi on the narrow gauge railway, operated by the Kenya & Uganda Railways; it was slow but extremely comfortable, the wood burning locomotives being driven by white engineers with African stokers. The journey from the coast to Nairobi took most of a day, the line passing through arid country which rose, en route, to some five thousand feet.

After interviews at HQ East Africa Command, the draft was

[By courtesy of PR HQ East Africa Command]

An RASC subaltern in the Kings African Rifles.

posted to different units and Major (later Lieutenant-Colonel) R W Armstrong RASC returned to Mombasa to join 39 Company EAASC – a four platoon Company with one platoon detached at Tabora in Tanganyika.

A few weeks later the unit moved to Moshi at the foot of Mount Kilimanjaro, the highest point on the Continent of Africa – 19,340 feet above sea level, where, 'the evenings were a delight with the setting sun reflected off the snowy peak. Cool breezes wafted down the mountainside giving relief after the hot days'. The Company remained only a short time at Moshi before moving to Athi River which was but a dried up wadi, except during the rainy season. Here the unit was joined by the detachment from Tanganyika which arrived with a quarter of its vehicles in tow. Six were immediately written off at £5 each as they were completely beyond repair.

Finally, 39 Company was stationed at Thika, some sixty miles north west of Nairobi when, until it was disbanded in January 1946, it was engaged on station duties for the KAR Regiments in

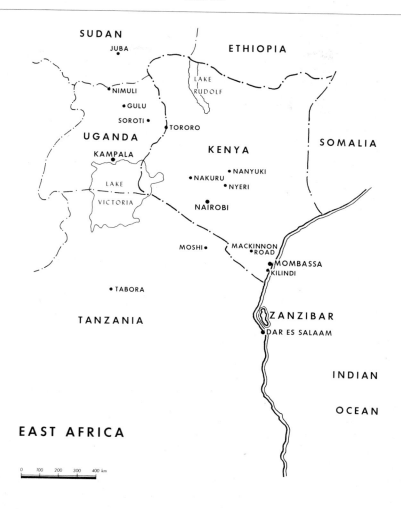

EAST AFRICA

0   100   200   300   400 km

the area. The CO was then posted to command 42 Company
EAASC with its HQ, Workshop and two platoons at Tororo with
detachments at Kampala, Nanuki and Juba. The Company's
primary work was the movement of East African troops then in
course of repatriation. These troops were mostly from the East
African Labour battalions which had been deployed throughout
Cyrenaica and Libya and had travelled up the Nile by barge as far

as Juba and then moved on through the staging camps there and at Nimuli, Gulu and Soroti. It was not uncommon for up to a thousand troops to be in the Tororo transit camp from where they were dispatched for discharge and return to their tribal areas. This work completed, 42 Company was disbanded, Major Thomas returning to the Depot at Nairobi where some four thousand African soldiers were awaiting discharge. Numbers gradually dwindled and the Depot was eventually disbanded in September 1946.

At this time, Water Transport services were essential to supply the needs along the Command's very considerable coastline as well as the adjacent islands. To meet this requirement, personnel were sent out from England from the RASC Water Transport Training Wing to form a cadre for the training of locally enlisted personnel. A number of boats were requisitioned for training purposes until deliveries could be made from the UK and South Africa of motor fishing vessels of 46-tons displacement, 48-ton high speed target towing craft and a large number of small beach landing craft.

Choosing the African crews presented problems and initial results were not too successful; however, sufficient recruits came forward from the coast and lake districts 'and within four months' recorded the first OC, Major C F Hill RASC, 'the unit was working smoothly as a Water Transport Company'.

The unit's value was soon proved in that it formed the only link between the mainland and the fortified islands in addition to carrying out the routine duties of target towing for coastal defence artillery, boarding launches for security officers and embarkation staff officers and supplying coastal areas with food when the rainy season made roads impassable to MT.

The East African Water Transport Company carried out vital work most efficiently. One of their greatest efforts was an unescorted voyage by four small 46-ton motor fishing vessels from Mombasa to Alexandria, a journey of some three thousand miles via Mogadishu, Dante, around Cape Guardafui, Aden, Port Sudan and the Suez Canal – where they were needed for urgent local transport work. The voyage took twenty four days and enough food, water and fuel was taken on board at Mombasa for the whole trip.

The command of the East African ASC units was by British officers and NCOs who were superimposed on matching establishments of African NCOs; this was necessary because the African soldiers were for the most part illiterate; few understood English and some not even Swahili.

A problem at this time arose from the complications of the ration scales. In Tororo, for example, there were special rations for Europeans, Asians – Hindu, Moslem and Goanese, African Christians and African Moslems. There were also an Italian POW company and two Chinese carpenters.

With this immediate post-war background, East African Command moved into its military future which involved the construction of the large base at Mackinnon Road, north of Mombasa, as the centre for the Strategic Reserve.

Of the RASC Companies assigned to the Mackinnon Road project, the first to arrive – from Palestine – was 51 Company which, whilst awaiting arrival of its vehicles, was accommodated at the Port Reitz RAF Camp where it was soon joined by another company, 4 Armoured Brigade Transport Company which had moved down from Palestine to Qassassin in the Canal Zone and re-equipped on an ad hoc establishment made up of a range of Class 1 vehicles of all types but with a predominance of tipper trucks. 'We finally organized ourselves', recalls Lt Col Ivor Thomas, then second-in-command of the Company, 'and had several hundred splendid National Servicemen posted to us and a very high quota of National Service officers of a particularly high calibre'. This unit sailed from Port Said to Mombasa in the *Empire Windrush* and on landing moved firstly to the RAF Camp and thence to tented accommodation near Killindi Harbour.

51 Company, when united with its vehicles, moved to Mackinnon Road, then but a small railway halt some sixty-five miles from Mombasa on the road to Nairobi and consisting of a disused aerodrome in the midst of a large tract of arid scrub desert with the nearest fresh water at the Tsavo river some seventy-five miles further westwards to Nairobi. The river water was not so fresh due to the silt; it was dull red in colour, the home of many crocodiles and much frequented by hippopotamus and elephants.

Sappers were already at work constructing pumping stations, pipelines and filter plants to ensure an adequate water supply to Mackinnon Road. The tank transporters of 51 Company RASC were immediately committed to carry all forms of earth-moving equipment and road construction plant. The whole Company was quickly and fully engaged in transporting labour, stores, water and

POL to sites. A Supply Point was also established and 4 Company RASC delivered fresh rations daily from the CSD at Mombasa. The task of the Corps was made extremely difficult by the road conditions in the area, badly corrugated earth roads made impassable in wet weather until improved a year later.

It was during these early days in the construction of the Mackinnon Road base area that personnel lived in banda type huts, just wooden frames covered with mats of dried coconut palm leaves with a door at each end. Early one day, in broad daylight, a full grown lion walked in the door of one of these huts and passing through slowly, went out of the door at the other end. It is said that the men in the banda stood perfectly still and watched the lion go through; however, within five minutes, the camp was on the hunt and not a single weapon was left in the armoury. The lion was seen many times and fired at without success. It was afterwards said by many in the Camp that the lion was less dangerous than some of the over enthusiastic big-game hunters. Finally, the RSM crept from a vantage point and made his way slowly along the side of a banda; before he reached the corner, the lion's head appeared. With his rifle at the ready and a round 'up the spout', the RSM squeezed the trigger; the lion fell dead due to this lucky shot!

4 Company had by this time received its ten ton vehicles and 242 Company also arrived from Palestine and relieved 51 Company. Thousands of tons of stores were moved each week. A Petrol Depot, with kerbside pumps, was built at Mackinnon Road together with a large barrack store and an abattoir, to be followed by a large Supply Depot with its own railway sidings, a cold store and a hospital. Nissen huts were erected for use as messes and dining rooms. Playing fields were cleared by bulldozers, then came a camp cinema, a large NAAFI and married quarters. Despite the initial conditions, the ensuing problems and setbacks, a great new camp had been constructed in less than two years.

Three months after regular runs had commenced on the Mackinnon Road, Lieutenant Colonel Ivor Thomas was posted from 4 Company to Athi River some twenty-five miles from Nairobi on the Kajiado Road in the Game Reserve to form an EAASC Depot and Training Centre. This was a large hutted camp – very isolated – a former 'open plan' prisoner of war camp for Italians, subsequently occupied as the Kenya Regiment Depot. The Camp was finally taken over as British reinforcements arrived to fill the key posts. The task of the Depot and Training Centre was to raise and form nine Special Establishment Transport Companies with British and African Officers and NCOs. Following basic training in foot and arms drill, they would be retrained as three ton vehicle drivers. The word 'retrain' was used as it was anticipated that ex-drivers MT would be enlisted and therefore this should be a reasonably elementary task. However, at this time, the ill-conceived Groundnut Scheme had just been launched, with wage scales and allowances far more attractive than those offered to the soldier. In consequence the Army found itself with a far greater number of completely raw recruits than had been envisaged. However, among those that did enlist were a number who had seen active service in Burma as NCOs with the King's African Rifles. They were immediately appointed drill instructors with the task of turning the raw recruits into soldiers, which they did with enthusiasm. The British element for the nine new companies – officers, WOs and NCOs – were slow to arrive from the UK. The younger subalterns were all National Service officers; they were described as excellent material, delighted to be in such a splendid country.

Problems in organizing normal courses in driving instruction resulted in the introduction of a safari run system which involved sending out a convoy of a number of trucks filled with some twenty to thirty men to each vehicle, led by an officer and a British NCO, on a journey of some thousand miles over lesser bush roads. This form of training actually worked, with the Askaris getting some two to three hours continuously at the wheel, but, recorded Lieutenant Colonel Ivor Thomas, it was too much for the young officers fresh out from home. The mental strain of five to six days out in the bush, miles from anywhere, the hazards of the driving conditions and with the troops indulging in 'camp fire parties' in the evenings. In consequence, additional British officers and NCOs had to be found to go out with each driver training convoy.

As soon as sufficient men were trained to form a Company, an OC was appointed and British and African Company Sergeant Majors were posted in. The unit formed up at the Depot where a ceremonial passing-out parade was held. Having taken over all the Company documentation from the Depot and drawn one or two vehicles from Nairobi, the new unit was ready to take its place in the life of East Africa Command.

In 1948, the DDST East Africa Command was Brigadier F A Shaw OBE who interviewed the draft of six RASC officers from the

QM fitting a Tarbouche.

[By courtesy of PR HQ East Africa Command]

Depot Battalion, then at Thetford, Norfolk, who disembarked from HMT *Scythia* at Mombasa in August. They were replacements for those whose service in Kenya dated from 1945–46. Among them was Major M F Horton RASC who was posted to the CSD at Nanyuki, then under command of the CRASC Nairobi – Lieutenant Colonel Lauder. This CSD supplied all units in the Northern Area having in turn been supplied by rail from the SRD at Kahawa.

By 1950 nine companies of the EAASC had been formed. The East African ASC Depot and Training Centre was closed down and, in a modified form, was amalgamated with the Kenya All Arms Depot at Nakuru. At this time, the EAASC Companies were in support of the six King's African Rifles Battalions which made up 30 (East Africa) Brigade.

Although East Africa Command, composed of the colonies of Kenya, Tanganyika and Uganda together with the Island of Mauritius, was a GOC-in-C's appointment, it had by 1952, become but an outstation of Middle East Command. The most Senior Staff Officer was at Colonel level and following the abandonment of the Mackinnon Road Project, the main task of the Command became the training of battalions of the King's African Rifles for service in Malaya. The only regular infantry in the

350

Command were colonial.

During the immediate post-war years, those serving in Kenya became aware of the existence and aims of the Mau Mau organization, an anti-white and anti-Christian body which had, as its aim, the driving out of the country of Europeans and all other foreigners by means of intimidation, murder and finally general revolt. The movement was supported almost exclusively by the Kikuyu tribe, although the Embu and Meru Tribes were, to a lesser degree, also involved. The Kikuyu, the largest and most intelligent of the Kenya tribes, originated in the Fort Hall district and spread northwards to Nyeri and to Kiambu in the south. Early in this century the Kikuyu in the Kiambu district was decimated by a smallpox epidemic which coincided with a severe drought and a plague of locusts. This resulted in the surviving Kikuyu abandoning the area and returning to the Fort Hall district. Subsequently the abandoned land was taken over, in all good faith, by white settlers, they being unaware that the Kikuyu considered that it was still their territory. Some years later, Kikuyu began to drift back to their former areas of residence in Kiambu, only to find the settlers well established. The latter were anxious to get more labour for their development projects and were willing for returning Kikuyu to settle down as their working tenants. It was these events which, as the years went by, formed the basis for the Kikuyu claims that the Europeans had stolen their land.

From 1949 onwards, ceremonial oath-taking ceremonies were conducted within the Kikuyu tribe; the oath was so worded that once taken there was very little risk of its disclosure to the authorities. In its early days, membership of the movement was voluntary but from 1950 onwards, pressure was brought on all Kikuyu to join. This pressure included not only physical violence and damage to property but even acts of torture and murder.

The movement grew and grew as its aims and objects became better known throughout the mass of the population and so progressed throughout 1951. In the following year the Mau Mau came out in the open to plan and murder people opposed to its aims and objects. At the same time some Europeans were murdered by Mau Mau fanatics.

The Kikuyu tribe which had sired the movement followed their convictions that the Europeans had stolen their lands in Kiambu and that the Missions which had been established were interfering with the traditional customs of the Kikuyu. Both these grievances were exaggerated and elaborated by Mau Mau agitators who, in gaining a hold over the tribe, made full use of the powerful influence of the oath-taking ceremonies.

These events led the Governor of Kenya to declare a State of Emergency in October 1952 and 1 Battalion Lancashire Fusiliers was flown down to Nairobi from the Canal Zone in support of the civil power in view of the serious situation which was developing. Political leaders suspected of being involved or assocated with the Mau Mau were arrested. Among them was one Jomo Kenyatta who, in December 1964, became the Country's first President when Kenya became a Republic.

As the months went by, there was no improvement in the situation and many murders were committed. Two well known and loyal tribal chieftains were assassinated and in March 1953 the Lari Massacre took place when, with the utmost brutality, over eighty Kikuyu, two thirds of them women and children, were murdered.

The Mau Mau activities were such that even the force of 39 Brigade of three British Battalions and 70 (East African) Brigade, composed of six battalions of the King's African Rifles was inadequate and sixteen months later, in September 1954, 49 Infantry Brigade with two battalions under command; The Royal Northumberland Fusiliers and 1 Royal Inniskilling Fusiliers were also sent to Kenya. A member of 4 KAR at that time was Idi Amin who was a Sergeant, later the President of Uganda. Attached to each British battalion was a detachment from the Kenya Regiment to help with language problems and to impart local knowledge. All members of this Regiment were local volunteer Europeans with a Regular permanent cadre.

A forest warfare battle school was established near Nyeri and here, in their new jungle green kit, the newly arrived troops set about their task of learning to operate in the territory of the Aberdare Mountains and Mount Kenya. The undergrowth below the tall trees was often of such density that it necessitated hours of hacking with machetes to clear a track through the forest. Higher up the mountain slopes the troops found themselves in the area where bamboo grew in profusion. There were also the moorland areas with great tufts of jungle grass. In addition to the hazards of nature, the troops were liable to encounter wild life such as rhinoceros and elephant, buffalo and hyena together with all the smaller species with which the country abounded.

The British battalions were, it was recorded, faced with 'a very fifth-rate enemy compared with the terrorists in Malaya. However, they possessed certain advantages over the security forces. They knew the country backwards, were quick and silent movers in the forest, had a fine intelligence service and were difficult to bring to battle'. The main problem of the security forces was to find the Mau Mau for as they became strong and more active, the Mau Mau withdrew into the Aberdare and Mount Kenya Forests or dispersed into the Kikuyu Reserve leading a normal existence until again concentrating to perpetrate a fresh act of terrorism.

In 1954 an independent field Squadron RE was sent to the Northern Frontier district of Kenya bordering the Republic of Somalia which, for some time, had been a troubled area with bands of armed Somalis crossing the border, driving out the inhabitants of numerous villages and taking possession, leaving the displaced occupants to move deeper back to safety in Kenyan territory.

In order to facilitate control of the area by the Kenyan Army and Police, the RE squadron was given the task of constructing a causeway across the Lorian swamps to replace one which had collapsed and also to construct a new road, a hundred miles long from the end of the causeway to Wajir through what was virtually virgin bush. Both tasks had to be completed, before the onset of the seasonal rains, in two months from the start.

The base camp for the operation was set up at Dadaab, an abandoned trading post, a few miles from the works site, only five miles north of the equator. In face of possible attack from the 'Shifta', as the raiding bands were called, the trading post area was converted into an extensive closed defensive perimeter.

The bulk of the stores and supplies for the project and the maintenance of those engaged were carried by the RASC but it was necessary for the convoys to be guarded by armed escorts. These were drawn from 3 RHA, 2 Scots Guards and 1 South Staffordshire Regiment.

The Aberdare Forest is made up of three belts, the tree belt rising to some 8,000 feet of semi-tropical forest and luxuriant undergrowth; the bamboo belt for the next 2,000 feet, the bamboo growing from thirty to sixty feet high; then came the moorlands, from which the peaks rose up to 11,300 feet covered with round tussocks of grass. The Mount Kenya Forest area was similar, rising to the base of the 17,000 feet Mount Kenya and then there was the difficult country of the Gura and North Mathioya River valleys running through steep, thickly wooded gorges.

The very nature of this country had led in the operations against the Mau Mau to the employment of an Air Despatch Detachment RASC, a small independent unit with some thirty British soldiers based on 37 Supply Depot East African Army Service Corps at Kahawa which, in September 1955, was commanded by Captain (later Lieutenant Colonel) Paul Fear who had succeeded Captain John Spurway. At that time, the role of the unit included provision of air despatch crews flying in RAF and Kenya Police Reserve aircraft and in packing supplies and stores at the depot to be despatched by the infantry battalions to their patrols in the forests on the Aberdares and on the slopes of Mount Kenya. Following the visit of the DST from UK, then Major-General Sir William Roe, the units flying role was given priority and the unit enjoyed an exciting few months with the Kenya Police, accompanying the pilots in Piper Tripacer and Cessna aircraft, free dropping bundles at below treetop level into small jungle clearings. The method employed involved opening the door of the aircraft, the air despatcher keeping it open with his right leg whilst balancing as many packages as possible on the leg ready for ejection either on a shout or a tap on the shoulder from the Senior Despatcher. In one fly-over DZ only one or two field packs could be dropped and so several round trips had to be carried out up to a maximum of six per day. Between September and November 1955, during the height of the operations, 20,000 lbs of free drops were made – 803 packs weighing 25 lbs each.

During Operation Bullrush mounted by a battalion of the Rifle Brigade, with the object of flushing out a large band of Mau Mau from a retreat they had established around Lake Naivasha, the Air Despatch Detachment flew in support of the operation in RAF Valetta aircraft. For his services at this time, Sergeant Vassey RASC was Mentioned in Despatches.

Although supply by air was required in certain areas, there was also the need for employment of animal transport and the services of 67 Animal Transport Company EAASC was available for all the battalions operating in the high altitude forests and mountains, but with only one Company to call upon, there was a need for economy in calling on their services.

A vital supply role was carried out by this EAASC company,

then commanded by Captain M F M Horner RASC, over terrain varying between mountain, moorland and dense forest, criss-crossed by precipitous gorges and tortuous rivers, at heights rising between 12,000 to 14,000 feet, operating from its base at Nanyuki, carrying rations, water, weapons and ammunition on the backs of its pack ponies and mules.

In 1955 most of the Mau Mau had taken refuge in the Aberdare ranges and the area of Mount Kenya following Operations 'Hammer' and 'First Flute', two large-scale actions which dealt heavy blows to the terrorists and in which 67 Company EAASC had been employed, but it was not known how the animals would react to high altitude load carrying. The first few days on the mountains were anxious ones for the unit, the animals grew lethargic and showed signs of losing condition. Gradually, however, they became acclimatized and, with the aid of an occasional tot of rum in their grain, completed their tasks successfully without suffering any ill effects, although when operating at these heights their loads were reduced from the normal 160 lbs to around a hundred.

It has been said that a loaded mule or pony can only get up a steep slope if a man can also do so without going down on his hands and knees, but in the Western Aberdares, one section of 67 Company ascended a precipitous 200 feet slope which no man could have climbed without using his hands. The animals took four hours to reach the top of the escarpment but they made it, their only aid being that they were shod with 'caulkins' – shoes with the ends bent to form studs.

Animal transport was subsequently attached as required to infantry battalions in sections of twelve. When allocated to a unit, the detachment reported for duty in three ton lorries, three animals to a lorry, complete with saddlery and seven days fodder.

The Battalions found animal transport invaluable for supplying isolated detachments and particularly the long range patrols and this led to short courses in pack transport and animal management being held for infantry NCOs at the Animal Transport Company HQ.

At the same time, a number of RASC subalterns were attached for short periods to KAR patrol groups in the forests where they learned the skills of the infantrymen.

In August 1953, Lieutenant (later Major) T E L Strange arrived in Kenya from 3 Division, then in the Canal Zone, with 77

Company RASC destined to support the operations against the Mau Mau. 'Our lack of experience in the driving conditions soon became very obvious particularly when the rains started', he recorded. 'The rate that vehicles were written off was alarming but this was not entirely the fault of the drivers; on corrugated "murrain" roads, the old three-ton trucks would literally shake to pieces'.

Lieutenant Strange commanded an RASC platoon in the operations against the Mau Mau for just under two and a half years, engaged in moving infantry around the Rift Valley to the Aberdares, to the Mount Kenya area and in the tribal areas around Fort Hall and Nyeri. During this period, the platoon covered over a million miles. 'From a young officer's point of view,' he subsequently wrote, 'the job was ideal as we were invariably deployed away from Company HQ. We would go up-country for anything up to six weeks at a time, completely self-contained, carry out a number of moves and then return to Kahawa, repair our vehicles, clean ourselves up and then go off again'.

The work of the Platoon was not without its hazards and it became the practice to put all the bits that became detached from the vehicles in one truck and on return to Kahawa, these were handed over to the LAD who would see what could be repaired. These items included superstructures, petrol tanks, spare wheel carriers, jerrican carriers, propshafts and other such items. On one occasion a vehicle that had been charged by a rhinoceros was brought back with part of its horn embedded in the back of the vehicle having penetrated the petrol tank and floorboards!

During the year, one platoon of 77 Company was involved in the operation centred on Nairobi which resulted in about 15,000 people being put into the Langata Detention Camp, the platoon being in support of the Royal Northumberland Fusiliers in the cordon operations.

In August 1955, Major W C Rees RASC joined GHQ East Africa Command and was detached to Nyeri to control the air supply to troops in the forests, a task carried out by a composite platoon of 77 Company RASC (MT). Their task was to pack supplies for free drops and to make these drops from Pacer aircraft flown by Kenya Police reservists; experienced pilots, most of whom in normal times being employed by East African Airways. It says a lot for the skill of the pilots that though they flew low enough to clip the tree tops, not a single aircraft was lost or badly damaged. The packing material was very elementary and consisted mainly of wood shavings, sawdust and hessian. It was a matter of trial and error in packing and despatch methods, but successful in that the troops received their supplies.

At the end of 1955, the ADST was Lieutenant Colonel H Lincoln Jones MBE RASC, his staff being Major T F B Low RASC, Major L Wright RASC, Major J R Butters RASC, Major (QM) W E Evans RASC and Lieutenant T Brattin RASC. The Fire Adviser was Warrant Officer Class 1 I Taylor and the Chief Clerk Warrant Officer Class 1 K Moore. 77 Company RASC commanded by Major W P de Beer RASC was at Kahawa, 92 MT Company EAASC at Buller Barracks, Nairobi was commanded by Major W R Orton RASC, 37 Supply Depot EAASC commanded by Captain J E C Stedham RASC was also at Kahawa and 70 Supply Depot, under command of Captain P J Davis RASC was located at Nanyuki. There were also 67 (AT) Company EAASC commanded by Captain M F B Horner RASC, the Air Despatch Detachment was commanded by Lieutenant (later Lieutenant Colonel) P Fear RASC, Major (QM) F G L Squibb was O i/c Barracks and the Warrant Officer in charge of 16 Army Fire Brigade was Warrant Officer Class 1 H Broadhead.

At this time, over seven thousand British troops were engaged in the operations against the Mau Mau together with some seven hundred RAF personnel, thirty members of the Women's Services and 22 Colonial Troops. In addition, there were 6,700 soldiers of the King's African Rifles together with 162 Somalis and 1,250 Arabs. To sustain this force, the Supply Depot at Kahawa issued a daily average of 4,800 rations to British troops and 2,500 to Africans. From the Depot at Nanyuki, 11,600 British rations were issued each day and 18,400 for Africans, whilst at Nyeri 20,500 rations were issued daily for African troops and a further 982 (average) to British.

70 Supply Depot EAASC, then at Nanyuki, situated on the equator on the slopes of Mount Kenya, was a small unit comprising a British officer, warrant officer and six ORs, an African Sergeant-Major, twenty African other ranks and several Asian clerks. The Depot served the varying number of units operating in the Nanyuki-Nyeri area and in the Northern Frontier Province. The climate in this area was described as 'idyllic', the depot being located at almost 7,000 feet, it was never too hot and it was necessary to have log fires after sunset. Within a half-hour's drive

in any direction, one could see herds of game ranging from giraffes to baboons and in the forest areas, it was not unusual to encounter buffalo, rhino and elephants. Frequent bush fires were a hazard, particularly when they approached the POL Compound and the local KAR battalion was often turned out to beat out the flames, which never got nearer than a hundred yards of the perimeter fence.

And so the Army continued to operate against the Mau Mau, pursuing them relentlessly in their hide-outs and wherever they conducted their terrorist activities; this lasted for four years. During this time, as a result of the successful operations which systematically destroyed the fighting elements of the terrorists, the British military commitment gradually decreased. The last British battalion to see action, the King's Shropshire Light Infantry, was withdrawn from Kenya in November 1956.

At the end of 1956, 70 Supply Depot was disbanded, following the rundown in the strength of the forces that had been engaged in quelling the Mau Mau activities but the unit reorganized to continue its role as the Composite Platoon of 93 MT Company EAASC, subsequently redesignated 93 MT Company KAR. The only practical difference between the Depot and the Composite Platoon was that civilian labourers were replaced by KAR Infantrymen.

In 1958 new barracks were built eight miles west of Nairobi at Kahawa and HQ 24 Infantry Brigade arrived to take occupation where they remained until July 1961 when the formation moved at short notice to Kuwait, 2 Coldstream Guards leaving behind a two company detachment. 19 Infantry Brigade arrived from Colchester to take over 24 Brigade's commitments in Kenya.

It was also in 1958 that Air Despatch provided support for the Mount Kenya Expedition during the International Geophysical year and during this time a world record altitude supply drop was established when supplies were dropped from a Pembroke aircraft from just over 17,000 feet to an area on the Lewis glacier at 16,300 feet above sea level.

Among the units which arrived in Kenya at that time was 60 Company RASC which was stationed 6,600 feet above sea level at Gilgil in the Great Rift Valley, the largest valley in the world. From here the Company exercised in the Kenya highlands, the coastal strip and in the desert conditions of the Northern Frontier Province. The Company also served outside East Africa at Sharjah in the Persian Gulf and in Aden and later formed part of 24

Infantry Brigade Group in Kuwait where it took over civilian transport of all types. April and May 1961 saw the Company employed on famine relief and again at the end of the year following the heaviest flooding ever known in the country. The Company was taken to East Africa by Major K H Crockford MC RASC who was succeeded in 1962 by Major C H Bavin RASC.

At this time, the ADST East Africa was Lieutenant Colonel V H Band RASC, the OC 92 MT Company KAR was Major Geoffrey Williamson RASC and Major Richard Blunt RASC followed by Major (later Lieutenant Colonel) Anthony Carr RASC commanded 93 MT Company; with the same Company were Captain (later Major) Robin Barton RASC whilst the TCO was Captain (later Colonel) John Bidmead. With 77 Company RASC (MT) were Lieutenant (later Colonel) Mike Finnis and Lieutenant (later Major) Tim Strange, whilst Major Robin Bulmer and Captain (later Major) John Huthwaite were then the OC and second-in-command respectively of the Animal Transport Troop KAR.

By 1961, two years before Kenya became an independent State within the British Commonwealth, and three years from its transition to a republic and the withdrawal of all British troops in 1964–65, the RASC element of the force was composed of the ADST and his staff at HQ East Africa Command in Nairobi, 60 Brigade Transport Company RASC stationed at Gilgil in support of 24 Infantry Brigade, 16 Air Despatch Company located at the RAF Station at Eastleigh and a Transport Office, a Barracks Office and a Supply Depot in Nairobi. In addition there were 91 and 92 Companies EAASC at Buller Camp, Nairobi, 93 Company EAASC and 'A' Troop (Animal Transport) at Nanyuki. Detached from 93 Company at this time was an independent Transport Platoon stationed at Jinja in Uganda in support of 4 KAR, the OC was Captain (later Colonel) P Mears RASC subsequently suceeded by Captain (later Major) A S Parkin RASC.

In the latter part of 1961 and early 1962, the Air Despatch Company working with the RAF were engaged in supplying civilians in those areas of Kenya and Tanganyika which had been isolated by flood waters. The ADST, Lieutenant Colonel G M Williams RASC, was the military representative on the Kenya National Disaster Committee. Supplies to the stricken areas were organized in cooperation with the Maize Marketing Board. Free dropping from RAF aircraft was the main method of delivery.

[By courtesy of RCT Museum]

RASC display at 1962 Army week East Africa Command.

Also in 1962, His Royal Highness the Duke of Gloucester, our Colonel in Chief, visited Corps units in Kenya and suitable events to mark the occasion were held. Kenya was an ideal country to display a wide range of Corps activities set in some of the most interesting country in the world.

It was in March 1963 that the first ever air maintenance exercise was held in Kenya and, for the first time, HQ East Africa Command moved out into the field, being located in the Northern Frontier District. 24 Infantry and the KAR Brigades were fully committed and the RASC established and controlled the airhead at Isiolo where Beverley aircraft loads were airlanded or airdropped for subsequent repacking and air dropping to forward troops from Beverleys and single or twin Pioneer RAF aircraft. Askaris of 91 Transport Company were taught some elementary packing and quickly learned to recover and sort air despatch equipment. The

Airhead Maintenance Area troops fed well, supplementing their issue diet with local game.

In 1963, the ceremonies marking Kenya's independence passed off without incident but some discontent in the ranks of the Armed Forces of the then independent territories of East Africa led to mutiny among elements of what had been the proud and efficient King's African Rifles. The main trouble spots were in Tanganyika and Uganda but there was also an incident within 5 KAR at Lanet in Kenya which was suppressed by 3 Royal Horse Artillery. In Zanzibar there was also considerable civil unrest.

The ensuing tension led, as a precautionary measure, to certain Askari manned units being encircled by British troops. Among these were 91 and 92 Transport Companies EAASC at Buller Camp which provided all the vehicles for resupply, Barrack Services, conveyance of school children and numerous other administrative tasks. In consequence, service support in Nairobi virtually ceased. However, the CRASC and the two Company Commanders convinced the GOC that their Askaris were loyal and the security cover was removed and the African personnel of these two units loyally and uncomplainingly returned to their duties.

During this period of tension, resupply was mainly by local purchase and this was carried out by an RASC Supply Depot Sergeant and an Officer and Warrant Officer of the Army Catering Corps who travelled as far afield as Dar-es-Salaam, Mombasa, Tabora and Zanzibar. There was also a major problem in arranging local procurement of POL and the positioning of 50-gallon drums of aviation fuels for use by light aircraft.

The rundown of British forces in East Africa was accelerated during 1964 in step with the creation of a wholly Kenyan Army. The CRASC, Lieutenant Colonel (later Colonel) K Andrews, supervised the disbandment and redeployment of the RASC units and the creation of the new Kenya Army Service units. 91 Transport Company EAASC was disbanded whilst 92 and 93 Companies EAASC were absorbed into the new force.

The supply tasks were slowly handed over but the procedure was somewhat complicated by the announcement of the reorganization of the Services in the British Army. It was however clear that the residual problems and advice regarding Supplies, Barrack Services and POL would be best dealt with by the RAOC element of BATTKEN (British Army Training Team Kenya) after February 1965 although this was five months in advance of the transfer of the responsibilities for supply to the RAOC from the RASC on the formation of the Royal Corps of Transport.

Some elements of the new Kenya Army were soon deployed in the Northern Frontier District of the country to combat infiltration by the Shifta. This area was frequently cut off by floods after the rainy season. Consequently, the resupply of these frontier area based troops became the first real challenge to be met and the ex-RASC transport units were hard pressed. They met their commitments with the help of the RAF.

16 Air Despatch Company RASC and 60 Mechanical Transport Company RASC were finally withdrawn and sent to Aden. However before 16 Company left, air despatchers formed Movement teams and after a short handover instructional period from RE Movements, assisted in the movement of Service personnel and families by rail and air. So the British Army left what, in Victorian days, had been 200,000 square miles constituting the Protectorate of British East Africa.

MAURITIUS

MAURITIUS, AN ISLAND OF 705 square miles, rising from the Indian Ocean some five hundred miles east of Madagascar, a Crown Colony for 158 years, and became an independent state within the Commonwealth in March 1968. The Corps has had links with the garrison dating back to its formation in 1810. Up to 1939, the garrison comprised a Heavy Battery RA and a Fortress Company RE with detachments of Royal Signals, RASC, RAMC, RAOC and RAPC.

In the immediate period after World War II, the Mauritius Garrison was serviced by 72 Supply Depot EAASC located at Vacoas commanded in 1953 by Major Robinson-Horley RASC who was succeeded by Major F T W Quelch-Wools RASC. The Depot was located on the plains in the middle of the island and was staffed by a small number of British soldiers plus an MT section of Mauritian enlisted personnel. The installation carried ninety days reserves of tinned foods and had contracts for the provision of fresh vegetables and fruit together with a small fresh meat section. An overflow of stores was held in a warehouse in Port Louis.

The Supply Depot could not be considered an aggressive unit but displayed outside the office were two antique French cannon which had been restored on instructions from the OC, including the manufacture of wooden cannonballs by the Depot carpenter. One morning, the OC decided that his newly restored weapons should be proof tested and one of the cannons was turned towards the golf course, charged with thunderflashes and loaded with a wooden cannonball. Unfortunately the trajectory was high and the charge more powerful than anticipated. The cannonball consequently went further than intended, over the compound wire and landed near a surprised Governor of Mauritius, Sir Hilary Blood GBE, KCMG having an early morning round of golf. It is not recorded whether the OC shouted 'fore', or whether the Governor considered this a novel way of paying compliments. The cannons were considered to have passed their proof test!

Mauritius was regarded as a congenial and pleasant station and, wrote Edward Faughman, one time RASC Depot Superintendent at Vacoas, 'There is no doubt that the greatest and most potent charm of the island was its people.'

RHODESIA/ZIMBABWE

RHODESIA, DESCRIBED AT the turn of the century as 'a vast region extending from the Transvaal and the Bechuanaland Protectorate to the Congo Free State and Lake Tanganyika and divided into North Eastern and North Western Rhodesia, north of the Zambezi and Southern Rhodesia, south of the River' – covers an area of some 580,000 square miles.

Southern Rhodesia was subsequently united with Northern Rhodesia and Nyasaland into a federation which lasted from 1953 to 1963. Nyasaland then became independent in 1964, as Malawi, and Northern Rhodesia as Zambia, whilst in November 1965 Southern Rhodesia made a unilateral declaration of independence. Rhodesia, as Southern Rhodesia was then designated, comprised Matabeleland, Mashonaland and Manicaland, in the part of the territory lying south of the Zambezi River.

Rhodesia's independence led to stormy relationships with Britain and to civil disturbances within the country. Finally, on the initiative of the British Government, a situation was reached which led to a 'ceasefire' between the rival factions and the deployment of a Commonwealth Ceasefire Monitoring Force in December 1979. This was to remain until the holding of elections to decide on the country's future in the following March. The operating of the Force was acknowledged as 'a unique and highly successful military undertaking which only the British Army could have done'. The part played by the Corps in this unique operation provides an excellent example of the flexibility and initiative displayed by junior officers and soldiers contending with conditions outside the realms of normal logistic patterns.

Major General J H B Acland CBE, who was appointed Military Adviser in overall command of the monitoring force, left Heathrow aboard a VC 10 in the first week of December taking with him Sergeant M Brennan RCT who had for some time been his staff car driver; on arrival they drove out to the initial talks with the leaders of the Zipra and Zanla organizations and the Rhodesian Forces.

It had been envisaged that the force would be administered

entirely by the Rhodesians and the RCT contingent was only a dozen men to carry out the initial reception of the force and thereafter to provide a liaison link between Force HQ and the Rhodesian Forces. However, as soon as the recce party arrived, led by Major J A Collar RCT, the Force Transport and Movements Officer, it was revealed that the Corps would be required to fulfil a wider role in the supply of a force scattered in 'penny packets' all over the country. The other members of the party were Staff Sergeant I Kidd, Sergeant Steeley and Lance Corporals Kennedy, Morton and Wilson, all from 29 Transport and Movements Regiment RCT.

The RCT contingent had no load carrying trucks but, as most of the roads in the bush areas had been mined and were liable to be washed away in the imminent rainy season, it became obvious that supply by air would, in any case, be necessary. In consequence, the RCT element of the force was increased by a forty-man detachment from 47 Air Despatch Squadron. Major Richard Morgan, then OC of 47 AD Squadron RCT, also went out to Rhodesia as OC of the Airhead Maintenance Area as the requirement for re-supply reached considerable proportions. He was subsequently awarded the MBE for his services during the operation.

The Lancaster House Agreement had set midnight of 28/29 December 1979 as the start of the ceasefire between the rival factions, to be followed by a seven day period when the guerrilla forces were to come in to sixteen assembly points where elements of the International Monitoring Force were stationed. By this time, 1500 officers and men from the UK, Australia and New Zealand had arrived in Rhodesia together with 180 vehicles with trailers and similar tonnage of freight. The force was rapidly deployed to thirty-nine different points in the bush where the detachments were required to monitor the arrival of the Rhodesian and Patriotic Front forces. This was done over a four day period starting on Christmas Day. By the end of the week, some 20,000 guerrillas had assembled, mostly with only what they stood up in. The Rhodesians then announced that they could not cope with the feeding and general maintenance of such numbers.

The re-supply problems, complicated enough just to cope with the needs of the 1500 strong Ceasefire Force, became an appalling prospect when, almost overnight, their responsibility jumped to some 23,500 men and women. Rations, cooking equipment, fuel, tents, blankets, clothing, medical supplies and even water were required. These stores began to pour into the Salisbury maintenance area where a hangar was soon filled together with four large marquees. Using seven C130 Hercules transport aircraft and six Puma helicopters, over a thousand tons of these supplies were prepared, packed, loaded and either dropped or airlanded by the air despatchers of 47 Squadron RCT working round the clock until 21 January 1980. During this operation 'flying low level for several hours, the view from the Hercules aircraft was breathtaking' wrote Lieutenant S Govan RCT, 'the miles and miles of bush bisected by occasional lazy rivers and dotted here and there with villages made an unforgettable sight.' Frequently, crocodiles were seen in the muddy water and in the clearings, elephants and rhinos . . .'

By then road transport had been organized by the RCT Force Transport and Movements Officer, eighty vehicles had been hired – trucks and trailers of different capacities and age. The vehicle fleet even included a furniture removal van and one enormous articulated 40-foot container-bodied truck pulling another 4-wheeled twenty-foot trailer. These vehicles and those of hired civilian contractors were used whenever and wherever road conditions allowed.

The distribution of all the basic stores and equipment was completed by the end of January and a road distribution pattern settled down to a weekly delivery round of thirty-five tons to fourteen areas from suppliers' warehouses in three main centres. Between the beginning of February and the end of the month, the RCT Movements organization in the Airhead Maintenance Area, located at the New Sarum Airforce base on the opposite side of the airfield to the civil airport complex, handled a hundred and sixty supply flights.

A few days before the elections to decide on the future government of Rhodesia, a contingent of four hundred British Police arrived in Salisbury to carry out the policing duties at the polling stations. Among them was PC Ranson, the father of Driver Ranson of 47 Air Despatch Squadron RCT who was on the tarmac to meet him. Polling lasted for three days starting on 27 February. It resulted in a massive win for the Zimbabwe African Nationalist Union – ZANU – led by Mr Mugabe. For the next few days the RCT with all other members of the Ceasefire Monitoring Force were confined to their accommodation whilst Mr Mugabe's chanting and singing supporters moved in crowds through the city.

However, the task of the Monitoring Force then being at an end, a speedy withdrawal was effected, the Corps Movement Staff being among the last to leave, an inevitable consequence of their role.

CHAPTER NINE
West Africa

In Burma in World War II, the Royal West African Frontier Force (RWAFF) had faced the greatest test in their half-century of existence, and their qualities of gallantry, loyalty and cheerful endurance had been tried as never before. They emerged from this test with great credit and enhanced traditions. That they were able to undertake operations of a kind no other formation could attempt was due not only to the qualities of the troops in general but to the magnificent work of the Auxiliary Groups who carried their head loads for long distances in most appalling country.

The use of carriers by West African formations in the hill jungles of Burma made them far more mobile than those relying on mules or other transport and, when supplied by air, remarkably flexible.

After the end of operations in May 1945 the first to embark for West Africa was 81 (WA) Division from India, but it was not until April 1946 that units of 82 (WA) Division began to take ship at Rangoon. The Division, however, did not complete embarkation until early in September.

The long time awaiting shipping was very trying for the Division, but there was not so much as a breath of an incident or lapse of discipline. In order that the Auxiliary Groups, transport and supply units of the African Colonial Forces (ACF) who took part in operations in Burma shall not be forgotten, the transport and supply order of battle which supported the two West African divisions is set out below:

81 Division	*82 Division*
1, 3 and 4 Auxiliary Groups	2, 5, 6 and 7 Auxiliary Groups
816, 817 Divisional Transport Company	825, 836 Divisional Transport Company
1780, 1781, 1782 Composite Platoons	1784, 1785, 1786 Composite Platoons
1, 4, 8, Field Butchery Sections	26, 29 Field Butchery Sections
Divisional Pack Bullock Company	

Note: An article entitled 'The Gallant Auxiliaries' was published in the February 1947 edition of the Corps Journal.

Reduction of the West African Forces began in 1946. The ACF ceased to exist and the gunners reverted to the RWAFF while reconnaissance regiments, engineers, signals and the ancillary units including transport and supply units, were disbanded.

The RWAFF in Nigeria was reduced to four battalions but, after a few months, 5 Battalion was reformed. In the Gold Coast all the war-time battalions disappeared, but 3 Battalion was reformed after disturbances in 1948. In Sierra Leone only 1 Battalion remained; the two Gambia Battalions were reduced to one company which formed part of the Sierra Leone Battalion and was at one time commanded by an RASC officer – Major (later Lieutenant Colonel) I H W Bennett.

The wartime RWAFF training school at Teshi, near Accra was retained to ensure common doctrine and methods of training in the units of the four contingents.

Nigeria and Gold Coast reformed both engineer and signal units as well as the ancillary services including West African Army Service Corps (WAASC) sufficient for the peacetime establishment. These units, descendants of the wartime ACF did not form part of the RWAFF but carried the name of the territory in which they were raised. In Sierra Leone, where prior to 1939 a small

RASC detachment was located, a Coastal Defence Regiment and the WAASC survived the return to peacetime soldiering.

The four colonies which together made up West Africa Command, had certain special features which need to be remembered in relation to the supply and transport services. Widely separated, each a distinct entity with its own problems, they had no rail communication between them and little road connection. The only practical means of getting from one to the other was by sea or by air. Nigeria is three times the size of the British Isles and the length of the coast line from the Gambia to the Niger about 2,000 miles. The spreading of the English language on the Coast where many major tongues and distinctly different dialects were spoken enabled Africans from whatever territory to communicate with one another.

The RASC standard component organization, introduced in 1941 was adopted by the RWAASC. At Headquarters West Africa Command the DDST was a Colonel and at this point it need only be said that, with the exception of Gambia, the WAASC was everywhere where the RWAFF was involved.

Apart from resettlement problems there was an incident at Lagos in 1948 when men of the WAEME Workshop staged a 'mutiny'. This was quite orderly: the troops simply fell in and marched on Government House. They were intercepted by the GOC who had no difficulty in getting them back to barracks. The trouble was mainly due to bad administration, including indifferent relations between officers, British NCOs and the African personnel. There was some unrest about the same time in an ordnance depot and in 88 Company WAASC, both at Lagos. The units of the RWAFF however remained contented and loyal in spite of the fact that HQ West Africa Command had blundered by insisting on the WAASC providing standard rations irrespective of the fact that, for instance in Nigeria, Northerners could not stomach southern forms of food and vice versa. West Africa was still a place where the improbable was normal and the impossible occurred often enough to make life interesting!

Major (later Brigadier) R A Nightingale RASC wrote the following account of his service in West Africa starting in 1950 which provides a facinating picture of service in Nigeria and Sierra Leone. It is of particular interest to the present generation of young officers and soldiers who are not likely to be posted to service of a similar nature. It also goes a long way to explain the dedicated attitude of the British Army in carrying out its duties in a British Colony.

'It all began at Blackbushe, a small airport in the north east corner of Hampshire, where a party of 34 military personnel and dependants, all bound for Lagos, emplaned in a civilian charter Viking aircraft operated by the Airwork company.

The first leg of the flight was to Gibraltar where overnight accommodation at the Rock Hotel had been arranged. The following day was a gruelling experience, particularly for the aircraft crew and dependants. Take-off was at 04.00 hrs local, our destination being Kano in Northern Nigeria. The aircraft had to refuel twice on this leg. This entailed landing on rough desert airstrips where the precious liquid was hand-pumped into the aeroplane from standard 44 gallon drums and while this operation was taking place the passengers found what comfort they could from the blistering heat under Arab matting shelters. That night was spent at a staging post, adjacent to Kano airfield which was really primitive, after the luxury of the Rock the night before, but everyone was too tired to complain. Take-off the following morning was delayed by a dust storm, almost two hours behind schedule we were eventually airborne, dry skinned, cool and heading for Kaduna where the aircraft was to refuel. On leaving the plane I was greeted by a particularly smart captain who introduced himself as 'your Northern District representative' and then went on to say that he was responsible for two transport platoons and elements of what until recently had been a supply platoon. Now up to this point I had thought my next appointment was to be supply orientated; had not the DST himself said experience of supplies was what I needed most. Anyway Kaduna was all of 600 miles from Lagos, so how could this fellow be so sure? Soon I would discover that the 'drums' in this part of Africa are frequently more reliable than any No 19 Wireless Set.

It was a very weary group that clambered aboard for that last leg of our journey. Shortly after take-off a sedative was needed for a lady who throughout the whole flight had steadfastly refused to be separated from the fur coat with which she had been advised to travel and now had become most agitated as to what might happen to her prized possession once she got to Lagos. As a result this passenger missed the first sighting we had of the Niger and the city of Ibadan and was eventually handed over, still fur wrapped, to a somewhat bewildered husband. Having discharged my final duties as the OC plane I was taken to the WAASC Officers' Mess at Apapa.

Waiting to go out to Nigeria I had a craving for the means to acquaint myself on the whole subject of the West Coast – a sort of interpretation of legends, climate, tribes, religions, territories, disease – in fact everything likely to help me survive in what not so very long ago had been referred to as the 'white man's grave'. It transpired that all officers about to serve with the RWAFF were introduced to an official mentor. Mine, a charming senior officer, the father of a lieutenant-colonel in my own Corps, had last served on the Coast when it was customary to wear a spine pad and topee by day and for officers to dine nightly in serge mess kit with a hard boiled shirt. Nevertheless he proved to be a wise councillor on matters concerned with the administration of native troops and his advice helped sort out many of the conundrums which lay ahead. Since all four colonies by now were family stations the incidence of 'woman palaver' was almost extinct.

My introduction to the social life of Lagos came in the form of an engraved 'stiffy' inviting me to dine at the home of the Colonel A/Q, the other guests being my new CO and his wife. There still had been no indication as to what my future employment was to be and it was not until the ladies had withdrawn that I learned my first task would be to preside at a Court of Inquiry being convened to look into alleged corrupt administration within a depot situated on the outskirts of Lagos. It was pointed out how this experience should give me a valuable insight into the sort of things that could occur.

The African eyed all military depots with envy, for stored beyond that perimeter fence was everything other than a gramophone that he needed to make the good life. Apart from the standard military bicycle, which legend would have, could not be pedalled fast enough to escape from a lion, there was a ready market waiting for everything and an abundance of 'brothers' to spirit away in a slumberous moment anything that could be had from iron work to desiccated yeast.

Courts have an irresistible attraction for Africans, they are occasions to be prolonged, embellished and enjoyed. The one that I was about to open was certainly no exception. At this particular depot a British store-keeper was in charge of each section. Apart from being responsible for receipts, care of stock and keeping the records he also supervised the selection of items that units indented for, their packing and dispatch; and in every respect was a general factotum and frequently a very harassed man. Indigenous assistants were a mixed blessing, for if honest, they were usually dull and often lazy, and if smart and intelligent, could be clever manipulators.

Their manner could be most disarming, and, what with their ingratiating ways and plausibility, they were generally difficult to cope with.

Ten days were spent studying the skilfully constructed chain of connections which an experienced hand had built up over an extended period. My senior member, an 'old coaster', initially welcomed an opportunity to come down to Lagos but then caused a furore when he learned that the daily proceedings were to continue far beyond the hour he was accustomed to take his sundowner. The junior member had an ambition to become a missionary, clearly he had never seen a cloven hoof and as the days passed I wished that I, too, were capable of thinking the best of everything and more particularly the best of everybody. This young officer experienced considerable difficulty over concentrating his mind on the evidence being given by a seemingly endless supply of witnesses, preferring, it seemed, to try and convert the Court Imam, a most majestic looking individual dressed in the manner which showed he had made a pilgrimage to Mecca.

The star witness to appear was a young negress. On entering the room she turned to a person whose presence was required by the rules of procedure and addressing him said: 'Hello honey – what's they all bin doin' to you?' Then turning to the court she angrily exclaimed: 'You'se all mighty proud now dat you'se done got me.' On being called to order she broke into tears and continually wailed: 'I'se done bin wronged – I'se done bin wronged.' By this time court orderlies and almost everyone present were in a fever of excited enjoyment, and the din they set up with their laughter and noisy comments about the prospect of some master being found out, held up the proceedings for quite a while. The 'old coaster' did little to help, whenever I ventured a line of questioning he was quick to explain, always condescendingly, that 'If I had known such and such, I surely would have realized how pointless my line of questioning was.' Fortunately opportunity arose that allowed me to deflate the fellow. Having been tasked to check a fist full of write-off vouchers and confirm their general correctness I then for some reason or other ran a double check on the documents and came across one voucher which purported that a 1½ cwt anvil had been – 'chopped by white ants'.

A few days later the proceedings were hand carried to District Headquarters. It was a beautiful morning and walking back to the officers' mess I met the CO: he was in spanking form and had obviously enjoyed his early morning exercise. He was intending to visit 88 Company and if the Inquiry was now completed would I like to go with him. The time taken to reach the company was spent discussing the problems that bedevilled transport operations in the Colony – the British element was more often than not under-posted, a situation exacerbated by the need to grant mid-tour recuperative leave. Although there was a captain at Kaduna the next senior officer, a lieutenant was nominally in command and also acting as the administrative and transport officer. In Lagos, the daily requirement for all types of vehicles invariably exceeded availability. A shortage of major assemblies, repair parts and traffic accidents accounted for the considerable number of vehicles that were off the road. Vehicle maintenance was based on the sixteen daily task system.

Apart from the shortage of British officers and NCOs the situation in the out-stations was generally much better. Reinforcements would shortly be arriving from the UK and there was the possibility that a captain could be cross-posted within the District also the first African to be commissioned into the WAASC was about to complete training at Buller and would join the detachment at Kaduna. After walking round the unit and commenting on how difficult it was to raise as much as a smile from the troops and the fact that the officers mess, unlike the anvil, really was being chopped by white ants, it was on to the maritime section of the company and back to Apapa. During the course of the morning it was easy to see the enormous potential of this company and a great pleasure to meet CSM Walshe and two British NCOs who were to play important parts in the units future, – CQMS Meyer RASC and Sergeant Smith REME. Later that day the CO asked how I would like to take on the company, and to this I readily agreed. Shortly afterwards the young officer concerned took over command of 88 Company.

Ikoyi had very much the appearance of an Indian cantonment, fine houses occupied by senior government officials and the upper crust of the business community, an excellent club with tennis courts and a golf course. 88 Company was situated in a large grassed area bordered by the race course, polo ground and barracks occupied by the Lagos detachment of the duty battalion. Offices, stores, single soldiers accommodation and the officers' and sergeants' messes were all of the standard wooden type with tin roofs having window spaces that were protected by either expanded metal or bars, with exterior shutters to keep out dust, rain and frequent invasions by flying ants – the latter when caught in large numbers were said to make chop. About half of the vehicles could be stabled under make-shift cover while the LAD occupied a small lock up compound in which the MT spares and tool stores was subsequently enveloped in a covering of barbed wire, until it eventually took on the appearance of a giant hedgehog.

The company comprised a headquarter platoon, five transport platoons each of 35 vehicles, relief driver increments, a maritime section including a coal bunkered 'T' class trawler, WAASC Fire Brigade and an LAD together with establishments for 32 British and some 930 locally enlisted personnel who were vastly different in their origins and cultures – from the northern territories the Hausa, from the west the Yoruba and the Ibo from the east.

88 Company was deployed over an area approximately 600 miles by some 340 miles with detachments at Apapa with HQ Nigeria District, Abeokuta, Enugu and Ibadan which were battalion stations and at Kaduna in support of HQ Northern Sub-District. Maritime section and the Fire Brigade were based on Lagos.

There was no official language which an officer joining the WAASC was forced to learn, all oral orders being given in English 'as she is spoke' in West Africa. In other words pidgin English, a form which enabled Africans from whatever territory to communicate with one another.

Among the many pressing problems of a new commander was seeking the means to break down the natural timidity and reticence of the great majority of his men. The Company or Detachment Durbar, with all present sitting in horsehoe formation faced by the company commander flanked by his senior African and British soldiers and possibly an Imam, was found to be an effective forum for two way exchanges and the making of important announcements. Within West Africa, command was exercised through what was said that commanded attention and understanding. In no way could this basic requirement ever be altered or compensated for. And ever present was a need for British officers and NCOs to be able to express themselves in clear, unmistakable and inspirational language. West African troops did not mistake the touch of sincerity nor fail to mark as unworthy of trust the man who paid only a superficial regard to matters which they deemed important.

So to listen well was the prelude towards pondering carefully and speaking wisely.

Enlistment was always voluntary in West Africa and the conditions offered by the Army sufficiently attractive to ensure there was no shortage of recruits. Standards of discipline were high. Wrongdoers, although they would invariably try every excuse and alibi imaginable, expected to be severely punished when caught, but also expected a fair chance to state their case.

African drivers normally took a year or eighteen months to become efficient, although for part of this time they were in charge of a vehicle, carrying out routine work as non-tradesmen. They learned to look after their vehicles chiefly by habit, and as an example of this it was a common sight on a wet day to see drivers, having returned from the days work, completely stripped and busy washing their vehicles – they had been taught to wash down after work each day and so nothing was allowed to stop them doing so. It seemed extraordinary and against the dictates of commonsense that the WAASC had been thought ready to adopt the daily task system of maintenance at a time when so many vehicles were off the road in need of repair and the static workshops were hopelessly overloaded. The company commander discussed with the army in a neighbouring territory the transport management practices the French had adopted with obvious good effect. The introduction of a similar centralized maintenance, inspection and repair system coupled with a reduction in the tasks that drivers were allowed to perform was all greatly assisted by the timely arrival in 88 Company of a well known Corps sporting personality and ex workshop officer Captain George (Darky) Hall RASC. A month of intensive effort produced a daily availability of 87 per cent and four weeks later the AF G 810 was showing that 92 per cent of the company's road transport was fit for duty. Lieutenant R A Graves RASC, an accomplished sportsman and an outstanding administrator, joined the company at about the same time and was followed by Lieutenant Justice Sey, the first West African commissioned into the Corps who added a whole new dimension to the station life of Kaduna.

To get to know the African properly one had to go to the bush with them and live amongst them, and it was there that the British officers quicky discovered each man's personality and were perhaps surprised to see that their platoon or company had exactly the same personalities as any British company: you found the funny man, the quiet man, those who were good at building night shelters, and a whole host of extras such as the ju-ju man, the hunter and others. On manoeuvres there were no tents and everyone lived in huts made by the troops from grass and branches, pleasures were simple and few and generally centred around a large camp fire which served as illumination for the entertainers but on cold nights tended to attract all manner of unwelcome guests.

In barracks and bush camp it was necessary to turn the troops to grass cutting practically every day, after morning parade. Armed with their formidable machetes they would form long lines and commence to move steadily forward cutting down the grass as they went. This showed the happy go-lucky African soldier at his best. As they worked, snatches of song and topical quips and jokes broke out up and down the line and by listening carefully it was possible to pick-up many interesting asides on matters of the moment.

Early one morning a deputation from the maritime section arrived to see the OC. They felt that he was paying too much attention to the MT and not enough to the maritime section. He readily agreed that this could be remedied by the River Class and General Service launch being exercised on the River Niger and by so doing it would enable the OC to visit an old friend who was an up-river District Officer. Nearing its destination the GS launch ran aground on a mud bank. Without thinking the OC ordered everyone apart from the coxswain and engineer over the side and he followed them to push her free. On arrival at their destination no mention was made of the incident but the following morning the OC enquired what had caused so much commotion in the chicken pen during the night? Only then did he learn that bathing in the river was more than a risky business, for alligators swarmed in the waters and were at times so bold that at night they would leave the shelter of the water and roam the compounds eating anything they could find including chickens.

Attempts at weeding out malpractice proved to be a most complicated task; petrol, stores and even lorries were spirited away as if by magic and no matter the degree of precautions taken at Ikoyi, including guards mounted by the duty battalion, the losses continued. The fact that no attempt had been made to breach the spare wheel and tyre store caused the OC to suspect that this plum-target was bound eventually to get a visit.

So, surreptitiously, a trusted African NCO moved nightly into the store to await possible 'thief men'. It may be hard to imagine, but many an African can shed the veneer acquired in civilized communities and revert to the savage in just about the same time as it takes him to divest himself of trousers and get into a loin cloth. The loss of a hand as far as is known was never reported but the stealing stopped and when the time came to hand-over the company, all vehicles and stores on charge were accounted for and present with the exception of two 3 ton Bedfords that had been stolen.

Not long afterwards, the same Company Commander was posted from 88 Company, to be OC WAASC Sierra Leone and Gambia District.

HQ WAASC was co-located with District Headquarters at Towerhill Barracks, the Independent Transport Platoon at Tinma Barracks, the Supply Depot, Bakery and Butchery at Murray Town with a small Petrol Depot on the outskirts of Murray Town. The Maritime Section which consisted of harbour launches, two Dickens Class GSL's including *Dombey* and the forty-eight foot, high speed launch *Laventi* were at moorings and the District Barrack Officer divided his time between Towerhill and Tinma. The LAD supporting the Transport Platoon and a pool of vehicles earmarked for the 'fly-in' brigade were also located at Tinma. The second-in-command was Captain V R Peters RASC, and Lieutenants Eric Lewis and Jim Morgan amongst the British element of the unit.

As a broacher of cargo the 'locals' held the palm, and so carefully concealed were all traces of pilfering that it was very rarely that the dirty work was discovered until weeks afterwards when cases were opened and checked. In taking over a unit under these circumstances it was very necessary to check every case and sack of supplies; strangely enough the contents of those which showed signs of having been tampered with were nearly always intact. Losses seemed to be inevitable, and 'writes off' large. Supplies, including contingency reserves, came either from the UK or were purchased under local contract. Practically all the produce bought in Freetown at some stage or other passed through the hands of Syrian contractors. Fresh meat stocks were held for the Army by the Freetown Cold Storage Company, on a cost per pound per day basis. Meat, ice packed and in sawdust was sent twice weekly by rail to units in the north including the training centre at Daru. Those who may have served in the colony will recall the consternation that arose when the train 'for Bo, she no agree to go'.

[By courtesy of Brig R A Nightingale]

Soldiers of the West African Army Service Corps on Exercise Bush Fowl 1953 being visited by General Sir John Harding and Major R A Nightingale.

The principal ingredient on the African ration scale was rice; this the Army for some inexplicable reason had long since contracted to purchase at prices that were generally in excess of those laid down by the Colonial Government.

By the time Brigadier R G W Melsome MBE became Commander Sierra Leone and Gambia District in late 1951, a plan, to concentrate the District WAASC in and around Murray Town had been endorsed by the DDST, Colonel F C J Goodyer-Pain OBE. This plan was swiftly put into operation. Permanent cold storage was added to the butchery section of 38 Supply Depot. A combined petrol and fuel depot was built. The LAD was rehoused and permanent thief proof storage for attractive items constructed. A new building also increased the availability of soldiers quarters. Under Regimental Sergeant Major Ogden's direction the Warrant Officers and Sergeants' Mess was completely refurbished. The headquarters moved to Tinma Barracks where an RASC Officers' Mess was established and No 5 Murray Town designated the residence of the OC WAASC. That so much was achieved in such a short time was in no small way attributed to the DCRE – Major Douglas Yendole MBE RE.

Trade standards achieved by WAASC soldiers selected for training as butchers, bakers, clerks and seamen were generally good, but most drivers compared with Jehu the son of Jehoshaphat spoken of in the Book of Kings as 'one who driveth furiously'.

All African troops, except recruits had 'wives' in barracks who cooked for, 'their lords', and kept the quarters and lines clean. A head woman, the magajia, was responsible for cleanliness of the lines as well as the dress, deportment and general behaviour of wives. These headwomen attended request day interviews and always accompanied any inspecting officer or other personage round their lines. They wore a sergeants' red sash, khaki drill jacket with sergeants' stripes and they saluted – and very well they did it.

The weeding out of malpractice again proved to be a most complicated saga, to the point that the District SIB investigator would have been well qualified for transfer to the Corps; but there were rewards, in twenty months the WAASC annual contractural budget was reduced by £200,000. The district rice supply was being drawn from the Government rice mill and vessel repairs and slipping had been transfered from a civilian yard to the Royal Navy.

In March 1953 WAASC units participating in Exercise 'Bush Fowl' were visited by The CIGS, General Sir John Harding (later Field Marshal Lord Harding). Drivers and Clerks who had been divorced from their accustomed duties to form porter platoons demonstrated in their tireless, cheerful and determined way the potential that had contributed so much to the mobility of the West African formations in Burma. The CIGS also showed particular interest in an improvised field bakery section which he saw at work and being transported – 'load for head'. Following an address to officers of the District the CIGS and GOC-in-C were entertained together with the District Commander in the WAASC officers' mess.

The annual visit of the Commander-in-Chief, South Atlantic in his flagship HMS *Bermuda* was always a very special occasion for the renewal of friendships and a full programme of sporting and social events. It was also a time when vessels of the WAASC marine section were in great demand for taking interested parties up the Skarejes to see what remained of the old church and the graveyard on Bunce Island.

A three year tour of duty entailed two return flights for UK based personnel with intra-district arrangements having to be made for those stationed in the Gambia. In mid-'53 a signal announcing the imminent arrival of a civilian operated Sunderland flying boat caused considerable consternation, particularly when it became known that this was to be no route proving flight but a real trooping operation. The fact that this type of aircraft had operated from Freetown during World War II did not help, since none of the wartime facilities had survived the intervening years. Protests based on the inherent dangers associated with a harbour landing at Freetown were of no avail. The RN did not wish to have any part in the reception arrangements which eventually devolved on the Staff Captain (Q Mov) and OC WAASC supported by the District Royal Signals officer. The primary consideration was policing the touch down and taxi path for drift wood, native canoes and fishing boats. Disembarkation entailed the transfer of passengers, including women, children and a baby in arms from the flying boat into harbour launches and thence to a general service launch (GSL), an arrangement made all the more hazardous by strong currents and the known presence of barracuda. Shortly after the first flight and much to the relief of everyone concerned, trooping reverted to land based aircraft.

A military review was held on the Freetown sports arena to mark the departure of His Excellency the Governor and Commander-in-Chief, Sir George Beresford-Stooke KCMG, the District Troops taking part were commanded by OC WAASC. During the review His Excellency presented Long Service and Good Conduct Medals to Staff Sergeant T G Potter and Sergeant H Bray of the RASC and congratulated Regimental Sergeant Major Ogden on the high standard of turn-out and drill of the WAASC.

The Coronation of HM Queen Elizabeth II (2 June 1953) aroused phenomenal interest throughout British West Africa. RWAFF contingents from the four Territories assembled at Coronation Camp, Accra before travelling to London as part of the forty-three thousand troops from overseas who took part. SLA/ 65163 Sergeant A F Gasama who represented SL and G District WAASC 'was much impressed by the occasion and the interest shown by the responsible military organizations and the British Public'. Within the District the occasion was marked by a parade and numerous sporting and social events.

In addition to Sergeant Gasama four other WAASC soldiers were awarded the Coronation Medal.

The Fifties saw the introduction of a number of constitutional changes leading up to the independence of the four Territories. The military forces ceased to be a charge on the Government of the United Kingdom and Headquarters West Africa Command closed down. New conditions and terms of service had to be introduced for all personnel seconded from the British Army which would be on a voluntary basis.

During the fifties considerable advances were made in the selection and training of potential officers. Successful candidates for regular commissions were sent to RMA Sandhurst; those for short service commissions to Mons OCTU at Aldershot and all earmarked for duty with WAASC attended a course at the RASC Training Centre.

An outstanding event was the visit of HM The Queen, moving from Region to Region with an entourage, baggage and a large Press party and carrying out visits to many places in each Region presented a difficult movement control problem. At the request of the GOC-in-C, the War Office sent out an experienced movement control officer – Lieutenant Colonel S J Cornfoot – who worked out a complete detailed programme for all Her Majesty's moves. In the event, everything over a period of 20 days went according to plan and Her Majesty's party was always punctual. In January 1957 HRH the Duke of Edinburgh visited Ghana and Gambia.

About this time Gambia decided to convert her small force into an armed constabulary and it seems that Sierra Leone had been contemplating a similar move. But during August 1957 the Sierra Leone Battalion was again called out in aid of the Civil Power, this time in connection with the disturbance arising out of the outbreak of illicit diamond mining. The fact that the police had failed to restore order in the Freetown riots in 1955 and the diamond disturbances of 1957 acted as a deterrent to any attempt to follow the example set by Gambia.

The Gold Coast became independent on 6 March 1957, and the troops were styled Ghana Military Forces.

In February 1958 the RWAFF was represented at the unveiling of the Rangoon War Memorial, where the names of 1,608 West African soldiers who had no known graves are recorded.

Also in 1958 the Governor General of Nigeria established a Federal Defence Council under his own chairmanship. The members were the Federal Prime Minister, the Regional Prime Ministers, the GOC and the Director of the Nigerian Naval Service. One of the activities of the Council was the preparation of plans for the establishment of a Defence Ministry when Nigeria became independent. A programme for making the battalions of the Queen's Own Nigeria Regiment more mobile, hard hitting and capable of sustained operations was approved by the Council in 1958. Sanction was given for the raising of a sixth battalion. Approval was also given for the establishment of a Training School at Kaduna as the RWAFF School at Teshi was closing down. On the 22 April 1958, after 60 years of distinguished service at home and abroad, the Nigerian Battery converted into a reconnaisance squadron. The Force also included an engineer field squadron, a signals squadron, an MT company and two hospitals.

A lack of knowledge of what entailed 'Barrack Services' and just how dependent the Force had become upon it presented the District Barrack officer Lieutenant Colonel I G Thomas RASC with the puzzle of finding anyone in the Public Works Department to take it on. Responsibility was however eventually transferred to the PWD who still flatly refused to have anything to do with the smaller items on inventory particularly those in married quarters. Finally, completely exasperated by the attitudes of everyone Colonel Thomas suggested that small items, having an estimated value of some £800 per quarter, be given to the occupants on 1 September 1958. To his amazement everyone agreed and this became the pattern for future handovers in other British possessions.

HRH the Duke of Edinburgh visited Nigeria in May 1959. On 19 May he inspected the Boys' Company at Zaria and on the 28 May took the salute at a Combined Services parade at Lagos.

During the fifties considerable progress was made in the building of new barracks and married quarters. Pay codes were overhauled and simplified, rates of pay were increased and pensions for long service instituted. On 1 October 1960 Nigeria became independent.

In the meantime GOC Nigeria had been made responsible for certain supervisory duties in Sierra Leone which were carried out by visits during 1958 and 1959. At this time the Sierra Leone Battalion was stationed:

Battalion HQ and three rifle companies	Freetown
One rifle company	Daru
Training company	Juba

On 27 April 1961 – Independence Day, HRH the Duke of Kent attended a searchlight tattoo preceding the flag raising ceremony.

Headquarters West Africa Command closed down in June 1956. Ghana severed its connection with the RWAAF on 6 March 1959 and the units became the Ghana Army.

By March 1960 the units previously belonging to the RWAFF were absorbed into the Royal Nigerian Military Forces, the Royal Sierra Leone Military Forces and the Ghana Army. The RWAFF had ceased to be an entity. It was eventually agreed that the formal date for the end of the RWAFF would be on 1 August 1960 and in the London Gazette of 2 August it was announced that General Sir Lashmer Whistler, Colonel Commandant of the RWAFF had relinquished his appointment.

In the meantime, HM The Queen had accepted appointments as Colonel-in-Chief, Royal Nigerian Military Forces, Royal Sierra Leone Military Forces and the Ghana Regiment of Infantry.

The many RASC Officers and NCOs who served with the WAASC and have happy memories of the cheerful West African soldier, will watch their progress with interest and pride.

And so we say 'Hail and Farewell' to the West African Army Service Corps and 'Allah shi dede ranika' to all ranks, past, present and future.

CHAPTER TEN
Aden and the Gulf

ADEN/RADFAN

SINCE ANNEXATION by the British in 1839, Aden with its
strategic position controlling the southern approaches to the Red
Sea and the Suez Canal, had been garrisoned by British troops.
The final break-up of the Turkish Empire following World War I,
the widespread effects of the Second World War, the growing
importance of Middle East oil supplies, and the tribal and national
rivalries in the Arab world, continued to contribute to both the
strategic importance and inherent instability of the Arabian
peninsula.

British Forces Arabian Peninsula (later HQ Middle East
Command) with its HQ at Aden, controlled the operational
commitments for all three services in the Arabian peninsula,
British Somaliland, the Persian Gulf and the Arabian Sea. This
wide span of command encompassed the then British Protected
States of Kuwait, Bahrain, Qatar, the Trucial States, as well as the
Colony and Protectorate of Aden.

Supporting the British and locally raised units in the area in
the late 1950s until the final British withdrawal from Aden in

385

November 1968, were a number of RASC (later RCT) units. A short resumé of the transport units may demonstrate the span of responsibility:—

2 Company RASC (2 Squadron RCT) came from the UK Strategic Reserve to Aden in 1958. A general transport unit, whose main task was the operational support of the infantry battalions of the Aden Brigade and support of the forces engaged in the Radfan and Dhala areas, some 60 miles North of Aden. The unit also had detachments in Muscat and Oman.

To fulfil its operational role in the rugged, climatic and geographical conditions 'up-country' and as a defence against the ever-present threat of mines and terrorists ambushes, the unit was equipped with a number of Stalwart vehicles (still under trials at this stage) and greater numbers of armoured and mineplated 3-ton Bedfords (commonly referred to as 'Bathtubs'). With the withdrawal from Aden in 1967, 2 Squadron moved to Bahrain.

16 Company RASC (Air Despatch) (16 Air Despatch Squadron RCT) was originally based in Kenya; this air despatch unit had 'A' Air Supply Platoon detached to Aden in 1961, and administered by 90 Company RASC. Based at the very large and busy RAF and civil airport of Khormaksar, their air despatch duties were vital to the resupply of units and detachments of the British

Left: *A Belvedere helicopter delivering supplies in the Radfan.*

[By courtesy of JPRS Aden]

Right: *Air despatchers Drivers Bates and Duck preparing loads for a Belvedere helicopter in the Radfan 1964.*

[By courtesy of JPRS Aden]

Army and British-led local units deployed on operations throughout the region, often in isolated and rugged positions in the hills or desert areas. 16 Company was the last unit to leave Kenya on the move to Aden, in December 1964. Loading and despatching from Beverley, Argosy, Twin Pioneer and Beaver aircraft and Belvedere helicopters, the unit was extremely busy throughout the whole period in the area. Their operations were not, however, limited to the Arabian Peninsula area, and in 1966 they undertook perhaps the longest ever air despatch sortie of 5,568 miles by Beverley to Botswana and a drop in response to an SOS from a mapping expedition on the island of Sokoros. On top of this, the squadron handled 200,000 lbs of freight during the Zambian operation in late 1966. They returned to UK in 1967 and were disbanded at Tangmere.

57 Port Squadron RCT/Joint Services Port Unit (formerly 57 Port Squadron RE) came over to the RCT in 1965 following the McLeod Reorganization when it changed from 'RE' to RCT. This lasted until mid-1966, when it was again re-titled the Joint Services Port Unit (Middle East) – (JSPU). It was a mixed Army and RAF unit of about 100 all-ranks, commanded by an RCT major. Its role was mainly supervisory as most of the military freight was handled by the Government Freight Agent, Luke Thomas and Company,

who were responsible for providing quay and ship labour, lighter-age, and ship documentation. The JSPU was responsible for overall supervision and control of work, calling forward all cargo, all documentation not done by Luke Thomas, and checking the latter's bills. In essence, it consisted of a headquarters, a lighterage troop with responsibility for one Z-craft, two RPLs, a harbour launch, a workboat, and some Uniflote. Additionally, there was a freight handling troop and a movement control troop.

The military part of the port of Aden consisted of three elements; HMS *Sheba* jetty, the military section of Ma'alla wharf, and the Obstruction pier.

By July 1967, preparations for the withdrawal of British troops from Aden were well under way. Already, units had dispersed to Bahrain and elsewhere, but it was at this time that the Port Unit was reinforced by elements of 17 Port Regiment RCT, 10 Port Squadron RCT from Singapore and 518 Company Royal Pioneer Corps, and included a port commandant, Lieutenant-Colonel J D Lofts MBE, who had overall control and was responsible for allocation of resources, including labour, craft maintenance and overall statistics, with two major units, the Joint Service Port Unit and 51 Port Squadron. Overall policy for all port operations was the responsibility of the Joint Movements Co-ordinating Committee (Middle East) which exercised its authority through two committees, the Port Committee, and the Port Working Committee.

It was as a result of the Aden civil unions harbour strike action that British servicemen took over the task of operating the port. At dawn on 1 July 1967, a party comprised of Royal Naval and Royal Marines personnel, as well as members of the JSPU, set out from Sheba and annexed two tugs, four barges, and three other ships by nailing orders/notices to their masts or hatches. The further requisitions following ten days later included water and oil barges. As LSLs were available so they joined the fleet for the withdrawal which consisted of four LSTs – *Tern*, *Fulmar*, *Petrel* and *Grebe*, four LSLs – *Lancelot*, *Galahad*, *Bedivere* and *Geraint*, and one LCT. Royal Naval reinforcements comprised boat crews and a taskforce of some fourteen ships, which included HMS *Fearless* and *Intrepid*.

During this five-month period of intense activity and military manning of the port, substantial quantities of stores and vehicles were handled by the JSPU:

Imports   – 11,500 tons,   65 vehicles
Exports   – 56,643 tons, 2,148 vehicles
Fuel imports – 10,886 tons.

The port was naturally a great focus of interest and there were a large number of visitors. The Commander-in-Chief, Admiral Sir Michael Le Fanu, paid several visits. On one occasion the C-in-C, an unconventional senior officer, arrived on one of our chartered ships unheralded and dressed in a shirt with no badges, shorts, a none-too-clean RM stable-belt, and 'floppy Joe' hat. He reported to the sergeant in charge of ship-working. The sergeant, thinking him one of the RM working-party, sent him to hump ammunition in the lower hold. After a time down there and being somewhat hot, the Admiral took off his hat while resting and exposed his fairly red hair. The corporal i/c gang seeing him standing still, called, 'Here, Ginge, over here; there's plenty of work to do!'

60 Company was the airportable transport unit of 24 Airportable Brigade and until 1964, was stationed in Kenya. Its move to Aden began during the Radfan Campaign (April-June 1964) when C Platoon, equipped with a mixture of long-wheelbase Land-Rovers, airportable Bedford RL 3-ton vehicles, Ferguson tractors and trailers, and commanded by Lieutenant F A Bush, and two sections of the Composite Platoon, commanded by Captain W J Horsfall, were detached to assist with the maintenance of supplies to and from Habilayn. The main body of the company moved to Aden under command of Major Ronald, in December 1964, when 24 Brigade redeployed there following the withdrawal from Kenya. The vehicles of A and B Troops were mineplated on arrival and were then gradually replaced by Mks I and II mineplated Bedfords. C Troop retained a partial airportability capability until late in 1965. The squadron was located in Normandy Lines, with two sections of Composite platoon detached permanently at Habilayn, and provided support to 24 Brigade, which was located at Little Aden for the replenishment of Habilayn and Dhala, and to Aden Garrison for Internal Security duties, such as Vulnerable Point guards, foot patrols and Vehicle Check Points. It also provided helicopter-handling teams for the forward movement of equipment and stores from Habilayn to detached infantry company positions.

Major C E Penn assumed command of the squadron in August 1965, This coincided with an increasing amount of civil

[By courtesy of Central Office of Information]

Unloading a Beverley at Thumeir airfield March 1965.

unrest and terrorist activity in the urban areas of Crater and Ma'alla and the squadron now began to provide an increasing number of soldiers and sub-units to assist the Aden Garrison Infantry battalions in their IS duties. At the same time, the up-country activity increased with convoys to Museimir and Abyan.

During 1966 a Mention in Despatches and a GOC-in-C's commendation were awarded to soldiers of the Combat Supplies Platoon for their work at Habilayn, and Driver Howes, who having learned colloquial Arabic at the Command Arab Language School, for his outstanding conduct as an interpreter at Al Mansura Detention Centre.

A sad ending to 60 Squadron in Aden was related to the Aden Police Mutiny of 18 June 1967, when a party returning from range practice came under fire from the Aden Police Barracks at Champion Lines and seven lives were lost. As a result of this action, Second Lieutenant Beard and Staff Sergeant Butler were Mentioned in Despatches for gallant conduct, the latter posthumously.

90 Company RASC (90 Squadron RCT) was raised for the third time on 1 December 1957 in Aden, with a largely locally

enlisted staff. It supplied staff-cars and administrative vehicles for Middle East Command and local units in Aden Garrison, but maintained a British-manned platoon/troop of 3-ton vehicles in support of Federation operations. This was a busy squadron which because of the large establishment of civilian labour, necessitated the British element being alert to any security problems. This was a particular problem during the whole of this period when much activity was being generated by terrorists against British Army camps. During the cool season, activity also increased for the staff-car troop; it was the favourite time for the annual influx of VIP visitors.

The squadron, like 2 and 60 Squadrons, became involved in IS duties and in particular, it provided Land Rover drivers for Aden infantry battalions, but a task which many will remember was the transporting of £100m of bullion for the Federal Treasury.

All the squadrons were to a greater or lesser degree involved in April – June 1964 in supporting operations in the Radfan, a rugged mountainous area some 60 miles north of Aden. A British

A convoy on the Dhala road from Aden

[By courtesy of RCT Museum]

force (RADFORCE) about a brigade strong faced the task of expelling Yemeni-backed left-wing guerillas from the area. The bitter fighting was supported by Corps units providing logistic support by road and by helicopter in most unfriendly terrain and climatic conditions. Uniquely, part of the logistic support was provided by RASC Army Emergency Reserve (AER) – the 'Ever Readies'. Two RASC/TA officers – Captain Adrian Stringer and Lieutenant Alan Woodward accompanied by ten RASC TA soldiers reinforced 2 Company RASC and participated in the dangerous resupply operations to the Radfan area.

Towards the end of 1966, the squadron moved from Seedaseer to join 2 and 60 Squadrons in Normandy Lines, and on the rundown from Aden the squadron moved to Sharjah.

It is probably fair to say that although some individuals may have enjoyed their service in Aden, particularly during the 1950s, before Communist inspired unrest became common, the British withdrawal in late 1967 was greeted with a subdued sigh of relief. As has been touched upon above, the RCT units were all heavily involved in the final rundown and at the end were either disbanded or transferred to other stations, ending a lengthy association with the area, which stretched back over a hundred years.

THE GULF

FOLLOWING THE 1967 withdrawal from Aden, one of the principal areas to be reinforced with an increased British presence, were the Gulf states of the Oman and the United Arab Emirates. The British interests in this area were basically two-fold – to maintain the stability of this oil-rich region, and to provide aircraft staging facilities for RAF flights to the region or passing through on their way to the Far East.

Bahrain, Kuwait, Oman, Abu Dhabi, Muscat, Sharjah, Dubai, are all familiar names to servicemen.

Until 1967 there were no regular, permanently stationed units of the RASC or RCT in the Arabian Gulf. On the evacuation of Aden, during the latter half of 1967, a British presence was built up in the Gulf, at the town of Sharjah, and on the island of Bahrain, two RCT squadrons were involved, 90 Squadron at Sharjah and 2 Squadron in Bahrain.

Up to 1967 the only military force in the Trucial States were the Trucial Oman Scouts, (TOS), a Foreign Office-sponsored and con-

GULF AND ADEN

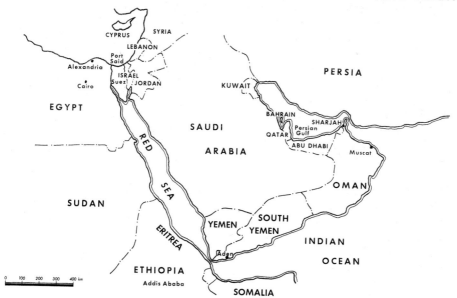

trolled army, trained and administered by the Ministry of Defence.

The TOS was a locally enlisted force with a number of seconded British officers and NCOs. The force consisted of five rifle squadrons and the normal back-up of administrative units. It had a supply and transport (ST) squadron, commanded by an RCT major with an RCT second-in-command, and three senior NCOs. The squadron sergeant-major was always an Arab; there was also an RAOC corporal for supply duties. The supply task was taken away from the squadron at the beginning of 1969. The RCT second-in-command also disappeared at the same time, and an RAOC captain set up a small ordnance unit.

The OC was also the Force Transport Officer and had the responsibility for ensuring that all transport in the TOS was correctly maintained. In addition to a vehicle fleet, the squadron had a dhow on permanent contract for the resupply of one rifle squadron which had a particularly bad land route, and for general sea patrolling to stop illegal immigration and gold smuggling. This

[By courtesy of Central Office of Information]

A convoy of Bedford RLs led by a Land Rover in Eastern Arabia

maritime fleet was increased by a second dhow and six Del Quay dories as the problem of illegal immigration increased during the 1970s.

The squadron was continually employed on operations and the resupply of the squadron outstations.

In 1969 a transport squadron was formed in the Abu Dhabi Defence Force (ADDF) and was commanded by an RCT major, who was the only British person in the squadron. Here the task was considerably greater, with the OC having direct control of the Force transport of well over a thousand vehicles. The Force was paid for and controlled by the ruler of Abu Dhabi. By the end of 1972 both posts in the TOS and ADDF had been 'Arabized'.

In addition to the Corps officers and senior NCOs attached or seconded to local forces in a transport capacity, there were and are former Corps officers serving as contract officers to these forces. A number of RCT officers also served as Desert Intelligence Officers

(DIOs), or as staff officers in the region.

The withdrawal from Aden in 1967 coincided with a build-up in the Gulf, and in particular in Bahrain. Both 2 Squadron, in Bahrain, and 90 Squadron in Sharjah, had originally come from Aden and now provided a support to the British forces in the area. HQ RCT Gulf was formed in Bahrain in August 1967, headed by a CRCT, (Lieutenant Colonel George Worsley). He was destined to be the one and only CRCT Gulf as the post was downgraded to OC RCT Gulf (a Major's post) in May 1969. At this stage there were some sixteen RCT officers and 370 RCT soldiers in the Gulf area.

In addition to the motor transport task in the area, a vital water transport function of resupplying the garrisons at Masirah and Salalah was carried out by LSL, with detachments from 17 Port Regiment RCT, equipped with two Mexeflotes. These resupply runs had to be carried out during the months September to March due to the hazardous monsoon conditions during the rest of the year. 73 Maritime Squadron, raised in November 1968 and based in Bahrain, operated a mixture of harbour launches, fast launches, RPLs, and the LCT *Arezzo*.

A gradual withdrawal of British forces from the Gulf in the early 1970s saw the disbandment of 90 Squadron in August 1971, the disbandment of 73 Maritime Squadron in December 1971, and the disbandment of 2 Squadron, also in late 1971 but 66 Squadron RCT in BAOR was immediately re-titled 2 Squadron RCT. For a short time there remained a small RCT presence in the area with the Military Advisory Team (Gulf) consisting of a seven-man transport section and two RCT Movements NCOs.

CHAPTER ELEVEN
The Caribbean

THERE IS NO DOUBT that of all the countries and stations where members of the RASC were represented after World War II those in the Caribbean area were amongst the luckiest. At least the author's research has revealed no complaints! Perhaps the nearest murmur came from an RASC Major based in Bermuda in 1951, deploring the cost of a haircut (5 shillings), the wages of a coloured maid (£3 a week for 6 days, mornings only) and a new Morris Eight (£369)!

From the map it can be seen where we were represented – albeit in small numbers.

BERMUDA

Up until mid-1953 a 200 strong British Army garrison was happily stationed on this tropical twenty square mile island some

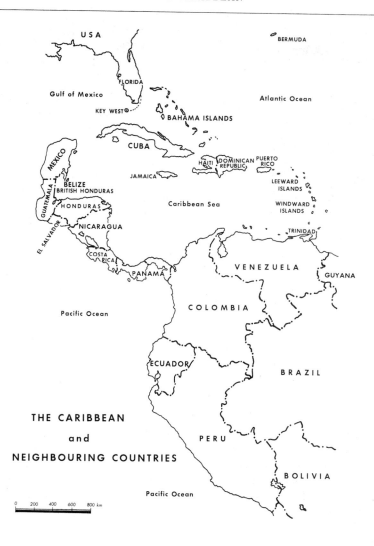

USA

BERMUDA

FLORIDA

Gulf of Mexico

Atlantic Ocean

KEY WEST

BAHAMA ISLANDS

CUBA

DOMINICAN PUERTO
REPUBLIC RICO

HAITI

JAMAICA

LEEWARD
ISLANDS

MEXICO

BELIZE
BRITISH HONDURAS

GUATEMALA

HONDURAS

WINDWARD
ISLANDS

Caribbean Sea

EL SALVADOR

NICARAGUA

COSTA
RICA

TRINIDAD

PANAMA

VENEZUELA

GUYANA

Pacific Ocean

COLOMBIA

ECUADOR

BRAZIL

THE CARIBBEAN

and

NEIGHBOURING COUNTRIES

PERU

BOLIVIA

Pacific Ocean

0   200   400   600   800 km

800 miles from Florida. In support of this garrison the RASC
was fully represented with an animal transport detachment
of twenty horses, a motor transport section of eight vehicles, a
water transport detachment with two launches, a Barrack Office
and a Supply Depot with Cold Store and Detailed Issue Depot – all
commanded by the unfortunate Major who complained about the

cost of living. As there was no perceivable threat to this peaceful island, the small British Army contingent was withdrawn in mid-1953.

JAMAICA

The British headquarters for the extensive Caribbean area was based in Up Park Camp in Kingston, Jamaica until 1962. Again a full, but small, RASC contingent were present to support the garrison. An HQ RASC commanded a Supply Depot and a small MT detachment with the larger Water Transport presence of 889 Company RASC (WT). This water transport unit controlled four harbour launches, four fast launches and a sea-going vessel *Oxna* used to transport supplies to the garrisons in British Honduras and later in British Guiana.

BRITISH GUIANA (NOW GUYANA), TRINIDAD, BAHAMAS, LEEWARD AND WINDWARD ISLANDS, BARBADOS, ANGUILLA

Although it is known that small British Army units were stationed in all the above locations during and immediately after World War II, little has been discovered by the authors of the RASC presence. It is known that with HQ Southern Caribbean in 1947 in Trinidad there was a HQ RASC, a Main Supply Depot, two Detailed Issue Depots (DIDs), an MT Section and an Area Barrack Office. There were detachments in British Guiana, Barbados, St Lucia, St Vincent, Grenada and Dominica with DID's and Barrack Stores in each island; also at Trinidad a small Water Transport Section run by HQ RASC. Further small commitments included Antigua, St Kitts, Nevis and Montserrat. This made an area 1000 miles long with relatively no breadth. In August 1946, however, most of the island locations were disbanded with the return to peace following World War II.

The UK based RASC staff consisted of only some four officers and twelve British soldiers, the bulk of the RASC staff were the eighty locally enlisted NCOs and soldiers.

With the formation of the Jamaican Defence Force in 1962, the British garrison left the island after 300 years colonial rule. The only British Army representation remaining for a further short period was at Staff level for the local force and the RASC continued to supply a Major, a Captain and some clerical staff.

[By courtesy of Lt APA Cole RCT]

A ferry crossing one of the many rivers in Belize.

BRITISH HONDURAS (BELIZE)

The former British colony in Central America, now better known as Belize, was garrisoned in the early 1950s by a British infantry battalion – and one RASC sergeant who ran a Supply Depot was responsible for local purchase of rations. In October 1961 peace was shattered by 'Hurricane Hattie', which caused extensive devastation throughout the Colony. Assistance from UK was flown in and included 142 Supply Platoon RASC, 32 Bakery Platoon RASC, and transport elements of 7 Company RASC, who laboured hard under atrocious conditions for many weeks to help restore the Colony to a more normal existence.

Today Belize is an independent country, with Britain retaining some defence obligations. The external threat from certain neighbouring countries require Britain to maintain a sizeable garrison in the country. Although no formed RCT unit is based there, the Corps is still represented with a water transport detachment and individual MT driver support.

CHAPTER TWELVE
The Falkland Islands

THE MOUNTING AND SUPPORT OF THE TASK FORCE in the South Atlantic in what has been described as the largest and most complex military operation since World War II, presented movements problems of enormous proportions. The lines of communication stretched 8,000 miles from the UK base, an average of 21 days sailing time. There was no contingency plan to retake the Falkland Islands and an operation of this magnitude outside Europe had never been foreseen.

The Falkland Islands, situated in the South Atlantic Ocean about 400 miles north east of Cape Horn, consist of two principal islands; East and West Falklands, together with numerous other smaller islands which, in total, cover 4,700 square miles. The island of South Georgia, some 800 miles south east of the Falkland

Islands, and the South Sandwich Islands are dependencies of the UK but have been administered from the Falkland Islands for convenience. The Falkland Islands were first settled in the eighteenth Century by British, French and Spanish settlers, but by 1806 the Islands had been abandoned. They were largely uninhabited until 1833 when Captain Onslow of HMS *Clio* occupied Port Egmont and raised the Union Flag over the Islands. Since then, they have been a British Colony. Today, the population is estimated to be about 1,850. They are mainly of British descent, with some 80% born on the Islands. The only town is Stanley, in East Falkland, with a population of just over 1,000.

On 19 March, in what in retrospect was an act of provocation, a small party of Argentine scrap metal merchants landed and remained illegally at Leith on South Georgia to dismantle stores from an old whaling station. Events during the next two weeks culminating in the fall of the Falkland Islands on 2 April and the invasion of South Georgia on 3 April, are well recorded and will not be repeated here. UK reaction was swift and decisive. On 5 April, within three days of the fall of the Falkland Islands, a Naval Task Force with 3 Commando Brigade embarked and sailed from the UK. Meanwhile, Ascension Island was being developed as a forward support base, using Wideawake Airfield to extend the limited facilities that already existed on the Island.

It was not until the night of 1–2 April that firm warnings were issued and plans for an amphibious operation were conceived. It was also at this stage that the Defence Situation Centre and Defence Operations Movements Centre (DOMS) were activated. Q(Mov)1 had already been tasked to advise on the availability of the LSL fleet and in those first few hours it was confirmed that four of the six Landing Ships Logistic (LSL) tasked by the Army, could be made available at short notice. *Sir Tristram* then off Belize and *Sir Bedivere* returning from Vancouver were to join the force later. The whole operation was code-named – Operation Corporate.

As the Task Force sailed south, the diplomatic situation worsened and, following the increased build-up of Argentine forces on the Falklands, it was decided to further reinforce the amphibious force, which by this time was approaching the Total Exclusion Zone declared around the islands by Great Britain, with 5 Brigade and a Headquarters Commanded by Major General J Moore. The consequences of deploying a further 3,000 troops were sorely felt in terms of available passenger shipping. The UK flag cruise liner fleet is not large and, with *Canberra* and *Uganda* already committed, the choice was narrowed to the *Queen Elizabeth 2* and a collection of smaller and less suitable ships, some of which were then cruising the Caribbean. After a number of high level discussions involving the Secretary of State for Defence and the Secretary of State for Trade with the Director of Movements (Army) in attendance, it was concluded that the only way of rapidly reinforcing the amphibious force was to take advantage of the speed (27 km) and capacity (3,250 berths) of the *QE2*. The flag ship of the British merchant fleet sailed for the South Atlantic on 12 May. 5 Brigade vehicles, stores and ammunition were carried South aboard *Tor Caledonia*, a Roll-on/Roll-off container vessel, and the *Baltic Ferry* and *Nordic ferries* together with a second Container Line helicopter 'carrier' *Atlantic Causeway*. This 'flotilla' sailed between 9 and 12 May together with many stores support ships, mine counter measure vessels and fuel tankers also requisitioned and committed during this period.

Over 50 vessels were taken up from trade totalling 673,000 gross registered tons. This fleet, extracted from some 33 different companies, represented one of the largest merchant fleets in the world and lifted over 100,000 tons of stores, 9,000 personnel and 95 assorted aircraft.

Ascension Island with its airfield was set up as a staging base. Airlift to and from Ascension and, in the latter stages of the conflict, extending further south to the Falkland Islands, was principally effected using RAF C130 Hercules and VC10 aircraft from the Air Transport Force. The journey to Ascension took some 11 hours by VC10 and 19 hours by C130 including a staging stop through Dakar or Freetown. By the end of June, some 5,800 passengers and 6,700 short tons of cargo had been airlifted forward. The RAF stations at Brize Norton and Lyneham were the principal mounting airfields and freight and passengers called forward by DOMS were swiftly processed by RCT movements staffs and the Cargo Allocation Centre. Commander-in-Chief Fleet also established a liaison staff at RAF Lyneham to control and record smaller items of naval stores loaded on available aircraft. Movement control at Ascension was maintained by an RAF Movements team, a detachment from 47 Air Despatch Squadron RCT and a Naval helicopter squadron. Because of the limitations of the jetty and port facilities on the Island, cargo and passengers were ferried to ships by helicopter. Later in the operation, an RCT movement control detachment was established to co-ordinate the movement and transit of Army units deploying and recovering through Ascension.

Marchwood Military Port, being the only UK port under military control provided a unique facility to mount operations rapidly whether pre-planned or unforeseen with a degree of security unobtainable in commercial ports. In a time of national emergency it can be freed from legal restrictions governing the movement and storage of ammunition and explosives. Therefore Marchwood was the ideal port from which to mount Operation Corporate. It was originally constructed in 1943/44 as a launching point for the Mulberry Harbour and the main facility is a single jetty designed to accept two ships. It is also the home of 17 Port Regiment RCT and the base for the LSLs.

At 0900 hrs on Friday 2 April 1982, Transport and Movements Branch UKLF was tasked to provide urgent transport assistance to move the assault packs of 3 Commando Brigade from depots at Kineton, Bicester and Donnington to shipping at Plymouth and Rosyth. Within 25 minutes, the first vehicles were on the move from 27 LSG Regiment RCT at Aldershot on what was the beginning of three and a half months of frenzied outloading activity. By 1700 hrs the same evening 140 vehicles were on the road and by the following morning this figure had reached 200. By this time Transport and Movements Branch had set up a small operations room next to the mounting centre in Headquarters United Kingdom Land Forces (HQ UKLF).

This proved to be only the beginning of a daunting and unprecedented challenge to provide the logistic effort required to go to war 8,000 miles away from the home base. At the start, the operation was mainly one of road transport, moving stores to ports and airfields. Amongst the RCT transport units employed were many Territorial Army units, the drivers carrying out their tasks with their customary vigour and enthusiasm. During this first week, as events were moving so quickly, and as it was not possible to use rail to supplement the military fleet, it became necessary to hire about 100 civilian 40 ft flat bed vehicles, but later, when there was sufficient time to plan ahead, trains were used for freight; British Rail providing an excellent service. HQ UKLF also had to identify the thousands of different items of stores which made up the ships loads and arrange their collection from the length and breadth of the country which was a formidable task by any standards. The fact that it was achieved in the very limited time available reflects great credit on the logistic units of all three Services.

When hostilities ceased Transport and Movements Branch HQ UKLF was tasked to organize the recovery and reception of 3 Commando Brigade Royal Marines and 5 Infantry Brigade, both by air and sea. This involved personnel, large quantities of equipment, munitions and stores, including Argentinian captured weapons, vehicles and ammunition.

The first RCT soldiers to become actively involved in operations on the Falklands came from 17 Port Regiment RCT, although the other Regiment of 3 Transport Group (LofC), 20 Maritime Regiment was also involved in supplying manpower cover in the Seaman employments. The Regiment's role was to provide specialist movement control and stevedore advice to cover the majority of the loading of ships in Southern England. Marchwood Military Port became a large holding area for equipment, mainly ammunition, to be loaded in Southampton docks. The Regiment was impressed with the smoothness with which requisitioned ships were prepared for operations in the South Atlantic and with the obvious expertise displayed by the Royal Navy and the cooperation of the Merchant Navy in providing the necessary additional crews and military equipment for each ship such as water purification plants, additional communications and armament. Each of the six LSLs had detachments of soldiers from 17 Port Regiment RCT on board consisting of Port Operator detachments and crews for Mexeflote, a 125 ft powered raft with a capacity of 150 tonnes. Additionally, the larger Roll On/Roll Off civilian ferries each took a detachment of 17 Port Regiment port operators and associated mechanical handling equipment to assist in cargo off loading. In all, the Regiment had two officers and 151 personnel deployed with the Fleet.

All elements of the Regiment received a thorough working-up period at sea off Ascension Island when the Fleet re-stowed its stores to reflect the expected plan. The Mexeflotes were launched and operated in sea states not normally encountered in European waters and for several days a continuous rearrangement of stores was carried out using Mexeflotes, the Royal Marine Landing Craft Utility (LCUs) and every available helicopter.

On the trip south from Ascension Island, further redeployment of stores took place whilst the Fleet was at sea. The complete transfer of stores front to rear in a loaded ship steaming in the

South Atlantic was no mean feat and was done by the onboard Port Operator detachments from 17 Port Regiment RCT. During this time, the plans for the operations at San Carlos were finalized and on each LSL the RCT detachment. Port Operators and Mexeflote crew, received training and practice in all aspects of LSL operating, especially in damage control, fire fighting, re-supply of ammunition to the anti-aircraft guns and as relief crews on those guns.

The initial landings took place at San Carlos on 20–21 May. All Mexeflotes had been carried as deck cargo as it was thought that the severe South Atlantic swell might tear off side-loaded equipment. The rafts were unloaded as the first air attacks came in and for the next two weeks the six Mexeflotes which finally arrived in the area continued to work by day and night, frequently under fire. As off Ascension Island, the Mexeflotes together with the Royal Marines eight LCUs and all available helicopters were the only way of getting stores ashore. One estimate suggests that Mexeflotes moved over 75% of all stores. Frequently the rafts were running under water with only the palletized ammunition visible. This allowed them to operate at payloads approaching 200 tonnes. Mexeflote crews normally work from their mother LSL which holds the spares for the two Mexeflote engines and the crews personal kit. Frequently LSLs left the war zone of San Carlos when they were not required for actual off-loading operations, leaving their Mexeflote raft to continue working all available shipping. The raft crews therefore lived off whichever ships they were operating from and the RCT Marine Engineers proved very competent in keeping their Mexeflote engines running. Two RCT officers from 17 Port Regiment provided liaison between the raft crews and the Landing Platform Dock Headquarters ship.

Apart from off-loading in San Carlos bay, LSLs were also used to ferry stores from the larger commercial ships further out to sea. In this case, for the first known occasion a Mexeflote raft was used as a bridge between the ramps of both ships whilst the Fiat Allis forklift truck ferried supplies over this impromptu ramp. The system worked well with the Fiat Allis being a most reliable piece of mechanical handling equipment, able to lift two ammunition pallets simultaneously. Once again the sea state of the South Atlantic frequently made this operation somewhat hazardous. During the San Carlos operations the LSLs received their share of battle damage. Two LSLs had unexploded bombs lodged in them and one of these two vessels, RFA *Sir Lancelot*, had a second bomb skip off the water, enter the ships structure, leave again and re-enter the water without exploding. The other ship, RFA *Sir Galahad*, had her un-exploded bomb craned over the side by Driver M Brough, RCT of 17 Port Regiment, into an inflatable craft full of cornflake packets to cushion the bomb! He was later awarded a Mention in Despatches.

Throughout this time the RCT Port Operator detachments, when not at work in the cargo holds, took their turn at fire fighting, ammunition re-supply and on more than one occasion, operated the ships anti-aircraft guns.

Later in the campaign two forward stores areas were operated by RCT detachments. That in the north at Teal Inlet was never challenged by the Argentinian airforce, but at the one in the south at Bluff Cove was attacked and both LSLs came under fire. One 66 ft Mexeflote raft working LSL *Sir Tristram* had almost completed unloading a cargo when the attack began. The Mexeflote returned

Unloading supplies from Ramped Craft Logistic and Mexeflote in Port Stanley.

[By courtesy of 3 Transport Group RCT]

to LSL *Sir Galahad* and made at least two trips to the shore with survivors. Sergeant Boultby RCT, the commander of the Mexeflote detachment, was awarded the Military Medal for his gallantry in this action. The RCT Port Operator crews on board both LSLs displayed great bravery and, with their detailed knowledge of the ship, in the smoke laden atmosphere, helped to guide many of their soldier comrades to safety. One ship's lifeboat from RFA *Sir Tristram* was manned by her RCT Port Operator detachment and went to the assistance of the less fortunate *Sir Galahad*. The regiment was lucky to have nobody killed, but suffered four injuries including a case of severe burns.

After the cease-fire, probably the first of the Task Force ships into Port Stanley was the LSL RFA *Sir Percival* and she proudly flew the Army Blue Ensign alongside her own RFA Blue Ensign as a mark of respect for the co-operation received from the RCT soldiers serving in all the LSLs. Detachments of 17 Port Regiment remained in the Falklands off-loading the large amount of stores required to lengthen the runway at Port Stanley, improve the accommodation and assist the Royal Engineers in their many tasks. Later Ramp Craft Logistic (RCL) manned by RCT soldiers were moved to the Falkland Islands as deck cargo on a heavy lift ship, and used to assist the Mexeflotes in ferrying supplies ashore and on inter-island work.

29 Transport and Movements Regiment RCT had a major part to play in mounting the Falklands operation. They provided Movement Control Check Points (MCCP) in unit lines throughout the UK; MCCPs at the mounting ports and Air Transport Liaison assistance at the airheads at RAF Lyneham and Brize Norton. In addition, individuals were tasked to augment movements staff in the MOD and HQ UKLF. The concurrent requirements of the various ports, airheads and units stretched the Regiment's resources in manpower to its limits. Movements representatives were also provided on board ships. Eventually the Regiment was to have 19 personnel embarked on ships. Their duties were liaison between ships crews and embarked personnel, consolidation and confirmation of stowage plans and maintaining a vested interest in Army requirements. Some tasks were more specific in nature. Lieutenant Byrne RCT of 59 Movement Squadron deployed as Liaison Officer to 5 Brigade and Staff Sergeant Higgs of 50 Movement Control Squadron was appointed to join HMS *Fearless* as a member of the Staff of the Commander Land Forces Falkland Islands.

Major R G Cockings MBE RCT was appointed Ships Commandant for the *QE2* and Captain G F Charlton RCT was Ships Liaison Officer on the *Canberra*.

All of the nineteen 'movers' aboard ships sailed into the Total Exclusion Zone, and with the exception of the *QE2*, eventually entered the Falkland Island waters and saw or experienced one form of action or another. Sergeant Steely RCT, who sailed with the MV *Elk* on 4 April, manned a Bofors gun and witnessed the attack on the *Atlantic Conveyor*. Many members of the Regiment established a close attachment to units during the conflict, some by design and some by coincidence. Sergeant Lewis RCT, for example, embarked with the LSL RFA *Sir Bedivere* on 27 April with Royal Marines on board. He disembarked with them at Ajax Bay, and worked with the Logistic Support Regiment RM while Ajax Bay was used as the Base Maintenance Area. It was towards the end of this phase that several of the ships were designated for hospital and prisoner of war duties. Sergeant Hillyard RCT who boarded the MV *St Edmund*, a British Rail Sea Link ferry, on 16 May reported his disenchantment when he had to give up his deluxe cabin with shower to Argentine General Menendez and Brigadier Joffre. The day the MV *St Edmunds* was due to disembark her troops, 14 July, was the date the Argentines surrendered. The *St Edmund*, which normally runs between Harwich and Hook of Holland, was probably the first Sea Link channel ferry to cross the Equator!

Following the Argentine surrender two members of the Regiment, Captain Charlton RCT in the SS *Canberra* and Warrant Officer Class 2 MacKenzie RCT on the MV *Norland* participated in the embarkation and repatriation of Argentine prisoners of war. This task completed, both ships assisted in the recovery of Task Force personnel from the Falklands to the UK. Warrant Officer Class 2 MacKenzie RCT, who remained with the *Norland* from 20 April until 15 October, received the CinC Fleets' Commendation in recognition of his service during the operation.

Warrant Officer Class 1 Roberts RCT on the MV *Baltic Ferry* and Sergeant Morton RCT on the MV *Nordic Ferry* managed to load their own Land Rover and trailer for their journey. When the Argentine forces surrendered, both disembarked from their ships at Port Stanley, with vehicles, and joined up with Corporal Stone RCT and Lance Corporal Allsop RCT taking up residence in an Argentine 20 foot container and forming the Air Transport Liaison Detachment at Port Stanley airfield. This was the start of our continuing commitment to what has now become the Joint Services Movement Staff Falkland Islands.

It was on 2 April, that 47 Air Despatch Squadron RCT became involved in Operation Corporate. There were a number of special forces contingency plans involving air drop and two air despatch crews were put at six hours notice to move. Also at this stage the use of airdrop for mail resupply to the Task Force was discussed. The Lindholme containers issued to the Squadron were completely inappropriate for the volume of mail to be dropped and so the Squadron found 200 Exocet boxes at Royal Navy Stores Depot Copenacre. These were boxes in which Exocet spares were delivered to the Navy from the manufacturer and with some minor air despatch modifications they made admirable waterproof harness packs. Finally, during this first week, with perfect timing, Joint Air Transport Establishment completed the trials of the new waterproof 1 ton container and the first were issued to the Squadron. On 16 April, Corporal Dargie RCT and his air despatch crew flew to Ascension and on 20 April the first airdrop of high priority stores was made to HMS *Invincible* and HMS *Alacrity*. For nineteen days the crews worked exceptionally long hours. Often they would fly a twelve hour sortie and on return, discover a number of newly arrived loads which, because of new priorities, had to be broken down, rebuilt and then loaded for the next sortie. Twenty-four to thirty-six hours work on the ground followed by the next twelve hour sortie became commonplace. They slept en route to the DZ and began another twenty-four hours work on landing. Four Air Despatchers of 47 Air Despatch Squadron RCT were honoured for their distinguished conduct in the Falklands campaign. Warrant Officer 2 P M Williams RCT received the MBE as did Warrant Officer 2 D Moore RCT; Corporal C J Holdsworth RCT received a Commander in Chiefs Task Force Commendation and Driver G J Hunt RCT received the Air Officer Commanding 38 Group RAF Commendation.

In the next two weeks life in 47 Squadron was very busy. Three AD crews were detached to JATE to learn how to lay mines by air despatch from a Hercules. AD crews were also sent with almost no warning to rig Sidewinder and other aircraft missiles at Brize Norton. As the Squadron was two officers understrength, Major D Hobbs RCT, OC Air Despatch Examining Team went to the USA to collect special stores. His task was to work out on the way back to the UK how to rig the loads for airdrop so that they

[By courtesy of RAF Lyneham]

Four Air Despatchers honoured during the Falklands war. WO2 Williams MBE: WO2 Moore MBE: Cpl Holdsworth, C in C Task Force Commendation: Dvr Hunt, AOC 38 Group RAF Commendation.

could be sent to Ascension without delay. Major Hobbs RCT and Sergeant Carter RCT later flew out to Ascension with the rigged loads and dropped them to HMS *Antelope* on 4 May. The first sortie to the Falklands in a Hercules took place on 16 May. No one knew with any certainty whether it would return. It needed two refuellings by Victor Tankers which were also refuelled once and twice respectively, which meant that five Victor Tanker sorties were flown to get each Hercules to the Falklands and back. A basic problem with In Flight Refuelling (IFR) was that in level flight a Hercules going flat out on full throttle could not reach the slowest speed of the Victor Tanker! This somewhat fundamental problem was overcome by all IFR being done in a. dive. The procedure started at about 26,000 ft and usually ended at about 8,000 ft, although slow fuel deliveries on occasion meant that the probe was withdrawn at 2,000 ft. During this dive the Hercules engines remained on full throttle and engine temperatures were alarmingly high, a number of engines being lost because of this. A further

410

danger on these sorties was that fuel reserves were marginal. In theory the reserve was enough, but unforecast 100 knot headwinds, Argentinian fighter activity, and tactical situations which required the Hercules to loiter at the DZ would all eat into fuel reserves. Several aircraft arrived back with little fuel. One flown by Squadron Leader Max Roberts RAF landed with 30 minutes fuel after a 26 hour sortie – 1.9% reserve.

During the second week of May the pattern of air despatch established itself with drops to both the Task Force and the Assault Group. It was also a week of incidents. At the beginning of the week, twelve 1 ton containers were flown to a DZ to be dropped to a frigate. When the first two were dropped, a killer whale surfaced and began to circle and play with the containers preventing the pick up crew from getting near them. This performance was repeated for ten of the containers, with the whale becoming progressively more possessive!. By now the aircraft's fuel state was critical and it started the long haul back to Ascension with two containers still on board. The second incident then occurred. A ramp seal failed and the aircraft could not repressurise. As there were insufficient oxygen masks to go round, the captain elected to fly back at 12,000 ft. The two remaining airdrop containers were not of British origin and their flotation devices were simply passenger lifejackets which air despatchers had inflated ready for despatch. When a cabin altitude of 12,000 ft was reached, three life jackets exploded causing some consternation until the cause was established.

Two more incidents led to modification in despatch techniques. Firstly, a container was lost because its 60 ft parachute did not open fully. On JATE advice all drop heights were raised to 700 ft and there were no further parachute malfunctions. The second problem arose when a sortie was cancelled because of thick sea fog in the DZ. Although both ships and aircraft could see each other on radar and a controlled drop was perfectly possible, it was doubtful if the containers could be found in the sea afterwards. JATE solved the problem and procured the required equipment in 3½ days! The solution was a Search and Rescue beacon fastened to the container, switched on just before despatch, and set to operate on a non-SAR frequency. The UHF homer of the Lynx helicopter could then locate the container which had a strobe visual beacon on top.

407 Troop RCT, an independent troop under command 27 LSG Regiment RCT was also warned for operations in support of 5

Infantry Brigade on 2 April 82. Under its commander, Lieutenant Paul Ash RCT it went to Sennybridge in Wales for two weeks to take part in a working up exercise with 5 Brigade which included 1 Welsh Guards, 2 Scots Guards and 1/7 Gurkha Rifles. This was a completely new Brigade formation, brought together for the Falklands operation, so they had little time to get to know one another and practise standing operating procedures. The troop practised, amongst other matters, driving and maintaining the Volvo over snow vehicles which were to prove so versatile over the muddy ground conditions in the Falklands. On 1 June 82, 407 Troop landed in San Carlos Bay to assist in the setting up of a Brigade Maintenance Area in support of 5 Brigade. Days and nights then merged into one another as the ceaseless work continued. Eager Beavers were used to off load the Mexeflote and landing craft. Volvo BV202 and requisitioned tractors were used to move the stores away from the beach and to set up dumps. Fuel became a serious problem as the consumption of the Volvo BV202 was high and there were many other calls on fuel supplies. Communications also became a problem, at one time Lieutenant

Typically difficult Falklands terrain. Military Vehicles are Volvo BV202 tracked vehicles operated by 407 Troop RCT.

[By courtesy of Commando Forces News Team]

Chinook helicopter working to a Mexeflote raft at Port Stanley. A requisitioned car ferry in the background.

[By courtesy of Lt Col RF Grevatte-Ball]

Ash had his troop split between Fitzroy, San Carlos, the *Nordic Ferry* and HMS *Dumbarton Castle.*

As the operation progressed the troop moved into Port Stanley and took over captured Argentinian vehicles, and with these helped to clear up the town of the mess left behind by the Argentinians.

As well as the RCT units which were involved in Operation Corporate, notable contributions were made by individual RCT officers and soldiers who were working on the staffs of headquarters or detailed for special tasks. Foremost among these was Colonel I S Baxter CBE who held the appointment of Colonel AQ HQ Commando Forces Royal Marines. He was responsible for the outloading and embarkation of the reinforced 3 Commando Brigade RM during the early part of April and then advised on the outloading and embarkation of 5 Infantry Brigade on 12 May. For the period 9 April to 30 May he also held the appointment of Chief

[Photograph by PR HQ UKLF]

Capt J G Greenhalgh DFC RCT. The Distinguished Flying Cross was awarded for his actions at Goose Green ferrying ammunition and evacuating casualties.

of Staff Commando Forces RM. As Colonel AQ of the Land Force Falkland Islands, he then assumed overall responsibilities for logistics support of the land force. He was one of the first members of the force to enter Stanley after the surrender, in order to give orders to General Menendez for the disarming and internment of his men. He was made a Commander of the Order of the British Empire for meritorious service in the South Atlantic.

Lieutenant Colonel I J Hellberg OBE RCT was Officer Commanding the Commando Logistic Regiment Royal Marines, responsible for the logistic support of the Commando Brigade and elements of 5 Infantry Brigade during Operation Corporate. He was made an Officer of the Order of the British Empire for his services.

Captain J G Greenhalgh DFC RCT commanded a detachment of Scout helicopters which went ashore with 3 Commando Brigade. During the assault on Goose Green by 2 Parachute Regiment, Captain Greenhalgh flew many missions in direct support of the operation, ferrying ammunition and evacuating casualties. He was continually exposed to enemy fire and, in particular, on the night of 28/29 May he was forced to fly into full view of the Argentine positions to evacuate severely wounded casualties. For gallantry he was awarded the Distinguished Flying Cross.

Major E L Barrett MBE RCT went to the Falkland Islands as second in command of the prisoners of war organization. He did outstanding work to prepare for the reception and holding of large numbers of prisoners and later was faced with the huge task of restoring logistic order out of the post-operational confusion. With only a small staff he established the framework of the force logistic base in the face of formidable difficulties – including appalling weather conditions and an almost non-existent local infrastructure. He was made a Member of the Order of the British Empire for meritorious service in the South Atlantic.

Major A Todd RCT was appointed GSO 2 on the Staff of the Commodore Amphibious Warfare and in that capacity sailed to the Falklands on HMS *Fearless*. On 7 June 82 he was awakened at 0230 hours and asked to navigate and lead two landing craft loaded with a company of 1 Welsh Guards from HMS *Fearless* to Bluff Cove, a voyage of about 40 miles which took them within six miles of Stanley and well within the range of Argentine 155 mm artillery. It was a splendid feat of navigation in strange waters at night trying to avoid outcrops of rock and kelp. He landed the Guards safely at Bluff Cove with enough time left to march to Fitzroy Sound by daylight. The following day Major Todd was standing on the Bridge of LSL *Sir Galahad* when it was attacked and set on fire. By his action and example many men, unfamiliar with the ships layout, were led to safety. On the day of the surrender, Major Todd escorted General Menendez and four other senior Argentine officers from Stanley to HMS *Fearless* with the original surrender document in his pocket. He was subsequently mentioned in despatches for gallantry.

Brigadier R E L Jenkins CBE and Brigadier D B H Colley CBE were both members of the planning staff at the Ministry of Defence and were appointed Commanders of the Order of the British Empire.

Colonel J D Bidmead CBE late RCT, the Deputy Assistant Chief of Staff Transport and Movements HQ UKLF played a vital role in the successful mounting of the force and logistic support of the Falklands campaign. He was also appointed a Commander of the Order of the British Empire.

Staff Sergeant W F Blyth BEM RCT was awarded the British Empire Medal for his work with G3 Transport and Movements of HQ UKLF.

There are many other stories of courage, fortitude and initiative displayed by those involved in Operation Corporate. The Corps has every reason to be proud of them.

Part II
THE ELEMENTS OF THE CORPS

13 · SUPPLIES

IN THIS CHAPTER, available space allows only for a brief description of the overall supply function of the RASC during the period 1945–1965. Mention of the activities of some specific RASC Supply Units is given in the chapters in Part 1. For those readers who may not be familiar with the system that served so well both in peace and war whilst it was the responsibility of the RASC, the following paragraphs provide a background to the various responsibilities and roles of the supply organization in this period. For those whose knowledge is greater, this brief description should in no way be taken as a diminution of the very important part that the supply organization played in the history of the RASC in the post World War II years.

At the height of the war, the RASC were providing rations for almost eight million mouths, with over four hundred different ration scales in countries as varied as Iceland and Egypt. This responsibility continued from 1945–1965 when under the McLeod reorganization the Corps was divested of its supplies role and the Royal Army Ordnance Corps took over the commitment. During the period, the size of the supply task diminished as the Army reduced in size and withdrew from many of the war time theatres of operations. At the same time as the Army became more static and the food situation in UK and overseas improved, the need for many of the more specialist supply units reduced. Eventually, some of them disappeared from the RASC order of battle and their functions were incorporated into the basic supply units.

The task of that part of the RASC concerned with supplies could be summed up as the provision, storage and regular issue of unit requirements of RASC supplies of the right quality and quantity at the right place and time. The term RASC Supplies covers all food stuffs contained in the various ration scales – referred to as rations – forage for animals, hospital nutritional requirements, disinfectants, water, rum, chemicals and insecticides.

From the peak requirement at the end of the war, the feeding strengths and diversity of ration scales dropped rapidly, but the British Army was still stationed world wide, and the problems of the aftermath of war, particularly in Europe, were considerable. Food rationing continued for some years in UK and no immediate improvement to the Home Service Ration Scale was possible. In BAOR, where the bulk of the British Army was still deployed, the task of restoring the feeding of this large occupation force to peace time fresh ration scales was considerable. In addition to the Army and RAF strengths, some 48,000 service families and

180,000 German labourers were being fed.

The RASC supply organization was however such that conversion from war to peace required little change, except in the size of units and installations involved. Again, the numerous operations which took place between 1945 and 1965 were capable of being sustained with rations from well established and proven organizations.

Up until 1965, the War Office, later the Ministry of Defence, branch responsible for supplies, was ST 6 of the Directorate of Supplies and Transport. The War Office was also responsible for the provision of supplies for the Royal Air Force and had been throughout the War. The Royal Navy were however responsible for their own supplies and indeed were to take over in 1966 from the Army, under rationalization of functions between the Services, the bulk provisioning of rations. The four main elements of ST 6 were concerned with:

ST 6 a	Provision
ST 6 b	Distribution
ST 6 c	Planning and organization
ST 6 d	Ration scales and allowances.

The Ration Scale is the basis against which all provision and issue of rations was and still is made. Scales for a daily issue based on an individual entitlement were produced to provide a well balanced, nutritionally sound and adequate diet, to keep the serviceman fit in the climatic conditions in which he was serving. Differing scales were provided to meet national and religious requirements with supplements for servicemen working under special conditions. In the post war years as our Colonial Forces were reduced and some withdrawal from overseas areas was possible, so the number of ration scales reduced. Improvements to the remaining scales was also possible as food became more readily available and rationing in the UK ended. Most scales had a cash element enabling units to buy items to achieve greater variety. These were normally to be obtained from NAAFI, who at various times were responsible for the issue of certain items of the ration scales. The part played by NAAFI/EFI in the issue of rations was carefully coordinated with the RASC function and RASC supply depots and NAAFI/EFI bulk issue stores were normally co-located. The extent of this co-ordination was marked by the fact that in operations overseas, NAAFI/EFI personnel wore RASC uniform.

Whenever possible in overseas theatres, fresh produce was obtained locally to reduce transport and import costs. Local contractors provided a wide range of fruit, vegetables, eggs, bread and meat. Quality and price control was a constant problem for the responsible RASC Headquarters, in maintaining the high standards required. The capability, reliability and often integrity of contractors in some areas left much to be desired, and only the most vigilant supervision and inspection produced the best possible ration, often under very difficult circumstances. That the standards were so well maintained speaks highly for the sound supply training of the officers and soldiers concerned.

The Army's reserves of rations at home and overseas were held in tinned or dried form and then had to be issued periodically to effect a turnover of reserve stocks. These tinned and dried equivalents had to be issued in lieu of fresh rations, e.g. biscuits in lieu of bread, corned beef in lieu of fresh meat, tinned or dried fruit or vegetables in lieu of fresh, and some of these 'in lieu' issues were more popular than others! Older soldiers will recall the unpopularity of PMP (Potato Mash Powder) and dried vegetables. Supply officers had to exercise considerable guile to get units to accept these and some other less popular alternatives. Certain items, such as hospital supplies and rum did not have a daily scale and were issued subject to special conditions of diet or climate as authorized by the medical authorities or force commanders.

In addition to the normal fresh ration scales, special ration packs, e.g. the 10 man compo pack, many of which were developed during the war, continued to play a large part in feeding the Army on operations and on exercises, when the issue of fresh rations was not always possible. The use of these packs, which were expensive, was and remains a temporary expedient until circumstances permitted the introduction of a suitable fresh ration scale.

The standard British compo and 24 hours packs did not always meet the requirement for special rations, and the operations in Malaya proved the need for flexibility in the provision of such rations. The start of the operations in 1948 produced an immediate need for special rations for Gurkha and Malay soldiers on jungle patrols, for which British special ration packs were not acceptable. ST Branch, HQ Malaya, set about improvising suitable packs within the requirement for an acceptable balanced diet at a reasonable cost and within the weight and bulk restrictions. The end products proved to be highly successful and a production line set up at the Main Supply Depot in Kuala Lumpur produced 80,000 rations a month in the specially designed local packaging. The packs were also issued to the civil police, and almost one and a half million packs were produced in Malaya before the task was passed to 4 Supply Reserve Depot at Singapore. Subsequently, a 24 hour FARELF pack was produced for British troops in the jungle, which was more suitable than the standard pack. Many technical difficulties were overcome in the production of these packs. Ingenuity and experience, e.g. 'deweevilization' of rice, shapes of tins, slaughter of meat in accordance with religious customs, in local conditions and resources proved invaluable in this rapid production within the financial limitations.

In the UK, development in food technology enabled the production of specially processed food, e.g. freeze dried products, to be considered for use in ration packs for varying climatic conditions, and experiments for such packs was a continuous process.

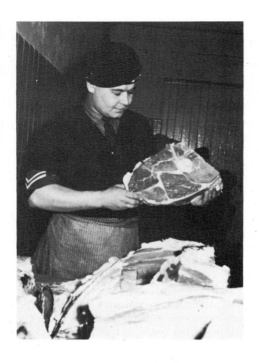

RASC Corporal Butcher

[By courtesy of RCT Museum]

The ration scale(s) for any particular theatre was the basis of provisioning of supplies either locally or from elsewhere. Overall responsibility for world wide provisioning rested with ST 6, but a number of other staff branches at the War Office and outside organizations played a vital part in forecasting the world wide requirements and producing a budget. These were:

a. The General Staff – Forecasts of strengths by areas and reserves necessary.

b. The Quartermaster Generals Staff – Staff direction.

c. Civil Service Finance Branch (QMGF) – Financial control of expenditure.

d. The Air Ministry – Forecast of strengths by areas for the RAF.

e. Ministry of Food (Later the Ministry of Agriculture, Fisheries & Food) – Provision of rationed food and nomination of countries from which other items should be obtained. The part played by Ministry of Food diminished as rationing and controls ceased.

f. Director of Army Contracts – Responsible for arranging Army supply contracts as necessary.

g. Chief Provision Officer (Food Supplies) – An RASC organization responsible for executive action to provision supplies worldwide on behalf of ST 6. Control of the Supply Reserve Depots in UK and implementing policy on behalf of ST 6.

h. Chief (WD) Analyst – Research and development of operational rations. Responsible with his staff for quality control, and for the technical examination of all foodstuffs, etc.
i. DMS Staff for nutritional balance and calorific value.

The calculation of global requirements of supplies was the first essential step in producing rations for the soldier and airman wherever he was stationed. This excluded items purchased locally by theatres. It was a somewhat tedious but well proven process carried out by ST 6, without the benefit of computers at that time. Briefly, the method employed for every theatre was to use the following formula for every item on each ration scale:

Daily ration scale of item × forecast strength of a theatre × frequency of issue in a 30 day period × number of months in the period under review, e.g. Frozen Meat (including bone) – 5 oz daily × 10,700 × 26 issues × 12 months

It is interesting to note that the scale in 1950 was 5 ozs of meat. By 1965, it had risen to 8 oz 'bone-in'. Some items on the ration scale were not issued every day, and meat is an example of this, only being issued on 26 days out of 30. On the remaining 4 days, offal (liver and kidney) and tinned meat was issued instead.

After arriving at the quantity required of each item as above, stocks held in a theatre were deducted, and the resultant figure was the quantity required to be provisioned. The length of the supply chain which governed operating stocks held, together with reserves, also had to be considered.

Requirements were scheduled by commodities and method of provision agreed with all concerned:

a. Ministry of Food who would indicate method of procurement in the case of rationed and controlled items, and for items purchased in bulk from overseas. The involvement of the Ministry of Food in a control capacity ceased when rationing and food controls in UK ended.
b. Chief Provision Officer who had overall responsibility for co-ordinating the procurement, and for subsequently ensuring that all requirements were received in UK or overseas.
c. Civil Service Finance Branch (QMGF) for financial surveillance.
d. Director of Army Contracts for making the necessary contracts with civilian suppliers.

There were in 1945, three RASC Supply Reserve Depots, at Hawkhead in Scotland, Barry in Wales, and Taunton in the South West of England. These were, shortly after the war, reduced to two, Barry and Taunton. These depots held the main stocks of rations, other than fresh items, from which the UK and overseas theatres were provisioned. They received their stocks by the process outlined above, and early in the period covered by this chapter were each holding 30 days reserve stock and 30 days maintenance stock based on a feeding strength of 500,000. In addition, the SRDs at Taunton and Barry held some 3,000,000 rations of

Mobile field bakery RASC

[By courtesy of The War Office]

10 man Composite ration packs and a comparable number of individual 24 hour ration packs. The maintenance of these special packs, which were packed at SRD Taunton, provided a considerable problem. Because of their cost, complete turnover was not economical, and examination of packs and repackaging was a continuous process, and special storage doubled the shelf life. Nevertheless one quarter of the stocks had to be turned over annually.

For convenience, and to save money, part of the supply requirements of overseas commands was met by direct shipment from producer countries, contracts having been made in the UK. All other items except those fresh products locally purchased, were shipped from the SRDs. The Supply and Petroleum Reserve Depot in Singapore held the rations and packed petrol reserves for the whole of the Far East.

A number of different types of RASC Supply units were involved in the handling, holding and issuing of supplies. Some issued in bulk to other depots, e.g. SRDs, and others issued in detail to individual units, e.g. Command Supply Depots. The latter often had Cold Store, Bakery and Butchery Units attached, and were specifically designed to meet the peacetime commitment. In field force formations, as found in BAOR for example, supply units on standard field force establishments existed in each formation to meet the war requirements. The most numerous of these were the composite platoons which existed on the scale of one for each divisional MT company and issued ammunition and POL in addition to rations. Normal day to day supply was however met by the static supply organization i.e. Command Supply Depots, and the integral field force units normally only functioned on exercises. For training purposes however, they were often attached to Command Supply Depots.

The most common type of supply unit was the command supply depot already mentioned, which appeared throughout the world tailor-made to fit the particular requirements. In 1950 there were still thirty six Command Supply Depots in UK, with a feeding strength of some 275,000. By 1963, the SRDs had been reduced to one at Taunton, and the CSDs to eight, with one static bakery. CSDs in UK and in overseas Commands were administered and controlled by the command in which they were located, and the S & T Branch at the HQ was responsible for provisioning. Most CSDs, in addition to holding and issuing rations also held and issued packed POL, and often ran static petrol pumps. In BAOR, the S & T Branch was responsible for administering the petrol rationing system by coupons for both military vehicles and civilian vehicles owned by military personnel.

As has already been indicated, a number of specialized supply units existed. These included bakery platoons, butchery platoons, cold storage platoons, port platoons, procurement platoons and embarkation supply platoons. These continued in diminishing numbers during the period. Of these units, bakeries, both static and field, existed in the largest numbers, and continued to provide bread throughout the period. However, because of the force requirement, the bakeries in BAOR continued to operate after all those in UK had closed where the requirement was met by civilian contract. A mobile field bakery was fully mechanized, with ovens, dough making machinery, water pumping and sterilizing plant and generating equipment, all mounted on trailers. With an establishment of 87 all ranks, it was capable of producing 30,000 lbs of bread a day. Those in BAOR operated in a static role alongside the CSDs when not required on exercises.

Butcheries which had been essential during the war to handle fresh meat, including slaughtering and dressing, ceased to be a general requirement after the war, when an unrestricted supply of frozen meat was generally possible. Sufficient butchers were retained on the strengths of CSDs to cut up and issue this frozen meat, or such fresh meat that continued to be issued in some overseas theatres. Band saws were introduced in Singapore enabling hard frozen meat to be jointed without defrosting, a problem in hot climates.

A longer term requirement existed in the Middle East, where meat was still obtained 'on the hoof'. A sad task soon after the war was the slaughter of some 600 surplus draught and riding horses. The meat was subsequently issued to POW. In the UK, the butchery in Aldershot was retained for the training of RASC butchers, and subsequently butchers nominated by MAFF, in the art of judging and grading of livestock on the hoof, and dressed meat. Because of the reduction in the number of butchers in the post war years, many changed their trade to Storeman, Supplies, and became skilled in their new trade, some reaching senior rank.

In 1960, as a result of a War Office working party, the specialized supply units which had existed to fulfil the various supply functions, were rationalized and a new structural establishment was introduced. Composite platoons in the RASC divisional regiments were not however affected. Included in this reorganization were the various types of petroleum units which, although they in most cases had worked alongside supply units, had separate designations, e.g. petroleum platoon, petroleum maintenance platoon. To carry out all these supply and petroleum functions, two new types of units were established. These were the Supply Platoon, and the Field Bakery platoon. Two of the original petroleum units were retained, the Petroleum Pipeline Platoon, and the Supply Laboratory. These four types of unit, covered all the duties hitherto performed by a much larger number of types of both supply and petroleum units. The Supply Platoon in particular became a very flexible unit and could handle either supplies of petroleum both in bulk or to issue in detail to units, or a combination of both functions. With the addition of an extra section it could also run a Cold Storage Depot. The new Field Bakery platoon could operate two types of equipment, the air portable or the mobile bakery equipment In the air portable role the platoon could bake 6,000 lbs of bread daily whilst in the mobile role 10,000 lbs. Additional sections could increase this capacity.

The soldier tradesmen in the supply units were storemen, clerks, butchers and bakers. These were specialist trades, and the storemen also covered both rations and petroleum. Training in supply and petroleum duties was carried out at 3 Training Battalion RASC, Ellis Barracks, Farnborough and clerks in 2 Training Battalion RASC which was located at Blackdown and subsequently Willems Barracks, Aldershot.

Unlike RASC soldiers, officers did not specialize in any one role of the many carried out by the Corps. Some, however, became more expert in a particular role than another, and this was aided by attendance at specialized courses. After initial training on commissioning, which gave a sound general grounding in all roles, 'in job' unit training in a particular role followed. Officers of the rank of senior captain or major subsequently selected for the Long Supply Course of 1½ years, would normally fill the more specialized supply appointments. Officers in bakery and butchery appointments were normally Quartermasters whose trade had been a baker or butcher, and were highly skilled.

From 1945 onwards, with the exception of Korea, most field force supply units continued to be located in BAOR, with the Divisions and Corps troops. Each divisional RASC company had its composite platoon, responsible in war for the issue of ammunition, supplies and POL, to units within its divisional area. These tasks were carried out on all exercises which were a major feature in BAOR in the early years after the war. A supply company, part of the Corps Troops Column RASC, existed in the Corps Maintenance Area, and was responsible for the issue in bulk

RASC Bakers

[By courtesy of RCT Museum]

of ammunition, supplies and POL to the Divisional RASC and in detail to Corps troops. In the latter part of the period whilst under the command of Major T A Danton-Rees (later Lieutenant Colonel) extensive experiments were carried out in the use of helicopters to carry supplies, ammunition and POL forward from the Corps Maintenance Area and this became a standard alternative procedure.

In July 1965, on the formation of the Royal Corps of Transport, overall responsibility for supplies and POL were passed to the RAOC. A cross section of RASC officers of all ranks up to colonel, totalling 345 most of whom were then currently serving in supply appointments, were selected to transfer to the RAOC. All soldiers in supply trades were transferred and many supply units were transferred complete with all their officers and soldiers. Thus, the supply skills that officers and soldiers of the RASC had cherished for so long and of which they had been so justifiably proud passed smoothly to their new Corps.

14 · PETROL, OIL
AND LUBRICANTS

UNTIL 1965, THE RASC was responsible within the Army, for the provision, storage and delivery to units of all petroleum products, with the exception of some oils and greases. ST2, a branch of the Directorate of Supplies and Transport at the War Office, controlled the petroleum organization for the Army in the period 1945 to 1965. It was supported by the petroleum branches at S&T Directorates in overseas commands and in the field by specialized RASC petroleum units or RASC units with a joint supplies/petroleum responsibility, e.g. supply platoons, field supply depots and composite platoons. Petroleum supply in the field had developed rapidly during World War II and the Army's POL consumption had also increased remarkably, as well as the variety of products.

The challenge of ever-increasing consumption in conditions as varied as those in Europe, the Middle East and Burma had been met with innovation and new techniques, and the arrival of the jerrican to replace the wasteful flimsy tin containers had ensured that supply matched consumption even in the most difficult terrain. Strategic pipelines had been laid in UK, the Middle East, Europe and India to take petroleum to bulk installations as far forward in theatres as possible. There, packing into containers took place, and ultimately it was the RASC driver in his lorry who was responsible for the delivery of packed petroleum to units in the field.

Specialized RASC Petroleum units existed in theatres with responsibility for the receipt and holding of bulk petroleum in tank farms. They also provided Petroleum Laboratories for quality control. Petroleum was either packed into containers direct from bulk at these installations, or taken forward in RASC road tankers for packing further forward.

In the forward areas, RASC Supply Platoons also had a petroleum function in that they handled all packed petroleum. They also had a limited packing facility from road tankers.

In divisions, the RASC divisional transport units were responsible for the carriage and issue of packed POL to all units in the division. The RASC composite platoons of the divisional transport units provided the technical function of receiving, holding and issuing petroleum, and stocks were normally held on RASC vehicles for immediate transport and issue.

[By courtesy of PR HQ NORTHAG]

Mixing flame thrower fuel in BAOR 1954.

OVERSEAS THEATRES

In 1946 major petroleum installations still existed in BAOR and the Middle East, but it was to be in Korea in the 1950s where the consumption rate of petroleum produced a major distribution problem. Before this though, a petroleum requirement of a different sort exercised the RASC Petroleum Organization in BAOR and this was the involvement in the Berlin Air Lift – Operation Plain Fare. This operation is covered in detail in Part I of this history, but it is appropriate to mention some facts here. During the airlift, 92,432 short tons, that is 8% of the total of all commodities lifted into the Western Zones, consisted of petroleum fuels transported in bulk in special tank aircraft. In July 1948, 31 planes were being employed based on the three airfields of Wunstorf, Schleswigland and Fuhlsbuttel. By the Spring of 1949, the daily lift of petroleum fuels was 500 tons. The maximum carried on any one day in July rose to 799 tons in 110 sorties using 5 types of aircraft – Halton, Lancastrian, Liberator, Lincoln and Tudor. When established, standard military bulk petroleum lorries of 800 or 1,750 gallons, were filled from rail cistern cars. A pool of pre-loaded lorries was maintained at the airfield and, when aircraft taxied to the loading point, one or two lorries would be called forward to the aircraft and the load transferred to the plane by 100 or 350 gallon-a-minute pumps through one or two 2 inch hoses some 80 feet in length. It was found that the 350 gallon-a-minute Carter pump, a 4-cylinder CI engine with a twin hose outlet, proved to be the most reliable. This was a form of petroleum supply 'not in the book' but which nevertheless proved totally effective under the circumstances.

British involvement under the United Nations flag in the Korean War from October 1950 saw the petroleum requirement met by more orthodox means, but the British were not involved in the actual provision

A bulk fuel installation in the Canal Zone.

[By courtesy of RCT Museum]

of POL, which was a United States responsibility throughout the campaign, except for some oils. Details are given in the Korean War chapter in Part I of this book and are only outlined here.

The exceptional item for which the British were responsible for provisioning was Oil C600 for gear boxes of Centurion tanks and, at a later stage, special oils and greases provided from the RAOC. All other POL was moved forward by rail in American 55-gallon drums and delivered direct to Brigade areas by the United States forces where it was taken over by the Composite Platoon of the Brigade RASC Transport Company in 29 Brigade. 27 Brigade drew POL from the nearest United States Army Class III supply point. In both these British brigades the RASC companies were responsible for the forward supply of petroleum to the brigade units.

When 1 Commonwealth Division Column RASC had been formed, during the period 1 January 1952 to 1 October 1952 some 11¾ million gallons of Mogas was issued from divisional petrol points. In addition, a further 1m gallons of diesel was dispensed. Generally, the United States 55-gallon drum was used throughout the campaign and the only jerrycans held in petrol points were a small reserve for use by the divisional RAC Regiment when on occasions they carried out a long range patrol.

Generally, handling problems were overcome by using a natural ramp down which drums could be rolled onto unit transport. One advantage was that the average 3-ton load consisted of a considerably greater amount of POL than would have been the case had jerricans been in use. During the winter months, the consumption of petroleum products was exceedingly high. The heating of dug-outs and tents was carried out by means of issue pattern or improvised stoves which burned petrol or diesel. In the coldest month of February 1952 the peak consumption of petroleum in the Commonwealth Division was 72,000 gallons issued from the divisional petrol point and the daily average for the month was 63,000 gallons.

The last of the major petroleum installations overseas operated by the RASC was in the Middle East. During the desert war in Libya the supply of petroleum to the 8th Army had required major petroleum installations to be established in Egypt, operated by specialized RASC petroleum units. A petroleum pipeline was built and maintained by the Army, a joint RE/RASC responsibility, from Ataka, a small port in the Gulf of Suez to Fort Agrud, about 17 miles south of Cairo. Several pumping stations were necessary along this pipeline which was approximately 100 miles long, to boost the flow of petrol. After the war, the pipeline was left open and made available to the various civilian companies who were endeavouring to re-establish their commercial markets. This pipeline was naturally very vulnerable to the raids upon it by wandering tribesmen who quickly found a fresh source of income by its illicit puncturing! In 1954, the Director of Supplies and Transport Middle East, Major General D H V Buckle, CB, CBE, was given the task of transferring this pipeline, which by then had become very expensive for the Army to run, to the Egyptian Government. The transfer was ratified on 1 January 1955 and General Sadat (later President of Egypt) was the Egyptian representative in these negotiations. An important outpost from the Canal Zone at this time was Aqaba at the head of the Gulf of Aqaba, which presented special problems. Here a garrison was maintained and a petroleum pipeline ran from tankage in Aqaba to an infantry detachment at Maon, the RASC detachment in Aqaba responsible for this installation and pipeline was also responsible for the other RASC services. King Hussein, the Commander in Chief of the Jordanian Forces took a keen and helpful interest in all activities emanating from Aqaba and was known personally to send assistance to broken down vehicles which he came upon on his journeys through the desert.

DEVELOPMENT OF EQUIPMENT

During the whole period up to 1965, there was continuous development of petroleum equipment. The British Army had large stocks of jerricans and development of mobile rotary jerrican filling machines was well advanced.

[By courtesy of PR HQ NORTHAG]

Hand operated jerrican filling machine 1954.

Such a machine was first designed in 1946. With the Royal Engineers a
fair stock of Second World War heavy type steel pipeline was maintained
with equally heavy booster pumps and bolted steel tanks. Various flexible
bags were developed for bulk supply of fuel and the Dracone towed
flexible barge was first taken into use in 1953. It was in 1961 that a
Dunlop-made tank was first accepted for Service use. Other developments
included the rolling liquid transporter, improvements to the bulk tanker
wagon and fabric tanks.

Though the 'Octopus' was used for jerrican filling throughout the
period, such developments as the Fulham filler and the Albro filler were in
use. But, by the end of the period, the principal machine was the mobile
automatic rotary jerrican filling machine. This equipment was capable of
filling 720 jerricans an hour and, mounted on a trailer, was self-contained
and driven by its own small diesel engine. Each of the three sections of a
petroleum platoon had a filling machine and a mobile automatic jerrican
washing machine which was capable of washing 750 cans an hour. With
this mobile equipment, two other complementary machines were provided; the portable decanting equipment and the portable loader stacker.
The portable vehicle refuelling equipment (PVRE), a steel 600-gallon
tank coupled up to a trade pattern, hand operated, metering column was

in use together with the transportable vehicle refuelling equipment (TVRE). This latter equipment consisted of a 1,000-gallon tank coupled to a meter and a pump which could be driven either by an external electricity supply or hand operated.

QUALITY CONTROL

The development of more sophisticated fuels, oils and greases demanded rigid quality control of products. POL performance properties had to be monitored to ensure that they were standing up to climatic conditions, chemical changes in the product and whether or not they were contaminated. RASC petroleum laboratories formed part of the quality control system which was directed by one of the sections of ST2. This system started with acceptance testing of all POL purchased by the War Office/ MOD or overseas commands and covered the testing of tanker cargoes, routine testing of stocks and investigation of cases of mechanical failure attributed to the fuel or lubricant. The RASC petroleum laboratory was scaled at one for the United Kingdom and one or two for each major overseas command. They were static units and their establishments included two mobile petroleum laboratories. A mobile petroleum laboratory was mounted on a 3-ton lorry chassis and equipped with benches, sink, Calor gas and essential apparatus and chemicals. Petroleum laboratories were commanded by RASC officers qualified in petroleum chemistry. Non-commissioned soldiers consisted of chemical laboratory assistants who attended an initial 4-month course in petroleum chemistry held at the RASC petroleum laboratory, Farnborough, and at Ministry of Supply petroleum laboratories.

TRAINING

To meet the demands of other specialist training in petroleum, the Army ran a variety of courses for both officers and soldiers. During the period, much of the control of this training was carried out by the Petroleum Training Company, 3 Training Battalion RASC under the direction of ST2. The Petroleum Training Company provided training for fitters petroleum, both in their initial trade training and subsequent upgrading. Officers in the main attended the Officers' Long Petroleum Installation Course which, during most of this period, lasted some 15 months and included a 10-month period of time receiving general training from British Petroleum at Llandarcy.

   In 1949, the RASC bulk training installation at Fleet was first constructed from salvaged materials. At that time, it had limited value, the equipment being outdated. In 1953, proposals for a major works service of rehabilitation and modernization were submitted and by July 1956 the installation in its new guise was in full use. It contained 5 groups of bulk tanks, each with its own transfer pump house, the main pump house and a main line pump unit, in addition to a booster pumping house, road and rail loading facilities, a packing plant and additional training equipment. It was capable of being stocked and operated with any two products and thus provided an excellent opportunity for practical training for specialist staffs.

EPILOGUE

In 1965, the RASC handed over its petroleum tasks of provisioning, storage, quality control and issuing to the RAOC. The RCT continues with the responsibility for the distribution of both packed and bulk fuel forward to units in the field. Within the operational area, the refuelling of armour from bulk tankers is now part of this system.

15 · BARRACK SERVICES

THE ANTECEDENTS OF RASC Barrack Services reach back to the late 18th Century when the time-honoured expedient of billeting troops gave way to the more efficient practice of housing them in accommodation specially built for the purpose. From then onward the efficiency, or otherwise, of Barrack Services had been a major factor bearing on the welfare and consequently the morale of the Army and never more so than during the period of peacetime National Service following the end of World War II, when less than adequate attention to such commonplace details as beds, bedding, light, heating and so on affecting soldiers' comfort could easily arouse front page criticism in the popular press.

The first links between the Barrack Department, as it was then called, and Supplies and Transport were created in 1870 but it was only in 1943, under the stress of wartime challenges, that Barrack Services became fully integrated into the RASC management structure. The Barracks side tended traditionally to remain a separate and self-contained entity within the Corps and there is no doubt that when the responsibility originally descended upon the RASC, it was more as a matter of military convenience than the reflection of any deep seated affinity with the other major functions of the Corps. Thus, despite its crucial role in the Army's peacetime administration, the workaday nature of the Barrack Service, when compared with some of the other many and varied activities of the RASC, seemed to many to be devoid of military glamour and over-vulnerable to an unfortunate but ribald association with sanitary matters. It is therefore ironic that as the post war era evolved and the Army, first as a mainly National Service and then as an all Regular force, settled down to a peacetime existence and sharing the national aspiration to improving living standards, the good name of the RASC in the eyes of the military public came very much to depend, for all its humble image, on the efficient performance of Barrack Services.

The present account covers only the two decades between 1946 and 1965, the latter being the year when Barrack Services passed to RAOC as one outcome of the McLeod reorganization. Throughout this period no fundamental changes took place in Barrack Service responsibilities which continued to be:

   a. to furnish camps, barracks, married quarters, hospitals, etc. with accommodation stores to scales laid down in War Office Barrack and Hospital Schedules and to ensure that such stores were held on proper charge by the user through the inventory accounting system; also to provide replacement and exchange facilities by maintaining stocks in suitably located Barrack Expense Stores.

b. to arrange for the supply of, and accounting and payment for, various fuels, gas, water and electricity for consumption on military premises.

c. to provide assorted contract services such as window cleaning, chimney sweeping, conservancy and funerals.

d. to supply various domestic consumables, colloquially known as 'Mis and Dis' (Miscellaneous Chemicals and Disinfectants) which included such items as rat poison, cleaning materials and humble latrine paper.

It should be stressed that Barrack Services did not itself control the bulk supply of the materials for which it was the retail distributor. Instead, it constituted the interface, and in times of shortage, the unfortunate buffer between the military customer and the various bulk procurement services involved. The source of all accommodation stores was RAOC (who in turn were coming to rely increasingly on MPBW as the procurement agency for this class of stores); electric lamps came from RE/MPBW and most 'Mis and Dis' items came from RASC Supplies. In some overseas stations, where local funeral contracts were not practicable, the latter range of items included coffins and shrouds. Shrouds, incidentally, seem to have been prone to misappropriation for use as curtains.

The basic unit designed to discharge the responsibilities listed above was, as ever, the Barrack Office, scaled originally to service an accommodation strength of 16–30,000 troops. As time went by, such large concentrations became fewer but the reduction in workload tended to be offset by wider geographical dispersion of units and the growing number of married quarters.

The area served by a Barrack Office was termed a Barrack Charge, presided over by an Officer in Charge of Barracks (O i/c Bks), supported by one or more Assistant Barrack Officers. Each Barrack Office had an appropriate staff of clerks and inventory, store and fuel and light accountants. The yardstick for determining the establishment of barrack inventory accounts tended to vary with the times but the scale generally accepted by 1959/60 was one for every six major units, or 60 minor units, or·200 married quarters.

In the static chain of command (and Barrack Services was essentially a feature of the static organization) a Major (Barracks) might be found on the staff of CRASC of a District, usually a commissioned quartermaster although there were exceptions; for example in 1963 the Major (Barracks) in HQ RASC BETFOR Trieste, was a regimental officer who doubled as O i/c Bks as well. At Command HQ, the staff of DDST would include an ADST or DADST (Barracks) depending on the commitment involved. The occupants of the appointments at these two HQ levels were commonly known as Command and District Barrack Officers respectively, titles which harked back to pre-1943 days.

At the top of the pyramid, ADST (ST 7) War Office administered the whole of Barrack Services on behalf of DST. Working in consultation with the 'Q' Staff on general policy matters and with QMG (Finance) on questions involving expenditure, his brief also covered Annual Estimates (Barrack Services were big spenders), technical practices and procedures, the upkeep of regulations and Barrack Schedules and by no means least, fuel efficiency for which there was a professional Fuel Technologist on his staff to assist him. ST7 found a ready source of technical expertise and advice in the Barrack Services wing of the RASC Inspectorate.

The Story of the Royal Army Service Corps 1939–45 records how Barrack Services responded successfully to the problems of the Army's enormous wartime expansion. The challenges which offered themselves at the end of the war were no less tractable. In December 1945 nearly 2.5 million troops, male and female, Dominion and Allied as well as British, were dependent on Barrack Services. Rather more than half this total were serving overseas (leaving aside those in India Command where Military Engineering Services (MES) carried out the function equivalent to Barrack Services). The support that had been provided throughout the war to the troops in UK and in permanent overseas stations had to be maintained but superimposed on this was the new task of establishing Barrack Services ab initio in the new British occupation zones of Germany, Austria, Trieste and Japan as well as re-establishing a presence in British territories such as Malaya, Singapore and Hong Kong only recently recovered from the Japanese.

This was a formidable commitment but it also coincided with the need to prepare for the post-war contraction of the Army which had already started in late 1945 and was to continue steadily into the early 1950s, despite minor reverses in the trend due to events such as the Korean War and the Suez Campaign. By 1953 the Army had shrunk to around 450,000 but the process of rundown still continued in response to pressure for defence economies and withdrawals from overseas possessions. By 1965 the number of men and women dependent on Barrack Services had dwindled to 214,000.

In spite of this decline in overall numbers, the Barrack Services effort per head of military population remained significantly greater than in 1939. The rundown of the Army left a widespread commitment to the custody of unoccupied barracks and camps over long periods. Eventually when decisions were made to mothball or dispose of them, there followed the heavy physical task of backloading the accommodation stores. Then, consequent upon the Sands reorganization of the Army in the late 1950s and the initiation of the long term barrack rebuilding programme a further abnormal task arose which entailed the stripping of old accommodation before demolition and the subsequent furnishing of the new construction arising in its place. As an example it is only necessary to visualize the implication for Barrack Services of demolishing Clayton, Buller and Mandora Barracks at Aldershot and re-equipping the site as the modern home of the RCT.

[By courtesy of RCT Museum]

Mobile Barrack Exchange Shop.

Meanwhile the Army's domestic standards were becoming more sophisticated. The austere but robust pre-war range of accommodation stores was progressively replaced by more attractive (though often less soldier-proof) patterns, supplemented by numerous innovations of which, in its day, the soldier's bedside mat was a notorious example. This all added to the volume of stores handling and accounting imposed on Barracks staffs. But the biggest single addition to the workload was caused by the very large increase in the number of married quarters built or hired for the Army. In 1945 there were 15,000; by 1965 there were 65,000 divided about equally between Home and overseas Commands.

This accretion over 20 years of 50,000 more married quarters was, according to the yardstick quoted earlier, equivalent in inventory accounting terms of 1,500 major units. Moreover Barrack Services was becoming much more closely involved in day-to-day married quarter administration. The original pattern was for married quarters to be located inside or adjacent to the barracks of the units whose families occupied them and which were responsible for all administration, especially for checking the inventory of contents on change of occupant (the legendary 'March In/March Out' ordeal dreaded by so many people). Units were also responsible for the periodical exchange of breakages and unserviceable items. However, this system was unsuited to the requirements of the large new married quarter estates appearing after the war, whose allocation and administration could only be done on a garrison basis. This led to the introduction of Married Quarter Administrative Staffs (MQAS) designed to relieve units of much of the workload, but later it became evident that there was duplication and overlapping of function between MQAS and O i/c Bks. As a consequence of a War Office Study initiated at DST's request in 1957 a policy of direct accounting for married quarters was adopted whereby families became directly accountable to O i/c Bks for the contents of their quarters and the Barrack Inventory Accountant was recognized as the key individual responsible on behalf of O i/c Bks for conducting March In/March Out checks without the need for a unit or MQAS intermediary to be involved.

This sensible shortening of the administrative chain was matched by the introduction, as offshoots of Barrack Expense Stores, of Married Quarter Exchange Shops to which families could resort for the direct replacement over the counter of their breakages and worn-out items. Binned lorries specially fitted out as mobile shops were also provided to service married quarters in remote and scattered locations. These innovations proved not only popular but also more economical and efficient than the previous system which all too often had presented the ludicrous spectacle of unit QM staffs moving from door to door delivering teacups off the tailboard of a first line 3 tonner.

In overseas stations, Barrack Services functioned in broadly the same way as in Home Commands but local factors often placed a different

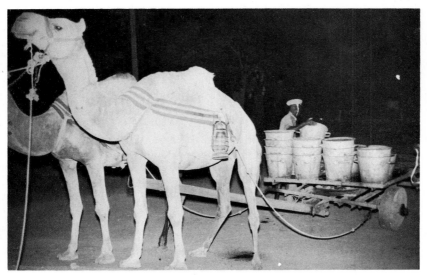

[By courtesy of Lt Col W Creighton]

An important aspect of Barrack Services in Khartoum – 'The Midnight Express'
honey-buckets!

emphasis on the importance of some of the services provided. For example in Bahrain there was little call for fuel for space heating but on the other hand water was so scarce as to cost more than in any other British Army station in the world. In Sudan, because sanitary services were primitive, the Barracks responsibility for conservancy was paramount. As the illustration shows, even camels were harnessed to the task.

Outside UK, Barrack Services' largest commitment lay in BAOR. The nucleus on which to build was provided by the town majors who had been set up in the wake of the Allied advance into Germany as local quartering authorities with power to requisition and de-requisition property. By 1946 the town majors had evolved into an organization of Quartering Commandants operating from Quartering and Barrack Offices for which their resources had been supplemented by a number of officers, mainly RASC Quartermasters, specially sent out from UK. The Quartering and Barrack Offices came under the wing of CRASC and the technical control of ST7 HQ BAOR. In due course the quartering role passed from RASC hands and an orthodox network of Barrack Offices remained.

Soon after settling themselves in, Barrack Services were kept busy dealing with the influx of families joining the occupation forces for the first time under 'Operation Union'. This involved requisitioning and furnishing large numbers of married quarters. The provision of furniture for officers married quarters was a new departure for the Army and a Barrack Schedule of Edwardian lavishness was drawn up in consultation with, and to some extent under pressure from the RAF. Whether as a result of this influence or not, the scale provided some slightly comic anachronisms, one being a housemaid's box reminiscent of black lead and brass fenders which was quite out of place in a German centrally heated environment. Another item was a Mrs Beeton style fish kettle big enough to cook a whole salmon, had such a luxury ever appeared on the BAOR ration scale.

In the major respect of married quarter fuel and light accounting BAOR practice was obliged to go its own way. In Home Commands, families wherever posible, were expected to make their own arrangements for the supply of fuel and light, but this was not practical in Germany, first because of the early problems arising from the occupation status and subsequently when this changed, the more permanent obstacles of language and the risk of bad debts. Thus the Army acting mainly through Barrack Services, always remained the intermediary between the German suppliers of fuel and light (as well as water) and the consumer in the married quarter, raising repayment charges, as applicable, against the latter. From this evolved a sophisticated system of standing charges and recovery at source on lines similar to the recovery of quartering charges. It stood the test of time and adapted naturally to the introduction in stations like Rheindahlen of district central heating schemes operated by the Army. It might be added that because of the harsher climatic conditions that prevailed in German winters, the fuel and light charges reflected an element of subsidy.

Turning to the manning of Barrack Services in its worldwide role, there was usually only a limited number of RASC regimental officers employed on Barracks work, mainly in staff-orientated capacities in the static command chain. There was a substantial civilian element among Assistant Barrack Officers and in Gibraltar at least, the post of O i/c Bks itself was a civilian one. But it was the RASC Commissioned Quartermasters who constituted the real backbone of Barrack Services. From over 800 (of whom some 200 were in UK Barrack offices) in 1946, their strength fell to an all-regular level of 107 by 1965. The Corps was doubly fortunate; first in being able to provide abundant scope for commissioned careers from the ranks; and second in the excellent talent among its warrant and non commissioned officers from which to select. It was always likely that any newly commissioned Quartermaster would serve most, if not all, his career in Barrack Services and Barrack Officers as a group were recognized as highly experienced professionals many of whom were formidable personalities well known among their contemporaries. Many rose to senior positions in the hierarchy and ex-Barrack Officers might be found in Personal Staff Officer appointments to generals from QMG downwards.

The expertise of RASC Barrack Officers was in demand when colonial territories were approaching independence, in setting up barrack service arrangements for the local armed forces after British withdrawal. The task required considerable patience and ingenuity to adapt British procedures to local conditions. Two officers who contributed reminiscences to this history had such experience, Lieutenant Colonel (Quartermaster) L D Darling MBE in the Malay Federation in 1953/54 and Lieutenant Colonel (Quartermaster) I G Thomas in Nigeria.

The bible for all Barrack Officers was Vol 5 of *Regulations for Supply, Transport and Barrack Services* (ST&B) supplemented by *Barrack Inventory Accounting, Fuel and Light Instructions and Sanitary Services*. These publications were unfortunately subject to fairly frequent detailed amendment and although reissued more than once, they were seldom completely up to date and usually needed to be read in conjunction with later ACIs or War Office letters.

The Army was, and still is, in a permanent state of organizational flux, but in 1957 the Sands proposals for defence economies initiated a decade of especially intense rationalization' fever which affected the Armed Forces at many levels. In due course the War Office was to disappear as a separate Ministry and re-emerge as a department of the Ministry of Defence. It was also to be the destiny of Barrack Services, among other RASC functions, to be transferred to RAOC.

The numerous studies carried out sought to simplify administration and reduce overheads. At the national level the objective was to achieve tri-service rationalization and to eliminate duplication in the logistic services of RN, Army and RAF as much as possible by centralizing procurement and supply of different classes of material in the hands of one or other of the services acting on behalf of all three. From outside the Ministry of Defence MPBW had made an early bid to take over solid fuel for the services but this was defeated on practical grounds. A more successful study resulted in the designation of the RAF as the common procurement authority for all accommodation stores. At District and unit level, various workstudy exercises took place. Those of concern to Barrack Services related mainly to aspects of inventory accounting and the distribution of solid fuel. It was often necessary to be sceptical of the schemes emerging from these studies. Some were unsound because they fudged lines of discipline or accountability or sought to introduce schemes specially tailored to different localities which would have cast administrative and procedural uniformity to the winds. Needless to say the job of the Barrack Office continued much as before.

In 1963 the Nye Committee on War Office Organization diagnosed, interalia, duplication and overlapping in the working of the Service Directorates and the Q Staff on the formulation of policy. The committee therefore recommended the separation of Service Directors from the War Office and the transfer of their policy-making functions to a 'Q' Staff enlarged to include staff trained officers from the services. The broad effects on the ST Directorate of the Nye Committee's recommendations are recounted elsewhere. When they were implemented in August 1964, ST7 disappeared and its last ADST (Lieutenant Colonel H Deighton) became the first AQMG Q (Maint)4. The central purpose of the Nye changes had been to simplify the transaction of business within the War Office but a side effect was to enable the interests and point of view of Barrack Services to be represented more strongly and with greater authority, inside the War Office 'Q' policy making machine.

Despite the spectacular nature of the Nye reforms and their impact on the higher management of the RASC, their occurrence tended to be obscured by the prospect of the much more sweeping changes in Corps responsibilities then under consideration in the McLeod Committee. The McLeod recommendations sought with obvious logic to bring an end to the old dichotomy existing within the RASC between its transport functions on the one hand and supply and services on the other. Thus, in July 1965, less than a year after the Nye changes had been introduced, Barrack Services was re-badged into the RAOC and Director of Ordnance Services assumed regimental and functional responsibility. Thenceforth the fortunes of Barrack Services belonged to the history of the RAOC.

16 · THE ARMY FIRE SERVICE RASC

THE SIGHT OF RASC personnel wearing the 'Red Roundels' of the Army Fire Service (AFS) surmounted by the Corps titles inevitably surprised many, caused eyebrows to be raised and invariably became the topic of conversation. Nevertheless there is nothing new about soldiers being employed on some form of fire duties. Fire parties and picquets are therefore well established and the Army has always been very conscious of the dangers of fire as a most destructive natural force. The AFS has a long history, the first military fire brigade being formed at Aldershot around 1864 and the early horse drawn manual and steam pumps were manned by infantry personnel, the drivers were provided initially by the cavalry and later by the Army Service Corps.

In the 1939–45 War the AFS rapidly expanded to approximately 7,000 officers and men serving in every theatre of operations, during which period the AFS was administered by a wing of the Pioneer Corps. As peacetime Commands and Districts were formed at home and overseas, specialist fire officers were appointed as advisers to Army Commanders, their staff and services.

On 1 July 1946 the whole of the AFS was absorbed into the RASC and the Pioneer Corps Fire Fighting Wing was disbanded. The Director of Supplies and Transport immediately tasked a study group to investigate the composition and role of the AFS and to produce a plan of reorganization, reflecting the reduced peacetime requirements. The recommendations of the study group were duly implemented and a considerable number of long overdue measures were rapidly introduced which resulted in streamlining the AFS and closely integrating it at every level within the command and control of the Corps. At War Office level a small branch within the Supply and Transport Directorate represented the AFS, elsewhere directors and commanders at each level represented the Service. Whenever possible Army Fire Brigades were grouped under the control of Army Fire Companies RASC and where this was not feasible they were classified as 'Independent Army Fire Brigades' with their own establishment. A small Army Fire Service Inspectorate was retained in the United Kingdom, British Army of the Rhine, Middle East Land Forces and Far East Land Forces. The various fire boat companies and sections originally formed to protect the Mulberry Harbour, major ports and waterways such as Hamburg and Suez were reformed under the RASC with a headquarters controlling two to three divisions each of three to five fire boat sections.

The general exodus of personnel on demobilization created man-

[By courtesy of The War Office]

Training in fire duties Cherry Tree Camp, Colchester

power shortages overseas and it became necessary to civilianize a number of United Kingdom Army Fire Brigades in order to release military personnel for overseas posting. These were designated RASC War Department Civilian Fire Brigades. Another important decision which was quickly executed was the closure of the Army Fire Service Depot and Training Centre at Catterick and the establishing of the Army Fire Fighting School RASC at Cherry Tree Camp, Colchester. The timber hutted block and open training areas provided excellent accommodation for specialist fire fighting training to be developed. The four corners of the square were concreted to take fire pumps and vehicles. Two whole buildings were used as instructional blocks, with each of the lecture rooms being set aside for specific purposes ranging from elementary fire extinguishers to pumps and hydraulics, ladders, breathing apparatus, building construction, ships and sprinklers. The large open training area was invaluable and met the requirements admirably. During this period in Colchester the whole training concept was reviewed and reorganized, and the staff underwent comprehensive Corps methods of instruction training which effectively ironed out the individual whims and mannerisms. This resulted in an exceptionally high standard of training being achieved which was regularly monitored by the RASC Methods of Instruction team.

For its size, the school's student throughput was very high. The main courses were a six week basic firemanship course for RASC National Service soldiers who were then posted to Army Fire Brigades, a nine week

444

intermediate course for RASC officers and NCOs, some of whom were posted to reinforce Army fire companies and brigades and two week All Arms Unit Fire Officers and NCO courses. As Army trades and peacetime substantive promotion was introduced, WOs and NCOs returned to the School to undergo a three day comprehensive assessment and trade testing. At the opposite end of the scale, six month RASC regular officers courses were introduced, students being earmarked for employment in the Fire Inspectorate or to command Army Fire Companies.

The staff and personnel of the School were also used in operational emergencies. They assisted in flood pumping and rescue work during the flooding of the Fens in 1947, and in Romford, Essex when they helped in controlling an extensive major rubber dump fire and other outbreaks of fire in the immediate vicinity. In addition numerous extensive realistic displays, demonstrations and exercises were conducted and there is little doubt that the school's concept of students actually tackling large fires was gradually adopted by many civil fire training establishments. Sometimes, however, realism became reality and this happened in 1949 during an 'At Home Weekend' when a fire rescue demonstration went awry and Sergeant Ronald Warwick RASC was subsequently awarded the George Medal for Gallantry. The extract from the official citation reads:

> 'Without any hesitation or thought for his personal safety, Sergeant Warwick mounted the escape and climbing at the double, passing through the flames and smoke reached Driver Reading and carried him down, again passing through the flames and smoke, to reach the ground safely. The contact of flames upon the steel fire escape had heated up the rungs so much that Sergeant Warwick's hands were severely burned when mounting and again dismounting, with Driver Reading's unconscious form across his shoulders. To the instant and gallant action of Sergeant Warwick, there is no doubt that Driver Reading owes his life, and his conduct and rescue are worthy of the highest traditions of the British Army and Army Fire Service'

In 1951 in order to eliminate training duplication and to promote professionalism, all fire training was then transferred to three local authority professional training schools, the Headquarters Station of Manchester City Fire Brigade who trained selected National Service RASC personnel for subsequent postings to Army Fire Brigades, Guildford Station of Surrey Fire Brigade for the training of RASC NCOs and All Arms Unit Fire NCO courses', and Maidstone Station of Kent Fire Brigade for RASC officers and All Arms Unit Fire Officers courses. A very small military staff of an officer and senior NCOs was established at each location to administer the students. From then on all AFS training was developed to Home Office standards by means of external professional training establishments. During 1957 it was decided to concentrate the training of AFS NCOs and men at the Surrey Fire Brigade Training School at Reigate. In 1960 the training of all officers and unit fire NCOs

Sgt R Warwick GM RASC
[By courtesy of The War Office]

was centralized at the Surrey Fire Brigade Training School, Guildford, which subsequently moved to Reigate. During this period the most far reaching innovation was the publication of *Regulations for Fire Services in the Army 1952*, a comprehensive manual on fire prevention and organization known as the 'Pink Book' and which has since been the yardstick for Fire Service Officers worldwide.

FAR EAST

In the Far East some twelve Army Fire Brigades were controlled by two Army Fire Companies RASC. One based initially in Alexandra Barracks, Singapore and redeploying later to Nee Soon controlled the training section and those brigades deployed throughout the island to provide cover for units and installations. These brigades were located at Nee Soon, Keat Hong, Kranji and Alexandra Barracks with one brigade over the causeway at Johore Bahru where the main vehicle depot was located.

The other company located at Kuala Lumpur controlled the brigades in Malaya, (less Johore Bahru) located in Kuala Lumpur, Taiping, Cameron Highlands, Seremban and Kluang. The brigades at Taiping and Seremban were closed in the early 1950s.

In Hong Kong only one brigade was established to cover the Ordnance Depot at Sham Shui Po, Kowloon.

MIDDLE EAST

In the Middle East, Army Fire Brigades were established to afford fire protection to the major military garrisons, depots and installations. AFS personnel consisted of a few British officers at command and formation level as Fire Inspectors or Advisers. A Warrant Officer Class 1 (Staff Sergeant Major) was the Superintendent of each brigade with a staff sergeant, sergeant, corporal and two soldiers for watchkeeping duties.

At the time of the absorption of the AFS into the RASC, an Army

Fire Service Training Depot for MELF was located in Polygon Barracks, Abassia on the outskirts of Cairo with 45 Army Fire Brigade located nearby. The only other brigade in the Cairo area was at Mena covering the RAOC Ammunition Depot with its storage in Mena Caves. Other brigades were at Port Said, Moascar, Suez and Tel El Kebir.

In 1947 HQ MELF and all other units in Cairo and Alexandria moved to the Canal Zone and as a temporary measure fire training was carried out at Dan Pinaar Camp. Soon afterwards the training was again moved to become a wing of the RASC School at Gebel Maryam south of Ismalia; fortuitously this location was on the Suez Canal which fed a large lake inside the camp thus providing an abundance of water for realistic fire hose training; in addition excellent permanent accommodation, lecture rooms and a drill tower were available. At this time 45 Army Fire Brigade moved to Fayid to cover GHQ MELF and Fayid Garrison; the Army Fire Brigade at Mena was disbanded.

All brigades were now concentrated in the narrow 100 miles long Canal Zone protecting the ports, garrisons, depots and installations. At Port Said brigades were located at Abbas Quay and Port Fuad. Other brigades were stationed at El Kirsh, Moascar, Fayid, Tel el Kebir, Geneifa, Fanara and Addabiya, the last providing to cover the Port Suez.

An important AFS post in the Canal Zone was that of the Warrant Officer Class 1 Staff Sergeant Major Fire Adviser Bulk Petroleum Installations who was located at Fort Agrud, the main site north of Suez on the Cairo road. Other installations were situated on the Great Bitter Lakes at Fanara and Nefiesha west of Moascar. All these locations were jointly operated by the Army and the Shell Company of Egypt where all the firemen were Egyptians under the technical control of the Fire Adviser.

In 1953 a disastrous fire occurred at the Command Ordnance Depot Geneifa involving a building containing the total stocks of clothing for the Middle East. During this period the Egyptians were being uncooperative and the fighting of all fires in the Canal Zone was left to the military. Consequently, as the fire developed, more and more Army Fire Brigade appliances from the length and breadth of the zone were mobilized and called forward to tackle the fire. Fire fighting was seriously hampered by lack of water near the incident and as the nearest static water tanks had been expended in the initial attack on the fire by the first appliances attending, water relays had to be organized from tanks located in other sections of this very large depot. At the height of the blaze so much water was being pumped onto the fire that it was running out of the building and bulldozers were called in to scoop large trenches into which the water was drained for it to be re-used. The entire building and contents were lost. The cause of the fire was attributed to spontaneous combustion of anti gas clothing.

At Headquarters East Africa Command, a Warrant Officer Class 1 (Staff Sergeant Major) Command Fire Adviser (CFA) was responsible for all fire matters including the technical efficiency of the Army Fire Brigades. He was visited annually by an Inspector Army Fire Service Middle East. The CFA was required to visit all units in the Command which embraced five countries in East and Central Africa namely, Kenya, Uganda, Tanganyika, Nyasaland and Northern Rhodesia in addition to the island of Mauritius.

Whilst very small AFS sections were formed as early as 1942, the first RASC Army Fire Brigade was established in Kenya at Mackinnon Road, north of Mombasa and was attached to 4 Company RASC (MT). This brigade arrived from Persia & Iraq Force (PAIFORCE) where it had provided fire protection for the Base Ordnance Depot at Shibah in Persia (now Iran). With the rundown of the depot, the brigade moved to Tahag in Egypt, then again to Mombasa.

On the run down of the logistic bases in 1952, the brigades at Mackinnon Road, Mombasa and Nairobi were disbanded and the brigade at Nanyuki moved to a purpose built fire station at the new Kahowa Base. In October 1952, the Mau Mau troubles started and numerous infantry battalions reinforced the Command. Despite the increased troop concentrations there were no increases in AFS personnel.

CYPRUS

In the early 1950s only one RASC Army Fire Brigade existed in Cyprus, this was manned by both military and local civilians and was located on the outskirts of Famagusta. The brigade afforded protection to the military installations in Karalos Camp, Famagusta, Four Mile Point and also responded to civilian fires throughout the Famagusta area.

The build up of Episkopi Garrison in 1955 warranted the formation of another Army Fire Brigade. Initially it was necessary for a Warrant Officer Class 2 and a Greek Leading Fireman to recruit and train local civilians, their first fire engine was merely a water bowser towing a trailer fire pump and they were accommodated in tents. Dhekelia Garrison also increased in size and importance and as no fire cover was available, a brigade section moved from Famagusta to Dhekelia and occupied a purpose-built fire station.

During the early days of the emergency, additional brigades were formed at Kikkos Camp and Lakatamia Ammunition Depot, Nicosia. Throughout this time the brigades were involved in many arson fires both in civil and military property. The NAAFI establishments were prime targets for explosive devices, many of which were crude home made designs. Fire Service military personnel were subjected to petrol bomb attacks at their homes, and were attacked by small arms fire whilst travelling to and from work or fire incidents. During these troubled times, although brigades were manned by mixed Turkish and Greek civilian crews, no problems arose and no Fire Service personnel were injured as a result of terrorist activities.

During the summer of 1956, military operations were hampered by forest fires of unusual severity. Troops engaged in the forests fought the fires with fortitude, yet the cost was high not only in terms of destroyed forests but also in the deaths of twenty two soldiers. The difficulties encountered were particularly hazardous because the mountains range up to six thousand feet in height and it was necessary to lay down firm guide lines on the methods of fire control thereby ensuring the safety of the personnel tackling the fires.

In addition to normal fire duties, the brigades were involved in riot situations and assisted the military in crowd control using jets of water. They also pioneered the use of coloured water which enabled the police to identify people once the crowd had been dispersed. The initial attempts with coloured water jets were from Bedford QL appliances carrying a light pump, the crew standing on the rear of the vehicle which was protected by a wire mesh guard.

During the Suez Crises of 1956, an RASC Army Fire Company of Army Emergency Reservists staged at Nicosia for a short period.

In the late fifties, a further Army Fire Brigade was formed at Ormedia to protect the ammunition depot located near Dhekelia, but the Nicosia brigade disbanded in 1960. At about the same time the brigade located at Famagusta was moved to Four Mile Point to cover the Ordnance Depot and Signal Unit. During this time the Cypriot civilian police fire service started training to provide cover for all major towns and not surprisingly, a number of Army local civilian fireman supervisory grades moved over to become the trained nucleus of the Cypriot Fire Service. This background enabled a very good liaison to be maintained throughout very difficult times. A number of British Fire Service officers also arrived in Cyprus on detached duty to assist in the building up of the new Civil Fire Service. Excellent cooperation existed between the Army and Civil Fire Service and on many large fires joint attendances were made by the brigades.

In 1962, the Army Fire Service was involved in a ship fire at Famagusta Docks, when fire broke out on the SS *Benicasim* moored there. The Famagusta civilian brigade were first to attend and requested assistance from the Army Fire Brigade. The ship's cargo included fertilizer in one hold and this was well alight. An initial attempt was made to extinguish the fire whilst the ship was in the docks, but the Harbour Master, being afraid that the ship would capsize and block the docks, ordered the ship to be towed out and beached. The ship was beached on the coast near Karalos Camp. Fire fighting was continued throughout with the aid of a Z Craft from the Royal Engineer Port Squadron. During the movement of the *Benicasim* the crew abandoned ship, the AFS personnel quickly secured a line, boarded the ship and claimed it as salvage. After some long protracted legal battles the AFS and military personnel involved in the incident received a share of the salvage money. It is likely that this may well be the only time that such a 'maritime salvage task' occurred in the history of the AFS.

BRITISH ARMY OF THE RHINE

The first AFS brigade landed in Normandy on D Day + 2 and as the military advance progressed so the numbers and deployment increased. The RASC inherited numerous Army Fire Brigades and sections many of which were in the throes of reduction, reorganization or disbandment. Many brigades were civilianized employing local labour and these afforded protection to the main depots and installations. At formation level RASC Fire Officers, Warrant Officers and Senior NCOs formed the fire inspectorate, advisory service and supervision.

On the move of HQ BAOR from Bad Oeynhausen to Rheindahlen, 41 Army Fire Brigade was relocated to afford protection to the new HQ garrison and surrounding area. The brigades comprised a Warrant Officer Class 1 (SSM) as Brigade Superintendent, 1 Staff Sergeant, 1 Corporal and 26 locally engaged German civilians manning two appliances. One of these, a Leyland Pump Escape, had a remarkable pedigree having first seen service in the UK, then the Middle East where it was captured by the Germans, re-captured by the British and eventually gave sterling service for many years at Rheindahlen.

In 1961, Mr A J G Chambers, ex Major RASC, returned as the first civilian Senior Fire Service Officer appointed Command Fire Adviser BAOR. He was initially supported by eight Fire Service Officers. These officers started an intensive programme of work to effect standardization and improvement to the overall efficiency of the Fire Inspectorate throughout the Command and weld them into an effective professional force. Under this direction all ad hoc local fire brigades located in military depots were brought within the direct control of the Army Fire Service RASC. Action was taken to uniform the personnel, regularize establishments, standardize equipment and training and improve efficiency.

BELGIUM

When the purpose built depots and installations in Belgium which constituted the Advanced Base British Forces were established, 128 Army Fire Company RASC was formed to protect the area. This was a unique situation which afforded the opportunity to institute a system of central

[By courtesy of Soldier Magazine]

A Leyland appliance of the Army Fire Brigade RASC Hamburg 1947.

fire control and a mobilization scheme to reinforce and concentrate fire resources as required. This was the last proper Army Fire Company to form and it comprised a small functional independent HQ commanded by a major with a captain as second-in-command, four double engined brigades and a total of about 130 military personnel. The brigades were deployed in the camps of the major units which were at Grobbendonk, mainly a fuel depot area; Tielen, the ammunition depot, Olen, the vehicle depot and Emblem the Ordnance depot.

As National Service ended so the brigades were partially civilianized and in 1960, 128 Company was disbanded. Some 120 local civilians were recruited, subjected to intensive training and those who were successful, completed the civilianization of the four brigades, a total of 176 personnel with a Warrant Officer Class 1 (Staff Sergeant Major) as Fire Adviser in overall control. These brigades became exceptionally proficient, to such a degree that they not only regularly won the BAOR technical efficiency trophy but a team from Grobbendonk also represented BAOR in the UK/BAOR Quiz competition and won the event two years running.

BRITISH TROOPS AUSTRIA (BTA)

Soon after the end of the war a Command Fire Adviser (CFA) was based at HQ BTA and three companies were located at Klagenfurt, Graz and Vienna. They occupied civil fire stations and manned a mixture of Bedford QL fire tenders and captured and requisitioned appliances. The fire crews were made up of British NCOs and Surrendered Enemy Personnel (SEP) who were awaiting repatriation but whose problem was finding their relatives. Two of these were pre-war professional soccer players and it was therefore little wonder that the Army Fire Brigade Soccer team was highly placed in the garrison league table.

Whilst Army Fire Brigades and sections were located to protect military installations and civilian property, the main risks were the petroleum depot at Klagenfurt, the Infantry area in Velden, the British Military Hospital at Lendorf, the petrol depot in Spital Villach and the Military Prison and displaced persons camps at Lienz. Ironically the brigade in Vienna was located in Schonbrunn Palace, the summer residence of the Hapsburg Family and had a detachment in the petroleum depot in the city slaughter house.

As the re-equipping, training and efficiency of the Austrian civilian fire service improved and increased and the number of Army Fire Brigades were gradually reduced, in 1952 the AFS comprised a CFA and assistant at HQ BTA with fire sections at Klagenfurt, Villach and the RE Field Regiment at Zeltweg. In 1955 all sections disbanded on the British withdrawal from Austria.

TRIESTE

In Trieste, the Army Fire Company and Brigade appliances were concentrated together to form a major fire station at the entrance to the docks, a unique position being flanked on the one side by the normal custom controlled access and on the other by American Military Police manning the military entrance. Furthermore the main railway station was nearby. The AFS, manning American Dodge and Bedford QL fire tenders, protected all military property and responded to civil calls in support of the local fire brigade which was in the throes of being reformed.

GIBRALTAR

In Gibraltar the AFS occupied the purpose-built fire station at Alemede Gardens. Its first RASC officer commanding was Captain K Hoare who eventually became the civilian Chief Fire Officer of Gibraltar City Fire Brigade. The AFS manned Leyland pump escapes and Bedford QL fire tenders. When the City Fire Brigade was formed the military element moved to Europa Point to form 15 Army Fire Brigade which was attached to 33 (MT) Company RASC. 15 Army Fire Brigade covered the military property at Europa Point, the Upper Rock area and the vast underground tunnel system.

CIVILIANIZATION OF THE AFS

In 1957 the Hull Committee recommended that whilst the AFS was an essential requirement within the Army, civilianization was recommended. Initially this was to be 60% civilian and 40% military, in the event however total civilianization took place between April 1961 and August 1962.

In June 1961, the Headquarters of the Army Fire Service was formed at The Barracks, Kingston-upon-Thames, Surrey. The Principal Fire Officer was responsible to the Director of Supplies and Transport for the organization and technical efficiency of the Army Fire Service and advising the staff and Services of the War Office on all fire precautions and fire protection matters relating to the Army. In addition, the Principal Fire Officer's responsibilities included research, development, introduction and approval of all fire vehicles and equipment used by the Army, advising the staff, units and Services on all fire matters, either in barracks or in the field, ensuring that all Army Establishments and affiliated bodies throughout the world received technical fire inspections at either bi-annual, annual or eighteen monthly intervals depending upon the establishment's fire risk, and representing the War Office on ten Government Committees.

In July 1962, a Fire Prevention Branch was formed at HQ Army Fire Service to assist the Principal Fire Officer in advising the Army Works Organization on all major projects being undertaken worldwide for the Army.

In November 1963, the Headquarters of the Army Fire Service moved from Kingston-upon-Thames to Beavers Lane Camp, Hounslow, Middlesex. In addition, the Principal Fire Officer became responsible for advising the Ministry of Public Building and Works on the Army's requirements in connection with fire prevention, fire equipment, water supplies, etc, in connection with new and modified building projects.

During this early transition period, considerable progress was made towards the attainment of improved professionalism. Fire inspection reporting systems were improved and amended to include fire survey schedules; Brigade operational procedures were updated and standardized and AFS officers started to attend courses in staff duties, fire prevention, aircrash and maritime fire fighting.

At this time the AFS had the responsibility for some 2,600 fire risks, inspections of which were undertaken by Command/District Fire Advisers depending upon their fire risk category and fifty seven Fire Stations with ninety nine Fire Appliances in selected garrisons and major installations throughout the World. Three of the stations provided crash rescue facilities for the Army Air Corps. The strength of the Army Fire Service at this time was 90 officers and 1,442 firemen. During the four-year period June 1961 to June 1965 the Army Fire Service attended 12,167 calls of which 9,657 were to fires and 2,510 to special services.

The role of the Army Fire Service has always been to provide close support to the Army in peace and war and during military operations at home and abroad, to provide mobile and static fire cover and a comprehensive fire advisory and fire prevention service. Its motto is 'SERVIMUS AD SERVANDUM' (We serve to save).

On 15 July 1965 as part of the implementation of the McLeod Report. The Service became responsible to the Director of Ordnance Services and thus ended twenty years RASC association with the Army Fire Service.

17 · CLERICAL SERVICES

In 1965 THE SUPPLY SERVICES were transferred from the Royal Army Service Corps to the Royal Army Ordnance Corps under the McLeod reorganization. The elements passed to the RAOC represented a number of rationalisation problems notably the transfer of the Supply, POL provisioning and storeholding branches, the Fire Services, Barrack Services and the takeover from the Royal Engineers of their Stores Provisioning function. Fortunately, included in the package was the means of ensuring that these tasks could be taken over and performed – the barrack officers, staff quartermasters, supervising officers and clerks of every rank and specialisation. All the products over many years of the Royal Army Service Corps' tried and proven system of clerical training.

The British Army had fought in theatres of operations stretching across the four continents of Europe, Africa, Asia and Australasia. Wherever the 'teeth' went, there followed the 'tail' leaving in its wake supply lines covering the globe like a gigantic spider's web. General, divisional, area and district headquarters had been established in each Theatre of Operations whilst installations for the issue of fuel, ammunition, food and water were dotted along the supply lines. Air despatch companies had been formed to supply airborne forces or to deliver food and equipment to men fighting in terrain no normal mode of transport could reach. Fleets of vessels had been established for the movement of stores and supplies within ports, up rivers and in some cases over areas flooded as a result of battle. All had one thing in common – clerical administration and support provided by clerks trained by the Royal Army Service Corps.

When hostilities ended, plans laid to prevent the errors of the mass exodus following the end of the 1914 war were implemented. 2 Training Battalion RASC at Willems Barracks, Aldershot, became the training centre for supply trades including clerks. Although some men joined the regular army during this time, the system was geared to the reception and training of National Servicemen who were still required to man the military installations worldwide. The aim of the Corps was to receive the National Service recruit and streamline his initial and trade training so that he was moved on to a 'working' unit as soon as possible. This meant induction at 5 Training Battalion, North Camp, Aldershot, for an initial five weeks military training followed by a move 'down the road' to 2 Training Battalion for training as a clerk. Clerks were taught the rudiments of typing, military office routine and the handling of office machinery, whilst courses in shorthand were available for clerks where

[By courtesy of The War Office]

RASC clerks under instruction.

this was a requirement, for example legal branches or personal assistants to staff officers at various levels. Training was also provided for the comparatively shortlived trade of Tactical Sketcher.

Upgrading courses were also a feature of this period, with wartime ranks threatening at any moment to be converted to peacetime substantive promotion, many NCOs and Warrant Officers intending to make the peacetime Army their career were endeavouring to obtain B1 and Chief Clerk grading without which, in addition to their Army First Certificate of Education, no promotion to higher rank was possible. Each clerk was required to be an efficient soldier as well as a tradesman; this required also the achievement of Military Proficiency Certificates at grades commensurate with their rank.

In 1947 occurred an event which was not only radical in its effect on world affairs, but produced a problem for the Corps which took some years to assimilate. Between 1923–1927 it had been decided that the Royal Army Service Corps would hand over its responsibilities in India to the Royal Indian Army Service Corps. This was completed in 1928 and from that time military clerks in India were trained and administered by either the RIASC or the Indian Army Corps of Clerks. In addition, the Indian Army Ordnance Corps had many clerks on establishment.

In 1947 India became independent with ensuing responsibility for her own armed forces. This required an agonizing decision to be made by the Anglo-Indians serving in the RIASC, IACC, or RIAOC, whether to remain in the newly established Army of India (if indeed they would be accepted), or whether to transfer to British Service. Many opted for the latter, although they had never served nor even lived outside India – there were naturally many problems for them to overcome. To make matters worse, the peacetime contraction of the British Army with its accent on the acquisition of qualifications for further advancement imposed constraints which many ex-members of the clerical elements of the Indian Army found difficult to meet. For some years after the independence of India, a period of turmoil ensued for these soldier clerks and sadly many who gave long, faithful and good service, particularly during the 1939–45 war, found British Service too exacting and were forced to leave. A number did overcome these difficult obstacles and remained to strengthen the Corps by their inclusion in its ranks.

It is perhaps interesting to note at this time that there was no official designation of Staff Clerks although the 'Staff Clerk Corps' founded many years before had been integrated with the Supplies Branch of the then Army Service Corps in 1899.

Although the myth of the 'Staff' Clerk is sad to abandon, it was nevertheless as 'Clerks-General Duties' that they edged their way up the promotion roll maintained by the Officer in Charge of Records, their only distinction being the 'S/' prefix which was shared with other members of the supply branch – butchers, bakers, storekeepers and petroleum

RASC clerks checking the documents of the draft.

[By courtesy of RCT Museum]

[By courtesy of The War Office]

Sgt W Craven, 60 Coy RASC Kuwait carrying out clerical duties.

operators. The Corps policy was to produce a many-faceted, military clerk versatile enough to serve one day in an MT company, barrack or transport office, the next to take his place in a 'G', 'A' or 'Q' Branch in a command headquarters at corps, division or brigade level or at War Office/MOD level. This last would test his versatility to the full as many and varied could be the role of the RASC clerks; a few examples will suffice – a Superintending Clerk (SSM) of an Army Board Member's Secretariat, a sergeant clerk in the Personnel Branch of his own Corps (AG8), shorthand writer in the office of the Director of Legal Services and always the clerical backing at junior NCO and private level for practically all other War Office branches.

The Officer in Charge of RASC Records did not encourage specialization amongst the clerical tradesmen although inevitably as peace imposed fresh constraints the specialist slowly but surely emerged and 'horses for courses' became the cry. As a result, although ideally a military clerk's training and postings should have been so ordered as to produce a complete, well-rounded Staff Sergeant-Major with experience of all branches of the Service, in practice this was not always possible. General officers have a habit of retaining clerks who have served them well and it would be a very courageous OIC Records indeed who refused the request of a 2 or 3 star general to take his Superintending Clerk with him to his new post!

Generally, however, the system worked well and by fitting round pegs into the appropriate hole the Corps built up a rapport with senior officers who knew that requests for clerks would receive prompt attention and the resulting product could be relied upon with complete confidence. This built up the image in the eyes of the senior hierarchy of the Army – who after all saw its product daily – of a Corps who could 'deliver the goods' at any time, anywhere.

One final example may serve to illustrate the ubiquity of the RASC Clerk – indeed not for nothing, was he described as being for 'General Duties'. To almost every country, Foreign and Commonwealth, a British Ambassador is accredited. The Military Attaché of such Embassies is supported by a clerical staff provided at that time by RASC Clerks and this in countries where often no other representatives of any other Service arm were present.

With the ending of National Service in 1959 and the restructuring of the Training Organization to meet the needs of all regular recruitment, 5 Training Battalion ceased to exist and recruits found themselves scheduled for three and a half months in Aldershot joining the Regimental Depot for a fortnight's documentation, medical checks, kitting and elementary military training, moving on to 1 Training Battalion for six weeks regimental training and finally taking a further six weeks trade training at 2 Training Battalion. Subsequent military and trade training was the responsibility of unit commanders, to whom the fourteen week product of this Training Centre was posted, although upgrading and other specialized courses continued to be available at 2 Battalion.

This mode was to continue until 1965 when, following the McLeod rationalization, the Clerks transferred to RAOC. It is perhaps interesting as a footnote to recall one of the particular problems which the 1,500 RASC Clerks of that time faced that the McLeod Committee solved. These represented a separate problem to the Committee as they could not logically be retained as functional to the new Royal Corps of Transport to be brought into being when the Supply functions were transferred. Various ideas were mooted including the possibility of allotting them to the RAPC, to the RAOC or to the Royal Corps of Signals. The last Corps was proposed in the belief that increasing mechanization and the introduction of electronic equipment into offices would demand from clerks, skills akin to those of some signal trades. In addition following trials in BAOR, it was known that divisional HQ companies would become part of the divisional signal regiment into which the Royal Signals were to introduce a new trade of staff operator which it was thought would reduce the clerk GD requirement. This was felt to be not altogether satisfactory particularly in respect of commissioning opportunities for GD Clerks who had traditionally such an outlet as barracks officers. As the Barrack Services were to be transferred to RAOC it was, felt logical that the clerks GD trade should go likewise.

The old clerk GD roll has been firmly split in two, one entitled 'Supply Specialist' and the other, at long last, proudly bears the name of 'Staff Clerk'.

Thus in 1965 the RASC handed over responsibility for clerks after more than 65 years, secure in the knowledge that the traditions of service forged during that period have been taken by those who changed their cap badges into their new Corps.

STAFF QUARTERMASTERS

During his campaigns before he became Commander-in-Chief India, Lord Kitchener carried a pad of message forms in his helmet. When orders were required he would merely remove the helmet, take out the pad, scribble a message and despatch it by hand of a 'galloper' to whatever part of the battlefield it was destined. This usually had the desired effect and the British Empire had cause often to be grateful to that mobile message centre.

From the 1890s, war and the administration of armies took on a different, more complex, approach. The inventions of the telegraph and the typewriter, linked with improved and faster means of communication, reduced the size of the world and meant that generals no longer needed to be in the firing line or indeed even within earshot of the battle. These shorter lines of communication brought about another problem. Generals who had been used to running their campaigns with only occasional interference from Whitehall had now, frequently, to look over their shoulders to argue, and often justify, their conduct to politicians and Commanders-in-Chief at home. This required a sharp increase in the numbers of staff officers and clerks at headquarters, with a corresponding upsurge in paperwork. A logical splitting of functions within these headquarters between 'G', 'A' and 'Q' followed and the comparatively small headquarters required for the fighting of the myriad minor colonial campaign's which characterized Queen Victoria's reign, burgeoned into a vast multi-faceted military office with proliferating sub-branches to accommodate the newly discovered methods of warfare. To handle these new problems, new methods were needed and the 'Chief of Staff' principle quickly evolved, requiring not only able, competent staff officers but a sub-stratum of professional clerks. Gradually the need grew for a commissioned officer with clerical experience to act as an interface between staff officers at all levels and their non-commissioned staff. The day of the Staff Quartermaster was beginning.

World War II firmly cemented the position of Staff Quartermasters throughout the military higher echelons and by 1945 these appointments had largely been rationalized. Each Headquarters had a Supervising Officer who specialized in office management and without whom the HQ would have slowly ground to a halt. Reception, distribution and despatch of mail, telephone services, employment of staff and general supervision of military clerical staff, office cleaning and sometimes even defence and employment platoons came within his orbit.

In the larger Army schools and training establishments, a Staff Quartermaster was usually established dealing with all the multifarious problems produced by a continual changeover of student population. If 'Office Manager' describes the Supervising Officer in a HQ then 'Bursar' should be the title of our second Staff QM. The Staff Officers within the War Office in the Department of Army Board and other General Officers, the Chief of the Imperial General Staff (CIGS), the Adjutant General, the Quarter Master General, Vice and Deputy Quarter Master Generals usually worked a 12–14 hour day for their Generals – all of whom seemed always indefatigable – and then went home to be on call at any time of the night to answer queries from staff officers charged with producing briefs or papers to a deadline. These Staff QMs had to be dedicated to survive the initial trauma, although many will tell you it rapidly became a way of life rather than a mere task. Even so, it was not until 1950 that steps were taken to regularise the appointments of staff quartermaster and it was only at this time that the actual title was used officially to describe the appointments for the first time.

In 1965, an era ended for the Corps. The responsibility for Clerical training having passed from RASC to RAOC, the Royal Corps of Transport is no longer required to train the men from whom the Staff Quartermasters are drawn. We can, however, look back with pride at the achievements of the Staff Quartermasters of the RASC, certain in the knowledge that their ghosts are looking over the shoulders of their successors with a nod of approval that the younger men have carried forward the legacy of tradition and service into their new Corps.

18 · ROAD TRANSPORT

During the Second World War the Army was equipped with a wide variety of mechanical transport of both UK and foreign manufacture. In fact by the end of the war an ever-growing proportion of our vehicles was of North American origin as a result of lease-lend. In 1945 the number of B vehicles in depots and units totalled some one and half million and, of those with units, some 40% were in the hands of the RASC scattered world wide from Aldershot to Inverness and Germany to Hong Kong.

Two fundamental problems faced the Army at that time from the mechanical transport point of view. Firstly how to reduce the holdings to meet the Army's revised post-war role, and secondly how to ensure that replacement vehicles of the correct type were available to replace ageing and foreign vehicles. Even before the end of the war the question of standardizing vehicles was raised by the QMG when in 1943 he called for a paper on the subject so that lessons learnt in the war might be taken into account for future planning. In order to follow the history of mechanical transport as it affected the Corps in the years since the war, it is simpler to take each of the main vehicles in turn from the motor cycle up to the tank transporter.

By 1945 there were some two hundred thousand motor cycles in service and many of these (Ariel, BSA, HarleyDavidson, Matchless, Norton, Royal Enfield, Triumph and Velocette) remained in service until they were gradually phased out and replaced by more modern machines. By the 1950s the two types in widest service use were the BSA 500cc and the Matchless 350cc. Both were inherently reliable having been proven over a number of years, but the ground clearance of the BSA was low and in cross country conditions this caused problems for many riders. Furthermore it was a heavy machine and needed a strong rider to achieve the best results. The Matchless on the other hand, although less powerful, was more agile across country but did not match the staying power of the BSA on the road. It was not until the mid-60s that the Army received completely new machines. The initial Army trials on four BSA 350cc and four Triumph 500 cc machines were concluded in 1965. Both types had major defects and further trials were completed with modified machines. By 1966 both machines were near to meeting the requirement and the BSA model, B40 as it was known, was accepted for service in 1967 and introduced on a maintenance basis. By the late 60s thoughts were being directed to the replacement for the B40 and in early 1971 it was decided that in future there would be no motor cycle specifically designed for

[By courtesy of JSPRS Hong Kong]

A selection of vehicles operated by the Gurkha Transport Regiment.

military use. This was part of an all-embracing policy for B vehicle procurement which is covered in greater detail later. In the event, it was subsequently agreed that two types of machine were needed for Service use; one for escort duties for use mainly on roads, and the other, a lighter machine, for general purpose use. After a review of the commercial field and subsequent trials, the Triumph Meridan Saint 750cc was introduced into service as the escort machine in 1978 and is in Corps use with tank transporter units. The contest between the lightweight contenders was less straightforward. In the end a late entry, the CANAM 250cc made by Bombardier of Canada, was the first choice. Some two thousand machines are to be introduced into the Army and despite a number of irritating faults in the first buy of 800, the machine's performance is good.

Turning to the lightweight vehicle, the ubiquitous Jeep served the Army well both during the war and in the immediate post war years. Spares for the vehicle after the cessation of lease-lend incurred dollar expenditure and it became necessary to find a suitable replacement from British industry. In the late 1940s the philosophy of a common range of military engines was conceived and subsequently the B range of Rolls Royce engine was born. There were three engines in the range, the B40, B60 and B80, and the first of these was selected to provide the power for our replacement for the Jeep. The resultant vehicle was the Austin Champ ¼ ton 4 × 4 and a limited number entered service in the early 1950s. The vehicle was not a great success as there were major problems both with the steering mechanism and the rear axle, nevertheless the Champ remained in service until the mid 1960s. At about the same time development started on the Land Rover. Its origins are often attributed to the then Technical Director of the Rover company who owned a Jeep for taking his sailing dinghy into the water. His Jeep reached the end of its useful life and he asked his firm to produce something similar! The first 100% Rover-built Land Rover with an 80 inch wheelbase, was produced in 1948 from a modified US Jeep where certain Rover units were fitted in place of American parts. Although the Land Rover was widely used in the United Kingdom, it was not until 1956 that it became officially adopted by the British Army. Both ¼ ton and ¾ ton versions were introduced in the initial stages and it was mainly the former that saw service with RASC units. The Land Rover has been subjected to changes and modification over the years and in 1965 the Rover Company began to develop an updated version known as the Series Two range. At the same time, the Army recognized the fact that the Rover had competitors and versions of the Austin Gypsy were tested at the MT Wing Army School of Transport. The Gypsy did not show up well and the Army continued with the well proven Land Rover. A ½ ton 4 × 4 Land Rover with a new austerity look came into service in 1968. Its introduction was as a result of the side-by-side loading requirement of the Land Rover in the RAF VC10 to make maximum utilization of the available payload in that aircraft. Both the weight and the overall width of the vehicle were reduced and the ½ ton Land Rover became an attractive addition to airportable regiments. Later in 1971, largely as a result of the Construction and Use legislation, the Series Three Land Rover was introduced into service on a maintenance basis and it is this vehicle which is in current use, mainly in the FFR (Fitted For Radio) version, in many Corps units today.

The predominant workhorse of the Corps, RASC and RCT, has been the 3 ton truck. Of the many varieties of 3 ton truck in the Army's inventory at the end of the war, some remained in-service for many years and in particular the Bedford QL and the Austin K5. A prime example of the former in the guise of an office truck was handed over in 1980 to the Army Transport Museum in Beverley where it is now on display to the public. So far as the Austin K5 is concerned, this vehicle was used as the experimental base for the B60 engine of the range of Rolls Royce engines referred to above. They proved very popular with units because the vehicles could be used for details outside the normal mileage limit for journeys! The experiment, however, was not deemed to be successful and the Rolls Royce venture was terminated. At the beginning of the 1950s steps were taken to replace these old vehicles and the vehicle manufacturers, Bedford, Commer and Ford, were asked to provide options; the two main contenders proved to be the Bedford RL and Commer Q4. In 1953, 11 Company RASC in BAOR was selected as the trials unit and their ageing QLs were replaced by 58 Bedford RL and 34 Commer 3 ton vehicles. The RL was the more successful of the two and became the general service mainstay of Corps activities. The Commer Q4 was not completely discarded and appropriate Corps units were issued with the Tipper version. In all, some 73,000 Bedford RLs, both military and civilian, were produced and updated through the years. In 1968 the RL was uprated to 4 ton capacity and no longer could the Corps use the endearing term '3 tonner' which for so long had been part of its vocabulary.

Even before the RL was uprated to 4 ton, plans for its successor were in preparation. In the mid 1960s the intention was that the RL's successor should have a 4½ ton capacity with a 5 ton emergency overload capacity; its degraded cross country performance with the increased payload was to have been accepted. Three manufacturers, Bedford, BMC and Commer produced options and subsequent trials at the Fighting Vehicles Research and Development Establishment (FVRDE) failed to find any particular model outstanding so all three options were put to user trials in 1965 in UK, BAOR, FARELF, MALTA and LIBYA. By 1967, the BMC contender, the Austin FJ, was excluded from the comparative trial due to continuous engine failures. In keeping with the then recent policy change by the Ministry of Defence from multi-fuel to tri-fuel (AVTUR/AVTAG/DIESO) the Bedford was fitted with a low compression engine, not capable of running on combat gas, which was almost the same as the commercial diesel design and therefore cheaper. The Commer was fitted with an inherently multi-fuel engine of an opposed piston two-stroke configuration. In both vehicles the body was designed with facilities for restraining loads and corrugated light alloy side panels to reduce the overall weight without loss of strength. Although both vehicles passed the technical acceptance stage, the Bedford MK was finally adopted and designated 4 ton rather than 4½ ton since it incorporated a steel body rather than the light alloy design originally proposed. Deliveries of the Bedford MK to Corps units started in 1971.

From concept to issue, the Bedford MK took some eleven years to materialize. This lengthy development cycle coupled with the high cost of military 'specials' led the Army Department to revise its procurement philosophy in the late 1960s. An Army Department Logistic Doctrine Committee paper was approved in 1969 which pointed the way ahead for the future family of B vehicles. The fundamental concept of the new philosophy was based upon three mobility levels:

[By courtesy of MOD CS (REPS)]

Alvis Stalwart High Mobility Load Carrier.

High — vehicles with mobility similar to Stalwart for the tactical resupply of forward units in certain situations.

Medium — vehicles similar to the former GS range capable of operating off routes away from roads and tracks and therefore needing all wheel drive.

Low — selected from those vehicles available on the commercial market for operation on roads and compacted tracks where only a limited off-the-road capability is necessary.

In general terms the degree of mobility depended upon the logistic environment in which the vehicles would have to operate. Forward of the Replenishment Park or equivalent, Medium or High Mobility capability would be appropriate whilst behind the Corps Rear Boundary, Low Mobility would be sufficient.

When determining high mobility vehicles, the Stalwart was used as an example and it was perhaps worthwhile to consider this vehicle in some detail. It was built by the Alvis Company in Coventry as a private venture in 1959. Earlier, an Armoured Corps officer conceived the idea, whilst employed as a Technical Staff Officer, of using the Saracen Armoured Car chassis to mount a load carrying body with a view to providing a high mobility load carrier for tank replenishment. He was unable to 'sell' the idea to the Army, so retired and joined Alvis. In the event the Stalwart was based upon components of the Salamander fire tender which itself had a chassis similar to that of the Saracen. The Stalwart is undoubedly the finest cross-country load carrying vehicle in its class in the world. Stalwart has a road speed of some 45 mph and a cross-country perform- ance virtually equal to that of the tank. It can cross a five foot ditch, climb a twenty plus degree gradient and has an eighteen inch ground clearance. It has an amphibious capability and a payload of some five tons. The Mark One version was introduced in 1961 and was widely used by the Corps in Aden. More Stalwarts, of the Mark Two version, were procured in the mid-to-late sixties and were deployed in BAOR to units of the Combat Arms as unit A echelon vehicles and to Corps units at second line. The Stalwart's high cost has precluded its issue as a replacement for all load carrying vehicles in the forward areas and in subsequent years, the question of its replacement has remained unanswered largely on financial grounds. It is currently expected to remain in Service use until the mid-eighties and certain vehicles are to be re-worked but without their amphibious capability which is both expensive to maintain and little utilized. One thing is certain, the need to replenish tanks and infantry units in forward areas remains a requirement and a vehicle such as Stalwart will be high on the logistician's shopping list.

At about this time, due partly to the onset of the Northern Ireland emergency, it became necessary to make an immediate purchase of 4 Ton vehicles to replenish Army stocks. Since increased production of the Bedford MK was not feasible, the Army were obliged to take a straight commercial chassis and cab option with a MK body. The resultant vehicle was designated the Bedford TK and is in wide use with the Corps as a general purpose vehicle in Garrison Transport Units and as a basic driver training vehicle. On 24 February 1971 the future B vehicle fleet requirements, based upon the philosophy expounded above, were pre- sented at the Military Vehicles and Engineering Equipment Establish- ment, Cobham, to a large gathering from Industry. Increasing tonnages to be lifted with reduced manning levels dictated that the largest capacity vehicle commensurate with the operational environment would be adopted. The individual vehicle capacity was related to both dead- weight tonnage and NATO pallet carrying capability. The basic vehicle of the new fleet is the 8 tonne/6 pallet medium mobility load carrier. This was to replace in Corps units, the 4 ton GS in first line, the 4 ton and 10 ton in second line and a proportion of the 10 ton vehicles in third line. Later it was accepted that the 4 ton vehicle would be retained to meet certain roles in the first line. The mainstay of the third line was to have been a 16 tonne/12 pallet medium mobility load carrier, however financial dictates persuaded the MOD to adopt the low mobility option instead and this would have the additional capability of carrying ISO containers. As might be expected the latter commercially based vehicle was the first of the new range to come into service in the form of the Foden 16 tonne. So far as the 8 tonne is concerned, the Army's link with the 'Bedford' continues and Vauxhalls are to produce this vehicle which is

[By courtesy of Central Office of Information]

10 ton AEC of 27 Regiment RCT, Bulford 1974.

known as the Bedford TM 4 × 4 8 tonne.

The absence of a 10 ton vehicle from the new range will be looked upon by some as a sad departure from tradition, but the fact that higher tonnages have to be lifted by the same number, or even less, drivers demand vehicles with a higher load capacity. The Leyland Hippo 10 ton 6 × 4 remained in service for many years after the war and from the early fifties the Army acquired relatively large quantities of the AEC Militant 10 tonners of both 6 × 4 and 6 × 6 configuration on a maintenance basis for the ageing wartime fleet.

In the 1960s, planning started for the replacement to the Militant, the Mark 1 as it became known, and two different options were considered. The first option, the Militant Mark 3, was of a 6 × 6 configuration and two of these vehicles commenced user trials with 2 Divisional Regiment RCT in mid-1966. The second option was a commercially based 6 × 4 vehicle and a number of trucks were ordered from AEC, Foden, Leyland and Volvo for user trials. A technical assessment team, led by FVRDE, was set up in 1969 to evaluate and report on the commercial contenders. Partly due to political pressures, the competition proved to be inconclusive and it was decided that the commercial option would be met by a 16 tonne LMLC in the new range of vehicles. However there was a need to replace at least some of the ageing 10 ton fleet where most of the vehicles were older than their drivers! Common sense prevailed and 300 of the Mark 3 Militants entered service with RCT units by mid-1975. These are however the last 10 tonners the Army will have as they are to be replaced by the new range of 8 tonne and

[By courtesy of Maj H B Stevens RCT]

Diamond T tank transporter in BAOR.

16 tonne vehicles referred to earlier.

To many of those who serve or have served in the RASC and RCT, the King of the road is the Tank Transporter. Until the 1960s the wartime American Diamond T 980/981 M20 tractor remained in service as the prime mover for tank transport trailers; the latter being mainly the Dyson 40 and 50 ton versions. Gradually Diamond T's were phased out and by 1964 replaced by new vehicles which were basically commercial vehicles modified to meet a military requirement. Among these new vehicles, the Scammell Constructor and the Thornycroft Antar were most common. The latter was a military version of the 'Mighty Antar' which had been designed originally for oil pipe transport in the Middle East to a specification laid down by George Wimpey & Co. Ltd. Three Marks of Antar tractor saw service with the Corps; the 50 ton Mark 1B ballast body version and the first articulated Antars with their semi-trailers, the 60 ton Mark 2 and the 50/60 ton Mark 3A. Dyson and Cranes manufactured the 50 ton transporter trailers whilst the 50 ton semi-trailers were produced by GKN, Sankey and Taskers. By the late 1960s thoughts were being directed to the replacement of the fleet in BAOR which was due to begin in 1972/73. In 1968 the aim was to carry a 55 ton tank, with a bridge classification of 80, with a marked improvement in performance and reliability over the current fleet. Following a re-appraisal of the BAOR requirement in 1969, however, the proposal to develop a new tank transporter tractor was shelved. Instead, the Antar was to continue as the prime mover for the foreseeable future and a new 60 ton semi-trailer, built to a military

[By courtesy of RCT Museum]

The first Thornycroft Antar delivered to the Army Sept 1951.

specification, was planned as an interim measure to replace the Dyson full trailer which was unsuitable for the carriage of Chieftain.

The 'go/no go' syndrome which has bedevilled tank transporter development since the war is illustrated by the cancellation of this proposed interim buy of semi-trailers in 1972. This decision was based on the grounds that the ideal longer term solution was to develop the tank transporter train as an entity instead of procuring the tractor and train separately. The General Staff Requirement for the new train was raised in 1976 with an in-service date of 1982 and this called for a semi-trailer of 55 tonnes. Meanwhile the Antar fleet, together with some of the semi-trailers were to be re-worked to extend their life until the new equipment entered service. By 1979 it became apparent that the battle weight of both Challenger and MBT 80 was to be in excess of 55 tonnes and an increase to the carrying capacity of the proposed Scammell Tank Transporter train was necessary. Two engineering models of the Scammell tractor started trials in 1979; one model was fitted with the American Cummings engine whilst the other was powered by a Rolls Royce engine of similar basic design to that fitted to the Challenger Main Battle Tank. The development was shelved in late 1981 but the project was re-activated in December 1982 and the new tank transporter, to be known as Commander, complete with its trailer, is expected into service in 1984/85.

Turning to Ambulances; perhaps the best known wartime ambulance was the Austin K2 and it remained in service into the 1950s. In the immediate post war years, various types of commercial model were adopted for use in support of hospitals and later static units. This practice has continued throughout the years. The military ambulance has been based upon a variety of 4 × 4 chassis and rigid bodies were fitted to both the ¼ and ¾ ton Landrover in the early fifties. Two-stretcher frames with canopies were fitted to the Jeep, Champ and Land Rover for use by field ambulance units of the Royal Army Medical Corps in forward areas and in 1954, 14 Field Ambulance in 2 Division in Essen had eight of each vehicle type for comparative purposes. The Rover model was finally adopted and there have been ambulance conversions on most Land Rover models ever since. For larger ambulances, capable of carrying four stretchers, both the Austin and Humber 1 ton were used, the former being developed originally as a RAF crash rescue vehicle. Whilst suitable for carrying four stretcher borne casualties, there was insufficient space for medical staff to attend to patient needs in transit. Purpose built 3 ton ambulances based upon the Ford Thames 4 × 4 chassis were produced by both Spurling and Mulliner and these afforded more space between the two bunks and more headroom between stretchers.

In the late sixties, when the forward control 1 tonne Rover was undergoing development as the Light Gun tractor, trials were carried out to assess the patient ride characteristics of the Rover 1 tonne prototype and its Swedish contender the 'Laplander'. There was little to choose between them and a final choice was avoided when it was decided that the future battlefield ambulance in forward areas would be armoured and an ambulance version of the Infantry APC, the FV 432, was produced. Field Ambulance units in BAOR are equipped with this vehicle which is gradually being replaced by the CVR(T) range of tracked vehicle ambulance version named Samaritan.

The logistic concept for casuality evacuation required the ability to load stretcher borne casualties into the cargo deck of load carrying vehicles. Additionally, military coaches can be converted to the ambulance role by removing the seats and fitting a specially designed stretcher framework. In the late seventies the need for a wheeled ambulance for use in forward areas was stated, and a 4-stretcher ambulance based on the Rover 1 tonne was developed. Field Ambulance units in the United Kingdom, including Territorial Army units, are equipped with this vehicle.

TRAINING

The history of training drivers for the complex range of vehicles that make up the Corps fleet is a major subject in itself and cannot be covered here. To illustrate the requirement for skills over and above those required for basic vehicle operation, three aspects of advanced training are touched upon below, radio, staff car and master driver. There are many others.

RADIO COMMUNICATIONS

In the immediate post-war years it was the motor cyclist who was the communications medium in most Corps units. This system continued until the early sixties when the increasing importance of communication in the logistic resupply system became apparent. The trade of Driver Radio Operator, as a secondary qualification, was established to cater for the increased communication commitment.

In 1964 the Signals Training Platoon was formed as part of 1 Training Battalion RASC in Buller Barracks, Aldershot, under command of Lieutenant Mike Patton, to provide radio training for the Corps. Its Instructional Staff comprised one lieutenant, one sergeant and six corporals tasked to train unit signals NCOs who were required to train radio operators in their own units. Corps communications were limited and the trade course was at basic level since the only set issued to and used by the Corps at that time was the SRC 13. On re-badging in 1965, the Signals Training Platoon became a Troop as part of 12 Driver Training Regiment RCT. By 1970 the instructional staff had been increased and the Corps undertook the training of its own B2 and B1 operators and regimental signal instructors, a task hitherto carried out in part by the Royal Engineers at the Royal School of Military Engineering at Chatham. In February 1977, as a result of new systems of re-supply and the advent of the Clansman range of radios, the trade of Driver Radio Operator was made a separate career employment qualification within the driver employment group. Later in the same year the Signals Training Troop left Aldershot and was incorporated in the newly formed Army School of Mechanical Transport at Leconfield as the Signals Division of the Advanced Training Wing.

The Corps regular driver radio operator establishment is some 420 all ranks, all of whom are trained at the appropriate level at Leconfield. The regular Army element of the Corps is equipped with the Clansman range of radios mainly the VRC 321 (HF) and VRC 353 (VHF) except for certain specialist units, particularly maritime units, where commercial radios are in use. Some Corps Territorial Army units still operate Larkspur equipments but are scheduled to get Clansman radios by the mid eighties. Territorial Army operators are also trained at Leconfield to ensure as far as possible uniform training standards.

The advent of the Clansman range of radios has greatly improved the standard of communications by Corps units. The need for the use of morse by Corps radio operators is often challenged and it was hoped that with the introduction of the Clansman range, morse would no longer be required. However the frequency allocations, coupled with the range over which many Corps units have to operate their radios, dictate that morse is often the only communication medium which will ensure messages get through the 'clutter', particularly at night.

STAFF CAR TRAINING

Staff cars and staff car drivers are emotive subjects and the Corps has been at pains to ensure that the standards of staff car drivers have remained as high as possible over the years.

Staff car driving is an acquired art where the obvious fundamental requirement is a high standard of driving. However personal attributes such as appearance, courtesy, resourcefulness, cheerfulness, reliability and good manners, to name just a few, are of equal high importance. In an effort to maintain a uniform standard a staff car course, predominantly for Corps and Womens Royal Army Corps soldiers worldwide, has formed a constituent part of the Corps' annual training programme. Up to the mid 1960s the staff car drivers course was held at 6 Training Battalion RASC, Yeovil, Somerset. For a brief period, whilst the new Buller Barracks was being built, the venue was Church Crookham in Hampshire with 12 Training Regiment RCT. The course later remained with that Regiment in Aldershot until it was transferred with basic driver training to the new Army School of Mechanical Transport formed at Leconfield, North Humberside in 1977.

Additional or in some cases alternative training is carried out in specialist staff car units such as 14 Squadron at Bielefeld, 22 at Wilton, 68 at Rheindahlen and 20 Squadron in London. In the last named, the training covers extensive route familiarization – not as extensive as that London taxi drivers have to undergo but sufficient to ensure that central London is well known before the drivers are permitted to drive Ministers and Senior Officers of the Ministry of Defence and Staff from Headquarters London District. They also provide the staff cars for Military overseas visitors, but most important of all, the cars for the Royal Family attending military occasions.

Up to 31 May 1967, 20 Squadron was the servant of the War Office and latterly the Army Department and Central Staffs from 1962. On 1 June 1967, 20 Squadron's responsibilities were extended to cover the whole Ministry of Defence and the assets in cars and drivers, previously serving the Navy and Air Force Departments were transferred to 20 Squadron. It is often said that 'old habits die hard' and the first few months of the reorganized commitment were fraught with difficulties, often as a direct result of inter-service jealousy.

The training of staff car drivers had been directed mainly towards improving driving standards and enhancing personal attributes. However in recent years this training did not meet the current needs of the Army, particularly in the field of security awareness and response to an emergency. Under these circumstances it is no longer sufficient to train good military chauffeurs. The modern staff car driver must be alive to the implications of security and sufficiently well trained to be able to react correctly in an emergency.

[By courtesy of JSPRS Hong Kong]

Staff cars outside Flagstaff House, Hong Kong.

For the future it is intended to operate a three tier system of Staff Car Driver. First the basic level where training takes place in units. Emphasis will be given to basic driving skills, courtesy drills and an introduction to security awareness. The second level is the Advanced Staff Car Driver where qualified basic Staff Car Drivers with a minimum of one year's staff car experience will attend a course at the Army School of Mechanical Transport where concentration will be directed to improving driving skills, including skid pan training, evasive driving, varied route selection, security awareness and recognition of potential threat. The final level is the Close Protection Staff Car Driver where RCT students attend a course held by the Royal Military Police with the emphasis on training the driver as a member of a Close Protection Team. Once so trained the graduate driver can be called upon to be a member of a Royal Military Police Close Protection Team driving high ranking personnel and VIPs who are considered to be 'at risk'.

Turning to the equipment aspect the variety of staff cars has been legion, from 'Monty's' Rolls Royce to Jaguar XJ6 in Washington and it is only in comparatively recent years that some measure of standardization has been achieved. In 1965 there were basically four grades of staff car:

Grade 1	Austin Princess
,, 2	Humber Super Snipe
,, 3	Humber Hawk
,, 4	Ford Zephyr

Staff car driver outside Horse Guards.

[By courtesy of PR London District]

By 1968 the grading was changed to:

Grade 1 Limousine	Daimler Limousine
„ 1	Rover 3.5
„ 2	Hillman Hunter
„ 3	Austin 1800

Being ever an emotive subject a special working party was set up by Principal Administrative Officers (PAOs) in 1979 and chaired by the Director General of Transport and Movements to consider the grading and allocation of staff cars for all three Services worldwide. As a result of this Working Party it was decided that only two grades of staff car were required:

Grade A	Ford Granada 2.3
„ B	Ford Cortina 1.6

By 1982 it was agreed that the Grade B replacement would be the Vauxhall Cavalier.

THE MASTER DRIVER RCT

Units throughout the Army are required, by the Directorate of Army Training, to have an appropriate number of their strength trained in various aspects of Mechanical Transport management and training. However it became apparent in the late 1960s that there was a need for a travelling expert to ensure that units had every possible assistance to maintain their standards. It was the Royal Corps of Transport who was asked to provide this expertise and the Master Driver was introduced in 1972. There are today some twenty-seven Master Driver appointments throughout the world – all warrant officers. Their role has expanded over the years and their responsibilities now cover five areas, MT Management, MT and Driver Training, control of Qualified Testing Officers and their re-testing, Road Safety and Health and Safety at Work in the MT environment.

To ensure the highest possible standard, their selection process is lengthy. All prospective candidates must be heavy goods vehicle driving instructors, qualified testing officers, professional MT operators, of senior rank and recommended for selection as Master Drivers in their annual confidential report once they have attained the rank of staff sergeant. Recommended Master Drivers are screened by a board at RCT Manning and Records Office before attending an assessment period, rather than a course, currently of six weeks duration, at the Army School of Mechanical Transport at Leconfield. During this assessment period, they are brought up to date on their future responsibilities but more importantly their attitudes are judged to ensure that they can gain unit commanders trust and confidence at their first meeting so that their advice is accepted right from the beginning.

The Master Driver RCT is a well selected, well trained and well motivated warrant officer and he has proved to be an excellent ambassador of the Corps in his dealings with units of all Arms.

BRITISH ARMY MOTORING ASSOCIATION (BAMA)

BAMA was authorized as an All Arms training medium in 1960. Whilst all Regiments and Corps have been expected and encouraged to take part in and assist in the organizing of events sponsored by it, it was the RASC which devised the concept of BAMA and spearheaded its early development by demonstrating its sound training principles. The RASC put BAMA on the map.

BAMA set out to make the training of Army drivers in its broadest sense more interesting and thus more effective. It was to do this by the introduction of the competitive element. At the same time it set out to enhance the standing of the Army among those civilians with whom competitors might come into contact. 'Be a Better Driver' – and show the Flag at the same time! These objectives were to be achieved in two ways. Firstly by running rally-based events for load carriers and Land Rovers, and blending military training norms with the internationally agreed rules for the conduct of civilian motor sporting activities. This was to form by far the largest part of BAMA's activities. The second way was to be in the guise of adventure training by taking part in major civilian events sponsored, whenever possible, by manufacturers.

It was as a result of international rallying experience that BAMA was first conceived. Its 'inventor' was Colonel M G M ('Bing') Crosby, OBE, MC, late RASC. In 1949 Major Crosby (as he then was) being a lifelong motoring enthusiast, decided to have a go at the Monte Carlo Rally as a private entrant. Unfortunately his car (a Bond Minicar) was ineligible, that sort of vehicle being considered by the Rally organizers to be not man enough for the job. So Major Crosby decided to follow the rally under his own steam, tackling the same hazards and enduring the same conditions as the competitors. This courageous effort resulted in far more publicity than might have been forthcoming had he been allowed to compete officially. It gave him an entree into motor sporting circles and enabled him to obtain the support and encouragement of people whose help was to be invaluable in later years. These included the competition managers of manufacturers and a host of others.

Above all, it encouraged him to develop his view that the Army could and should extract training benefit from competitive motoring. In 1951–52 Lieutenant Colonel Crosby found himself in Korea with time to develop his plans. His objectives were: official recognition of BAMA with full Staff backing throughout the Army, a slice of central and local training budgets, and official registration as a Motor Club at home and abroad. To do this it was necessary to win friends and influence people. The best way to do that was to demonstrate the intended methods of operation and their benefits. Colonel Crosby's next posting was to Germany where he lost no time in lobbying manufacturers to supply cars for entry in international rallies. As BAMA did not yet exist and 'Crosby's Circus' of drivers had no official standing, British firms were reluctant to help; but greater success was achieved with Opel and to a lesser extent with DKW. Comment in the motoring press regarding the use of foreign cars by British Army teams in international events resulted in Standard-Triumph lending a sympathetic ear and some cars! This arrangement lasted for about four years until 1959, during which time teams had been entered for three or four major international rallies a year. This experience resulted in the build-up of a cadre of experienced drivers which was to stand BAMA's credibility in good stead when in 1960 it was able to start discussions with a British manufacturer on a proper footing. It should be remembered that even in those days international rallying was an expensive business and that with no official funds available, places in the Army team had not only been allocated on the basis of skill and experience but also on the ability of the individual to pay his whack. Perhaps it was no coincidence that officers from the nearby Guards Brigade predominated in the early international teams. A further point was that until 1960 very few soldiers possessed competition licences, or the experience to qualify for them.

Success in demonstrating the scope for innovation in the training of drivers 'in the round' was much more rapid. The 2 Division Driving Championship in 1956 attracted a lot of attention in Germany from senior officers of all arms. Numerous similar events were instigated by RASC officers during the following three years in BAOR, in France and in the

UK, culminating in Exercise 'Southern Cross' in 1959. Cynics in high places were converted and doubting Thomases won over. Even so, there were lingering suspicions in some minds that the whole BAMA concept was a deep-dyed plot being hatched for the sole benefit of the RASC. However the composition of the international car rally teams in which RASC members were very much in the minority, and the fact that the majority of the participants in 'Southern Cross' and its precursors were from other arms went some way towards allaying these doubts. By the summer of 1959, Colonel Crosby was Commandant of the Army MT School at Bordon. The School was then a truly All Arms Establishment and apart from the Commandant, there was only one other RASC officer on the training staff. Still no BAMA; intimation was received that War Office approval was likely upon presentation of a formal case. An Army Council Instruction was published. BAMA existed. Central and local funds were now available. A new appointment of 'Secretary BAMA' was added to the MT School Establishment to coordinate the activities of local BAMA secretaries in RASC HQs worldwide. Doors opened; Vauxhall Motors provided three cars to do a year's rallying and gave full backing. They did this for three years providing a new set of cars each year. Then it was Rover's turn. They supplied three East African Safari 3-litre cars, and so on.

There were two main tasks following the authorization of BAMA. First, to advise all Home and Overseas Commands on the setting up of local committees, and generally to get things going. Secondly, to organize the first Army Driving Championship which was to take place in the Autumn of 1960 in the UK. This entailed Commands (including BAOR and Northern Ireland) running preliminary heats; also briefing UK Commands in associated requirements. Not least was the procurement of trophies for the winners. The RAOC Directorate wrote to all the manufacturers of vehicles and accessories used by the Army. The response was surprising as was that from Commands, Formations and Regiments, so that when the Vice Chief of the Imperial General Staff (VCIGS) presented the trophies at the Finish at Bedford ('To be returned next year please'), there seemed few who did not get something. Thus it was that Colonel Crosby was able to see BAMA home and dry before he moved on. The first Army Driving Championship had been an outstanding success. The fact that it had been run on the orders of the Military Training Directorate of the War Office through the agency of the all arms MT School and with the full cooperation of G(Training) at Commands/ Divisions removed any remaining uncertainties in the minds of entrants and ensured a fully subscribed turnout (60 three-tonners and 120 Land Rovers and trailers with three men on each vehicle). The success of this event also ensured that the Championship would become a regular event in the training calendar. Time was needed to digest the lessons learned and it was therefore 1963 before the second major event was held. It was mounted in Germany and was known as Exercise Roadmaster 1, or the Rhine Army Driving Championships. The pattern was then set for a Roadmaster to be run each year. Each alternate year it was to double as the Army Driving Championship. These were to be 4-day events reaching parts of Germany not normally visited by the British Army and making use of the training areas of other NATO Armies. The race tracks at Nürburgring and Hockenheim were also incorporated for special tests. The skills tested were not limited to driving. As stated earlier, BAMA aimed to train the driver in the round. The firing of weapons, physical endurance, swimming, orienteering in the dark together with self-sufficiency and iniative were all put to the test and included in the scoring. All units were encouraged to make use of the BAMA concepts, (incorporated in a training manual) wherever in the world they might be. By 1962, BAMA Committees had been set up under the auspices of the local G(Training) wherever British troops were stationed. It must be added that in many cases the day-to-day job of organizing events or providing technical advice and expertise often fell to the lot of the local RASC Headquarters.

Initially the appointment of Secretary BAMA at the Army MT School was filled by a serving officer but was later converted to a Retired Officer post. The first retired officer incumbent was Lieutenant Colonel James Low who firmly made his mark as the Army's BAMA expert and was a stalwart of the organization for more than a decade.

When Colonel Low retired, his place was taken by Colonel Bob Sherville (late RMP) and the post was transferred in 1977 to the newly formed Army School of Mechanical Transport at Leconfield. In the late seventies and early eighties external constraints have reduced BAMA activities but the Army Driving Championships have survived and are still held regularly.

The Army Motor Cycling Association (AMCA) was formed in 1937 but was put into abeyance in 1941. It was reconstituted after the war in 1947. The President is the Quarter Master General and the sponsor is the Director General of Transport and Movements on behalf of the Director of Army Training. The activities of the Association are a recognized form of military training for all arms to promote skill in motor cycle riding, rider initiative and machine maintenance. As such the Association is in no way a social or sporting club. The fact that it is called an Association is to regularize the Army's position and membership in relation to the Federation Internationale Motorcycliste so that the Army and Royal Marines may participate in civilian events. It is therefore affiliated to the Auto Cycle Union which controls motor sport in the United Kingdom.

19 · WATER TRANSPORT

IN 1945 AT THE END OF hostilities in North West Europe, the RASC commanded a large fleet of vessels, both military and RASC Civilian Fleet manned. Military Motor Boat Companies were serving at Hamburg and Antwerp and there were even large fleets in Burma and the Eastern Mediterranean. Nearer home there were Water Transport Companies at West Mersea; on the Isle of Wight; at Plymouth and Salcombe in the West Country; at Rothsay on the Isle of Bute in Scotland; and at Portsmouth and Sheerness.

For the invasion of Japan a large fleet was assembled at Yarmouth, Isle of Wight, under Headquarters, 42 Water Transport Group, commanded by Lieutenant Colonel Groves RASC. Several holiday camps in West Wight were requisitioned as barracks, together with three of the Victorian coast defence forts. Norton Holiday Camp near Yarmouth housed the Headquarters and Quartermaster. Savoy Camp provided the Officers' Mess and accommodation for 81 Harbour Launch Company. Brambles Chine Holiday Camp provided accommodation for 395 Fast Launch Company while Cliff End Fort was the home of a second harbour launch company. Fort Victoria on the sea edge, now demolished, became the navigation and engineer training school. Nearby were the workshops, the buildings of which still stand. The jetty, now in a sad state of dilapidation, could take up to four vessels alongside for repair despite frequent damage from passing ships. Golden Hill Fort, between Yarmouth and Freshwater, became the Regimental Training School.

Yarmouth Harbour was filled with RASC military vessels which had returned from Normandy to form part of the fleet to go to Japan. Vessels not berthed in the harbour were moored on buoys laid offshore for almost a mile East and West of Yarmouth pier. While the fleet was assembling, 395 Company RASC (Ambulance Launch) was formed at Yarmouth to man twelve specialist ambulance craft for the invasion. This Company was commanded by Major Archie Campbell Crawford RASC, formerly a Royal Navy destroyer officer, who had gained invaluable experience commanding a motor boat company at Normandy. The launches provided were Royal Naval Fairmile 112 ft B type Motor Launches (MLs). This design had done superb work in coastal convoy escort duties throughout the war. It was planned that they should sail as a squadron to Japan, to evacuate casualties from beach heads. These vessels required a much higher standard of navigation and seamanship than that necessary for the coastal motor boat companies.

In November 1944 the first two MLs, 166 and 167, were taken over from the Royal Navy in Scotland. Aboard, the RASC crews learned how to operate them and of their remarkable seakeeping qualities. A training voyage from the Isle of Man to Stranraer, in a Force 11 gale, instilled confidence in these fine vessels. After completion of training, both vessels sailed south for conversion into Ambulance Launches. After conversion the Ambulance Launches were handed over to 935 Company RASC (Ambulance Launch). The Royal Navy provided refuelling facilities and Coastal Force Bases were nominated to carry out major repairs. 935 Company RASC (Ambulance Launch) had a complex job dealing with both Royal Navy and Army administration. The summer of 1945 was spent gathering the ships together, manning them and training deck crews and engineers for August, the planned month of sailing.

Captain O M Watts' Navigation School at Warsash near Southampton was used to provide navigation training. To adapt the vessels to Army requirements, the MLs were altered internally. The wardroom aft was converted into a twelve berth sick bay and a deck house was built above to accommodate a further ten stretcher cases. The new wardroom was positioned under the bridge. The vessels were powered by two Hall Scott Defender 650 hp petrol engines and wing tanks were fitted on deck to increase cruising range. They had a maximum speed of 23 knots and cruising of 18 knots. These were perhaps the most pleasing and satisfying vessels the RASC ever had.

The vessels were formed into two divisions named after locks on the Thames. Their names were: A Division: *Chertsey* (HQ Ship), *Boveney*, *Abingdon*, *Clifton*, *Benson*, *Bray*; B Division: *Goring*, *Cleeve*, *Boutlers*, *Cookham*, *Culham* and *Caversham* (not completed). Training was carried out in ML 171, commanded by Captain C Gill (the Sea Training Officer), who had also been transferred from the Royal Navy. She was constantly training at sea to develop the much higher skill in navigation and seamanship needed. After basic training the ambulance launches worked up on Naval manoeuvres. Shortly before the intended sailing date two young Lieutenants of the Royal Navy joined the Company as navigators. As by now RASC officers and warrant officers were well experienced this caused considerable leg pulling. However during the week prior to sailing for the Far East the first atom bomb was exploded and on 15 August 1945 war with Japan ended. Departure of the Company was cancelled and thus ended what could have been a most interesting chapter in RASC Water Transport history. Great disappointment was felt throughout the unit as it had been proved that RASC officers and soldiers were fully able to run such vessels; nevertheless VJ night at Yarmouth was marked by tremendous celebrations.

Shortly after VJ Day, while the units were relaxing, a requirement arose for two fire tender vessels for duties in Singapore. The two vessels selected and equipped for firefighting, were the 90 ft Ex Naval Motor Fishing Vessels (MFVs) 1501 and 1514 stoutly built of wood. They were

fine seaboats and were commanded by Captain A Barr RASC and
Captain Tom Wood RASC both of 135 Company RASC (Ambulance
Launch) very experienced seamen and navigators. This became the first
long ocean voyage to be made by vessels commanded and crewed purely
by serving Army personnel. It was most successful with calls being made
at Gibraltar, Malta, Port Said, Suez, Aden, Karachi, Bombay, and
Colombo prior to Singapore. Only minor repairs were necessary during
the whole voyage.

Action now moved to the Eastern Mediterranean based on Port Said
and Port Fouad in Egypt, the homes of 697 Company RASC (Motor
Boat) and 698 Company (LST Administration). Commanded by Lieuten-
ant Colonel Dunlop RASC who was followed by Lieutenant Colonel
Richards RASC, these companies operated a total of 140 vessels together
with an extensive workshop and a floating dock. Amongst the vessels were
six Fairmile ML's some of which were built locally or in India – *Sonning*,
Sunbury, *Iffley*, *Mosley*, *Marsh* and *Shepperton*, the pride of the RASC Middle
East Fleet. *Shepperton* was adapted for use by the Commander-in-Chief
Middle East Land Forces (MELF), comfortably equipped and fitted with
a radio to keep in touch with GHQ when at sea. She made many voyages
to Greece, Crete, Cyprus and the Dodecanese Islands, as well as to
Tobruk. The remainder were standard Fairmile B, but with the naval
armament removed. To supplement these vessels, high speed target
towing launches were sent from the UK to operate, the 'Spud Run'. This
task was taken over from the Royal Navy and involved supplying the
newly liberated islands with fresh food.

It subsequently developed into maintenance of communications and
the delivery of mail and rations to support the indigenous islanders.
Amongst the vessels used for this task was the 250 ton steamer *Lord Plumer*
(known affectionately as 'Plum-Plum'), carrying scars from the siege of
Malta. She was commanded by Captain 'Tubby' Taylor and became an
inter-island ferry, carrying up to one hundred passengers as well as sheep
and goats.

As well as in Egypt, water transport maintained a substantial
detachment in Greece until 1950 based on the Company in Port Said.
Normally two Fairmiles and a 61½ ft MFV were stationed in Piraeus
Harbour. These vessels had mixed crews of RASC officers and soldiers,
German POW's awaiting re-patriation, and Greek civilians locally
employed. They were used to support the British Military Mission to
Greece and were employed in communication and cargo duties around
the Greek coastline and islands, as during the period of the Greek
Communist Terrorist Campaign, most inland communications had been
cut off. ML *Sunbury* (557), commanded by Captain John Bell RASC, ex-
Indian Navy, was the Launch allocated to the General Officer Commanding the British Military Mission. In addition it was involved in a number
of operational and intelligence tasks, such as coastal patrols. On

Christmas Eve 1948 *Sunbury*, with an officer from Naval Intelligence aboard, was dispatched in a snowstorm to Kalamata on the South Coast of the Peleponese to search for a Dakota thought to have crashed inland, which had been carrying British despatches. On arrival it fell to the lot of a very young Second Lieutenant Mike Hughes RASC to accompany the Greek Army search party into the bitterly cold mountains. It was his task to search through the wreckage and through the twenty six mangled and charred bodies of the passengers and crew. Unfortunately the terrorists had already been on the scene and mule tracks showed that they had plundered most items of value, including clothing from the bodies. They had however missed a number of gold sovereigns and the search filled a sack with sundry documents, including Communist party papers of considerable value to intelligence. Second Lieutenant Mike Hughes walked back through the mountains to Kalamata with his Greek Army escort and handed over the items recovered to the Naval Intelligence Officer, Lieutenant Commander Bathurst RN; subsequently gaining a commendation for his efforts.

During this period, the RASCV's *Sunbury* and *Marsh* (commanded originally by Captain 'Toddy' Todhunter RASC and subsequently by Captain Jim Haddrell RASC) were frequently loaded with a jeep lashed on deck over the fuel tank space; and despatched to remote parts of the coastline with heavily armed British Military Mission 'Advisors' to the Greek Army. Warrant Officer Bill Gardener in *MFV 221* and subsequently *MFV 210* carried regular cargoes between Piraeus, Salonika and Crete. On one voyage, returning from Crete, the machinery failed and jury sails were rigged. The MFV was eventually found and taken in tow by a Greek Naval LST.

Warrant Officer Class 1 "Orra" Gardener, a benevolent giant became a well known figure around the Greek Coast. On one occasion, King Paul of the Hellenes, also well over 6 ft, spent some time chatting to him.

Greece in the post war period, was Water Transport's first contact with the LCT Mk IV, which was later to play such a major role. A Naval LCT, detached from the Amphibious Warfare Squadron at Malta became the 'chummy' ship and gave much needed material support. All was not plain sailing in the aftermath of the war and one should remember the fate of RASC Drifter *Lucien Gougy* (*MFV210*) the last of the Fleet craft to be lost due to hostilities. This 160-ton vessel commanded by Sergeant Trewherne with a crew of eleven left Salonika bound for Piraeus with Brigadier Hards as the only passenger. Soon after departure a storm with heavy seas and a blizzard developed, reducing visibility. On approaching the island of Skiathos where it was known that the Skiathos Inner Channel was mined although the Outer Channel was clear, and uncertain as to his whereabouts, Sergeant Trewherne posted extra look-outs. When the blizzard eased it became apparent that the vessel was entering the mined channel. Sergeant Trewherne immediately turned the vessel but there was a

*A Sergeant Navigator at work
aboard an LCT Mk VIII.*

[By courtesy of The War Office]

tremendous explosion and the *Lucien Gougy* sank quickly by the bows. No-one below decks escaped.

Corporal Carrigan, ultimately the sole survivor, was thrown into the water with Sergeant Trewherne and the cook, Private Hardy; the latter was half-conscious with a very severe head-wound. A strong swimmer, Corporal Carrigan found them a spar and a badly damaged Carley float, and did what he could to help them. Sadly both succumbed to the cold and exposure. During the night, Corporal Carrigan was washed up on the beach where he lay unconscious until found on the following morning. Shortly after the sad loss of *MFV 210* and the end of the Greek hostilities, the two ML's sailed to Malta to be handed back to the Royal Navy, bringing to an end another memorable era in Water Transport History.

The period from 1946 to 1956 was one of gentle run down throughout the RASC Military and Civilian Fleet. From 1946 the Fleet was administered by ST3, a department of the Director of Supplies and Transport situated at Kingston-on-Thames which included the Fleet Administrative Unit under the Fleet Superintendent. The Technical Inspectorate and Fleet Repair Unit REME, was responsible for all maintenance and repairs.

With the disposal of many vessels, changes took place; Fleet Repair Unit RASC, later REME, moved to Portsmouth in 1958 and 1 Boat Stores Depot moved to Barry, South Wales shortly before the Suez Campaign. Changes were also made in the training organization which became part of 1 Training Battalion at the RASC Training Centre, Aldershot. Captain 'Skipper' Woods, late Merchant Navy, and Lieutenant Tom Stibbards, late RN, became responsible for technical aspects of training on the deck and marine engineering side respectively.

The first major task after the end of the war was the redistribution of stores and equipment world-wide. Due to the scarcity and expense of merchant shipping it was decided in 1946 that the RASC Civilian Fleet should take over seven LSTs from the Royal Navy. These were named after distinguished Corps officers. Their names were, *Evan Gibb, Charles Macleod, Maxwell Brander, Snowden Smith, Humfrey Gale, Reginald Kerr, Frederick Glover.*

The LSTs were the largest landing ships used during the war with an overall length of 345 ft and a beam of 54 ft. They were driven by triple expansion steam engines. They had bow doors with a ramp and could beach on slipways. Since the ships ceased to be Naval vessels they required added accommodation to comply with Board of Trade regulations and to bring them up to Merchant Navy standards. Alteration was a long job but on completion of refits five vessels sailed for the Middle East and two for the Far East. These are the largest vessels so far operated by the WD Fleet.

During the evacuation of Palestine RASCV's *Humfrey Gale* and *Evan Gibb* made fifteen voyages each between Haifa and Port Said, lifting between them over 26,000 tons of vehicles and stores. Similar work was done world-wide until 1952 when the ships were handed over to the North Atlantic Steam Navigation Company and subsequently in 1961 to British India Steamship Company, tasked by the War Office direct. The RASC then had no further concern with their administration although subsequently one transferred to the Royal Fleet Auxiliary (RFA) under the name *Empire Gull* and, tasked by Q (Mov) I, moved ammunition from Marchwood Military Port to Zeebrugge until finally retired in 1978.

Meanwhile the ambulance launches were disposed of and HQ CRASC and 42 Water Transport Unit disbanded at Yarmouth. 935 Company was redesignated 985 Training Company RASC (Water Transport) and moved into Golden Hill Fort near Freshwater. Fort Victoria was retained with the workshops whilst the holiday camps were returned to their owners. The two Motor Boat Companies and the Fast Launch Company were disbanded. It was at this depressing time that Captain 'Toddie' Todhunter, Captain Doubleday and Captain Hunter with former military crews of 935 Ambulance Launch Company RASC took over three LCTs Mk IV from the Royal Navy. They sailed to Jersey to assist in the dumping of thousands of tons of German ammunition into the Hurd Deep north of Alderney. The vessels were based at St Helier in company with other Mk III and Mk IV LCT's taken over by the RASC Civilian Fleet. The RASC Fleet also continued dumping operations in LCTs in other areas of the United Kingdom, particularly out of Cairnryan, in Scotland.

From 1946 therefore the LCT's began to play a major role in RASC military and civilian fleets. The major dumping programme continued at Port Said, Egypt, where four LCTs, (named ADCs – Ammunition Dumping Craft) of 697 Company were based, working constantly dumping ammunition from the Canal Zone into deep water north of Port Said. German prisoners of war and transitees were used as labour. Whilst dumping was in progress fishing used to take place by using grenades and a story is told of an officer and seaman who put off in a dinghy from their

LCT to collect some fish for lunch. Inadvertently the seaman dropped a grenade with the pin out into the bottom of the boat, which he reported to the officer. Spectators on their ship saw two bodies leap into the sea and swim frantically. With a loud explosion the dinghy blew up but the soldier retrieved a piece, which he handed into the stores in exchange for a new boat! During the dumping, an ML was employed as escort against possible attack by Palestine terrorist vessels. Another important task for these vessels was the evacuation of British Forces from Palestine. In addition to large quantities of vehicles and stores, huge loads of petrol contained in leaking 'flimsy' cans were moved at great risk from Haifa to Egypt. The cook of one LCT which was loaded with high octane petrol, prepared meals on a primus in the dinghy towed some distance astern.

Three LCTs Mk IV were permanently stationed in the Far East as part of 37 Company RASC (Water Transport) re-established on the island of Pulau Brani in Singapore Harbour. During the Communist troubles in Malaya these vessels were used for transporting military stores quickly and safely by sea to Prai river, opposite to Penang Island, and other ports on the west coast of Malaya, and to ports on the east coast of the peninsular.

Meanwhile in the United Kingdom a requirement had arisen for a vessel for long distance sea training. There were in existence in Training Company a military manned fleet of six 61½ft Motor Fishing Vessels (MFVs), two 75 ft MFVs, one 90 ft Fire Float (disposed of in 1946) six Dickens General Service Launches (GSLs), Class 1, four Dickens GSLs Class 2, thirteen 36 ft, Harbour Launches (HLs), two Rover Class Fast Launches (FLs) and one 68 ft High Speed Target Tower (HSTT).

None of the available vessels proved suitable due to expense or shortage of accommodation; so in 1947, *MV 1502* a 90 ft MFV formerly a fire boat was taken over by 985 Training Company RASC from the War Department Fleet in Portsmouth. The fire pumps were removed and the hold was converted into trainees accommodation. This vessel, renamed the *Yarmouth Navigator* has served the RASC and RCT ever since, suffering periodic changes in structure as requirements changed. She is still (1982) the RCT navigation training vessel.

For seamanship training, a 61½ft MFV already in service was renamed the *Yarmouth Seaman*. She is still to be seen in the Solent under private ownership. Originally both, vessels were manned by RASC soldiers but in 1959 due to manpower shortages both vessels transferred to the Civilian RASC Fleet.

Both vessels voyages took them across the English Channel to the Channel Islands and West to ports in the West Country. These trips were interspersed with exercises with the Royal Navy and patrols off coastal ranges while firing took place. Many RASC warrant officers, sergeants and soldiers had considerable experience in LCTs Mk III and IV, with the ambulance launches and on other sizeable requisitioned vessels such

[By courtesy of Central Office of Information]

Maritime Engineers at work on LCT engines.

as *Blue Bird*, a 600 ton ocean going yacht. These formed the nucleus of the training fleet.

The military motor boat companies disbanded in 1948 and the fleet continued to decline until a further run-down hit the RASC Civilian Fleet in 1956/57 when coastal gunnery was abolished and the coastal batteries of the Royal Artillery dismantled. With their abolition went target towing, a task which had been in existence for eighty years. There was always a risk of a mistake resulting in a shell landing on the towing launch instead of the target. It was a highly important task which asked for excellent seamanship and good vessel handling. The RASC Civilian Fleet gave first class service to the Royal Artillery in their task of defending our shores, especially during the early part of the Second World War when the *RASC Sir Walter Campbell* was used in Iceland to tow targets for the Royal Artillery Coast batteries firing in bad weather.

The end of this task together with the completion of the ammunition dumping commitment by LCTs and coasters such as *Sir Evelyn Wood* and the *Marquess of Hartington*, from Cairnryan caused big reductions in RASC Civilian Water Transport Companies all round the United Kingdom.

Finally, 71 Company RASC based at HM Gun Wharf Portsmouth which was reduced to a detachment in 1958 alone remained, together with 45 Company RASC, Menai Bridge, North Wales. Water Transport

Companies overseas remained in reduced form. So by September 1957, Water Transport had reduced to a few RASC Civilian Fleet manned vessels, small overseas commitments, a training element on the Isle of Wight and a company and a workshop at HM Gun Wharf in Portsmouth.

THE ERA OF THE LCT MK VIII 1956–1965

During the first rumblings of the Suez crisis in September 1956 the decision was taken in the Chief-of-Staffs Committee that the Army would organize and run shipping to provide logistic backing to purely army operations.

General Sir Gerald Templer, then Chief of the Imperial General Staff decreed that the Army would take over, control and operate its own LCTs. The Royal Engineers and the Royal Army Service Corps were invited to undertake the project. Both Corps agreed, the Royal Engineers based on their experience with Z-craft in the Middle East and the RASC on their years at sea with Water Transport. The RASC were particularly enthusiastic and Major General W H D Ritchie CB CBE, who was the Director of Supplies and Transport, readily accepted the project. Major General G N Bond CB CBE, the Inspector RASC, himself a fine sailor, was able to give the necessary encouragement to the takeover and operation of LCTs Mk VIII under the concept of a general transport company afloat.

The Water Transport WOs, NCOs and men formed the basis of the crews available to Major Dennis Cuff RASC who was appointed to raise 76 Company RASC (LCT) on 5 October 1956 at Yeovil in Somerset. The first problem was to find officers to man the vessels and the net was widely cast by the War Office (AG8). The first two officers were Captain Tony Charles, ex Royal Indian Navy and Lieutenant (QM) W E Gardener. They were soon joined by other Regular and National Service officers with previous sea experience; Army or civilian.

Meanwhile a lone LCT Mk IV-ADC 408 commanded by Master J G Scott RASC Fleet was manned with volunteer members of the RASC Civilian Fleet. Loaded with 200 tons of composite rations she departed from Plymouth in company with an LCT Mk VIII, 4086 Master J Bayliss, also RASC Fleet manned together with a trawler, for Suez to join the RN Mediterranean based LCT squadron. On 6 November they sailed from Famagusta to Port Said and took part in the supporting operations. ADC 408 returned to UK at Easter 1957. LCT 4086 returned via Cyprus and Malta with a mixed cargo of tomatoes, gun barrels and cars to Barry Docks; subsequently laying up at Port Penrhyn in March 1957.

On 19 January 1957, after refit in Whites Shipyard in Southampton, LCT 4061, the Headquarters vessel, arrived at Portsmouth and secured to No 3 buoy, under command of Major Cuff RASC with Second Lieutenant David Jones RASC, the first First Lieutenant to be appointed. She was joined on 22 January by LCT 4097 commanded by Captain John Woodford RASC, an ex-Merchant Navy officer, with Lieutenant (later Lieutenant Colonel) Tim Street RASC as his First Lieutenant. During the next few days they were joined by LCT 4041 Captain Tony Charles RASC with, as First Lieutenant, Lieutenant (later Major) Mike Randall-Smith RASC and LCT 4128 Major Frank Millar-Essen RASC who subsequently received Captain Peter Barnard RASC as his No 1. The remaining 3 vessels, LCT 4062 (Captain Bill 'Orra' Gardener RASC), LCT 4002 (Captain Mike Weston RASC with Second Lieutenant Malcolm Price RASC as his first Lieutenant) and finally LCT 4074 (Captain Reg Meads RASC) all joined after various difficulties in their respective dockyards so that by the end of February 1957 76 Company RASC (LCT) was ready for operations.

The unit 'tail' had meanwhile moved from Yeovil to Southsea Castle where it took up residence in a Nissen hut within the battlements. The ships companies lived on the ships while unmarried soldiers awaiting berths or employed ashore lived in the Royal Naval Barracks. The active support of the Water Transport Workshops REME under Major Joe Beckett REME based at HM Gun Wharf, Portsmouth, did much to improve the mechanical efficiency of the ships. This was difficult as the LCTs Mk VIII were very different from previous RASC vessels. The RASC knew the old type of LCTs well and it was widely believed that the LCT Mk VIII was only a larger and more sophisticated model. It was soon appreciated that the RASC had jumped into the big ship business and there were many lessons to learn. These vessels were of registered tonnage 1017, gross length 231 ft, beam 38 ft, maximum beaching draught 6.3 ft, cargo capacity 300 tons, speed 8 knots, range 4000 miles, with a crew of two officers, one Captain, one First Lieutenant, twenty six soldiers including warrant officers and non-commissioned officers.

Each vessel had the full RN Medium Frequency/High Frequency (HF) radio outfit and was required to operate within the RN radio network. It was found necessary for the Royal Corps of Signals to provide two operators per ship together with a sergeant and corporal for repair work and a warrant officer as squadron signals officer. They very soon reached full RN and MN proficiency. From the very beginning all branches of the Services worked in complete harmony and demonstrated to the Royal Navy that the Army could run ships up to Naval standard. At War Office level there were a number of civil servants well qualified in marine engineering and with considerable knowledge of the problems of operating War Department ships. Their assistance, cooperation, guidance and patience contributed much towards organizing the unit. The longest serving and best known and loved of these was Captain (Merchant Navy) 'Winkle' Beard. Born in 1908 he joined the RASC Civilian Fleet in 1937 with his Masters Ticket. He was appointed a Master in the Fleet in 1939 and after war service in Italy and serving as Master Superintendent,

Hong Kong, he was appointed Fleet Superintendent RASC Fleet in 1959 finally retiring in 1973. Sadly he died in 1977 and many serving and retired officers attended his funeral. He was succeeded by Captain W H Stoodley MBE, ex Merchant Navy as the Army Department Maritime Inspector. By March therefore the RASC had seven LCTs Mk VIII in full operational commission and tasks were urgently sought to provide employment.

OPERATIONS IN THE HEBRIDES

It was then that 76 Company RASC (LCT) became involved in Operation Hardrock, the setting up and maintenance of the now well known Guided Weapons Range in the Hebrides. Operations in Hebridean waters and on the island of St Kilda provided a challenge impossible to ships other than landing craft, as no port facilities existed. The project was under Air Ministry control as at that time Guided Weapons were RAF controlled. Time was short so LCTs 4002 and 4041 were sent North in March 1957 with instructions to reconnoitre Oban, South Uist and Benbecula in the Outer Hebrides for suitable landing places. A beaching in Village Bay, St Kilda, was also to be attempted. The weather prevented this until mid April but on the afternoon of 15 April 1957, LCT 4002 (Captain Weston RASC) sailed from Lochboisdale, South Uist round Barra Head and after the RAF reconnaissance party from 5004 Airfield Construction Squadron RAF was put ashore, Operation Hardrock commenced.

The operation required the LCTs to put men, stores and equipment ashore over the beach at St Kilda, so that the RAF could build roads to the top of the island, build an accommodation area, and set up radar and other electronic equipment for the surveillance of the Guided Weapon Range. The Range Head was to be established on the Island of Benbecula. The Island of St Kilda at that time had been uninhabited since 1932. It resembles an extinct volcano crater rising from the sea fifty miles out in the Atlantic, West of the Outer Hebrides. One side of the lip of the crater is broken away and forms Village Bay. It is here that the only possible beaching place exists, as on the other sides of the island the cliffs rise directly out of deep water, including Conachair the highest cliff in the British Isles. By mid-May the LCTs were employed on a gruelling schedule from the military port at Cairnryan to Lochboisdale, Cairnryan, South Ford (between South Uist and Benbecula) and St Kilda.

The pressure of work until mid September, when the weather makes the task impossible, was very hard on both ships and men. The ships were not equipped with radar and it had been agreed by the Army and the RAF that a number of calculated risks would be taken. One of the biggest hazards was being trapped in bad weather in Village Bay, St Kilda, where sudden winds of up to gale force quickly place a ship in danger and a terrifying sea builds up. This has happened only once when on 21 May 1957, LCT 4041 was driven ashore and but for the fine seamanship of her Captain, Captain Tony Charles RASC and of Captain Peter Barnard RASC by then commanding LCT 4128, together with the excellent efforts of LCT 4128s crew, the stranded ship would have become a total loss. They struggled for three days and nights to save her after she had been driven onto the rocky beach by gale force easterly winds and a heavy sea. She was holed in several places and the steering flat and part of the engine room were flooded so that no power for the winches was available. Captain Peter Barnard, having been advised of the situation by radio, steamed to Village Bay and under dangerous conditions succeeded in geting a wire aboard and towed LCT 4041 off the beach at high water. It was not known if she would float so the crew were ordered off, Captain Tony Charles RASC, Lieutenant Mike Randall-Smith RASC the First Lieutenant and a corporal only remaining, to cut the towing wire if necessary. They found she floated and could be towed so, in a heavy swell and with a 20° list, they made for Ayr on the Clyde. From then on the hazards of St Kilda have received the respect due to them. A trip by the author Hammond Innes to St Kilda aboard LCT 4062 with Captain Ian Peradon formed the basis of an incident in his book *Atlantic Fury*.

The ships frequently operated in thick weather but the build up was complete by the time the RAF handed over to the Royal Artillery at the end of the summer of 1958. All the ships moved South each Autumn for major refits.

The winter refits 1958/59 were in preparation for the big task of 1959, the move of the Guided Weapons Wing of the School of Artillery with its equipment and vehicles to Benebecula for the opening of the range. This move heralded the first blast off of the 'Corporal' missile in this country.

Four ships were loaded at the Joint Services Amphibious Warfare Centre at Hamworthy, Poole on 6 April 1959 and, after inspection by the Director of Supplies and Transport, sailed North to the Island of Benbecula under command of Major Cuff. The movement of Royal Artillery equipment, the rockets, fuel, and all stores and men, now became the main task of the squadron so the mainland operating base for this was moved to Rhu, a hard at the entrance to the Gareloch which has good road and rail communications with Glasgow. Navigation was basic and the only aids available were the ships compass, charts and a sextant. No echo sounder or radar was fitted in the early days, and Radio Direction Finding (RDF) was inoperable due to the LCTs magnetic field. Hebridean mists and the fact that St Kilda could remain invisible in the mist even on quite clear days caused many anxious moments. Operations in the Hebrides have continued without break ever since then.

In 1959 76 Company RASC (LCT) was divided into two flotillas – Scottish waters and South of England, one being commanded by Major

Jimmy Haddrell RASC and the other by Major Tony Charles RASC. In 1960 four ships operated in the Hebrides all summer, the flotilla in Scotland being commanded by Captain Tim Street RASC; with Major Tony Charles RASC commanding in the South. This flotilla always included at least one vessel based at Instow to work with the Amphibian Training Wing RASC, 18 Amphibious Squadron RASC and Fording Trials Branch REME at Fremington/Instow.

Meanwhile Water Transport entered a new phase of world-wide LCT operations with the fitting out, training of crews and sailing of three ships to Singapore to replace the three elderly LCT Mk IV mentioned earlier. The refits included the addition of a boat deck forward of the bridge together with lifeboats and davits. The bridge was extended to the ships sides.

Lieutenant Colonel Cuff MBE RASC, handed over command to Lieutenant Colonel Jimmy Spicer RASC and took charge of LCT 4073 (*Ardennes*) with Lieutenant Brian Middleton RASC as No 1. After various delays in civilian shipyards, she sailed in a snowstorm down channel in early January 1960. She arrived safely in Singapore, having called at Gibraltar, Malta, Cyprus, Aden, Bombay and Colombo en route. This Army operated LCT excited much comment. Then on 19 September 1960 LCTs 4085 (*Agedabia*) (Captain Mike Hughes RASC), and 4086 (*Arromanches*) (Captain Hugo John Leech RASC) sailed under overall command of Major Haddrell MBE. On arrival these three vessels formed 3 Division of the Squadron based at 37 Company RASC (WT) on Pulau Brani.

1960 was the busiest year so far as it also included Exercise Holdfast, an operation which tested the squadron to the full. The Company had been redesignated 76 Squadron RASC (LCT) during 1959/60. 16 Parachute Brigade with a large tonnage of vehicles and camp equipment was to be landed by air on the island of Sylt, off Schleswig-Holstein. The Squadron was tasked to carry out an amphibious operation with and under command of the German Navy. However, at the last moment the aircraft were withdrawn and the delivery of all the stores had to be carried out by the LCTs. A squadron HQ was set up ashore at Harwich in radio contact with the Commanding Officer who moved onto LCT *Antwerp* (Major Tony Charles) and controlled the Squadron at sea between Harwich and Hernum, Sylt. As a result of an accident at Hernum LCT *Antwerp* was replaced by LCT *Arezzo* (Captain Tim Street RASC). The move to Sylt was completed, but as no final plan had been received the two LCTs – *Aachen* (4062) Captain Ian Peradon and *Arezzo* (4128), forming the UK Squadron – loaded with 7 RHA at Sylt, then sailed to Kiel via the Kiel Canal to come under command of the Commanding Officer of the German Amphibian Squadron, Korvettenkapitan Kretschmer, the famous U Boat Commander of the Second World War. The two LCTs berthed in the berth earlier reserved for the *Scharnhorst* and

Gneisenau. The next night they were joined by two squadrons of German Landing Ships Motorized (LSMs) and at first light the assault on the beach at Eckenforde commenced with the Germans beaching first, getting badly stuck and blocking the beach. The squadron made a perfect beaching; unloading and clearing within 4½ mins. The LCTs returned to Kiel where they reloaded; subsequently carrying out the whole withdrawal of the forces from Sylt and Hamburg. 76 Squadron RASC (LCT) was involved in this exercise for almost two months and stood the test well in every way. Command and administrative procedures and the maintenance techniques, together with endless training in navigation, summer and winter, combined to prove that 76 Squadron RASC (LCT) had 'arrived'. After short winter refits, work again started in the Hebrides in late February 1961.

Some weeks later a request was made by the Air Ministry to assist in placing heavy radar equipment on the northernmost island of the Shetland Group which had been reconnoitred by Lieutenant Colonel Jimmy Spicer RASC and Major Haddrell RASC, during the previous winter. Owing to bad weather, they had been marooned at Balta Sound where they had gained some idea of conditions to be expected. The advice of the Admiralty was to keep away from the area until June but the equipment was required urgently and National Defence requirements justified the risks. Captain Hugo John Leech RASC, who had recently returned from Singapore, was chosen for the job. The cargo was loaded on the Clyde and, despite delays when the ship had to seek shelter from the gales, the cargo was put ashore at Balta Sound on time: the round trip of 1000 miles completed without mishap.

Throughout the period 1958–1961 other interesting missions included the movement of Staff College vehicles and stores to Ouistreham, France for the annual Battlefield Tour; exercises in Northern Ireland, visits to the Channel Islands, Scilly Islands and the Normandy beaches; the movement of AFVs to and from Pembroke, South Wales and Exercise Soft Line on behalf of the War Office. 76 Squadron was redesignated 46 Squadron, in 1961 and was always at seven days notice to join the Royal Naval Squadron in the Mediterranean. One result of this Middle Eastern requirement was the conversion in 1959/60 of LCT *Audemer* (4061) into the Squadron Headquarters Ship, by the addition of extra accommodation on the existing flag deck. This produced a top heavy looking profile, but did not affect the ships seaworthiness. *Audemer* became affectionately known as the 'Gosport Flats' or the 'Greyhound of the Gunwharf' finally becoming the last military manned LCT Mk VIII to be paid off.

As early as 1958 the pattern of the year had taken firm shape; consisting of very heavy tasking during the Spring, Summer and Autumn, with refits taking place from November to March. This programme enabled crews to be trained, given leave and time to re-equip the LCTs during the winter months to ensure fitness for the coming season. This framework has continued right up to 1982. Refits and docking in naval or civilian yards were organized by Fleet Repair Branch REME. Before refit, all stores apart from essential sea items were laid out in one of the vast sheds in Hilsea Lines, Portsmouth or nowadays at St George Barracks Gosport. Whilst a tedious and laborious job, it ensured that ships equipment started the following season in first class condition.

The garrison on St Kilda had to be maintained during the winter so the RASC Fleet manned the ex-Royal Navy steam T-class Trawler *Mull* which took out passengers, mail and fresh rations to the island. She was a good seaboat but uncomfortable in bad weather. As communication with the shore was insufficient, *Mull* was fitted with a 20 foot surf boat named *Puffin*. This type of craft was originally designed for use by fishermen off the beaches of West Africa. She had three rollers built into her steel hull for landing up on a beach and was driven by a water jet. She was successful and robust and was used until the *Mull* was paid off. A contract helicopter service now undertakes the job.

OPERATIONS IN THE FAR EAST

The original deployment of LCTs Mark VIII to Singapore in 1960 was to form 46 Squadron RASC (WT), 3 Division to replace the LCTs Mark IV which had been in FARELF since the end of World War II. The tasks included movement of RA batteries from Singapore to China Rock range for firing practice; amphibious exercises and stores moves to Terendak and Penang through the Malacca Straits on the West Coast; and to Kuantan and the beaches on the East Coast in the Merang Trenganu area. The LCTs also assisted in the setting up of a tank range in British North Borneo based on Tendu to allow practice firing.

46 Squadron RASC (WT) had British officers and SNCOs and Malayan other ranks (MOR). In practice MOR included Chinese and Indian nationals of Singapore. They were excellent crews once a routine was established and maintained their ships to a very high standard. Their only problem was a belief in ghosts which prevented them from doing, or made them do, strange things. One particularly awkward spirit used to hold down men attempting to get out of their bunks to come on watch!! *Ardennes*, *Arromanches* and *Agedabia* were the three Malayan manned ships. In 1962 Confrontation developed in Borneo which provided an immediate operational role for the vessels in maintaining Brunei by sea from the Labuan airhead. There was neither a main airport nor a deep water sea port at Brunei in those days; re-supply being via Brunei River to the Public Works Department Hard just south of Brunei Town. Ardennes commanded by Captain Tony Todd RASC was the first ship into Brunei after the revolt in 1962 and took a unit of Gurkhas to restore order and

establish a curfew. Other tasks included working the Rajang river to Sibu and passages to Tawau and Kuching.

As the pressures of confrontation increased the workload, two further LCTs were depatched from UK on 18 February, the HMAVs *Arakan* (Captain John Venmore RASC) and *Antwerp* (Captain Mike Randall-Smith RASC). Both had British other rank (BOR) crews and formed a second squadron. In 1965, on rebadging to RCT, the LCTs were formed into 74 LCT Squadron RCT with three Malayan manned ships and 75 LCT Squadron RCT with two British manned ships. Both squadrons being commanded simultaneously; at first by Major Tony Charles and later by Majors Brian Middleton and Randall-Smith.

1964 saw additional involvement in Thailand in support of Operation Crown, a RE airfield construction project at Ubon. 1966 onwards saw considerable involvement in sea dumping of Japanese bomb stockpiles dug out of the jungle in Penang. The LCT being based with the RAF Air Sea Rescue Unit at Glugor. In 1967 *Ardennes* Lieutenant (later Lieutenant Colonel) Chris Armstrong and Second Lieutenant Roy Potts carried out the Balambangan project to establish a live firing range on a deserted island off the North tip of Borneo to test SS 30 missiles.

Defence Reviews in the late sixties heralded the withdrawal from FARELF by 1970 so the LCTs were sold locally. An unsuccessful attempt was made to transfer *Ardennes* and *Arromanches* to the Singapore Navy but six months after handover neither ship had moved and both were subsequently sold on the civilian market. It is believed they were later run as logging barges in Borneo with Chinese civilian crews. Those who served in the LCTs in FARELF will remember the period as near idyllic days. Conditions on board were enjoyable, particularly on the Malayan manned ships with their Chinese cooks and stewards. Confrontation was a 'gentleman's' war for those at sea, and although three 20 mm Oerlikons were fitted to each LCT they were never fired in anger. Nonetheless the LCTs worked long hours and did a great deal of sea time. They made an immense contribution to the operations and the Commonwealth Brigade camp at Terendak on the West Coast of Malaya owed much of its build up and maintenance to LCT support.

On 23 November 1965 two more LCTs were required for overseas service in the Persian Gulf and at Aden for the evacuation. The vessels selected were HMAV *Arezzo* (4128), commanded by Major Tony Pheby RCT and HMAV *Agheila* (4002) commanded by Captain Chris Rawlinson. *Arezzo* was stationed at Bahrein in the Persian Gulf whilst *Agheila* remained at Aden and did much clearance of stores and equipment. She then undertook a voyage to Durban for the Rhodesian Security Forces and became the first Army LCT to cross the Equator. On completion of the Aden evacuation she returned to Portsmouth under command of Captain John Venmore RCT being the only foreign based LCT to do so. However *Arezzo* was not to be outdone. Due to the need for an extended refit it was decided that she should be docked in Singapore so in 1969 she changed places with *Antwerp*, both ships undertaking amongst the longest non-stop LCT voyages on record. Each voyage was 3250 miles taking eighteen days at sea at an average speed of ten knots, and involved only the second crossing of the Equator by Army LCTs.

An unusual task for *Andalsnes* (Major Pheby RCT) was the carrying of a landing craft within a landing craft. A new 72 ft Ramped Powered Lighter (RPL) had been completed in Berwick-on-Tweed. She was sailed to Rosyth and there loaded onto *Andalsnes*, fitting comfortably. She was conveyed to Portsmouth where she was lifted out onto the water by the 500 ton crane in the Dockyard. The RPL then sailed to Marchwood Military Port, her base.

In 1967 *Andalsnes*, commanded by Major Hughes RCT, sailed to Zeebrugge and on to Tromso, Northern Norway with soldiers and vehicles, as part of a winter exercise. This was the first voyage into northern Norwegian waters. On the return voyage to UK, she had trouble with her stern shaft bearings and had to be docked in Stavanger where her ships company were looked after admirably by the Royal Norwegian Navy.

Whilst under command of Captain Paul Boyes she carried out two further voyages to Norway. The first voyage was to carry four SRN6 Hovercraft of 200 Hovercraft Squadron to Northern Norway for an evacuation exercise. This was done by fitting beams across the tank deck combings on which two hovercraft rested. The second voyage was an official visit to her namesake town of Andalsnes. The ship and her company were given a splendid reception by the Mayor and townsfolk. An amusing incident happened in 1960 when ships badges were being designed for each LCT. The then vessel captains wrote to Mayors of the towns after which their ship was named, for permission to adopt the town coat of arms. Andalsnes did not have one so the Mayor sent in a shoulder badge of Andalsnes girls school choir as a possible solution. This showed the Rhomsdalhorn, a high mountain behind the town which was adopted for the ships badge. The original badge is displayed in the Officers Mess, Gosport.

By late 1965, due to the number of LCTs which had been sent overseas, there was difficulty in meeting the tasks required, in particular the all important maintenance of the Hebrides. By good fortune however the Royal Navy were still operating HMS *Rampart* based on Portsmouth. As she was underworked, it was arranged that she should be transferred to the RCT and in 1966 she was taken over by a military crew under command of Captain David Hammett and renamed HMAV *Akyab*. She differed from the other LCTs in that her forecastle had been raised and her ramp replaced by an LST ramp to allow larger vehicles and equipment aboard. To give better vision forward, the RN had raised the bridge and placed it upon a lattice structure. However, owing to its weight and high centre of gravity it was a liability. She was fitted with an extra large winch aft which was capable of hauling in the anchor cable at a good speed, which could not be done by the older type of electric winch on the other LCTs. Unfortunately, it gave constant trouble even to the makers. There were also hydraulic ram operated bow doors. Her design however left its mark and her high bow was incorporated in the LCLs now in service.

Before passing on to the next period mention must be made of RASC Fleet operations in the Caribbean and Bermuda, which started with the formation of 889 Company RASC (Water Transport) at Port Royal in Jamaica on 23 September 1946 and have continued in various forms ever since. Water Transport maintained its base in Jamaica carrying out a variety of tasks between Fort Clarence, Port Royal, Palisadoes, Fort Nugent and Kingston; in addition to ammunition dumping, target towing, sea rescue and VIP movement. The RASCV *Catania* weathered many tropical storms on her runs between Jamaica and British Honduras (now Belize), Nassau on New Providence Island in the Bahamas and Turks Island; originally commanded by Captain E J V Armsden and crewed by local Jamaicans from Port Royal. Other vessels stationed there included the Steam Target Tower *Abercorn* and the ML *Ernest Taylor*. The vessels continued to operate until the closedown in 1962. At the same time a detachment in Bermuda which included the Governor's launch the RASCV *Helford* under command of Mr Houghton, a civilian mate who had been in charge of WD launches since 1915, provided local communications. In British Honduras the Governor's Launch and the Nuffield Launch *Lord Nuffield*, under command of the Garrison RASC Officer and skippered by Junior NCO's of Water Transport, took part in numerous supply operations along the coast in support of operations against bandits, and were used for minor amphibious operations in the country south to Punta Gorda and Monkey River, up until the middle 1960s.

WIDENING THE SCOPE: 1965–1976

Although it was not appreciated at the time, the Mcleod Report, which resulted in the formation of the Royal Corps of Transport from elements of the RASC and the Royal Engineer Transportation branch, was a major turning point for Water Transport. Prior to 1965, Water Transport had in effect consisted of a number of semi-independent small units spread round the world, under the command and control of the various local Headquarters; carrying out independent tasks. From amalgamation however, Water Transport became part of a single organization tasked by Q (Movements) I, Ministry of Defence (Army) with the main task of supporting the movement of stores to, from and within UK and North West Europe.

The immediate result was that 17 Port Training Regiment RE based at Marchwood Military Port on Southampton Water discontinued its purely training aspect and re-emerged as 17 Port Regiment RCT with a full operational role. The lighterage portion of the Regiment (471, 472, 473 and 474 Lighterage Troops of 51 and 52 Port Squadrons), although organizationally separate, was manned by soldiers who became part of the Water Transport trade structure. In time, cross-fertilization very much improved the expertise of both the sea-going and the port-operating side. Port Operations are dealt with in the chapter on Port Operating. Lighterage, the LCTs, Fleet Squadron and the various units still serving abroad, form the Maritime component of the RCT. This was extended by the formation and inclusion within 20 LCT Support Regiment RCT at Gosport of 200 Hovercraft Squadron RCT based at Browndown. The Hovercraft are not covered here but for most of its life the squadron was included within the Maritime Organization. Thus by January 1966, Water Transport at home had grown from independent operations to a cohesive entity formed by 20 LCT Support Regiment RCT together with 17 Port Regiment RCT.

Abroad, 33 Maritime Regiment RCT was formed with under command 10 Port Squadron RCT and 37 Squadron RCT (Water Transport) based at Pulau Brani. The varied small craft of 33 Maritime Regiment operated in all Malaysian waters from the sophisticated port of Singapore with its modern facilities to the winding jungle bordered rivers of Borneo. 10 Port Squadron was based at Tanjong Berlayer at the narrow Western entrance to Keppel Harbour where the squadron provided the lighters and freight handlers for the military port. 37 Maritime Squadron commanded by Major Geoffrey Williamson RCT on Pulau Brani provided the craft for harbour communications and regular passenger and vehicle ferry services. The tasks in Singapore waters are best described in relation to the craft which fulfilled them. 10 Port Squadron controlled Z craft, ramped powered lighters, (RPL), tugs and barges. 37 Maritime Squadron controlled ramped cargo lighters, (RCL) harbour launches, general service launches and fast launches of the Derby and River classes.

10 Port Squadron and 37 Maritime Squadron maintained detachments in Borneo at Brunei, Kuching, Tawau and Sibu from the start of Indonesian confrontation. The detachment of 10 Port Squadron lived and maintained itself on the waterfront in Brunei in converted offices belonging to the Port Authority. This detachment had a freight handling section, two RPLs and, attached from 37 Maritime Squadron, an RCL. They also operated the Brunei Government vessel *Nakhoda Manis* which was built on the lines of the Z craft, until it was handed over to the Royal Brunei Malay Regiment, which formed a Maritime Section commanded by an RCT Officer. The tasks and loads varied but the main voyage was the daily return maintenance trip to Labuan resupplying Central Brigade with stores and rations. Other trips took craft along the mangrove lined

local rivers, the Limbang and Temburong, or to small villages across Brunei Bay – Lawas, Sipitang and Weston. The vessels were not equipped for long coastal passages, but RPLs in suitable weather completed runs of up to a hundred miles from their base to meet operational requirements, north east up to Jesselton and South West down to the entrance of the Baram river.

Although the Majority of loads carried were on wheels, which saved time by cutting out double handling, LCTs had to be offloaded at Sapo Point in Brunei Bay. Besides routine tasks there were occasional unusual details, from moving live goats for the Gurkha Dashera festival to carrying drilling equipment on repayment for Government sponsored prospecting projects. Government medical teams were frequently moved to isolated villages in the river complex and on one occasion some 150 tons of prefabricated huts were moved to Limbang. At Kuching, the busiest port in Borneo from a service point of view, 10 Port Squadron operated two RPLs backed up by a freight handling section. The Port Commandant controlled the detachment's activities and a combined control office in the port ensured close co-operation. RPLs carried out regular weekly journeys round the coast to Lundu, a distance of 60 miles, and up the river to Simanggang, a distance of 100 miles, to resupply troops in forward positions. There are sand bars at the mouths of the rivers Lundu and Lingga and journeys had to be carefully timed so that vessels could cross these bars within two hours of high water. Craft then off loaded and returned to base as soon as the tide permitted. Tawau on the East coast of Borneo was very close to the Indonesian border which bisected Sebatik Island a few miles across the bay. The border ran through a river complex of wild swampy mangrove country for many miles and the only way for troops to reach their patrol areas and be resupplied was by boat or, in some places, by helicopter.

A GSL supported by three Harbour Launches from 37 Maritime Squadron and a Uniflote from 10 Port Squadron were responsible for carrying the resupply requirements to the main forward bases at Kalabakan and Wallace Bay. During 1965/66 those vessels logged over 32,000 miles carrying 9,000 passengers and 1,600 tons of stores. The Uniflote proved invaluable for carrying vehicles, loads of fuel in 45 gallon drums and miscellaneous heavy cargoes to inaccessible locations. It also played its part in assisting local estates by moving heavy plant when certain areas were declared prohibited zones. There was also a detachment of two 44½ ft River Class launches operating from the inland river port of Sibu which however closed in July 1966.

Back in England, within 17 Port Regiment, the four lighterage troops developed differing roles. 471 Troop and 473 Troop dealt with vessels, including the operation of the RPLs and Towed Flexible Barges (TFBs) or Dracones, with their associated tugs and workboats. 472 and 474 Troops took over operation of Mexeflotes; large pontoons, built up on a brick system which could reach 120' long by 56' wide at their largest; powered by two giant Harbourmaster outboard engines. These Mex-eflotes, allocated to Landing Ships Logistic (LSL) and secured to their sides or disassembled and secured on board, travelled all over the world to carry out specialized lighterage tasks in remote areas. Their operations are covered under Port Operations although they were, and are, manned by seamen and marine engineers of the Maritime branch.

During the seamen's 6 week strike in 1966, Marchwood Military Port, commanded by Lieutenant Colonel (later Brigadier) J D Lofts MBE RCT and operated by 17 Port Regiment RCT, began the movement of priority military stores and ammunition across Channel to Zeebrugge and Ostend which since then has developed into a major role for Maritime units. The LCTs began their freight cross channel operations which became a most important role. In 1968 with the second seamen's strike, container traffic through Marchwood Military Port began on an ad hoc basis. From small beginnings container operations have grown to become one of the three major Maritime tasks. By pure luck LCTs Mk VIII proved to be ideal for ISO Container shipping. Most LCTs were able to carry thirty-two 20' ISO containers – a thoroughly cost effective method of shipping them. In January 1966 therefore, the pattern of the next 11 years became settled with LCTs in UK running cross channel trips to Belgium, delivering tanks within North Europe and continuing the Hebrides maintenance. Fleet Squadron RCT, the civilian fleet, still based at HM Gunwharf, Portsmouth provided range-safety and clear-ance all round the British Isles, together with exercise support and training vessels. The four lighterage troops at Marchwood provided sheltered water port support, a Dracone re-fuelling capability and operational support for the withdrawal of forces from the remaining colonial outposts.

Overseas, with the disbandment of the Singapore based units, a mixed military and local civilian detachment was retained in Hong Kong to support operations against the Chinese Communists and small detachments remained in Cyprus, Aden and Malta.

After the withdrawal from Aden HMAV *Arezzo* (4128) was disposed of in the Gulf and HMAV *Agheila* (Captain John Venmore RCT) returned via Malta and Gibraltar to continue service with 20 LCT Support Regiment RCT in the UK, arriving at Portsmouth on 7 December 1966; the only LCT Mk VIII to return from abroad. Later, as part of the RCT civilian fleet she became the last LCT to remain in service. Also in 1966 the Queen graciously approved that Army vessels commanded by commissioned officers should be designated Her Majesty's Army Vessels (HMAV).

A heavy programme started in 1967 when the obsolete Centurion tanks in Germany were replaced by the new Chieftains. Large numbers were loaded at Marchwood Military Port and discharged at Antwerp, the old tanks being recovered. Three large 'dolphins' were erected off Marchwood Hard to allow LCTs to moor securely whilst discharging and loading the tanks. This continued right through to completion in 1970 when the task was replaced by one of ferrying out the new Chieftain tanks for Iran from Marchwood Military Port to a heavy lift ship moored in Cowes Roads.

In the early evening of the 10 October 1969 HMAV *Abbeville* was in collision with the Dutch Coaster 'Phoenix'. HMAV *Abbeville* was leading a convoy of four LCTs, *Agheila*, *Aachen* and *Andalsnes*. Having set sail from Portsmouth at 0730 on 10 October, the convoy was nearing the Dover Straits, the weather towards early evening was calm, with fog patches; visibility varying from 50 yards to ½ mile. All vessels were proceeding independently, but by chance in line ahead. At approximately 2139 hours *Abbeville* reported on the radio, that she had collided with another vessel; a further report from *Abbeville* stated that the other vessel had sunk in about five minutes. One life was lost on the *Phoenix*, but no Army casualties were sustained. *Abbeville* was badly damaged in the bow door area, but proceeded into Dover next day, the other three LCTs continuing their voyage to Gothenburg. This was the worst disaster in Water Transport since the loss of MFV *Lucien Gougy*.

From 1946 the units in the Solent Area had come under command of Portsmouth Garrison until it was replaced by Solent Garrison. The Landing Craft unit under its various titles remained under command until Solent Garrison was replaced in its turn by Headquarters Maritime Group RCT based at Ravelin House, Portsmouth, commanded by Brigadier P H Henson OBE with Lieutenant Colonel George Athey RCT as SO1. The Group was disbanded in April 1968 and replaced by the new HQ 2 Transport Group, initially based at Salisbury but later moving to Bulford, until disbandment in 1977. The final closure of an Army Headquarters in Portsmouth raised an interesting problem. Since the Civil War, Portsmouth, as opposed to Portsea, had been a military garrison town. For many years indeed the Army garrison protected the towns people against the depredations of the Naval press gangs. Thus the Senior Army officer was also, ex officio, the Military Governor of the Ancient Fortress of Portsmouth and the Keeper of the Keys of Portsmouth. One of his few duties, which are purely ceremonial, is to present the Keys of Portsmouth, symbolic since there are no gates, to Her Majesty the Queen on the occasions of her official visits to Portsmouth. After considerable discussion this duty passed to the Commanding Officer of the Regiment at St George Barracks Gosport, who now has the privilege of presenting the Keys to the Queen. He also retains a number of other ceremonial duties although the Keys themselves are now kept in the Portsmouth Guildhall. On the 1 February 1971, 20 LCT Support Regiment RCT was reformed in St George Barracks, Gosport into 20 Maritime Regiment RCT and subsequent Commanding Officers have held the dual appointment of Station Commander, Portsmouth/Gosport Station and the ceremonial duties of Governor of the Ancient Fortress of Portsmouth and Keeper of the Keys.

To illustrate the variety of work for which LCTs were used in this period two voyages to Norway should be mentioned. In September 1974 HMAV *Abbeville* (Captain Roy Potts RCT) visited Tromso to load the fuselage of a Halifax bomber which had been shot down in the attack on the German battleship Tirpitz. The fuselage had been raised almost complete from a depth of 90 ft in a remarkable state of preservation. It was unloaded at Felixstowe and conveyed to the RAF Museum, Hendon. Also in 1974 HMAV *Audemer* (Major Simon Birch MBE RCT) joined with a Royal Naval Diving Team from HMS *Daedalus* and sailed to Norway to collect a Skua Divebomber of the Fleet Air Arm which had crashed in a lake during an attack and had been salvaged. It was taken to Lee-on-Solent Hard, where HMAV *Audemer* beached and the fuselage was taken ashore to become an exhibit at the Fleet Air Arm Museum, Yeovilton. In addition the LCTs were used in clearing projectiles from Maplin Sands. Another event in 1974 hall-marked the standard of shiphandling which RCT officers had reached. The Iranian Navy had two new landing ships *Larak* and *Henga* built by Swan Hunter. They were a new departure and no experience in handling them was available to their captains. It was therefore arranged through MOD Sales that Major Simon Birch MBE RCT should join their first ship *Larak* for a fortnight to instruct the Captain how to handle and beach his ship. This took place in the Solent and Channel area, the final test taking place in Warbarrow Bay, Dorset where the captain himself successfully beached his ship and discharged a number of tanks in front of several Iranian senior officers. There was much jubilation aboard afterwards. A few weeks later Major Murray Jones RCT, another experienced LCT Captain, visited Iran to help the Captain of the *Henga* in the same manner.

Despite these interesting side line jobs the main tasks were more and more concentrated into BAOR and Hebrides maintenance and the LCTs Mk VIII were worked harder the older they became.

By 1976 it had become clear that the LCTs Mk VIII, of which there were still four in commission, HMAVs *Agheila*, *Audemer*, *Abbeville* and *Antwerp*, had reached the end of their operational life and should be replaced by modern vessels. Although HMAV *Audemer* remained in commission until February 1978 and HMAV *Agheila* was transferred to 18 Squadron RCT (as the RCT Fleet Troop had been re-named); the launching of the new Landing Craft Logistic, HMAV *Ardennes* commanded by Major Tony Pheby RCT, by Her Royal Highness Princess Alice, Duchess of Gloucester at Brook Marine, Lowestoft on 29 July 1976 heralded the end of an era.

As will have been clear from this short history the RASC and RCT had for many years operated Water Transport with mainly second-hand vessels either supplied by the Royal Navy or taken over from the RAF or civilian sources; or from the RE on formation of the RCT. Indeed, since the delivery of the MLs in 1945 to be ambulance launches, only the command and control launches (CCLs) and an Atlantic 21 were designed and built for the RCT as entirely new vessels. However by 1976 all the RCT vessels, both home and abroad, were ageing badly. Many of the GSLs and LCTs were over thirty years old and, despite the first class efforts of Fleet Repair Branch REME, a devoted team under Mr Alan Blight, many of the craft were barely seaworthy. Finally a near disaster at Rye made it quite clear to all that the crisis was nigh.

MOD (Transport 2), especially when headed by Colonel R N Harris MBE, set out to modernize the fleet and replace all existing craft with vessels more suited to modern operations. The vessels which were to be replaced were first of all the aged LCTs Mk VIII of which only HMAV *Audemer* (Major Peter Robyns RCT), HMAV *Agheila* (Captain Andy Paterson RCT) and HMAV *Abbeville* (Captain Paul Boyes RCT) were still operating in UK waters by mid 1976. As far back as 1968 it had been questioned whether there was a need for the ships. In 1969 Major General P F Claxton CB OBE, Transport Officer in Chief (Army), started investigations into the type of ship needed and the Ministry of Defence (Navy) produced a design for a considerably larger version of the LCT Mk VIII. A great deal of finance and thought was put into the project. The Royal Naval LCT Mk VIII was a highly adaptable ship capable of sailing in oceans or shallows, with a cargo capability both simple and extremely flexible where everything from a ramped lighter to a motor cycle could be carried in any weather. The original design was masterly in simplicity and effectiveness. The manoeuvring ability was remarkable. The LCTs Mk VIII were however slow by modern standards with a maximum speed of 8½ knots. The first consideration was the bow design. The choice was between a sharp and streamlined shape to give more speed or a ship which was simply an updated version of the well tried LCT with more comfort.

This question however was resolved by the voyage of HMAV *Abbeville* (Captain Simon Birch RCT) in October 1974 when she sailed in good weather from Harwich bound for Tromso. She had reached the middle of the North Sea when the weather forecast deteriorated suddenly to a severe North Easterly gale. Captain Simon Birch kept the ship on course at a much reduced speed before deciding to run for the Dutch Naval Base of Den Helder. This required the ship to be turned, producing the highly dangerous possibility of broaching; by this time the wind had reached storm force with steep forty foot waves running. After watching

[By courtesy of Mr M Lennon]

HMAV Ardennes *(Landing Craft Logistic)*

the seas, he selected a less vicious wave and turned the ship onto her southerly course. She manoeuvred faultlessly and reached Den Helder safely. The high bows had thoroughly proved themselves, as no green water had been shipped into the tank deck apart from spray, which cleared through the storm ports. On being asked what the conditions were like on the day, one of the warrant officers said: 'Well Sir, it is the first time I have ever seen soldiers on their knees saying their prayers'.

As a result of this voyage the LCT hull design was adopted in principle, retaining the buoyant bluff bows capable of lifting to any sea. This decision was supported by tank tests carried out by the Royal Navy which, however, proved that due to shallow draft requirements it was not possible to obtain more than 10 knots.

The main task for the new LCLs was to continue maintenance of the RA Ranges in the Hebrides, but they would be required to carry out other tasks as decided by the Director of Movements (Army) and thus were to be able to operate in the Atlantic Ocean off the West coast of Scotland, the English Channel, the North Sea and both flanks of NATO. They were to be shallow draft vessels capable of ocean navigation with a pay load of 350 tons and able to beach and dry out with a load of 250 tons. No type of ship capable of doing such work was in existence. The main difference from the LCT Mk VIII was in the machinery. The LCT Mk VIII had four engines (two on each shaft) but the new LCL had two, thus reverting back to the original system of the LCT Mk IV. This decision immediately eliminated the complicated gear trains in delicate casings which proved such a difficult problem in the last days of the LCT Mk VIII. The machinery was to be bridge controlled thereby relieving the engine room staff. The accommodation especially needed improvement. The crews of the LCT Mk VIII had earned their 'hard lying' money but the modern soldier now deserved something better and more akin to Merchant Navy practice. Taking into account all the requirements, a speed of 10 knots was the theoretical maximum. Final authority was given for the building of the new ships by the Quartermaster General.

The Director General (Ships), who provides ships for the three Services placed a contract with Brooke Marine Ltd, Lowestoft on 6 September 1974 and work began. During the design and building, further tank tests on a large working model of a LCL were carried out at the Admiralty Experimental Establishment which found that raising the poop deck by a metre would considerably help her seakeeping qualities, a fact borne out in practice. Major Tony Pheby RCT was appointed the Army Project Liaison officer and subsequently to command of HMAV *Ardennes* as the first ship was named. He started work at Portsmouth but soon moved to Brooke Marine where he worked closely with the firm, the Royal Navy and the Army over various construction problems.

The overall length of the LCL is 240 feet with a beam of 42 feet. The hull is stronger than the LCT Mk VIII and is fitted with a heavy winch aft which handles the heavy anchor. The ship is propelled by two × 1200 hp Blackstone Mirlees engines giving a speed of 10 knots. At the after end of the engine room is a sound proof control room which protects the watchkeepers from the high pitched roar of the engines. A large galley, fitted with up to date machinery and a good dining room for the soldiers has been provided. There is simple, but comfortable cabin accommodation for everyone, and use has been made of space under the catwalk for additional sleeping berths for passengers. The wheelhouse, above the accommodation, is impressive, with all navigational aids and safety instruments, a shapely funnel – a sizeable mast with radar platform emerges from a bevy of ship aerials. A full size bow door mock up was constructed at Lowestoft to determine the general shape and detail of the bow structure, the ramp and bow door. Due to the urgency of replacing the LCTs Mk VIII, which were by then thirty two years old and becoming dangerous as well as expensive to maintain and repair, the building of the LCLs went ahead as fast as possible. The great day arrived on 29 July 1976 at Lowestoft when HMAV *Ardennes* was launched by Her Royal Highness Princess Alice, Duchess of Gloucester. It was a fine breezy day. The launching was faultless followed by a happy luncheon during which Princess Alice was presented with a teak garden seat as a souvenir; made by the firm at her request. Fitting out continued and trials of all types took place before HMAV *Ardennes* finally sailed for Portsmouth and was commissioned at HM Gun Wharf, the home of the RCT Fleet.

Back at Brooke Marine work was started immediately on HMAV *Arakan*; the Army Liaison Officer's task being taken over by Major David Nicholas RCT who was to command her on commissioning.

At the same time it became necessary to update and replace the vessels of the Fleet Troop RCT at HM Gun Wharf. For some years their major task had been range clearance which had been greatly increased in importance with the advent of large numbers of yachts whose skippers and crews were not interested in chart warnings and whose navigational knowledge is too often very slight. Around the coast of Britain there are a number of ranges where gunnery practice takes place out to sea. Whilst firing is in progress a danger area is created for a considerable distance off shore. As these ranges are mainly used by the Army, the RCT Civilian Fleet is responsible for warning ships and persuading masters of vessels or yachts approaching the area to alter course and keep clear. In most cases they readily comply but occasionally no notice is taken and firing has to stop until the vessel has sailed clear. Firing takes place on shore if the weather is clear quite regardless of sea conditions. The major ranges are at Shoeburyness, Hythe, Lulworth, Eskmeals and in the Outer Hebrides. For this purpose it is necessary to have fast launches with good seakeeping capabilities which are also fully reliable as they operate entirely on their own when detached from Portsmouth, although still under command of 20 Maritime Regt RCT.

For some years the task was carried out by the old RASC Inshore Target Towing Launches and the 50 ft General Service Launches, none of which had the speed required to intercept modern yachts. They were also ageing steadily and since they were built of wood it says much for the standard of maintenance that the Civilian Fleet were able to keep the launches going. It was therefore decided to build a new class of range launch. These were the Command and Control (C&C) launches of glass fibre construction with Cummins diesel engines, on a standard 48 ft Keith Nelson hull. Their main problems were the noise factor, constant fuel trouble and cramped accommodation. Nevertheless, good work was done by the crews who covered all the ranges with these launches in conjunction with their elder sisters. Soon the sea ranges developed into a permanent and highly important requirement of the armament industry and Defence Sales where no lapse could be allowed in firing programmes through insufficient or unserviceable range safety launches. A further investigation by Transport 2 took place in conjunction with Director General (Ships) and a new class of 15 metre Range Safety Launch recently came into service which have proved excellent in all respects. All were to be named after officers and soldiers awarded the Victoria Cross. For use in the Atlantic off the Outer Hebrides RCTV *Alfred Herring VC* a fine 24 metre Air Sea Rescue type launch has been built and brought into service and a second, destined for Cyprus, is undergoing trials. Thus after a long period of uncertainty and financial stringency the RCT Fleet now possesses an array of launches fully suitable for its present important role of range safety.

Mention must also be made of the new fibre-glass harbour launch which has replaced the old wooden and aluminium ones. With the increased range safety tasks, the RCT Fleet Troop took on other wider responsibilities.

Perhaps one of the greatest compliments which has been paid to the RCT Civilian Fleet in recent years was the request made by the Royal

[By courtesy of PR HQ UKLF]

Range safety vessel Sir John Potter.

Aircraft Establishment Farnborough for sea assistance in its research work. A highly important project had been undertaken requiring the use of an ex-naval inshore minesweeper. The work required specialized techniques which had been developed over a long period, and needed a crew fully familiar with procedures at all times. The vessel was manned originally by Royal Air Force officers and airmen who changed period- ically due to postings, courses and other service requirements. This changeover became unacceptable in view of the work to be undertaken. As the RCT Fleet could provide regular crews it was agreed that the RCT should take over the ship and train for the work to be carried out for trials as needed. The ship was named *Richard George Masters VC* who, as an ambulance driver of the RASC during the 1914–1918 War, received that award for recovering numbers of wounded soldiers under fire with his motor ambulance. As he had died some years previously, his sister was able to name the ship at a ceremony held on HM Gun Wharf Portsmouth. RCTV *Richard George Masters VC* was commanded by Captain F Bourne, RCT Fleet who steamed many thousands of miles with her on this task. She was subsequently paid off as her hull became suspect after 30 years service and was no longer economical to maintain but was soon replaced by a stern trawler still in service.

In 1977 the RCT Maritime Branch took part in two very major and exciting events. On 6 April, 'The Maritime Troops of the RCT' received the Honorary Freedom of the Borough of Gosport.

The Mayor of Gosport had first approached 20 Maritime Regiment RCT at the end of 1976 to find out whether the Regiment would be able to accept the Freedom. The Regiment accepted with alacrity and were slightly embarrassed when, shortly after, firstly the Lord Mayor of Portsmouth and then the Mayor of Salcombe, Councillor Leslie Stone, also approached the Regiment with the same offer. However the Mayor of Gosport had asked first and on 23 February 1977, at a special meeting of Gosport Borough Council, The Maritime Troops of the RCT were admitted to the Honorary Freedom of the Borough of Gosport. The name was selected due to the impending change of title, as on 1 March 1977 the Regiment was re-titled the Maritime Detachment RCT. Due to the LCT sailing programme only a small percentage of LCT crews could be released to take part and 52 Port Squadron RCT from Marchwood and a platoon of newly trained soldiers made up the parade. Unfortunately the Mayor was unavoidably absent on the day so the Deputy Mayor, Councillor T R Keith, accompanied by the Representative Colonel Commandant, Major General W Bate CB OBE and Lieutenant Colonel T C Street RCT, the Commanding Officer, took the salute. After the parade the troops marched through the town with bayonets fixed behind the RCT Staff Band. In the final event of the day the Maritime Detachment RCT presented the town with an Edwardian silver inkstand for which all ranks in the unit, both military and civilian and many of the wives and staff as well as former members of Water Transport and ex-maritime officers had contributed.

The next major event of 1977 was the Queen's Silver Jubilee Review of the Fleet at Spithead on 15 June. Due to shortage of RN vessels discussions had taken place with the Royal Navy culminating with a formal invitation to the remaining LCTs Mk VIII to attend. Unfortunately, due to pressure of work, only HMAV *Audemer* (Captain Peter Robyns RCT) could be made available. She arrived late the week before the Review, direct from the Hebrides, and had only five days to prepare. Most RN ships had six months. The crew did magnificent work and in the view of the Royal Navy she was the best turned out vessel in the Review. This was a notable event, as it was the first time that one of Her Majesty's Army Vessels, commanded by a serving Army officer with a properly constituted military ship's company, had taken part in such an occasion. She was the oldest ship on the Review, just beating the much publicized *HMS Reclaim*. The following year she was paid off after the commissioning of HMAV *Arakan* which added to the lustre of her crews hard work in bringing her, from being constantly at sea, to a standard which, earned many compliments and provided a worthy platform from which Major General P H Benson CBE the Director General of Transport and Movements, Lieutenant General Sir Anthony Farrar-Hockley GBE KCB DSO MC, Commander South East District and a number of senior officers were able to cheer Her Majesty the Queen from the flag deck. There were 21 'stars' aboard and the painting of the occasion by Major B V Wynn-Werninck (late RASC) is in Buller Officers Mess.

If ever a ship went out with a flourish HMAV *Audemer* did when on the night of 24 April 1979, shortly before being paid off, the vessel now commanded by Captain Roy Potts RCT, answered a Mayday signal from the Sail Training Ship *Sir Winston Churchill*. There was a severe Northerly gale blowing at this time which had caused the training ship to drag her anchor off Cowes. She went aground just before high water on the mudbank of the Shrape bordering the breakwater. She was in danger of being badly damaged by heeling right over as the tide receded. HMAV *Audemer* was approaching Egypt Point when the message was received and being the only available ship in the area immediately went to help. On arrival off Cowes Captain Roy Potts worked her in as far as he could and anchored by the bows. A very confused and heavy sea was running off the harbour which prevented an inflatable dinghy from the training ship reaching *Audemer* with a line. Shortly afterwards the Harbour Master with his heavy launch was able to do this. Cable was soon made fast and TS *Sir Winston Churchill* was winched off to safety. Had any further delay occurred she would have stuck fast and undoubtedly heeled over at low tide, flooded and been lost or very severely damaged. For this fine rescue Captain Roy Potts received a Commendation from the GOC South East District.

Shortly prior to this, HMAV *Audemer*, then commanded by Major Peter Robyns RCT was sailing up the Irish Sea bound for the Clyde when she was asked by HM Coastguard to make contact with a vessel which had sent out a 'Mayday' signal. She altered course and found a Danish coaster rolling in the swell having run out of fuel two days previously. She had no power for propulsion, lights or services. There was a fair sea running so a line was passed and the vessel was towed to Milford Haven forty miles away. After some time salvage money was paid to the ship's company by the Ministry of Defence.

In 1979 the Maritime Detachment RCT reverted to the title 20 Maritime Regiment RCT and settled down once more to routine operations only interupted by the presentation of the Keys of Portsmouth to the new Lord Mayor by Lieutenant Colonel John Flood RCT. HMAV *Ardennes* (Major Guy Yeoman RCT) completed her first stint in Scotland with a successful annual inspection by Brigadier J D Lofts MBE ADC and followed it with a trip to Antwerp and participation in the NATO exercise 'Agate Exchange' which involved a trip to Korsor where the Royal Danish Navy arranged the landing. Subsequently she did a run to Jersey to convey home the outgoing Lieutenant-Governor and Commander-in-Chief on his retirement. Meanwhile HMAV *Arakan* (Major David Nicholas RCT) ran the Marchwood Military Port to Antwerp supply run with ISO containers prior to replacing HMAV *Ardennes* in Scotland.

Abroad, 10 Port Squadron continued with harbour duties using a RPL and workboats at Akrotiri in Cyprus dealing with a wide selection of vessels. RCTV *Hyperion* was transferred from Fleet Troop for range duties.

LCT Mk VIII 4097 (later HMAV Andalsnes*) arriving at Portsmouth on commissioning,
January 1957.*

In Hong Kong, 415 Maritime Troop RCT continued to operate a
LCM Mk VII, two GSLs, two harbour launches and three RPLs. The
Troop was based on Stonecutters Island which forms the apex of a rough
triangle within Hong Kong's harbour about twenty minutes sailing time
from the mainland. The vessels were operated by a small staff of RCT
seamen, navigators and marine engineers who trained the Chinese
soldiers in the art of seamanship and safe operations of the small fleet. The
vessels were employed carrying out regular sea-border patrols for illegal
immigrants; on inter-island ferry services and on a wide variety of supply
tasks in support of tri-service requirements. As a direct result of the
patrols for illegal immigrants the decision was made to replace the RPLs
by RCLs. This new class of craft the Ramped Craft Logistic (RCL) was
designed in the United Kingdom. So far two have been built by Brooke
Marine, Lowestoft, RCTV *Arromanches* and *Antwerp* and three others are
on order for delivery in 1984/85, although the RPLs remain in service.
These vessels are larger than their predecessors but are still capable of
being lifted and transported by suitable cargo ships. At present, they are
operating in the Falkland Islands, providing coastal transport and the
discharge of merchantmen anchored off Port Stanley in the huge task of
refurbishing the Islands after the Campaign.

The first RPL to be deployed to Belize, RCTV *Medway*, arrived
aboard HMS *Fearless* in February 1977, the LPD flooding down some
twelve miles off the coast allowing the RPL to navigate her way through
the coral reefs to Belize City. The craft was employed resupplying the
company base in the south of Belize in the Toledo District. In the early
stages she carried a portable refrigeration plant on deck to transport

[By courtesy of Lt Col T C Street]

HMAV St George

perishable foods. In July 1977 relations with Guatemala deteriorated sharply, an attack was forecast for the night of the 7 of July 1977, and the Joint Theatre Plan (JTP) was implemented to reinforce the Garrison, in practice doubling its size to 2000. The southern company became a battle group split between Salamanca and Rideau Camps. The RPL resupply increased in importance to supplement both road and air movement. A major building programme required large tonnages to be moved south and needed a second RPL. RCTV *Kennet* arrived by heavy lift ship in December 1977. In the Autumn of 1977 the Quartermaster General, General Sir Patrick Howard Dobson GCB, personally intervened to persuade Tate and Lyle, the owners of the Belize Sugar Corporation plant at Corozal in the north of Belize, to allow the RPLs to be refitted on their slipway. 1979 saw the provision of a harbour launch to further supplement the Maritime Detachment. Soldiers were provided from 17 Port Regiment on six month tours up until the Falklands crisis when the commitment became a 3 Transport Group responsibility shared between 17 and 20 Regiments.

The task of supplying Battle Group South has been the principal commitment for the duration of the RPLs deployment. It is a 12 hours passage of reasonably difficult navigation with coral reefs and severe electrical storms as the principal obstacles. The country is extremely primitive and metal rusts rapidly in the very humid climate, increasing the maintenance difficulties for already ageing craft. Living in Airport Camp near Belize is basic and crowded but adequate for field conditions. Most crew members much prefer to be at sea even though there is no air conditioning aboard an RPL.

1981 was a landmark year in the history of Water Transport. 20 Maritime Regiment RCT celebrated its 25th Birthday with the Commissioning of HMAV *St George*, designed and built to replace the Royal Fleet Auxiliary operated LSL *Empire Gull* on BAOR ammunition supply runs. On Thursday 1 October 1981 at a ceremony attended by the GOC South Eastern District Lieutenant General Sir Paul Travers KCB, and conducted by the Chaplain General The Venerable Archdeacon W F Johnston QHC MA, and with the cake cut by Mrs Pat Allen, wife of the DGTM, *St George* provided an expansion of the maritime role into conventional ships and a new task providing the maritime BAOR maintenance commitment for movement of ammunition. This was part of the secure L of C policy initiated by General Jackson when QMG in the mid seventies. She is proving an excellent ship, having been built by Appledore Shipbuilders at Bideford, a yard with whom Maritime has much experience over many years refitting LCTs. She has a high standard of crew comfort and for the first time providing individual cabins for the whole crew, a far cry from LCT days.

1982 will always be remembered for the Falklands campaign, and although 20 Maritime Regiment RCT played no part in the action the campaign resulted in a dearth of logistic shipping available for BAOR maintenance, and increased the pressure on LCLs. On reoccupation of the Islands 73 Squadron RCT was formed at Port Stanley. This will be an ongoing commitment for the Regiment for the foreseeable future, increasing the already high separation rate from their families faced by maritime soldiers. The bonus has been an establishment increase to the trade structure, a lot of acting promotion, and considerable responsibility for handling Mexeflote's and work boats by junior NCO's who responded magnificently to a demanding workload, in often appalling conditions, with good humour and resourcefulness.

The years 1976–1983 have seen continued re-equipment of 18 Maritime Squadron with the 15 metre Talisman class launches. The QMG, Lieutenant General Sir Paul Travers KCB was present to watch Lady Travers name a launch after him on the 8 July 1982.

HMAV *St George* (Major Andy Paterson RCT) made her first Mediterranean passage in September to ship the annual ammunition scale to Cyprus. It was the first time the ship had been continuously at sea for more than 48 hours and gave her the first real opportunity to shake down into sea watches and try out her autopilot.

The Water Transport element of the Corps offers an interesting and varied experience to those who serve in this branch of the RCT. Apart from the vital function fulfilled by the Maritime units, the work at sea provides a stimulating life and the opportunity to travel extensively. The soldier 'sailors' have earned themselves a very high reputation with their Royal Navy and Merchant Navy compatriots who they frequently work alongside.

512

20 · ANIMAL TRANSPORT

DURING THE 1939–45 War, vast numbers of horses and mules were used in mountainous and jungle areas, notably in the Italian and Burma campaigns. At one time there were some 30,000 operating with the Allied Armies in Italy and in the Far East some 2,000 were flown into the Chindits airheads behind the enemy lines in Burma. Since then the Animal Transport (AT) units of the Corps have been run down until they disappeared from the United Kingdom with the disbandment of H Squadron RCT at Aldershot in 1972 and finally with the disbandment of 414 Pack Transport Troop RCT in Hong Kong in 1976.

In post war operations, until the advent of the helicopter in a logistic role, the mule once again showed that it was superior to the motor vehicle in supplying troops in mountainous areas and they proved their ability in operations in Hong Kong, Kenya and Muscat and Oman.

In the United Kingdom, approximately 1,500 ponies on the strength of the four companies of 5 Pack Group, of 52 (Lowland) Division, based in the Highlands of Scotland, together with the mules of the mountain artillery were sold off at various horse sales throughout the country. Overseas the mules and horses from the animal transport companies in the different theatres were disposed of in a similar manner.

There only remained, in the United Kingdom, the Transport (Animal) Training Wing (later to become H Squadron RCT) in Aldershot, and overseas a few horse transport companies on the Continent and one in the Canal Zone. The main function of the Training Company in Aldershot, was to keep alive the techniques of animal transport and to train officers and NCO's for units overseas. In addition to running courses for this purpose, at that time and for many years after the War, all junior officers entering the Corps were given a certain amount of equitation and pack transport training as part of their Junior Officers Course. Most of their riding school work was undertaken on early morning rides. These rides were not always appreciated by every student at the time but certain incidents have been the subject of after dinner stories in Corps messes for many years since they occurred. The names of individual equine characters are still often repeated. To name one in particular, Phantom, may bring back memories to some of the more senior readers. A grey mare, about 15.2 hands, she was in the Training Company in the late 1940's and early 50's, who whilst being a perfect lady, had the disconcerting habit of attempting to lie down in every puddle and wet patch of mud within sight. This habit made her of great help to instructors, who generally waited until about halfway through a course,

when the most obnoxious student would have made himself apparent. No mention would be made of Phantom's habits. At that time it was permissible to ride along the tow path of the Basingstoke Canal. The class would be taken out on a hack with the desired student riding Phantom in the middle of the file of riders. At a certain point the canal would be forded, the instructor checking slightly in front to give Phantom some encouragement and invariably down she went in about three and a half feet of water. This resulted in a rather wet, sometimes very cold and always very subdued young officer on the ride back to Buller. At the conclusion of the course, a two day pack transport exercise was held with each student leading a pack horse. The exercise included a night march over the roughest country that could be found. This training ensured that all junior officers at least had some knowledge of the basic principles of animal management and pack transport, should they at any time be posted to an animal transport unit.

Overseas, the long rein horse transport companies were eventually disbanded, the last being that in the Canal Zone. However, in the latter part of 1949, 81 Troop RASC (Pack Transport) was established in the New Territories of Hong Kong, and in the early 1950's a pack unit was formed in Kenya for work during the Mau Mau operations. In 1958 a small unit of 200 pack donkeys was also formed on a temporary basis for work on the operations in Muscat and Oman. All of these units had local soldiers as animal transport drivers but the officers and most of the NCOs were British. The majority of the latter were animal transport specialists who had served with the Horse Transport Company in Aldershot but

Left: *Horse Transport Company RASC on exercise near Aldershot*

[By courtesy of The War Office]

Right: *Horse Transport Company RASC Aldershot*

[By courtesy of The War Office]

some, in particular the officers, were from other branches of the Corps, who had attended courses. One such course for both officers and NCO's, was of ten weeks duration and included instruction in equitation, pack transport, animal management, long rein driving and veterinary first aid.

In addition to courses for the RASC/RCT, many were run for other Arms. These included short pack transport courses for the Special Air Service, Parachute Regiment and any unit who might make use of animals in this capacity at any time. Courses were also run for the Army Saddle Clubs Association. These were of six weeks duration, both elementary and advanced and helped to encourage riding as a sport throughout the Services. Students, male and female, came from all branches of the Army as well as a few from the Royal Navy and the Royal Air Force.

Apart from its training functions, H Squadron RCT, as it eventually became known, performed much excellent work in keeping the Corps in the public eye. A first class display ride toured the Country for many years and undertook engagements at agricultural and horse shows, tattoos and twice at the Royal Tournament. The Squadron also more than held its own in military equestrian sports amongst the much larger mounted ceremonial units. The RASC/RCT Coach was horsed and largely staffed by H Company/Squadron. The history of the Corps Coach itself has been the subject of a separate book published in 1972.

During the rebuild of Buller Barracks, the Squadron moved to Beaumont Barracks, Aldershot. However, by the time the foundations of

515

[By courtesy of The War Office]

Horse Transport Company at Tweseldown.

the new stables had been laid, it was decided by the authorities that pack transport was unlikely to be required by the British Army in the foreseeable future and H Squadron was disbanded in 1972.

The British cadre of 81 Troop RASC (Pack Transport) was established at Colchester in May 1949 for operation in the New Territories of Hong Kong at the time of a large build up of forces in the Colony when the Chinese Communist Armies were approaching the border. The cadre consisted of a captain as officer commanding, supported by a subaltern, a warrant officer class II, a staff sergeant for administration, one sergeant and three corporals. There was also a farrier sergeant, a corporal saddler and two junior ranks of the Royal Army Veterinary Corps (RAVC). After some delay the cadre sailed from Southampton on the Troopship *Orbita* and after a five week voyage finally arrived in Hong Kong in the middle of September. The numbers had been increased by the addition of an officer and staff sergeant RAVC who had been taken on board at Singapore.

The cadre took over a few huts at Sek Kong on what had been a government experimental farm, in fact a crop of rice was still being harvested. A few marquees were erected and the arrival of the Hong Kong soldiers from the Hong Kong Military Service Corps and the mules was eagerly awaited. However, there was further considerable delay and in the meantime eight horses were taken over from the Hong Kong Jockey Club as riding animals. These were Australian and ex-racing ponies, not ideally suited to the task in hand. They were transported in a Landing Craft Tank (LCT) from Hong Kong island and disembarked in Castle Peak Bay, from where they were ridden to Sek Kong. Unfortunately, the OC was an early casualty when the horses were first worked alongside the Sek Kong airstrip, where he was bucked off and broke a thigh. This resulted in a temporary OC having to take over for several months.

Eventually, on 18 January 1950, about eighty Hong Kong soldiers were posted in from the Training Centre in Lyemun Barracks and on the same day a ship arrived from Australia with fifty mules on board and docked in Kowloon harbour. Unfortunately the Hong Kong soldiers had been recruited before the arrival of the British cadre, who had therefore no say as regards their suitability for work with mules. As a result, most were Hong Kong City born and never knew a mule existed before they saw one. In addition, the purchase of the mules had been left to an Australian stockman and most had hardly seen a human being before being rounded up in the bush. They had been cramped together in pens of five on the open deck for over a month, the ship having sailed to Hong Kong via Japan. The one stockman had merely given them a little hay and water and the heavy seas and pitching had resulted in a number of open head wounds. Three had died of tetanus on the voyage. According to the contract the mules were broken to lead but in fact, only three had had so much as a halter on before embarkation. The officer commanding and troop sergeant major, full of confidence that the animals could at least be led, reported to the ship's captain who wanted to know how long disembarkation would take. The OC reckoned about half a day but the captain who had seen the stockman loading in Australia, thought this rather an optimistic assessment which, indeed, proved to be correct. The Hong Kong soldiers, whose first sight of mules this was, refused to go near them but six or seven British other ranks from the infantry were coerced to assist. It did in fact, take two days to disembark and transport the animals to Sek Kong. They had to be dragged off the ship down a gangway and towed and driven, four men to each through the main streets of Kowloon to the railway station. Several tradesmen's roadside stalls were demolished in the process. From Kowloon they were taken by rail to Tai Po and then driven in a herd to Sek Kong. About thirty were taken on the first day and the remainder on the following. At Sek Kong a picket line had optimistically been erected. However, as the mules had never been tied up before, this proved useless. They were kept in a herd and it was about ten days before the last was rounded up and driven into a corral, newly constructed by the Sappers.

Gradually, the Hong Kong soldiers were encouraged to go nearer to the mules and eventually turned out to be quite good muleteers. No chances were taken with future recruitment and recruits were selected from the villages where they had at least handled water buffalo. Two mules were always taken along with recruiting parties so there could be no illusion as to what the potential soldier would have to work with. The mules, after much hard work on the part of the few British ranks, were broken and within about three months approximately 50% could be

517

worked fairly reliably with infantry.

Most of the remainder could be worked on supply, carrying loads such as rations and ammunition which did not suffer too many ill effects by being bucked off a few times. After about six months almost all could be worked carrying infantry loads. One exception never submitted to the idea of working for the Army and eventually had to be put down. Almost before the first batch of mules were finally broken, a further seventy to eighty arrived from Pakistan. The Australian animals, apart from being absolutely wild were also a very mixed bunch, varying from 12.2 to 15.2 hands high and all ages, from a yearling to one rising twenty. The Pakistani mules had been purchased by a RAVC Veterinary Officer and a party from the Troop had escorted them on their voyage. They were all about 14.0 to 14.2 hands and four and five year olds, handled from foaling, broken to lead and indeed bred for the Pakistan Army. They proved much easier to break, to saddle and load and were soon in work. They were never, however, quite so hardy or had so much stamina as the Australian animals.

As the first batch of Hong Kong soldiers had arrived from the Training Centre on the same day and had just completed their basic training, it was not apparent who would be suitable for promotion. This fact made much extra work for the British element but gradually one or two of the local soldiers showed themselves as being of NCO material. About six were eventually promoted to Lance Corporal and Corporal.

After the first eight to nine months the unit became an efficient Pack unit with varied roles mainly that of providing the first line transport in the difficult terrain near the border of the New Territories and Red China. The larger mules carried loads of up to 300 pounds but the smaller mules were restricted to 160 pounds. Loads varied from the daily maintenance requirements of the infantry units situated in the border areas, the radios and batteries for them and their gunner observation post communications, to the 4.2 mortar and their ammunition plus the sapper defence stores. They also carried the equipment and medical stores for the joint military/civil police penetration patrols.

Aid to the civil community was also undertaken varying from the evacuation of the occupants of a village situated in the area of the new Lan Tau reservoir to moving materials for District Officers building paths to isolated villages. 'Heart and minds' activities were also undertaken. Thanks to the early efforts made in this field, there is now in 1982 a thriving Horse Society and Pony Club affiliated to the British Horse Society and Pony Club of Great Britain. Even after disbandment in 1976, some of the mules were given a reprieve by being taken into use by the Royal Hong Kong Jockey Club as mounts for the handicapped of the Colony.

The unit was redesignated 81 Company RASC (Pack Transport) in 1955, and changed to 29 Company RASC from 1962–1965. On the

[By courtesy of JSPRS Hong Kong]

414 Pack Transport Troop RCT with helicoter fuel.

change of cap badge in 1965, it became 29 Squadron RCT, its strength being 72 mules and 136 men. Finally it was redesignated 414 Pack Transport Troop RCT on 15th July 1965 and remained so until disbandment in 1976.

Over the years a number of amusing incidents occurred. For example, in November 1961, HQ Hong Kong Land Forces organized a military tattoo in honour of Her Royal Highness Princess Alexandra visiting the island. Part of this display was a mounted skill at arms demonstration including tent pegging. The OC, Major A R Grimshaw RASC was mounted on his grey ex-racehorse, a notoriously difficult animal. Having had a number of years on the race course, the horse pulled like a train. On the OC's first run the horse set its mouth against the bit and charged, totally ignoring the pegs and headed for the rather ornate gate that served as an exit from the arena. The NCO on the gate closed it and some wag in the audience shouted 'I hope he's got a ferry warrant 'cos that horse ain't going to stop'.

In 1961 during an exercise in support of the 2/10 Gurkha Rifles, one of the mules fell from the bank into a very large and ripe night soil pit. It was carrying the observation post party's radio and batteries. The mule fell upside down and was in danger of drowning and when the Troop Officer, Lieutenant A R M Adams RASC arrived on the scene, the only thing to be seen was the hooves and the mule's muzzle which was being pulled by the reins out of the slime by Sergeant Paddy Young. At this time most of the Chinese handlers, British and Gurkha troops had retired up wind to a safe distance. Sergeant Young asked Lieutenant Adams to sit on the edge of the pit and keep pulling the reins whilst he sat on the other side with his feet on its belly so that he could cut the girth and surcingle. Mules are remarkable animals in that they do not panic when trapped. However, once free they get out as quickly as possible. Therefore once Sergeant Young freed the load the animal let fly with all fours, pulling Messrs Young and Adams inwards, both passed in mid air and landed head first in the night soil pit. No one came to their aid.

Also in 1961, the Commander 48 Brigade decided to hold a review of all troops in the Brigade for the Governor. The aim was to have the Brigade lined up in full battle order on Sek Kong airstrip in the late afternoon, wait for darkness and then let the crowds arrive. The Governor was to arrive by car and would be given a mounted escort by the company. Meanwhile, all the troops would be waiting in the darkness, including 120 mules and three horses, the horses being ridden by Lieutenant A R M Adams RASC, Captain R Currer-Briggs RAVC and Troop Sergeant Baxter. Several daylight rehearsals took place, then the full dress rehearsal was ordered for the night but one before the event. The Brigade Major failed to inform the OC, Major A R Grimshaw RASC that maroon rockets would be fired from behind the 'mock-up' castle walls to start the proceedings.

On the night of dress rehearsal, the mules and horses were lined up in front of the tanks of the Royal Scots Greys, HRH Captain the Duke of Kent being on parade with his squadron. The maroons were fired into the air but came cascading down onto the top of the middle rank of mules, they of course panicked and shot forward into the front rank – many of the machine guns, ammunition boxes and mortars hitting the handlers of the front rank of mules. All the mules took off up the airstrip causing pandemonium amongst the Gurkha Infantry. Lieutenant Adams, the Troop Officer and his horse went over backwards and the horse finished up on top of him in a monsoon ditch.

It took three ambulances to clear what looked like a battlefield. Some thirteen soldiers were injured, one with a fractured skull. It took nearly 48 hours to find all the mules – many carrying the support weapons for the Brigade Group. However, with two handlers to every mule and needless to say, *no* maroon rockets, on the big day all went well and the horses, mules and muleteers conducted themselves with exemplary behaviour.

So came the end of an incredibly long association between men and horses. Many of those who served in AT units continue to argue that we still need the horse in military operations. The record of the helicopter in the Falkland Island and operations in other difficult terrains sadly kills any argument. Apart from their training and recreational value, the horse is no longer the answer to a logisticians prayer in those parts of the world where the terrain is too difficult for motor transport. The rotary wing aircraft has revolutionized operations of this nature, but as in so many other spheres, life isn't as much fun!

21 · AIR DESPATCH

IN 1945, WHEN THE Royal Army Service Corps became the officially designated parent Corps for supply by air, there was available a vast fund of knowledge of organization and methods which had developed in two main streams to meet the dissimilar requirements of the 14th Army in Burma and the 2nd Army in North West Europe.

To follow the developments and changes which have taken place since the end of World War II and which are still in progress, we need to recall briefly the organizations which were in being when the war ended. They have survived the test of time because they were products of experience in the hardest of schools and it is not surprising that in those elements of the system which have survived the rundown of the Army, albeit with frequent changes of name, the basic functions and method of operation have remained remarkably consistent.

In Headquarters 14th Army, control of air supply was vested initially in a staff branch 'Q' Air. As the operations in Burma became more intensive, 'Q' Air was replaced by a new Headquarters known as Army Air Transport Organization (HQ AATO). This new staff organization was responsible to HQ Allied Land Forces South-East Asia (ALFSEA) for the operation and efficiency of supply by air, and air movement and transportation.

HQ AATO controlled Rear Air Maintenance Organizations (RAMO's); lieutenant colonels commands, which were not RASC/ RIASC units although some were commanded by RIASC officers.

HQ RAMO had a small staff including some service representatives, who in the case of the Corps were a DADST and a Capt (S&T). It commanded air despatch companies, general transport companies, petrol platoons and Royal Pioneer Corps labour units and other service detachments as required.

At the receiving end of the organization, stores were handled by Forward Air Maintenance Organizations (FAMOs) which were GHQ troops. Unlike RAMOs, FAMOs were not controlled by HQ AATO but were allotted to, and under command, of the formations they served.

The factors influencing the development of air supply in Europe differed from those in FARELF in that:

a. Supply by air was the exception, rather than the rule.
b. The distances to be overflown were comparatively short.
c. Well established ground communications existed.
d. There was a requirement to resupply by parachute, large airborne formations, for relatively short periods.

To meet the 2nd Army requirement in Europe an Air Despatch Group was formed which had under command two CRASCs (AD) each of two AD Companies, a CRASC (Transport Column) of four to six general transport companies and a Petrol Depot. Two Airborne Divisional Companies RASC were attached, as were Ordnance and Pioneer units, as required. The Group at its peak was approximately 5000 strong. Some idea of the difference in scale between the two theatres can be gained from the fact that by March 1945 10,000 soldiers had been trained in air despatch in FARELF.

In Europe there was no real equivalent of the FAMO. A formation was responsible for the reception of its own maintenance but 'air freight reception units' were formed on the larger airfields to clear aircraft of bulk freight. Following the war it was decided that a common organization was required for the task of air supply and this was based on the organization which operated in FARELF.

The controlling headquarters retained the name of AATO but the despatching organization RAMO became the Rear Air Supply Organization (RASO). Although similar in organization to a RAMO the RASO was an RASC headquarters working on an establishment similar to that of a transport column. Because his command included units of other arms the OC was designated 'Commander RASO' instead of CRASC.

The RASOs task was to carry out the programme allotted by HQ AATO: to hold and maintain buffer stocks; to call forward, pack, load and despatch supplies and to emplane formed bodies of troops. HQ RASO was designed to command one or more AD companies and attached personnel as required, eg RAOC, RAMC, RMP, RPC, NAAFI, etc.

Forward Air Supply Organizations (FASOs) working with RAF Mobile Staging Posts were responsible for the reception of supplies on forward airfields and the supervision of their control and distribution. The FASO also co-ordinated the back loading of returned stores, salvage, casualties and prisoners.

Unlike the FAMO, FASO's were under command of AATO, and also differed in that they had neither transport nor labour on their establishments. They were in effect, a controlling headquarters commanded by a Major RASC with a small staff including two Captains and some administrative personnel. The provision of transport and labour was the responsibility of the formation being served. While it was prudent to plan for large scale operations, as the Berlin Airlift was soon to prove, in practice only two air despatch units survived the post war reduction in the Army.

749 Company (AD) based in UK with detachments in Aden, Egypt, and Cyprus served the needs of the Middle East while 799 Company (AD) with detachments in Burma, Hong Kong, Borneo and Malaya covered the Far East.

[By courtesy of Capt R Nicholson]

Heavy drop from a Hastings during Suez operations 1956.

749 Company (later to become 47 Company) consisted of an Air Duties Platoon, a Training Platoon and an MT Platoon, and its command and control was sufficiently unusual to be of interest. Although an operational unit it was part of the RASC Training Centre (presumably because of its training role) and also under the local command of Salisbury Plain District (SPD). However, neither the Training Centre nor SPD played any part in operational tasking which the Company received from HQ Transport Command RAF via Station Operations RAF Abingdon.

In fact it was normal for the Operations Officer of 749 Company, Captain (later Lieutenant Colonel) D R Black, to deal direct with the RAF up to MOD level without going through any Army headquarters.

Although this state of affairs would be unlikely to receive Staff College approval it is recalled with pleasure by the then members of the unit who enjoyed a degree of autonomy seldom experienced at company level. However, June 1948 and the Berlin Airlift in which 749 Company, 68, 950 and 955 Companies took part saw the return of the 'big battalions' with an HQ AATO commanding RASO's operating from the base airfields in the British Zone of Germany and also exercising technical command of a FASO at Gatow airport on the outskirts of Berlin. Details of this major operation can be found in Part 1 of this Book.

In the Far East, after operations in Burma and Java which are also covered in detail in Part 1, 799 Company returned to Singapore in 1948 and after initial concentration at Selarang Barracks three platoons moved to Nee Soon Camp for employment on MT duties. The fourth platoon remained at Selarang to carry out air despatch training at RAF Changi.

In June 1948, when the emergency was declared in Malaya, one platoon was sent to Kuala Lumpur initially for MT duties. The air despatch requirement grew steadily until, by the end of 1949, the Kuala Lumpur detachment had increased to a captain, a subaltern and nine sections, and later in 1950 to 16 crews.

In September of that year the unit number was changed to 55 Company. At this time there was a large detachment at Kuala Lumpur and Company HQ with the residue of one platoon based on the RASC School (Far East) at Nee Soon. Air Despatch units, it would appear, have a predilection for Training Centres/Schools!

In 1952 the part of the Company in Singapore gave up its MT role and concentrated on the largely quartermaster function of holding and issuing supply dropping equipment to the large detachment in Kuala Lumpur and the small one which had been established at RAF Changi to support civil engineering operations in Borneo. No doubt there was some good reason for the Company HQ remaining in Singapore until 1954 although the main company effort and operational task was clearly based on Kuala Lumpur, but for many onlookers it was at the time, and still remains, an unsolved mystery.

1960 was a time of expansion in the air despatch world and a time once again to provide new titles for old functions. 1 Army Air Supply Organization (AASO) (commanded initially by Lieutenant Colonel L Barker-Simpson MBE and later by Lieutenant Colonel W C Grierson MBE MM) was formed at Watchfield with under command 47 (AD) Company, the Air Despatch Training Wing and later a new unit, 22 (AD) Company. The HQ AASO was established to deploy up to three Air Supply Control Sections each consisting of a Major, a Captain and a small staff. Thus tidily combined in one establishment was the capability to perform the functions of what had previously been called a RASO and FASOs.

As we shall see when we look at AASO activities in the Far East, Air Supply Control Sections could also be used for other purposes. Expansion continued in 1960–61 with the formation of 3 AASO, (Lieutenant Colonel B H J O'Reilly MBE) for service in the Far East and 16 (AD) Company (Major J O'Brien) bound for Kenya and Aden.

In an account which of necessity consists mainly of unit titles and dates we offer a short story of a day in the life of 1 AASO. This true account concerns the first visit to an AASO by a Quartermaster General. Acutely conscious of his unit's aerial role the Commanding Officer was determined that his visitor, a distinguished airborne soldier should arrive by helicopter. His staff, veterans of UK winters, who for a week previous had groped their way to work with the aid of white sticks and powerful torches were equally determined that the General should be provided with a more predictable means of transport. After numerous changes of plan and taking advantage of a fleeting break in the weather the Commanding Officer prevailed and announced to his staff that despite their defeatism and timidity the QMG had been picked up by the Army Air Corps at

RAE Farnborough and was en route. At that moment the phone rang and a penetrating female voice was heard to say 'Are you No 1 ARSO? will you accept a reverse charge from a helicopter pilot who is phoning you from a callbox near Wantage?' Later that day, as the inspection party proceeded at a snail's pace through dense fog, the QMG, tongue in cheek suggested to the CO that the limp state of certain flowers outside the barrack huts was due to weak bladders and the long walk to the toilet block. This was vigorously denied. A young Lance Corporal was summoned and asked by the General 'Where do you go at night when you want to relieve yourself?' The NCO who was clearly taken aback by this very personal question sprang to attention and replied 'Swindon, Sir.'

Later as he approached his car the distinguished visitor was heard to say to his aide, 'I don't know what it is about air despatch but it makes them all mad – from Lance Corporals upwards.'

In October of 1961 the Training Major of 1 AASO (Major P E Gray MM) was attached to the RAF Transport Command Examining Unit (TCEU) for two months to join it for its visit to Singapore and Malaya. His terms of reference left ample scope for interpretation and during this attachment he began to devise the Air Despatch Categorization Scheme which, albeit much modified, is still in use. Categorization, now a well established and accepted part of AD life, had a painful birth as few looked with favour on a system which required proof of efficiency at six monthly intervals. Early in 1962 Major Gray, in the face of considerable opposition from the air despatch world and a noticeable lack of enthusiastic backing from his sponsors, launched the RASC Categorization Scheme on a 'publish and be damned' basis. His first attempt to examine and award a category took place in Cyprus with the late Warrant Officer Class 1 Peters (then a Corporal), cast unwillingly in the leading role. His failure was impressive but from this unpromising beginning he subsequently became a staunch supporter of the Categorization Scheme and the second member of the Corps to earn an A Category. The first A Category had not unreasonably been awarded by the examiner to himself! .

The initial 8 weeks grew into a continuous attachment which lasted until March 1963 when Major Gray was reinforced by two Warrant Officers Class 2 (H Carver and J O Atkinson) to form the Air Despatch Examining Team. Warrant Officer Class 2 Carver, who joined the Team in Singapore promptly fell into a monsoon drain and candidates for the oral 'ground examination' took their test at his bedside. At about the same time in Singapore a joint Service organization was formed boasting the impressive title of Far East Land Air Warfare Training Centre (FELAWTC). It was an organization which doubtless found favour with the Inspector of Establishments as it drew its staff from officers already gainfully employed in other posts. Under a Commandant, otherwise the Group Captain Station Commander, Seletar, were two Chief Instructors provided by CO 3 AASO and the Wing Commander Flying, Seletar, while an Air Supply Control Section provided a Senior Instructor and all remaining instructional staff. As the first senior instructor Major M D Isherwood was ruefully to observe 'Seldom before had so many commanded so few.'

In 1966 an Air Despatch Group was formed at Watchfield. In this case the practice of providing new names for old functions was reversed by the use of an old title with a new role. The Group's charter limited its responsibility to the technical control of air despatch systems and air despatch units. The lack of a command function was a cross which the Group Commander, Colonel R A Nightingale MBE had to bear, but nevertheless under his leadership the Group was able to exert an influence on air despatch matters quite out of proportion to the size of its small staff.

Fortunately the Group was in being to direct the fight for air despatch at a time when takeover bids were in fashion and when persuasive (but usually ill informed) staff papers appeared with monotonous regularity proposing the transfer of responsibility for parachute resupply to the RAF or any interested Corps.

On the 13 June 1966 SCAO set up a Working Party under the Chairmanship of the Deputy Director of Army Staff Duties to investigate a suggestion that:

'The present air despatch organization is too lavish in present conditions of manpower stringency'.

After a preliminary meeting, and an Air Despatch briefing led by Commander Air Despatch Group Colonel R A Nightingale MBE, a static and airborne resupply demonstration was attended by the Working Party on 5 July 1966 at RAF Benson and RAF Watchfield. AOC 38 Group RAF roled 2 Hastings, 3 Argosys, a Beverley and 2 Wessex helicopters for the airborne activity. Major A J Gidley was responsible for the static demonstration.

The working party next met on 10 August to consider firstly a position paper prepared by an aspiring agency claiming a transfer of function could result in a 27% manpower saving and secondly the AD Group response to questions arising from the demonstrations.

The report by the SCAO Working Party on the Air Despatch organization endorsed the requirement for a Training Squadron and a proposal, to incorporate the mission performed by Air Liaison Sections in a series of new and more cost effective Air Despatch establishments.

The establishment for an Air Despatch Training Squadron subsequently to become the Air Despatch Wing of the Army School of Transport, was approved on 24 February 1967 and located at RAF Tangmere. New establishments were also approved for the HQ of an AD Regiment, Squadron and Troops.

A Working Party, under the Chairmanship of Major E A Kynaston assembled at Watchfield to 'Design a Group 'B' Air Despatch Trade

Structure, compatible with the RAF Categorization Scheme and which also gave credit for Crew Commander and Checker qualifications'. After several days discussion there appeared no way that a meeting of minds could be achieved. Commander A D Group had anticipated this impasse and promptly 'grounded' the whole working party. Thirty hours later, all the contentious points had been ironed out and the aim, perhaps helped by the proximity of the school holidays, was accomplished.

RCT Training Directive No 8 promulgated the general principles which would in future apply in the RCT to all officers, warrant officers and senior NCOs serving in AD units, as well as Despatch Crew Commanders. Officers would qualify for AD pay in the same way as their soldiers, provided they were categorized to command air despatch crews. The additional work load arising from these changes would be undertaken by two new grades, the Master Air Despatcher and the Qualified Air Despatch Instructor, for whom a new brevet was approved.

In January 1968 the Air Despatch Group and the Maritime Group were disbanded to provide the manpower cover for the newly formed management branch Transport 4, with Colonel Nightingale at its head and his two Air Despatch Group Majors, M D Isherwood and H O'N Drew on strength. The subsequent arrival of Lieutenant Colonel P E Gray MM led to observations that the Air Despatch Group had not disbanded but simply changed its name; but the activities of Transport 4 is another story. In 1965, with the formation of the Royal Corps of Transport, 1 and 3 AASOs were redesignated 14 and 15 (AD) Regiments respectively but their functions were unchanged.

In 1968, with the rundown of the British presence in the Far East, 15 (AD) Regiment was disbanded and although 14 (AD) Regiment was to survive for a further eight years the post war peak had been passed for air despatch. In 1968 air despatch training became the responsibility of the Army School of Transport – a role the School retained until its Air Despatch flag was hauled down for the last time on 31 March 1976.

In 1976 responsibility for the dropping of vehicles and plant, known in the airworld as 'heavy drop' was transferred from RAOC to RCT and 47 (AD) Squadron took over 24 medium stressed platforms (MSPs) and all ancillary equipment from 16 Parachute Heavy Drop Company RAOC, which disbanded. This additional role which greatly enhanced the Squadron's responsibilities and workload was undertaken without an increase in its manpower establishment.

47 (AD) Squadron is part of 29 Movement Control Regiment. As it is the last surviving air despatch unit its organization is described in some detail. The Squadron consists of a Headquarters Troop, and two Air Despatch Troops. The Headquarters Troop has four elements; a Supply Dropping Store (SDS) controlled by the Squadron Administrative Officer, an Operations Cell consisting of a Captain who is also the Squadron 2IC, two Warrant Officer Class 2 Master Air Despatchers, two

Sergeant Air Despatchers and a Corporal Clerk; a Training Wing manned by a Captain, a Warrant Officer Class 2 Master Air Despatcher, a Staff Sergeant and Sergeant Qualified Air Despatch Instructors, a Corporal Air Despatcher, Assistant Instructor and a Corporal Clerk and a pool of transport and mechanical handling equipment the drivers of which are found on a rotational basis by the Air Despatch Troops. Each Air Despatch Troop consists of an officer and 43 and is capable of providing 7 air despatch crews.

When an operation is mounted the Headquarters Troop Training Wing provides the manpower for a Load Control Cell and when necessary other tasks. It is difficult to equate the operating procedures of this small unit to those used in the heady days of AATO, RASOs and FASOs or the activities of the relatively strong Air Despatch Regiments. But although names may change and the detail of establishment vary, the basic requirements established in World War II remain the same and must be fulfilled. It is necessary to plan and launch the operation from the base airfield. This task started with AATO and RASO. It was carried on by HQ AASO and HQ Air Despatch Regiment. The capability exists, albeit on a much reduced scale, in the operations cell of 47 (AD) Squadron. The link provided by FASO/Air Supply Control Section is still required and on Operation Corporate at Ascension Island we find the Master Air Despatcher of the Training Wing, a one man FASO, receiving the incoming stores and sending them forward. While off the Falkland Islands on *HMS Fearless* two Qualified Air Despatch Instructors from the Training Wing were engaged on ship to shore helicopter operations. Flexibility is the name of the game. Or as Professor Parkinson might have put it 'Air Despatchers expand to carry out the task to be done.'

The weight, shape and size of air despatch loads and the type of parachute in use at the end of World War II had been influenced mainly by:

    a. The physical capability of the air despatch crew.
    b. The size and shape of the aircraft cargo door.
    c. The proximity of the tail plane.

To ensure that loads did not float or glide into the tail plane (or pass so close beneath it that the parachute could snag) a density of at least 30 lb per cubic foot of load and a ratio of longest to shortest side of not more than 4:1 was required.

In Europe a roller conveyor system was designed and introduced to reduce time spent over the dropping zone in anti aircraft fire and although this enabled the crew to despatch a complete load of containers in a matter of seconds, door size and shape and density and weight continued to limit what could be dropped.

But in the late 1950s the introduction of the Beverley aircraft with its high tail and huge aft loading opening removed almost all constraints and paved the way for new equipment and systems.

In the description of equipment development which follows the shift is always toward larger parachutes and heavier loads, sophisticated and in many cases automatic despatching systems and lower dropping heights.

Equipment

At the end of the Second World War the Air Despatch organization was left with a good range of efficient air drop containers compatible with the aircraft of the day. The main ones were:

    a. The Mk 5D Container (SEAC Pack).
    b. The CLE Mk 3 (Bomb Cell Container).
    c. The Airborne Pannier.
    d. The Mk 7 Strap Set.

The Mk 5D Container (SEAC Pack) was designed and manufactured in India for use in the Burma campaign and is still in use today (1982) there being no better container designed to meet its particular qualities. It is made entirely of canvas reinforced with six webbing straps to form a harness. Four loops are attached to the harness to form carrying handles which are so arranged that they can be attached to the saddlery of a pack animal. The mouth of the container is secured by a tie like a kit bag.

The parachute is attached to the harness on the opposite end of the container to the mouth. To absorb the shock on landing a percussion head made of canvas, filled with suitable material is tied to the mouth end of the container. The percussion head can also be fitted inside the container but this reduces the load capacity.

To give the container rigidity and keep the sides square (essential for good stacking and speedy despatch) stiffening boards are used, pieces of thin plywood are ideal.

The first parachute used with the Mk 5D container was the 18 foot cotton Mk 2, which was replaced firstly by the Irwin Mk 1A 18 foot nylon parachute and finally by the GQ utility 18 foot viscous rayon parachute.

Two versions of the Mk 5D container were produced. The original measured 38 × 14½ × 14½ inches and with its percussion head and jute sack lining weighed 20 lbs. The later model which has an identical weight measures 32 × 18 × 13 inches and is designed for loads up to 185 lbs.

For despatch the containers were stacked three high in the door (usually of a C47) and arranged in a fan shape so that nine packs in three stacks of three could be ejected in one run over the DZ. 22 inch static lines were tied to the aircraft floor and parcel ties were used to keep the packs together until they had fallen past the tail plane.

Later the introduction of despatch boards and the later model pack enabled a stack of six to be ejected simultaneously and onto very small DZs. This was and still is a very accurate method of delivery of easily handled supply packs. Aircraft like Hastings, Beverley and Argosy, manned with double crews, could get twelve packs out on each run over a DZ and flying figure of eight circuits could quickly replenish the dropping zone. A similar double door despatch is in use from the Hercules aircraft.

The Bomb Cell Container CLE Mk 3

The bomb cell container was originally used for dropping small arms to parachute troops. The first model was designed to hold 12 rifles and 1,000 rounds of ammunition, but as the techniques progressed it was adapted for all types of supply dropping. The container could be fitted to many types of fighter, bomber and transport aircraft, and was used for the last time with the Twin Pioneer.

Fitted with an R type parachute the container could be dropped from high or low altitudes; when dropped from high level a delay device operated the parachute at the correct altitude. It was unpopular with ground troops because it often buckled on impact and was difficult to open when time was at a premium. The CLE Mk 3 helped utilize aircraft payload to the full and the Hastings aircraft could carry 20 CLE containers under its wings and belly at the same time as a full internal load of paratroops or 28 Airborne panniers and drop the lot in one run over a DZ.

The container was made mainly of sheet metal and constructed as two halves of a cylinder, hinged together down one side. The two halves were locked together by an internal locking belt fitted along the inside of the closing edge of one half. At one end of the container a bulkhead was fitted to form a parachute storage compartment 8 inches deep. The R type parachute fitted into this compartment and was secured there by snap hooks onto D rings. At the landing end of the container an easily replaceable dome shaped metal cap provided a percussion head designed to buckle on impact and absorb shock. The loaded container had an all up weight of 500 lbs, 400 lbs of which was available for stores and packing material.

The container was carried in the 500 lb universal carrier designed for 500 lb bombs. The carrier cradle had arms fitted with adjustable, quick release clips to encircle and secure the container. A metal lug welded on the cradle tube attached the container to the aircraft bomb carrier mechanism.

The RASC/RCT were responsible for packing the containers and fitting the cradles. RAF armourers were responsible for fitting the CLEs to the aircraft. The containers were released by the RAF crews in the same way as bombs. On big aircraft like the Hastings the CLEs were dropped by an automatic mechanism which once set in motion released the containers in pairs at an interval of 0.3 seconds until the last pair automatically switched on the green light which was the signal for the despatch of the internal load of parachutists or panniers.

The Airborne Pannier

Before its adoption for air supply operations the Airborne Pannier was normally used by RAOC as a storage container. For air supply it was used initially with the 'R' type parachute and later with the GQ28 foot utility parachute. It was ejected from the aircraft by air despatchers pushing trains of panniers over roller conveyors. The panniers were coupled together in pairs and in air despatch jargon 'twinned or daisy chained'. The parachute of the top pannier of each pair was attached to the aircraft and the parachute of the bottom pannier was attached to the top pannier. When the top pannier parachute deployed the deceleration deployed the parachute of the lower pannier.

The pannier, which was similar to a large laundry basket, was of rectangular construction of wicker in two halves. The top half telescoped over the lower half. The top half had a strand of rope interwoven round it forming loop handles at each corner. Two webbing straps attached to the lower half passed over the top half to secure the container with quick release buckles.

To assist movement over the roller, the bottom pannier of each pair was fitted with either a plywood base board or wooden runners. To facilitate the attachment of a parachute, a harness was fitted to each pannier. When empty the pannier weighed 25–30 lbs and it could be loaded to an all up weight of 500 lbs. Bell and light location devices were fitted to the panniers for night operations.

While ideal for supply dropping, the airborne pannier was time consuming to manufacture and bulky to store or transport when empty. A collapsible pannier was tried out but was not successful and in 1958 a collapsible plywood box made by the Granby Box Co was introduced but this was a poor substitute and never replaced fully the Airborne Pannier.

The Airborne Pannier was dropped on roller conveyor from C47 Dakota, Valetta, Hastings, Beverley and Herald aircraft and as single or pairs of containers out of many other aircraft including Twin Pioneer, Beaver and helicopters.

Harness Packs

Various pre-packed materials, equipment, or components which are issued boxed or canned (or contained in special-to-type containers) can be prepared for dropping as harnessed loads known in air despatch as Harness Packs.

The advantages of such packs are the low cost of air drop equipment; awkward shapes can be catered for; quick and easy access to supplies after dropping. Harness packs may be dropped from fixed wing aircraft or helicopters, over the sill of rear loading aircraft, through the side door, from bomb bays or as external wing or belly loads.

Mark 7 Strap Sets

The Mark 7 strap set was designed for use with loads which would not fit into standard types of containers and could take packages up to 8 cubic feet capacity and up to 120 lb in weight. The sets which consisted of three webbing straps each 9 foot in length, and fitted with quick release buckles were used with the 18 foot cotton parachute.

Straps Securing Airborne Freight

This was a simple multi purpose strap in heavy green webbing for strapping stores together into manageable bundles before the harness was fitted. Operations in Malaya increased the demand for Harness Pack drops and the Airborne Pannier Harness used in conjunction with Straps Securing Airborne Freight was widely used. This method of rigging harness packs became the standard method world wide and continued until the mid 1960's. 1.5 inch Manila rope was also used world wide to supplement the stock of pannier harness. In the early 1960's a Universal Harness was introduced for harness packs and this is the current recognized equipment for that task. It consists of a fixed cruciform item of heavy webbing with parachute attachments sewn into it and expendable webbing which is cut to the required length and passed round the loads to form a pack of the required size. As loads increased in size and complexity due to the introduction of bigger aircraft and demands for larger and more varied equipment to be air dropped were received, a new strap set was added to the harness pack equipment list. These sets are available in 3, 6, 8, and 24 foot lengths to cater for harness loads in the weight range 1,000–2,500 lb.

One Ton Container

The One Ton Container, developed in 1956 from the United States A 22 Container, was a natural step in the evolution of containers, and was designed to make best use of rear delivering aircraft such as the Blackburn Beverley. That aircraft, the Argosy and currently the C 130 Hercules were capable of carrying 16 one ton containers which could be dropped singly, in pairs or any combination of pairs up to 16. The containers are despatched manually by the Air Despatcher air crew or automatically by an auto gravity system set in motion by the RAF aircrew.

The one ton container, which consists of a plywood base board, a harness set, canvas sheets and parachute attachment straps, measures 52 × 43 inches at the base board and can be loaded to a minimum of 30 inches and a maximum 60 inches in height. The container is designed for loads in the weight range of 1,000–2,300 lbs.

During operations in Borneo, in which the 1 ton container was used extensively, the high wastage rate and time lag between the drop and the return of containers to the air despatch unit resulted in a critical equipment shortage. To offset this shortage a 1 ton rope harness was

[By courtesy of MOD 0514]

One ton container despatched from an Argosy.

devised using 1½ inch manila. Rope had been used before to supplement the stocks of airborne pannier harness but not for loads in the 1 ton container range. Rope presented certain problems not the least of which was the fact that its strength was not governed by a British Standard. The safe working load of a webbing strap or a piece of nylon breaking cord was guaranteed. The breaking strain of rope was an estimate and two examples of apparently identical rope could fail at quite different loads. Trial and error, with the emphasis on the latter, revealed that rot proofed rope failed at significantly lower weights than untreated rope, and the dropping zone party credited with this discovery ran for their lives as concrete filled ammunition boxes fell like a shower of lethal hailstones. Large numbers of rope containers were used during the Borneo operations, the loads a rope could safely support were established by experience and it became 'respectable'. However, in the interests of flight safety, tested and predictable material will always be preferred and rope will remain an emergency alternative.

With the introduction of new materials and the increase in cost of the older materials a new container was introduced in the 1970's which conformed to the same dimensions but was made from a nylon net construction. This proved strong and the maximum weight was increased to 2,500 lbs for each container. Initially one ton containers were dropped on 42 foot parachutes using 'static line first' techniques; from 1970 on, the 60 foot 'canopy first' parachute was used and this permitted both the drop height to be reduced and the accuracy of the drop increased. During the 1970's a revolutionary parachute was introduced by GQ Defence Equipment for loads in the 1,000–2,500 lbs range and this simple, low cost, field replaceable parachute made of polypropelene is called ADUX or Unicross. There are many variations of the one ton container, its delivery system and parachutes, the latest creation is a special cardboard, waterproof container, conforming to the standard dimensions, and designed for the resupply of ships at sea, oil rigs etc. This proved invaluable during the operations in the Falkland Islands. One ton containers were also used as slung loads for helicopters in lieu of nets.

With the introduction of the one ton container a new generation of Mechanical Handling Equipment (MHE) was required to move it. This MHE, which itself had to be airportable, was required in the packing areas, for aircraft loading and on the drop zones to recover the containers to distribution points. This requirement was met over the years by the Massey Ferguson FE 35 tractor with its unique trailer, later by the Clark Ranger forklift truck and then in 1969 by the specially developed Eager Beaver train consisting of a 4,000 lb all wheel drive, all wheel steering, rough terrain forklift truck and two 5 ton collapsible trailers.

Other containers and delivery vehicles
Over the years a wide variety of delivery containers and methods have been developed including the following which are not in development date order.

ISRG Multi Packs – small manpackable containers for clandestine troops. The multi pack, designed for some aspects of the resupply of clandestine troops consisted of four small, linked packs which were secured together by a built in webbing 'parcel tie' to produce a neat pack which would fall clear of the aircraft tail plane and which was heavy enough to deploy its parachute. As the parachute deployed the parcel tie was released allowing the four small containers to hang vertically one below the other. As each container touched down the weight on the parachute was reduced giving the last container to arrive a soft landing. Delicate and easily damaged stores such as radio valves could be safely dropped using this method.

Wing Bundles – special harness packs for delivery as external loads from the Beaver aircraft, used with a special round parachute designed for external loads. Four special harness packs could be carried by the Beaver aircraft as external loads, two under each wing. To ensure that the slip stream could not deploy the parachute prematurely a parachute with a pin secured mouth was necessary and a modified type R fitted the bill perfectly.

Derby Sack – This was a loaded sack within a loose sack which was free dropped from a low altitude without a parachute. It was a very economical method of delivering stores such as grain which could survive impact with the ground and, using tail gate aircraft, up to four tons could be dropped during each pass over a dropping zone.

Jungle Line – A 200 foot line was fitted between pack and parachute thus enabling the pack to smash through the jungle canopy to within reach of a patrol while the parachute was still above the tree tops. This method eliminated the need for a clearing and avoided the loss of supplies lodged in the jungle canopy and out of sight or out of reach of those on the ground. The order to drop was given by the ground party to the aircrew.

A, B & C Boxes – These were wooden boxes, locally made, for dropping a multitude of supplies mainly in the Far East and Middle East. Each box was fitted with a rope or webbing harness, D rings and the appropriate size of parachute.

Awkward Loads. Loads which cannot be despatched through the aircraft side doors and which will not fit into 1 ton containers are classed as awkward loads. These are despatched over the roller conveyer fitted on the aircraft lower door.

Tailgate Loads. The description Tailgate is used for special loads for Royal Marines, SAS, etc and includes raiding craft, demolition equipment and light vehicles. These loads are rigged, loaded and eventually despatched by Air Despatchers over roller conveyer fitted to one side of the bottom door only. The other side of the door is kept clear of roller conveyer to enable the equipment users to free fall and follow down their loads using steerable parachutes.

Wedge Loads. When this system is used a wedge shaped floor section is fitted to the lower half of the Hercules door to permit loads to be delivered over the ramp with only the upper door open. This permits up to 3,000 lb (including parachute) to be dropped on the same dropping zone and at the same time as a full aircraft load of parachutists exit through the side doors.

Heavy Dropping

Although the dropping of Jeeps, trailers and small guns had been possible from the belly of the Hastings and the bomb bays of the Halifax aircraft, it was not very practical and most items of that nature had been delivered by glider until rear loading aircraft entered service.

The introduction of rear loading aircraft and the ability to drop loads from these aircraft in flight inevitably improved the heavy drop capability and new techniques have continued to be evolved.

Until 1956, when the Beverley entered service, British troops depended on the loan of the American C 119 Fairchild Packet (The Flying Box Car). Heavy dropping of items such as ammunition, rations, water, fuel etc was always the task of the RASC/RCT Air Despatchers, but the heavy dropping of vehicles took a different path.

The dropping of vehicles is a complicated and specialist task but the rigging and derigging of these vehicles has to be the responsibility of the user. An Air Maintenance Company RAOC was set up to store heavy dropping equipment, to issue it to the users (Airborne Forces), install it in the aircraft and if necessary jump with the drop to salvage valuable equipment. This unit was called 2 Air Maintenance Company RAOC later renamed 2 Airborne Company RAOC and finally 16 Para Heavy Drop Company RAOC.

Heavy dropping equipment developed as follows:

AATDC Platform. This was a wooden platform for use with supplies or vehicles dropped from the C 119 and Beverley aircraft. The platform was inexpensive, simple but fragile. It could deliver a Jeep and trailer or 8000 lb of stores using the extractor retarder system. The Beverley could drop two platforms.

Boscombe Down 8,000 lb–11,000 lb Platforms (stressed supply platform) This well constructed piece of equipment also used the extractor retarder system and was used for supplies rather than vehicles. It was dropped from Beverley, Argosy and Hercules. The equipment, being chiefly made of wood, could not stand up to the opening shock of the 'Reefed Mains Extraction' system (introduced in the early 1970's to reduce the drop height and increase accuracy) and therefore became obsolete. With one exception the entire platform stock was subsequently destroyed, a short sighted action in hindsight because it would have made an ideal slung load pallet for the Chinook helicopter introduced six years later; the sole surviving stressed supply platform was used for that purpose.

Medium Stressed Platform (MSP) This splendid platform, designed for the heavy dropping of vehicles and cargo up to 18,000 lbs all up weight, was built by Aircraft Materials Ltd the design being influenced by the REME. The platform is of metal construction with interchangeable parts, and has been continually improved and updated over the years. Originally designed for the extractor retarder system it was converted in the early 1970's to the reefed mains extraction system. This equipment has been dropped from the Beverly and Argosy and is currently in use with the Hercules which can carry and drop two. It can also be adapted for use by most foreign aircraft having suitable cargo compartment and payload. The platform can be recovered by helicopter and has an alternative use as a general purpose helicopter slung load pallet for use with the Chinook.

Heavy Stressed Platform (HSP) This heavier and larger version of the Medium Stressed Platform is used for heavy plant vehicles such as bulldozers and airfield construction equipment. Only a small number of these platforms have been built and they are controlled by the Joint Air Transport Establishment (JATE). It was dropped originally from the Beverley aircraft and is still in use with the Hercules aircraft. One rigged platform is a complete aircraft load. Because the rigging task is highly complicated, the right to rig and check was retained by AATDC and was eventually transferred to JATE.

Ultra Low Level Air Drop (ULLA) This very accurate system of aerial delivery is for cargo dropping and consists of up to three heavy duty sledges which are extracted from the aircraft by brake parachutes. ULLA can be dropped accurately on straight roads, runways or firm flat ground and a three sledge drop can deliver up to 42,000 lb in one run over a dropping zone. It was dropped by the Beverley and Hercules aircraft. Providing extraction takes place at or very close to the critical height of 15 feet it is possible to deliver fresh eggs by this method without a subsequent omelette. The system is currently 'on the shelf' for use if required.

When ULLA trials were in full swing, alarming news reached the air despatch world concerning USA experiments with an ULLA 'peoples pallet' sometimes referred to, like a well known brand of aftershave, as 'ULLA for men'. Serving readers may be relieved to learn that enquiries reveal no further USA interest in this exciting mode of personnel transport and that the last remaining 'peoples pallet' with its 36 rear facing seats has found a home in the Museum at McGill Airbase, USA.

In the early 1960's 1 AASO pioneered a system of operating helicopters at Air Heads and main dumps for both out loading and in loading operations. This system for the operation of Logistic Support Pick up Areas had been adopted by our allies and is even more important today with the introduction of new and larger helicopters with enormous lift capacity. Helicopter support operations have never been the sole responsibility of the AD units but because of their unique association with aircraft and their very high standard of selection and training Air Despatchers have always been the undisputed leaders in this field. Special equipment has been developed for use with helicopters.

Nets

The 1,000 lb net developed for use with the Sycamore and early Whirlwind helicopters was a small rope net attached to the aircraft hook by a wire grommet. As its name suggests it could carry 1,000 lb of stores. The 3,000 lb net was a larger nylon net fitted with a stirrup for attachment to the aircraft hook. This net was used with the Whirlwind and later aircraft including the Wessex, Belvedere and Puma. An example of its capacity was 72 Jerricans or 72 × 10 man compo boxes and it could be used in clusters to obtain best use of aircraft payload, (the Belvedere could lift 6,000 lbs). A 5,000 lb net replaced the 3,000 lb net in the late 1970's. This was a nylon net of knotless construction with a similar stirrup to the 3,000 lb net and an increased capacity. It was designed for use with the Puma, Wessex and Chinook helicopter (Chinook can lift clusters of nets up to 8 at a time). The 5,600 kg net introduced in 1980 for use with Chinook Helicopter was a flat net and broke with the tradition of having round shaped or octagonal nets (the Chinook can lift two of these).

Slings

The one ton pallet sling was designed at the AATDC in the late 1950's and named the Royle Sling after its designer Major R. Royle RASC. This sling consisted of two beams held together by elastic bungees and suspended from four cables terminating in a shackle. The beams were dropped under the overhanging edges of a standard NATO pallet and held there by the bungees. The 3,000 lb general purpose sling set was developed by Aerolex Company of Camberley and consisted of three two legged slings and six 15 foot chains with a 10,000 lb sling connector to hold them together. Each sling has two 9 foot legs made from steel cable, each leg fitted with a chain lock into which the chains are fitted and which facilitated the adjustment of the length of chains. This set was and still is used for a multitude of different loads varying from vehicles and guns to defence stores. The 4,600 kg sling set and 11,300 kg sling set are made from textile fibre and are a revolutionary type of four legged sling developed in the UK for use with a wide variety of loads and intended to meet the requirements of the Chinook Helicopter.

Development and Trials

Development and acceptance of helicopter slung load equipment has always been the responsibility of the AATDC/JATE and until recent years the Helicopter Section of that establishment, like the Air Drop Section was always commanded by an RASC/RCT Major with a detachment of Air Despatchers. The department is now commanded by an RAF Squadron Leader assisted by a Lieutenant RN but still with a detachment of RCT Air Despatchers.

Supply dropping from Helicopters

It is of course quite possible to drop supplies by parachute from helicopters and this task is the responsibility of Air Despatchers. Helicopters dropping supplies by parachute were used operationally in Borneo and Northern Ireland. Wessex Mk 5's of the Royal Navy were used in Borneo and both Army Air Corps and Royal Marine Scout helicopters were used in Northern Ireland to carry out drops into Carlingford Lough for resupply to RN vessels. (The Scout is fitted with a special chute to get the packs over the skid during despatch). 47 Air Despatch Squadron in 1981/82 carried out over 60 supply drop sorties with US Army Chinook helicopters dropping loads up to 1,500 lbs. On all supply drops from helicopters, the parachutes have to be modified so that the static line goes down with the load and does not trail outside the aircraft.

Although the numbers employed in Air Despatch duties have decreased, the quality of the men and the high level of skills that they achieve remain undiminished. As the technology in aircraft design evolves so must the techniques and methods of air delivery. In spite of the great store of knowledge and experience that now exists in Air Despatch it became evident in the Falklands campaign that the need for original thought and innovation was still as necessary as it was in the past, each new requirement needing either a new technique or a modification of an old one. The contribution made by 47 AD Squadron to the success of Operation Corporate is both a tribute to them and to the long tradition of excellence established by their predecessors.

22 · AIRBORNE FORCES

In the immediate post war period 1st Airborne Division was involved in the Greek Civil War and then the operations in Palestine to counter the activities of the Jewish terrorist organizations. With the division of Palestine and withdrawal of the British Mandate the Division was withdrawn and disbanded, its equipment being stored in the Tel-al-Kebir Ordnance Depot in Egypt. 1 (Airborne) Divisional Column RASC was also disbanded.

The 2nd Parachute Brigade was moved to Germany where it became an independent brigade group and was renumbered 16 in order to retain the numerical association with the former 1st and 6th Airborne Divisions. The supporting 63 Parachute Company RASC, formed from the three RASC companies of 1 Airborne Division when they were withdrawn from Palestine, was stationed at Neumunster, Schleswig Holstein and later at Hildesheim and comprised:

63 Parachute Company RASC (Parachute Brigade Group)

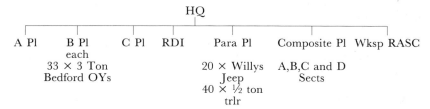

HQ						
A Pl	B Pl	C Pl	RDI	Para Pl	Composite Pl	Wksp RASC
	each					
	33 × 3 Ton			20 × Willys	A,B,C and D	
	Bedford OYs			Jeep	Sects	
				40 × ½ ton		
				trlr		

With a total establishment of about 350, over half of whom were parachutists, RASC officers and soldiers also served with the Brigade's 23 Parachute Field Ambulance RAMC and as staff officers, drivers and staff clerks in the Brigade HQ. During its tour in Germany 63 Parachute Company provided detachments at Celle and Wunsdorf airfields for the 'Berlin Airlift' operation.

In the UK in 1948 the newly re-formed Territorial Army included 16 Airborne Division with its HQ in London. The HQ of the Divisional Column RASC was at Southall, Middlesex collocated with 562 Company RASC. The other two companies were 560 at Tottenham and 561 at Uxbridge. The CO and Adjutant were regular officers; the RSM, permanent staff instructors and a small cadre of drivers were regular soldiers. All other posts were filled by TA volunteers. The organization of these companies was similar to the regular company except that they were on war establishment and had a smaller composite platoon. The parachute course for the TA was compressed into two weeks to meet their limited training availability, but included the eight qualifying jumps.

Also in the UK was the RASC element of the Parachute Training Support Unit based at Cardington who, together with the RAF, were responsible for the locating and supporting of balloon detachments primarily for parachute training for the TA parachute units. There was also a strong RASC airborne presence in the Army Air Transport Development Centre (AATDC) at RAF Old Sarum, both for the development of equipment and teaching unit instructors the techniques of airborne and airportable operations.

In November 1949 16 Independent Parachute Brigade returned to the UK and was stationed at Aldershot with 63 Parachute Company RASC in Clayton Barracks.

Following the nationalization of the oil companies in Abadan, Persia in June 1951 the Brigade was sent to Cyprus in the Royal Navy aircraft carriers HMS *Warrior* and HMS *Triumph*. 63 Company was stationed initially in Karalis Camp on the north side of Famagusta (a former Palestine Illegal Immigrant camp). Subsequently it moved to a new tented camp at '4 Mile Point' on the Nicosia Road.

In October 1951 King Farouk abrogated the Anglo Egyptian Treaty and at 24 hours notice 16 Brigade was sent into the Canal Zone by air in Royal Air Force Hastings and Valetta transport aircraft. Only light scales of equipment were taken and new vehicles were drawn on arrival. Many of the 'new' vehicles were recognized as those which had been handed in by the disbanding 1st Airborne Divisional Column half a decade before. The Brigade remained in the Canal Zone for a full 3 year tour, training and taking part in internal security operations. 63 Company RASC was stationed initially at Fanara before moving to another new site at North Camp Moascar. The main change in 63 Company in 1952 was the rebadging to REME of the workshop officer and his tradesmen as 'REME Phase 2' came into being. At this time resupply was by parachute with airborne panniers (made of wicker) or containers light equipment (CLE) which were carried on bomb beams. Vehicles and equipment were parachuted with complicated 'kits' again carried on the bomb beams.

1954 saw the return of the Brigade on the troopship *Empire Fowey* to the United Kingdom. They were later stationed at Aldershot with 63 Company going into Waterloo Barracks (West) (now the school and married quarters on the west side of Gun Hill). New vehicles were drawn up including ¼ ton Landrovers for the Parachute Platoon.

In August 1956 16 Parachute Brigade Group embarked at short notice for Cyprus to preposition for any eventuality following the nationalisation of the Suez Canal by President Nasser. 63 Parachute Company RASC, who were on exercise in Dorset, had 48 hours notice to embark on the aircraft carrier HMS *Theseus* at Portsmouth. On arrival in

[By courtesy of RCT Museum]

Airborne forces exit from a Hastings.

Cyprus the Company made a new camp on the Troodos Road outside Nicosia employing airborne initiative and self help to lay cement floors and install electricity and refrigerators. During the long build up for the operation, reservists arrived to make the Company up to war strength. During this period the Company was employed on anti EOKA operations, C Platoon, who were reservists, and Parachute Platoon earned a Commander's Commendation for their conduct of a night troop lift.

For the parachute assault on 5th November 1956 on Gamel Airfield at Port Said during the Suez operation, one Sergeant and nine men from the Company dropped with the 3rd Battalion, the Parachute Regiment. Weapons captured during the fighting can be seen in the Corps Museum.

The main body of the Company followed on by sea, for the most part without their vehicles, and arrived in Port Said just before the cease fire. In order to fulfil its task the Company had to requisition a large number of civilian vehicles and these ranged from Cocoa-Cola vans to air conditioned buses. For the next month the Company maintained the Brigade and in early December, along with the rest of the Force, withdrew to Cyprus and then to the United Kingdom.

In the summer of 1958 civil war erupted in Lebanon and as a precautionary measure to having to restore order in that area, the Parachute Brigade was flown to Cyprus at short notice. On the 14th July King Hussein's position in Jordan came under threat following a coup d'etat by a military junta in Iraq. Stability in the Middle East depended to a large extent upon responsible leadership in Jordan and on the 16th July the King appealed to Britain for help. The Parachute Brigade started flying into Amman on the 17th and by the 20th the entire Brigade, less one battalion, was deployed around the airfield. 63 Parachute Company was extremely busy during the period, not only in providing conventional support for the Brigade but also by running a very busy airhead. The Brigade withdrew from Amman once the position was stabilized. This withdrawal was completed by 29th October and 63 Company returned to UK.

Throughout the fifties and sixties elements of the Parachute Brigade were deployed for various operations in places such as Aden, British Guyana, the Radfan, Borneo and the Persian Gulf. In most cases small detachments, ranging from a troop to a few drivers, were also deployed to give support.

On the 1961 reorganization of the Territorial Army, 16 Airborne Division was reduced to a brigade of four battalions – numbered 44 Parachute Brigade (TA) with its HQ in London. 562 Company RASC (TA) was the supporting RASC unit.

At the formation of the RCT in 1965 the existing regular and TA units were redesignated as Squadrons and their composite platoons became RAOC combat supply platoons.

Following the Defence Review in 1967, the manpower of the regular parachute force was reduced. The most drastic savings were made among the logistic units when the Parachute Logistic Regiment was formed consisting of:

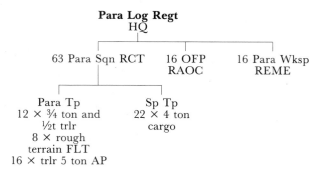

63 Squadron's conventional transport was also reduced. The Combat Supply Platoon was amalgamated with the Ordnance Field Park and the Workshop with 16 Parachute Workshop. The Parachute Logistic Regiment was made to work in spite of the fact that it had a limited (36 hour) ability to sustain operations. In 1971 with other units of 16 Brigade, 63 Parachute Squadron was the first unit of the Corps to do public duties when they mounted the Bank of England Guard.

With the integration of 38 group RAF and 16 Independent Parachute Brigade to form the Joint Air Transport Force (JATFOR) in Aldershot, a closer liaison was established with the RCT Air Despatch Units.

In August 1969, 63 Squadron RCT was rapidly deployed to Belfast to support 39 Brigade in aid of the civil power. The Squadron not only provided 1st and 2nd line support but also produced a most effective IS Troop. The Squadron left four months later but they were the first of many Airborne units to be deployed to Northern Ireland. In 1972 the Squadron was again deployed but this time as part of an independent rifle company for another successful Op Banner tour.

16 Parachute Brigade was disbanded by the 1976 Defence Review; and the Parachute Logistic Regiment ceased to exist after 1st April 1977. With it went 63 Squadron leaving the only regular parachute element of the RCT with 47 Air Despatch Squadron although not wearing a red beret. The number 63 is kept in being in one of the squadrons of the Depot and Training Regiment RCT. At the time of disbandment it was perhaps appropriate that Major Jack Matthews was the OC having joined the Company from Boys Service in 1959 and continuing to serve until 1971 when he was the Squadron Sergeant Major.

44 Parachute Brigade TA was disbanded in 1978. The supporting 562 Squadron RCT (TA) was re-roled as a Heavy GT unit supporting the UK (Regular) armoured regiment and TA and regular artillery regiments.

During this time, the RASC and RCT provided officers to command the Airborne Forces Selection Company (P Coy). Majors Philip Bulpin and Mike Thompson took their turn with officers of the Parachute Brigade. There has also been a strong connection between the RASC and RCT and the Special Air Service where at one time five RASC or RCT officers were serving together.

The airborne RASC and RCT companies and squadrons operated in the same way during parachute operations. The unit was split between an airborne element and the land and sea tail. The airborne party consisted of elements of the HQ, Composite or Combat Supply Platoon and tradesmen from the Workshop together with the Parachute Platoon reinforced from the Transport Platoons as necessary. The airborne element was responsible for the marking and clearance of the supply dropping zones (DZs). A number of light vehicles, trailers and tractors would be dropped with the airborne element which together with any captured vehicles would be used to collect and distribute the combat supplies.

Resupply parachute equipment, which had started with panniers and CLE 'Bombs', developed into the 1 ton container and supply platforms culminating in the ultra low level 'sleigh' ULLA which was extracted by parachute at zero feet.

With the diminished parachute role for airborne forces in any envisaged conflict, the techniques of air supply is still maintained by 47 Air Despatch Squadron RCT.

23 · COMBINED, AMPHIBIOUS AND JOINT OPERATIONS

The three types of operation dealt with in this chapter are:

Combined Operation – An operation conducted by forces of two or more allied nations acting together for the accomplishment of a single mission.
Amphibious Operation – An attack launched from the sea by naval and landing forces embarked in ships or craft involving landing on a hostile shore.
Joint Operation – Any operation in which elements of more than one service of the same nation participate.

The early part of this chapter is concerned with the amphibious aspects of joint operations. Joint operations were few and far between until the early 1960s. Airborne Forces and Air Despatch operations are covered in their relevant chapters.

In spite of the important contribution made by the Corps and the number of Corps units that have been involved, representation in joint headquarters and planning staffs has been negligible. Even during the war there was only one Corps post within Combined Operations HQ for a short period from August to December 1943, when there was an Assistant Director of Supplies and Transport. There was a Deputy Director of Supplies and Transport who also commanded the RASC Wing of the Combined Operations Experimental Establishment at Westward Ho! He also represented Combined Operations Headquarters on committees concerned with research and development where Corps expertise was essential. He was the sole representative of the Corps in the Combined Operations Centre in North Devon. The Centre was redesignated Amphibious Warfare Centre on 1st June 1951. The first RASC member of the Directing Staff of The School of Amphibious Warfare at Fremington was not appointed until 1956 when Major A (Sandy) Thomson RASC assumed the appointment. Soon after this the School moved to Poole in Dorset and then in June 1957 it amalgamated with the School of Land/Air Warfare at Old Sarum to become the Joint Warfare Establishment. It was not until November 1965 that the post was upgraded to Grade 1 level, that of AA and QMG (Logistics). Retitled GSO1 (Logistics) in November 1968 it remained so until July 1982 when the establishment finally closed having joined up with the Joint Service Staff College, later the National Defence College at Latimer.

In the climate of Defence cuts in the late 1970s and early 1980s and the tremendous contribution made by the unit towards the training of officers in joint techniques and the expertise of the permanent staff, it is a matter of great concern that this establishment should close just at the moment that the Falkland Islands campaign was brought to such a successful conclusion. The doctrines worked out and taught at JWE and its predecessors proved highly successful.

Before considering the RASC units to be found specifically in amphibious roles it is important to consider the United Kingdom Defence Policy of the early post war years. For example in 1950, the Directive to the Chief of Combined Operations was:

'To preserve and develop the technique of landing a force of up to a brigade group across beaches against light opposition. To study the technique of the maintenance and withdrawal of a considerable force across beaches when normal port facilities are not available. To advise Port Emergency Planning Staff on the application of combined operations techniques to the problem of assisting the civil authorities in embarking or disembarking cargoes by improvised means. To study the technique of operations larger than a brigade group in conjunction with the United States of America'.

The Combined Operations Handbook defined RASC responsibilities in a combined operation as:

a. The provision of amphibians for transferring stores from MT/Stores ships to a transhipment area or direct to depots in the beach maintenance area.
b. The provision of lorries for transferring stores, etc from beached coasters, landing ships and craft, or from a transhipment area to depots in the beach maintenance area.
c. The provision of amphibians for the evacuation of casualties from the beach area to ships.
d. The establishment and operation of depots in the beach maintenance area for supplies (including medical comforts, disinfectants and possibly water), petrol oil and lubricants (including RAF fuels). These depots will issue to Naval, Army and Air Force units and possibly to the civilian population.
e. The provision of fast launches for the control of amphibians.
f. The provision of craft for ferrying Royal Engineer (Transportation) personnel between ships and shore.
g. The provision of personnel for general technical supervision of the loading and unloading of RASC supplies.

The RASC units responsible for carrying out these tasks formed part of an Army formation known as the beach brigade. 264 (Scottish) Beach Brigade Column RASC (TA) was formed in 1948 for this purpose.

RASC participation in combined (joint) units in the United Kingdom was fairly limited. The RASC Wing of the Combined Operations Experimental Establishment at Westward Ho! was already in existence in 1945 and amphibious units continued to serve in that area until the move of 18 (Amphibious) Squadron RCT to Marchwood in March 1971.

[By courtesy of The War Office]

A Landing Vehicle Tracked (LVT) Mk 3 (USA) at Westward Ho! 1960.

Also in the field of amphibious trials there was the Amphibian Squadron RASC, a squadron belonging to the Amphibious Wing of the Specialized Armoured Development Establishment Royal Armoured Corps. This squadron was based at St. George's Barracks, Gosport and carried out most of its tasks in Stokes Bay. Specialist training of RASC amphibian drivers was carried out at Towyn, Merioneth, Eckenforde Brucke, Germany and in the Canal Zone where 101 Company (GT Amphibian) RASC was stationed on the edge of the Bitter Lakes and equipped with Neptunes and DUKWs.

Outside these trials and training units there was no Regular Army RASC amphibious unit in the UK Order of Battle until 116 Company RASC was formed at Cairnryan, Stranraer in Scotland in May 1951. There were two TA amphibious companies in 264 (Scottish) Beach Brigade (TA) and 102 (Amphibious) Transport Column RASC (TA) which were formed in 1948. There was also one amphibious transport company RASC in the Supplementary Reserve RASC.

The Combined Operations Experimental Establishment was tasked by the Chief of Combined Operations to 'Carry out trials as directed by COHQ on problems of the assault, follow up and build up and the suitability of military and naval equipment used in amphibious warfare and defence against landings. Suggestions should be made for modifications or improvements to all types of equipment used in amphibious warfare'.

The RASC Wing at Westward Ho! had easy access to the beaches and Taw/Torridge Estuary where almost every conceivable condition of beach, tide, sea and hinterland was available. The staff was composed of a mixed bag of skills led by a major with a captain and subaltern RASC and containing navigators, marine engineers, watermen, barge engineers,

[By courtesy of Mr Baguly]

A Neptune (UK) landing vehicle Tracked.

drivers amphibian and drivers MT, backed up by civilian clerks and drivers, a total of three officers, twenty six soldiers and seventeen civilians.

Apart from vehicles and equipment on trial, basic vehicles held on establishment or loan ranged from a Scammell tractor and Rogers trailer for moving equipment and vehicles overland. Landing Vehicle Tracked Marks I, II, III and IV. Amphibian 2½ ton 6 × 6 (DUKW), Trailer Amphibious 2½ ton (Duckling). Amphibian Tracked M290 (Weasel), various amphibian prototypes including the Terrapin, Argosy and Neptune plus the standard range of load carrying vehicles and two harbour launches.

In addition to carrying out trials on its own account, the Wing provided support to the other wings in the establishment in carrying out their trials and so were involved in almost every aspect of development. Demonstrations of equipment and techniques were mounted for the School of Combined Operations and the Combined Operations Signals School located at Fremington and close liaison was kept up with the Fording Trials Branch REME located at Instow.

Apart from its military activities the unit often found itself engaged in providing support to civil authorities ranging from Lynmouth Floods 1952 and East Coast floods of 1953 to delivering supplies to people and stock isolated by blizzards on Exmoor. The unit was disbanded on 31 May 1955.

The Amphibian Squadron RASC at Gosport was engaged on trials of a more specialized nature in that it was almost entirely employed on trials with tracked amphibians (LVTs) and the support of trials of Duplex Drive (DD) tanks. The squadron was a sub-unit of the Amphibious Wing of the Specialized Armoured Establishment Royal Armoured Corps, with its HQ at Woodbridge, Suffolk. This HQ moved to Tidworth, Hampshire in 1947. As a result of reorganization within the RAC the RASC Squadron came under command of 3 Royal Tank Regiment when this unit took over trials responsibilities on 1 April 1948.

The RASC Squadron, accommodated in St George's Barracks, consisted of a headquarters, two LVT sections each with three LVTs, a launch section and one LCT Mark IV. Tasks carried out by the Squadron included firing from LVTs, positioning of navigational aids, station keeping and track propulsion requirements. The squadron was disbanded in 1948. It is of note that the two RASC officers in the squadron in 1947 were both holders of the Military Cross, Major J A Abraham MC RASC and Captain R J Butler MC RASC.

The first Regular Army amphibious unit to be formed after the war was 116 Amphibious Company RASC. The unit, commanded by Major J A Abraham MC RASC, consisted of a standard MT company headquarters and four amphibian platoons each of sixteen DUKWs. Cairnryan was a most unsuitable place for the unit and in March 1952 the unit was moved to Fremington, the natural home for any amphibious unit. Its first major task that year was assisting in the training of the Z Reserve drivers allocated to 264 (Scottish) Beach Brigade Column RASC (TA) almost none of whom had ever been in a DUKW or LVT let alone driven one! However after about six days most of the Reservists were driving alongside coasters moored in the estuary with great aplomb. An annual event of this era was Exercise Runaground. This took place at Eastney, Hampshire and was a demonstration to show amphibious techniques to students of military colleges and similar establishments. The unit was reduced to a cadre of three officers and 37 other ranks with effect from 1st June 1954. It was redesignated Amphibian Training Wing RASC in February 1960 with the task of basic and upgrading training for drivers amphibian for the Regular and Reserve Army.

The last amphibious unit to be formed was 18 Company (Amphibious General Transport) RASC. Major J F Heathcote RASC, who had previously served in 116 Company and the Amphibious Wing of the Specialized Armoured Development Establishment, formed the unit at Fremington in June 1958. It was organized with a headquarters, two amphibious platoons and a REME workshop. A half-troop of the unit was sent to Singapore and based at Pualu Brani Island under command of 37 Company RASC (Water Transport).

During the period February 1958 to March 1960 a detachment was sent to Christmas Island for Operation Grapple, the testing of the British nuclear device.

In August 1956 was formed one of the shortest living amphibious units. 303 Company RASC (Amphibious Transport) with a headquarters and two amphibious platoons to take part in the Suez operations. It never left Fremington, being reduced to platoon strength in November 1956 and disbanded a month later.

Along with other amphibious units during their existence, 18 Company took part in many operations in aid of the civil authorities. One

[By courtesy of Central Office of Information]

DUKW of 18 Company RASC in the North Devon surf 1964.

of the most local occasions was operating a ferry service across the River Torridge at Bideford when the ancient bridge was damaged by floods. 10,700 people were carried in five days. In 1968 the Squadron was put under command of 17 Port Regiment RCT but remained at Fremington. Its major overseas commitment was taking part in Exercise Cunningham, the last of the major port operating exercises to be held and which took place near Flushing in Holland. In 1971, the squadron was re-roled, as by now there was a requirement for only one troop of DUKWs. The troop moved to Marchwood near Southampton and became part of the establishment of 17 Port Regiment RCT.

In 1973 the decision was made to phase out the DUKW and in April 1974 a final swim past was held at Marchwood. The salute was taken by Admiral of the Fleet Earl Mountbatten of Burma KG, PC, GCB, OM, GCSI, GCIE, GCVO, DSO who in his speech later declared that he had been personally responsible for the introduction of the DUKW into the British Army. DUKWs continue to be operated by the Royal Marine Amphibious Trials Unit at Instow who operate the last remaining UK holdings of DUKWs in support of the trials taking place there.

Amphibious units were to be found in several other parts of the world; BAOR, Middle East Command and South East Asia Command.

Their role was mainly administrative and there is no record of their being used in an assault operation in these theatres. With the restoration of communications, normal land and water vehicles and craft came back into use and the amphibious units were disbanded and the vehicles put into storage. Often they were hurriedly brought out again to deal with the results of natural disasters such as the floods in the Low Countries in 1953, but these occasions were few and far between.

Apart from the air dropping methods of delivering men, equipment and supplies there have been great advances in air movement and the consequent rundown of sea movement. This has meant that new logistic systems have evolved and new types of units have been required to operate them. Furthermore, changes in NATO policies have required new methods of deployment of international forces and these have to have special logistic support. Four major RCT units with their special organizations have grown up as a result and between them they are all involved in joint, combined and amphibious operations. These units are the Logistic Support Battalion, Allied Command Europe Mobile Force (Land), 20 Maritime Regiment RCT, 29 Transport and Movements Regiment RCT and 17 Port Regiment RCT.

LOGISTIC SUPPORT BATTALION AMF(L)

The first of these units based at Bulford, Wiltshire with the task to produce and control a comprehensive logistic organization designed to sustain the AMF(L) in extremes of political/economic and geographic environments.

The Logistic Support Battalion AMF(L) was formed in 1977 as a direct result of restructuring 27 Logistic Support Group Regiment RCT, the regiment which had been responsible for providing logistic support to the AMF(L) since the regiment's formation on 15 July 1965 when it took over the responsibility of providing the HQ element from HQ RASC Aldershot District. Prior to this reorganization, logistic support for the AMF(L) was largely provided by 4 Divisional Column RASC based in Germany. In March 1967 the additional task of providing a transport squadron was imposed. This AMF(L) support was only one of the roles of the regiment and although with the evolvement of logistic methods and the appointment of a commanding officer for the newly titled Logistic Support Battalion AMF(L) the role was still being filled by the second in command of 27 Regiment. It was not until 1st April 1977 that the unit came into a separate existence. It consisted of Battalion HQ, 42 Squadron RCT, AMF(L) Workshop REME, 263(A) Field Cash Office RAPC. It had under command also 150 Squadron RCT, a non AMF(L) unit which it lost on deployment but taking under operational control at that stage 50 Movement Control Squadron RCT, and 16 Field Ambulance RAMC, AMF(L) Company RAMC.

The second of the specialist units employed in joint and combined operations is 29 Movement Control Regiment RCT based at South Cerney, near Cirencester in Gloucestershire. This ex-Royal Air Force Station provides excellent accommodation for the unit's role apart from the high standard of personnel accommodation and a pleasant situation. The unit itself is one of the youngest in the Corps with its present organization dating only from 1981.

The relatively short history of the Regiment began in 1970 at Prince Maurice Barracks, Devizes, with the formation of 29 Movement Control Regiment RCT. It was created at the time of the formation of United Kingdom Land Forces Headquarters (UKLF) and United Kingdom Mobile Forces (UKMF) to assist with the rapid deployment of our forces from the United Kingdom. However, the facilities at Devizes were inadequate and, in September 1971, 29 Movement Control Regiment moved to RAF South Cerney, subsequently renamed Duke of Gloucester Barracks. At the time of the move the Regiment consisted of 50 Movement Control Squadron RCT and the Air Mounting Centre. In July 1976, with the disbandment of 14 Air Despatch Regiment RCT, 29 Regiment was named 29 Transport and Movements Regiment, and the Air Mounting Centre reformed to become 55 Air Mounting Squadron. 47 (AD) Squadron RCT was also put under command. In 1982 59 Squadron was formed to provide the Movement Control support to the UKMF.

Today 29 Transport and Movements Regiment is responsible for Air Despatch support for operations and exercises involving all three services (including heavy drop); all training for the Air Despatch trade; the provision of movements expertise to Allied Command Europe Mobile Force Land (AMF(L)) in direct support to NATO; and for the provision and direction of operational Movement Control resources allocated to HQ UKLF and the UKMF. It also provides assistance with airportability training and testing for those units with an airportable role or on Spearhead call, as well as processing units through the Air Mounting Centre.

It is difficult to give a clear overall picture of the extent of the Movements commitment carried out by 29 Regiment, but, suffice to say that each year some 20,000 passengers, 10,000 vehicles and well over 6,000,000 lbs of freight are moved by air and sea alone.

The third of the units concerned with joint operations is 17 Port Regiment RCT which is covered in detail in the Port Operations chapter of this book. In addition its important role during the Falklands is covered in that chapter. The fourth unit, which by virtue of its role is mentioned in this chapter is dealt with in the chapter on Water Transport.

[By courtesy of PR HQ UKLF]

Derigging a load from Chinook aircraft.

MISCELLANEOUS UNITS

Other joint units in which the Corps has contributed or has been represented include the Joint Services Combined Booking Centre (JSCBC) in London, the Joint Service Air Trooping Centre (JSATC) in London, the Joint Air Transport Establishment (JATE) Abingdon, the Joint Experimental Helicopter Unit (JEHU) and Army Air Transport Development Establishment (AATDC) both at Old Sarum and the Army Detachments serving aboard the Landing Ships Platform (LPD) HMS *Intrepid* and HMS *Fearless*.

Over the past 37 years there have been many other units and individuals that have been engaged in these joint, combined and amphibious operations. They range from the units that existed only during the period of the Berlin Airlift and dealt with in that section, to individual officers and soldiers filling staff and extra regimental employment posts in Commando Brigade Headquarters, Carrier Borne Ground Liaison Sections, 38 Group RAF and so on. A great contribution has also been made by the Territorial Army in such units as 264 (Scottish) Beach Brigade Column RASC (TA), 102 Column RASC (TA) the Port Operating Squadrons RCT (TA) and 495 Movement Control Liaison Unit RCT (TA) which provide the liaison officers in NATO national headquarters mostly speaking the language of the country, be it Danish, Dutch or German.

The youngest unit in which the Corps is represented is the Joint Helicopter Support Unit. The advent of the heavy lift helicopter produced a requirement for a unit to provide specialist ground handling for all helicopters but particularly the Chinook. It was decided that the Joint Helicopter Support Unit should be made up of personnel from the Royal Corps of Transport and the Royal Air Force with support from the Royal Electrical and Mechanical Engineers and the Army Catering Corps. Two units were formed to assist the Support Helicopter Forces, one in support of 1 (BR) Corps, the other UKMF(L) and are known as JHSU(G) and JHSU(UK) respectively. JHSU(G) became operational on 1st April 1982 with JHSU(UK) obtaining operational status on 1st July 1982. Although collocated at RAE Farnborough under the administrative control of 27 LSG Regiment RCT the units will eventually deploy to RAF Odiham and RAF Gutersloh. The units' job is to select, operate and defend landing sites and to organise any passengers and loads for the helicopter lift. Although capable of working with any type of helicopter it is the Chinook, with its heavy lift capability, that requires JHSU support. The unit ensures that the aircraft's potential is used to the full by preparing safe loads of the correct size/weight in respect of the task to be done.

The unit has been involved in a number of major exercises in both UK and Germany and was heavily involved in Operation Corporate. The JHSU was deployed to both Ascension Island and the Falkland Islands. During a nine week period on Ascension Island approximately 2,000 helicopters were 'hooked up' lifting an estimated 10,000,000 lbs of freight from the Island out to the south bound ships. On the Falkland Islands a small JHSU detachment went ashore during the hostilities to support the one Chinook that survived the sinking of the *Atlantic Conveyor*. Two RCT members of JHSU were also on the *Atlantic Conveyor* when she was hit but both thankfully survived. After hostilities ceased, replacement Chinooks arrived and the JHSU detachment was increased to 20 men. Many loads were rigged for lifting, some for the first time ever and all flew without serious incident. Examples of lifts are: 150 sheep carcasses, 40 foot ISO containers, 4 × 1 tonne Land Rovers, Harriers, Puma, Sea King and Chinook helicopters, tons of mail and general stores, CVR(T)s and fuel containers.

Whatever the task, the Corps contribution to all these types of operations has been magnificent, and it can be said a major contribution in the successful conclusion of those operations often performed in the same active conditions as teeth arms. Who will forget the young driver who operated the crane used to remove the unexploded bomb from the LSL *Sir Tristram*, or the crews of the mexeflote pontoons ferrying equipment ashore during the Falkland Islands reoccupation?

It is inevitable that a good many RASC/RCT posts and activities that are termed 'Joint' will not have received a mention in this section. To produce a complete list is nigh on impossible. It is safe to say that wherever the Army is operating with the Royal Navy or Royal Air Force it is almost certain that the Corps will have a presence.

24 · AVIATION

INTRODUCTION

DURING THE 1939–45 WAR THE RASC had played its part in providing pilots for the Glider Pilot Regiment, indeed the history of the Regiment records that Lance Corporal L Morris RASC was their first volunteer, closely followed by two more soldiers of the Corps. After the war the Glider Pilot Regiment was quickly run down and by 1949 had reduced to a single squadron based at RAF Netheravon, where it shared the airfield with 749 Company RASC (Air Despatch).

The outbreak of the emergency in Malaya and of the Korean war highlighted the need for light aircraft for tactical and liaison duties. It had also become increasingly apparent that the massed glider assault was no longer tactically possible. The Glider Pilot Regiment was re-roled to provide Light Liaison Flights equipped with the Auster and they started operating alongside the established Air Observation Post (AOP) Flights of the Royal Artillery. The AOP Flights were Royal Air Force units with RAF technical ground crew. The non-technical ground crew were soldiers, and all the pilots, who were trained to fly by the RAF, were officers of the Royal Artillery. Although under overall RAF control for technical matters the flights, and in some cases squadrons, were deployed in direct support of the Army and formed part of the normal order of battle. They had gained a most distinguished reputation during the war and extended a generous welcome to the new light liaison flights. The remaining pilots of the Glider Pilot Regiment who were suitable were converted to the Auster and in addition, officers and NCOs of all Arms were invited to volunteer for service with the light liaison flights. Officers of the Corps were immediately attracted to the new role and were strongly encouraged to apply for flying duties by some senior officers who, anticipating the part suitable aircraft could play in battlefield logistic support, foresaw the need to establish a cadre of young officers with practical aviation experience.

In the early and mid 1950s many officers and a few senior NCOs served in the light liaison flights throughout the world. Much of this flying was on active service in Malaya, Korea and Cyprus and it was during this period that a solid foundation of experience was gained which enabled the Corps to play a major part in the subsequent expansion of Army Aviation.

The experience of the United States Army in Korea confirmed the value of helicopters in combat and in April 1955 the Army sponsored the formation of the Joint Experimental Helicopter Unit (JEHU) as a joint Army/Royal Air Force unit. The then DST, Major General W H D Ritchie CB CBE, played a major part in bringing JEHU into existence and six of the original seven Army pilots were RASC. The Operations Officer, Adjutant, RSM and the great majority of the Army element of the ground crew were also found by the Corps. The unit was equipped with Sycamore Mark 14 and Whirlwind Mark 2 aircraft. The remainder of 1955 and the first half of 1956 were devoted to work-up, training and trials. During the period the new qualification of Helicopter Crewman was authorized for RASC personnel.

The theory of helicopter operations was to be put to the test sooner than had been expected. On 14 August 1956 JEHU was placed on standby for Suez and mobilization was completed by 25 August. The 'E' for experimental was dropped from the title and the Joint Helicopter Unit embarked on HMS *Theseus* at Spithead on 1 October 1956. Re-embarking on HMS *Ocean* in late October they sailed for Malta on 27 October and from there to Suez on 3 November.

JHU played a major part in the assault on 6 November and then switched to casualty evacuation and resupply tasks. 340 sorties were flown, many under fire, before the unit disembarked to El Gamil on 8 November.

Despite this undoubted success in battle the unit, as a joint Service organization, was to have a relatively brief existence. On return from Suez, 1957 saw them training in BAOR. On Exercise New Harpoon II the Whirlwind Flight, operating from a simulated Forward Maintenance Area (FMA), maintained an isolated brigade group for several days exclusively by helicopter. Using six aircraft an average of fifty tons a day was moved. In 1958 training and trials continued and elements of the unit were again on active service when, in November, the Whirlwind Flight deployed to Cyprus. They took part in operations against EOKA until the ceasefire in March 1959.

The Ministry of Defence decision to hand support helicopter operations to the Royal Air Force and disband JHU came without warning in mid 1959 and caused much bewilderment and distress to a unit that had achieved a great deal during a short but extremely active existence. In all twenty-two officers and a large number of warrant officers, NCOs and soldiers of the Corps served in JHU during the four years. Some pilots left the Service shortly afterwards for the attractions of civilian aviation and others transferred to the permanent cadre of the newly formed Army Air Corps.

THE ARMY AIR CORPS

With the formation of the Army Air Corps on 1 September 1957 responsibility for Army aviation, except for some residual matters including provisioning, base repair and instructor training, passed from the Royal Air Force to the Army. The formation of the Corps acknowledged the requirement for close battlefield support and the increasing importance of the helicopter as the equipment of the future. The permanent cadre of the new Corps attracted several RASC officers of high calibre. Many other RASC officers volunteered for the initial four years flying tour before returning to regimental duty.

THE INTEGRATION SCHEME

Early in the 1960s approval was given for a major expansion of Army aviation. It had been long argued and increasingly accepted that the light military aircraft, either rotary or fixed wing, was no more than a tool – albeit a particularly sophisticated and expensive one – that should be an integral part of the equipment of units of most of the teeth and supporting Arms. The factor that enabled the tool to be used to its full effect was the relevant military experience and professional skill of the pilot, who should come from the Arm concerned. Unit flights, or air troops and air platoons as they were called, were to be formed in most armoured, armoured reconnaissance, field artillery and engineer regiments and in some signal regiments and infantry battalions. The Army Air Corps would continue to provide reconnaissance flights at brigade and divisional level operating the larger Westland Scout helicopter now coming into service. At theatre level, where the role was primarily a logistic one in the widest sense, the flights were to be manned by RASC.

The arguments for and against the proposals were many and complex and, amongst others, manning considerations played a significant part. Not all regiments had been enthusiastic about letting their young officers and high quality NCOs be seconded to AAC for a period of at least four years, especially when many of the NCOs and some officers subsequently applied for transfer to the permanent cadre. By enabling them to fly with their own regiments it was argued that commanding officers would have a positive incentive to release them for training. Another argument was more tortuous. There were those in the Army, who having so recently gained control of their own aircraft, feared that in some future period of retrenchment and rationalization they might once again be forced to cede control back to the Royal Air Force. By splitting the aircraft throughout the Army it would make any such transfer of responsibility much more difficult.

Those opposed to the integration scheme, including many very experienced officers within Army Aviation, argued that aircraft were

becoming increasingly complex and expensive and that proper professional standards could only be maintained by centralized control. Not
surprisingly this school of thought was particularly opposed to the
formation of RASC Flights, where the tactical arguments for integration
were less cogent and where future generations of larger aircraft would
have a greater role to play in battlefield logistics. These aircraft and the
skills required to operate them were held to be the proper perquisite of the
permanent cadre at the AAC and an important part of their career
pattern. Within the senior elements of the RASC there were also some
reservations. It was thought that to become too heavily involved would
call for a disproportionate share of scarce resources and there were also
doubts that the existing command structure contained sufficient expertise
to manage this new mode of transport. Other influential senior officers,
foremost among whom was Brigadier R A J Eggar CBE, then serving in
the War Office as Brigadier Q (Operations) of the Quartermaster
General's Department, argued forcefully that the coming Royal Corps of
Transport could not be the all purpose transport service the Army
required without being fully involved in logistic military aviation. It was
to be to the credit of all concerned that, once the decision had been taken,
virtually everyone involved forgot the arguments and got on with making
the scheme work. The few who still resisted tended to receive little
sympathy from the majority regardless of their parent capbadge.

RASC/RCT FLIGHTS

The first RASC Flight to form was 30 Flight RASC in the Far East. Under
command of Major J S Riggall RASC it formed on 8 April 1964 at Kluang
in Malaya from the existing Beaver sections of two AAC Flights of 656
Squadron AAC. The Borneo campaign was in progress and most of the
squadron was deployed in Borneo and Brunei. Aircraft were scarce and in
constant demand, so it was not possible to allow the usual period of work-
up on the formation of a new unit. Indeed the first operational sortie was
flown at 0800 hrs on the day of formation. The new flight commander, on
landing back from the sortie, signalled the DST and was able to claim,
with a truthfulness not always possible in such messages, that his Flight
'had commenced forming today and was operational with immediate
effect'.

Technically 30 Flight was the theatre flight in direct support of
Headquarters Far East Land Forces. In practice five of the six aircraft
were in Borneo, split between Brunei and Tawau and heavily involved in
every type of close support for units spread along a thousand miles of
frontier with Indonesia. The aircraft was the De Haviland Beaver AL
Mark 1. Designed and first built in the late 1940s by De Haviland of
Canada, it was a private venture built for the owner operator in the North
and North West of Canada and intended for operating in rugged bush

[By courtesy of Colonel J S Riggall]

130 Flight RASC flying over LCT Arakan *on the Brunei River 1964.*

conditions without sophisticated engineering support. It was simple, strong and extremely reliable, characteristics which made it ideally suited to military operations and the demanding conditions of terrain and climate in Borneo. One REME aircraft technician, usually a junior NCO, with a little unskilled assistance from his pilot was all that was normally required to keep a single aircraft, stationed many hundreds of miles from its workshop support, operational thirty days in a month. The Flight was to fly well over 13,000 sorties during the campaign without losing a single aircraft through mechanical failure and the incidence of technical malfunction was remarkably low.

Performance and equipment were also equal to the task. The Beaver was powered by the Pratt and Whitney Wasp Junior, a nine cylinder, supercharged, air cooled, radial engine developing 450 brake horse power at sea level and driving a two-bladed Hamilton Standard constant speed propeller. It was a single engined high wing monoplane, of all metal construction with a fixed undercarriage and steerable tail wheel. The cabin was large, with a flat unobstructed floor and large removable doors on either side. The seats were easily removable allowing room for two stretchers or half a ton or more of cargo. Four passengers and their full kit could be carried in the cabin and a fifth in the co-pilot's seat. Four bomb racks, two under either wing, could be fitted. Each rack carried a maximum of 250 lbs and although bombs were not available, they could be used to carry wing bundles of stores. These could be dropped by the pilot, using the bomb release controls, either singly, in pairs, or as a salvo. This was a useful, although little used, alternative to despatching loads manually from the cabin. The bomb racks were also capable of carrying the 4 inch reconnaisance flares. These were used occasionally for target marking but more frequently for night illuminating, when it was usual to supplement the four flares on the bomb racks by carrying a generous supply in the cabin and despatching them by hand. The F95 camera, a sophisticated electrically operated hand-held camera, could also be plugged in and operated by a crewman from either the co-pilot's seat or the cabin. The radio fit, essential to effective operations, was initially limited to VHF and the Army B.47 but after modifications comprised:

STR 38   – a VHF set providing 360 selectable frequencies in the range 118 to 135.95 mc/s

PRT 170 – a UHF set providing 12 pre-set frequencies in the range 225–399.9 mc/s

B47   – an Army VHF/FM set covering the frequency range 30 to 56 mc/s. This could be replaced by the B48, a similar set in use by the Royal Artillery, with the frequency range 26 to 38 mc/s

Sunair – an exceptionally effective light weight crystal controlled HF set.
T14R   When used with a trailing aerial extended it provided communications in conditions when all other sets were ineffective because of technical limitations

Maximum all up weight of the Beaver was 5,100 lbs with an overload of 5,400 lbs for take-off when operationally necessary. The aircraft had good short take-off and landing (STOL) characteristics and could operate out of 400 yard strips at maximum overload under almost all conditions. At sea level, even on the hottest days, more than 250 yards was rarely needed, even in still air. The major limitation was the landing roll when using forward airstrips that were soaking wet. The poor braking surfaces meant that the aircraft often needed a longer distance than for take-off. When a stiff wind was blowing, unusual in the Far East except in the vicinity of a tropical storm, there was never any difficulty. The Beaver on occasions operated from the aircraft carriers of the Far East Fleet and both landing and take-off, with the carrier (by steaming at an angle to the wind) providing 20 knots or more of wind over the flight deck 'fine on the port bow from red one-zero', presented no technical difficulties, although it was invariably an exhilarating experience.

Normal cruising speed was 110 kts and when using the 75 gallons of fuel in the three fuselage tanks, the planning endurance was three hours with a comfortable reserve left for emergencies. By using the two wing tip tanks, which carried an additional 18 gallons each, planning endurance was increased to five hours. A ferry tank, with a further 75 gallons, could be fitted in the cabin. This gave up to eleven hours flying at normal consumption at sea level and was used when aircraft were ferried between Singapore and Borneo.

The Beaver then, was equal to the many tasks it was required to perform. Distances were considerable and in Borneo, except for isolated patches of cultivation along the coastal strip where there were a few roads, all communications were by air or, where these were navigable, by river. The Short Range Transport Force of the Royal Air Force consisted of Single and Twin Pioneer fixed wing aircraft and Belvedere, Wessex and Whirlwind helicopters. The disembarked squadrons of the Royal Navy had Wessex and the Army Air Corps Scout and Sioux helicopters and one or two remaining Austers. All aircraft were in constant demand and the most rigorous tasking system was applied with every bid subject to meticulous screening. 30 Flight, with their particularly versatile and serviceable aircraft, found themselves undertaking the full range of tasks from long distance communication flying to close reconnaissance. By far the largest amount of time was spent on lifting troops and stores to the forward company locations, a role that in any other theatre would have fallen to the brigade companies of the divisional column. There were many other tasks as well. Passenger, visual, and photographic reconnaissance sorties were flown in considerable numbers, as were casualty evacuation flights. In East Brigade area, at Tawau, many air observed shoots were carried out for the guns of the Royal Artillery and ships of the Royal and Commonwealth Navies. VIPs were constantly being flown to all locations and supply dropping, usually to isolated patrols of the Special Air Service and Border Scouts, were a less frequent but enjoyable task.

The demand for aircraft support was so great that the Flight was soon reinforced. Firstly the War Maintenance Reserve aircraft was released, a most unusual step even on operations, bringing the Flight to seven aircraft and shortly afterwards a further three aircraft were sent out from the United Kingdom. These came from 3 Division via Cyprus, where they had spent a short period with the United Nations Force and were then flown on to Aden by Captain C F L Wastie RASC and Captains J H Ingram AAC, himself a former RASC officer and A D Ashley AAC. From Aden they were shipped to Singapore by aircraft carrier and, after reassembling, flown on to Borneo. The journey, via the Sudan, was at the time the longest undertaken by a flight of Army aircraft. It was not to be exceeded until 1970.

On 15 July 1965, 30 Flight RASC was retitled 130 Flight RCT. It remained in Borneo until the completion of the campaign in 1966 and then withdrew to the Flight Headquarters at Royal Air Force Seletar in Singapore. The HQ had moved there from Kluang in Malaya soon after formation in 1964, where it had joined 3 Army Air Supply Organization, later to be retitled 15 Air Despatch Regiment. At least one aircraft had always been based there providing support for HQ Far East Land Forces, 28 Commonwealth Brigade and other headquarters and units stationed in Singapore and West Malaysia. Demand for aircraft support was as heavy as it was in Borneo and although the type of tasks were not quite as varied, the Flight was kept very busy indeed. Many operational sorties were flown, mainly reconnaissance, when the Indonesians landed on both the East and West coasts of the Peninsula in 1964 and 1965. With the withdrawal from Borneo the Flight was able to provide detachments in Laos, where a single aircraft provided transport for the Ambassador at Vientiane, and in Nepal. Both detachments provided extremely demanding and interesting flying conditions and were eagerly sought after by the pilots.

In January 1967 a decision was taken by Transport and Movements Branch Headquarters Far East Land Forces, to set up a scheduled passenger and freight service between Singapore and Central Malaya. The route was from RAF Seletar to Kuala Lumpur stopping at Kluang, Terendak, and Paroi. At each place passengers and freight would be set down and taken up. There was to be one north bound flight on Monday, one south bound on Friday, a return flight on Wednesday and two return flights on Tuesday and Thursday of each week. Five seats were available for booking by intending passengers; with baggage, freight and brief cases the aircraft resembled a village bus. Soon after the service commenced the advantage of routing Signals Despatch Service (SDS) by air, rather than under guard on the night express, was recognized and this element was added to the schedule. The success of this service depended upon establishing and maintaining a reputation for reliability. Coincidentally the north east monsoon of 1966–67 was the worst that the Malayan Peninsula had experienced for many decades but despite the difficult flying conditions the schedule proved most successful.

The Royal Air Force had for several years maintained a single aircraft detachment in Laos based on the airfield at the capital, Vientiane. The aircraft was a Single Pioneer and it provided air travel for the British Ambassador and his staff in a country which had hardly any roads. The Royal Air Force were anxious to give up this detachment and an initial approach had been made by the Air Officer Commanding 224 Group in August 1965 to see if the Flight was interested in taking on the commitment. At the time no aircraft could be spared from the Borneo operations but the situation had now changed. The first aircraft was detached to Vientiane on 26 August 1968 and initially the pilots for this detachment spent six weeks in Laos and were then relieved by another pilot from Singapore.

At the time of its introduction the Vietnam war was at its height and the communist and royalist forces in Laos were locked in a desperate struggle. Roads hardly existed and even the few there were were constantly subject to ambush. The only safe means of travel was by air.

The Americans were in Laos in large numbers, although they remained anonymous by cloaking their extensive air activities under the disguise of two civil companies named Air America and Continental Air. One company was concerned with flying agents in and out of strips throughout Laos and Vietnam and the other in aerial resupply of royalist forces. Many of the airstrips that the Flight's aircraft used were surrounded by Pathet Lao forces, and were well defended by anti-aircraft weapons. Approaches could only be made from altitude, followed by a steep descending spiral into the strip; similarly, departures required a steep climb out in a small safe circle until sufficient altitude was gained to avoid hostile fire. Certain strips in remote areas changed hands repeatedly and it was essential to receive the most up to date briefing at the Air America operations room immediately before undertaking any sortie. The detachment remained the responsibility of 130 Flight RCT until their withdrawal from the Far East in October 1970. After this date the aircraft remained in Laos as an independent detachment serviced directly from Middle Wallop, until 1 August 1975. It was finally withdrawn after the fall of Saigon, Pnom Phen and Vientiane to the communist military forces. The last pilot, from December 1972 until August 1975, was Major P Shield MBE RCT. He had been a founder member of 30 Flight RASC in April 1964 and the last commander of 130 Flight RCT. For his services in Laos he was awarded the MBE.

The second detachment established about this time was in Nepal. This aircraft was attached to the Gurkha Recruiting Depot at Dharan in East Nepal, although it was based about twenty miles south of the camp at a DC3 airstrip at Biratnagar. The aircraft was provided to enable pension paying and recruiting teams to move more easily in a country that had no lateral means of communication, other than by air. From a flying point of view it provided a challenge for a light aircraft pilot, perhaps unique in aviation. The Himalaya range is not only the highest in the world, but also its profile is exceptionally steep. Only sixty miles separate the Ganges Plain, which is generally no more than 1,000 ft above sea level, from the crest of the range at over 26,000 ft. In those temperature ranges the Beaver's operating altitude was limited to 10,000 ft. Flying became an interesting compromise between valley floors and ridges that were known to be within the aircraft's capabilities. Since the weather for ten months of the year was dangerously unpredictable, with no meteorological forecasting service at all, this detachment stretched a pilot's skills to the limit. Intense haze or cloud persisted for much of the year and ground navigation aids were very limited and often inaccurate. Ferrying aircraft that required major servicing between Singapore and Nepal and – to a lesser extent – between Singapore and Laos, provided a challenge in itself. Both detachments routed via Phuket and Bangkok, the Nepal aircraft then continuing via Rangoon, Calcutta and Katmandu. The round trip took twelve days. As with the other detachment the pilots from Nepal

[By courtesy of PR HQ FARELF]

Six Beaver aircraft of 130 Flight RCT on their way to UK prior to disbandment in Sept 1970.

rotated every six weeks. With six pilots in the Flight, of which two at any one time were on detachment, the ever present demands of the schedule, all the other routine communication flying, and the need to train and remain current in the other skills, placed a considerable demand on all the pilots of the flight.

The final sortie flown by 130 Flight RCT was the unescorted ferry flight home from Singapore. The aircraft, flying in loose formation, departed RAF Changi on 29 September 1970 and arrived at Middle Wallop, Hampshire on 20th October. Led by Major P Shield MBE RCT they routed via Phuket (Thailand), Rangoon (Burma), Calcutta and Nagpur (India), Karachi (Pakistan), Sharjah (Gulf States), Isfahan and Tabriz (Iran) Ankara and Izmir (Turkey), Naples, Nice and Bordeaux to Hurn airport near Bournemouth and finally to Middle Wallop. There they were met by the Transport Officer in Chief (Army) and many old members of the Flight. After a formation fly past and brief ceremonial parade 130 Flight RCT formally disbanded. The flight took seventy five flying hours and covered over 7,000 nautical miles. It is believed to be one of the longest formation flying sorties on record. With the exception of the lead aircraft, which undertook the navigation, it was all single pilot operation.

The second RASC Flight to form was 31 Flight RASC retitled 131 Flight RCT in July 1965. Under command of Major P G C Child, a former RASC officer who had transferred to the permanent cadre of the Army Air Corps, this formed at Royal Air Force Wildenrath in BAOR on 16

November 1964 from 12 Independent Liaison Flight AAC. The Flight was equipped with a section of three Beavers and a section of three Sud-Aviation Alouette 2c helicopters. The Flight was under command of HQ 1 Wing AAC for aviation matters and formed part of CRASC Munchen Gladbach, later 23 Regiment RCT, for all regimental matters. Tasking was through the ST Directorate (later Transport Branch) HQ BAOR and the role of the unit was to provide support for HQ BAOR, HQ Northern Army Group and units of Rhine Area. Flying in North West Europe, with poor weather conditions for much of the year and crowded air space with constant civil and military traffic, called for a different type of flying skill with much emphasis on instrument flying and the ability to follow complex and demanding procedures both en route and in terminal areas. Much of this type of flying fell to the Beaver.

To enable the aircraft to operate in this environment a range of navigational aids had to be carried in addition to the standard radio fit. These aids included Mark 8 Decca Navigator, Radio Compass, and a Fan Marker. Later, long range navigational equipment known as VOR with azimuth instrument landing system (ILS) was also fitted. The Mark 8 Decca was an area navigational system. A receiver in the aircraft interpreted signals from a master and three slave ground stations. The pilot was presented with an instrument display showing his position to an accuracy of within 200 metres. A moving chart display supplemented the instruments and charts could be obtained of any required area within the extensive Decca coverage, at a scale most suited to the type of sortie. The radio compass, which was also fitted in the Far East Beavers, indicated the relative bearing from the aircraft of a ground based medium frequency (M/F) radio beacon. Positioned throughout the world these beacons were being gradually replaced by more advanced equipment but were still in widespread use as the standard navigational aid for civil aircraft.

The Fan Marker, another ground based beacon, indicated visually on a dial on the instrument panel and aurally through the pilot's headphones, when he passed overhead or in the immediate vicinity. Although initially of limited use, when the aircraft were eventually fitted with an instrument landing system (ILS), the fan marker became an integral part of the system. The ILS enabled a pilot, by following the signals transmitted from the ground, to maintain the centre line of the runway down to the minimum safe approach height for any given airfield. There was no glide path indicator as such fitted and the pilot had to judge his rate of descent with care.

The instruments alone however were only one half of the picture. The pilots themselves had to be fully trained to fly blind 'on instruments' and hold a valid Instrument Rating. This rating scheme, which was common to all three Services, consisted of three levels of expertise known as White, Green and Master Green – the name being derived from the colour of the authorization card carried by the pilot. He started with a

White Card and as he became progressively more experienced advanced to Green and then Master Green. Each stage was subject to stringent initial examination both theoretical and practical. There were then regular periodic checks to ensure that the required level of skill was being maintained.

This range of equipment, coupled with the skills of the pilot, enabled the Beaver to be flown by day or night in all but the very worst weather conditions along the airways of Europe. There were only two major limitations. The first was because the aircraft was not equipped to carry oxygen. This restricted the operating height to 10,000 ft and meant that winter flying had often to be undertaken at a flight level subject to severe turbulence and airframe icing. The second limitation arose through the establishment of the Flight, which allowed for only one pilot an aircraft. During busy periods a second pilot was not always available to double crew an aircraft tasked to fly into terminal areas with a high traffic density, such as Paris, where the work load on a single pilot was exceptionally demanding and called for intense concentration. Only the more experienced pilots could undertake these sorties solo and if a second pilot could not be spared a tasking occasionally had to be refused.

The rotary wing section of 131 Flight RCT initially consisted of the French built Sud-Aviation Alouette. Seventeen of these aircraft had been purchased as an interim measure pending the introduction of the Scout in quantity. It was a five seater helicopter with a range of 350 nautical miles and represented the ideal light utility machine. It had both an internal and external carrying capacity and had been sold widely all over the world. In British Army service it proved most reliable, and despite its lightweight construction, adequately robust. Some of the original aircraft were still in service with the AAC in 1973. As a liaison aircraft its main limitation was the lack of navigation aids and a full blind flying panel, which restricted its use to fair weather flying.

The Alouette was replaced by the Westland Scout in the middle of 1965. This aircraft was a single engined general purpose helicopter originally designed for the Services by Saunders Roe. Powered by a Nimbus Mk 105 free turbine engine rated at 710 shaft horse power which drove a four bladed main rotor and a two bladed tail rotor, it represented a significant advance in performance and sophistication over the smaller Alouette. The flying controls were conventional with the collective and cyclic pitch servo-assisted by power from a hydraulic system with provision for reversion to full manual control. The Scout was fitted with skid landing gear and could be equipped for a variety of roles including troop carrying, casualty evacuation, internal and external freight carrying, winching and air to ground firing. First introduced into service in 1961 it proved to be a robust aircraft, well liked by pilots and passengers. Designed for easy maintenance it had initially suffered considerable teething troubles, which had been aggravated by a severe shortage of spare parts. Once these were overcome it gained an increasingly sound reputation for reliability. Although cleared for instrument flying it did not have any of the navigational aids fitted to the Beaver and was therefore less suited to long liaison sorties in bad weather conditions. For other types of sortie, with the inherent advantage of the helicopter in the ability to operate away from airfields and airstrips, it complemented the Beaver well and the Flight seldom had to refuse a tasking on the grounds of unsuitability of equipment.

Although trained to undertake the full range of military aviation tasks the principle role of the Flight was passenger carrying and flying VIPs was an almost daily occurrence. On two occasions the unit had the very rare privilege of flying a Head of State, when first the President of the Federal Republic of Germany and then HM The King of the Belgians were flown in Scouts during visits to the British Army of the Rhine. In addition to their normal routine the Flight had the unusual task during the three years 1965 to 1967 of mounting a detachment in West Berlin for a period of two weeks every six months. The requirement arose when the West German Bundestag decided to meet in West Berlin. The Russians signalled their strong political objections by frequent overflights designed to cause maximum disruption to the proceedings. Of the occupying Powers only the Americans had helicopters stationed in West Berlin and the British Military Government were asked to provide a token presence of military helicopters to exercise our rights and discourage the Russian flights. This task fell on 131 Flight RCT until a permanent AAC Flight was eventually established in West Berlin. The Beaver was allowed to operate along the air corridor over East Germany and did so on occasions, but the Scouts were not cleared for this. As a result the detachment was deployed and recovered by RAF aircraft. This necessitated very considerable stripping, including removal of the main rotors and the skids, in order to fit into the restricted cargo hold of the Argosy. This regular detachment represented a most enjoyable change from routine duties and was eagerly sought after by all ranks.

The last RCT Flight to form was 132 Flight RCT. Under command of Major C F L Wastie RCT this formed at Middle Wallop from the Beaver and Auster Sections of 6 Liaison/Depot Flight AAC on 1 March 1966 and was originally titled 132 Flight AAC but with RCT personnel. It was re-titled 132 Flight RCT on 1 April 1967. The Austers were replaced by three more Beavers in May 1967 and the Flight moved to Old Sarum in early June that year. Under command of HQ 2 Wing AAC their role was that of War Office and Theatre Fixed Wing Flight providing operational, exercise and liaison support to all units in the United Kingdom sphere of operations. This area covered a similar region to 131 Flight RCT and stretched from Norway in the north to Turkey in the Near East. The unit found themselves operating, either as a flight or in single aircraft detachments, in a dozen countries throughout Europe and the Mediterranean. The skills required covered the whole spectrum from full airways procedures to tactical close support and the majority of the pilots were on their second and sometimes third flying tour, thus ensuring they had the necessary level of expertise.

THE END OF THE INTEGRATION SCHEME

The integration scheme was to finish in a most unexpected way. The worsening economic difficulties of the 1960s, culminating in the crisis of 1967 when sterling was sharply devalued, gave an added impetus to the rigorous and protracted review of defence spending being undertaken by the Government. The outcome was a fundamental change of policy including withdrawal from East of Suez and a major reduction in the size of the Services. Army Aviation was to be particularly heavily hit. The planned expansion was drastically curtailed and at one stage the very existence of the Army Air Corps as a separate cap-badge was threatened. In an attempt to achieve economies of overheads the RCT, in common with the other major Arms, was instructed to prepare a paper showing how it could sponsor Army Aviation from within existing resources. Our case, sound though it was in many respects, was rejected on two fundamental grounds. Firstly it was argued that the principle future role of a much reduced AAC was to provide close battlefield fire support. It followed logically that it should be sponsored by an Arm such as the Royal Armoured Corps or Royal Artillery. The second reason was more mundane, but in the climate of the time carried equal if not greater weight. It was shown that the existing career structure of the RCT was already one of the worst in the Army and by far the worst of the major Corps. It was therefore quite impracticable to provide acceptable promotion prospects to a small, but proportionally heavily officered, new element.

In the event the Army Air Corps survived as a separate Corps but the integration scheme itself was abandoned, principally because it could not make the most economic use of the reduced resources. Over the next few years the unit flights were gradually phased out. Of the three Corps Flights 132 at Old Sarum retitled as 132 Aviation Flight in October 1969, although it was to remain commanded by successive RCT officers until just before it finally disbanded in January 1974. 131 Flight in BAOR retitled as 131 Aviation Flight in January 1970. 130 Flight, the only flight to do so, remained a Corps unit throughout its existence, flying home to disband in October 1970.

OTHER ARMS

Although this is primarily an account of the Corps involvement in aviation it should be remembered that several other Arms served in RASC and RCT Flights. The non-technical ground crew, including the aircraft crewmen and driver operators, were from the Corps but the engineering support, typically about half the strength of a flight, were aircraft technicians of the Royal Electrical and Mechanical Engineers. Carefully selected and subjected to a long and detailed technical training, they epitomized the best of their Corps. Unlike the Royal Air force, where each trade was separate, they were dual trained as either engine and airframe specialists or as electrics, instrument and radio specialists. This policy made particularly effective and economic use of scarce high quality manpower and meant that it was often possible for a detachment to be mounted with a single technician in support. Even the Nepal detachment, over 2000 miles from base, only required two technicians to keep it operational. In its early days the Far East Flight also had two successive Chief Petty Officers from the Fleet Air Arm in charge of the flight workshop. Very experienced, the first one had been rated as a Petty Officer for over twenty years, they both adapted quickly to Army ways but none the less brought a refreshingly 'do it yourself' approach to keeping aircraft serviceable when problems arose and spares were in short supply. 130 Flight RCT also had a Royal Army Ordnance Corps photographer on establishment who was equipped with a darkroom mounted on a 3 tonner chassis. He was in constant demand to fly photographic sorties and immediately after landing, would process the results in his vehicle, often working in temperatures of 120°F. There were also technical storemen from the RAOC in each of the three flights.

PILOTS

Not all the pilots were from the Corps either. A RCT pilot, having completed his flying training at Middle Wallop, would not necessarily be posted to a RCT flight. He would instead be sent where he was most required at the time by Army Aviation. Similarly some experienced permanent cadre AAC pilots and pilots from other Arms on their first tour with Army Aviation flew with the Corps Flights. This was particularly so of the NCO pilots, the majority of whom were from other Arms. This cross flow of pilots throughout Army Aviation, although it could be argued that in theory it was against the basic concept of the integration scheme, was in practice a source of strength. It not only made the best use of the resources available, but did much to defuse any lingering hostility to the scheme itself. It eased career planning difficulties for some warrant officers and senior NCOs of the permanent cadre and compensated for the initial uneven flow of young Corps pilots. To correct this was a lengthy process. The lead time from applying for flying duties, through the selection procedure to the completion of flying training was often in excess of two years. At the start of the integration scheme the Corps had available for each command vacancy several suitable senior pilots but a relative

*Sergeant D Phillips RCT 131
Flight RCT 1966.*
[By courtesy of Central Office of Information]

shortage of more junior officers and NCOs. Had the integration scheme lasted longer than it did the supply would have met the demand, although it is doubtful if the correct balance of NCOs to officers would ever have been achieved. Despite the high quality of the RASC and RCT groundcrew the Corps never succeeded in meeting its quota of NCO pilots.

In this the RCT was not alone; many other cap-badges had similar problems and throughout Army Aviation the ratio of officer to NCO pilots was always higher than the establishment allowed for.

During the 32 years from 1950, when the first volunteers joined the Glider Pilot Regiment in their new role, to the end of 1982 144 members of the Corps gained the qualification 'pl' as a light aircraft pilot or 'ph' as a helicopter pilot. Many of them qualified as both. Of the total 117 were officers and 27 Senior NCOs. Of these 28 officers and a number of SNCOs subsequently transferred to the permanent cadre of the Army Air Corps and made flying their career. Despite the abandonment of the integration scheme and the loss of the Corps Flights a steady flow of young officers and NCOs have continued to volunteer for flying duties. On 31 December 1982 26 serving RCT officers, one warrant officer and one senior NCO were qualified as pilots.

25 · HOVERCRAFT

THE SERVICES IN GENERAL and the Corps in particular have always monitored technical developments to assess their military potential. The advent of the Hovercraft was no exception and as it was patently first and foremost a means of transport, it was not surprising that the Corps became involved with this unique concept very soon after Sir Christopher Cockerell had first demonstrated the potential of the air cushion as a form of suspension.

In January 1962 a tri-Service unit was set up at the Royal Naval Air Station HMS *Ariel* (later re-named HMS *Daedalus*) at Lee-on-Solent to carry out an evaluation. Included in the Army element of the Inter Service Hovercraft Trials Unit (IHTU) was a small number of RASC officers and soldiers who were to become the pioneers of the military hovercraft. These men learned, with the help of the newly formed British Hovercraft Corporation, but largely by trial and error, how to pilot and navigate the first generation of hovercraft, which at that stage were civilian prototypes only slightly adapted to meet military purposes. Global interest in hovercraft spread quickly and the earliest trials in conjunction with the manufacturers were carried out not only in the United Kingdom but on the Danube, on the ice in Sweden and across the sands of El Adem in North Africa.

The first major military trial, however, was to be carried out in the Far East. In July 1964, the Joint Service Hovercraft Unit (Far East) was formed and included two RASC officers (Major R N Harris and Captain P A Beacon) and two RASC soldiers as machine gunners. Together with crew members from the other two Services, they were tasked with evaluating the craft in a wide variety of roles from straight forward logistic support of ground forces deployed in Eastern Malaysia to the more sophisticated task of coastal patrolling in all weather, by day and night, off Singapore. To cope with these tasks, the craft was fitted with transistorized marine radar, HF, VHF and UHF radio, lightweight armour plating and a ring mounted 7.62 mm general purpose machine gun.

Two hovercraft, SRN 5s, were shipped out as deck cargo to Singapore, arriving in mid-January 1965. After a seven week work-up period in Singapore, the Unit moved to Tawau in Sabah for the start of operational trials in the Borneo Campaign. The hovercraft were used in support of ground forces deployed along the coast and on the banks of the rivers above an extensive delta complex. The Unit soon became familiar with the local area and aware of the presence of Indonesian forces who were established near the international border a few miles away. The craft were integrated into the logistic supply organization of Headquarters East Brigade. Important lessons on the problems of control at high all up weights and the design limitation in regard to the craft's ability to carry awkwardly shaped or high density loads were learned but it was quickly proved that the craft was invaluable in the rapid deployment of troops to various points in the area. The first attempts at night operating, which was to become such a valuable facet of military hovercraft operations, were carried out at this time. Further exercises were carried out by day and night with a Royal Marine Special Boat Section, as was some preliminary work with the Commando ship HMS *Albion*.

On completion of the trials in Tawau, the craft moved to Sibu on the 28 August 1965. Sibu is on the banks of the Sungei Rajang in Sarawak. The task here was to assess the ability of the craft to operate over river rapids and to establish its ability to complete long river journeys inland and distant from an operating base. The longest journey undertaken at this phase of the trials was some 310 miles to the village of Long Jawi. The journey which included crossing the treacherous Pelagus Rapids was achieved in 11½ hours at an average speed of 37½ knots: this compared favourably with the 8 to 10 days necessary to complete the journey by conventional river craft! After the Rajang trials the craft were redeployed to Southern Malaysia and tasked in the Naval role of coastal patrolling.

The final work undertaken by the Joint Services Hovercraft Unit (FE) was a series of overland trials carried out in Thailand. A base was established at the Marine Police Depot on the banks of a river a few miles south of Bangkok, and the overland performance trials took place approximately 100 miles away across the Gulf of Siam on the Eastern side of the Thai Peninsula. A comprehensive and convincing series of tests and demonstrations was carried out without technical difficulty and, after nearly a year away, the craft re-embarked for return to the United Kingdom. The Joint Services Hovercraft Unit (FE) was disbanded, after the final accounting and report writing had been completed in April 1966. An interesting aspect of this trial was the exceptionally rapid development which took place in producing the new version of the hovercraft – the SRN6 Mk 11 – in time to equip 200 Hovercraft Squadron RCT which was formed only seven months after the completion of the FARELF trials. This was due to the excellent feedback from FARELF to MOD and thence to the manufacturers. This enabled equipment improvements on the new version to be brought in at a far greater speed than is normally possible.

Shortly after his return to his parent unit, the Inter-Service Hovercraft Trials Unit, Major Harris was again detached, this time to the Canadian North West Territories, charged with carrying out further trials with an SRN 5 in Arctic conditions. The hovercraft used was one of those which took part in the Borneo campaign, refurbished for the Arctic trial. It was broken down and flown direct into the Canadian Arctic in two RCAF C130 Hercules. Sir Vivian Fuchs was amongst experts consulted before this trial, which proved to be a very exciting period of the development. These trials were jointly sponsored by the British Ministry of Defence and the Canadian Research Board. It became quickly apparent that the Hovercraft was very much at home on the ice and rolling tundra. The extreme low temperatures caused some problems, associated with the stiffness of materials which would have been flexible in normal temperatures. Successful tests over rough sea ice with its associated pressure ridges, willow covered tundra and frozen lakes were achieved. In one cross-country run a ridge of hills some 150 feet above sea level were crossed by using the many lakes in the area as steps. On another occasion, a journey of some 60 miles was made out over the ice in almost zero visibility conditions to locate and rescue the crew of a snow mobile vehicle which had broken down. In this rescue, the skill of the navigator and his proficiency in using the transistorized marine radar were of the utmost importance. The major phase of these cold weather trials was a journey some 400 miles up the Mackenzie River via Inuvic, Arctic Red River, Little Chicago and Fort Good Hope, ending at Normal Wells. The aim was to prove the feasibility of using hovercraft during the Spring break up, when no other surface movement is possible.

For the first 300 miles all went according to plan despite the comparative scarcity of up-to-date information on weather conditions. The craft then ran into packed and tumbling ice. Due to the juxtaposition of the fuel dumps, the craft was beyond the point of no return and the crew had no alternative but to press on for another 30 miles before being able to seek shelter in the tranquillity of an unfrozen creek, thus reducing the risk of doing irreparable damage to the craft and possibly the crew. Camp was set up on the banks of the river and the crew waited for conditions to improve. They were visited by an inquisitive but fortunately harmless brown bear, a family of beavers kept them under almost constant observation and a pair of Whisky Jacks (Canadian Jays) were their constant and hungry companions. Stores were dropped to them by a supporting helicopter and the occasional wild duck was shot to augment the meagre rations. Once conditions had improved, the craft again ventured out into the river ice and completed the journey to Normal Wells. This concluded the Arctic trials and Major Harris returned to the United Kingdom, where he was subsequently awarded the MBE for his services with hovercraft.

There was Royal Corps of Transport representation throughout the life of the Inter Service Hovercraft Unit and in October 1969, two RCT officers, Major G G Blakey and Captain D K Patterson undertook another major trial. This was carried out in Africa and aimed to observe and assess the performance capabilities of hovercraft on a difficult and prolonged journey with a minimum of maintenance and repair facilities; in the event, it turned out to be the longest journey ever undertaken by hovercraft, a record which stands to this day. The craft used was a civilian

SRN 6, modified to meet the trial requirements: these included the addition of long range fuel tanks to carry an additional 400 gallons of fuel, the removal of the aft seats to provide a storage area and the strengthening of the boundary members. External storage bins were also added. Perhaps the most appreciated modification was a device on the door which enabled it to be held partially open when under way, ensuring a strong through draught.

The route took the craft over a variety of surfaces; swamp, sand, bush, rice fields, roads, rapids and rivers, which ranged from the great straight Oubangui to the tiny, twisting Lagone. For most of the journey, the craft was carrying a heavy weight penalty and regularly started the day's journey with a two ton overload – more than 50% over the designed payload. High ambient temperatures also detracted from the performance and noon camp temperatures on occasion exceeded 120°F. Nevertheless, the mean speed throughout the journey was over 30 mph and on the straighter rivers towards the end of the journey, where the stores load had been reduced, the mean speeds increased to 50 mph.

The first leg of the journey was from Dakar in Senegal to St Louis. From St Louis the expedition followed the River Senegal to Kayes in Mali. Although the river journey provided little of technical interest, a diversion of over 40 miles of swamp, marsh and savanna was made into Mauritania. No handling problems were experienced and skirt wear was negligible although some difficulty was encountered with navigation. At Kayes, the craft was dismantled, with some difficulty, and loaded on a train for the journey southwards to Bamako, the capital of Mali. Here the craft was re-assembled and set off on the great River Niger. Thence the craft travelled to Lake Chad, by way of Timbuktoo, and then southwards, through the Congo, to complete the journey at Kinshasa. Many lessons on · the overland capability of the hovercraft, its performance in high ambient temperatures and river driving techniques were learned. Apart from one igniter plug failure, there were no mechanical failures throughout the journey.

At this time, a military hovercraft trials squadron had been in existence for some three years, having been formed in November 1966. 200 Squadron RCT was equipped with four SRN 6 Mk 2s, an extended version of the SRN 5, but capable of carrying 30 men. Early in 1967, the Squadron moved into new purpose-built accommodation at Browndown and was immediately in business, demonstrating its craft at a number of major and minor exercises. The charter of 200 Hovercraft Trials Squadron was quite simply to evaluate the military uses of hovercraft in all types of climates and terrain. Air cushion technology was still in its infancy at this stage and performance under stress and extremes of heat, cold, dust and dampness, in a military environment, had yet to be properly assessed. At this time, the value of hovercraft for military purposes appeared to be indisputable. The performance of the SRN 5s with the Inter Service Hovercraft Unit had already established the logistic role of the hovercraft and the United States Navy had also used SRN 5s as fast offensive patrol craft in the Mekong Delta in Vietnam. 200 Squadron's task was to build on the experience of IHTU and the United States Navy, so that it could recommend in due course the size and shape of hovercraft or units to be included in the Army's regular order of battle. There seemed no doubt at that time that a regular hovercraft unit would be justified, when the apparent advantages over more conventional forms of transport were considered.

The Unit consisted of a Squadron Headquarters, two Hovercraft Troops each of two craft, and a Workshop provided by the Royal Electrical and Mechanical Engineers. The first Squadron Commander, Major Stanley Ball, was a graduate of the Royal Military Collge of Science and had been a hovercraft pilot in the Inter Services Hovercraft Unit. His Troop Officers and the Squadron Sergeant Major were also qualified craft drivers, thus effectively doubling the Squadron's official driver strength of 4 – one for each craft.

Early in 1968, the Squadron embarked with its four craft for the Far East. It was established at the old Japanese slipway at HM Naval Base Singapore in June. There then followed a fascinating and astonishingly varied series of trials throughout the Far East. The craft proved its versatility in beach operations and as a true amphibian scornful of the obstacles to normal craft or vehicle progress presented by mangrove swamps and inpenetrable sub-surface weed. It performed efficiently as an assault craft, emerging smoothly from the bowels of a docked ship or landing ship and making at high speed for the shore.

After trials in Japan and Hong Kong, the Squadron took part in a major exercise – Exercise Coral Sands in Australia. This was an important amphibious exercise which included 3 Commando Brigade Royal Marines, HMS *Albion* and Australian units. All craft performed well under considerable pressure, operating continually at high speeds and with heavy loads, mainly at night using navigational radar. Ship-to-shore journeys which would have taken 4 or 5 hours using conventional craft were made in a quarter of that time; the official trial report says that even in rough seas 'Marines arrived on the beaches showing no evidence of fatigue or discomfort'.

After further minor trials in Malaya, Thailand and Bali, the Squadron returned to Browndown at Christmas 1969 to start the NATO phase of its existence. The balance sheet for the Far East tour showed a healthy credit, not only in terms of operational success but also of goodwill. The squadron had broken new ground and several countries had taken a keen interest in its military – and commercial – possibilities.

The outcome of the NATO trials were crucial for the Squadron's future. Successive Defence Reviews had underlined the increasing import-ance of the British NATO contribution and the hovercraft had to prove its

[By courtesy of PR STRATCO]

SRN6 in Istanbul at the entrance to the Bosphorous.

worth in the vastly differing types of terrain on NATO's flanks to have a chance of survival in the Army's future order of battle. The central region was quickly eliminated as an area for operating hovercraft, as conventional vehicles are cheaper and more effective for the support of ground forces in this type of terrain. The extremities, however, offered exciting new possibilities and NATO's flank protection force, the ACE Mobile Force, was keen to try out the Squadron. Under a new Squadron Commander, Major Mike McKindoe, 200 Hovercraft Trials Squadron took part in Exercise Deep Express in Greek and Turkish Thrace in 1971; the hovercraft was found to be highly effective during operations in the marshy coastline and deltas for up to 60 miles inland. Nevertheless, it had to be admitted that they could only claim their speed as an advantage over cheaper, conventional craft performing similar tasks in this region.

The Northern Flank, however, was a vastly different story. The sheer beauty of Northern Norway's mountains and fjords in winter masks one of the most forbidding climates in the world. In winter, it is permanently dark and temperatures of up to 30° of frost are commonplace. In these conditions, a man can become badly frost-bitten before realizing it, and contact of exposed skin with metal results in loss of the outer layer of that skin. Helicopters are grounded for 50% of the time during the winter months and the water freezes inland in most of the fjords and along parts of the coast for some way out to sea. Much of the possible operational area is impassable even on foot. In January 1971, the Squadron, now under the command of Major Blakey, deployed to Norway for a four month series of trials and exercises. It was here that it was shown that military hovercraft, hitherto assessed as extremely useful, had finally come into their own. Unbounded enthusiasm is not usually a description to be applied to a report on a piece of military equipment, but comment on the hovercraft arctic weather performance comes as near to lyrical as a reasoned military assessment will allow. Consider the problems faced by a force commander in this region: the threat is from the north but the east-west ranges which span the territory are barriers to north-south movement. The fjords cut deep into the mainland – Lingen Fjord runs to within a few miles of the Swedish border – but they cannot be used by conventional craft in the depths of winter because they are wholly or partly frozen over. The opposing commander of course has the same problems, but he has a preponderance of men trained to live and handle their equipment all the year round in arctic conditions. He also has the great advantage of being able to choose his time and place to strike. In these conditions a NATO commander needs two things: early information of his enemy's main point of strike and tactical mobility with which to counter it. A small opposing force landed fit and fresh and at the right time and place could produce results out of all porportion to its size, an ideal task for hovercraft as 200 Squadron proved. To quote from the exercise report: '109 soldiers (of the Norwegian Army) and their support weapons, bergen rucksacks, reindeer skins as bedding, skis and sledges were embarked in four SRN 6 Mk 2 hovercraft and driven to an assault beach 15 miles down the coast. It was assumed that the beach was lightly defended. The assault was made just before last light. The four craft hit the beach simultaneously, running about 100 metres inland. All infantry and equipment were disembarked within 28 seconds and the craft had withdrawn clear of the beach in less than 2 minutes from coming ashore. It would not have been possible to land infantry at the point selected by normal landing craft due to off-lying rocks and shallow water. This exercise successfully demonstrated the hovercraft's unique ability of crossing shallow water coming well inland and landing men dry-shod in extreme conditions'.

Other lessons were being learned. The SRN 6 Mk 2 with its enclosed cabin was ideal as a troop carrier, but assault troops operating out of range of heavy artillery need light vehicles and close support weapons. They need these things quickly, particularly if the weather denies them the assistance of close support aircraft. There was an urgent need for a hovercraft with an open deck capable of carrying a tracked over-snow vehicle of the type used for arctic operations or a light sled mounted field artillery piece with its crew and limber. Procurement action was initiated and eventually two of the old SRN 5 craft were modified to provide a central open well deck, flanked on either side by a small cabin for the pilot and crew. These craft were designated SRN 6 Mk 5. Into the open deck a gun with crew and limber or an over-snow vehicle with crew and trailer fitted snugly. Alternatively, 50 troops could be carried but they would lack the warmth and comfort provided by the enclosed cabin of the SRN Mk 2. At the same time, the Squadron gained two small hovercraft, Cushion Craft CC 7s. These were small, highly manoeuvrable vehicles with two semi-enclosed centrifugal fans mounted on the stern of the craft, one on each side of the passenger cabin. The air jet provided by these fans provided both lift and forward propulsion and resulted in a considerably quieter performance than the much bigger SRN 6. It had a payload of 5 fully equipped troops and was ideal for such tasks as surveillance, coastal reconnaissance, beach survey and landing clandestine raiding parties in hostile territory. The northern flank trials marked the end of the overall trials programme for 200 Hovercraft Trials Squadron. Since its formation in 1966 the Squadron's craft had travelled nearly a million miles and visited 19 countries. It had taken part in countless exercises, trials and demonstrations. The time had now arrived for the reckoning. There was no doubt in the minds of the Army's hovercraft enthusiasts, a number of them senior officers in influential positions, that hovercraft could make a decisive contribution to tactical mobility within NATO.

A blueprint for an operational squadron was prepared, this was to consist of 9 craft in two troops of four and one in reserve and was to be an expanded version of the existing Trials Squadron. However, in 1974, the axe fell: the Ministry of Defence announced that the military hovercraft project had to be abandoned for reasons of economy. 200 Hovercraft Trials Unit was to be disbanded as was Army representation at the Inter Service Hovercraft Unit. There is no doubt that the conclusion of the Army Hovercraft Committee's final report, which recommended the formation of an operational squadron had been sympathetically and carefully considered and equally little doubt that had the money been available it would have been acted upon. It is ironic that both our American allies and the Warsaw Pact, having learned the lessons of operating military hovercraft from the British Army in general and the Royal Corps of Transport in particular, now have a large number of operational hovercraft in their order of battle.

There are still many who believe that, in time, and as technical advances are made, military hovercraft will find a place in the British Army. Whatever the ultimate verdict, the officers and men of the Royal Corps of Transport who, in the 12 years between 1962 and 1974, were the pioneers of military hovercraft made military and transport history.

26 · THE GURKHA TRANSPORT REGIMENT

The Gurkha Army Service Corps (Gurkha ASC) was formed on 1st July 1958 in Singapore and Malaya as an integral part of the Brigade of Gurkhas.

The formation of the Regiment under command of Headquarters Royal Army Service Corps 17 Gurkha Division/Overseas Commonwealth Land Forces was beset by many unusual problems. Not least, the Gurkha soldiers had little or no experience of vehicles, driving, or RASC operating procedures and few spoke English. Also, the British Command and Training team, although widely experienced in mechanical transport and Corps procedures, knew nothing of Gurkha Brigade customs and did not speak Gurkhali. Even some of the soldiers did not speak Gurkhali very well since it is the language based on Nepali, that is taught to all Gurkhas recruited into the Brigade! The Brigade of Gurkhas itself gave the Regiment every possible assistance to get off to a good start. The RASC British Officers, posted in to fill company appointments, were sent on the Gurkhali Language Course held at the Brigade of Gurkhas Depot at

No mistaking who is on parade!

[By courtesy of Lt Col D M Ivison]

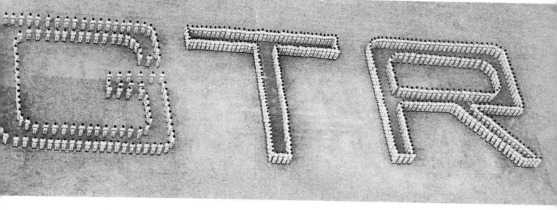

Sungei Patani, in Northern Malaya. This was followed by attachments with either 2/2nd KEO Gurkha Rifles, 2/10th PMO Gurkha Rifles or the Depot to gain experience of working in a Gurkha environment. These attachments were invaluable and thoroughly enjoyed, though it was heard that not everyone had expected jungle training and operational patrolling to be such an integral part of their preparation for company transport tasks with Gurkha drivers!

One of the first arrivals was the Gurkha Major, a Queen's Gurkha Officer (QGO), Major (QGO) Prembahadur Ghale MBE who transferred to the Regiment from 1/6th QEO Gurkha Rifles. He arrived at the RASC School, part of the Far East Training Centre, in Nee Soon, Singapore at the same time as our first Liaison Officer, Major (later Brigadier) John Whitehead 7 GR whose close association with the Regiment was subsequently to span 22 years. The Gurkha soldiers to form the new Regiment were selected from all ranks and ages from the infantry regiments of the Brigade of Gurkhas. The infantry battalions recruit from either East or West Nepal. The drivers therefore included Gurungs and Thapas from West Nepal, and Rais and Limbus from the East. This tradition persists today for the Regiment contains men from all parts of Nepal. The clerks however were mainly recruited from Darjeeling in North East India, although now all clerks for the Brigade are recruited from Nepal.

The QGOs and the Senior Ranks of the raising Cadres for 28 MT Company Gurkha ASC and 30 Infantry Brigade Group Company Gurkha ASC arrived at the RASC School Nee Soon in Singapore in August 1958 where they immediately began training. This was completed by December 1958 and they in turn became instructors for the junior NCOs who by then had reported to the School. In early 1959 the second group of RASC British Officers and Senior NCOs joined the Regiment after completing their language course and subsequent training attachments with 1/7th DEO Gurkha Rifles, 1/10th PMO Gurkha Rifles and the Depot.

The Composite Platoon of 30 Company was the first unit of the Regiment to be formed at Kluang in Johore, Malaya in April 1959 and it began gaining experience in its operational role in the field by supporting 62 Supply Depot RASC. In June 1959 the raising Cadres of 28 and 30 Companies moved from Singapore to their new home in Batu Pahat Camp and Balaclava Lines, Kluang respectively, where they joined newly formed REME Light Aid Detachments (LAD). Their initial task was to establish both camps, some 25 miles apart, for the arrival of our first soldiers and in early August the men, soon followed by their families, moved into specially erected tented and hutted camps. Both companies were formed on 1st August 1959. Meanwhile, on 1st July 1959 the raising Cadres for 31 and 34 Companies assembled in Nee Soon.

The first recruits were received from the Depot in November 1959. This batch consisted of fifty four men recruited directly from Nepal and a further forty from Boys Company training at the Depot. Driver training began immediately and soon it was a familiar sight to see a Bedford QL lorry with L plates being driven along the roads of Johore and Singapore accompanied by the high pitched whine of its transmission. A sight regularly seen at Kluang was a 3 ton vehicle lurching to a halt in the middle of a roundabout, usually with a 'Gora' (British rank) as the instructor: the explanation usually was, 'All I said sahib was "sida janu" (go straight)'. The 'Kamikaze' drivers of the timber lorries and taxis along the Malayan roads soon realized that they had formidable opponents to contend with and a mutual respect was quickly established. Considering the inexperience of the driving instructors, it was remarkable that the accident rate was no more than one per 6,000 miles.

In July 1960, 28 and 30 Companies completed their initial training and 28 Company sailed to Hong Kong on the troopship *Nevasa* arriving on 10 September to replace 8 Company RASC. 30 Company remained in Malaya as the MT Company of 63 Gurkha Infantry Brigade and was soon employed in direct support of operations against the communist terrorists during the Malayan Emergency.

In May 1960 the raising cadres of 31 and 34 Companies Gurkha ASC moved from Nee Soon. 31 Company, commanded by Major R C Thorpe, went to join its newly formed Composite Platoon, commanded by Captain R N Ablett, in Buller Lines Kluang while 34 Company under command of Major E W Henderson moved to Batu Pahat which it initially shared with 28 Company. The training teams established for 28 and 30 Companies remained in situ to assist. Both 31 and 34 Companies were officially formed on 1st August 1960.

MT Training was carried out by the British personnel posted to the companies, the men of the training teams, and by the RASC School at Nee Soon. The first person to attend a course in the United Kingdom was Capt (QGO) Kunjalal Moktan of 30 Company, who distinguished himself by obtaining an A grading at the Army Mechanical Transport School at Bordon from 23 April to 4 June 1960 and he is reputed to have been the first Gurkha to have obtained an A grading on a course in the United Kingdom.

Driver training was carried out by the companies and also at the Depot Brigade of Gurkhas during recruit training. Instructors were sent from the companies to the Depot to assist. It was almost a case of the blind leading the blind as some of the men sent as driving instructors had less than one year's driving experience, having passed out from the Depot the previous year.

For many years Headquarters Royal Army Service Corps 17 Gurkha Division had been in Seremban but in October 1959 it moved to Kluang. It must have been a fairly turbulent time for the Headquarters because in March 1961 they returned briefly to Rasah Camp, Seremban before settling into Paroi Camp, in October 1961. B Platoon, 34

Company, joined them in Paroi Camp on 31st October 1961 to provide transport for Seremban Garrison.

Headquarters Gurkha ASC itself was formed on 1st July 1960 by the redesignation of Headquarters RASC 17 Gurkha Division/Overseas Commonwealth Land Forces. The RASC Officers forming the first Regimental Headquarters were:

Commander	Lieutenant Colonel I R Elliot RASC
Second in Command	Major W S Compton RASC
Senior Supply Officer	Major L G Howe RASC
Adjutant	Captain A R Bain RASC
Gurkha Major	Major (QGO) Prembahadur Ghale MBE GASC

The affiliation of the Gurkha Army Service Corps to the Royal Army Service Corps was graciously approved by Her Majesty The Queen in December 1959. To commemorate the occasion the officers of the Royal Army Service Corps presented the Regiment with a Silver Rose Bowl. This was formally presented on a parade at Kluang on 18 August 1960 by Brigadier R A J Eggar OBE, the Director of Supplies and Transport, Far East Land Forces. The bowl was received by the Major General Brigade of Gurkhas on the Regiment's behalf and handed over to the Gurkha Major, Major (QGO) Prembahadur Ghale MBE GASC.

During 1960, Her Majesty the Queen graciously approved the Regiment's badge which was described as: 'An eight pointed star in silver, thereon a scroll inscribed Gurkha Army Service Corps, issuant therefrom a wreath of Laurel all in gold, overall two Kukris in saltire, the blades silver, the hilts gold, ensigned with the Royal Cypher in gold'. Her Majesty also approved the Regimental buttons as: 'a scroll inscribed Gurkha Army Service Corps, issuant therefrom a wreath of Laurel, over two Kukris in saltire ensigned with the Royal Cypher in gold'. Orders for the manufacture of the badges and buttons were then placed and in due course they were received in 1961. The Commander of the Regiment presented badges and buttons to the Malaya and Singapore based companies at parades held in December 1961. 28 Company in Hong Kong also received its badges at the same time. The Regimental black malacca cane with silver knob embossed with the Regimental badge and silver ferrule was taken into use by all officers on 1st June 1961.

The Regiment was proud to learn that CQMS F W Healey RASC had been awarded the BEM in the 1961 Queen's Birthday Honours List.

THE REGIMENT SETTLES DOWN 1960–62

Although Regimental Headquarters (RHQ) had been given the new title of Headquarters Gurkha ASC, the Commander was 'double hatted' and retained the responsibilities of Commander RASC 17 Gurkha Division.

Regimentally, matters of discipline, dress, establishments, pension, promotions and postings were centralized in Seremban with the companies detached in Kluang, Batu Pahat, Singapore and Hong Kong.

On arrival in Hong Kong, 28 Company settled into Whitfield Barracks alongside Nathan Road, the Oxford Street of Hong Kong. In its MT role the Company had three platoons each equipped with the standard complement of 20×3 ton task vehicles plus 2×3 ton in reserve. The company also had a heavy section of 10 ton vehicles and a section of two tank transporters with trailers. The transporters provided an awe inspiring sight along the narrow roads of the New Territories as they carried out their annual major task of rotating the Colony's stockpile of Centurion tanks between Sek Kong and Kowloon. The steep and winding Route Twisk up the slopes of Tai Mo Shan was a great challenge to men and vehicles. Equally challenging was the drive along Nathan road and the manoeuvre to get into Whitfield Barracks.

The Company also provided second line support on Colony deployment exercises and was tasked with the provision of transport for Internal Security (IS) operations and in aid of the civil community. In early September 1962, Typhoon Wanda struck Hong Kong making 78,000 people homeless. The Company was employed round the clock to provide support for the victims: in 6 days over one million hot meals were carried.

Soon after its formation in July 1960, 30 Company in Kluang began training as an infantry brigade group company with three standard platoons and an additional composite platoon. However, one and a half platoons were quickly moved to the Depot to assist with driver training. Even this redeployment was short lived because in March 1961, the Regiment was advised that 30 Company would be moving to the UK the next year to support 51 Gurkha Infantry Brigade (Air Portable). Commanded by Major A G Bell, the Company moved in 3 phases: the advance party by air in April 1962, the main body by sea on the troopship *Nevassa* on 4 May 1962, and the rear party by air on 24 May 1962. They settled into Jellalabad Barracks, Tidworth with minimum turbulence.

Only fifteen Gurkha personnel were permitted to be accompanied by their families, who, having mastered the intricacies of pounds, shillings and pence and accepting that the UK climate was different, settled down rapidly.

The Brigade was to form part of the United Kingdom Strategic Reserve and 30 Company therefore needed to be trained for two roles: firstly as an Air Portable Brigade Company and secondly as a Brigade Group Company to operate the second line resupply chain under nuclear conditions in BAOR. The air portable requirement brought additional vehicle holdings of sixteen Massey Ferguson tractors and thirty-two trailers with corresponding quantities of equipment such as lashing chains and nets for underslung loads. These roles were so different that within the company establishment two entirely different organizations were evolved. The term 'switch' was introduced and soldiers had to be trained to operate in both roles and organizations. Whilst supporting different exercises during 1963 the Company was required to 'switch' four times in seven months.

The tour in the United Kingdom appeared to be a catalyst towards bringing again the Brigade of Gurkhas into 'full' membership of the British Army and showed once more how well the soldiers were able to adapt to tasks normally done by their British counterparts. It gave them a wider experience of military life and greater self confidence. They had better accommodation, rations, scales of equipment as well as better rates of pay.

News of the return of 51 Brigade to Singapore because of Indonesian confrontation was a disappointment to all and the company packed its equipment, returned its vehicles and flew to Nee Soon Camp during February and March 1964 to reorganize as an Infantry Brigade Group Company. It is worthy of note that the Commander RASC 3 Division, Lieutenant Colonel (later Brigadier) T A K Savage MBE finished his farewell 'Special Order of the Day' with the commendation 'You leave behind in this country a reputation second to none and in 3 Division you will be remembered with affection and pride'.

31 Company moved into Nee Soon Camp Singapore on completion of its initial training in November 1961 as the Infantry Brigade Group Company in support of 99 Gurkha Infantry Brigade Group. It provided vehicles for IS operations in Singapore and general transport details in the Nee Soon Garrison area. One platoon was also trained in specialist bridging tasks, a role normally undertaken by specialist RASC bridging companies and elements of the company were deployed on exercises in Malaya, including Exercise Trumpeter in support of 29 Commonwealth Brigade. In addition, a close link was maintained with 3 Army Air Supply Organization for the training of tractor and fork-lift drivers in the air loading role. This training proved fortuitous because in December 1962 the Company was deployed on operations into North Borneo. Revolts always come at inconvenient times and this was no exception. The news arrived during an excellent Headquarters 99 Brigade Officers' Mess dinner night attended by the company officers. The meal had finished but the after dinner merriment was curtailed as the officers departed early to await orders. The Brunei Revolt had started.

Major A W Blackmore and Captains R C C Cooke and R D S Marston were in the advance party which left on 10th December 1962 for Labuan Island. Leading elements of the main body followed in an RAF Shackleton on 12th December and included Captain P G Honeyman RASC and Lieutenants D J Turner RASC and R C A McAllister RASC with 32 British and Gurkha soldiers. The group flew to Brunei Airport in an RAF Shackleton which unfortunately landed them in error and then had to make a rapid departure as the airport was under curfew. In order to reach Labuan Island, to the west of Brunei, the stranded passengers were shepherded aboard an RAF Beverley which was on a resupply flight.

All units were being deployed through Labuan and so the Composite Platoon established the initial Resupply Point (RP) on the island. Flexibility was essential as the pace of work increased, and accounting became somewhat relaxed. While Captain R C C Cooke set up the main resupply dump on the edge of Labuan airfield, Captain R D S Marston and a section of the Composite Platoon, augmented by selected soldiers from the transport platoons, were detached into Brunei Town itself. This split proved too great a burden however and reinforcement had to come from 28 and 34 Companies and the Composite Platoon of 3 Company RASC based in Terendak Camp, Malacca, Malaya. REME support was provided by 31 Company Workshop, who sent fitters and light scales of equipment on the initial deployment flights. The heavy equipment followed by sea. By the time the company was fully deployed, only a small rear party remained in Nee Soon to look after the families leave parties, documentation, pay and the unit lines.

Resupply from Labuan was achieved by three means: air drop, air landing and by sea. Supplies were broken down from bulk and delivered to the RASC Air Despatch Section who prepared them for air drop or air landing. In some instances accounting for stores delivered by air was difficult since rear and forward areas were on peace and war time procedures respectively. A NAAFI bill for Christmas turkeys dropped into a Scottish regiment's forward location circulated for months because no one would accept responsibility. Resupply by sea was done using the company's 4 ton vehicles and the RASC Maritime fleet of Landing Craft Tank, Ramp Powered Lighters and a Z Craft. The 4 ton vehicles were loaded at Labuan and delivered to the port where they were put on board the vessels. The drivers remained on the island while the craft sailed to and from Brunei Town on a return journey lasting some 6–9 hours depending upon the vessel speed, wind and tide.

In Brunei the vehicles were loaded by 31 Company Composite Platoon, unloaded at the Forward Supply Point, reloaded with returnable stores and returned onto the craft to be taken back to Labuan. This cycle started at 0600 hours when the vehicles were taken for loading and finished with them back on the vehicle park empty by 1730 hours. The men remaining on Labuan were employed as Land Rover drivers, providing a military light vehicle service, driving the remaining 4 ton vehicles, unloading stores from the docks or on training. Continuation driver training of the new recruits arriving from the training platoons of 34 Company was a top priority, in addition education and trade training courses were run and finally many soldiers were taught to swim. Swimming training was undertaken as a result of a directive issued by the

Director of Operations because of a number of drownings which occurred during the operations.

Although the Brunei revolt ended in December 1962, units continued to be operational and 31 Company did not withdraw from Borneo to regroup and retrain until November 1963. The company had carried the Regiment's name in the operational theatre for over 12 months and in recognition, Major A W Blackmore RASC and Captain R D A Marston RASC were Mentioned in Despatches and Staff Sergeant Corless was awarded the BEM.

Compared with the other three companies, who were located well away from RHQ and operating in independent and exciting environments, 34 Company was something of a 'Cinderella'. Despite the lack of glamour in its tasks of garrison details and regimental training the latter was especially important to the success of the Regiment. Every new recruit driver passed through the company which was responsible for setting the initial driving standard. The receipt of 200 recruits in November 1962 posed such a task that additional driving instructors were detached from 28 and 31 Companies to assist. It was not surprising that as the years passed many of the best shots and sportsmen found themselves at some time driving on garrison details in Kluang.

After four years of service, the Regiment was by the end of 1962 operating in widely differing roles in four different theatres. The standards achieved so far had more than justified the efforts of those who supported the Regiment's formation.

It was also towards the end of this period in 1962, that through the initiative and efforts of Lieutenant Colonel I R Elliot RASC and Captain D M McIlvean RASC, the Gurkha ASC Association was formed. The first reunion was held in the UK in September the following year.

The Association has thrived over the years and continues to provide a focal point for both British and Gurkha ranks in the UK.

CONFRONTATION 1963–1966

The Indonesian Confrontation dominated the Regiment's activities over the next four years. All companies were involved although the weight of the commitment fell on 30 and 31 Companies. In 1963 the Federation of Malaysia was formed comprising Malaya, Singapore, Sarawak, Sabah and Labuan Island, whilst Brunei remained an independent state. Subsequently, Singapore also chose independence in 1965.

In March 1963, RHQ moved from Seremban back to Kluang where it remained for the next seven years. Apart from changes in personalities, the period of confrontation found the Headquarters leading a settled life.

By now, 28 Company was well established in Whitfield Barracks Hong Kong and began to develop additional expertise as the Brigade Group MT Company in support of 48 Brigade. This included transport support for both the Garrison and IS operations as well as the heavy lift capability with the tank transporter and 10 ton sections. Some men were detached to the companies operating in Borneo but apart from this minor involvement, the Indonesian Confrontation hardly affected 28 Company at all. However, in 1963 the first of many cuts to hit the Regiment throughout its history reduced 28 Company to 2 platoons. Fortunately, it was possible to minimise the redundancy by cross posting men to the other three companies.

31 Company's return from Borneo in November 1963 only gave it a brief respite. On 6 January 1964 the company was off again, this time to join 30 Company in the East Malaysia theatre where both companies provided the majority of the land transport support until the end of confrontation. Initially, a forward detachment of two platoons, with two armoured cars and fourteen Land Rovers and trailers was deployed to Kuching in support of 99 Gurkha Infantry Brigade. The Composite Platoon followed on 24 January 1964 to Tawau in Sabah under command of Lieutenant F R Falle. Both 30 and 31 Companies were based in Nee Soon Camp, Singapore with 30 Company occupying the transit lines which consisted of attap huts built in 1939 to last five years! Unfortunately for them, the company's Gurkha families had to be housed in Majeedee Barracks, South Johore while new quarters were built for them next to the unit lines.

The two companies were kept very busy. On operations, they rotated on a six monthly roulement programme in support of the three brigade areas. Back in Nee Soon, Singapore District tasked them with daily transport details and troop lifts before they had even had a chance to draw breath. The six month 'rest' in Nee Soon also had to be used for intensive individual training to ensure that the soldiers were qualified for promotion and did not fall behind their contemporaries in 28 and 34 Companies. Operational training was essential as they were also tasked for an Internal Security role. 31 Company provided both a platoon in the infantry role to secure Nee Soon Village and transport to lift 2/10th PMO Gurkha Rifles from Johore during the Singapore riots in 1965. The company also provided the Guard at Singapore Base Area and soldiers to work on the Gurkha Composite Ration Pack production line to replace the Chinese female staff who went on strike.

31 Company, based in Tawau and Kuching, was first relieved by 30 Company in June 1964. 30 Company deployed into five locations. Commanded by Major J B Massey RASC, the tactical headquarters was based in Brunei Town at the Forward Administrative Complex with Headquarters 51 Brigade. The Composite Platoon moved into Tawau, while B Platoon went to Seria, a town 80 miles south of Brunei where they were tasked to provide transport for the furnishing of the new Gurkha battalion location. The other two platoons took over from the 31 Company detachment in Kuching supporting 99 Brigade. Meanwhile, the

30 Company Workshop replaced that of 31 Company on Labuan Island and the two workshops continued to change every six months with their companies.

In Kuching, the companies provided general transport support in the form of load carriers, light vehicles, troop lifts, and operational re-supply convoys travelling over 100 miles into the hinterland. In the areas where the road ran close to the Indonesian frontier, these convoys had a scout car escort provided by the armoured car regiment.

30 Company ended its own first six month period in November 1964. The Composite Platoon was withdrawn to operate in Brunei Town and B Platoon moved from Seria to Brunei Town having completed its task and driven 150,000 accident free miles. However, 31 Company found they had no operational role with the East Brigade or in Tawau and Major Blackmore was authorized to move his tactical headquarters to join the majority of the Company in Kuching. Operations in the West Brigade area on the other hand were intensifying and in January 1965 a Royal Marine transport platoon was placed under command of 31 Company. Later the Marines were replaced by a platoon of 1 Company RASC (Infantry Brigade Group) from Colchester.

When 31 Company handed over to 30 Company in June 1965, the attached platoon of 34 Company in Brunei Town returned to Kluang to be replaced by A Troop, 34 Squadron in June 1966 in Kuching. So the roulement continued until June 1966 when 30 Squadron took over for the last time.

On 16 September 1966, Confrontation ceased and the task of withdrawing troops and equipment through the airports and docks began. The run down continued until the end of the year with 30 Squadron rear party returning to Singapore in January 1967.

34 Company continued to play an important supporting role during this period. At the beginning of 1963, the company was based in Kluang with B Troop detached to Seremban. (B Troop returned to Kluang with RHQ in March the same year). Gradually, as confrontation developed, the company became increasingly involved providing convoys to lift battalions deploying to the operational theatre. However, its general transport and driver training tasks continued. The company was itself deployed on operations in West Malaysia as a result of the Indonesian parachute landing in Labis, Johore during 1964. It provided the troop lift to deploy 2/10th PMO Gurkha Rifles from Malacca and the back up transport during the operations. In 1965 a platoon was detached to Brunei Town under command of 31 Company for six months and in 1966 a further troop was deployed, this time to Kuching under command of 30 Squadron. All of the Company/Squadron soldiers were operational in either East or West Malaysia and many in both and, as a result, earned the Malaysia Clasp for the 1962 General Service Medal.

Towards the end of Confrontation, however, the future of 34

[By courtesy of Lt Col D M Ivison]

The Gurkha Transport Regiment on parade.

Squadron began to take on a more positive direction when it was decided in 1965 to form an All Arms Mechanical Transport Training Wing (AAMTTW). This Wing, under the direct supervision of the Second in Command, Major P I Attack MBE was also to include a Regimental Education Wing. Accordingly, in 1966 Captain P E B Daniel was moved from 30 Company to Kluang and tasked to expand the MT Training Wing. The Regiment's first RAEC officer Captain E Brodie was appointed at the same time.

Despite five years of confrontation, the Regiment continued to establish its own traditions, entertain visitors and support training exercises. Highlights of Regimental life such as Kasam Khane parades (when the recruits swear allegiance to the Queen and the Regiment) and commissioning ceremonies still took place. The squadrons entered into all activities wherever they served.

Three major Regimental events during this period are worthy of note. During 1963 it was announced that the Regiment was to be honoured by the appointment of Captain (QGO) Jarnabahadur Rai GASL as a Queen's Gurkha Orderly Officer for 1964–65. In November the same year the Regiment's first Gurkha Major retired and was appointed in the rank of Honorary Lieutenant. His successor, Major (QGO) Kunjalal Moktan GASL came on promotion after a very successful tour as the Senior Queen's Gurkha Officer (SQGO) of 30 Company.

In 1965, as a result of the Macleod Reorganization the RASC became the Royal Corps of Transport (RCT). It was intended that the

Regiment would be renamed on the same date in July 1965. However, it was then discovered that a staff branch of Headquarters, Far East Land Forces had failed to seek the necessary approval of Her Majesty The Queen. All arrangements therefore had to be postponed and the Regiment was eventually redesignated on 1st November 1965. The Gurkha ASC became the Gurkha Transport Regiment (GTR), Companies became Squadrons and Platoons became Troops. Unlike the RASC, however, the Regiment did not lose all of its Composite Platoon personnel. Composite Platoons were renamed Combat Supply Troops and, although the majority of British personnel were rebadged RAOC, all the Gurkha personnel were rebadged GTR.

Of course Regimental accoutrements also had to change. The flag which was three panelled: old gold, indigo blue and white with the Regimental crest superimposed on the centre blue panel, was replaced by an indigo blue flag with a Regimental crest superimposed in the centre. The former RASC old gold and blue lanyard was replaced by the plain blue No. 3 pattern lanyard also worn by RCT personnel, whilst the officers changed to a plain blue unknotted lanyard with a long loop. The RASC forage cap with GTR badge was retained for wear by British and Gurkha officers, but the Gurkha ASC shoulder titles were changed for GTR shoulder titles made of black metal. The old gold flashes for wear with hose tops or stockings were retained.

As a very young regiment, the GTR had been exposed to an ever changing operational environment and as happens now throughout the RCT, responsibility ultimately rested on the shoulders of the driver. It is he who has to find his way to the correct place at the correct time, meet his user and be able to communicate with him in English and complete whatever task he is given. The Regiment's name was made by the splendid service given by the soldiers during these five testing years.

At the end of 1966, the Regiment was at its peak. It had served world wide, was respected by all for its efficiency and panache, and should have been able to look forward to a promising future. However, this was not to be. The rumblings in Whitehall had already started and plans were well advanced to drastically affect the Brigade of Gurkhas and with it the GTR. Redundancy was upon the Regiment.

THE THREE R'S – REDUNDANCY, RIOTS AND REMOVALS – 1967–69

By the end of 1966 the Regiment's strength was 1,268 including the Nepal leave increment and men on Extra Regimental Employment (ERE). The Redundancy order directed that by December 1969 the strength was to be reduced to 806. Although this represented an enormous loss of over 36% it had to be viewed against the cuts forecast for other units of the Brigade of Gurkhas. The second battalions of 2nd KEO, 6th QEO, 7th DEO and 10th PMO Gurkha Rifles were listed for disbandment together with the

Gurkha Military Police, 5 Gurkha Dog Company and the Gurkha Independent Parachute Company. Like GTR, the Gurkha Engineers and Gurkha Signals were to lose squadrons.

The task of selecting the men to go was a difficult one. The process had to be fair and select men not only from every rank but from all years of service. The Regiment was the youngest in the Brigade with only nine years service and over half its soldiers had been recruited during that time. This meant that soldiers were nominated to go after only a few years service and many were less than 20 years old. It is difficult for anyone who has not been associated with the Brigade of Gurkhas to appreciate the numbing shock caused by redundancy. All young men recruited into the British Army had achieved one cherished ambition: that they then could expect at least 15 years service and a pension. This was now to be denied them. Fortunately, redundancy was initially planned in three phases and this at least enabled the youngest nominations to be sent on the last phase and thus to just qualify for the lowest rate of gratuity.

Unfortunately, however, as redundancy planning progressed the total number of men to go was increased leaving GTR with a forecast strength after Phase 3 of 733, a loss of 535 trained soldiers. The effects of this on the Regiment were very great. 30 Squadron disbanded and 31 Squadron was reduced to two troops but took the training element of 34 Squadron under command. The remainder of 34 Squadron disbanded. Inter squadron postings took place for those in the disbanding squadrons who were not nominated for redundancy. Even then the cuts were insufficient and the Regiment was forced to plan a fourth phase. Eventually redundancy ended when the GTR establishment of April 1972 was set at 420. Of the men nominated for Phase 4, 43 were reprieved and posted to 1/2nd and 2/2nd KEO Gurkha Rifles when it was decided not to disband their second battalion.

In step with redundancy came news of the Gurkha Welfare Appeal. Previously, welfare in Nepal for the Brigade's ex-servicemen and families had been met by annual contributions from serving soldiers and other charitable donations. With the reduction in the Brigade it was realized that this system could not sustain the continuous welfare requirements. An appeal to raise £1 million was established. In addition to generous donations from personnel in the Regiment, each squadron was tasked with raising funds by means of fetes, raffles and similar events.

Although redundancy hung over the whole Brigade like a dark shadow, life in the Regiment continued in Kowloon, Nee Soon and Kluang. In 1967, Major P I Attack MBE became the first second in command to be appointed as Commander GTR. In the same year, in recognition of his excellent service as a Corporal in East Malaysia, Sergeant Kale Gurung of 30 Squadron was awarded the BEM in the New Years Honours List. That year also saw for the first time a central Regimental Dashera, the major Gurkha religious festival, with strong contingents from the squadrons under the control of the Gurkha Major in Kluang. This was attended by all squadrons including a contingent from 28 Squadron.

In April 1968, Major (QGO) Kunjalal Moktan retired as an Honorary Lieutenant after five years as Gurkha Major. News came after his retirement that he had been awarded the MBE in the 1969 New Year Honours List. Also in the same list Warrant Officer Class 2 Gangaram Chhetri had been awarded the BEM. Both medals were presented during an investiture at the British Embassy Kuala Lumpur on 24th November 1969 and Honorary Lieutenant Kunjalal Moktan returned from India to receive his award. The Regiment was again honoured when Captain (QGO) Aite Gurung was appointed as a Queen's Gurkha Orderly Officer for 1969.

October 1969 found the new Gurkha Major, Major (QGO) Jarnabahadur Rai MVO organizing his first Dashera spectacular. All was going well until a slight wave ruffled the mill pond. Shortly after the sacrificial bull had been purchased, the Gurkha Major arrived hot and flustered to report, 'Sahib, the bull it's gone! The bull has escaped to the jungle!!' Search parties were despatched with haste and some time later it was reported that the bull had been found. Since no irate local farmer came into the lines it can only be assumed that the correct bull was found, or that its replacement was inferior to the one lost!

Life in Hong Kong for 28 Squadron GTR in 1967 was a little more hazardous. On 13th May the squadron was recalled from annual training camp and heavily committed in support of IS and border operations against communist inspired unrest throughout the Colony. Support was given to the 2 Queens and 1 Welch in Kowloon and Hong Kong, while another detachment operated with 48 Gurkha Infantry Brigade in the New Territories. An escalation of the border situation in July led to a full troop being deployed with 48 Brigade where it remained until the end of the year carrying out general duties, resupply and patrols in support of the three Gurkha battalions.

A more settled routine after the unrest was disturbed in April 1969 when many Gurkha soldiers reported sick with stomach pains and breathlessness. Lead poisoning was diagnosed and at one time forty soldiers were seriously affected and others suffered mild pains. To keep the Colony second line fleet operating the Regiment despatched men from the other squadrons to assist. Eventually the lead was located in chilli powder but it was not until November that sick parades were down to manageable proportions.

Hong Kong was and always will be a place of change so perhaps it was not surprising that 28 Squadron GTR celebrated its ninth year in the Colony by a move of camp. Whitfield Barracks in the centre of Kowloon was required for development by the Hong Kong Government. The alternative agreed on was Sham Shui Po Camp which had been notorious as a Japanese prisoner of war camp after the fall of Hong Kong in 1941. The camp was divided by a busy main road with messes and Gurkha family quarters on one side and the squadron lines on the other. The camp was located by the harbour and next door to the Kowloon pig abattoir with its continuous noise and smell. Overhead the flight path to Kai Tak airport added to the bedlam of life in Kowloon. The squadron also shared the camp with 56 Squadron RCT and 415 Maritime Troop RCT of 31 Regiment RCT.

In the knowledge that 30 Squadron was to be disbanded, and having the unenviable task of folding up his unit, Major J D English in Singapore welcomed back the Squadron rear party on the RFA *Kittywake* from Kuching in January 1967. Initially the squadron returned to the transit camp lines but, as a result of the Army's overall plan for the reduction of all forces in the Far East, permanent accommodation became available within the camp and the squadron moved. The gradual disbandment of the squadron commenced with soldiers being sent on resettlement courses and then pension, or being posted to other squadrons.

The first elements to be disbanded were the Combat Supplies Troop on 13 August 1967, followed by B Troop on 1 November. Although the Squadron was disbanded, those remaining continued working with pride and professionalism and recorded 160,000 miles accident free driving during Exercise Picot, on the roads of Singapore and Malaysia which was a fine achievement. A fitting finale for this proud squadron was the occasion of the Regiment's 10th Anniversary Parade. This was held in the early morning of 31 August 1968 and consisted of a vehicle parade and march past held on Punjab Square, Nee Soon. The Major General Brigade of Gurkhas, Major General A G Patterson DSO OBE took the salute. At the end of the parade, while the remainder of the Regiment presented arms, 30 Squadron slow marched through the ranks to the strains of 'Auld Lang Syne' before marching off to the very apt tune of 'Great Little Army'. Effectively its disbandment was complete although the official date was not until 30 November 1968.

For 31 Squadron GTR it was also a time of upheaval, adjustment and training at all levels. Men of all ranks were sent on redundancy but were replaced, as 30 Squadron GTR ran down, by those not nominated for redundancy. So 31 Squadron GTR was able to continue its role as the Brigade Squadron of 99 Gurkha Infantry Brigade until the latter too was disbanded and the squadron became a general transport unit.

Early in 1967, 34 Squadron GTR absorbed the Gurkha Mechanical Training Wing when the Far East Training Centre in Nee Soon closed down. In order to identify its now all arms training role for the Brigade of Gurkhas, the squadron was redesignated 34 Training Squadron on 1 August 1967. During the initial phases of redundancy the Squadron was losing men without replacement but still required to provide garrison transport and a fully committed training wing. Over 400 students were trained in 1968/69 and more than 640 the following year. Unfortunately, the Regiment lost its own Education Officer and had to share one with the Gurkha Engineers. Nevertheless, the Education Wing flourished and provided a very necessary facility for the Regiment.

REDEPLOYMENT AND SURVIVAL 1970–1971

The two year period of 1970–1971 was a difficult one for the Regiment. Amidst the upheaval created by the run down of the British Forces in the Far East, the RHQ and one of its remaining squadrons redeployed into the completely new environment of Hong Kong requiring a very different form of transport support. Gone were the days of the Malaysian deployment exercises, with their long Lines of Communication and the need for copy book RCT resupply systems. The congested roads of urban Hong Kong and Kowloon, and the winding roads of the New Territories required different skills.

Fundamentally the Regiment's employment changed, from operating in direct support of the Gurkha Brigade, with minimal involvement in the supply of daily transport in conjunction with the RCT, to producing transport in support of an integrated Colony system. The Transport Control Organization was under direct control of the CTMO at Headquarters British Forces with Transport Control Offices based in 29 Squadron RCT for Hong Kong Island, and 56 Squadron RCT for Kowloon and the New Territories. With the arrival of 31 Squadron, in the New Territories in 1971, the Squadron Operations Captain became double hatted and assumed the responsibility of Transport Control Officer, New Territories.

The regiment in 1970 was commanded by Lieutenant Colonel A G Bell, who like the previous commander had also been promoted from the second-in-command appointment. The Commander was 'double hatted' in that he was also Commander RCT 17 Gurkha Division/Malaya District. He had two staffs, one in the Headquarters at Seremban and the other with the RHQ in Kluang. Commuting twice weekly to Seremban by the Beaver flight was an accepted part of life. The run down in Kluang continued during the first half of 1970 and the Regiment eventually departed by air and Landing Ship Logistic (LSL). Twelve years residence in Kluang came to an end and the regiment said goodbye to that pleasant friendly station where it had lived amongst so many friends, civil and military, expatriate and local. The Officer's Mess closed its doors in style with a Ladies Dinner Night, Regimental Dinner, Cocktail Party and a last 'Hash Mash Pash Thrash' of the Kluang Hash House Harriers, which had been formed and supported throughout its existence by members of the Regiment.

The RHQ and MT Training Wing moved together to Hong Kong and left a small rear party in Kluang commanded by Captain J A Collar to hand over the camp at a cost of only £8 after a tenancy of twelve years.

The move of the Regimental Headquarters from Kluang heralded a change of Commander. Lieutenant Colonel A G Bell remained in his appointment as CRCT 17 Division/Malaya District and Lieutenant Colonel P C Bowser RCT took over his third hat as Commander, he was already the Chief Transport and Movements Officer, Hong Kong and Commanding Officer 31 Regiment RCT.

On arrival in Hong Kong on 17 July 1970 the RHQ established itself with 28 Squadron and 56 Squadron of 31 Regiment RCT in Sham Shui Po, while the MT Training Wing moved into Sek Kong South Camp in the New Territories. However, the Education Wing was divorced from the MT Training Wing and moved to Sham Shui Po Camp. The British Education Officer, Captain T A Groom RAEC departed before the move and handed over responsibility to Corporal Lalbahadur Rai. Lalbahadur accomplished the move with great success and as a result was awarded the BEM.

28 Squadron GTR completed the move of its Gurkha families to Jubilee Buildings, Sham Shui Po Camp in 1970. As a result of his untiring efforts during the protracted move of the squadron, the SQMS Staff Sergeant R Owens was awarded the BEM. The unit was now established with a squadron headquarters, two troops, one heavy and one 4 Ton, supporting 51 Infantry Brigade and a half troop in Brunei supporting the garrison there. In Kowloon, the squadron often found itself on both sides of an exercise, providing friendly force transport on one hand and producing men for the enemy on the other.

As the run down of British troops in Singapore neared completion, 31 Squadron GTR was employed in back loading stores and equipment to the airport and docks. Finally, Major G M Roberts had the task of moving his own squadron from its comfortable lines in Nee Soon, saying farewell to the many friends that had been made after the squadron's twelve years of residence and resettling in Hong Kong. A farewell parade was held in Nee Soon on 18th June 1971 and the Commander Singapore Area, took the salute. The squadron main body boarded the LSL *Sir Lancelot* on 15th July and arrived at the Sham Shui Po jetty on 19 July 1971 where they were met by a band and a welcome in the Gurkha Officers' Mess. The squadron took over Sek Kong South Camp and were tasked to provide first line support for the Training Depot Brigade of Gurkhas (recently moved from Sungei Patani in Malaya) and second line transport in the New Territories. 31 Squadron GTR also assumed administrative responsibility for the MT Training Wing, renamed the Gurkha Mechanical Transport School (GMTS), who provided all the driver and MT trade training for Brigade of Gurkhas units. In due course 31 Squadron GTR also took over the Tank Transporter Section.

Regimentally, survival was the name of the game. It had been rumoured in the Ministry of Defence and confirmed in Hong Kong that the GTR might be replaced by an additional RCT squadron. The problem was how to meet the requirement, not only for a transport squadron with a full field force role in support of Internal Security operations, but also to provide an organization to meet routine administrative tasks on Hong Kong Island, in Kowloon and the New Territories. The GTR could not meet all these tasks alone, nor was there justification to retain two RHQs, i.e. for both the GTR and RCT.

Having three hats, Lieutenant Colonel P C Bowser was able, as CTMO, to submit a counter proposal recommending a combined HQ 31 Regiment RCT/HQ GTR with 31 Squadron GTR taking on the routine administrative tasks in the New Territories, as well as the MT School. 28 Squadron GTR would continue with its field force tasks, and the balance of general transport and specialized duties would be carried out by the RCT elements in Kowloon, the New Territories and on Hong Kong Island. To take on the staff tasks of transport and movements for the Colony and other stations such as Brunei, Korea, the British Gurkha L of C and those elements left in Singapore, a Transport and Movements Branch would be set up in HQ Land Forces.

It was a long and hard fought battle with both the staff and financiers, and there was a good deal of internal opposition to the use of Gurkha soldiers in routine administrative tasks with minimal time for military training. After producing the 'blue print', Major General D G T Horsford CBE DSO as Deputy Commander Land Forces and Major General Brigade of Gurkhas had to be convinced that it was a viable plan and worth his while surrendering Gurkha Infantry posts to keep the Regiment alive. Thankfully, once convinced, he was GTR's staunchest ally and it was due to his support that the Regiment survived at this very critical time.

The combined RHQ was established in Sham Shui Po Camp in 1971. It had one commander, two seconds-in-command, one adjutant, one Gurkha Major, two Regimental Sergeant Majors and two orderly room staffs. Naturally there were the initial teething problems, but it quickly settled down into an efficient organization. The RHQ commanded the following units:

31 Regiment RCT	29 Squadron	(Lyemun)
	56 Squadron	(Sham Shui Po)
	414 Pack Transport Troop	(Lo Wu)
	415 Maritime Troop	(Sham Shui Po)
GTR	28 Squadron	(Sham Shui Po)
	31 Squadron	(Sek Kong)
	Gurkha MT School	(Sek Kong)
	Brunei Troop	(Brunei)

28 Squadron GTR having formed in 1958 and moved to Hong Kong in 1960 found themselves in direct competition with another squadron of

[By courtesy of Lt Col D M Ivison]

Queens Gurkha Officers of the GTR

the Regiment for the first time. The impact of a nearby RHQ was felt in many aspects of regimental life and operations.

On 14th March 1971, Major (QGO) Jarnabahadur Rai MVO retired as an Honorary Lieutenant and Major (QGO) Giriraj Chhetri became the new Gurkha Major. In November 1971 Captain (QGO) Aite Gurung MVO was promoted and achieved the distinction of not only becoming the first Gurkha Major from the Regiment to serve at ERE, but the Regiment now had two Gurkha Majors serving at the same time.

In 1971 the first ever full regimental parade took place on the occasion of the unit's Fitness for Role inspection. This was held at Sek Kong and the salute was taken by Major General D G T Horsford CBE DSO, Major General Brigade of Gurkhas.

Perhaps the Regiment, with a sound organization and a worthwhile job to do, could now look forward to a reasonably secure future.

HONG KONG SERVICE — 1972 ONWARDS

The reader must remember, at the beginning of this period of the history of the GTR, that although there was only one RHQ, the Commander still wore two hats and had both 31 Regiment RCT and the GTR to command.

In September 1971 Lieutenant Colonel D B H Colley MBE RCT took command but Lieutenant Colonel P C Bowser RCT remained in Hong Kong as CTMO.

At this time RHQ 31 Regiment RCT provided the coordination and operational control for both regiments and RHQ GTR looked after purely Gurkha matters. Initially the commander and adjutant wore the uniforms of both RCT and GTR when they visited the respective units. This brought back memories of cadet training when they usually had to change uniforms more than once a day. This situation was resolved eventually in 1976 when 31 Regiment RCT and 56 Squadron RCT disbanded.

Sham Shui Po, the home of over half of the Regiment, will remain in everyone's memory as the epitome of 'the fragrant harbour'. Not only was the camp bordered by a large abattoir but all the flotsam and rubbish from the large resettlement areas of Laichikok, Mongkok and Yaumati seemed to collect on the water front. The screaming and snorting of pigs, coupled with the smell was a continual source of discomfort to the soldiers and families. The squeals and smell caused consternation to the staff during the visit of HRH Princess Anne to the Colony in 1972. Nothing could be done about the smell but it is understood that there was a good reason to have a Pipe Band playing between the abattoir and the landing stage!

By close liaison with Headquarters Brigade of Gurkhas, Gurkha Record Office and 7 GR who were the first Gurkha battalion to complete a UK tour, the regiment was able to send a Staff Sergeant, Corporal, Lance Corporal and four drivers as a non-established section with the MT Platoon of the UK battalion. This section provided a small outlet for a few GTR men to serve in the United Kingdom. The other popular employment away from Hong Kong was with the 28 Squadron Brunei Troop consisting of a British Captain, as Transport and Movements Officer, a QGO and sixteen Gurkha other ranks. This Troop was assisted by two RCT Traffic Operators and was responsible for all transport and movements for Brunei Garrison and second line transport support. In addition the Regiment also provided personnel throughout the British Gurkha Line of Communication, in a few posts in the United Kingdom and at the Training Depot Brigade of Gurkhas. A final outlet for the soldiers to gain valuable experience was in support of the Gurkha battalions on exercise in Australia, Brunei, Fiji and Malaysia.

Once the Regiment had begun to settle down, Kasam Khane (swearing in) parades which had lapsed during the turmoil created by confrontation and redundancy, were re-introduced. The first of these was held in conjunction with the Major General Brigade of Gurkhas parade in 1972 and included another historic event. It was the last occasion the Regiment paraded in the renowned Gurkha shorts. The shorts were designed so that the measurement around the bottom of the legs was the same as that round the waist and were worn starched rigid. Gone were the days when the sahibs could compete a circuit of the athletics field without spoiling their creases. Commissioning parades were another feature of regimental life. These are conducted in accordance with Headquarters Brigade of Gurkhas Standing Instruction No 16 and may only be taken by Major General Brigade of Gurkhas, the Commander Gurkha Field Force or the Brigadier Brigade of Gurkhas. The Regiment's first soldier, who had enlisted directly into the GTR, to be commissioned was Warrant Officer Class 2 Yambahadur Khan who was soon followed by Staff Sergeant Dipakbahadur Gurung, Staff Sergeant Balkrishna Rana and Warrant Officer Class 2 Motiparsad Ale all promoted to Lieutenant (QGO). Motiparsad Ale had also gained the distinction of being the Regiment's first champion recruit on passing out from recruit training.

In sport the Regiment established itself as a worthwhile competitor. Because of its dispersion and long hours of work it was necessary to enter competitions as Minor Units. The only Regimental team was the soccer team, for the Nepal Cup. The winning of this much coveted prize eluded the Regiment but at the lower level the squadron teams did well. Khud (hill) racing continued to be the strongest event and either 28 or 31 Squadron GTR annually took the honours. A new sport in Hong Kong at this time was orienteering and Captain J R Cawthorne, the Administrative Officer of 28 Squadron GTR, was in the vanguard with his team. Basketball, being a game that can be played throughout the year, provided many hard and close fought battles between the squadrons of both Regiments with the honours for top places usually being equally divided between RCT and GTR squadrons. Being a transport regiment, it was not surprising that motor rallying came to the fore. Captain J A Fraser, the Assistant British Instructor at the Gurkha MT School, trained a successful team in 31 Squadron GTR.

In 1973 the regiment's dress changed to No 6 Dress which was worn on the parade held in October to say farewell to Major General P G Turpin CB OBE on completion of his appointment as the first Colonel GTR. He had been in the appointment for ten years and as a memento the regiment presented him with a silver statuette of a Gurkha soldier. The Colonel of the Regiment presented the regiment with a signed photograph of Her Majesty Queen Elizabeth II. It was with great pleasure that the Regiment received the news that Major General D G T Horsford CBE DSO had accepted the appointment as our second Colonel of the Regiment.

On 4 March 1974 Major (QGO) Giriraj Chhetri retired as an Honorary Lieutenant Gurkha Commissioned Officer and handed over to Major (QGO) Aite Gurung MVO who had completed his tour as the Gurkha Major at Paklihawa, Nepal. Giriraj Saheb had taken over shortly after the turmoil of the Regiment's move from Malaysia and had the difficult task of moulding the Regiment together. Unbelievable as it was, the Commander also handed over in the same month, and on 29 March Lieutenant Colonel H L A Mitchell RCT assumed the appointment from Lieutenant Colonel D B H Colley MBE RCT. Throughout his tour Lieutenant Colonel Colley had commanded two regiments of different ethnic groups with a strong element of British ranks. Within the Colony he had been responsible for pack transport, maritime vessels and general road transport, including tank transporters. He had seen the end of redundancy and set the Regiment on its new path.

Despite the gradually increasing workload on the squadrons, they could still in those days complete two two-week camps training each year. One was devoted to practising RCT skills while the other was a dismounted camp and concentrated on infantry skills with some adventurous training included. Both squadrons were also required to train in helicopter handling skills although 28 Squadron GTR had the helicopter handling task.

It was during one of 31 Squadron GTR camps on Lantau in August 1973 that Driver Birbahadur Pun, unaided, rescued two Gurkha soldiers from the wreckage of their vehicles which had gone over a cliff. For his prompt and brave action Birbahadur received the Commander British Forces Commendation. In a similar Commendation, Driver Asman Rai was congratulated for his coolheadedness when the brakes of his coach failed as he was driving down Route Twisk in the New Territories. Asman averted a major tragedy by manoeuvring his vehicle round the tight and treacherous bends to safety.

In March 1975, the Regiment were required to provide the British Korean Honour Guard contingent. This was the first time that a Brigade of Gurkhas Corps unit had provided the contingent, which was commanded by Lieutenant J Longland, and consisted of 19 Gurkha soldiers provided from 28 and 31 Squadrons. The task of the Korean Honour Guard contingent was to support the United Nations Force in South Korea, together with United States Army and South Korean military elements. This was a new venture and involved a lot of work from all concerned. The two main problems were the uniforms which had to conform to United Nations requirements in Korea and the drill. The US Army had developed highly complicated drill movements which must be perfected before contingents arrive for their tour of duty. Nevertheless, the Korean Honour Guard provides a valuable opportunity for soldiers to travel and gain experience outside the daily routine.

In 1975 a reduction in the number of British troops serving in Hong Kong was announced. On 31st December 1975, 414 Pack Transport Troop was disbanded. Resupply to the more inaccessible parts of the New Territories subsequently had to be done by helicopter. This placed a greater requirement on the regiment which was tasked to have a Joint Air Training Establishment trained British officer on its strength at all times to cope with special lift requirements.

The 1976 New Year Honours List brought recognition to the Gurkha Major for his many years of dedicated service and he became Major (QGO) Aite Gurung MVO MBE. This award heralded an eventful year. Due to the reduction of British troops in Hong Kong the Royal Artillery Barracks in Borneo Lines Sek Kong were vacated and in March 1976, 31 Squadron GTR moved from their quiet Romney huts in

South Camp into the modern accommodation and the hustle of North Camp the other side of Sek Kong airfield.

As a result of the continuing rundown of British troops, Headquarters 31 Regiment RCT and 56 Squadron RCT were disbanded later in the year and under a new establishment dated 1st September 1976, GTR retained the following command and control structure. RHQ was badged and manned by GTR throughout.

RHQ	(including 415 Maritime Troop)
28 Squadron GTR	(including D Troop 29 Sqn)
29 Squadron	
31 Squadron GTR	
GTR Workshop REME	(with sections detached to Squadrons)

28 Squadron GTR took over the Transport Control Office (Kowloon) from 56 Squadron but although it became firmly committed to daily driving tasks, the Squadron retained the Regiment's only true field deployment and operational capability.

On 23rd November 1976 the Gurkha Major changed over. Captain (QGO) Kishnabadur Tamang was promoted to take over from Major (QGO) Aite Gurung MVO MBE. Aite Saheb retired as a Honorary Lieutenant after 33 years service and in the middle of a hectic period before departure presented his personal kukri to the British Officers' Mess and his medals to the RCT Central Medal Collection at Buller Barracks.

In December 1976 it was time to move again and RHQ, 28 Squadron moved away from the squeals of the abattoir to the squeal of brakes along the busy roads of Kowloon, outside Gun Club Hill Barracks. The barracks had been vacated by 1 BW and the accommodation was spacious and air conditioned. There was a delay in the move of the Gurkha families as new quarters had to be built. Temporary accommodation was provided in the Osborn Barracks British family quarters.

For the next two years the camp looked like a builder's yard whilst the QGOs' Mess and the family complex were built. Eventually, after completion of 116 quarters, a Mandir (temple), a school and a families hospital, Gun Club now boasts the best family complex in the Brigade. The complex was formerly opened by the Commander British Forces on 9th April 1979. The Regiment's new home was magnificent as it provided the necessary focal points for the regiment: its own British Officers, QGOs' and Gurkha WOs' and SNCOs' Messes.

The Regiment had long nurtured the idea of forming its own Pipes and Drums. Since the GTR was the only Regiment or Corps in the Brigade of Gurkhas without its own musicians, it was felt that every effort should be made to produce a GTR Pipes and Drums. Over the years a few pipers and buglers had been transferred to the Corps but a band had not been formed. In 1977 three pipers were transferred from 6 GR and the Commander, Lieutenant Colonel D M Ivison, and the Quartermaster, Captain (QM) M F Bohan RCT, commenced the enormous task of obtaining the accoutrements and forming the Pipes and Drums.

The foundation to the regiments's Pipes and Drums was eventually secured when the Pipe Major, Sergeant Balaram Rai, transferred from the Queen's Gurkha Engineers. Balaram had long been associated with piping and with his expertise he was able to train the pipers who had transferred and new pipers who were dual (tradesmen) as drivers and pipers. The Pipes and Drums are not included in the GTR establishment and while it is difficult to dual train drivers as pipers and drummers the effort is well worthwhile.

For his untiring efforts in all fields but especially during the move from Sham Shui Po to Gun Club, Captain (QM) M F Bohan was awarded the MBE in the 1978 New Year Honours List.

On 4 March 1977, amid the chaos of building, Lieutenant Colonel H L A Mitchell RCT handed over command to Lieutenant Colonel D M Ivison RCT including some additional responsibilities. The Commander was appointed Camp Commandant and the Local Defence Area (LDA) Commander and also required to run a Gurkha Transit Centre to facilitate the move of Gurkha personnel. The new Commander had joined the Regiment on its formation and served in all squadrons, as the Adjutant at RHQ, and as Officer Commanding 28 Squadron.

In January 1978, the Regiment's fourth squadron was formed. Headquarter Squadron was raised to alleviate the excessive administrative work load on 28 and 29 Squadrons and at the same time introduce a better command and control structure. The Operations Major was appointed as OC Headquarter Squadron and under his command he had: an Administration Troop consisting of the Quartermaster's department with its cooks and storemen, and the clerical staff in the Headquarters; 415 Maritime Troop RCT and the Brunei Troop. The Commander, Second-in-Command, Adjutant, Gurkha Major and Regimental Sergeant Major formed the RHQ which was administered by Headquarter Squadron.

The redeployment of units in Hong Kong also affected the Royal Air Force. The helicopter squadron based at Kai Tak was reduced in size and redeployed to Sek Kong in the New Territories during 1978. This move affected the transport support required from 31 Squadron GTR and resulted in an increase to the establishment of a third troop.

March 1978 saw the last performance of 29 Squadron RCT motorcycle display team on the Army issued BSA 350 cc motor cycles. The team had started in a small way in 1976 with Corporal Wong Chun Hung as leader with four motorcycles and riders. By 1978 their enthusiasm had spread and they were ten strong. The limitation was the BSA motorcycle but in March 1978 the Hong Kong Jockey Club donated a generous grant which purchased seven Yamaha XT 500's. On 2nd September their premier performance on the new motorcycles was given at 28 Squadron GTR Annual Fete. This highlight of their year was followed by an invitation to entertain the crowds in Macau before the start of the Macau Grand Prix. In 1981 the Display Team performed at the Edinburgh Tattoo.

The final visit of the Colonel of the Regiment, Major General D G T Horsford CBE DSO was to Dashera in October 1978. He relinquished his appointment on 4 November 1978 after five years in which he had become intimately involved in the Regiment's affairs. Brigadier P I Attack MBE agreed to be the next Colonel and the Regiment welcomed for the first time a previous commander of the Regiment in the appointment.

As Gun Club Barracks began to settle down to normality, the 28 Squadron GTR Saracen Troop, taken over from 31 Squadron GTR in 1976, became increasingly involved in many unit and Colony exercises. One notable occasion was in support of 1/2nd GR on a demonstration during the visit of their Colonel in Chief, HRH Prince Charles. Driver Padambahadur Thapa was spoken to by the Prince who commented on his good standard of driving. Even Gun Club itself and the family quarters were used once or twice for staging Internal Security training.

On 1 July 1979, the regiment came of age. To celebrate their 21st Birthday a cocktail party was held for three hundred and fifty people, followed by a Beating of Retreat in Gun Club Hill Barracks. The Pipes and Drums of the three Corps: Queen's Gurkha Engineers, Queen's Gurkha Signals and Gurkha Transport Regiment combined to provide over fifty musicians on parade. It was a magnificent display coordinated by Major D V Pilley RAEC the GTR/Queen's Gurkha Signals Regimental Education officer. The Colonel of the Regiment with Lieutenant Colonel D G Mortlock, a previous commander, and Brigadier J Whitehead MBE ADC, who had been the Regiment's first liaison officer and was then the Brigadier Brigade of Gurkhas, were all able to attend.

Lieutenant Colonel D M Ivison RCT completed his handover on 9 October 1979 during the Dashera celebrations. The new Commander, who had previously served with 30 Company Gurkha ASC and 34 Training Squadron GTR, was Lieutenant Colonel P E B Daniel RCT.

December 1979 saw another change in the appointment of Gurkha Major. Major (QGO) Kishnabahadur Tamang retired as a Lieutenant (GCO) and was succeeded by Captain (QGO) Kulraj Limbu.

This period was also one of heavy operational involvement. Boatloads of Vietnamese refugees were arriving daily and from China, large numbers of illegal immigrants were trying to enter the Colony by land and sea. Considerable assistance from the Forces was required by the civil authorities and the Regiment was heavily involved. 415 Maritime Troop RCT was deployed with its Ramp Powered Lighters which were used as holding pens for illegal immigrants captured by the Royal Navy and Police launches as they tried to swim from China or, as ferry craft to move large numbers of refugees or illegal immigrants. The troop was also required to have men trained in the use of Rigid Raiders (small boats) but this task was eventually given to the Queen's Gurkha Engineers. Both 28 and 31 Squadrons were deployed to provide troop lifts and 28 Squadron was required to deploy its search light sections to floodlight either certain border areas or Lo Wu Station when the illegal immigrants were being returned to the Chinese authorities. 29 Squadron had a detachment of interpreters permanently deployed with border battalions. The battalions were fully extended and they willingly accepted sections from all four squadrons operating in an infantry role.

During 1979 and 1980, GTR were closely involved with Operation Drake. This was a two year expedition to circumnavigate the world and complete a large number of challenging but useful community and scientific projects. The expedition chairman was General Sir John Mogg GCB CBE DSO DL and the leaders included Lieutenant Colonel J N Blashford Snell MBE RE. The Regiment's first involvement was when Driver Diliram Limbu, 28 Squadron, was selected to join the expedition boat *Eye of the Wind* and completed the initial phase of the operation from London to Panama. The second involvement was in Hong Kong where the Regiment provided transit and additional support facilities during phases six and seven of the 'operation' in Papua New Guinea and Suluwesi. It was during this time that contact was made with the expedition leaders and Lieutenant R J Bacon, 29 Squadron RCT, was selected to lead the diving team during the Suluwesi phase.

In March 1980, the Regiment welcomed back Captain (QGO) Yambahadur Khan MVO who had just completed his tour of duty at Buckingham Palace as a Queen's Gurkha Orderly Officer and the Regiment's fourth Korean Honour Guard were deployed under command of Lieutenant G T Collinson until May. It was during this guard that the Regiment's Pipes and Drums completed their first formal parade. The support and efforts of the Commanders, Quartermasters, Pipe Presidents and Pipe Major had borne fruit. The GTR Pipes and Drums paraded on 26 April on the Korean Retreat Ceremony for the lowering of the United Nations, Republic of Korea and United States flags and troops from the United States, Britain, Korea, Thailand and the Philippines took part.

The pace of life in Hong Kong continues to be hectic as is inevitable in such a busy metropolis. The Gurkha Transport Regiment with it's unique blend of Chinese, British and Gurkha soldiers serving harmoniously side by side remains one of the few outlets for RCT service outside Europe. In the 2½ decades of it's existence, the Gurkha Transport Regiment has successfully combined the renowned military virtues of the Gurkha soldier with the professional transport expertise of the RCT, as well as incorporating the skill of the Chinese soldier. Service in Hong Kong will continue to provide a challenge – as well as being enjoyable.

27 · THE CORPS TRAINING ORGANIZATION

By THE LATE 1940s the post war National Service Army was established and the various training organizations had been reorganized to cope with the influx of young men who needed to be trained for just two short years service. Such training had to be comprehensive enough to enable them to be effective soldiers for those two years, but at the same time should not take up more time than was strictl, necessary.

The Director of Supplies and Transport was responsible to the Chief of the Imperial General Staff for the training of the Corps, which he exercised through his ST8 Branch at the War Office. All basic and centralized trade training was the responsibility of the Commandant of the RASC Training Centre.

The Royal Army Service Corps was then responsible for supplies, petroleum, transport, barrack and fire services, and clerical services. All RASC officers were required to be trained to undertake any RASC duty and to be able to assume the next higher rank on mobilization. Although, obviously, some acquired more expertise in some subjects than in others, as a general rule officers were not allowed to specialize.

Soldiers were generally grouped into either the supply or transport branch, their regimental numbers identified them with a prefix S/ or T/. They were primarily required to develop their military skills in weapon training and fieldcraft and then be proficient in their trade. NCOs, like the officers, were expected to be prepared to accept the next higher rank in war and to be trained in leadership.

The Officers School ran a wide range of courses to train officers from initial commissioning to senior major and lieutenant colonel. They also organized courses of instruction for officers of the Territorial Army and Army Emergency Reserve.

National Service recruits, after being allocated to the RASC, joined 5 (Selection) Battalion in Oudenard/Blenheim Barracks in North Camp, Aldershot, where they stayed for two weeks for selection to trades and basic military training. Those selected as MT drivers, after completing their military training, were trained to B3 driver trade standard over 14 weeks at one of the two Driver Training Battalions, 6 at Houndstone Camp Yeovil or 15 at Blandford Forum. These driver training Battalions also ran staff car courses and driver upgrading courses. The WRAC Clerical and Driver Training Company was located at Yeovil. On completion of their training, drafts were sent either direct to their Home or Overseas Commands or through the Depot.

The clerks, who were the second largest trade group in the RASC, together with tactical sketchers, were trained at 2 Training Battalion RASC, located first at Blackdown then later at Willems Barracks, Aldershot. All other technical tradesmen, with one exception, were trained at 3 Training Battalion RASC at Ellis Barracks, Farnborough (now the site of the new Rushmoor Municipal Offices). These trades included butchers, bakers, laboratory assistants, firemen who were first trained as drivers, marine engineers, petroleum operators and store-keepers. The firemen, after training as drivers, were qualified at the Army Fire School at Colchester.

Until REME phase 2 began in 1952, RASC vehicle mechanics were also trained by 3 Battalion RASC. Exceptionally, from 1949, seamen and subsequently navigators who were trained at Golden Hill Fort on the Isle of Wight, came under 1 Training Battalion RASC at Aldershot.

Up until 1948 4 Training Battalion RASC, based at Blackdown, trained driver specialists as tank transporter operators, landing vehicle tracked (LVT) drivers, amphibious DUKW drivers and armoured personnel carrier drivers. Later this role was given to training wings attached to 19 Tank Transporter Company in UK, 7 Tank Transporter Column in BAOR and 116 Amphibious Company at Fremington in North Devon. The LVT was later discontinued and APC driving became an RAC task, until the advent of the Northern Ireland operation when the

Boys Company 1 Training Battalion RASC at weapon training.

[By courtesy of RCT Museum]

[By courtesy of Lt Col I H W Bennett]

Passing out parade, Officer Cadet Company, Buller Barracks 1949

RCT once again started to drive APCs.

47 Air Despatch Company RASC at Watchfield was responsible for training all ranks in air despatch duties.

The bulk of basic and regimental training took place at Aldershot at 1 Training Battalion in Buller Barracks. The Battalion then comprised six training companies including officer cadets; junior soldiers; animal transport; regimental training (for some regular recruits, drill certificate and senior rank courses), and mechanical transport.

After 1949 its responsibilities also included the Water Transport Company at Freshwater, Isle of Wight. Later, the RASC Method of Instruction Team and the TA Training teams were established with 1 Training Battalion. A Junior NCOs Cadre course was also set up at Freshwater.

HQ Army Emergency Reserve (AER) had a number of changes in location, including Blandford and Crowborough, and again to Grange Camp near Bedford. It was responsible for administering and training the RASC units of the AER.

The Depot RASC started in 1947 on an airfield at Coney Weston near Thetford before moving in succession to Colchester and then to Old Park Barracks Dover in 1950, Bordon and Newton Abbot, until it finally settled in Aldershot. The Depot was concerned with the administration and holding of officers and soldiers on posting, discharge and transfer, for the movement, documentation and kitting of drafts and individuals bound for stations overseas, and the general administration of personnel in transit. To avoid the expense and inconvenience of sending soldiers home for courses, RASC Schools were set up in the larger overseas commands. These included Gebel Marian in Egypt, Nee Soon in Singapore and 4 Training Brigade RASC (BAOR) which formed in July 1945 at Lippstadt in Germany. An amusing incident occurred when the Brigade moved in to 'Flak Barracks', now called Churchill Barracks. The Barracks had been previously occupied by displaced persons who, before quitting them, removed everything movable and broke nearly everything else. Our advance party, faced with dirt and disorder, ordered the local Mayor to send 300 frauleins to the barracks forthwith. These young ladies arrived gaily dressed in their best frocks, and after it had been conveyed to them that the services required by the British Army were somewhat different from those previously rendered to the SS troops, they were each given a bucket, brush and a bar of soap, and mopping up operations began. An amphibious training wing, located at Eckenforde on the Baltic, was added in February 1947. All these schools had much the same sort of role, providing training for special local conditions.

All the training units in the United Kingdom had mobilization roles, and it was planned to expand the training facilities to cope with the greatly increased numbers that would be required in war.

The RASC Training Centre would concentrate on officer, officer cadet, senior rank and WRAC driver and clerical training. The two driver training battalions were to become training brigades: one responsible for supplies, petroleum, clerks and fire training whilst the other brigade covered water transport, specialist driver and air training.

The late 1960s saw the end of National Service, and a return to an all regular standing army.

A feature of this new organization was the increased reliance on civilian instructors, particularly driving instructors, and the expansion of the Junior Soldiers Company into the Junior Leaders Battalion which was in line with the need for a steady input of young regular soldiers; the warrant officers and NCOs of the future.

About this time, the RASC assumed responsibility for the Army MT School at Bordon, formerly the Royal Artillery and Infantry MT Schools, although overall control remained with the Director of Army Training. This School was designed and equipped to provide courses for officers and NCOs of all arms who were required to manage MT in their units. Driving and motor cycle instructors were also required to pass the appropriate instructors course at Bordon before taking up their duties, and courses were provided in the driving and handling of specialist infantry vehicles. To ensure an overall continuity of standards in MT driving techniques and management, a travelling team was added to visit formations and units worldwide.

The training of specialists was taken over by two newly formed organizations: HQ Water Transport Group and HQ Air Despatch Group, which was later to become 1 Army Air Support Organization. An amphibious training wing was formed at Fremington and tank transporters remained with 19 Tank Transporter Company.

In the overseas commands the RASC Training Schools were disbanded or integrated into local units as the number of stations were reduced and the increasing use of air transport made the training facilities in the United Kingdom more readily available.

Shortly after this major reorganization, the Corps had to turn its attention to a more significant change brought about by the recommendations of the McLeod Committee on the rationalization of the Services. On the 15 July 1965, The Royal Army Service Corps was formally disbanded and the Royal Corps of Transport raised in its place. The RASC was divested of its responsibility for supplies, petroleum, barrack services, fire and staff clerks, all of which were transferred to the Royal Army Ordnance Corps together with many officers and soldiers who were trained in these duties.

The newly raised Royal Corps of Transport assumed responsibilities for the distribution of combat supplies, all road transport, water transport and air despatch duties from the RASC and in addition took over from the Royal Engineers responsibilities for port operation, railways and Movement control.

The charter for the new Transport Officer in Chief now included responsibility for all Transport and Movements matters and placed the Army MT School under more direct control. The RCT also took over the Royal Engineers Transportation Training Centre at Longmoor which became The School of Transport:

1966 was a particularly busy year for the Corps. The problems associated with the formation of a new Corps and the assumption of new responsibilities were immense, and no more so than in the training organization at Aldershot. To add to these problems, the decision had been taken some time previously to move the HQ RCT Training Centre and its colocated units, less the Horse Transport Squadron which moved to Beaumont Barracks, from Buller Barracks to Queen Elizabeth Barracks in Church Crookham, while the old Buller Barracks was pulled down and rebuilt as part of the overall Aldershot Military rebuilding programme. It was a prodigious task vacating a barracks which the Corps had occupied since 1859 and it reflects great credit on those who managed the move as well as continuing, almost uninterrupted, the training.

During this period both 6 and 12 Training Regiments RCT were responsible for basic recruit and driver trade training. 11 Training Regiment RCT constituted the Depot, Horse Transport and Recruit Reception and Selection. After the initial processing of the newly joined recruits, they were posted either to 6 or 12 Training Regiments. In the Autumn of 1968 the Ministry of Transport extended the Heavy Goods Vehicle licencing scheme to include three categories of licence. This was to have a significant effect on the conduct of our driver training. Although the Services had Crown exemption which allowed drivers to hold licences under the age of 21, there remained a considerable restructuring of the driver training syllabus, and the period of training was lengthened to take in the additional instruction required on a laden vehicle. Service formations and units were required to have Qualified Testing Officers

[By courtesy of MOD OS 14]

Syndicate discussion during Joint Movement Staff Course at Buller Barracks.

(QTOs) who were authorized to carry out HGV testing. These were trained and classified at the MT Wing of The School of Transport who, to take up the backlog, classified some 1,900 in the first year.

Meanwhile, as a result of a major Defence Review the numbers of adult recruits coming into the Corps were much reduced, and it was apparent that we could no longer justify two driver training regiments. Accordingly in 1968, 6 and 12 Training Regiments were amalgamated at Crookham, the new regiment retaining the title of 12 Training Regiment RCT.

In November 1969 the Headquarters RCT Training Centre and 11 and 12 Training Regiments moved back to their newly rebuilt home in Buller Barracks. Between then and the early 1970s other changes took place in the training organization; all as a result of the gradual retrenchment of the Army as a whole.

The Horse Transport Squadron was disbanded in March 1971, marking the end of an era in Corps history, and the remaining HT Squadron in Hong Kong was reduced to troop strength as the advent of the helicopter reduced their role. At the same time 11 Training Regiment assumed responsibility for the basic recruit regimental training whilst 12 Regiment became a driver training regiment. The Maritime and Air Despatch Group Headquarters had already been disbanded and their training wings transferred under the direction of the Commandant, The School of Transport at Longmoor.

In the late 1960s it was appreciated that the established strength of the TA of 250,000 was not compatible with either our wartime needs or our ability to recruit, now that the National Serviceman's reserve commitment had been reduced. On 1st April 1967 the TA and AER were reorganized into the Territorial and Army Volunteer Reserve (T and AVR) having a total strength of 60,000 consisting of independent (old TA) regiments and sponsored (old AER) units. So far as the RCT were concerned, they included the former RE Transportation Units transferred in July 1965. Despite this radical reduction the new TAVR was to become more effective than the former TA units which, many thought, had depended for too long on their war experienced individuals. The onus of the TAVR changed from home defence to overseas (mainly BAOR) reinforcement. With their new role came new equipment, the same as the regular army, and a new emphasis on training. The RCT now had eight 'independent' regiments, most commanded by regular officers, and four 'sponsored' regiments with other minor units and specialist pools of experienced senior officers and senior ranks, a total establishment of 10,000 RCT; the second largest TAVR reinforcement to BAOR. The RCT Central Volunteer Headquarters (CVHQ) establishment at Bedford was increasd to meet this commitment. It also later became responsible for the basic military training of both the independent and sponsored units.

During the first half of the 1970s three factors were bearing on the Army driver training organizations. First there grew a number of mutual assistance agreements between the various army driver training units in the Aldershot area in order to cope with fluctuations in recruiting. At the same time there was increasing pressure from the Local Authority to reduce the amount of driver training in the urban areas surrounding

Trainee drivers and their instructors at the Army School of Mechanical Transport

[By courtesy of Army School of MT]

Aldershot. Secondly, it was decided that the MT Wing of the School of Transport should be rehoused at a surplus RAF airfield rather than re-building the School in Bordon or Longmoor. Thirdly there was an economic need to rationalize tracked vehicle training and Bovington was the preferred choice. The Transport Officer in Chief (Army) Charter was, therefore, further expanded to make him responsible for the centralized basic wheeled vehicle driver training of all arms and services except RE and REME while the Director Royal Armoured Corps became respon-sible for all arms tracked vehicle training.

The airfield finally chosen for the new Army School of Mechanical Transport was Leconfield near Beverley in Yorkshire, renamed Norman-dy Barracks, with a detachment at nearby Driffield for junior soldiers driver training. These reorganizations resulted in further adjustments to the RCT Training Organization. The basic driving of the RCT soldiers and juniors, was removed from 12 and Junior Leaders Regiments, and carried out at Leconfield. The RCT Officers' School, the technical training of non MT employments and Publications Section were moved to Buller Barracks to occupy accommodation vacated by the driver training regiment.

In the years between 1965 and the establishment of the training organization as it exists today there have been great advances in instructional technology. The RCT, in line with the other arms and services has not been slow in keeping abreast of these developments. The increase in the quantity and complexity of our equipment in recent years has been so great, that soldiers are required to be trained in exacting skills to the highest standard of competence so as to use it effectively. While ensuring that high standards are met, individuals cannot be allowed to spend any longer in training than is strictly necessary. In March 1971 the RCT Training Development Team was formed at Longmoor. Its aim was to examine in detail the content of our trade training and the standards of achievement that was expected of men of various rank, age and experience. This resulted in the acceptance throughout the Corps of the 'systems' approach to training which was earlier promulgated by the Director of Army Training. The system is designed to break down every phase of training into 'training objectives' so that each individual's state of training can be monitored as well as ensuring that syllabi contain no more than is required for each stage of training. Other unrelated matters have all had their effect on the training organization. The raising of the school leaving age in 1973 from 15 to 16 years affected recruitment into the Junior Leaders Regiment. Happily, the shorter training time did not reduce the standard of entry and the junior units are always in great demand with vacancies allocated up to a year ahead of time. The RCT Junior Leaders Regiment moved from Norton Manor Camp to a former RAF Station in Colerne in Wiltshire, in April 1978 the Station was renamed Azimghur Barracks. Norton Manor Camp was later re-opened

[By courtesy of Central Office of Information]

Corps of Drums, Junior Leaders Regiment RCT 1970.

to house the Junior Soldiers Infantry Battalion. The Corps held some key appointments in it including the Adjutant's post.

On 1 June 1980 two RCT junior soldiers squadrons became part of the unit. These were later disbanded as the size of the Junior Army was reduced. 59 Squadron RCT was disbanded in August 1981 and 34 Squadron RCT disbanded exactly one year later thus ending the Corps' long association with Norton Manor Camp, Taunton.

An Army Board decision to integrate the Womens Royal Army Corps into the general army trade structure has resulted in WRAC officers and junior ranks attending at all our courses. In 1980 CVHQ having moved to Prince William of Gloucester Barracks, Grantham, another former RAF station, was reorganized and·redesignated RCT TA Depot and Training Centre. It now has very much wider responsibilities for all aspects of TA training including that of the Independent Units.

As a Corps the RCT must always be prepared to meet the ever changing operational demands of the Arms it supports. To do this the training organization must be flexible in meeting the challenge of new techniques and skills in preparing officers and soldiers for their tasks in peace and war. The fact that they succeed was never more evident than when the RCT provided a large element for the South Atlantic Task Force. Well trained officers and men slipped easily into their war roles and contributed in no small measure to the success of that operation.

28 · THE RESERVE ARMY AND CADET FORCES

It is difficult to acknowledge adequately the debt that the United Kingdom owes to its Citizen Soldiers in two World Wars. There is little doubt also, that the majority of the population and a large number of serving officers and soldiers today are unaware of the essential contribution that is made by the TA to the overall viability of the Army in its major roles. It is now almost impossible to mount any reasonably sized operation should this prove necessary, without the embodiment of the Reserve Army. Even during the Falklands operation in 1982, although not called out, Reserve Army personnel voluntarily assisted in the movement of personnel and stores to docks and airfields.

It is not the purpose of this section to cover the period 1946–82 in detail. To do it justice would require a book in itself. In any case material is hard to come by. The publication *Citizen Soldiers* covering The Royal Engineers Transportation and Movements and the Royal Army Service Corps 1859–1965 by Colonel G Williams, published by the Institution of the Royal Corps of Transport in 1969 is an excellent summary of that period but again, it does not claim to be a complete history.

In his introduction to *Citizen Soldiers*, Major General D H V Buckle, CB, CBE, writes –

> 'Whether driving horses or operating railways, controlling vehicles or manning installations, improvising supplies or extinguishing fire, commanding, planning, flying or navigating, the performance of our voluntary soldiers is indeed worthy of permanent record.
>
> The Corps and its antecedents have sometimes in the past been slow to realise that the Regular element has been the essential leaven of the citizen soldier upon whom it is wholly dependent in emergency. After two world wars, there is no longer any lack of realization. Now however, the nature of war and the status of the nation have both changed and it is hard to foresee what commitments the Army and the Corps may be called upon to undertake. But there is one forecast that can safely be made. The Corps will still be dependent on its volunteer element which will become even more closely integrated with its professional counterpart.'

That was written in 1968, some two thirds of the way through the period under review and just after the biggest blow to their morale that the TA had ever received. It is pleasant to record that not only the spirit of volunteers and their voluntary service remains unchanged, but their role now is also absolutely clear. Every volunteer in a Corps unit has a clearly defined wartime role and is an essential element in the order of battle on mobilization. This applies equally to the evergrowing female element in our Corps particularly in the sponsored units.

Before launching into the post 1939–45 war period, it is as well to recall the antecedents of the present day TA units. Although the TA only came into existence as the Territorial Force on 1st April 1908 under the Territorial and Reserve Forces Act 1907, its origins go back centuries, when ancient peoples formed bands armed with clubs to defend their territory. We have since those days, had the National Levy of the Sixteenth century, the Trained Bands or Militia (not formally disbanded until 1953) which were the forebears of today's volunteer forces, indeed the oldest regiment in the British Army is a Territorial Regiment, the Honourable Artillery Company (HAC).

1859, at the time of the threat from France, is the year that saw the birth of a good many of our present day TA units from which the RCT can trace its roots. The first unit was composed entirely of officers and called The Engineer and Railway Volunteer Staff Corps and was formed in 1865. It still exists as a reserve unit of the Royal Engineers. The RASC lineage is rather more obscure. There is evidence of ASC badges appearing in units of volunteers towards the end of the 1880s, the first recorded ASC Transport unit was raised in 1885 at Stockbridge, Hampshire, when a transport company was raised for the 1st Hampshire Volunteer Battalion. Similar units were raised in Herefordshire, Kent and London and were in operation before the South African War.

Although no volunteer units served in South Africa, many ASC volunteers served in Regular ASC units. It was not until the first six divisions were formed later in the UK under the 1907 Act that the first transport and supply columns came into being.

The period 1908–1945 is not covered in this book. Suffice to say that volunteer ASC and RASC units played their part in the TA embodied for both world wars and suffered the cuts and reorganizations that occurred during that period. There was however one event that should be noted which was the advent of the Supplementary Reserve (SR) and the first Royal Engineer Railway Units (SR) formed in 1924. There were already individual RASC (SR) officers but it was not until 1932 that one brigade company RASC (SR) was formed to serve in Anti-Aircraft commands. The second part of this chapter is devoted to the Sponsored TA as the SR has now become, but firstly an examination of the Independent units, from their re-creation in 1947.

INDEPENDENT UNITS

The political situation worldwide after the end of the 1939–45 World War soon came to the point where the reconstitution of the TA became necessary. 1946 was a year of planning in the War Office in which the Territorial Army and Voluntary Reserve Council was much involved. 1st January 1947 was the effective date of the reconstitution and the date on which the appointments of Divisional and Brigade Commanders were announced. Unit commanding officers and Regular Army permanent staff instructors were announced on 1st February 1947 and general recruiting started on 1st April 1947. At this stage the TA was to be entirely composed of volunteers, conscripts completing their fulltime service would come into the TA in three years time and serve for three and a half years.

The composition of the TA was six infantry divisions, two armoured divisions, one airborne division and five anti-aircraft groups plus some non-divisional units including a beach brigade. To meet the RASC tasks in these formations, the RASC raised a column headquarters for:

3 corps troop columns	9 anti-aircraft group columns
6 infantry divisional columns	2 tank transporter columns
2 armoured divisional columns	9 transport columns
1 airborne divisional column	1 amphibious transport column
1 beach brigade column	

The number of units raised was:

24 infantry divisional companies	3 general transport companies
8 armoured divisional companies	3 tipper companies
5 independent infantry brigade companies	3 tractor companies
2 independent armoured brigade companies	4 tank transporter companies
3 parachute brigade companies	4 amphibious general transport companies
29 anti-aircraft command transport companies	1 fast launch company
18 artillery transport companies	3 supply companies
7 heavy general transport companies	Port, supply and petroleum platoons for the beach brigade.

Recruiting started off slowly. There were no summer camps in the first year and most drill nights were taken up with recruiting, organizing and establishing the social life of the units. This was no surprise since it was realized that few of those who had just finished their war service would wish to come back into a total military atmosphere so soon. It would take a while before people began to miss the life and the comradeship that obtains in the Services. By August 1948 the overall TA strength was just over 51,000. RASC columns were only at about company strength, but as a result of prodigious efforts, camps that year were realistic and hard working and it was realized by everyone that this was a serious business and as the word passed round, recruiting improved.

The two major events of 1950 were a change in the order of battle of the TA and the first intake of National Servicemen. Generally speaking the introduction of National Servicemen worked well. Apprehension on both sides was largely dispelled by the keenness and efficiency obtaining in most units on the one side and the surprising smartness and willingness of the new intakes on the other. There were naturally a few 'bad hats' but they were very much in the minority. The majority settled down to complete their liability and many volunteered for Territorial service, continuing to serve after National Service ended, leaving only when reaching retirement age.

In 1954 the first major overseas exercise involving the TA took place. Exercise Winch, a logistic exercise in which stores for BAOR were moved through Zeebrugge and adjacent beaches. 264 (Scottish) Beach Brigade TA with its RASC column containing amphibious companies, general transport companies, a fast launch company and port supply and petroleum platoons participated. Many valuable lessons were learned as a result, some of them unpalatable but nevertheless invaluable in view of the reorganizations that were just ahead.

The first major change occurred in 1955. Not only did a good many units change their role but many disappeared altogether. Indeed the TA's role as a whole underwent a major change. No longer was it recruited and trained to support the Regular Army in overseas operations and to support Anti-Aircraft Command and Coast Defence Artillery Command; it was to become mainly a Home Defence organization, not in its traditional sense but in support of the Civil Defence organization.

Only two infantry divisional columns RASC were to remain in their overseas role, 43 (Wessex) and 53 (Welsh), the remaining seven were reduced and earmarked for Civil Defence support. 264 (Scottish) Beach Brigade (TA) was re-roled to become 4 (Scottish) Port Task Force and with it its RASC column. Anti-Aircraft and Coast Defence units were disbanded.

The effects of the Suez operation in 1956 were hardly felt in the TA as it was the AER that was principally committed; that aspect is not covered here. The TA Jubilee Year 1958 was the next milestone and most RASC (TA) units were involved in local and national celebrations including two Royal Reviews. The first in Hyde Park London in June where a detachment of three hundred RASC Territorials from units throughout England, Wales and Northern Ireland took part. The second in July was held in Kings Park Edinburgh where all Scottish RASC (TA) units were represented. Many other RASC (TA) personnel helped with transport and administrative support throughout the UK.

The changes that occurred within the Reserve Army in 1961 had little effect on the RASC (TA). It was the AER that was mainly affected and a similar situation obtained during the changes in 1962. The withdrawal of National Service only made units more united and the introduction of the 'Ever Readies', The Territorial Army Emergency Reserve, with the enhanced bounty, drew little support from within the RASC (TA).

The next major event that took place was the reorganization of the Army logistic support services as a result of the McLeod Report but again the impact on RASC (TA) was limited apart from the rebadging ceremonies that took place as close as possible to the Regular Army date of 15th July 1965.

1967 is a year that will long be remembered by those who were serving in the TA at that time. Not only were there huge cuts and reorganizations but the title was changed to 'Territorial and Army Volunteer Reserve' (TAVR). The word 'Territorial' in the new title was originally planned to be discarded in favour of 'Army Volunteer Reserve', but it was retained after a country wide outcry. There were four main categories, I and II forming the 'Volunteers' and liable for call out for service worldwide and III and IV only liable for call out in defence of the United Kingdom. As far as the RCT was concerned there were only two Category I units, 562 Parachute Squadron RCT(V) located at Southall, Middlesex and 490 Movement Control Troop at Bedford. The remaining category IIA units in the Corps were:

    150 (Northumbrian) Regiment RCT(V)
    151 (Greater London) Regiment RCT(V)
    152 (Ulster) Regiment RCT(V)
    153 (Highland) Regiment RCT(V)
    154 (Lowland) Regiment RCT(V)
    155 (Wessex) Regiment RCT(V)
    156 (Merseyside and Greater Manchester) Regiment RCT(V)
    157 (Wales and West Midland) Regiment RCT(V)

The 1967 reorganization caused many old established units to disappear and consequently many loyal and long serving Reservists to be retired. At first there was a lot of bitterness directed towards the Regular Army and particularly to those who were personally involved in the details of the reorganizations and amalgamations especially the selection of Reservists who were to man the new units. Few realized what a painful undertaking it was to the headquarters concerned in making these decisions. There can be no doubt however that whatever else was affected in the TA, the enhancement of the TA's role in reinforcing the order of battle of the British Army and BAOR in particular, had reached a new era of mutual responsibility and understanding. The one Army concept was now in being!

Further reorganizations took place in 1969, 1971 and 1974, but again they did little to affect the Corps units that grew out of the 1967 reorganization. The main change of 1969 was that of nomenclature when the category IA were called Group A (Independent) Units and the IIA units became Group B (Sponsored) units. The title 'Territorial Army' was restored in 1979.

That is not to say that there were no important changes affecting units and individuals throughout the period. Right up to the present day units have changed their mobilization roles, their organizations and seen great improvements in vehicle and equipment holding. Units in some

[By courtesy of WO2 N K Reed RCT]

Pipes and Drums 153 (Highland) Transport Regiment RCT (V) on tour in BAOR.

cases have benefitted greatly from intakes from other arms suffering under the cutbacks. The Pembrokeshire Yeomanry, the Fife and Forfar Yeomanry, the Royal Artillery and the Royal Tank Regiment have all contributed sub-units and individuals to the present day independent RCT regiments.

In 1982 all the regiments formed in 1967 are still in being although their roles may have changed. 562 Squadron is no longer an independent parachute unit but a standard MT squadron under command of 151 Regiment.

The role of the ATS/WRAC (TA) in Corps units has fluctuated considerably over the post-war years. In the fifties and early sixties, they were in considerable numbers particularly in AA Command. Reductions in the TA disposed of all WRAC(TA) by 1967 but it is pleasant to record that once again regiments are being allowed to recruit women.

The deployment of the independent RCT TA regiments is given at Annexe 'A' at the end of this chapter.

SPONSORED UNITS

In the 34 years since the reconstitution of the Reserve Forces there have been several changes in the title of the Sponsored Reserve. Supplementary

Reserve in 1950, then Emergency Reserve and now Territorial Army (Sponsored). In the case of RCT sponsored reserve units this is a most logical title because the only real difference between the two types of reserve is the training commitment. Originally, there was a considerable difference, as there still is in some Corps, in that units and individuals in the Supplementary Reserve units were almost entirely specialist and staffed by specialists in that unit's role, a role that was not normally required in the Regular Army Order of Battle, for example, some railway or petroleum units. The object was to gather together volunteer experts from civilian sources and to train them to perform their tasks in a military environment when a national need arose. It was wasteful in money and resources to maintain these units full time or to recruit and train TA units from scratch.

This form of reserve commitment was generally encouraged by private industry and commercial firms and worked extremely well before 1939. After 1946, the nationalized firms were also encouraging when the majority of the UK population were still defence minded. Many firms granted extra leave with pay to members of their staff whilst carrying out their reserve training and many units and sub-units were formed within private companies. Sadly, attitudes have changed over the years and generally speaking, support from industry and commerce has dwindled and, regrettably in some cases, TA membership is actively discouraged. There are a number of recent cases on record where individuals have been offered the choice of resigning from the TA if they wished to stay with the firm, and, whilst it may not be official trade union policy, individuals have been encouraged by shop stewards to resign from the TA because it is not in the best interest of the local 'shop'. In the harsh light of present economic difficulties there are limits too in what even the most enthusiastic firms can do to give extra time off.

All this means that the concept of sponsored units has changed and, in addition to military training, it has become necessary to carry out basic and continuation trade training. This has even included basic driver training although this has to be kept to the minimum. Only in one unit, 275 Railway Squadron, has it been possible to maintain the old system. One of the most fruitful sources of good recruitment is ex-servicemen and women who find that they are missing the qualities of life they found in the Service and are able to find it once again doing part-time service. Their previous training and experience in The Royal Navy, the Army or Royal Air Force is invaluable, particularly when measured against a raw recruit. This new concept has meant a greatly increased burden on the permanent staff of the TA Depot and Training Centre plus an increase in material and equipment for training, a point rarely appreciated outside 'sponsored' circles.

At the present time, responsibility for all detailed aspects of recruiting, equipping, training and administering sponsored RCT reserve units is held by RCT TA Depot and Training Centre located at Prince William of Gloucester Barracks, Grantham, Lincolnshire. Once again, the full circle has been achieved in that the first post-war title was Supplementary Reserve Depot and Training Centre RASC. When it was decided to reintroduce Supplementary Reserve, the RASC set up, on 8 June 1950, a permanent Cadre for the administration of RASC (SR) Units. The cadre of three officers and six soldiers (all clerks) was attached to 15 Training Battalion RASC at Blandford Camp, Dorset. They had no equipment, borrowed office space and were mainly concerned with recording the volunteers from information supplied by the Record Office. Lieutenant Colonel J E Williams OBE RASC formed the Supplementary Reserve Depot and Training Centre RASC at Blandford on 26 July 1951 with an establishment of permanent staff consisting of six officers and thirty soldiers. Limited training was started with approximately sixty SR officers and 3–400 soldiers, called up for training in 1951. From 1951 until 1963, TA and SR units were strengthened by National Servicemen completing their reserve liability of 3½ years. Although a great many of these willingly performed their training liability, some were most unwilling and posed an unwanted additional burden on permanent staff and units. Since the run out of the Army General Reserve, gaps in reserve units on mobilization are planned to be filled by Regular Army Reservists.

The unit moved to West Camp, Crowborough, Sussex in March 1952 and the first trainees started arriving in April, the numbers increasing rapidly. Trainees reported on Saturdays for two weeks throughout the summer. West Camp was in several ways unsuitable for its role. Situated only one mile from Crowborough through which the only access route passed, it lacked sufficient hardstanding, the surrounding area was unsuitable for vehicle training, the local population consisted of many retired professional people in expensive houses, who did not take kindly to the mass of soldiery in its midst nor were the local hosteleries geared to cope. Colonel Williams relates an amusing reason for one of the misunderstandings. The lane from Crowborough to the camp was sparsely residential, completely unlit and bordered by fields in which farm stock was kept. Complaints came in from the locals regarding the noise made by the soldiery returning in large numbers late at night. Investigation by a tried and trusted sergeant-major revealed very little drunkenness but a large number of 'town' soldiers who were very frightened of the dark and strange noises from the fields, singing lustily all the way back in order to bolster their courage. Quite a number of present day Reservists doing their sentry duty on exercise in a German forest will recognize the feeling! However, an explanation to the locals and a quiet word with the Reservists during one of their instructional periods went a long way to improving relationships.

Due to an Army reorganization, the first redesignation became effective on 6 April 1953. The title SR disappeared to become AER, (Army Emergency Reserve), and the unit became HQ AER Depot and Training Centre RASC. In September 1954, the strength of the permanent staff was some twenty officers and about 150 soldiers with 1,000 officer and 25,000 soldier reservists in the following units:

10 transport columns	1 amphibious company
3 supply groups	1 air despatch company
3 petrol groups	1 tank transporter company
1 water transport group	1 pack transport company
4 fire companies	

Considerable help was given by other RASC training organizations. Water transport units went to the Water Transport Unit at Golden Hill Fort, Yarmouth, Isle of Wight, Petroleum units to the Petroleum Reserve Depot at West Moors, Dorset, Supply units to 3 Supply Reserve Depot at Taunton, Somerset and so on. The transport columns were the greater problem due to the already mentioned unsuitability of the local countryside and inadequate roads in the Crowborough area. Although a considerable amount of training was carried out locally, units were also based at Clifftop Camp, Dover which was a tented camp.

Command changed on 28 August 1954 when the post was upgraded and filled by Colonel W Horsfall, OBE. He vividly describes the problems of mixing the volunteer and the unwilling National Service reservist. Although only a small minority of the latter bitterly resented being called out for training, they managed to make life difficult for all at times. Losses of and damage to stores and equipment was high. Equipment and clothing taken home was used for all sorts of purposes and was unserviceable at the next training session even if it was not lost and, in the circumstances prevailing at the time, financial recovery was difficult.

One of the camp boundaries was an unfenced public road, a perfect escape route for those Reservists who decided that they wished to leave early and without passing the guardroom. That particular problem was easily resolved by digging a ditch and fencing it, the task being carried out by Reservists, of course! Another boundary was formed by a 1,000 × 400 yard wooded valley with a drop into it of about 200 feet. One Saturday afternoon, this valley was swept by fire and when it had burnt itself out some 300 men were tasked to search the area. About 2,000 items of missing equipment were discovered, including tentage, jerricans, knives, forks and spoons, trestles and tables, steel helmets, tin plates, etc. The piece de resistance was a 4 ton vehicle missing for the past two years or so.

In September 1955, the unit moved to Grange Camp, Bedford. Apart from the easier access to the training area in East Anglia, including Coney Weston Camp which was particularly suitable for training transport columns, the facilities at Bedford were a great improvement on those at Crowborough. The Quartermaster's department had adequate accommodation and the Reservist sleeping and ablution areas were vastly better. Other advantages included easier access by road and rail and most important, as Bedford had for many years been the depot of the Bedfordshire and Hertfordshire Regiment, the population was more used to soldiers and their recreational habits. Indeed the town made the unit most welcome and a very happy and fruitful relationship was created in Town and Country which continued until the unit departed twenty-one years later in 1976.

The move heralded improvements all round apart from the camp itself. Training became more varied and morale improved to such an extent that National Service Reservists started signing on as volunteers and many are still serving. The year of Suez meant that many reservists were called out, the majority being mobilized at Bedford. A magnificent job was done by the permanent staff aided by some reservists brought in to assist and some 6,000 passed through in seven days. History does not relate the standard of messing, but it should have been good as the reservist messing officer was Captain Graham Kerr, ACC (AER) later to become well known as television's 'Galloping Gourmet'.

A story that well illustrates the attitude of a good many of the reservists concerns the officer posted to an MT company in Cyprus and being the owner of a one man business in Wales, when asked what was the most difficult task he faced, as a result of his call-up stated 'Convincing my wife that I was very sorry that it had to be'. Another important event for the reservist in 1956 was the appointment of three Colonels (AER). These were Colonels 'Spider' Wheeler, Henry Slack and Hugh Williams. Not only did these officers provide an invaluable link in the Regular Reserve chain, they established the 'Troika Club' now the 'Waggon Club' which still meets regularly at Buller and in August 1982 had a membership of 154.

In 1961, there was a sharp cut in the number of reservists required and by 1962 the number was reduced to about 100 officers and 1,000 soldiers manning:

2 transport columns	1 amphibious company
1 petrol group	1 fast launch company
2 supply companies	1 air-despatch pool

The next major event was the despatch to BAOR for the first time of RASC AER units carrying out their annual training. In 1964, a motor ambulance company commanded by Major (now Colonel) Colin Brice and a supply platoon commanded by Captain (now Major) Ralph Alford served alongside their regular counterparts on exercise. Their professionalism was an eye-opener to many. It is no surprise to those who have served with these men to hear that recently the Chief of Staff HQ BAOR was amazed to discover that one of the watchkeeping officers in the operations room at the HQ was in fact a Reservist.

In 1965, the implementation of the McLeod Report was the next

[By courtesy of Maj A P Stringer RCT (V)]
'Ever Readies' of the Territorial Army on the Dhala road Radfan 1964.

major upheaval. The report proposed, among other far reaching recommendations, that the Reserve Movement and Transportation functions
administered by the Transportation Centre RE at Longmoor, Hampshire
should be absorbed into the new RCT. After much discussion and camp
recces, it was decided that the RASC system of administering and training
the AER as a self-contained unit and separate from the other Corps
training regiments and units should continue. The only other Corps to use
this system was the Royal Signals. It was also decided to continue using
Grange Camp, there being no other available camp as suitable or more
conveniently situated. It was only achieved after a lot of argument and
uninhibited action by the then Commandant, Colonel Peter Pearman and
his staff. The new organization at Bedford, HQ AER RCT, consisted of
the Headquarters, Training Wing, and Administrative Wing supported
by an LAD REME and staff by fifteen officers and 200 military and
civilian staff. The former RASC and RE Reserve units now badged RCT
were:

> 101 Regiment RCT (AER) of two MT squadrons and one amphibious
> squadron
> 104 Regiment RCT (AER) of two MT squadrons and one maritime
> squadron
> 2 Railway Group RCT (AER) of three railway regiments, one railway
> squadron and a transportation pool

5 Port Group of two port regiments, two independent port squadrons
and HQ 3 Port Task Force (AER Element)
Four Movement Control Regiments
One independent Movement Control squadron
Two Movement Control increments

The total strength was 4,000 of which over 2,000 were based at
Longmoor and together with a detachment from Bedford remained there
until early 1967.

Rebadging parades were held both at Bedford and Longmoor. The
salute at Bedford being taken by Major General W H D Ritchie, CB,
CBE, Honorary Colonel of 101 Regiment RCT (AER) and at Longmoor
by General The Right Honourable Lord Robertson GCB, CBE, KCMG,
KCVO, DSO, MC, Honorary Colonel of Railway and Port units.

The reorganization of 1967 as with TA units, caused tremendous
turbulence, some disappointments and an enormous amount of paper
work. Each individual had to decide which category of the Reserve he
wished to belong to (I, IIA, IIB, III or IV), transfer to the other Corps or
discharge. As a result, ninety-six officers and 958 soldiers became
redundant whilst some twenty officers and a large number of soldiers were
taken on from other sources. On the effective reorganization date of 1
April 1967, HQ AER RCT became Central Volunteer HQ RCT and the
ORBAT RCT (T & AVR), all Category IIB except 490 Troop which was
IB was:

160 Regiment of four MT squadrons and two artillery troops
162 Movement Control Regiment with three MC squadrons
163 Movement Control Regiment with four MC squadrons
490 Independent MC Troop
491 and 495 Movement Control Increments
280 Independent MC Squadron
275 Railway Squadron
HQ Port Task Force
270 and 271 Port Squadrons
264 Amphibious Squadron
265 Maritime Squadron (Fast Launch)

The first training year 1967/68 was devoted mainly to military training at
Bedford which also allowed the reorganized units to 'shake down' and
personnel to get to know each other. Conversion courses were also
necessary particularly for those new to Movement Control duties. Apart
from the railway squadron and the qualified civilian HGV driver
volunteers in MT units, this period saw the end of the old SR/AER
concept of the civilian expert in uniform as far as the RCT was concerned.
This was particularly the case amongst the officers, where only one or two
were specialists from civilian equivalent posts. In the following year unit
training was carried out in a number of diverse locations, Penhale in
Cornwall, BAOR, Cyprus, Malta and there was even a small detachment
in the Persian Gulf.

[By courtesy of HQ TA RCT]

TA recruits during a casualty evacuation exercise.

It was also in 1968 that the scope of training within CVHQ widened in that training facilities were offered to TAVR Category IIA (ex-TA and independent) units at Grange Camp. Apart from undertaking the initial training of recruits for RCT and other Corps, provision was made for the use of accommodation and pool vehicles and equipment for complete Category IIA units and sub-units. It is interesting to note how this facility has over the past fourteen years developed into the present fully integrated recruit training organization.

The Corps was amongst the first in the field in this matter of centralized training of recruits. Its many advantages include the lifting of the heavy burden of recruit training from independent units who have a high turnover, permanent staff instructors can be maintained at a very high standard and have the advantage of the best possible facilities and, not least important, the 'cross fertilization' between the two categories of recruit. This era also heralded the centralization of training for officers and soldiers in category IIB (previously SR/AER). It had been the practice to send out training teams from CVHQ to various locations throughout the country in order to set up training camps for units in the area where the maximum number of that unit's personnel resided. With the cuts in the number of units and the resultant mix of the personnel it became necessary to run these courses at Bedford itself. Again, this resulted in considerable savings in equipment and allowed better use of available instructors. Given the magnificent accommodation now occupied at Grantham, this must give the Corps the optimum conditions for producing efficient Reserve Army units with high morale, plus a superb centre for all the independent units when they require it, but more of Grantham later.

One of the few disadvantages of the concentration at Bedford was the poor state, by modern conditions, of the accommodation in Grange Camp and the high cost of maintaining this 1939/40 temporary camp. No maintenance funds were allowed to be spent on Kempston Barracks across the road where the instructional accommodation in use was literally falling down, some parts actually being declared unsafe.

Government policy in the late sixties and early seventies was to alienate Service land in towns and cities for use by local authorities and it was decided to move CVHQ into a deserted Ordnance Depot at Marchington, Staffordshire. The only possible recommendation for being there was that it was only thirty miles from the notional centre of England at Meridan and could genuinely be said to be central and it had plenty of wild real estate! It was only after a personal visit by the then Transport Officer in Chief, Major General Peter Blunt, that disaster was avoided but it was a close run thing. The architect had actually started work on designing the many new buildings required and the conversion of the remainder. Fortunately, it was soon after this that in August 1974, Royal Air Force Spitalgate at Grantham was declared available. This Womans Royal Air Force (WRAF) Depot was still occupied when the preliminary reconnaissance by the then Commandant CVHQ, Colonel J S M Walker and the SOI Administration, Colonel A R Price RCT took place. A decision to recommend acceptance was arrived at in about ten minutes, much of this time being taken up with admiring the inmates as well as the property!

Having assessed the accessability to the rest of the United Kingdom (UK) by road and rail, the decision to move the unit to Grantham was quickly made and the necessary works services put in hand. It was with great regret that CVHQ ended its association with Bedford and Bedfordshire. Saddest of all was losing the majority of the devoted and loyal civilian staff who had been such an important element in the successful running of the unit.

Colonel A G Bell and his staff moved to Grantham in October 1976 with only a short break in the training programme. Spitalgate Aerodrome was established in 1917 with 3 training squadrons of the Royal Flying Corps and was mainly used as a training establishment. In 1937 it became part of Bomber Command, in 1938 an advanced flying training unit, in 1948 an RAF Officer Cadet Training Unit and in 1954 the Womans Royal Air Force Depot. It will be appreciated that the environment is excellent by Army standards.

On 21 May 1977, the barracks was formally named Prince William of Gloucester Barracks by the Colonel-in-Chief, HRH Princess Alice, Duchess of Gloucester. Two years later on the 1 June 1979 CVHQ was redesignated the RCT TA Depot and Training Centre (CVHQ) and on the reorganization of HQ UKLF in 1982 opportunity was taken to give the RCT TA its own exclusive one star command headquarters. On the 13 April 1982 Brigadier Bernard Courtis set up at Grantham HQ RCT TA, a Headquarters of the Field Army, having under command:

> a. A sponsored group of RCT units consisting of four regiments and thirteen minor units, including road transport, railway, port and movement control units, with an establishment of some 3,000 including 250 officers of whom 17 are Lieutenant Colonels TA.
> b. The Depot RCT TA under comand of a regular RCT Lieutenant Colonel and having the specific responsibility for the special to service training and interests of the eight independent RCT TA Regiments and other independent RCT volunteers serving in other units.

The Commander RCT TA not only issues detailed Corps policy for the Volunteers on behalf of the Director General of Transport and Movements (DGTM). He is also responsible for formulating the individual training standards to be achieved by the officers and soldiers and advising the Commander Field Army on RCT TA matters and organization. The Depot RCT TA provides centralized courses for all RCT volunteer recruits, a whole range of WO, NCO and specialised courses; and training and administrative facilities for complete units to undertake individual training during annual camps. The Depot RCT TA also continues to act as the recruiting, administrative and training sponsor to the RCT TA sponsored group of units.

The first WRAC (TA) to join the Sponsored Units were transferred from RE (Tn); (AER) Mesdames Weeks, Wood and Bartlett were transferred from 75 Movement Control Regiment Royal Engineers (AER) to 163 MC Regiment RCT (V) when the RCT was formed. They were joined by Mesdames Power, Bailey (now Notley) and Powley when the WRAC disappeared from many Independent Units in 1967. The 'Terrible Six' as they were sometimes called were fully integrated into the Regiment and were expected to carry out exactly the same tasks as their male contemporaries. So successful were these early 'female movers' that the Regiment is now over 50% staffed by WRAC (TA) and it is responsible for an essential role in the UK movement plans. Their contribution to the operational efficiency of the regiment is beyond praise.

In 1982 the sponsored units based at Grantham were:

160 Transport Regiment and three squadrons
161 Transport Regiment and four squadrons
162 Movement Control Regiment and three squadrons
163 Movement Control Regiment and six squadrons
265 Port Squadron
275 Railway Squadron

280 Movement Control Squadron
495 Movement Control Liaison Unit
496 Movement Control Liaison Unit
400 Artillery Troop
420 Artillery Troop
421 Artillery Troop
422 Artillery Troop
491 Traffic Regulating Centre
492 Traffic Regulating Centre
493 Traffic Regulating Centre
494 Traffic Regulating Centre

These units all have important tasks to perform on mobilization, their performance, be it in the United Kingdom or Overseas in a NATO force, is in no doubt.

Although organizations and their names change over the years the formation of HQ RCT TA marked a significant development in the evolution in the control of RCT TA for it brought under one senior Corps officer the two types of volunteers, sponsored and independent and with it an overdue visible recognition of the vital role which the TA plays in the mobilization orbat of the Royal Corps of Transport.

No chapter in the RCT Volunteers would be complete without mentioning the essential role which the Colonels of Volunteers RCT have played in advising the Regular on the Volunteer and in advising the Volunteers on the Regular. A debt of gratitude is owed by the Corps to them for their successful efforts in creating a better mutual understanding of the strengths and limitations of both the Regular and the Volunteer. Their names are recorded at the back of this history.

CADET FORCES

INTRODUCTION

The Army Cadet Force can trace its origins back to around 1859 when junior volunteer forces came into being alongside the adult volunteer battalions which were then forming throughout the country under threat from France. Some leading schools formed volunteer units of their own, the forerunners of the Combined Cadet Force, but these were part of the adult force and would have been operational had the occasion arisen.

About this time Miss Octavia Hill formed a band of boys from the streets, modelled on the Army, to instill standards of cleanliness and decent behaviour. Thus there were two factors in the formation of cadet units; firstly the military needs of the country and secondly the desire to help boys in the sociological conditions of the nineteenth century.

Since those early days the Cadet Forces have grown and developed into the fine organization that exists today.

ARMY CADET FORCE

As can only be expected, the end of World War II and the continuing reduction of the Armed Forces over the years plus national attitudes brought about a decline in the interest and numbers joining the ACF. On the other hand quality remained as high as ever and, for those serving, offered a more varied career. Whilst the objectives have not changed, both in fitness and individual training, the many facilities available have greatly increased the scope of training and the varied weapons and equipment now in service has increased the interest in purely military training. Perhaps the most important part of the later years has been the greater interest shown by the Regular Army in the cadets and the scale of help provided by individual Regular and TA units.

There is no doubt that the experience a boy gains in a cadet unit often points towards a career in the Regular Forces. It must be a matter of great pride to those involved in the organization of cadet units that in 1980 well over half the intake in Junior Soldiers and Junior Leaders Regiments served previously in a Sea Cadet, ACF or ATC (Air Training Corps) unit. It is particularly noticeable that in our own Junior Leaders Regiment at Colerne many of the junior NCOs and prize winners are ex-cadets.

The number of Army cadets has fluctuated considerably over the years naturally rising in times of national need. In 1982 there were upwards of 44,000 13 to 18 year olds serving in 1,600 detachments in 69 counties of the United Kingdom. 8,000 adults are currently engaged in running the ACF. It is interesting to compare the strengths over the past years; in 1923 there were 49,000, in 1930 51,000 and in 1939 there were 170,000.

The establishment of the Cadet Training Centre at Frimley Park in Surrey in 1959 has meant a great deal to the cadet movement. It trains instructors in their duties, runs courses for officers, is a conference centre and, not least of all, sets a very high standard to be followed throughout the movement.

The number of units badged RASC/RCT and/or sponsored by Corps Regular or TA units has varied considerably since 1945. Changes have, in the main, been due to reorganizations within the Regular or Reserve Army. As in the early days of the movement, it is clearly best for the cadets to be badged the same as their sponsor if they are to gain the maximum benefit from belonging to the 'family'. This rule has to apply almost entirely to static Regular establishments and TA units as opposed to a field force unit which is likely to move at short notice. A lot also depends on the attitudes shown by sponsor unit commanders and by Corps senior officers and headquarters. Cadet unit fortunes vary directly with the interest shown in them from above and this has varied enormously over the years. One great advantage Corps badged units have over some other Arms and Services is the availability of transport in sponsor units for both instruction and administration but this is often sponsor units for both instruction and administration but this is often offset by the lack of time that can be allotted to cadet matters. There are at present 81 ACF detachments badged RCT.

COMBINED CADET FORCES

In 1948 it was decided to rationalise the position of school cadets. Schools which kept boys over the age of 17 and with a minimum strength of 60 cadets were invited to join the newly formed Combined Cadet Force with its tri-service organization, that is possibly having sections of all three Services and commanded by an officer of any of the Services with a single headquarters.

The aim of the CCF is to provide the framework of a disciplined organization within which and through which there may be developed within boys qualities of endurance, resourcefulness, self-reliance, leadership and responsibility and a sense of public service, in the belief that these things are of profound consequence to the stamina and stability of the nation, in civil as well as in Service life, in peace as well as in war.

The specific function of the Service training in the programme of the CCF is not only to contribute to the development of the attributes described above but also to give all cadets a background knowledge of Service methods and conditions and to assist and encourage those boys who have a special interest in a service career to become officers in the Regular, Territorial and Reserve Forces or to serve in civil organizations of national importance.

The latest known strength in the United Kingdom is 44,000 cadets with 1,700 officers and a training and administrative staff of 177. There are 7 RCT badged CCF contingents.

ANNEXE A   INDEPENDENT REGIMENTS RCT (TA)

150 (Northumbrian Transport Regiment RCT (V)
Headquarters   –   Hull
216 Squadron   –   Tynemouth
217 Squadron   –   Leeds
218 Squadron   –   Hull
219 Squadron   –   Doncaster
Band   –   Hull
Predecessors post 1945   5 AA Group Column RASC (TA)
                                            42 Division Column RASC (TA)
                                            49 Division Column RASC (TA)
                                            50 Division Column RASC (TA)
                                            66 Regiment RCT (TA)
                                            103 West Riding Column RASC (TA)
                                            Royal Artillery

151 (Greater London) Transport Regiment RCT (V)
Headquarters   –   Croydon
210 Squadron   –   Redhill
                                            Workshop REME Sutton

631

		one troop Croydon
		one troop Clapham
215 Squadron	–	Grays
		two troops Leigh-on-Sea
240 Squadron	–	Barnet
		one troop Hitchin
		one troop Slough
562 Squadron	–	Southall
		one troop Dulwich
		one troop Bow
Predecessors post 1945		16 (Airborne) Division Column RASC (TA)
		23 Corps Troops Column RASC (TA)
		44 Division Column RASC (TA)
		54 Division Column RASC (TA)
		56 Division Column RASC (TA)
		105 Transport Column RASC (TA)

152 (Ulster) Ambulance Regiment RCT (V)

Headquarters	–	Belfast
211 Squadron	–	Londonderry
		one troop Ballymeney
220 Squadron	–	Belfast
Pipes and Drums	–	Londonderry
Predecessors post 1945		68 Regiment RCT (V)
		112 Regiment RCT (V)

153 (Highland) Transport Regiment RCT (V)

Headquarters	–	Dunfermline
212 Squadron	–	Perth
		one troop Aberdeen
		one troop Dunblane
230 Squadron	–	Edinburgh
231 Squadron	–	Dunfermline
239 Squadron	–	Cupar
		one troop Kirkcaldy
		one troop Leven
Pipes and Drums	–	Dunfermline
Predecessors post 1945		3 AA Group Column RASC (TA)
		51 Division Column RASC (TA)
		51/52 Division Column RASC (TA)
		69 Transport Regiment RCT (TA)
		123 Transport Column RASC (TA)
		Fife and Forfar Yeomanry
		Scottish Horse
		Royal Artillery

154 (Lowland) Transport Regiment RCT (V)

Headquarters	–	Glasgow
221 Squadron	–	Glasgow
222 Squadron	–	East Kilbride
225 Squadron	–	Edinburgh
		Workshops REME Grangemouth
251 Squadron	–	Troon
		Workshops REME Dalny

Pipes & Drums   –   Glasgow
Predecessors post 1945   –   3 AA Group Column RASC (TA)
         51/52 Division Column RASC (TA)
         52 Division Column RASC (TA)
         123 Transport Column RASC (TA)
         264 Beach Brigade Column RASC (TA)
         Queens Own Lowland Yeomanry
         Ayrshire Yeomanry
         Royal Artillery

155 (Wessex) Transport Regiment RCT (V)
Headquarters   –   Taunton
232 Squadron   –   Plymouth
         one troop Tavistock
233 Squadron   –   Southampton
         one troop Weymouth
         one troop Portsmouth
245 Squadron   –   Bristol
         one troop Reading
395 Air Despatch Troop   –   Swindon
Predecessors post 1945   43 Division Regiment RASC (TA)
         4 AA Group
         Aldershot District Column RASC (TA)

156 (Merseyside and Greater Manchester) Transport Regiment RCT (V)
Headquarters   –   Liverpool
234 Squadron   –   Birkenhead
235 Squadron   –   Liverpool
236 Squadron   –   Manchester
238 Squadron   –   Bootle
         one troop Southport
Predecessors post 1945   22 Corps Troops Column RASC (TA)
         42 Division Column RASC (TA)
         102 Transport Column RASC (TA)
         Duke of Lancasters Own Yeomanry
         40 RTR
         41 RTR

157 (Wales and West Midlands) Transport Regiment RCT (V)
Headquarters   –   Cardiff
233 Squadron   –   Swansea
224 Squadron   –   Carmarthen
         one troop Haverfordwest
         one troop Lampeter
237 Squadron   –   West Bromwich
         one troop Stoke-on-Trent
Predecessors post 1945   48 Division Column RASC (TA)
         53 Division Column RASC (TA)
         Pembrokeshire Yeomanry
         4th Battalion Welsh Regiment

633

29 · THE MOBILE CIVILIAN TRANSPORT GROUPS AND MT UNITS OF THE MIXED SERVICES ORGANIZATION IN BAOR

INTRODUCTION

Following the complete collapse of Germany at the end of World War II, the victorious Allies were faced with the daunting task of administering their respective Occupation Zones. Debris had to be cleared, public supply facilities, housing and factories had to be rebuilt. The transport network of railways, roads, canal, river and ports had to be reopened and airports and bridges had to be repaired. Vitally important goods, particularly food, coal, and building materials, had to be transported for troops, civil population, prisoners of war and refugee camps; timber had to be cut; attractive and important goods and places had to be guarded; telegraph and radio communication systems had to be re-established. The harvest had to be gathered. Many thousands of tons of army equipment, weapons and ammunition awaited collection and destruction.

Grinding through the dust and rubble of the battered countryside of the British Occupation Zone of Germany in late May 1945 could be seen many hundreds of vehicles bearing, not the colourful heraldic signs of the Corps and Divisions of 21 Army Group, but a simple white-lettered 'DG' and a number. They were driven by tough-looking individuals clad in a curious mixture of German Wehrmacht and British Army uniforms. They were the Dienstgruppen (DGs) or Service Groups formed from the Prisoners of War in British hands and tasked to support 21 Army Group and the British Military Government.

The term Dienstgruppen unit was used to denote certain German working units which had an authorized establishment. They were always placed under command of a British headquarters or unit (parent unit). They could be used anywhere, for any type of work. There was no restriction on the hours of work other than the physical limitations of the men. They had the status of disarmed troops, that is, they were not entitled to any of the privileges of protection afforded by the Geneva Convention.

About 100,000 ex-Prisoners of War were employed in the various sorts of labour, transport, engineering and watchman units of the DG.

Just how many DG transport units there were is not known exactly but it was probably around 45. There were several in each of the Corps Districts, attached to RASC companies and under control of DDSTs Corps, CRASCs Divisions and the commanding officers of Army and Corps Transport Columns RASC. The composition of the Groups varied considerably, but each was several hundred strong and was divided into a number of subgroups. They were originally entirely ex-Wehrmacht military groups with their own officers and NCOs from the former German Army and Luftwaffe units. Doctors and orderlies from the Wehrmacht Medical Service were attached to give medical cover. Later on, refugees and displaced persons were also formed into transport units.

Seen originally as an expedient to help in the administration and reconstruction of the Zone, the direct descendants of these units are still serving the British Army nearly forty years later. Their history is an essential and integral part of the Corps in BAOR and this chapter can only cover the highlights of their fascinating story. In some cases, individual histories tell in minute detail of the events, personalities, equipment and barracks that have shaped them; for others, there may be only a passing reference to a disbandment or amalgamation presenting a tantalizing glimpse into the past. Two of the most complete and typical histories are held by 604 and 632 Mobile Civilian Transport Groups RCT (now in Dortmund and Bischofshafen near Herford respectively) – both have been drawn on heavily. They are by no means unique and contributions from many other unit histories have also been used to support and fill out details.

TRANSPORT UNITS OF THE DIENSTGRUPPEN

There were many virtually intact German Army units marching from the East into British Prisoner of War Camps in the Schleswig-Holstein area to avoid capture by the Russians. Among them were 450 men from Corps Group von Stockhausen of the Panzer Division 'Gross – Deutschland'. Nearly 90% of the men had been recruited from areas then under Russian domination and they had no immediate wish to return. When they were offered the opportunity to serve as a Dienstgruppen Transport Unit, they volunteered immediately. The first 'Supervisor' was their Colonel, Oberst Roeckner. In July 1945 he led them from their camp at Krokau/Eutin as 304 Wehr Transport Company via delousing, rekitting and a final check at Bramstedt, to 'freedom' in a barracks at Hiltrup near Munster. By 17 August 1945, they had already collected 150 vehicles from a Dutch Airfield near Venlo. Canadian Fords, Chevrolets and Bedford trucks and a variety of German motorcycles were distributed on a basis of 33 vehicles to each Sub-Group. Later 3-ton Chevrolets from 67 Company RASC were taken over. Spares were desperately short and the shortage of tyres was so acute that, at any one time, one Sub-Group was off-the-road. Until December 1945, the men wore their black Panzer uniforms with rank insignia, awards and decorations. These were later replaced by field-grey and semi-civilian dress, and dark-brown dyed battledress blouses and trousers were issued in the Summer of 1946. Supplies were short and men were virtually confined to their barracks often without shoes or boots. They were paid at between 1½ and twice their old Wehrmacht rate and, although food was desperately scarce, an arduous duty ration was agreed in recognition of the long hours and demanding work.

The unit history of 632 Mobile Civilian Transport Group RCT also recalls these early days when the German Parachute Transport Column No. 21 remustered virtually man for man as a Dienstgruppen to operate as the Corps Supply Company, Ems Command in Laak on 14 May 1945. Under the command of 51st Highland Division, the unit consisted of nearly 800 men with five platoons and two workshops under the direct supervision of Major F K Freese, the former Commander of the original Parachute Battalion. In February 1946, the company re-roled as German Transport Column 666, equipped with 3-ton cargo vehicles and a platoon of troop carrying vehicles.

DG Transport Units were used on practically any task. These included the transport of coal for hospitals, clothing, furniture, ammunition, engineer and military equipment, building materials and even the collection of peat. Perhaps the saddest details of all were the carriage of refugees and returning prisoners of war from the East. These included Operation Shuttle which was the transfer of prisoners between the American and British Zones; Operation Exodus in September 1945 which involved the removal of 19,000 disarmed Wehrmacht soldiers from the British Sector of Berlin to the British Zone in Western Germany; and Operation Dolomite, also in September 1945, for the exchange of prisoners between the British Zones of Austria and Germany. From time to time vehicles were exchanged and most units had a variety of American, ex-German Army, Canadian and British vehicles. Gradually, as the British Zone settled down into manageable Districts, the DG units were refined and standardized in structure and their miscellaneous vehicle fleets were rationalized, using some of the large quantities of British vehicles made available by the run-down of what had, by now, become the British Army of the Rhine.

In the Spring of 1946, the de-Nazification of the DGs began. Because there were comparatively few Nazis in the old German field-force, this process was quickly done. By then, DG units were in good spirit and endeavoured to bring a measure of normality to their social life. One of the most pressing problems was the reunification of families separated by war or the political divisions of Europe. The units quote many examples of successes and in one instance an Assistant Superintendent Schade spoke to a newcomer in his unit canteen with the result that he was able to trace first his uncle, then his sister and finally his mother in 1953/54. Although naturally popular with the local populace, units often met considerable hostility from stone-throwing Dutch on the trips to Venlo. Also in 1946, military titles within the DG were abolished and the supervisors were renamed Managers, Under-managers, Superintendents, Foremen and so on, but the reality of the German command remained and the units continued to largely administer themselves under the watchful eye of their various RASC sponsors.

THE GERMAN CIVILIAN LABOUR ORGANIZATION

On 31 July 1947 all members of the Dienstgruppen were formally discharged from their military service because the Russians had requested the 'disbandment of still-existing German military units'. The following day, 1 August 1947, they were redesignated as part of the German Civilian Labour Organization (GCLO). Units were retitled, 304 Wehr Transport Company became 504 GCLO. The men were offered contracts generally valid for about a year.

Unemployment and shortage of food in civil life encouraged most to stay on with service accommodation, heating and rations for 5 Reichmarks a week. Most of the men were, in any event, desperately hoping for a political normalization that would give them the chance to return to their former homes. At this time, a formal British Supervisory Element (BSE) (usually a RASC Major, one other officer, a senior NCO or two and a RASC Workshop Supervisor, usually a Mechanist Sergeant Major (MSM)) was established to control the transport service GCLOs. 302 BSE GCLO (Tpt), for example, controlled 504, 505 and 512 GCLO. Day-to-day running of the units remained very much in the hands of the German supervisors until early in 1948 when a RASC Major, Lieutenant/ Captain and a MSM were appointed to each GCLO Transport unit to provide direct supervision and control. The number of groups was also gradually reduced mainly by amalgamation. Because vehicles were in poor condition following their war-time service and with spares, particularly tyres, in short supply, the DG/GCLO units began to build up that tradition of good vehicle husbandry which even today is carefully cherished and much admired.

The prime task of the DG/GCLO Transport Units remained to assist in restoring the German economy and the resettlement of the vast number of refugees and deportees which had flooded into the country. Amongst the many undertakings of this difficult period was the Berlin Airlift. GCLO Transport Units provided the vital links between supply depots, railheads and the airfields and movement of supplies on the airfields themselves. The enthusiasm with which the GCLO workers of all categories supported the West German end of the Airlift operation is something which all who saw it will never forget.

Those serving in those days remember them with great pride and recognize very clearly the genuine efforts made by the British to restore their dignity and a reasonable standard of living to the German populace. Translated from the chronicles of one DG unit on its dissolution in 1947 were the following poignant and revealing words:

'So ended a two-year journey, full of cares and duties, of joys and sorrows, of ironies and deep meanings, after much effort for the women and children, after difficult labours for rebuilding within our own country and for the tasks of the British Zonal Authorities. The 'Former members' are proud of their Dienstgruppen, even though the British called them the "donkey workers". They were a test of one's remaining energy, of patience, of one's convictions and faithfulness. The experiences of the DG included much personal and national misery but also personal and national hope. Days which one hopes will never come again but from which the memory of a community not without a sense of pity remains unforgotten. Time heals many wounds. In one's memory, the bad things fade; the good and worthwhile experiences remain. Most satisfying is the memory of duties clearly of use to our own people. And quietly, of our comrades who gave their lives in this service and never got to the hoped-for finish.'

The GCLO Groups offered steady employment, accommodation and, above all, food to a large number of the German population. Some Germans were envious of the standard of living enjoyed by the GCLOs and the British Control Commission had to step in to prevent threatened cuts in rations and allowances which had been agreed in new contracts. Once the German 'Economic Miracle' began to get under way, however, the GCLO with its long hours (a 72-hour week was normal) and comparatively low pay soon began to suffer from comparison and the numbers employed began to fall. The change from Reichmarks to Deutschmarks also brought uncertainty and contracts were for short terms of 6 to 24 months. Ill-discipline, even a minor traffic accident, could result in almost instant dismissal. There remained always a hard-core of ex-Wehrmacht soldiers to whom the DG/GCLO had become a way of life and who prized the comradeship still to be found within the units. From about 1948, command of GCLO Transport Units was vested in the 'Static' CRASCs in BAOR. When, in 1948, the decision was taken to reform combat Divisions in BAOR, GCLO Transport Units were lent to Divisional CRASCs to make up their Columns for major exercises, a situation which continued even after British Companies were formed in 1949. At least one Divisional CRASC expressed the view that he would have preferred to keep his GCLO!

As a postscript to this period, von Brockhusen, a member of the original Corps Group von Stockhausen which had surrendered in 1945, returned from captivity in Russia and was promptly re-enrolled as Personnel Manager/Administrative Superintendent of 504 GCLO. His grandfather was rather well known – von Hindenburg!

TRANSPORT UNITS OF THE GERMAN SERVICE ORGANIZATION

On 21 October 1950, a further reorganization was undertaken, and retitling to the German Service Organization (GSO). Despite a reduction in units, a better structure of pay and work conditions was introduced together with stricter control of recruitment which favoured single men. A new and better uniform was issued and new grades, (staff superintendent, superintendent) replaced the GCLO titles. The aim was to present the GSO in a better light in the eyes of the civil population as Government employees in uniform. 504 GCLO became 504 Motor Transport Unit GSO and, like many other similar units, were committed to British Army exercises. Because of their wartime experience and the number of ex-Wehrmacht Officers in supervisory grades, they soon earned a reputation for faultless performance in what had become a mainly British National Service Army. In 1952, the Workshop Sub-Groups were also redesignated to REME Workshops (and the MSM to ASM) in recognition of REME Phase 2.

MOBILE CIVILIAN TRANSPORT GROUPS

The GSO was restructured as part of the Civilian Working Group (CWG) in 1957. Those elements that had a mobility commitment formed the Mobile Civilian Groups (MCGs) and the GSO Transport Units became Mobile Civilian Transport Groups (MCTGs), taking the same numbers as their predecessors. Pay and conditions of service were now more nearly equated to those generally pertaining in the Federal Republic of Germany and were governed by a formal Tariff Agreement to which the British Forces were but one of the several employing parties (the others being the remaining NATO Sending States, eg USA, Canada, France, Belgium and the Netherlands. Federal German Labour and other Laws were now applied to the CWG employees, albeit with some slight relaxations in recognition of their 'mobility' (the right of the employers to redeploy units to new locations and participate in exercises). The title 'BSE' was dropped and the British Army supervisors were written directly into the unit establishments. By then the British staff had been run-down to an OC (RASC Major), CQMS RASC and REME ASM.

The next few years saw a gradual, but highly significant, change of emphasis in the role of the MCTGs. From being largely operational transport in support of the RASC in the field, they increasingly assumed responsibility for the operation of Garrison administrative and welfare transport. An important change was in 1960 when the MCTG took over the buses established for school children, family administration and the newly introduced air trooping, previously held on Station Staff establish-

[By courtesy of MOD CS (REPS)]

School bus service provided by MCTG units in BAOR.

ments and driven by Directly Employed Labour (DEL) drivers. From then on, these buses with the RASC (and later on RCT) badges became one of the most familiar sights around the British Garrison towns. MCTGs continued to provide a good deal of 3rd-line transport support to 1 British Corps and its constituent formations and units. Most MCTGs also retained a vital role in the event of a period of tension and would expect to operate ambulances, coaches and cargo and specialist vehicles in a variety of tasks not always compatible strictly with their status as civilians.

In 1963 MCTGs were renumbered with '6' prefixes (for example 532 MCTG became 632 MCTG). The unit organization remained largely unchanged, each unit having from two to four sub-groups plus a REME Workshop. The formation of the RCT in 1965 saw the end of the static CRASC and the establishment of the BAOR Transport and Movements Regiments RCT, under whose command the MCTGs now came. The RCT Freight Service, which started in BAOR in the late 1960s, was (and still is) operated to a large extent by MCTG vehicles and drivers. The personality structure of the MCTG changed over the years. The number of ex-Wehrmacht members gradually declined; some had already returned to the fold by joining the Federal German Bundeswehr on its formation, and others retired because of age or infirmity. Some of those founder-members still remain, many of them now in the senior CWG management positions of Staff and other Superintendents. Staff Superintendent (formerly Major) Freese MBE was one of the several awarded the MBE in recognition of their services.

New members came in of varying quality, depending on the state of the German labour market. A number joined simply to evade national conscription and at the height of the economic boom years of the 1960s and 70s, recruiting was poor and morale within the MCTG correspondingly low. The slow-down in the German economy in the early 80s reversed this trend. The CWG employee clearly valued his job and there was little difficulty in finding men to fill the comparatively few vacancies which arose. The survivors of an almost non-stop round of reviews, cuts, restrictions, streamlining and financial stringency, the MCTG have earned an almost Darwinian reputation for evolving and adapting to change.

At the end of 1982 there are 12 MCTGs operating in BAOR. Each is tailor-made for its role and unique in its own way, but all perform quietly and unassumingly tasks which are vital to the BAOR community well-being. Indeed, for most of the thousands of BAOR soldiers and their families, the MCTG *is* the RCT; the buses which meet them at the airport on arrival in the Command, take their children to school, their wives to the NAAFI and the Wives' Clubs, the ambulances which take them to hospitals, are driven by the 'Green Men' of the MCTG or the 'Mojos' of the MSO. Even for many thousands of TA soldiers, their first experience on exercise in BAOR is to be driven from the airfield in the white buses of the MCTG by a taciturn veteran of the Wehrmacht or a fresh-faced young German for whom the war is but a piece of history. It would be difficult to find a single Garrison Commander in BAOR who would agree to any reduction at all in the service he gets from the MCTG. They provide a range of transport support from school coaches to ambulances, from fuel tankers to tippers, minibuses and road-sweepers. They still have a role to fulfil in a time of tension but these tasks have now been selected to be compatible with the civilian status they enjoy.

The MCTGs can look back with pride on a long and honourable past with work well done.

MT UNITS OF THE MIXED SERVICE ORGANIZATION

The origins of the Mixed Service Organization also lie in the period immediately following the Second World War, at a time when many servicemen, civilians and ex-prisoners of war from the countries of Eastern Europe found themselves in the British Zone of Germany.

The majority of these people were Polish or Yugoslavian but there were also many from the Baltic States of Latvia, Estonia and Lithuania. Few wished to return to their homelands which had come under Russian influence and communist control. So was born on the 29th of December 1946 the Civilian Mixed Watchman Service (CMWS) and the Civilian Mixed Labour Organization (CMLO) later renamed the Mixed Service Organization (MSO).

The essential difference between a Mixed Service Organization (MSO) Unit and Mobile Civilian Transport Group (MCTG) is the ethnic derivation of its members. Whilst DG/GCLO/GSO units were manned by men of German nationality, MSO Units were staffed entirely by people of non-German origin. In later years, most MSO Units gradually became cosmopolitan organizations, but they managed to retain the character given to them by their founder members. Although formed for rather different reasons and at a later stage than the DGs, the development of the MSO followed a similar pattern. A particularly significant difference was that CMLO/MSO carried personal weapons for unit defence, received military training and had a clearly defined operational role in direct support of military field formations.

The history of the struggles of the Polish people and their contribution to the allied war effort is well known and it suffices to record only Ernest Bevin's remarks to the House of Commons on 22 May 1946:

> 'As for those Poles who do not wish to return to Poland it is our aim to demobilise them as quickly as possible and to arrange for their settlement in civilian life either in Great Britain or overseas. It was, I thought, the desire of the House that I should do that, and treat them, having played their part, almost *pari passu* with our own people with whom they have fought'.

Several mainly Polish manned transport units were formed at Cuxhaven in 1947 and 1948; particular records exist of the raising of 312, 317, 321 and 322 Transport Units. They owe their origins to Colonel Karol Zeimski who was the Senior Polish Liaison Officer with the British Army in Germany in 1946. With the newly-formed Polish Combatants Association, he discussed with the British Army how best to absorb the Poles from the various camps as a component of the British Forces.

The early history of 321 CMLO shows that after training at Cuxhaven, it moved to Flensburg in 1949 and later to Catterick Barracks Bielefeld in 1950. Its establishment was approximately five hundred all ranks and consisted of a headquarters, four transport Platoons, Workshops Platoon and a spare Platoon without vehicles. Platoons were based on the RASC brick system of 33 task vehicles. A Platoon was equipped with 3 ton trucks, B Platoon drove ambulances, and C and D Platoons operated fuel tankers. Detachments of the unit served in Oldenburg, Osnabrück, Bünde, Lübecke, Nordeney and Minden. The unit was under the command of HQ RASC Bielefeld. At the start, this pattern was similar for all units, but there were two major exceptions.

Both 312 and 317 Transport Units CMLO RASC formed at Unterlüss in the Autumn of 1947 and trained at Cuxhaven as general transport units but in May 1948, 317 Transport Unit moved to Hamm where it took over the vehicles, equipment, quarters and task of 15 Company RASC. It was then redesignated 317 Tank Transporter Unit and, by the end of 1948, the men had mastered the Diamond T and its Dyson Trailer and started work in their new role – a role destined to continue without break until the 1980s. 312 Transport Unit was also reroled with tank transporters and eventually redesignated 612 Tank

[By courtesy of PR HQ 4 Div]

A detachment of 612 Tank Transporter Unit MSO with Mart II Antar loaded with Chieftain tanks.

Transporter Unit (MSO) RASC.

It is known that 322 CMLO (a Polish-manned unit) helped in this training of yet another CMLO, but in this case manned by displaced persons from the Baltic States. The history of the Baltic units is less well known and it is important to have some understanding because it helps to explain the astonishing loyalty of such units to the British Army. Despite their full independence in 1920, the Baltic States were invaded and then annexed by the Soviet Union in 1940 in a well managed election. The rapid advance of the Germans following Operation Barbarossa was aided in part by a spontaneous rising of the people in all three States. During the next two years many of the men and youths of the countries enlisted or were conscripted into the armed forces. Some served in German units, others in national units – of which possibly the best known is the 'Latvian Legion'. For more than two years these forces fought on what was probably the hardest front of the Second World War, always short of equipment and rations and often fighting through appalling climatic conditions. As the Red Army advanced, many of the women and children were evacuated to Germany often by sea in appalling cramped conditions and subject to attack by the Allied Air Force. Some formations of the Baltic States armed forces managed to withdraw almost intact to Germany; others were surrounded and continued to fight in isolation until they were overrun or until the capitulation of May 1945. It is of note that partisan groups continued to operate against the Russians in Latvia until 1949.

Immediately after the war, Germany (and Austria) was a mass of displaced humanity. Not only had the German Army taken many thousands of East European prisoners who had no wish to return to Soviet domination but the Allies had captured many Axis prisoners who now also had no desire to return to homelands newly occupied by the Russians. These numbers were swollen by large numbers of refugees. In 1946 the responsibility for these people was handed to the United Nations and they were declared Displaced Persons (DPs). Programmes were started to encourage DPs to emigrate but clearly not all wanted to go, and any emigration programme would clearly take a long time to effect. In the meantime, there remained the problem of housing, clothing, feeding, employing and paying them. At the same time the Allied Control Commissions were faced with the problem of carrying out the occupation duties of defence and administration of the Allied Zones at a time when demobilization was in full swing and military manpower was becoming scarce. Both problems could be tackled by inviting ex-soldiers among the DPs to enlist in para-military units in the same way as the German DG/ GCLO. From the outset the idea proved to be a success, and it was gradually expanded. Protests were made by the Soviet Union that the Allies were arming and training anti-communist units made up of nationals from countries where there was an elected Communist Government for the sole purpose of attacking the Communist Bloc. The units were therefore named the Civilian Mixed Service Organization (CMSO) and military titles were discarded in favour of civilian titles (Superintendent, Warden, etc).

In July 1948, a number of Baltic DP Camps in Niedersachsen and Schleswig-Holstein were visited by Major D C Collins RASC, who suggested that the men might like to join a transport group that was being formed to provide support for the British Army. There was no shortage of volunteers. On 5 August 1948, 505 men (including 396 Latvians, 48 Lithuanians and 25 Estonians) arrived at 53 Civilian Mixed Depot Osnabrück where, in tented accommodation, they were documented, medically examined, clothed and equipped. By 14 August 1948 a basic organization had emerged and Franciskas Marcinkus was provisionally appointed as the Chief Superintendent of what was to become 323 Transport Group, Civilian Mixed Labour Organization. On 19 August 1948 the unit moved to Cuxhaven where it was attached to 322 Transport Group (a Polish unit) and training began in earnest. The next two months were hectic. Many of the men had never seen a motor vehicle before the war, yet by 20 October 1948 training was completed and 323 Transport Group CMLO was ready for work. Initially the unit was deployed in the Mönchen-Gladbach area with Headquarters at Hellenabrunn, three detachments at Viersen, one at Krefeld and one at Boisheim. Two months later the unit was on the move again when it reported to Bochum, for retraining on a new range of vehicles, where it remained with two sub-units detached to Viersen until 1951. 323 Transport Group did not remain static and the long awaited emigration programme was soon in full swing. Many Displaced Persons were sailing to seek a new life in Australia, North America and the United Kingdom. Among them were men of 323 Transport Group and by 1949 the unit strength had dwindled to an established strength of 400 men. In 1951 the unit moved to Bielefeld, where it was located in Harrogate Barracks. Many of the buildings were derelict, accommodation was cramped, and parking space inadequate, but, although the unit did not at the time know it, this was to be their home for the next 30 years. The story of 323 Transport Group is typical of all these early MSO units. The men were issued with battle-dress dyed dark-blue with silver rank insignia and appropriate years of service badges and clasps were awarded from time to time. Soon a familiar sight on exercises, they were affectionately known as 'Mojos' by the British Soldiers.

Thus the raising of these and many similar units provided not only employment and purpose, but dignity and a new life for those who had lost home, family and livelihood. Even after later emigrations to North America, the United Kingdom and Australia by thousands of refugees, many hundreds remained in the service of the British Army. For many, the only home they were to know would be a British Army barrack-room. To their units and their British officers and senior ranks, they brought their national spirit and customs, great variety of national food and drink, an untiring enthusiasm for apparent routine and a disconcerting but unstinting loyalty in the face of almost continual cuts and financial stringency. The great majority still serve on, or have retired with the status of German citizen, and many now have German wives and families. Few have returned, other than for very brief and limited visits to their homeland. Recognition of their loyalty and service has resulted in the award of MBEs to a number of Staff Superintendents and Superintendents.

To return to 323 Transport Group, the unit celebrated its tenth anniversary in 1958. No-one expected to serve for so long a period with the MSO. For most, it had been simply a temporary employment whilst they, along with the rest of the world, found their feet. The earlier expectation had been for a two-year contract, but here, although depleted in strength (establishment of only 218), they were resilient enough and willing to continue as a unit entity. This was despite two major events to affect the unit in 1958. The first event was the formation of two MSO Platoons of 91 Company RASC (now 14 Squadron RCT) which established a 'rival' Baltic unit to share Harrogate Barracks. The second event was the decision for the (by then considerably depleted) MSO Staff Band from the original MSO Depot to become an integral part of 323 Transport Unit. The Band, under Superintendent Ferninands Heinrichsons, had a very high reputation and played at many Regimental Dinner Nights and Unit Parades, giving both open-air and radio performances. For some years the

[By courtesy of PR HQ BAOR]

617 Tank Transporter Unit MSO being inspected by the Burgermeister of Sennelager accompanied by Maj Gen P Blunt MBE GM.

unit was able to benefit directly from having its own show piece band. In 1959 the unit title was changed to 323 MT Unit RASC, assuming the title of a unit which had operated trains in England during the First World War and which had been a Cypriot Animal Transport Unit during the Second World War.

The passing years brought many changes. Still in Harrogate Barracks, it is no longer a purely Baltic unit but contains representatives of seventeen nations who work together with no difficulty. As one of the last remaining MSO Units, 623 MT Unit has gained many members from disbandments of units in other branches of the MSO (such as defence companies and labour units). In October 1977 as a result of the proposals of the Stephenson Committee, the MSO element of 14 Squadron RCT were returned to the unit and formed C and D Sub-Units. Between 1 November 1977 and 31 March 1978 twenty-two members of the MSO were received from 621 MT Unit MSO on its disbandment, thus bringing together again after thirty years, founder members of the Civilian Mixed Labour Group units formed from the DP Camps of Schleswig-Holstein and North Germany.

The Polish tank transporter units have seen many changes; from their early days of the Diamond T, the units were later equipped with Antar and semi-trailer. They established an unprecedented record for professional skill and slick operating that became a hallmark of the whole tank transporting fleet. In 1976, 617 Tank Transport Unit MSO, established to carry one complete regiment of tanks in a single lift, was organized with HQ, HQ Troop, three tank transporter troops (each 20 task vehicles and semi-trailers), a 10-ton troop of 33 vehicles and a REME Workshop. In addition to the founder members, a number of non-Polish East Europeans were enlisted. The fiercely proud Poles, however, maintained their national spirit and customs throughout this period and as a mark of respect the Polish Eagle was adopted by 7 Tank Transporter Regiment as a Regimental insignia. To this day, a tiny silver eagle is worn on the mess kit of senior ranks and officers in recognition of the contribution to post-war tank transporting by the Polish MSO. Eventually both units were unable to sustain recruiting from MSO sources and British soldiers (UK Trained Adult Males (UKTAM) were used to replace the MSO in a process that became known as UKTAMisation. 612 Tank Transporter Unit became 16 Tank Transporter Squadron RCT on 1 January 1973 and on 7 July 1982, 617 Tank Transporter Unit was redesignated 617 Tank Transporter Squadron RCT. Both units retain an MSO component and maintain the proud traditions handed down to them from their founder members of the old Polish Army. MSO Tank Transporters have carried many thousands of AFVs; as examples, in 1981, 2,375 and in 1982, 3,049 vehicles were lifted. They continue to do so to this day, saving substantial sums of money in movements costs in other areas, contributing a vital service and generally adding to the efficiency of the Force.

30 · AUXILIARY TERRITORIAL SERVICE/WOMEN'S ROYAL ARMY CORPS

At the height of the Second World War there were over 200,000 members of the Auxiliary Territorial Service (ATS) serving with the Army in 124 different trades and employments, of these over 17,000 served with the RASC. The close rapport, first achieved by the Queen Mary's Auxiliary Army Corps in the First World War with the ASC, continued during the Second World War with the ATS and provided the foundations for the mutual respect and co-operation which exists between the RCT and the Women's Royal Army Corps (WRAC) today.

The primary role of women in a military environment has traditionally been to provide the necessary administrative support to enable men to be released to fight battles. Thus, although in 1945 women were serving in all the overseas theatres of war, the majority were employed in base areas. Those members of the ATS serving with the RASC were in the main employed as drivers, clerks, cooks, orderlies and storewomen, although the complete list includes such diverse trades as carpenter and joiner, coachtrimmer, hairdresser, tinsmith, tailoress and petrol issuer. At the end of the war the ATS was still running its own training centres for drivers and clerks under the sponsorship of the Directorate of Military Training. These drivers were trained on a ten week course which included a thorough grounding in maintenance. Those with a bent for mechanics had special training to enable them to qualify as driver mechanics. After some time in the trade, for those who displayed the necessary qualities, there was the opportunity to qualify as ATS driving instructors. The clerks were trained on an eight week clerical course before being posted to units. By 1947 the ATS drivers and clerks basic training was being run at Horsley Hall, Gresford in North Wales.

The ATS began to run down in June 1945 with the start of demobilization, but a small efficient service remained embodied for full time service until the formation of the WRAC on 1 February 1949, the last members of the ATS being absorbed into the new Corps by the middle of 1951. The advent of the WRAC as a Corps of the Regular Army brought in its wake many changes, not the least of which was the acceptance of the principle of joint training for men and women, a slow process of evolution which continues to the present day. Their role was defined thus 'The Women's Royal Army Corps provides replacements for officers and men in such employments as may be specified by the Army Board from time to

Sgt Nancy Williams ATS Western Command 1945

[By courtesy of The Imperial War Museum]

time'. It was decided that amongst the employments to be filled by members of the WRAC would be those in the driving and clerical trades – both sponsored by the RASC.

The WRAC driver and clerical training establishment moved from Gresford by way of Puddlestone Camp, Winterbourne Dauntsey to become part of 6 Training Battalion RASC at Yeovil in 1954. Despite being part of an RASC regiment complete integration of training was still a long way off. The course syllabi were drawn up jointly by the RASC and WRAC Directorates. WRAC driving instructors continued to be trained and employed until the mid-1960s when civilian driving instructors assumed this role, which coincided with the arrival of the Mini as the driver training vehicle. On the clerical side the tradition of instruction being carried out by WRAC warrant officers and NCOs continued, with some assistance from the men!, until after the RAOC assumed the responsibility for clerical training in 1965. No statistics are held but many marriages resulted from friendships made at Yeovil and the sons and daughters of these marriages are to be found serving amongst the young NCOs and soldiers of the RCT and WRAC today.

The members of the RASC at 6 Training Battalion participated enthusiastically in WRAC Corps Day celebrations (Princess Royal's Day) and greeted Her Royal Highness when she visited the unit in 1962. Her Royal Highness took the salute at a drive-past of vehicles driven by both men and women. In their turn the members of the WRAC paraded with the RASC for their visiting generals and on one occasion in 1963 provided

[By courtesy of MOD OS 14]

WRAC Staff Car Driver

a WRAC Company to march in the RASC Corps Week Church Parade in Aldershot. In 1962 also, the Battalion provided a combined RASC/ WRAC driving display at the Bath and West Show, the outstanding feature of which was a race through obstacles when blindfolded WRAC drivers were talked through the course by their male colleagues. The audience were said to have been astounded to discover that some of the drivers were students in their last week of training. Such was the feeling of togetherness that one WRAC officer in recalling the day that the RASC disbanded and the RCT formed said recently: 'I cried buckets on the day, I can see the flag coming down now. It was the end of an era, I felt I was losing something rather precious that could never be captured again.' All ranks participated in joint celebrations on the rebadging day and the All Ranks Dance remains a vivid memory for all who attended. For the servicewomen though there was little apparent change. The clerks whose training had become an RAOC responsibility remained at Yeovil until the closure in 1969 when they moved to the Duchess of Kent Barracks in Aldershot to live whilst completing their training at the RAOC Trade Training School at Blackdown. They subsequently moved into purpose built accommodation at Blackdown in 1971. In 1969 the RCT amalga-mated 6 and 12 Training Regiments RCT and the Camp at Yeovil was closed. It was the end of an era.

For the next eight years the driver trainees lived in the Duchess of Kent Barracks, Aldershot and were trained by 12 Training Regiment RCT. 'L' plated Minis containing three WRAC privates and their civilian instructors became a familiar sight on the Hampshire roads. The close cooperation between the two Corps continued during this period, the WRAC feeling very much part of 12 Regiment despite living in a WRAC Barracks. In 1977 the wheel turned full circle with the formation of the Army School of Mechanical Transport at Leconfield. The recruits once again live in the unit in which they train and, in common with many of their predecessors in the ATS, train initially on a disused airfield.

What happened to the recruits trained by the RASC and RCT when they passed out from Yeovil, Aldershot, or Leconfield? The clerks were posted to serve with Headquarters and units all over the world from Bangkok to Berlin, Cairo to Kuala Lumpur, Aden, Cyprus, Gibraltar, Bad Oeynhausen, Moenchen Gladbach, the list reflects the military campaigns since 1945 as well as the United Kingdom base organization. Some clerks returned to Yeovil as instructors, some served as clerks in RASC and RCT units and others never visited the scene of their trade training again, but all retain happy memories of those days. It is interesting to note that in 1954 in an article from East African Command in Nairobi, an officer stated that of the thirty six WRAC other ranks on station 'We tend to have a high proportion of NCOs, sometimes filling RASC (clerical) vacancies.' The drivers were posted out to 70 Company RASC at Hounslow, 68 Company RASC in Germany, to serve with the Royal Artillery at Larkhill, the Royal Armoured Corps at Bovington, the Royal Engineers at Chatham and many other units. The jobs they are called upon to do have remained much the same over the years. In 1945 the ATS drove staff cars, ambulances, lorries, jeeps and trucks. In fact, as one contemporary writer said 'everything non-armoured that goes on wheels'. In 1982 the WRAC driver drives staff cars, ambulances, Ford Escorts and Minis, Land Rovers, 4 tonne trucks and coaches.

The advent of the legislation regarding heavy goods vehicle and public service vehicle licences in 1973 affected the role played by the WRAC driver. WRAC drivers were not trained to drive 3 ton trucks to HGV 3 standard as part of their basic course, this skill had to be taught in units and consequently for a time only a few drivers obtained their HGV3 licences and to the chagrin of many they were no longer allowed to drive trucks. This was partially rectified on the move to Aldershot when those trainees who showed promise were given the opportunity to qualify as HGV drivers. During the firemen's strike in 1977/78 selected WRAC HGV drivers in London drove 'Greengoddess' fire engines. Today all drivers trained at Leconfield sit both the normal driving test and the HGV 3 test as part of their training. WRAC drivers wishing to obtain a PSV licence to enable them to drive coaches are given the opportunity to apply for the relevant course. Indeed qualified WRAC drivers regularly drive 55 seater coaches around Berlin. A number of auxiliaries in the ATS were qualified as motor cyclists and with the return of the motor cycle to RCT units at least one WRAC sergeant has recently taken the necessary tests to qualify herself in this skill. It was from 68 Squadron RASC in 1957 that the first female drivers were sent as part of a convoy to SHAPE HQ just outside Paris to drive senior officers and leading scientists observing a NATO exercise. This is thought to have been the first time since the Second World War that women were entrusted with such a task. The decision by the RASC to include WRAC drivers in the convoy was considered to be a great honour by those participating. Today it is accepted as part of a normal day's work for WRAC drivers to drive VIPs on exercises in the field. The RCT squadron commander rarely even pauses to consider the sex of the driver when tasks are detailed.

The ATS driver received training in first aid and of coure always carried her respirator. The WRAC driver is trained, as is the RCT driver, in first aid and nuclear biological and chemical (NBC) drills and in Germany takes part in exercises wearing her NBC kit. An officer who was present on 68 Squadron RCT's first mixed training exercise in NBC kit in 1971 recalls having to put two drivers in each cab as a single girl wearing a respirator could not see to reverse her vehicle. The same officer remembers vividly being driven by a girl whose hands kept slipping on the steering wheel because she could not grip it properly whilst wearing NBC gloves. Skills and kit have thankfully improved since then. The WRAC ambulance drivers have over the years carried out their duties efficiently and with the minimum of fuss despite often very difficult conditions. WRAC ambulance drivers assisted in the evacuation of the wounded to hospital following the bombing by the IRA of the Parachute Regiment Officers Mess in Aldershot, and their quiet competence and unflappability was commented on by those who witnessed their actions.

The formation of the WRAC was complemented by the raising of WRAC (TA) units and the incorporation of members of the Corps into mixed TA units. Each WRAC (TA) battalion (there were three in Scotland alone) had a driver company. The WRAC were assisted in the training of their drivers by the RASC and there are many recorded tributes to the help given. In 1951, 315 (Scottish Command) Battalion WRAC (TA) noted that they had been given every help and assistance by 52 (Lowland) Divisional Transport Column with their driver training. B Company, 328 (Ulster) Battalion received assistance with their driver training from 26 Company RASC. This help was not restricted to purely WRAC (TA) units for in the same year 916 (Mixed) Anti-Aircraft Company RASC recorded that at their annual camp at Braunton, Devon, their WRAC drivers all made good progress in their training and took part in combined exercises, night convoys and map reading exercises. In 1952, 4 Anti-Aircraft Group Column RASC wrote of their WRAC drivers 'Our main purpose is to train drivers for ambulances and staff cars and many of our women have now changed their civilian employment so that they can drive all day'.

It was in 1952 also that the first of the exercises which were to become an annual event in the South West for the WRAC (TA) drivers

WRAC Officer of the RCT in NBC clothing

[By courtesy of 2 Lt Cecilia Davies MA WRAC]

was held. The weekend exercise was hosted by 15 Driver Training Battalion RASC and run by 311 (Southern Command) Battalion WRAC (TA) who were thankful for the 'thoughtfulness of our hosts in making up our beds for us'. By 1955 all arrangements for the competition, by now called the South West District (TA) Driving Competition were being made by 15 Battalion. In 1959 the exercise was redesignated Exercise Night Owl and in that year no fewer than twenty seven teams of WRAC (TA) participated. Indeed it is doubtful whether the WRAC (TA) drivers in the South West would have been as well recruited and trained but for the willing help given to them by 15 Battalion, of whom 2 Dorset Transport Platoon WRAC (TA) said 'No WRAC (TA) unit could receive greater co-operation and support'. This co-operation was not confined to the South West, which area has been quoted as an example of the cordial relationship which existed between the two Corps. To balance the picture one last story from the North. In 1960, 318 (Cumberland and Westmorland) Independent Company WRAC (TA), a newly formed unit, had six trained drivers on strength. This number was increased to twenty-two within a year thanks to the 'expert tuition received from members of 502 Company RASC (TA)'.

1967 saw the demise of the TA and the formation of the T & AVR. Sadly all WRAC units were disbanded and none of the initial posts given to the WRAC in the T & AVR were with RCT units. At the time of writing there are once again members of the WRAC serving with RCT (TA). The numbers are small and none of the servicewomen on the strength of independent TA units are employed as drivers. They are all enlisted for pay and clerical duties. Two of the officers do though fill troop commanders posts. The major role for WRAC (TA) employed with the RCT (TA) is with sponsored units and their role is covered elsewhere in this book.

What of the future? In 1977 a Working Party studying the future employment of the WRAC reported to the Army Board and as a result several changes affecting the employment of WRAC with the RCT, amongst other Arms and Corps, were implemented. To enable these to take place the role of the Corps was re-defined as 'The WRAC is to be organized and trained as an integral part of the Army, to carry out those tasks for which its members are best suited and qualified so that it will contribute to the maximum efficiency of the Army as a whole'. The RCT offered to open up the employment category of clerk RCT to women, an offer which was quickly accepted by the WRAC – after all, clerk TMT and RASC (MT) had been an ATS trade. It was proposed that these young women after training by the RCT and a spell working as RCT clerks should be considered for employment as movement controllers. Although happy to accept members of the WRAC as clerks the idea of their becoming movement controllers was resisted by some members of the RCT on the ground. How they asked could a WRAC corporal possibly operate on the quayside in Antwerp or on a railway siding in the middle of Germany in all weathers and at all hours with no other female for miles and minimal supervision? The answer was, of course, that the right type of servicewoman can and does. Those members of the ATS who turned their hands to whatever was asked of them in 1940 and the men of the RASC with whom they then worked could have enlightened today's young men had they been consulted! Although the number of WRAC movement controllers is small, they proved their worth at Marchwood during the recent Falklands conflict, by, in the best traditions of their Corps, carrying out their duties alongside the men in supervising the smooth outloading of shipping. The clerks RCT and movement controllers remain members of the WRAC but their postings and promotions are the responsibility of the RCT Manning and Record Office.

Whilst the decision to employ WRAC in RCT trades was being taken, the RCT passed a critical eye over its officer establishment and identified a number of posts which could be filled by suitably trained officers of either sex. These posts ranged from those requiring second lieutenants to those filled by lieutenant colonels. It was accepted that the RCT could employ a small number of female officers within its ranks. These officers remain 'cap badged' WRAC and wear WRAC uniform but undertake jobs previously only carried out by RCT officers. They attend the RCT young officers course before being posted to RCT units in subaltern's posts. One of the first of the officers accepted for permanent employment with the RCT applied to do so after a tour as the Assistant Adjutant of the Logistic Support Battalion AMF (L) which is commanded by an RCT officer. She then held a troop commander's post in 62 Transport and Movement Squadron RCT in Berlin and is currently a captain with 17 Port Regiment RCT at Marchwood. Since transferring to the WRAC/RCT she has completed both the Troop Commanders and RCT Captains Courses as well as a Junior Officers Port Operating Course.

The future looks good and those auxiliaries who went to war with the ATS in 1939 have every right to feel proud that the traditions of service that they helped to form are still being carried on by the young officers and servicewomen of today. Those members of the WRAC serving with the RCT do live up to their Corps motto:

'Suaviter in Modo, Fortiter in Re'
(Gentle in Manner, Resolute in Deed).

31 · MOVEMENTS

INTRODUCTION

The Royal Corps of Transport assumed responsibility for Movements from the Royal Engineers on its formation under the McLeod reorganization in 1965. The Movements organization was a going concern with a high reputation for efficiency. At that time, with all the other problems involved in the launching of a new Corps, Movements was left to continue more or less as before and, although organizational changes were made in conformity with the RCT regimental system, it tended initially to be treated virtually as a separate and specialist activity. Some two hundred Royal Engineer officers had transferred to the RCT and many were Transportation trained, or were specialists in port operations or movements. Rather fewer had railway experience. In the case of the Royal Engineers soldiers who transferred, some, especially the senior NCOs were skilled in railway or port operation, and provided a sound nucleus of experience and knowledge in these fields, but the majority were Movement specialists, vital to the day-to-day movement of the Army.

The Army Movements task includes the Q(Movements) staff functions and executive Movement Control responsibilities other than unit operational movement in the combat zone. The Movements organization carrying out these functions is referred to as the 'user'. The 'user' is responsible for co-ordinating the available movement resources, be it road, rail, sea, inland waterways or air, into a co-ordinated plan which achieves the optimum usage of these resources in carrying out the operational requirement in the shortest possible time. The agencies responsible for the technical efficiency and physical operation of these resources is referred to as the 'operator'. Naturally the success of any movement plan, large or small, depends upon the maximum consultation, co-ordination and co-operation between the 'user' and the 'operator'.

The main principles of Movements agreed by America, Britain, Canada and Australia (ABCA) were:

    a. Centralized control to the highest level at which it can be effectively exercised.
    b. Movements will be regulated.
    c. Movements will be fluid and flexible.
    d. Maximum utilization will be made of carrying facilities.

Thus the focal point of control of world-wide movement rests in the Ministry of Defence where each Service has its own Director of Movements.

ORGANIZATION

At the formation of the RCT, and up to 8 May 1978, the Army Movements staff was headed by a Major-General, Director of Movements (Army) at the War Office, later Ministry of Defence. The Deputy Director post of Brigadier was abolished in 1966. Until 8 May 1978, the Director reported to the Quartermaster-General direct but, since then, and in the new rank of Brigadier, his staff have formed part of DGTM's Logistic Executive (Army) staff and the reporting chain was changed accordingly. In 1971, the Director of Movements assumed full responsibility for Movements finance.

By 1980 the principal changes to this establishment were:

a. In Q(Mov)1, 1a and 1c Sections combined to form a new 1a Section, and
b. The Colonel Q(Mov)2 appointment had been removed and the branch was then headed by an AQMG.

It was during the early '70s that two important developments occurred. The Director of Movements took over from the Deputy Quartermaster-General responsibility for transport policy, and he also became responsible for the control of Movements finance which, by 1973, was in the region of £31M annually. These historic changes simplified the channels of responsibility for transport in that the Transport Officer in Chief became responsible to only one staff Director for both transport and movements; and the responsibility for Movements finance speeded up decision making within the Ministry of Defence and in Directorate of Movements itself.

The organization in the Ministry is, with the exception of finance, generally reflected in the various Chief Transport and Movements Officers (CTMO) and other subordinate commands in headquarters at home and overseas. As far as possible, responsibility has been delegated from the Ministry of Defence to lower formation headquarters and, up to 1977, in the case of freight, to the Army Freight Organization. Movements is inevitably a Joint Service matter and particularly in the Ministry of Defence.

The various staffs and committees were formed from members of the single service Directorates, together with representatives, as required, from other Departments and Agencies. The senior committee was and still is the Defence Movements Coordinating Committee of which the Director of Movements (Army) is the permanent Chairman.

Returning to 1965, Q(Movements) staff were located at all command and general headquarters, both at home and overseas. The Movement Control Service was based on these headquarters and capable of deploying and operating whenever and wherever a Movements requirement existed. Planning was based on Movement Control Units (now Royal Corps of Transport) being located at places where control could be best effected. These included ports and beaches, railway stations and marshalling yards, airfields, road and inland water transport regulating points, base depots and service installations. An example of the organisation in overseas Commands was that of Far East Land Forces. At the time of McLeod in 1965, the Movements organization was already well established and providing the support needed for the Borneo operations.

The Army Movements staff in the Far East was organized on a system comparable generally throughout overseas commands before the McLeod organization.

The joint services nature of movement was also clearly illustrated. At Headquarters Far East Command, there was a Joint Movements Coordinating Committee composed of senior Movements staff, officers of the Royal Navy, Army and Royal Air Force and the Divisional Sea Transport Officer, Far East. The Committee was not in permanent session and met as and when required. It was responsible to the Commander in Chief and was chaired by the Senior Movements Staff Officer.

HISTORICAL SURVEY

As with many departments in the Ministry of Defence, although progress is continuous, much planning is long term and the time scale, particularly for the introduction of new equipment or methods is measured in years rather than days or months. Financial limitations as always are a major factor particularly in non-operational situations. So it is with Movements.

Fortunately though, Movements is also very much a day-to-day business dealing with operational or routine movement of personnel or freight and has an immediate impact on the user of the many resources involved.

For this reason, this historical survey is linked to the tours of the Directors of Movements at MOD, to highlight the operational, routine and progressive action over which they exercised influence whilst in office.

It was Major General P G Turpin, CB, OBE, who had assumed his appointment in 1963, who was responsible as Director of Movements (Army) for seeing our Corps accept its Movements task in 1965.

As the first RASC officer to be Director of Movements, and having previously been Director of Supplies and Transport, when the McLeod reorganization was being considered, he was ideally placed for guiding the reorganization as it affected Movements. Most of his officers in the Directorate at that time were ex-Royal Engineers. A few officers were from other Arms, as indeed there were in other movement appointments away from Whitehall.

The training of officers and soldiers for Movements work within the newly formed Corps did not proceed with very great speed, due in large measure to the availability of well trained ex-Royal Engineers, who had been absorbed very smoothly into the new Corps.

There were however, at this time numerous discussions between the Transport Officer in Chief and the Director of Movements on all aspects of officer and soldier training, within the Royal Corps of Transport, and the basis for training in Movement techniques in the new Corps was formulated.

During General Turpin's tour of office, regular air trooping between India, Hong Kong and Singapore was developed for Gurkha movement. This provided a significant step forward from the old sea route to and from Calcutta. It was to be some time though before the airlink to Nepal could be established, avoiding the need to transit Gurkhas and their families at Barrackpore, Calcutta and the long and tedious journey by surface to Nepal.

With the introduction of air trooping from the UK the last of the troopships, the *Nevasa* and *Oxfordshire*, serving the Far East had been taken out of service.

The considerable shipping responsibilities of Movements did not however diminish with the removal of the troopship element. During the same period as the *Nevasa* and *Oxfordshire* were being withdrawn, entirely new vessels were coming into service to replace the Landing Ships Tank (LST) for use by the Army. By 1967, six Landing Ships Logistic (LSL) were in service. These remarkable vessels of some 5,000 tons gross are capable of carrying a squadron of tanks or equivalent 'B' vehicles, and for short sea voyages, up to a battalion of infantry with all their equipment. The operational tasking of these vessels was vested in Director of Movements (Army) through Q (Mov) 1, and until March 1970 these vessels were operated by the British India Steam Navigation Company, using British Officers and Asian crews. The Board of Trade, Sea Transport Branch was responsible for operating the contract.

From the moment of their coming into service these vessels proved their value. At an early stage, the *Sir Lancelot*, the first of line, which came into service in 1963, was used as a substitute for the air lift of Gurkhas to Hong Kong, when a shortage of fuel restricted the air lift. Since that time, their use has covered a wide range of both operational and maintenance tasks worldwide.

It was also during General Turpin's tour of office that the important agreement in principle was reached on the replacement for the Landing Craft Tank (LCT), but it was some years later after much discussion that the new Landing Craft Logistic (LCLs) were approved and brought into service.

In October 1966, Major-General P G Turpin CB OBE handed over to Major-General Sir John Potter KBE CB who had been the first Transport Officer in Chief (Army) on the formation of the Royal Corps of Transport.

The most significant operational movement task in General Potter's time was the withdrawal from Aden. This presented certain unique problems. Not only was there prevarication over the timings for the start and completion of the evacuation, but the Movements staff had to contend with the banning of overflying of the Sudan and Saudi Arabia. This resulted in greatly increased distances to be flown with consequent reductions in payload. It is recalled that flights to and from the United Kingdom via Teheran resulted in aircraft on occasion losing touch with various navigational aids. Another major factor was the closure of the Suez Canal in 1967 when some of the ships with stores homeward bound from the Far East were trapped in the southern end of the Canal and stayed trapped until the Canal was reopened eight years later in 1975. The cargo of some of the ships included ammunition. The Blue Funnel *Agapenar* proved to be a major hazard as she was carrying Sea Cat Missiles which after a period of one year were declared sensitive by a UK Surveyor. After diplomatic exchanges, they were discharged and destroyed. With the closure of the Canal and the subsequent long sea route around the Cape, there were very many fewer ships in the Aden/Gulf area available to assist with the sea lift out of Aden. Major General Sir John Potter remembers an event which was never publicized, and that was the assistance which a couple of Russian ships gave to the British Forces at that time!

It was during 1967 that several studies were started on the advantages and disadvantages of switching from the traditional cargo arrangements for the carriage of military stores, to movement by ISO container, especially to and from the Continent. The fairly substantial savings to be achieved in the fields of cost and handling time soon became apparent but there was conservative response within the Ministry of Defence at that time, due to concern at making such a major change of policy. However, ultimately as a result of a major presentation to senior military and civilian staff at the Ministry of Defence early in 1969 a start was made in the use of ISO containers for freight movement.

Over the following few years under the direction of succeeding Directors of Movement, there was to be a dramatic increase in containerization for the carriage of freight worldwide. In 1969 a start was made on the movement of stores direct from Base Ordnance Depots in UK to depots in BAOR, using the services of the Government Freight Agent and civilian road and shipping agencies. This cut the time of movement and reduced losses considerably. The speed of this movement was such that quite early in the development of the use of ISO containers for the movement of all stores (less ammunition), a daily container service for Red Star high priority items was introduced. Stores were collected at one selected depot in UK and sent direct to the required depot in BAOR.

At this time also it was agreed that when the current MFO (unaccompanied baggage of individual servicemen and their dependants) air contract to BAOR ended, this would be replaced by containerized movement. The Royal Navy took responsibility for movement of MFO baggage using their depot at Deptford, which at that time had spare capacity.

In 1970 the direct movement of unit stores and MFO for unit moves between UK and BAOR was containerized. Containers were provided at barracks in UK or BAOR, and with Movements assistance, containers were loaded by units. Customs examination was provided at destination barracks and the whole process of the move of unit stores and MFO was made speedier and more secure. Developments since that time have allowed movement by containers worldwide.

Major General Sir John Potter was relieved on 20 October 1968 by Major General J R Reynolds CB OBE ERD. One of the major achievements during his tenure of office was effectively making Ministry staffs aware of the practical movement problem inherent in the BAOR reinforcement plan and associated mobilization plans. Until 1969, little regard had been placed on the timescale and the movement resources available and a very detailed Joint Service Movements study was necessary to bring out the shortcomings and the risks involved. The lesson learnt was the need for the Joint Movement planners to work directly and closely with MOD Central and General Staffs, a lesson which has been of benefit on many occasions throughout the remaining period of this history.

During the period that Major General Reynolds was Director and Chairman of the Defence Movements Coordinating Committee, a significant paper to the Principal Administrative Officers (PAOs) was prepared on the feasibility of establishing a Joint Movements staff under the Chief of Personnel and Logistics. It failed, but only after a great deal of discussion and study, and the Joint Committee continued in being as the means of achieving movements coordination between the Services.

At this time also an important change in the operating of the six LSLs took place. In March 1970 responsibility for both crewing and operation passed from British India Steam Navigation and the Board of Trade, to the Navy Department, and the vessels became part of the Royal Fleet Auxiliary. A long link with British India Steam Navigation, which started with troopships was then broken, but some of the ships officers transferred to the Royal Fleet Auxiliary, and the very close ties which the Army users had with the officers and crew were maintained. Responsibility for tasking the LSLs continued to rest with Director of Movements (Army).

On 5 March 1971, Major General W Bate CB OBE DL became Director, having previously served in the Ministry as Director of Administrative Planning (Army) and Chairman of the Defence Administrative Planning Staff.

During his tour, there was a reduction in the British Army's overseas commitments which was accompanied by a series of emergencies in various parts of the world. This inevitably involved a good deal of contingency Movement planning and execution. Typical examples of these operations include the run-down of Malta and Singapore, emergencies in Anguilla and Belize, famine in Nepal and the setting-up of the training area in Suffield, Canada. It was also during this period that the first major reinforcement of Northern Ireland in the continuing emergency there was carried out. This was code named Operation Motorman and involved a complicated movement operation which was executed efficiently and at short notice. These events brought into focus, once again, the close links which must be established and maintained between the operational and planning staffs and the Movements staffs. In the Ministry of Defence, improved machinery for consultation, planning and for the conduct of operations was firmly established and the Director of Movements, for the first time, became a member of the Defence Operations Executive. The division of responsibilities between MOD and UKLF were also established and operating procedures evolved. These developments were extended into the area of mobilization and reinforcement for operations in Europe which were beginning to emerge as our Priority 1 defence commitment for the future.

Movement planning for the reinforcement and maintenance of BAOR took on a new look. Movement agencies were becoming more varied and sophisticated and NATO infra-structure projects for 'roll-on' – 'roll-off' capabilities and similar developments in continental ports were initiated. The development of these plans and resources began to minimize the restrictions hitherto imposed by the Channel barrier between the UK and the Continent. Thus the concept of 'One Base' became the basis on which logistic support to our forces on the Continent would be developed.

For the 'One Base' concept to be successful, there was a need for essential movement resources such as shipping, containers and above all, a sizeable UK port to be entirely under military control. This led to the retention of the six LSLs (*Sir Percivale, Bedivere, Galahad, Geraint, Lancelot* and *Tristam*) which would otherwise have been under serious threat as our worldwide commitments declined. For example, the requirement for three LSLs operating in the Far East as late as 1969 was reduced to one LSL on a periodic basis thereafter.

The refitting of the *Empire Gull*, the last LST in service with the Royal Fleet Auxiliary and which was finally decommissioned in 1978 was dedicated to cross-Channel movement. The decision was taken to build two new LCLs, the *Arakan* and *Ardennes*, after a determined effort to justify the requirement based largely on the need to maintain the missile ranges in the Hebrides. Agreement was also obtained to extend and modernize the military port of Marchwood, helped to some extent by prevalent strikes in civilian ports which demonstrated the vulnerability of our Lines of Communication (L of C) if we were ever entirely to rely on civilian resources.

Containerization was continuing to develop in the Movements

world and after suitable trials, agreement was obtained to purchase a number of MOD containers and tractors and trailers to be operated entirely under military control. All these developments have made considerable progress over the past decade and will continue to do so, so far as financial resources permit.

During the period the air L of C for the Gurkhas, started in 1966, was extended to include links between Brunei and Hong Kong and between Hong Kong and Nepal. This is a story in itself. Previously, the Gurkhas and their families were moved from and to Nepal by surface means having been flown to Calcutta. The journey involved a long stay in a very austere transit centre in Barrackpore, near Calcutta, followed by movement over a long, tenuous and very crowded railway through Eastern India to the borders of Nepal. The overall transit time could last for several weeks and, taking into account the administrative backing needed to support this system, it was expensive in money and manpower. Clearly, the most sensible arrangement would be movement by air direct from Hong Kong and Brunei through to Katmandu; and air movement within Nepal to the two Gurkha depots in Dharan and Pucklihawa. This concept involved many complications. The most important were – political agreement to the RAF overflying India and landing in Katmandu; the use and reliability of the very limited number of Nepalese aircraft within Nepal; the establishment of suitable transit arrangements in Katmandu; reactions to the impact on the Indian economy; and the closing of, and the disposal of equipment from the Barrackpore Transit Camp. Eventually, agreement was reached on all these issues and the air L of C was firmly established, much to the benefit of the hitherto long-suffering Gurkhas and their families.

In the UK, various improvements were achieved in the movement organization including the reorganization of the Army Freight Organization which controlled the overall movement of army stores, the introduction of the Priority Freight System on 1st April 1973 for the movement of urgent stores by road between UK depots and distribution points and developments in the system and organization for the movement of personnel by air.

The organization in the MOD Movements Directorate saw only minor changes, but a very important development, as mentioned earlier, was that the Director became responsible for the Army Movement vote which meant that his finance branch answered to him and he, in turn, answered to the Permanent Under Secretary (PUS) (Army). This oiled the machinery and serious difficulties over financial problems were virtually eliminated.

The Joint Services nature of movement has already been stressed and no history of Movements would be complete without some coverage of Joint Service cooperation. During this particular period, RAF aircraft became the dominant agency for personnel movement, although char-

*Air Transport Liaison Officer
(ATLO) Lyneham – Maj A
Rowley RCT*

[By courtesy of Central Office of Information]

tered aircraft were used, in the main, between the UK and BAOR. It was perhaps understandable that the RAF Movements considered themselves responsible for the planning and control of air movement; on the other hand, about 85% of the movement of personnel by air was generated by the Army. This conflict of interests sometimes led to difficulties over matters such as the chairmanship of the DMCC, the use of departure and arrival airfields preferred by the Army and the composition and command of air movement staffs at RAF and civilian airfields. Nevertheless, air movements is essentially a Joint Service matter and these demarcation disputes did not seriously damage the overall effort, especially as liaison and cooperation between the Army and Air Movement executive staffs were excellent.

However, one disappointment was a failure to integrate or rationalize the more common services such as the RAF's Early Bird system for priority stores with the Army's Priority Freight system. Conversely, an example of totally successful tri-service coordination at this time was the re-supply by sea of maintenance stores, equipment and vehicles to the RAF airfields at Salalah and Masirah in the Gulf. This was achieved by the use of two civilian ships on hire to the Royal Navy, the *Hebe* and the *Baccus*, and tasked by the Army through their chairmanship of the Defence Freight Movement Sub-Committee.

Major General V H J Carpenter CB MBE who had been Transport Officer in Chief, assumed the Directorship on 1st October 1973. During his tenure of appointment, we saw Turkish forces invading Cyprus. The British reinforcement of Cyprus was one of the biggest for a considerable period. As a joint operation, it was most successful and it was probably the first operation where the Chairman of the Defence Movements Coordinating Committee attended the Chiefs of Staff meetings as a standard procedure.

During this period, there was continuing interest by Army Districts in the United Kingdom to achieve preferred airfields for the movement of troops to and from Germany. This problem is of continuing interest; the Royal Air Force know the Army preferences and do try to assist wherever this is possible. However, the occasional disappointments do cause concern within Districts and difficulty is experienced in understanding the RAF's known main base operating principle.

It would be apt at this time to mention increased movement to and from Northern Ireland from both Germany and the United Kingdom. The various uses of shipping, particularly LSL and LCT to meet specific reinforcement situations were unsung at the time but, nevertheless, well executed operations were models of their kind. From 1969, routine and operational movement between Northern Ireland (NI) and the mainland settled into a pattern where units from the mainland moved by surface routes accompanied by their vehicles either by LSL or civil ferry and BAOR units flew direct on RAF aircraft under Operation Banner and drew their vehicles from a pool retained in NI. Later, MOD sponsored

Movement controllers at Dusseldorf airport. – Capt Brett and Sgt Horton.

[By courtesy of Central Office of Information]

personnel moving between NI and the mainland had the option of travelling on the BA Belfast/Heathrow Shuttle and this concession was eventually extended to include unit moves to and from their permanent locations.

In support, the RAF have been operating R & R flights since 1973, mainly through RAF Gutersloh, with 1 to 2 flights each way, every week.

The intensity of movement operations between NI and BAOR fluctuated to meet the ever changing force levels from the 1972 high of 21,776 regular soldiers to a 1980 level of 12,484 with some 50% being roulement units who change over every four months.

Major General V H J Carpenter recalls that, during his period in office, the position of the Director of Movements (Army) at Major-General level was a much discussed subject. Fortunately, at that time, such events as the reinforcement of Cyprus helped to convince all concerned that there was merit in keeping the appointment at this level. He remembers how advantageous it was in his dealings with other senior Army Staff Officers. It was whilst he was Director of Movements that the trade of Traffic Operator started to prove its effectiveness. This is probably the most significant addition to the range of Corps trades which we have made since 1965.

It was in December 1975 that Major General F J Plaskett CB MBE became Director and he held the appointment for 2½ years before passing the specific responsibilities to Brigadier N I B Speller MBE. Major General Plaskett then became the Director General of Transport and Movements and thus retained overall responsibility for the tasks of the Director of Movements (Army) on the establishment of the Logistic Executive (Army). Thus for the first time, there was a single Director responsible for both Movements and Transport.

From 1975 to 1980, a number of policies came to fruition, and together with the special operations which occurred made this another interesting movements period.

The development of the 'One Base' concept for the resupply of BAOR was based to a great extent on direct resupply from UK depots and establishments. Before 1978, the container distribution system was largely dependent on commercial movement facilities which, from time to time, were disrupted by industrial disputes. It was decided, therefore, that, in order to safeguard the logistic supply of BAOR, a dedicated military container distribution system should be introduced to complement the commercial service. This system has now the capacity to move 200 containers per month between UK and BAOR in each direction, including the ability to roadhaul the containers on trailers within UK and BAOR.

In June 1978, a regular pattern of LSL sailings was established with departures from Marchwood and Antwerp every four days. In addition to containers, the LSLs are able to carry heavy A, B and C vehicles in the tank deck and lighter vehicles on the vehicle deck. Space is regularly allotted to the other two Services. Whilst this is basically a RO/RO service, a number of containers can be carried on the vehicle deck within reach of ship's gear for discharge overside in military or commercial road transport.

MFO UNACCOMPANIED BAGGAGE

A new system of moving unaccompanied baggage of individual Servicemen and their dependants was introduced in 1979 under which the Government Freight Agent (Hogg Robinson (GFA) Ltd.) took over from the Royal Navy as the MOD's agent for the movement of baggage:

    a. Within UK (when associated with movement to and from overseas).
    b. Between UK and NW Europe.
    c. From UK and NW Europe to all overseas destinations within NW Europe.
    d. Elsewhere the Service Movements Staff continue to be responsible for movement from and within their theatres.

Between the UK and NW Europe baggage is moved in special vehicles on a through running basis, usually within a transit time of 14 days. In addition to the normal service, those personnel moving direct from one residence to another take advantage of a 'Removal' type service operating from door to door.

For movement between other theatres, the GFA or overseas Movement staff arrange shipment by commercial vessel, using container services whenever possibe. In the case of certain 'Remote and inaccessible areas' baggage is moved by air.

RESERVE ARMY

Hard on the heels of the major logistic reorganization which transferred movements functions from the Corps of Royal Engineers to the newly formed Royal Corps of Transport in 1965 – the reserve soldiers thus affected were subject to a further organizational upheaval in the following year when the Army Emergency Reserve became the sponsored sector of the TAVR.

The units concerned comprised four under-recruited Movement Control Regiments, one independent Movement Control Squadron and two associated staff increments, all of which could trace their origins to the Longmoor based Movement Control Groups of the 1949 Supplementary Reserve.

The significance of the role which these RE badged units were cast, in the two decades prior to 1965, was to be widened by the contributions that they were to make in the subsequent two decades – not only to the smooth transition and welding of movements within their new Corps home, but also to the Army's logistic capability in its NATO role.

From 1966 to 1979, the movements element of the Reserve Army comprised two sponsored TAVR MC Regiments (162 with BAOR role and 163, including a WRAC element, with UK role) plus an independent squadron (280) and two special MC liaison units – all administered by the Central Volunteer Headquarters at Bedford (formerly HQ AER RASC) and from 1976 – Grantham.

Whilst the inexorable Army system of career development strictly limited the periods in office of all regular appointment holders in Movements – this did not apply to the Reserve movers – many of whose service records showed continuous annual training in movements units over periods of ten to twenty years. As late as 1970, at least one commanding officer in these units had continuous service since holding a Q(Mov) staff appointment in the 39–45 War.

The continuity of involvement in annual training exercises in UK and on the Continent created standards of professionalism that were recognized by the staffs of all the British and host nation Services with which contact was made.

Mastery of their craft – movements – overlaid with the effects of positive leadership in the regimental context, combined to produce an elan readily recognizable, infectious, and always contributing beneficially to whichever form of military environment applied – Corps affairs, TAVR functions, NATO occasions and the myriads of personal contacts and friendships between individual volunteer movers at all rank levels and their counterparts in both the regular and part-time sectors of our own and allied forces.

RHODESIA – ZIMBABWE

In December 1979, in Operation Agila, a Commonwealth Liaison and Monitoring Organization was deployed to Rhodesia following the ceasefire agreement which ended the civil war. The majority of the force, comprising approximately 1,000 men, 300 vehicles and trailers and 400,000 lbs of freight was processed through South Cerney and the Air Transport Liaison (ATL) detachments at RAF Lyneham and RAF Brize Norton. The USAF provided two C5A sorties which enabled the deployment of helicopters with minimal breaking down. At Salisbury, Rhodesia a Joint Movements Staff was established in which the Army representative was also the Force Transport and Movements Officer. Movements responsibilities included UK-Rhodesia air movement, surface and air internal movement for both personnel and supplies. When the Monitoring Organization was withdrawn in March 1980, all personnel, helicopters and essential freight were returned to UK by air; the balance of non-essential freight and vehicles were returned by rail and sea in containers.

NEW HEBRIDES – VANUATA

Following a revolt in the island of Espiritu Santu in the New Hebrides (now Vanuata) group of islands, in June 1980, elements of the Spearhead

[By courtesy of Maj M B Brett]

RCT Movements staff on exercise in Vanuata – Capt Brett, Sgt Solaini and LCpl Mitchell.

battalion group, together with 80,000 lbs of freight and 25 vehicles and trailers, were deployed to the New Hebrides by air from England in Operation Titan. The Force Movements Officer, was provided by 29 Transport and Movements Regiment RCT and he was supported by an ATL detachment of four. The force was withdrawn mainly by air in August 1980 but, again, use was made of containers by sea for low priority freight with considerable savings in aircraft hours and money.

Both Operations Agila and Titan proved the value of retaining the AMC facility of South Cerney.

EXERCISE CRUSADER 80

In September 1980, Exercise Crusader 80 was held. It was designed to practise mobilization, UK home defence and reinforcement of the British Forces in Germany linked to field training. A total of some 32,000 troops, nearly 9,000 vehicles and trailers were deployed and it was the biggest movement of British troops on one occasion since the end of the Second World War. Some 16,100 men and women, including 7,300 Territorial Army troops, moved by sea, and some 15,900, including 12,200 Territorial Army troops, by air. The Movement Control Organization was reinforced by some extra 500 men and women and three sea transit centres were utilized for the sea movement. Air movement took place through 10 British airports, flying into four Continental airports.

OPERATION CORPORATE 1982 – THE FALKLAND ISLANDS OPERATION

The activation and training of Movements Staffs for Crusader 80 – the major movements exercise for the reinforcement of BAOR held in 1980, undoubtedly helped in the mounting and support of the Task Force in the South Atlantic in what has been described as one of the largest and possibly the most complex military operation since World War II. Movements problems of enormous proportions had to be resolved using lines of communication stretching 8,000 miles from the UK base. There was no contingency plan to retake the Falkland Islands and a Priority 2 operation of this magnitude had never been envisaged.

On 19th March 1982 in what in retrospect was an act of provocation, a small party of Argentine scrap metal merchants landed and remained illegally at Leith on South Georgia to dismantle stores from an old whaling station. Events during the next two weeks culminating in the fall of the Falkland Islands on 2nd April and the invasion of South Georgia on 3rd April are well recorded and will not be repeated here.

Not so well known are the difficulties of reinforcing the Falkland Islands' Garrison prior to the invasion. Reinforcement at short notice by air was not possible because of the limitations of Port Stanley airfield and the distances involved. Reinforcement by sea would have had to be carried out well in advance, as the Falkland Islands are some 21 days sailing from the United Kingdom at 15 knots.

In the event, local sea and air superiority gave Argentina complete freedom of action and, in the immediate weeks after capturing the Falkland Islands, the Argentinian ruling Junta rapidly reinforced the Garrison to a strength of approximately 12,000 personnel. United Kingdom reaction was swift and decisive. On 5 April, within three days of the fall of the Falkland Islands, a Naval Task Force with 3 Commando Brigade embarked and sailed from the UK. Meanwhile, Ascension Island was being developed as a forward support base, using Wideawake Airfield to extend the limited facilities that already existed on the Island.

Just prior to Operation Corporate the Ministry of Defence Joint Services Movements Staff in support of operations had been reshaped with special emphasis on the Defence Operations Movements Staff (DOMS). In essence the Directors of Movements Army and RAF became Co-Directors of DOMS and had a seat in the Chiefs of Staff (COS) Committee. This matched the seat the Chairman Defence Movements Coordinating Committee (DMCC) has in a non-operational situation. The new Co-Directors of DOMS replaced the previous Co-Directors of DOMS at Colonel and Group Captain level who now became Deputy Co-Directors. During the mounting of the operation, Brigadier R E L Jenkins CBE the Director of Movements (Army) sat in the Army Co-Director DOMS seat.

Below the Chiefs of Staff, the operations of the three Services are coordinated by the Defence Operations Executive (DOE). This Committee is chaired by the Vice Chief of the Defence Staff (Personnel and Logistics). The members are the 2 Star officers responsible for operations in each Service, together with a number of ex-officio members. The Defence Operations Executive looks after the implementation of contingency plans, Joint Theatre Plans and other operational related questions and has direct contact with the Transition to War Committee.

Finally in the crisis management chain is the Defence Situation Centre (DSC) and when fully operating it houses the Central Defence Staffs and in separate but adjoining rooms, the operations staff of the Navy, Army and Air Force. So, although the staff of the three Services are not integrated, they are collocated and can easily keep in touch with one another under the coordination of a Controller provided by the Central Staff.

In order to carry out its wide ranging role, the Defence Situation Centre is supported by other staffs including DOMS which is an integral part of the Defence Situation Centre and therefore at the centre of all operational planning.

The staff of Defence Operation Movements Staff (DOMS) is split into three shifts and each shift has a Joint Movements Section, an Air Resources Section and a Sea Resources Section. The main task of DOMS was to plan operational movement by deciding detailed priorities of movement within the framework of the Defence Operations Executive (DOE) requirement and then allocating, coordinating and tasking to best effect the available service and civil movement resources. It advised the COS and the Defence Operations Executive on all operational movement matters and monitored the broad progress of all the major movement plans.

The first indication of a need or intention to deploy forces to meet the perceived threat in the Falklands only became aparent to the Movements staff on 1 April 1982. During that day, two meetings of the Defence Operations Executive (DOE) were called but even then the emphasis appeared to lie on the suitability of Port Stanley airfield to accept C130 (Hercules) aircraft. It was not until the night of 1/2 April that firm warnings were issued and plans for an amphibious operation were conceived. It was also at this stage that the Defence Situation Centre (DSC) and Defence Operations Movements Staff (DOMS) were activated.

On 2 April (the day of the invasion) a hastily convened session of the Naval Staff Advisory Group (NSAG) sat to consider the options open for the deployment of a naval task force including 3 Commando Brigade. Q(Mov)1 had already been tasked to advise on availability of the LSL fleet and in those first few hours it was clear that four of the six LSLs could be made available at short notice. *Sir Galahad* was due back from an RM exercise in Norway on 4 April. *Sir Geraint* was at Devonport preparing for refit. *Lancelot* and *Percivale* were in or due in home waters by 3 April from routine BAOR maintenance tasks. These vessels eventually sailed with the leading element of the Task Force. LSL *Sir Tristram*, then off Belize and *Sir Bedivere* returning from Vancouver were to join the force later.

At that early meeting, it was appreciated that a major airlift would be impracticable. The problem then thrust at the naval and defence movements staffs was that of finding suitable Ships to be Taken Up From Trade (STUFT) to fill the gap between RN amphibious force vessels and the size of the force to be deployed. Bearing in mind that the line of communication stretched 8,000 miles from the UK base, and the sea route south would involve an average of 21 days sailing time to the stormiest seas in the world, with winter gales expected at any day, the selection of suitable ships was not amenable to an easy or obvious solution. As if the problems of getting there were not enough, consideration had to be given to the way in which an amphibious force could be landed in such hostile climatic and military conditions.

The only possible staging base available along the 8,000 mile L of C was at RAF Wideawake on the South Atlantic island of Ascension (ASI), some 4,000 miles from UK and a further 3,500 miles distant from the Falklands. It was neither practicable nor cost effective to establish a full forward operating base at ASI but the airfield did offer the facility to save shipping time by flying personnel and stores there for loading onto ships passing en route for the Falklands.

3 Commando Brigade comprising some 3,500 men and vehicles together with 60 days War Maintenance Reserve (WMR) stocks (that is 4,000 short tons of freight of which 3,500 tons comprised ammunition) was mounted from Devonport/Marchwood and Southampton in April in HMS *Hermes*, HMS *Fearless* (LPD) and the four LSLs. The SS *Canberra* was taken up from trade on 4 April and sailed on 9th April carrying 2,065 passengers from 3 Commando Brigade and 2 Parachute Battalion which had been placed under command. MV *Elk* was loaded at Southampton with over 2,000 tons WMR. LSL *Sir Tristram* joined the amphibious force later at ASI where elements of 40 Commando joined her having been flown out from UK. SS *Uganda* was requisitioned at Naples and fitted out at Gibraltar to sail as a hospital ship on 19 April.

As the political and diplomatic initiatives failed to produce results, it became increasingly apparent that the deterrent function of the Task Force could well be transformed to a more active role. The Chiefs of Staff approved plans for the deployment of an Army reinforcement force which became known as '5 Brigade Slimline'. This slimline brigade consisted of an infantry battalion group (3 Parachute Battalion) and supporting arms which embarked on the North Sea Ferries ship MV *Norland* and the European Ferries RO/RO vessel MV *Europic Ferry* which left UK on 25/26 April. The ill-fated container ship *Atlantic Conveyor* departed on the same day having been converted to carry 6 × Harriers, Chinook and Wessex support helicopters plus tentage to provide a 3,000 man camp. As the Task Force sailed south, the diplomatic situation worsened and it was decided to further reinforce the Amphibious Force which by this time was approaching the Total Exclusion Zone (TEZ) with the remaining element of 5 Brigade and a two star Headquarters.

The consequences of deploying a further 3,000 troops were sorely felt in terms of available passenger shipping. The UK Flag cruise liner fleet is not large and, with *Canberra* and *Uganda* already committed, the choice was narrowed to the *Queen Elizabeth II* (QE2) and a collection of smaller and less suitable ships, some of which were then cruising the Caribbean. After a number of high level discussions the QE2 with a passenger capacity of 3,250 and a speed of 27 knots was taken up and sailed for the South Atlantic on 12th May. 5 Brigade vehicles, stores and ammunition were carried south aboard MV *Tor Caledonia*, a RO/RO container vessel, and the *Baltic* and *Nordic* ferries together with a second sea Containers Line helicopter 'carrier' *Atlantic Causeway*. This 'flotilla' sailed between 9th and 12th May.

On 20 May, eight more support helicopters and four RAF GR3 Harriers were shipped out on the *Contender Bezant* to replace losses suffered in engagements in the TEZ. A final consignment of Harriers and helicopters was despatched aboard the *Astronomer* on 8th June. Later sailings included the *Laertes*, used to carry stores and munitions, the *Rangatira* carrying Army and RAF support personnel (largely RE), and the *Cedarbank* and *Strathewe* which between them lifted support stores, heavy engineer plant and equipment needed to reconstruct and extend the Port Stanley runway. Two Ramp Craft Lighters were also loaded on *Strethewe* for use in the Falklands to augment the rather sparse ship to shore lighterage hitherto available only in the form of LCM and LCVP from the landing ships (*Fearless/Intrepid*) and six Mexeflotes despatched with the LSLs.

Over 50 vessels were taken up totalling 673,000 gross registered tons. This fleet, extracted from some 33 different companies, represented one of the largest merchant fleets in the world and lifted over 100,000 tons of stores, 9,000 personnel and 95 assorted aircraft.

The necessity to take up ships from trade with very little forewarning and certainly no pre-planning, was a particular problem. Two basic options were open: charter or requisition, and since most of the UK merchant fleet was busy earning its keep, the prospect of short notice charter on commercial ventures was not a hopeful proposition. Cruise liners such as the *Canberra* and short range RO/RO vessels like the *Norland, Nordic* and *Europic* ferries were booked for the summer season and most of the cargo vessels which could have been used were operating under commercial contract. The only way of obtaining the use of these ships was to resort to requisition under the Royal Prerogative, a system used during the Suez Campaign. This became the prime method for securing ships though it was possible to obtain some vessels under charter terms. Such a vessel was the *Rangatira* which was lying at Falmouth as a disused floating hotel when taken up and made seaworthy to meet the Ministry of Defence requirements – much to the appreciation of her owners.

As the operation progressed, DOMS and the Director of Naval Operations and Trade (DNOT) developed a set of procedures which became the routine method of obtaining and tasking vessels. Once a firm requirement for shipping had been established, a meeting was held to set out action to be taken. Chaired by DNOT under the aegis of DOMS, all relevant military and naval departments attended, together with representatives from the Department of Trade and the owners. At the meeting, the operational role, the fitting out requirements, the composition of the crew and naval party to be embarked and the load to be carried were covered. The detailed timings of deployment and the fitting out port and loading ports were also decided. Following this meeting, a STUFT signal was sent out.

Having specified these requirements, the detailed loading assessment was established by DOMS according to the operational requirement and bids for movement which had been received. These bids were arranged in an order of loading and unloading priority by the operational commander – and eventually passed by signal to the loading authority.

DOMS retained control over all loading of ships taken up for the movement of passengers, vehicles and freight and, in conjunction with Department of Trade, conducted a rough pre-stow staff check to establish what cargo would be carried by each vessel. The detailed pre-stow exercise was carried out by the loading authority (in most cases United Kingdom Land Forces (UKLF) but occasionally Joint Services Movements Coordinating Committee (JSMCC) Devonport before actual loading commenced thus keeping cargo shut outs to a minimum.

Once a ship had been fitted out, often with helicopter decks, water distillation floats, ship to ship refuelling gear and a special communications package, and loaded – operational command was passed from MOD to CINCFLEET who issued sailing instructions. On departure, the loading authority passed sailing signals specifying what was actually aboard on completion of loading and finally DOMS were kept informed of any stowage changes occurring aboard major vessels on passage by embarked movement control officers and detachments.

Airlift to and from ASI, and in the latter stages of the conflict extending further south to the Falkland Islands, was principally effected using RAF C130 Hercules and VC10 aircraft from the Air Transport Force (ATF). The journey to ASI took some eleven hours by VC10 and 19 hours by C130 including a staging stop through Dakar or Freetown. Freight and passengers were ferried forward to RV with the Task Force in what grew to be the biggest military airlift operation conducted by UK since the Berlin Airlift of 1948/49.

The RAF stations at Brize Norton and Lyneham were the principal mounting airfields and freight and passengers called forward by DOMS

SSgt W Blyth BEM. The British Empire Medal was awarded for his work in movements during the Falklands campaign.

[By courtesy of PR HQ UKLF]

were swiftly processed by RAF movements staffs. CINCFLEET also established a liaison at RAF Lyneham to control and record smaller items of naval stores free flown on available airlift. Movement control at ASI was maintained by a United Kingdom Mobile Air Movements Section (UK MAMS) Team, a detachment from 47 Air Despatch Squadron RCT and RN helicopter squadron. Cargo and passengers were ferried to ships by helicopter (there being no suitable jetty or port facilities on the island). Later in the operation, an Army movement control detachment was established to coordinate the movement/transit of Army units deploying and recovering through ASI.

From the outset the Movement Control Centre at Andover was heavily involved in the planning and execution of the movement of freight for the Falklands force. The commitment of 29 Transport and Movements Regiment RCT based at South Cerney throughout the whole operation was intensive. In particular, movement control support was made available for the loading of MVs *Elk* and the *Canberra*, and some members of the Regiment accompanied the Force as well as detachments from 47 Air Despatch Squadron RCT and 17 Port Regiment RCT. All units of 3 Transport Group RCT and Marchwood Military Port played a vital part in the mounting of the operation not only in an advisory capacity but in the movement and loading of personnel, ammunition and equipment. Once again Marchwood Military Port proved its value in that it guaranteed an operating base which not only was able to respond rapidly to changing requirements and priorities, but which also allowed freedom from constraints, particularly those relating to the movement of ammunition which can be very difficult through civil ports. All this activity was coordinated and arranged by the Movements Staff at HQ UKLF responding to the Director of DOMS.

675

32 · PORT OPERATIONS

ON THE FORMATION OF the RCT in July 1965, one of the functions taken over from the Royal Engineers was Port Operations. Until that time the RASC had been responsible amongst its other roles for water transport and this role continued in the RCT. It was therefore inevitable and natural that there should be an overlap in the organization of these closely associated functions, when the RCT became responsible for both. Royal Engineer Port Units and RASC Water Transport Units, hitherto carrying out two separate functions were variously regrouped under the generic term – Maritime Units. This chapter is concerned with the Port Unit elements and touches on Water Transport only where there is overlapping as a result of the reorganization.

The tasks of Port Operation, in addition to the landbased facilities, added a variety of vessels to the previous RASC worldwide Water Transport fleet. These included specialist craft such as tugs, ramp powered lighters (RPLs) and training vessels. In addition the task of operating Mexeflote was taken over.

Mexeflote consists of three standard pontoon units: a bow section with an adjustable ramp, a centre section and a stern section. These can be rapidly connected together to form ramped lighterage rafts, causeways and jetties for use in sheltered waters. The name is derived from the Military Engineering Experimental Establishment (MEXE) where the equipment was developed in the early 1960s.

The equipment can be built up in water in which the waves are not more than two feet high and can operate in waves four to five feet high. A raft is powered by two heavy duty outboard motors, which are bolted on, and it is used for ferrying vehicles and stores from a ship anchored or moored offshore, to a beach or hard. A causeway consists of rafts without power units, connected together to bridge the water gap between the bow ramp of an LSL, or ramped craft and the shore. The length of a causeway depends on how near to the shore a vessel is able to reach.

Two 120 foot by 24 foot rafts can be carried suspended along the sides of an LSL; they can be operated as two ferries or formed into a causeway with, if necessary, other rafts.

The Landing Ships Logistic (LSL), which initially were operated on behalf of the Army Department by the British India Steam Navigation Company and later by the Royal Fleet Auxiliary, are tasked worldwide by the Director of Movements (Army), and controlled on his behalf by RCT Movements staff who took over the responsibility from the Royal Engineers. Apart from the provision of Mexeflote detachments on the

LSLs though, the most important effect of the introduction of LSLs into service was the eventual expansion of the port facilities at Marchwood, near Southampton for the handling of these vessels. This has led to the establishment of the military Line of Communication (LofC) to BAOR through Marchwood.

The many changes in organization outlined in this chapter might seem excessive, but in the main were due to the need to reduce manpower, as overall commitments diminished for the Services as a whole. The introduction of new vessels, including the Landing Ships Logistic (LSLs), Landing Craft Logistic (LCLs), Ammunition Ship Logistic (ASLs) and Ramped Craft Logistic (RCLs) (RCT manned), the new movement techniques involving International Standard Organization (ISO) containers and associated equipment, the development of Marchwood as an operational port, and the operational experiences of Borneo, Aden, Libya and Cyprus, have all contributed to necessary changes, resulting in improved efficiency and economy in port operations.

From the onset, the growing importance of ports in a logistic role was quickly apparent. In July 1965, 17 Port Training Regiment, Royal Engineers, at Marchwood was redesignated 17 Port Regiment RCT. The dropping of the word 'training' gave the first indication of the intention to develop Marchwood into an operational military port. The prototype Landing Ship Logistic (LSL), *Sir Lancelot*, launched in 1963, was by now in commission undergoing troop trials worldwide, developing Mexeflote operations. 17 Port Regiment was commanded at the time of the transition by Lieutenant Colonel G J Athey RCT.

At Longmoor the first six RASC officers to receive formal port, railway and movements training attended 26 Long Movements and Transportation Course, together with six RE officers who underwent a change of cap badge at half-time. These were the last officers awarded the 'Tn' qualification.

HQ Maritime Group RCT was formed at Ravelin House, Portsmouth to command all port and maritime units in UK, whilst 20 Maritime Regiment RCT was located at Gosport to operate the Landing Craft Tank MK VIII (LCTs). 18 Amphibious Squadron RCT operated a full squadron of DUKWs (wheeled amphibians) as an independent unit located at Fremington. The next five LSLs were laid down, but Marchwood, although operational by role, made only occasional genuine shipments.

On 15 July 1965 at Tanjong Berlayer in Singapore, 10 Port Squadron RCT assumed its new title when the Corps took over the responsibility for port and additional maritime matters from the Royal Engineers, and in October, 33 Maritime Regiment RCT was formed and took under command 37 Squadron RCT (Water Transport) located on Pulau Brani and 10 Port Squadron. During most of this year also the Borneo operations were still continuing with their demand for port and maritime support.

In Singapore, Port Operations were handled by the Joint Services Port Unit (Far East) (JSPU (FE)), which was formed in the port initially to handle RN cargoes arriving and departing on other than RN ships.

The JSPU(FE) was responsible for sea movement in and out of the Base of Singapore including the military port at Tanjong Berlayer, the hards at 43 BAD, RAF Seletar and for Army and RAF cargo shipped through the Naval Base.

Through these facilities the JSPU(FE) handled about 21,000 tons of cargo per month, representing hundreds of thousands of packages together with a wide variety of aircraft, all before the days of containers.

Lieutenant Colonel J D Lofts MBE (later Brigadier) RCT assumed command of 17 Port Regiment in 1966 and proceeded to develop the concepts of modern port operating with purpose built LSL ships and the wonderfully versatile Mexeflote pontoon equipment. A Joint Service Port Unit and 425 Troop deployed to Aden to assist in the withdrawal, and were joined by RHQ and 51 Port Squadron RCT commanded overall by Lieutenant Colonel (later Brigadier) John Lofts MBE RCT. They were joined by a detachment of 10 Port Squadron RCT from Singapore. Although the shipping used was mainly commercial and conventional, the first LSLs joined the operation and instantly proved their superiority for military purposes while the LSTs plied between Aden, Bahrein and Dubai. The operation proved the concept of a Port Squadron organized on a composite basis with both stevedoring and lighterage capabilities, working as a squadron group.

In the RAF route stations at Masirah and Salalah independent Freight Handling Troops operated the ports on a rotational basis.

A further catalyst to the development of Marchwood's operational role was the massive strike of the Union of Seamen of the summer of 1966, which brought British shipping to an almost total standstill for some six weeks. LSLs and LCTs started to use Marchwood for the movement of priority military cargo which hitherto had been shipped commercially.

A commercial freighter was acquired for use as Marchwoods principal training aid and named *Marchwood Freighter*. She replaced the elderly and outdated *Empire Stevedore*.

With the proved operational experience of Aden, 51 and 52 Port Squadrons were organized in 1967 on an identical composite basis, each with its own plant and lighterage. The operating pattern adopted was for one squadron to operate Marchwood Military Port in all respects for a period of four months, leaving the other squadron to undertake overseas exercises and complete its military training. The last of the fleet of six LSLs came into service in this year. Two LSLs remained in home waters establishing the first voyages of ammunition, vehicles and military supplies to BAOR, and provided regular support for winter and summer United Kingdom Mobile Force exercises. The remaining LSLs started a programme of resupply voyages to and within the Middle and Far Eastern

678

theatres. Marchwood was now established as an operational port.

Maritime Group RCT developed into 2 Transport Group RCT, moving to Bulford and commanding transport in addition to maritime units.

At Marchwood, to separate training from port operations, 53 Port Training Squadron was formed to meet the training commitment.

The summer of 1968 saw another national dock strike. Marchwood again proved an invaluable asset by providing the only open route for priority military cargo. For the first time ISO Containers were exported on LSLs and LCTs. Much improvization was necessary to handle the containers. Large commercial mobile cranes had to be hired to handle the containers and to operate a make-shift container park.

52 Port Squadron first operated as a composite squadron for the recovery of troops from Exercise Overdale in BAOR in October. It then carried out the redeployment of 6 Infantry Brigade and 36 Heavy AA Regiment RA from BAOR to the United Kingdom, subsequently mounting Exercise Bold Adventure through Marchwood Military Port to Esbjerg where they completed the operation in February 1969 using two LSLs.

18 Amphibious Squadron, while remaining at Fremington, came under command of 17 Port Regiment. To improve the quality of training, the Maritime Wing was created as part of the Army School of Transport. Located at Marchwood, it controlled 53 Port Training Squadron together with 81 Maritime Squadron at Gosport.

The spring of 1969 saw the last Regimental Group sized port operating exercise. Called Exercise Cunningham and commanded by Lieutenant Colonel (later Brigadier) Peter House RCT it took place in Holland near to Flushing. It comprised the whole of 17 Port Regiment, 18 Amphibious Squadron RCT and those surviving components of the Reserve Army Port Task Force including 270 and 271 Port Squadrons RCT (V). Some 1,600 port and maritime soldiers were on the ground. LSLs and LCTs were committed as were two chartered commercial ships carrying ammunition. Afterwards 428 Freight Handling Troop took part in the unloading of German armoured vehicles and cargo at Pembroke Dock for the annual training at Castlemartin.

The workload of Marchwood Military Port continued to expand and detachments aboard the LSLs visited all parts of the military world. RCT detachments were formed on both of the Landing Platform Docks (LPD), HMS *Intrepid* and HMS *Fearless*. These were both sponsored by 17 Port Regiment.

Over the beach operations were put firmly on the map in a fine demonstration of beach capability by Exercise Waggon Trail held at Browndown Beach near Gosport in June 1969.

53 Port Training Squadron RCT, under command of the Maritime Wing, was redesignated Port Training Squadron RCT.

On 1 January 1970, 52 Port Squadron RCT deployed to Tobruk for the Libya withdrawal operation. It remained there from January to March inclusive. Major Robin Barton RCT was appointed Port Commandant Tobruk. Further confirming that the composite organization was best suited to port operations, the party comprised Squadron Headquarters, a Freight Handling Troop, a Lighterage Detachment operating Mexeflote and a detachment of 17 Field Workshop REME.

The Port Squadron evacuated the stores and equipment of RAF El Adem and that of the local Army Garrison and sponsored organizations. The LSL fleet was committed in turn, operating to the UK, and the LST *Empire Gull* plied continuously to Cyprus or Malta. Chartered commercial shipping was also employed on occasions for hazardous cargo. A feature of the operation was that while the shipping and equipment were completely modern, the range of cargo was totally 'break bulk' without palletization or unit load.

Seventeen service and three commercial ship sailings evacuated a total of 38,902 tons of cargo. The final act of British withdrawal was made on 28 March with the simultaneous sailing of the LSL *Sir Geraint* and the LST *Empire Gull*. Resulting from the Libya withdrawal operation, Major R H G Barton was awarded the MBE in the 1971 New Years Honours.

In early 1970 the Royal Fleet Auxiliary assumed the operating responsibility for the LSL fleet and the LST *Empire Gull*. It was many months before the smart 'Blue Band Margarine' livery of the British India Steam Navigation Company, the traditional operator of troopships, was eventually replaced by uniform navy grey. More than one ship was interrupted during her painting programme and proceeded on her way in a piebald condition.

A further national dock strike took place during 1970. Approximately 300 containers were routed through Marchwood and again commercial mobile cranes had to be hired to handle them. By now containers were not the novelty they had been in 1968 as containers in small but increasing numbers were becoming a regular feature of many sailings. Nevertheless, the strike served to underline the importance of the military port and the need for specialized container handling equipment. Other operations included the shipment to Gibraltar of 15 skid mounted 'mobile' homes, each 37 ft long which called for new and unusual techniques with rollers.

Towards the end of 1970, due to the rundown of British Forces in the Far East, 33 Maritime Regiment RCT was disbanded and the responsibility for all port and maritime matters passed to 10 Port Squadron RCT which during the year celebrated its centenary in the sense that the first Corps unit to be designated number '10' was formed in 1870: 10 Company ASC. A parade of all ranks was held during which Brigadier D W E Hancox, the IRCT, presented the Centenary Shield and Scroll.

By 1971, the limitations of Marchwood with an ever increasing throughput were now most evident. A major preoccupation was the

[By courtesy of Central Office of Information]

LSL Sir Galahad *at Marchwood with an RCT work boat in the foreground.*

production of the initial justification and plans for the redevelopment of the port. On 10 June 10 Port Squadron was disbanded with the rundown in the Far East. In order to retain the number of one of the oldest squadrons in the Corps, 59 Port Squadron located in Cyprus was redesignated as 10 Port Squadron.

With the rundown of the Far East, those LSLs employed directly and indirectly with that theatre returned to home waters and Marchwood during 1972. Extra moorings had to be put in for those occasions when the jetty was fully occupied. By now a RO-RO pontoon facility had been constructed in the South berth to Class 60 standard. This was a great help for vehicles loading and discharging but did not permit one tank to tow another off an LSL, for recovery. All difficult unloading still had to be carried out by Mexeflote through the LSLs rear door.

As Exercise Cunningham had been the last Port Task Force exercise so Exercise Busy Truce became the last Port Squadron Group Exercise.

52 Port Squadron departed for Esbjerg, Denmark complete, with under command 'A' Troop, 18 Amphibious Squadron RCT and elements of 270 Port Squadron (V).

The next major events were Operations Grasscutter and Motorman in early 1972. Called at very short notice on a Friday evening 52 Port Squadron activated Marchwood Military Port for Northern Ireland support. Five of the six LSLs were involved and very large quantities of troops and equipment were outloaded through the port.

In June the first of the joint Anglo-German port exercises Symphonie '72 took place. This was carried out by 51 Port Squadron in conjunction with some 160 men of the Federal German Armed Forces. During the exercise 1,000 tons of ammunition were moved by DUKWs and by LARCs of the German Navy.

From September to December 1972 52 Port Squadron under command of Major Tim Street RCT stood by in RAF Gan to assist in the Uganda withdrawal: its task was to run RAF fuel through the reef to the mounting airport at Mahé in the Seychelles.

Det 51 Port Squadron under Captain Wyn Winskell RCT carried out the evacuation of Malta using four Mexeflotes in conjunction with JSPU Malta in early 1973. The principal task was the backloading of RAF ammunition which was accomplished by commercial ships and LSLs.

During February and March 1973 52 Port Squadron took part in the 24 Airportable Brigade Exercise Sun Pirate in the Caribbean including the British Virgin Islands and Barbados.

In 1973 18 Amphibious Squadron left Fremington in a change of role. One troop of DUKWs only was retained in service, which joined 17 Port Regiment at Marchwood. The remainder of the squadron reverted to a MT role.

The LST *Empire Gull*, brought back from the Mediterranean in 1970 was refitted in 1973 to comply with safety regulations and entered regular service between Marchwood and Antwerp as an ammunition carrier. This freed more LSL capacity for the re-supply of BAOR, exercises, MOD sales and service worldwide. Little by little larger plant able to handle containers was acquired and the 'Khaki Container' now appeared upon the scene.

The decision to phase the final troop of DUKWs out of service in 1974 was much regretted by the maritime world. Their final swim-past and parade in April, however, was a red-letter day in Marchwood's history. Admiral of the Fleet, Lord Louis Mountbatten, took the salute and in an address admitted to his own responsibility in the acquisition of the Marchwood site for the development of Mulberry Harbour construction and for the provisioning of the ubiquitious DUKW, so versatile in amphibious operations.

At Marchwood, much effort was concentrated during 1975 into developing and presenting the long drawn out case for the redevelopment

[By courtesy of 3 LE(A) Tpt]

An aerial view of Marchwood Military Port.

of the military port. The culmination was a presentation to the QMG's Study Period, Exercise Armed Athene III, which constituted the biggest port and maritime demonstration the port had ever seen.

In Scotland, Port Unit Rhu was set up to mount the re-supply of the Outer Hebrides and St Kilda. The Landing Craft Tanks (LCTs) and now the Landing Craft Logistic (LCLs) operate from there for most of each year, supplying the Hebrides rocket range on South Uist and Benbecula.

Later in the year elements of 51 Port Squadron deployed to Cyprus for the withdrawal operation resulting from the Turkish invasion. Much of the cargo returned through Marchwood by LSL and commercial charter. A feature of this operation was the landing at Marchwood of some 2,000 private cars, which with the attendant stream of Customs Officers and hopeful owners resulted in a peak of congestion. Major David Hammett RCT earned the MBE as a result of his efforts to secure the evacuation of personnel and vessels from the port of Famagusta. This withdrawal completed the main run down of overseas dependencies and heralded the operation of the main BAOR L of C as the primary port task.

During 1976, 17 Port Regiment made a major contribution to the Anglo French and German Forte series of biennial logistic exercises. For 'Forte 76', 51 Port Squadron conducted a logistic beach operation at Merville-Franceville-Plage on the coast of Normandy, near to 'Sword Beach' of the 1944 D Day Landings. BAOR maintenance cargo carried by LSL, LST and LCT was diverted and landed over the beach. The cargo, which included ammunition, vehicles and engineer stores, was subsequently cleared to BAOR by road and rail.

The continuing gradual acquisition of container handling equipment, vehicles and trailers resulted in the start of a semi-regular through running container service to BAOR and Marchwood became an established link in the lines of communication to BAOR. The upgrading of the RO-RO at Marchwood's South Berth from Class 60 to Class 100, together with improved ramp profiles also greatly improved operations with commercial type equipments and A vehicles.

In March 1977, Headquarters 3 Transport Group RCT (Lines of Communication) was formed at Marchwood with Colonel P K A Todd OBE as its first Commander. The Group managed the dedicated line of communication to BAOR and left the RHQ of the Port Regiment free to concentrate on its operational task.

At the same time 17 Port Regiment RCT was redesignated 17 Port and Maritime Regiment RCT. The Marchwood Administrative Squadron RCT became 53 Port and Maritime Support Squadron RCT and came under command of Headquarters 3 Transport Group.

Again in 1977, 51 Port Squadron RCT carried out a UNFICYP tour in Cyprus and a Maritime Detachment of 17 Port and Maritime Regiment with two ramped powered lighters was established in Belize.

April 1978 saw the start of the Military Container Service (MCS) through running to BAOR with scheduled LSL sailings from Marchwood every four days. The range of container handling equipment now permitted commercial standards of operation with a properly stacked container park. A capacity of some 200 containers each way per month was established. The capacity of the port was now sufficient to cater for all priority military cargo. Organizational changes at the same time within 17 Port and Maritime Regiment reorganized the two Port Squadrons on a functional basis: 51 Port Squadron – Lighterage; and 52 Port Squadron – Port Operations, Plant and Military Container Service (MCS). This led to economies in maintenance and equipment management and a Port Squadron Group could be organized on a brick system as required.

In June the second LCL, HMAV *Arakan* was commissioned. Both LCLs henceforth were used for cross channel container operations when available.

The RFA LST *Empire Gull* was withdrawn from service after thirty years and sailed sadly for the breakers yard leaving only a nostalgic whiff of steam and a stuffed gull in a glass case.

The Headquarters Maritime Wing was disbanded but the two training divisions, Port and Maritime, remained.

The remaining Reserve Army support of 17 Port and Maritime Regiment was rationalized with the formation of 265 Port Squadron RCT (V) which was henceforth to be the Regiment's permanent Reserve Army Squadron.

[By courtesy of Lt Col T C Street]

The Keys of the Ancient Fortress of Portsmouth being offered to HM The Queen by Lt Col T C Street RCT.

17 Port and Maritime Regiment RCT was honoured in 1979 to receive the Corps Unit Efficiency Award.

In March the designation of the major units reverted to former practice; 17 Port Regiment RCT and 20 Maritime Regiment RCT both regained the titles changes in 1978. 53 Squadron adopted the shortened designation of 53 Port Support Squadron and 408 Priority Freight Service Troop RCT, stationed at Bicester, came under command of 51 Port Squadron RCT.

The training vessel *Marchwood Freighter* was sold for scrap in May. The need for basic practical training facilities for Port Operators was in future to be met by commercial charter as necessary.

A second, Class 100 RO-RO facility was constructed at Marchwood's North Berth. At long last, Marchwood had the capability of conducting two LSL RO-RO operations simultaneously.

The arrival in the military port of a 120 ton DEMAG mobile crane provided the capability of loading containers directly to the top deck of an LSL. This greatly reduced the need for commercial hire, and increased the theoretical capacity for containers on the L of C through Marchwood to BAOR to some 300 each way per month.

The acceptance of two Composite Port Squadron Groups in the

plans for the Royal Marines in the Northern Flank and for UKMF operations, confirmed 17 Port Regiment's operational role for the foreseable future.

In February 1981, 53 Port Support Squadron came under command of 17 Port Regiment.

The entry into service in mid-summer of the Ammunition Ship Logistic (ASL) HMAV *St George* gave the L of C its first purpose built ammunition carrier, replacing the scrapped LST *Empire Gull*. The *St George* provided a regular ammunition service to BAOR in compliance with all the latest safety requirements at about twice the speed of her illustrious predecessor. The ASL can carry approximately 700 tonnes of paletized ammunition and creates further LSL capacity for use on other tasks. *St George* joined 20 Maritime Regiment RCT.

Opportunities for a regimental exercise are rare in a Regiment that exists to support others, but Exercise 'Canute' did permit 17 Port Regiment to practise every aspect of a full scale logistic beach operation. It was held in 1981 at Brownsdown and was supported by every type of in-service logistic ship.

The summer of 1981 also saw the entry into service of the class leader of a new type of coastal and ship-to-shore lighter. Called a 'Ramped Craft Logistic' (RCL) the class of eight vessels is to be known as the 'Mulberry Class' in perpetuation of Marchwood's association with Mulberry Harbour and the D Day landings. The RCL, which is eventually to replace the RPL, is a lighter of 96 tonnes payload, able to carry containers and vehicles anywhere in the European theatre. The class leader was named *Arromanches* by the Mayor of Arromanches at a ceremony in Marchwood in November to cement further the relationship of Marchwood with the Normandy coast and the events of 1944. *Arromanches* and her sister ship *Antwerp* joined 51 Port Squadron RCT and commenced regular operations after the completion of satisfactory troop trials.

1 April 1982 was to be the start of the real test for Marchwood Military Port and its operation. What followed was to bring into perspective all the work that had been done over the years to establish a viable operational military port. This date, which will long be remembered, was the start of 'Operation Corporate' – the Battle for the Falklands. The part played by 3 Transport Group (Lines of Communication) and 17 Port Regiment RCT is described in the Falklands Chapter in Part 1 of this Book. Suffice it to say here that the parts which they played both in the mounting of the operation in UK, not only from Marchwood, but also from civilian ports and the operational landings on the Falklands were vital contributions in the success of the logistic backing for the operation and so an appropriate high note on which to end this chapter.

33 · RAILWAYS

IN 1965 AS PART OF THE McLeod reorganization, the operation of military railways passed from the Royal Engineers to the Royal Corps of Transport. Regrettably, it was a diminishing responsibility and in the period from 1965, the railway organization has been reduced drastically to meet the differing needs of today's Army. At the present time, with the demise of the Longmoor Military Railway (LMR), the actual operation of military railway systems is confined to major depot sidings in the UK and BAOR. The training of RCT personnel for railway operation is now also restricted to BAOR, with a dependence on Reserve Army personnel to provide a greater contribution in a time of emergency. Nevertheless, the railway element of the RCT still has important functions to perform, particularly in BAOR. Whilst the scale of operating may have reduced, the control of railway traffic is still an essential requirement for logistic success and is today being achieved by a blend of railway and movement skills that exist in the RCT.

The Royal Corps of Transport inherited from the Royal Engineers various railway facilities at home and abroad. None of these was particularly large and some were no more than a single siding. The most impressive, without a doubt, was the Longmoor Military Railway which had the dual function of being the practical military railway trade training school and of serving various rail-connected depots in the vicinity. The great majority of other railway operating duties concerned the rail-served depots. Before we examine the various railway facilities it may be appropriate to explain inter-corps railway responsibilities.

INTER-CORPS RESPONSIBILITIES

The Royal Engineers had been responsible for construction, maintenance and operation of military railways. With the advent of the Royal Corps of Transport these functions were split, railway construction and maintenance (civil engineering tasks) remaining with the Royal Engineers, motive power and rolling stock maintenance (mechanical and electrical engineering tasks) being given to the Royal Electrical and Mechanical Engineers and railway operating alone being undertaken by RCT. As in Sapper days, the Royal Signals retained responsibility for installation and maintenance of communications. From 1 April 1967, the Ministry of Public Buildings and Works (MPBW) became responsible for the maintenance of railways (way and works). MPBW became part of the Department of the Environment (DOE) on 1 December 1970 and, in

[By courtesy of Central Office of Information]

A diesel engine hauling a passenger train at Longmoor 1965.

1972, became the Property Services Agency (PSA), still part of DOE.

MILITARY RAILWAYS – UNITED KINGDOM

16 Railway Regiment RCT

Two quite separate organizations existed to operate military railway installations in Great Britain. One was 16 Railway Regiment which operated the Longmoor Military Railway and provided locomotives and rolling stock for the Marchwood Military Railway. Both the LMR and MMR were manned by soldiers although the Permanent Way Gangs, the Signal Fitters and a few jobs in the Operating Department and Workshops at Longmoor were civilians. The Regiment was disbanded in April 1969.

Longmoor Military Railway

Lieutenant Colonel D W Ronald RCT and Major R J Carter (Retd) have written an excellent and comprehensive history entitled *The Longmoor Military Railway* published by David & Charles of Newton Abbot, and it is not intended to repeat their account. However, the present survey would not be complete without a passing mention of the only real Military Railway that has existed in the period under review. It was a 'real' railway, albeit in microcosm, for it had some 60 miles of track, main and branch lines, scheduled passenger and goods services, a great variety of locomotives and rolling stock, blockposts ('signal boxes') and fixed signals, well equipped locomotives – and carriage and wagon workshops and most of the features one would expect to find in the infrastructure of a civilian railway. And yet, paradoxically, it was not a real railway in the legal sense for its construction had not been authorized by Act of Parliament, Light Railway Order or Military Tramway Order. In general terms, this did not much matter as it was a military installation on military land. Where the anomaly did become apparent was at level crossings with public roads for here it was necessary for trains of dubious status, if they existed at all in the eyes of the Law, to hinder the passage of legal road traffic. It must be admitted that the LMR was not often challenged over this legal nicety but the double line crossings at Longmoor and Oakhanger were singled in the last years of the existence of the Railway.

The official closure ceremony of the Longmoor Military Railway took place on 31 October 1969. Towards the end, traffic increased as railway stores were moved out of Longmoor Camp itself and a certain amount of Royal Engineers equipment was relocated from the Engineer Stores Depot in the former Apple Pie Camp on the plateau overlooking Greatham Village. With final closure and the lifting of the line by George Cohen Sons & Co Ltd, between October 1971 and August 1973, Longmoor and the School of Electrical and Mechanical Engineering at Borden were cut off from railway communication, as was the Engineer Stores Depot. In the latter place were stored large items of Engineer Stores and, in particular, Heavy Girder Bridge sets. Very soon, the problems of moving these around the country by road were being felt; not only was it a slow business but suitable lorries had to be found, and the move of a bridge set from Longmoor to Stirling might start with the empty lorries coming to Longmoor from as far afield as Taunton.

Closure of the LMR created problems of quite a different nature for a group of civilians. In 1967 the well known artist David Shepherd, having bought a British Railways Standard Class 4 MT 4–6–0 steam locomotive, was wondering where to keep it. Approaches to the Military Authorities at Longmoor produced permission for this loco and his later acquisition, a standard 9F 2–10–0, to be stabled there. Mr. Shepherd was not alone in buying steam locomotives from BR and two Southern Railway 4–6–2 and an IMS 2–6–2 tank engine were awaiting rehousing at Nine Elms. These locomotives and an industrial 0–4–0 saddle tank were also permitted to be kept at Longmore due again to David Shepherd's intercession with sympathetic senior officers. Several locomotive preservation groups were by now tenants at Longmoor and it soon became obvious to them that the

Longmoor Military Railway was exactly what the British Army had carefully developed it to be, an ideal, small but complete system. In the field of railway preservation word travels fast and when, at about the time that their locomotives were arriving at Longmoor, these groups heard of the decision to close the LMR they very quickly decided to make a bid to purchase it.

A bold scheme was drawn up to use the LMR for running preserved locomotives and rolling stock and for the Longmoor area to become a place to keep and run old road vehicles. The military airstrip in Gypsy Hollow would enable historical light aircraft to fly in and out. Such a scheme would produce a unique transport museum and the Association of Railway Preservation Societies put forward its ideas at discussion with MOD (A) in January 1969. Major General E H G Lonsdale, CB, MBE, MA, was chairman of the Longmoor Trust, a body set up to create the 'Longmoor Steam Railway and Southern Transport Centre' as the working museum was to be called. Besides the ARPS, The Transport Trust also supported the scheme. By the end of 1969, however, MOD (A) indicated that the proposals were unacceptable for several reasons, not least of which was that they still needed Longmoor Camp and the military training areas surrounding it. The Army offered the last 1½ miles of line from Liss Forest Road to Liss to the ARPS as this was outside the training area. The ARPS accepted this offer, a provisional lease was drawn up in April 1970 and planning permission was sought for developments at Liss. Unfortunately the people of Liss did not share the enthusiasm of the preservation bodies and opposed planning permission. Seven residents raised £9,100 in a successful bid to buy this last piece of line, thus ensuring that trains would not run here again.

So ended the story of the Longmoor Military Railway which had its origins in 1903. Generations of Railwaymen had trained there and its name is well known to this day largely because so many British Railways staff, not to mention people in many other callings spent two years there as National Servicemen. It was, in some respects, a working museum of railway relics throughout its existence, with most of its rolling stock and many of its locomotives being bought secondhand from railway companies great and small throughout the country. At the same time it was capable of prodigious efforts and smart work. Frequent and varied were the trials conducted on the LMR, not only with locos and rolling stock, but also, for example, with structures, methods of working, and signalling. Many thousands of people visited Longmoor on its Open Days and they would join with military railwaymen everywhere in declaring the railway world a poorer place without the LMR.

A sequel to the account of the private locomotives at Longmoor is that David Shepherd, by way of thanking his hosts, painted a splendid picure of the famous LMR 2–10–0 'Gordon' hauling a passenger train in typical moorland scenery south of Weaversdown. He permitted a limited edition of two hundred prints to be made specifically for the military railwaymen and those directly associated with Longmoor.

Mr. Shepherd took great pains to ensure that the print faithfully reproduced the colouring of the original, rejecting three proof printings that would have deceived an eye less discerning than his own. The result was a most lively and evocative picture that adorns the home of many a military railwayman.

This generous gesture was very gratefully received and the valuable original oil painting now hangs in the Corps Headquarters Officers' Mess at Buller Barracks, Aldershot.

Marchwood Military Railway

Situated on the west bank of the River Test, opposite Southampton Docks, is Marchwood Military Port. Here the vessels of 20 Maritime Regiment RCT and the Landing Ships Logistic (LSL) of the Royal Fleet Auxiliary (RFA) load and discharge cargoes for many destinations.

Until the closure of the Longmoor Military Railway, the remaining total of 5.63 miles of track, linking the Port and its facilities to the British Railways Southampton – Fawley Branch, was known as Marchwood Military Railway (MMR). Its locomotives and rolling stock were 'on the books' at Longmoor but, as with 'Chittagong' at Liphook, they were permanently allocated to Marchwood. In steam days locomotives bore the same livery as LMR locos (blue, lined red with cream lettering, red coupling rods and buffer beams, black wheels with white tyres, black frames and smokebox). Locomotives and passenger coaches bore the legend MMR.

With the closure of the LMR, Marchwood became the responsibility of 1 Railway Group RCT, now Army Department Railway Staff (ADRS), and lost its 'Military Railway' title.

Three Ruston & Hornsby 275 hp. 0–6–0 DH locomotives are based at Marchwood loco shed, currently (Feb 82) AD 423, 425 & 432. Beside some heavy shunting duties these locos run a scheduled passenger service over the line between the quarters and the jetty.

Liphook

Some three miles east of Longmoor lies the village of Liphook where, adjacent to the British Railways station, lies the former No. 2 Engineer Stores Depot (2 ESD) which was later to become RAOC COD Liphook. This Depot had a track layout amounting to 2.58 miles which was shunted by an Army diesel locomotive. As the Depot was so close to Longmoor, the loco was part of the LMR stock but was permanently detached, only appearing at Longmoor (via Liss, the next BR station south) when in need of heavy repair. For at least ten years the loco allocated to Liphook was 829 'Chittagong' (formerly 'Basra'), a Drewry/Vulcan Foundry-built 0–4–0 DM, works numbers DC 2175VF5256 of 1945. Before 1956 this loco carried fleet number WD 72220 and is now AD 222.

Railway operations ceased at the Liphook Depot in May 1970.

1 RAILWAY GROUP RCT

The above organization was responsible for military railway operating in the United Kingdom depots. In July 1965 this amounted to regular activity in 53 locations throughout the land and assistance at several other places such as Royal Ordnance Factories and Proof & Experimental Establishments as required. At the time of the formation of the Corps this Unit assumed its sixth title in the 23 years since its formation in May 1942. Strictly speaking '1 Railway Group RCT' was a resurrection of the third (1945) title with a new suffix.

At the end of the Second World War the establishment of this Unit, then known as No. 1 Railway (Home) Group RE although '(Home)' was dropped from the title in 1945, was 2,400 military personnel. Once peace had returned and traffic reverted to normal levels, it was decided to scale down the size of the manpower establishment and replace soldiers with civilians. By 1964 the only regular uniformed member of the Unit was its Commanding Officer, a Colonel (late RE), although eight NCOs formed an attached increment, mainly for supervision of Royal Pioneer Corps permanent way tasks.

When the RCT moved into the Group Headquarters at Beavers Lane Camp, Hounslow, the unit consisted of some 760 civilians, responsible for working 37 Army depots with another 17 served by British Railways and, in one case, by a private company.

RAILWAY WING, ARMY FREIGHT ORGANIZATION

The next change in administration was to involve the Headquarters in moving further into London, where the staff took up residence in Empress State Building. This upheaval, which took place in March 1971, was brought about by the Group's inclusion in the Army Freight Organization and its new title was Railway Wing, Army Freight Organization.

ARMY DEPARTMENT RAILWAY STAFF RCT

Six and a half years later, on the formation of the Logistic Executive (Army), normally referred to as LE(A), they moved again and found themselves occupying part of the former Royal Air Force Station at Andover, Hampshire. Another change of name accompanied this removal and the Unit is now called Army Department Railway Staff (ADRS) which title they adopted in March 1977, before the Headquarters moved to Andover in September of that year.

Turning our attention to the depots, and remembering that when the RCT took over responsibility for No. 1 Railway Group there were 53 railway installations amounting to a little over 400 miles of track, it is of interest to see how these figures have been reduced in the intervening years by the withdrawal of railway facilities from, or closure of, some 27 locations and 128 miles of track.

These closures include two of the last locations operating narrow gauge (600 mm) layouts. Barlow and Burnhill both had standard gauge sidings as well but these were for trans-shipment traffic delivered and picked up by British Rail locomotives and the work of the depots was carried out by the well known Ruston & Hornsby and Hunslet loco-motives of the 'clockwork mouse' variety.

Another but unconnected point of interest at Barlow, a short distance South East of Selby, is that the original airship hangar, dating from the days when dirigibles were based there, was in use as the main storage and maintenance building in the Depot continuously until closure of the Returned Stores Depot (RSD) a few years after railway operations ceased.

Narrow gauge operations continue to be associated with the RCT at the Ordnance Explosives Stores Depot (OESD) Eastriggs, near Gretna Green, Dumfriesshire and on the ranges at Lydd, sharing Romney Marshes with that other narrow gauge concern, the world-famous Romney, Hythe and Dymchurch Light Railway. The latter also joined the Army during the Second World War but that is another story.

Bicester, in Oxfordshire, is the site of a large Central Ordnance Depot served by a sprawling network of sidings arranged round two large loops known as Craven Hill and Arncott. This large complex, amounting to some 44 miles of track, is connected to the former Oxford to Cambridge line of BR, at Bicester London Road.

Traffic for the depot is quite heavy and six locomotives of two classes are allocated for this work. Also of interest is the fact that the 32nd Central Workshop REME, the Group Central Railway Workshop of old, is located at Bicester. For this reason one may normally find several locomotives from 'foreign' depots here for overhaul. These may be seen in traffic on the depot lines running-in after attention in the Works before returned to their home depots.

On the two 'loops' or main running lines, traffic is controlled by the Regulator System which is a method of block working peculiar to certain of our depots. In each loop is located a Regulator who sits in front of a large diagram of the depot and is in telephone contact with suitably situated control points (numbered boards) along the line.

As permission is given for a train to pass between two points the Regulator moves a peg, annotated with the train details, to occupy the relevant section of the diagram, thus indicating that no other movement may be made in that section until the train is reported clear of the section at the next control point. In practice, when traffic is light enough to allow, train movement through two or more sections may be permitted. This is a very simple and easily understood system which is ideal for application in military depots where traffic is relatively slow moving. Two Blockmen (railway signalmen) are employed in Bicester by ADRS to man the two blockposts ('signal boxes') which control traffic at each end of the 2-mile single line joining the two loops. Five passenger coaches form a small part of the 213 vehicle holding. Two of them, the ex London Transport Tube cars AD3028 and AD3030, are awaiting disposal, AD3018 is an inspection and VIP coach while the other two are known as the 'Winter Coach' (AD5308) and the 'Summer Coach' (AD5319). These two vehicles are used on what is known as the 'Whistle Stop' train which enables works teams to be taken to certain locations where they use the coach as their place of work. AD5308 is equipped with gas heating and electric lighting while AD5319 has only got heating.

A proper scheduled passenger service has long since ceased to run.

Only one depot is bigger than Bicester in terms of mileage and that is Command Ammunition Depot (CAD) Kineton which, with 63.18 miles of track is almost exactly the same size as the erstwhile Longmoor Military Railway. But there the similarity ends; functions and layouts differ greatly. The functional aspect is highlighted by the fact that although Kineton is served by the same number of locomotives as Bicester and, in track miles is almost half as big again, its rolling stock holdings are only a quarter of Bicester's. The nature and destinations of its traffic, however, involve the use of much more BR stock.

AD Bramley is the third largest depot in Great Britain with 30.45 miles of standard gauge track. ADRS now operate this depot on an agency basis for the United States armed forces who have become the tenants. As at Bicester, its traffic also is controlled by the Regulator system but in this instance communication between the trains and the Regulator is by means of radio, hence the Regulator being referred to as the Radio Controller. Two locos are presently working in this depot.

In terms of mileage, after the 27.52 miles of Eastriggs (24.11 miles narrow gauge), comes CAD Longtown with 24.79 miles, operated by three locomotives.

The Royal Engineers depot at Long Marston has 20.12 miles of railway left after handing over some track to the scrap merchants, Birds, in whose hands many BR steam locos have fallen to the cutter's torch, along with the few Army ones. AD wagon repairs are carried out here and this depot is about to relinquish control of one of the last two semi-active steam locos on Army metals. When 0–6–0ST AD98 Royal Engineer leaves the three diesels in charge and goes for preservation elsewhere, a similar move will be made from the Proof & Experimental Establishment Range at Shoeburyness, last home of AD92 'Waggoner' in Army service. The description 'semi-active' means that these two saddle tank engines have only been steamed for special events such as the Aldershot Show and various 'open days' since the end of regular steam working.

Shoeburyness has four diesel locos, including the former LMR Sentinel 0–8–0 DH 'General Lord Robertson', to operate its 20 miles of track. Here a lot of work is done with rail-mounted cranes which are required to lift heavy items, such as gun barrels, when setting up the experiments which are the primary function of this facility. Two particularly interesting items of railway equipment are kept here; an enormous 200 ton rail-mounted gun and a coach, referred to as 'The Kitchener Coach', built in 1898 for the Saukin-Berber Railway. It is alleged that Lord Kitchener used the coach during his campaign in the Sudan. This is possible for although we know that the Sudan Railways, based on Kitchener's 576 mile military railway from Wadi Halfa to Khartoum, completed in the period 1897–1899, are built to 3 ft. 6 in. gauge, the Saukin – Berber Railway was a Standard gauge project. However, there appears to be no proof that the Great Man ever did ride in the coach.

In any event, from Sudan to Shoeburyness, it has come and now carries VIP visitors to the Proof & Experimental Establishment (P & EE) even if its history is not quite as illustrious as we are led to believe.

As at Bramley, Shoeburyness was provided with three London Transport Tube cars for its passenger services. They arrived in November 1961 and have subsequently been sold out of service.

There are a further seventeen locations with fifty-six miles of track employing a total of sixteen AD locos.

MILITARY RAILWAYS – OVERSEAS

Singapore

Outside the United Kingdom the RCT found itself responsible for railway operations in Belgium, Germany and Singapore. The trend here has been similar, a shrinking Army and severe financial stringency have taken their toll abroad as well as at home. On the withdrawal of British Forces from Singapore the unusual depot line serving the Ordnance Depot and Engineer Base Installation (EBI), between Ayer Rajah Road and Tanglin Halt on the Malayan Railway (Keretapi Tanah Melayu), was closed and its assets dispersed. In order to connect with the KTM this was, of course, a metro-gauge system. Motive power was provided by two interesting 0–6–0 saddle tank engines, each bearing no less than three fleet numbers:

000016, Yard No. 144, S.L.7 Blt Avonside, Bristol 2030 of 1929 Blr No. 2181
000017, Yard No. 145, S.L.8 Blt Avonside, Bristol 2031 of 1930 Blr No. 2182
They had two outside cylinders, 18″ × 12″; wheel diameter 2′11″; axle load ca. 7t; coal capacity 1 ton; water capacity 670 gall. Tractive effort at 80% of boiler pressure was 8,290 lbs. These locos had worked on the Singapore

Naval Base railway which had been closed some years before by the Royal Navy.

An amazing incident, though doubtlessly not for the man involved, happened at the loco shed here one morning when the early turn fireman went to prepare his engine, which had been left in steam overnight. In order to rake out the ashpan he descended into the gloom of the pit and was about to start work when he noticed, by the glow from the open ashpan doors, that he was not alone. His companion was a large snake! Luckily for him this reptilian railway enthusiast was not a deadly hamadryad but a docile python which had discovered a convenient way of keeping warm overnight. The creature was captured alive and was thenceforth kept in a wire cage, inside which it was provided with a suitable tree trunk over which it would drape itself, just beside the loco shed in the adjacent Medical Depot, overlooking the scene of its adventure.

The Engineer Base Installation (EBI) was one of the locations of the only other RCT railway activity in the Far East. Of an original requirement for eight Tank Carrying Railway Wagons (TCRW), equipped with standard and metre gauge bogies, six were built by Gloucester Carriage and Wagon Co, for metre gauge only and two for dual gauge. Of the former, three were sent to EBI while the other three were sent to Bangkok for trial over the Royal State Railways (RSR) of Thailand.

Thailand

At Mae Nam (Bangkok Docks) they were ready to meet a Centurion Mk V Main Battle Tank (MBT) when it arrived from Singapore aboard the 75 Sqn RCT Mk VIII Landing Craft Tank (LCT) L 4073 *Ardennes*. The tank was discharged direct to the deck of one of the TCRW by the huge floating crane *Archimedes*, on 26 April 1966. On the leading TCRW was mounted a large timber frame from which projected light wooden 'fingers' which described the outline of the MBT. With train speed suitably reduced it would easily be seen if these 'fingers' fouled any structure as they would break off and the train could be stopped before any damage was done. This careful planning prevented the sort of announcement which Public Relations (PR) men only dream about when they have dined unwisely – 'The Royal State Railways regret to announce the cancellation of all trains to the East for the next two months. This is due to a British Army tank being embedded in the bridge over the Mae Nam Mun'.

Early the following morning the train began its 568 km journey from Bangsui, a suburb of Bangkok, to Ubol Rat Thani in the East of the country. Generally things went well; the newness of the wagons resulted in some equipment being stiff and difficult to work and the failure of a slack adjuster caused the brakes to drag on one wagon which resulted in the axle boxes running warm, but there was no real problems. The RCT

Officer-in-Charge enjoyed 780 miles of colonial splendour travelling in the Officers' Saloon and the local population was greatly entertained. The natives of Ubol particularly were treated to a demonstration of the Centurion being discharged and re-loaded, very gingerly, over the rickety, sleeper-built headramp of their station. The waggons acquitted themselves well, weight transference and bogie spring deflection being well within limits.

A casual enquiry of the Inspector in Charge of the train as to why there was a man standing beside each of the many bridges in the east of the country elicited the reply that Communist insurgents enjoy blowing up bridges. If the lonely, unarmed sentinel were not there, the train would not proceed without explanation. The Royal Train is the only other one to which this special consideration is accorded.

The trials train did not return directly to the docks but diverted over the Paet Riu branch line before terminating in Bangkok (Mae Nam).

Belgium

After the Second World War, during which there had been intense military railway activity through the Low Countries, it was decided to concentrate to the east of Antwerp the widely scattered RAOC facilities and group them, with certain RE, RASC and other depots, in an area called Advanced Base. This complex was built up from 1951 onwards in the neighbourhood of the towns and villages of Berlaar, Broechem, Emblem, Geel, Grobbendonk, Olen and Tielen. Nine depots were rail served and the RCT took over railway responsibility for them in 1965. Most have now been closed.

79 Railway Squadron RCT, based in MonchenGladbach, Germany, was the unit tasked to operate the depots, provide locomotives from the BAOR fleet and to train engine drivers and shunters. Locomotives used were interchangeable with locos in BAOR depots but normally the loco allocation was only changed when it was necessary to take one away for general overhaul.

BAOR

Training Military Railwaymen

When it was decided to close the Longmoor Military Railway, alternative arrangements for the training of military railwaymen had to be made. Although nothing comparable to the LMR existed, 79 Railway Squadron had its own facilities at MonchenGladbach in Germany, where the Unit made use of the railway layout of the former German airfield which is now a Royal Army Ordnance Corps vehicle depot. This squadron was then responsible for the railway operation of all the Army and Royal Air Force rail-served depots and airfields, the maintenance of the Commander-in-Chief's Diesel Train and a fleet of locomotives and rolling stock which

[By courtesy of Central Office of Information]

A young RCT officer in 79 Railway Squadron in Germany.

included the BAOR Ambulance Trains and the military stock of 'The Berliner', the train which runs between Brunswick and Berlin. Although a certain amount of this maintenance work, especially the C in C's Diesel Train and the 'The Berliner' stock, was done under contract by civilian workshops, the size of the fleet was large enough (a total of 33 locomotives, 38 coaches and 215 wagons) for a small REME workshop to be an important part of the Unit. The responsibility of this Workshop was first line maintenance and repairs. The Unit already had a minor training role which was to teach the rudiments of practical railway work to personnel of other units (mainly RAOC soldiers of the various depots) to enable them to shunt wagons in the event of the civilian engine drivers or shunters employed in these depots being absent for sickness or on leave. It was also necessary to teach Movement Control tradesmen how to load and secure vehicles on trains using both the British Army's unique Ramp Wagon (WGR) and more conventional facilities such as end and side-loading platforms, docks and ramps. A suitable course was therefore run, usually two or three times a year. Occasionally there was a need to teach a newly recruited civilian to be an engine driver or shunter in one of the depots, a task which was performed when required.

The availability of these features and facilities persuaded those responsible that 79 Railway Squadron offered the best potential as the future training unit for railway trades.

The Squadron, which had been formed on 1st May 1952 as 79 Transportation Squadron Royal Engineers, was disbanded between 30 June 1956 and 1963 when it reformed under the title 79 Railway Squadron RE (BAOR). A change of suffix in 1965 gave the Unit its present title and in 1970 a move within 17 Base Vehicle Depot RAOC, its home location, to more spacious accommodation enabled it to prepare for its additional role of Trade Training. The famous Signal School Model Railway from Longmoor was imported, classrooms were prepared and instructors posted in.

Until 1970 the railway trades employed by the RCT were:

Operating Department	Trade Group	Classes
Brakesmen & Shunter	B	3 & 2
Blockman	B	3, 2 & 1
Traffic Operator	A	3, 2 & 1
Locomotive Department	Trade Group	Classes
Fireman, loco	B	3, 2 & 1
Railway Engine Driver (Steam)	A	3, 2 & 1
Railway Engine Driver (Diesel)	A	3, 2 & 1

The closure of the LMR reduced the number of railway tradesmen required, not only because Longmoor's tasks were phased out but also because there were no steam locomotives in military service in Europe, the new base. Nor were there any blockposts ('signal boxes') abroad, to be manned by Blockmen. The new trade (or 'Employment' as the term was shortly to become) of Railwayman, introduced on 1 April 1971, embraced all the necessary skills inherent in the six former trades and, as a Group A Employment, represented very good value even if it could be argued that the Railwayman Class 1 could not be as skilful and experienced a man as a top class tradesman in each of the former trades.

The first training task of the new Training Wing was to conduct special conversion courses for all the regular railway tradesmen by introducing Railway Engine Drivers to blockposts and Traffic Operators to the footplate. In general terms this programme went well. As on British Railways, there existed a noticeable professional rivalry between the Locomotive and Operating Departments although as Brothers-in-Arms, this was not so pronounced amongst soldiers as it was outside the Service. In the event almost all was 'sweetness and light', a tribute to forbearance and understanding.

275 Railway Squadron, Royal Corps of Transport (Volunteers)
The original trades were retained for the TA soldiers of 275 Railway Squadron RCT (V) who got their steam experience on the various preserved railways to which they went. Eventually the two specifically steam trades were dropped as it became apparent that the railways which

were ever likely to be operated by military railwaymen had changed from steam to diesel traction. In the meantime they had enjoyed several camps on such fascinating systems as the Festiniog Railway, the North York Moors Railway and the Nene Valley Railway, the latter complete with European steam locomotives and rolling stock. We like to think that these adventures were mutually beneficial. Certainly Mr. Garraway of the Festiniog seemed pleased with his extended permanent way and the Welshpool & Llanfair Light Railway would have had a much greater problem with their bridge over the River Banwy had it not been for the professional help of 507 Specialist Team, Royal Engineers, the construction unit attached to 275 Railway Squadron RCT (V).

As this unique Territorial Army Squadron would join its Regular Army sister squadron in the event of hostilities, it is important that the men of both units should be taught from the same book. The view is occasionally expressed that, as 275 Railway Squadron's men are mainly recruited from British Railways, there must surely be little that the regular railway soldiers can teach them about railways. In fact there is a lot.

British Railways have become very much more sophisticated, particularly in the last fifteen years or so, as their equipment and methods have been changed to equip themselves for high speed operations with diesel and electric traction. A BR signalman in a modern power box may not actually see a train in an eight hour shift and he will be controlling traffic as many as thirty or more miles from his location. The driver of a High Speed Train is as far removed from shunting operations in and around warehouses as the booking clerk or the person who 'regrets to announce...' Complex timetables prepared by a computer are more easily compiled than those by the individual with graph paper, ruler and pencil. There is also a natural tendency for the civilian railwayman to be more parochial in outlook than his Army counterpart.

For these and other reasons there is a continuing necessity for courses to be run for the TA railwayman as military railway operations are very basic indeed but nevertheless there is a particular way of going about them. A bonus for the Regular Army is the updating in modern railway operating methods which is the natural outcome of a fortnight's exchange of ideas during annual training.

79 Railway Squadron's other tasks were not neglected while all this new activity was going on. Since 1965 the RCT have been responsible for operating a number of rail-served depots in BAOR. The number involved is usually referred to as 32, but as two depots share the same general location in two cases, it would be more accurate to say that 34 depots were involved. There were an additional four depots in Berlin but these were not a direct responsibility of 79 Railway Squadron due to the different status of Forces in that city. As it was, all four depots were (and the remaining one is) worked by the Ost Havel Eisenbahn. In Belgium there

*Army Department diesel locomotive
'Carr' of 79 Railway Squadron
RCT.*

[By courtesy of MOD CS (REPS)]

were an additional nine depots (ten if one accepts the colocation argument). The squadron was responsible for railway operation in these 44 depots including, where necessary, the provision of AD locomotives and training and testing of drivers and shunters to ensure their professional competence. Twenty of the depots in West Germany were worked by civilian railways for the Army, half by the Deutsche Bundesbahn (German Federal Railway) and the other ten by private and local authority railways. In one case a Kleinbahn (literally 'small railway') uses Army locomotives to serve one of the depots. This unusual arrangement has obtained for several years and is recognized in the terms of the contract. This railway has no locomotives of its own based in the location in question and, in the event of a problem, the Army is obliged to provide another loco.

BAOR has not been granted immunity from financial stringency and ten depots with fifteen kilometres of track have been closed since 1965. In three cases, by continuing to pay a very modest annual maintenance fee, the British Army has been able to retain the option to re-open a once-closed depot.

After closure of the one depot in 1975, the track was lifted and neatly stock-piled. One may imagine the surprise of those in charge when they noticed one morning that their pile of track was missing. Someone had stolen almost one kilometre of permanent way material. After an enquiry the miscreants were caught.

Several of the depots have been reduced in size during the period under review, due more to building programmes than to redundancy, and one new depot has been opened. One depot has been increased in size.

An enterprising way of saving money has been introduced in suitable locations by taking in lodgers. Known as 'Joint Users', certain civilian firms have moved into redundant facilities within a depot and maintenance costs are shared. So far this has been arranged in four depots.

Although the RCT was not responsible for it, a 600 mm, Decauville narrow-gauge railway did operate in one of the depots, its track forming common crossings with the RCT standard gauge in three places. Unfortunately the depot is now vacant and nine of the Rail Motors 'Simplex' 2¼ ton locomotives were shipped back to Great Britain on RFA LSL *Sir Galahad* from Antwerp to Marchwood on 7 January 1980. Two of them LOD/758000 and 758220, are now at East Riggs and the remainder are at Lydd for refurbishing and storage.

79 Railway Squadron is in charge of a fleet of locomotives and rolling stock. There have been some changes in this fleet since 1965 a few of the more important ones are noted here. The Commander-in-Chief British Army of the Rhine/Commander Northern Army Group had at his disposal an interesting two-car diesel train set in which to tour his Command. As far as can be established it was built by M.A.K. of Nuremburg in 1935 and spent a certain amount of time in Lithuania before being captured by the Germans in 1942. It became General von Manstein's mobile headquarters and was bombed by the Allies in Berlin in 1945. Rebuilt by M.A.K. in 1953, it became the British Commander-in-Chief's train and was used by many prominent people. As it grew older it became increasingly difficult to keep in good order, especially in respect of mechanical spare parts, but the most telling point against it was that it had a top speed of only 100 km/h, and fitting it in amongst high speed trains on the main lines created severe problems and some embarrassment, for the Deutsche Bundesbahn officials did not wish it to be felt that they were being uncooperative with the General. Eventually it was sold to Mr. De Lille, a well-known enthusiast and collector of locomotives, of Maldegem, in Belgium. The transaction took place on 16 November 1978.

The unit consists of two cars, a driving motor coach equipped with a 360 hp M.A.K. diesel engine and hydraulic transmission, and one driving trailer car.

Unfortunately many of the records relating to locomotives between 1965 and the present day have been destroyed, thus one can give only an outline of what has happened.

It appears that there were 32 locomotives allocated to BAOR in 1965. Between then and now there has been a steady reduction in numbers and, as the fleet has become older and less reliable, that rate of withdrawal has increased, exacerbating the already difficult task of keeping fit locomotives in traffic. The year 1981 saw the Squadron's holdings reduced to twelve. A recent announcement by the QMG has, however, assured the unit's future – a future that, until early 1982, had hung in the balance. With the promise of new locomotives and a strengthening of morale now that the shadow of disbandment has gone, the squadron will be able to recover from the present parlous situation and considerable financial savings will be made with the reduction of locomotive hiring and repair. The introduction of new and reliable motive power will obviously lead to improvements in service and a renewed pride in the task so vital to BAOR.

With the new main battle tank comes the task of transporting it and the RCT has been looking at its equipment to see how it is suited to this job. The introduction of new Ramp Wagons is the likely outcome.

By jacking up this wagon with a central, manually-operated, in-built screw jack, removing one wheelset, and lowering the wagon to rail level, it becomes a ramp up which tracked vehicles climb in order to reach the decks of Warflat trains when no suitable head or side-ramp is available.

In the early 1970's the American Army decided to replace its ambulance trains. These had been purpose-built by German carriage works and were very much better equipped than the British Army's stock which consisted of ordinary Deutsche Bundesbahn (DB) (German Federal Railway) coaches modified in a somewhat austere manner for the task. These vehicles were also rather old, one at least dating from 1934 and the others not much more modern. OC 79 Squadron proposed that we obtain the American trains and hand back our own to the Federal Government. This was arranged and in October 1974, the Squadron took delivery of the 36 coaches involved. These have now been augmented by twelve converted B4YG coaches from DB which were bought in 1978. With this equipment the unit is able to run eight ambulance trains with additional stock on hand either to form more trains or augment those planned.

The squadron maintains a fleet of 140 Warflats (WGF) on which to carry armoured vehicles. Over the years since their introduction in 1940 the wagons have been widened and strengthened and look quite a lot different to those running in UK. They are capable of carrying the heaviest British tanks in use.

79 Railway Squadron also has eight fitted Guard Vans (FGV) equipped with cooking stove, sink, bunk beds and other basic accommodation requirement for military guards protecting classified consignments.

Before moving on to another activity one should mention the unique position in which the Officer Commanding 79 Railway Squadron finds himself. Under German Law, organizations which undertake railway operations must nominate a suitable person to be held responsible in law for the safe conduct of those activities. The Chief Transport and Movements Officer BAOR therefore nominates OC 79 Railway Squadron to the appointment of Eisenbahnbetriebsleiter, a singular title for an RCT major. He is thereby responsible for the safe operation, construction, maintenance and repair of all Army Department railway equipment, rolling stock, sidings and permanent way. Not to be entered into lightly by those of a nervous disposition!

Mention was earlier made of the rolling stock for 'The Berliner'. Although the six coaches are held on the ledgers of 79 Railway Squadron such is the distance from the unit base and such is the nature of the operation that day-to-day administration of this rolling stock is undertaken by 62 Transport & Movements Squadron RCT (Berlin).

'The Berliner' is the last of the British Military express passenger trains still running in Europe. After the Second World War, and before the era of regular air trooping there had been: 'The Blue Train', not to be confused with the rather more exotic 'Train Bleu' of the French Riviera, 'The Red Train', 'The Yellow Train' and 'The Crossed Swords'.

Since its inauguration in 1945 'The Berliner' has run in and out of Berlin through the Helmstedt – Magdeburg – Potsdam 'Corridor' daily, except for Christmas Day, and the period of the Soviet blockade of Berlin in 1948–49. Funding is provided by the 'Berlin Budget' and the train exercises the British Army's right of access by railway through this 'corridor' 364 days each year. It is therefore more significant than a useful and civilized means of travelling to and from Berlin and the West. (The Americans and French have their trains to Berlin, also.)

From 1945–1960, the train ran between Berlin and the Hook of Holland as a sleeping car express, but with the advent of air trooping, the through service to the Hook of Holland was reduced to two days a week, terminating at Hanover on the other five days. Connections westward from Hanover to the Hook of Holland were provided by 'The Red Train' via the Paderborn area and 'The Blue Train' via the Bentheim area. The twice-weekly through train travelled through the Ruhr area. There were, of course, appropriate balancing workings in the opposite direction.

From 1963, with the introduction of a comprehensive air trooping service, the train was reduced to its present form. Departing Berlin-Charlottenburg at 0842, 'The Berliner' is scheduled to arrive at its destination, Brunswick (Braunschweig) at 1228. This somewhat pedestrian schedule allows for examination of the Deutsche Reichsbahn locomotive and exterior of the train, the checking of documents by the Soviet Duty Officer at Marienborn and the changing of locomotives (Deutsche Reichsbahn for Deutsche Bundesbahn or vice versa) at Helmstedt.

The schedule also permits excellent meals to be served in the dining car. Catering on the train is provided under contract by the Compagnie Internationale des Wagons Lits et de Tourisme (CIWLT) and four crews of six cooks and stewards share the duties week by week. As in normal messes, meals are provided free to those travelling on duty and no more than the appropriate element of the daily ration allowance is charged to people travelling on leave. On discovering this and the fact that certain palatable wines are also available on board at concessionary rates, a British journalist recently felt that it was his duty, pro bono publico, to tell all. His fearless revelations appeared in one of the more popular British newspapers. 'The Berliner' is still running.

The return working departs Braunschweig at 1600 and arrives in Charlottenburg Station at 1945.

Since 1965, 'The Berliner' has been the responsibility of the RCT and 62 Transport and Movement Squadron RCT (Berlin) ensures the smooth running of the train from an administrative point of view. This Unit provides the Train Conducting Warrant Officer (TCWO), who travels on the train and deals with problems en route. 62 Squadron personnel also man the Movement Control office on Charlottenburg Station, checking documents, giving advice and directing the dispersal of passengers by road transport which is also provided by the Squadron. Ordering extra rolling stock to strengthen 'The Berliner', often necessary when complete units move, is also a 62 Squadron duty as is liaison with the other train staff and their unit. Besides the TCWO and the CIWLT catering crew, the Squadron must ensure that the following staff have been appointed and briefed; OC Train, Russian Interpreter, military guard of five soldiers to defend the train if necessary – they also act in a general security capacity, a Postal and Courier unit NCO responsible for mails and, until made redundant by more sophisticated equipment in 1981, a Regimental Signaller from 229 Signal Squadron (Berlin).

The train is normally formed of five coaches, viz: a staff coach to accommodate the train staff, a restaurant/kitchen car which also houses emergency rations in case of protracted delay, one first class and two second class coaches. The last three belong to Deutsche Bundesbahn as do any strengthening coaches added for unit moves. Of particular interest to us are the staff coach and the restaurant/kitchen car for these are two of the six 'owned' by the RCT.

Friday 19 April 1974, was the occasion of the 10,000th round trip, and suitable celebration was made with the General Officer Commanding Berlin (British Sector) and several senior officers and guests embarked. The Director of Movements (Army) flew in from England to celebrate the event and to enjoy the special arrangements made by OC 62 Squadron.

34 · MILITARY AID TO CIVIL MINISTRIES (MACM) OR COMMUNITIES (MACC)

IN PEACETIME the Services may be called upon to aid the central or local government in times of an emergency. This aid may be extended to the communities of allied or friendly nations with the agreement of our own central government, also occasionally to commercial companies for unusual tasks. Emergencies may be caused by natural or artificial disasters or because of industrial action in a critical area of the economy. In principle, however, the Services will normally only be employed to reduce or eliminate the danger to life or the health of individuals or communities. Economic charges are sometimes raised against the user by the Service or Services concerned. Military Aid to Civil Ministries (MACM) does not include military or policing operations against subversive groups such as were encountered in the Malayan or Northern Ireland emergencies. MACM operations are usually confined to the Regular Army and it is unusual for the Territorial Army to be directly involved, although both their equipment and accommodation are frequently used.

The RASC and RCT, because of their functional characteristics, are ideally suited for the aid of many disaster situations and have been employed over the last 37 years on many occasions. A summary of those in which the army has been employed are listed in Annex 'A'. In overseas commands it has not been possible to list all the occasions where troops have helped because many of the operations were given little publicity or were overshadowed by and merged with other operations or international aid contributions. The following incidents are therefore intended to illustrate the various types of involvement and do not claim to be a comprehensive account of all aid given to Civil Ministries by the Corps in the time frame 1945–82.

In the decade following the end of World War II, there were a number of strikes in the transport industry, in particular in the docks, the London food distribution organizations and by road transport firms. Some of these threatened the well being of the community, especially at a time when food was still rationed. There was a comparatively large standing army in the UK which was readily employed in relieving the population of the worst features of the industrial unrest. Every district had at least one MT company which could be employed on such tasks. Both 6 and 15 Training Battalions RASC, which had all military instructors, were

[By courtesy of RCT Museum]

DUKW's of the Amphibian Training RASC rescuing civilians during the 1946 floods in the Welshpool area.

used for major transport tasks. The more specialist functions were met by the RE port, beach, railway and movement control units.

During the war years 1939–45 little work had been done to keep the streams and rivers rising on Exmoor clear of debris and as a result of heavy rains in August 1952 there was a massive build up of water behind the many obstacles in the river beds. On 11th August the rain had been particularly heavy and persistent. The sheer weight of water built up behind the obstacles caused them to give way and a massive flow was created. In its path to the river mouths it caused much damage, washing away bridges, property and livestock.

Lynmouth, situated as its name implies, was not only at the mouth of the river Lyn but at the bottom of two steep valleys and it caught the full impact of the huge flow of water. Bridges, buildings complete with occupants, buses, cars and cattle were swept away out to sea. Buildings left standing along the edges of the river had debris piled up to first floor level.

Two military units particularly suited to provide assistance were close by and both contained sizeable Corps representation. These were the Amphibious Warfare Centre in the Fremington/Instow/Westward Ho! area and 264 (Scottish) Beach Brigade (TA) in camp at Braunton. Parties from both these units were on their way to the scene before dawn and composed of representatives from the arms and services most needed. Royal Engineer Field and Transportation, Royal Signals, RAMC, RMP, REME. Tank transporters driven RASC carrying engineer equipment, 4 × 4 vehicles particularly useful in negotiating the damaged countryside and last but not least the RASC DUKWs. The DUKWs could not be used in the immediate area of the disaster because of the sheer weight of water, but were put to good use rescuing people and cattle in flooded areas around the Moor.

There is no doubt that the immediate response provided by these local units, soon to be reinforced from further afield contributed enormously to the effectiveness of the whole rescue operation. It was very heartening to find that, of the many Z Reservists called up to train with the Beach Brigade that year, quite a few volunteered to stay on after their call up period in order to give their services in their own time.

A similar event occurred on the East Coast when the combination of an exceptional high tide and a full storm in the North Sea caused extensive flooding in the Spring of 1953. The sea defences were severely breached, while many ships were swept from their moorings and sunk. Whole communities had to be evacuated and thousands of livestock were destroyed. Many transportation and transport units were involved in the evacuation, maintenance of essential services and repair of the dykes and bridges. In particular, 18 Company RASC, then a water transport unit stationed at Gun Wharf, Sheppey Island, in the midst of the disaster area became heavily involved. This Company had to evacuate its own married quarters and rescue and repair many of its own vessels. It then provided support for the community which included a water bus service for the children of Chatham, the distribution of milk and fresh food to individuals and communities cut off by the floods; and even the evacuation of the dead. 116 Company RASC (Amphibious GT) was also heavily involved in the rescue of people and animals, using their DUKWs from Fremington.

An example of the simple sort of overseas tasks in which the Services help the expatriate community occurred during the Suez Operations in 1956. This was given the code name 'Op Diplomat'. An increasingly hostile Egyptian population caused some 600 British nationals, led by the Ambassador, to be evacuated from Egypt to Capuzzo in Libya on 10 November 1956. The Garrison in Libya received, fed and accommodated these individuals before transporting them to RAF El Adem from where they were flown to Blackbushe airfield in Hampshire. A simple operation involving the RASC transport, supply and barrack staff but the speed and efficiency with which it was conducted avoided hardship and danger to the evacuees concerned.

On the maritime side, the RCT LCT *Audemer* operated as a yacht haven and dinghy park for service yachts during Cowes Week 1966, following the withdrawal from service of the last Royal Navy LCT.

From August 1967 to July 1968 the RCT FARELF took part in a sea dumping programme designed to remove a large quantity of World War II Japanese bombs, mines and torpedoes from Penang Island using Mexeflote and an RCT LCT.

In May 1967 all RCT units in Hong Kong were involved in transporting units and stores in support of the Civil Authorities to counter the widespread disturbances in both Hong Kong and Kowloon. Also during the year HMAV *Andalsnes*, commanded by Captain Robin Melvin,

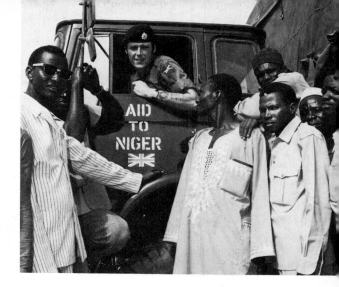

Aid to Niger 1974.

[By courtesy of PR HQ UKLF]

assisted BBC Television in the making of a film 'Old Man of Hoy'. While the Z craft *Zara*, based at Marchwood was used for the carriage of fire fighting equipment during an emergency at the Fawley Oil Refinery. 17 Port Regiment RCT also chartered *Mexeflote* to Taylor Woodrow to recover a crawler crane from its Solent site and an RPL to Limmer and Trinidad to move ready-mix asphalt to the Isle of Wight.

After exceptionally heavy rain in the West Country on the night of 10/11 July 1968, there was again extensive flooding and several road bridges were swept away. 18 Squadron's amphibians were deployed on flood relief operations, while 60 and 65 Squadrons, 17 Port and 6 Training Regiments were employed in lifting bridging material from Engineer Depots at Longmoor and Long Marston to the bridge sites. In September it was the turn of the South East where both regular and reserve army units were used after exceptionally heavy rain on 14 September caused widespread flooding. 151 (GL) Regiment RCT (V) tasked vehicles from 210 and 215 Squadrons RCT (V) while 20 Squadron RCT from Regents Park was also committed, followed by two troops from 27 Regiment in a bridging role and 17 DUKWs now of 17 Port Regiment RCT. Tasks included evacuation of families to emergency centres, resupply of troops taking part, sandbag filling and transporting, towing from danger points, operating water pumps, ferrying of equipment and stores for emergency centres and the rescue of flooded vehicles.

In the Gulf, the LCT HMAV *Arezzo*, commanded by Major R Melvin, made regular runs between Bahrain and Sharjah. During one sailing she answered an urgent call for assistance from the German master of the Iranian fishing trawler MV *Matragh* to put down a mutiny. She located the trawler and within a few hours had put an armed party aboard and escorted her to a rendezvous with a naval vessel at Bandar Addis. The commander and crew were commended on their timely action.

For the Investiture of HRH The Prince of Wales on 1 July 1969, a two span heavy girder bridge for the Caernarvon Corporation was carried by 65 Squadron in forty lifts over nine days. Camp stores also had to be transported and sixty personnel carriers (military coaches and TCVs) provided on the Investiture Day. Movement control detachments from the Corps covered road routes and railway stations.

415 Maritime Troop, Hong Kong was employed in the autumn of 1970 to deploy 1 DWR to Lantau Island to assist the civil police to search out escaped convicts.

55 Air Despatch Squadron RCT and 33 Maritime Regiment RCT were involved during the same year in disaster relief in East Pakistan (now Bangladesh) after severe floods following the Monsoon.

From 30th September to 31 October 1970, a composite medical unit, Ferrieforce, was deployed from Cyprus to Jordan as part of an international Red Cross relief to that country following the battle to drive the Palestine Liberation Organization (PLO) from Jordan. In addition to a small transport element in Amman, 30 Regiment RCT in Cyprus concentrated the Force at RAF Akrotiri, assisted in loading the aircraft for the initial move; and moved casualties from returning aircraft at Kingsfield airstrip to BMH Dhekelia. (101 sorties with 1200 passengers and 830,000 lbs of freight.)

Although not strictly MACM, during the 1970 Dock Strike the Marchwood Military Port came into its own, handling all Service priority container traffic to BAOR. Four Army Landing Craft Tank (LCT) and the RFA Coaster *Robert Middleton* were involved moving 366 containers in three weeks. Loading and discharging rates reached a record of twenty four 20 foot ISO containers from an LCT in 3 hours.

On 23rd October 1970 the tanker Pacific Glory (70,000 DWT) was in a collision close to the Isle of Wight and it caught fire and went aground threatening an oil pollution disaster in the Solent. The Board of Trade put SOLFIRE into action which included men from 17 Port Regiment RCT operating the six detergent spray units mounted on tugs, first in the Solent and later in Torbay and Rotterdam to where the tanker was towed. In all the soldier seamen spent a month at sea both operating the equipment and standing watch on the tugs.

On 17th August 1971, Typhoon 'Rose' struck Hong Kong. Over 100 people were killed and extensive flooding and wind damage was done throughout the Colony. 31 Regiment RCT and the Gurkha Transport Regiment were involved in the clearing operation including the rescue of numerous pigs stranded by floods in the New Territories.

Earlier in the year 414 Pack Transport Troop in Hong Kong were involved for three weeks in moving materials for a school playground into the inaccessible Sai Kung Peninsula.

In January 1972, the Hong Kong Maritime Troop were again in action with ramped powered lighters (RPL) and landing craft mechanized (LCM) ferrying firemen trying to save the former passenger liner *Queen Elizabeth* (Seawise University) which was on fire in the harbour –

710

unfortunately without success.

In July and August 1972 another Dock Strike confirmed the value of Marchwood which met all the Joint Service and NAAFI freight movement to Germany and Northern Ireland, some of it with improved timings.

In February and March 1973, a force of four Hercules transport aircraft and two air despatch troops were deployed to Nepal to operate from two forward bases dropping grain to inaccessible famine stricken areas. Some 2,160 tons of grain were distributed by air drop by 1 April meeting the Nepalese Government's requirements.

Later in the year 51 Port Squadron RCT from Marchwood were tasked to move a 145 ton Reactor measuring 90 feet in length and 17 feet in diameter from the Heavy Lift ship *Gloria Maria* berthed in Southampton to Calshot Power Station where it was to be landed en route for the Fawley Esso Refinery. A four string wide Mexeflote was made and took 1½ hours to cross the Solent at a steady three knots for a successful landing and eventual construction.

In March 1975, Operation Slant was mounted when the dustcart drivers of the City of Glasgow were on strike. For four weeks an ad hoc transport regiment of 65 Squadron RCT and two ad hoc District Squadrons removed rubbish from the areas which were likely to become a health hazard. The actual collection and loading was made by a Scottish Infantry Battalion (1 RHF followed by 1 KOSB). Vehicles provided were from Territorial Army training scales, both the infantrymen and the drivers commuted daily from Edinburgh although their HQs, formed initially from the regular staff of 154 Transport Regiment RCT (V) and in April from 153 Transport Regiment RCT (V) remained in Glasgow. When the strike ended 42,000 tons of 'emergency' refuse had been moved.

From November 1977 to January 1978 the firemen all over the UK went on strike over a pay dispute. All three Services provided emergency cover with 'Green Goddess' Civil Defence fire engines under the direction of senior fire officers on a regional basis. The RCT contribution was mainly as individuals who were employed as appliance drivers. The Army School of Mechanical Transport provided a Military Control HQ for the Humberside Authority. Many, indeed most, TA Centres were used as 'stations' which reduced the ability of the reserve army to train.

In the winter of 1979/80 the Corps was alerted for a series of transport strikes including oil tanker drivers, road haulage and ambulance drivers. The only actual committal was in Northern Ireland where the roulement transport regiment (4 Armoured Division Transport Regiment RCT) took over and operated civil fuel tankers for a short period. The UK Line of Communication units were heavily used throughout the winter months and all transport units spent much time planning and preparing for emergencies during this Winter of Discontent.

In Hong Kong the Gurkha Transport Regiment was involved

Right: *26 Sqn RCT with 'Green Goddess' fire engines during the firemans' strike in Northern Ireland Christmas 1977.*

[By courtesy of PR HQ N Ireland]

Left: *Driver 'Jonah' Jones takes over a civilian tanker in Northern Ireland during a strike in 1979.*

[By courtesy of RCT Museum]

during 1979–81 in support of the infantry in controlling illegal immigrants both from China and Vietnam. Helicopter handling teams were provided and stores for the rebuilding of the border fence were positioned. 415 Maritime Troop assisted the Royal Hong Kong Police in coastal patrols.

In the winter of 1980/81 27 Logistic Support Group Regiment RCT prepared for another firemen's strike which did not take place. The following winter, 66 Squadron together with the regular and some TA members of 156 Transport Regiment, were involved in transporting salt from Cheshire for road clearance in Wales during a particularly hard winter.

RCT units provided transport support for the units guarding civil prisons during the 1981 Prison Officers' strike.

These emergencies and incidents, and many others like them, serve to illustrate the way the Corps has been called to the aid of civil ministries and communities since 1945. It has invariably risen well to any challenge or task that it has been given. In particular, the cheerful, resourceful and efficient way in which our soldiers have coped with a wide variety of difficult, sometimes dangerous tasks has reflected great credit both to themselves and to the Corps.

ANNEX 'A'

35 · REGIMENTAL AFFAIRS

THIS CHAPTER COVERS THOSE aspects of the history of the RASC and RCT which may generally be described as 'family matters'. It has long been appreciated that the continuation and well being of 'the family' is a basic essential of Corps morale and therefore its performance.

Although this factor is now fully recognised, official support does not necessarily mean total financial support and many officially recognized regimental activities have to be funded wholly or partly from Corps funds.

The agency now responsible for the management of regimental activities is Regimental Headquarters RCT. Its raison d'etre and progress to its status in 1982 is discussed below.

REGIMENTAL HEADQUARTERS ROYAL CORPS OF TRANSPORT

The 1950s saw the beginning of a steady campaign of manpower cuts in the Army and it became apparent that serving personnel could no longer be employed in sedentary jobs. It was appreciated by the Army council that the continuation of regimental activities was essential to the traditions and morale of the Army and therefore if the Army's manpower did not stretch to the staffing of regimental committees, civil servants paid from public funds would have to be provided.

In 1960 Regimental Headquarters for all corps and regiments were authorized. Establishments were approved, the staff being paid from public funds. Prior to this date, all regimental activities were controlled by committees either from serving officers or voluntarily by retired officers, or a combination of both, any expenses being provided from Corps funds.

RHQ is the focal point of RCT regimental activities and exists to co-ordinate Corps domestic affairs. These cover Corps funds, Corps property, the Corps Journal – *The Waggoner*, The Corps Technical Journal – *The Review* and the RCT Officers Handbook, museum, library and medal collection, Corps history, records, archives and memorials, policy aspects of the Headquarters Mess, the Band and the administration of Old Comrades and benevolence. RHQ provides the Corps' specialist staff which ensures the maintenance and safeguarding the regimental traditions. It provides a secretariat for the Colonels Commandant and the head of the Corps for the exercise of their control over these domestic regimental matters. RHQ is able to give the required advice on all these subjects quickly and unequivocally, because of the continuity of its staff.

These tasks are carried out mainly through the following committees:

Committee of Management – Institution of the RCT
Museums, Memorials and Publications Committee
Central Sports Fund Committee
Professional Activities Advisory Committee
Officers' Dinner Club Committee
Central Property Fund Committee
Aldershot Institute Rebate Fund Committee
Band Committee
Headquarters Mess Committee
RCT Museum Trust

The senior appointment in the staff of RHQ RCT is that of Secretary, a Retired Officer Grade II, the first incumbent being Colonel J R Burgess TD from 1960 to his untimely death in harness in 1972. His successor was Brigadier D W E Hancox who filled the appointment from 1972 to 1982. The present incumbent is Brigadier B G E Courtis.

The RASC/RCT Association is an integral part of RHQ RCT and is responsible for the administration of Association branches throughout the United Kingdom and the operation of the RASC/RCT Benevolent Fund. From 1927 to 1944 the Association was run by a Secretary but from 1945 onwards the post became that of Controller when it was held by Colonel H M Wright, OBE. In 1952, Brigadier Farquharson-Roberts CBE took over until 1960 when Colonel E (Jock) Marshall OBE assumed the appointment. He was followed by Colonel R F Discombe OBE from 1975 and then by the present incumbent Brigadier D Cardle who took over in 1981. The responsibilities and activities of the Association are discussed in a later section of this chapter.

THE INSTITUTION OF THE ROYAL CORPS OF TRANSPORT

Before 1910 there was in existence the 'Army Service Corps Dinner Club' which in that year was reconstituted as the 'Army Service Corps Club' having added to its financial responsibilities the Corps Band, the Army Service Corps Journal, the Point-to-Point and Cricket. In subsequent years other sports and games were added to this list. After the 1939–45 War the Club assumed control of *the Review*, the Museum and certain other Corps activities.

Financial support was provided by voluntary officer membership, although in practice nearly all regular officers joined, the rates of subscription being based on rank in the case of serving regular officers. In the cases of retired officers and those of the various reserves and those who had served on temporary or emergency commissions in both wars, a level rate was fixed without regard to rank. No financial assistance was provided from public funds and the Honorary Secretary, who was usually the Buller Mess Secretary, received only a small honorarium classed as expenses.

In 1950, the then Director of Supplies and Transport, seeking means to improve the financial situation, ascertained that the Royal Artillery and the Royal Engineers, because they had Institutions, were entitled to an annual War Office Grant of £500. He therefore took action to have established an organization to be entitled 'The Institution of the Royal Army Service Corps' to be governed by a Council.

The first meeting of the Council of the Institution was held on 21st July 1951, the key appointments made on that occasion being:

President	:	Lieutenant General Sir Humfrey Gale
Vice President	:	Major General Sir Reginald Kerr
Hon Secretary	:	Major General Sir Cecil M Smith

All these officers were Colonels Commandants and the Honorary Secretary had just retired as Director of Supplies and Transport.

The institution assumed responsibility for all the academic activities of the RASC Club. It did not take over activities of a sporting or social nature and the Annual Dinner from which the Club had originated became the responsibility of a Committee financially answerable to the Club.

At the third meeting of the Council in February 1952 it was decided that a permanent paid secretary was necessary and Brigadier C Mc I Delf, an employed retired officer, was appointed at a small remuneration; he continued to function until 1957 when he was replaced by a serving officer, Major A F Brigden RASC.

Major General Sir Cecil Smith KBE, CB, MC relieved Lieutenant General Sir Humfrey Gale, the President, who had completed his tour as Colonel-Commandant, in the same year. Hitherto, the RASC *Journal* (now *The Waggoner*) had been independent of the Institution but at this same meeting, 1957, it was brought under the wing of the Institution. The two organizations, the Institution and the RASC Club, were administered entirely separately but the Institution did not take direct subscriptions from officers; instead it drew a lump sum from the Club.

On the formation of Regimental Headquarters in 1960, the staff being paid from public funds, RHQ RASC became the Secretariat for both the Institution and the Club and the Institution was no longer entitled to an annual grant of £500. By 1962 it was becoming an increasing burden to administer two organizations with two sets of controlling committees, having in many cases the same members and requiring two separate series of meetings. Therefore at the 24th meeting of the Council of the Institution it was decided, with the agreement of the RASC Club, that the two should amalgamate and the final Institution Annual General Meeting was held on 29th April 1963. It was agreed that the title of the RASC Club should be retained but that the Institution should be kept alive within the Club by the continuation of responsibility for mainly academic affairs through the medium of two committees, the Museums, Memorials and Publications Committee and the Professional Activities Committee.

On the formation of the Royal Corps of Transport on 15 July 1965, the title of the RASC Club was changed to RCT Officers Club. After this formation, the two committee concept was maintained until 1969 when the late Colonel James Burgess, the first appointed Secretary, Regimental Headquarters RASC produced a thoughtful paper pointing out that under the existing reorganization there was no single controlling body which could make financial and other decisions affecting not only the Club, but the Institution and various other committees, e.g. the Central Sports Fund Committee (which had taken over responsibility for Sports and Games from the Club) and the Central Property Fund Committee. The lack of such an over-riding authority caused confusion, duplication of effort and waste of time in committees resulting in delay to final decisions. The paper therefore proposed that the Institution should be reconstituted as the governing body for all Regimental affairs of the Corps.

In 1972 the Transport Officer-in-Chief (Army) set up a committee to consider this question of central control. The report of this committee by and large accepted and recommended for action the proposal outlined in the Burgess paper and the report was approved at the final Annual General Meeting of the Club on 10th May 1973. Consequently the Institution of the RCT was not merely restored to the status that it had held prior to 1963, but absorbed all the responsibilities of the RCT Officers Club whose title disappeared.

The governing body became known as the 'Council for the Regimental Affairs of the Royal Corps of Transport'. It is responsible for the coordination of all RCT Regimental activities and in particular for the direction of the Institution of the RCT in accordance with its objects and rules.

THE REGIMENTAL ASSOCIATION

Starting Anew in 1945

With the end of the 1939–1945 War some of the work then in progress became redundant, notably the schemes to help prisoners of war.

On 23rd April 1945, Colonel H M Wright OBE assumed the duties of Controller and he at once set about adjusting the organization of the Association to suit peace time conditions. An Honorary Secretary was appointed to each of the UK Command Committees and the possibility of establishing branches in the most important towns and cities in the UK was considered. By the end of 1945, forty entirely new branches had been established to add to the then existing thirty branches that had survived the war and the organization was well on towards founding one hundred branches. To speed up the work of giving relief, local Imprest Accounts with funds allotted from the Benevolent Funds were established and based on the chairman of District Zones or on the larger branches. Association HQ was on the move again and new, more suitable premises had been purchased at 6 Queensberry Place, Kensington. It is a tribute to the founders of the Association that it came out of the 1939–1945 era largely unscathed. The objects, management and organization of the Association had stood the test. However, peace-time conditions, structural changes in the Forces, new social concepts and financial pressures brought about changes in the Association from 1945 onwards.

Organization

In 1945 the Executive Committee recommended that the management of the affairs of the Association be vested in a Committee of Management presided over by a Chairman to be elected annually. They also recommended that an Annual Conference be held to which all Branches would send a representative and that the policy of the Association would be determined by resolutions passed at this Conference. The Senior Colonel Commandant of the RASC was to preside at the Conference as President of the Association. In 1946 the Committee of Management revised the Rules of the Association which allowed for the appointment of a General Purposes and Finance Sub Committee to carry on the routine business of the Association. The first Conference was held in London on 25th June 1947 with Major General M S Brander CB OBE MI Mech E presiding, and fifty-two branch delegates attended. It was at this meeting that the decision was made to change the name of the Association from 'The Royal Army Service Corps Regimental Association' to 'The Royal Army Service Corps Association'. The change simply reflected common usage. It was also decided that in future the expenses of branch delegates attending the conference would be borne by Association Headquarters. Up to 1960 the Association had met all its own administrative charges, salaries, rents, and the like. 1961 was a key year in that it was the year in which the RASC Association Headquarters became part of the RASC Secretariat, a proposal made by the Army Council for all Regimental Associations. Vesting date was 1st April 1961. The effect was that the staff became civil servants but continued to work for the Association as in the past. The change had been argued over and debated at length since many members were worried that the Association might lose some of its independence through the change. Having been assured on that point and having accepted that financial savings would accrue as there would be no salaries to meet, and no accommodation and heat and light charges, the change was accepted.

There was however a reservation that if the new system was found to be to the extreme disadvantage of the Association then the Association could revert to its original organization. The favourable effect on Association funds is noticeable from this period and in part must be attributed to the change. On 1st June 1961 Association Headquarters moved from Queensberry Place, SW1, to the Duke of York's Headquarters in Chelsea.

1965 was a bitter sweet time for in that year the Royal Army Service Corps was no more and in its place rose the Royal Corps of Transport.

The change was largely a functional one revolving around yet another reorganization of the Army, but it meant much to older members that their old well loved Corps was no more. In fact the change made little impact on the Association – matters went on as before albeit under the new title of The Royal Army Service Corps/Royal Corps of Transport Association. In 1966 the then Transport Officer-in-Chief, Major General E H G Lonsdale CB MBE ruled that the RCT regimental tie as we now had it could be worn by any member of the Corps past or present if he so wished. At the same time the 'old tie' of the RASC should not be worn by those who had joined the Corps since its designation as RCT. It followed that those who had served in both Corps could wear both ties. In 1968 the Headquarters was moved to Regents Park Barracks in Albany Street, London NW1 followed by yet another move in 1975 to Aldershot in the administrative shadow of the RCT Training Centre. Because of tradition and for a variety of practical reasons the move from London was not popular with everyone. But it proved to be a wise decision and a sensible precaution in the face of the cost cutting and retrenchments that were looming on the horizon.

The number of Association branches has varied over the years. Of the 37 that existed before the war, 30 survived and were reinforced by a host of new branches immediately afterwards. In 1946 there were 104, in 1947 130, 1948 137 which was the peak. After this numbers remained fairly constant at around 120 branches, until a steady rundown started in the early 1960s and by 1964 numbers were reduced to about 100. By 1973 they were down to 76 and the current figure is 75. In spite of this decline it is heartening that there are many more branches in 1980 than there were in 1939. It is also a matter of note that the Life Membership cost at the outset in 1927 was three guineas (£3.15), it now stands at £3.00. Annual subscriptions during the period have risen from 3s.0d. (15p) to 30p, a bargain by any standard!

Social Events

Stemming from one of the objects of the Association, 'to foster esprit de corps', comes the organization of social functions. These gatherings are of the greatest importance to the Association in that they present opportunities for members to renew friendships. Events occur regularly at branch and regional level; this section comments briefly on the national events, the Dinner Dance, the Rally, the 'Northern Get Together' and the Efficiency Award.

There had long been an Old Comrades Dinner Club which catered for members and ex-members of the officers' and sergeants' mess. That club was wound up in 1927 when the Association was born. Stag dinners were organized by the Association before the Second World War but they could not be revived immediately in 1945 due to rationing. The first dinner after the war was held in the Horticultural Society Hall,

Westminster on 30th October 1948, some 850 members attending. The chief guest was Field Marshal Sir William Slim. No regular pattern for the dinner emerged until 1955, it appears to have taken turns with the Rally, when a Dinner Dance was held in Lyons Corner House, Coventry Street, London in November 1955. 550 members, their wives and friends attended and many hundreds were disappointed since the seating capacity was limited. There is little doubt that the pinnacle was reached as far as the dinner dances were concerned at a series of dinners arranged at Derry & Toms Restaurant, Kensington High Street (now Marks & Spencers). They regularly attracted 800–900 people and many more would have attended had the room capacity allowed. It is a matter of regret that Derry & Toms closed in 1971 and sadly the Dinner Dances from then on were very much less well supported. Various other places have been tried with mixed results but if the proof of success is in the numbers attending then the successful formula achieved at Derry & Toms is still evading the Committee of Management.

It was consistent with the deep camaraderie that existed after the Second World War that the membership were heavily in favour or holding a Rally in London. The first of many took place in the Royal Albert Hall on 19 November 1949. It was an outstanding success and the pattern was set for all future rallies. The programme is normally in two parts, the first half consisting of a pageant and a parade of standards from various Branches followed by a celebrity performance and the Corps Band is always present to accompany the artists and entertain with a programme of music. The second half is devoted to dancing. In 1949 it was Mr. Billy Ternent's band together with a cabaret. Nearly 5,000 members attended. Rallies were held in general every second year until 1977 when the pattern moved to every third year. The decision was a natural consequence of falling attendances, down to around 2,000 in 1980, and to increased costs. For many years the Rally had paid for itself but in recent years, losses have been substantial culminating in 1980 in a subsidy of over £4,000. The strength of the Rally always lay in the strong support it obtained from its older war time members: regrettably such events have little appeal for the young as is borne out by the fact that all other equivalent war-time based rallies have ceased. It is a simple fact that times, people and social customs change and it makes no sense to continue blindly with an event that is not supported by a reasonable number of the membership, apart from the fact that the Royal Albert Hall about one-third full is an unattractive proposition.

In an effort to popularise the Association away from the South, an RASC Association Northern Region Activity was held in April/May 1964 culminating in a Church Service at York Minster. 900 members attended. It was some time before the idea was taken up again, not until 1971, when Major R A Smart of the Edinburgh Branch organized a Dinner Dance at Blackpool in the Metropole Hotel. It became known as the 'Northern Get

[By courtesy of RCT Museum]

HM The Queen Mother with Major General W Bate CB OBE DL at the Field of Remembrance Ceremony, Westminster Abbey 9 Nov 1978.

Together' and continued under the direction of Major Smart on a year on year off basis until 1980 when he relinquished the task.

Finance

In the early years there was considerable thought given before a maximum of £5 was spent on benevolence; that sum is very low in comparison with the grants in aid of around £100 that are being made regularly and indeed daily in the 1980s. It speaks much for the diminishing value of the £1 but it reflects even more the judicious handling of the funds by the Administrative trustees who have maintained the real worth of the fund and the financial aid given remains realistic in terms of need. Annual grants exceed £100,000 and the fund is now worth over £800,000, it has to be said that it is increasingly due to the voluntary one day's pay scheme by serving soldiers towards benevolence.

It has already been mentioned that the Association has two funds, the Association Fund and the Benevolent Fund. Adjustments to the Benevolent Fund occurred when the Compassionate, Memorial and the small Canteen Funds were merged in 1969 under a scheme prepared by the Charity Commissioners. These Benevolent Funds had achieved charitable status in the early 1920s with the tax savings that brought. The

Association Fund on the other hand did not achieve charitable status until 1978.

The funds were generally in good shape immediately after the War in 1945 but they did come under some strain when they began to show regularly an excess of expenditure over income. The losses were not excessive but they were such that the Committee of Management sought to put them in better order.

It is difficult to isolate the reasons why the funds are now in good shape. Both funds now reflect regularly an excess of income over expenditure and the stepping stones to that welcome situation could be said to be when the funds were put in the hands of a firm of professional investors, Charterhouse Japhet, when the Association Headquarters' expenses became public which reduced overheads dramatically, and, as has already been mentioned, by the introduction of the voluntary day's pay scheme towards benevolence by serving officers and soldiers. This now means that the Corps can in most cases look after its own compassionate cases without outside aid from other charities. That was not always the case.

Benevolence

If every other conceivable activity in the Association ceased, save that of benevolence, the Association would still be very much worth while. The work done by the Benevolent Commitee on behalf of the Association is, to paraphrase its object, 'to benefit in such way or ways as the Committee thinks best, officers, warrant officers, non-commissioned officers and private soldiers who are serving or who have served in or been attached for service to the RASC/RCT and the wives, widows, children, grandchildren and other dependants of such who find themselves in financial difficulty.' It was estimated that there were in the UK in 1980 around one million who qualified for aid from the Benevolent Fund. A national study by an independent organization concluded that the peak of requests for benevolence would be reached in 1990 when many who had served in the Second World War would reach an age when the physical and mental state of many might be such as to call for help, not forgetting their wives and other dependants. Already there are increasing pressures on the fund.

The problem of inflation is the only present shadow on the horizon. Its effects are particularly severe on the Association Fund since investment income is currently fairly static whilst costs continue to escalate. It means simply that whatever money the Association has, it buys less and less. The Benevolent Fund on the other hand is in part inflation proofed as the one day's pay scheme mirrors the inflation proofing of the serving soldiers pay. In broad terms the Benevolent Fund is holding its own in terms of purchasing power – but only just.

A tribute needs to be paid to the various Committees and to the Administrative Trustees of both Funds for their sterling work in keeping the Funds in good order so that the aims and objectives set in 1927 can still be achieved. The dangers are there but there is every reason to suppose that they can be kept in check.

Accident Benefit Insurance Scheme
In 1955 an Accident Benefit Insurance Scheme was introduced. At that time for one shilling (5p) ex-service and serving members between the ages of 16 and 65 could receive certain benefits. As far as serving soldiers were concerned the scheme only covered them when not on duty, the argument being that they were already well covered by the Services if they were killed or injured on duty. The Association was also able to arrange general insurance on an agency basis with the Legal and General Insurance Company, that service has since lapsed.

The Benefit Scheme worked so much in favour of the insured that in 1959 some changes were made in the benefits paid but the fees remained unchanged. In 1963 the benefits available were extended in that members could, if they so wished, take up five units of insurance against the previous one. Each unit cost one shilling.

The Scheme has remained popular and it now embraces members from 16 to 70 years of age and attested junior leaders from age 14. A serving member who contributes to the day's pay scheme automatically gets 30 free units of insurance, a maximum benefit of £3,000. Non-serving members get one free unit with their annual membership fee of 30p with the right to buy up to 29 additional units if they wish. The worth of the Scheme is reflected in the statistics – particularly in recent years. In 1981 £20,000 was paid out mainly to serving personnel killed in traffic accidents. This is an unwelcome statistic but it shows that the fund meets an important need.

Employment
A great deal of excellent work was done immediately after the War by the Association Headquarters and by Branches to find employment for soldiers leaving the Service. Very gradually specialized organizations have emerged that have taken on that role, mainly the Regular Forces Employment Association. That organization has offices throughout the United Kingdom and the Association works very closely with it. Some jobs are still found through the Association Headquarters on behalf of those who have specifically asked for an ex-soldier of the RCT.

Presentations
The Association has always been very keen to promote the well-being and efficiency of the Corps. In the late 1950s it presented to the Corps the Association Efficiency Cup to be awarded on an annual basis to the Regular Unit deemed to be most deserving of it. In more recent days a shield to be awarded to the best Army Cadet Force or Combined Cadet

Force RCT badged unit was presented and now to the best young Regular soldier of the year, a replica of the silver trophy presented to Her Royal Highness, Princess Alice on her 80th Anniversary by the Corps and to which the Association made a substantial contribution.

THE CLAYTON TRUST FUND

After the death in 1933 of Lieutenant General Sir Frederick T Clayton KCB, KCMG, late Army Service Corps, and in acknowledgement of his most distinguished services to the Army Service Corps and Royal Army Service Corps throughout his long life, it was decided to establish the Clayton Memorial. Subscriptions were then invited from all who had served with, or knew personally, General Clayton, and a total sum of £171 3s 6d was received from individual and collective subscriptions.

A retired officer who wished to remain anonymous realized that the appeal could not possibly result in the raising of any large sum, on account of the rates of subscription. In order therefore to create a more substantial amount of capital the anonymous donor transferred securities to the Fund amounting to some £3,000.

On Corps Sunday 1934, a memorial tablet which had been purchased by Lady Clayton was unveiled in St George's Church, Aldershot and The Clayton Trust Fund was formally established on 26 March 1935.

The original objects of this Fund were as follows:

a. Promotion of the mental and physical efficiency of all ranks serving in the Corps.
b. Provision of grounds for outdoor exercise and sport with the necessary equipment.
c. Purchase of land and buildings.
d. Maintenance, repair and decoration of other ranks' messes.
e. Provision of medical assistance for past and present members of the Corps and for their dependants.
f. Provision of almshouses for those under medical care.
g. Any other charitable purpose for the benefit of the Corps as a whole.

These original objects have now been widened to assist in the financial provision of amenities for the good and benefit of all ranks of the Corps as the Council of the Trust think fit.

In addition the Trust has provided prizes for articles published in the Corps Review and for the best RCT soldier at the Army Apprentices College, the Junior Leaders Regiment RCT and other establishments.

THE REGIMENTAL MUSEUM

In September 1944 the *RASC Journal* printed two short paragraphs to declare the intention of starting a museum in Buller Barracks. It was to be

[By courtesy of RCT Museum]

Field Marshal Lord Montgomery of Alamein presenting his war time Rolls Royce to the RASC Museum in June 1964, accompanied by Brigadier J R Reynolds OBE ERD.

founded for the purpose of collecting objects of historical interest connected with the Royal Army Service Corps and its predecessors.

Previously, military artefacts, trophies and medals appeared to have been kept in messes or privately by members of the Corps and as one would expect, the largest collection of such items was already in Aldershot, in the RASC Headquarters Mess.

The collection, which began in 1944, was eventually housed in the old mobilization store buildings, adjacent to the riding school, and it soon became a great attraction and centre of interest to recruits and old soldiers alike. The recruits had their first introduction to Corps history during their first visit to the museum and during Corps Week, many an old soldier reminisced over some ancient custom or artefact.

With the rebuild of Buller Barracks plans were laid down for a permanent custom-built museum, and when HQ RCT Training Centre, 12 Regiment RCT and the Depot Regiment returned to Buller Barracks in 1969, a new museum was occupied.

The new museum was well designed for those who considered that museums should not be cobwebbed shrines, but that they should be light and airy, and emanate not a dark past but indicate a bright future. In the ten years to follow, conservation became the watchword of all museums and controlled artificial lighting and atmosphere have in a short time, closed all windows to light and extremes of temperatures.

None of this, of course, diminishes what is now a fine collection and

725

it is attractively displayed and added to continuously, through the generosity of those closely connected with the Corps and by those whose enthusiastic interest in tradition ensures that our heritage is gathered together. From time to time, purchases are made from auction-room sales and in recent years, a fine collection of Military Train badges was obtained. Amongst the most prized exhibits in the museum are a very fine Royal Waggon Train jacket, which enhances the Waterloo case and a beautiful gilt and enamelled casket in which is contained the document conferring the honorary freedom of the Borough of Southampton on General Sir Redvers Buller, VC. The Corps' unique collection of transport artefacts are loaned to the Museum of Army Transport, Beverley, E Yorks.

Corps archives exist as part of the museum complex and material of varying degrees of importance is continually being added. The archives are open to recognized researchers and there is an increasing interest in squadron/company history from the respective units. Some unit histories are well written and up to date, others are almost non-existent, and in both bases it is evident that well written notes for *The Waggoner* form a basis of information for the missing years.

THE WAGGONER

The Waggoner, the journal of the Royal Corps of Transport continues to cover Corps activities, the work of the Institution and the news of the Regimental Association. It aims at promoting esprit de corps and presents a picture of life in the Royal Corps of Transport for those interested in Corps activities and traditions.

The regimental journal was founded in 1891, and although its style changes in keeping with the times, it remains a sound source of information for Corps history students and the contemporary history of the Corps continues to be written in its pages.

THE RCT HEADQUARTERS' MESSES

The RCT Headquarters Officers' Mess is located in Buller Barracks. Major Corps functions are held in this mess. It also serves as the mess for the day-to-day residents of Buller Barracks. Being the home and regimental depot of the Corps, it is appropriate that a fine collection of silver is held there and this creates a fine display on social occasions. It is a custom of the Corps that young officers, on first joining the Corps, make a contribution towards the purchase of an item of silver which remains permanently in the Headquarters Mess. This is done when officers are on their Troop Commanders Course, previously named the Junior Officers Course. The names of all contributing officers are inscribed on the item and such a collection of silver and names is part of our history and tradition; the first item so presented is dated 1889.

THE STAFF BAND OF THE ROYAL CORPS OF TRANSPORT

Although the Band of The Royal Corps of Transport and its predecessors has been in existence since 1799, it was not until 1938 that it received official status. Up to that point it was wholly maintained from Corps funds principally by the Officers. Early in the Band's history – that is early 19th century – a musician was enlisted to organize the musical element of the Band's duties. There was no training for Bandmasters or standardization of drill and procedure, so that each band of the Army consisted of the instrumentation decided by the leader of the band – usually a sergeant. At this time all members were enlisted soldiers who played their instruments in a spare time capacity, and the leader, usually a Continental, started using the title Bandmaster but still with no official rank. Each Bandmaster of the Army decided on his instrumentation, pitch and music and it is a safe assumption that no two bands could play together without considerable rehearsal and adjustment. This state prevailed until the 1850s culminating in the cacophony at the time of the Crimean War when the bands massed for the playing of the National Anthem in Hyde Park in front of Queen Victoria. From this came a directive that all bands would be standardized, a task undertaken by the Duke of Cambridge who arranged the purchase of Kneller Hall in Twickenham as the home of Military Music.

So a new page of band history started in 1857 when courses were set up to train Bandmasters who were granted the rank of Warrant Officer Class 1. Additional courses were instituted to train young musicians and the more mature members as future Band Sergeants. Also a prescribed instrumentation and general standardization were introduced but all bands were still maintained at Regimental expense. This was not a happy situation, where the Army was virtually telling commanding officers how they had to spend their money.

It took a long time for an official establishment to be laid down limiting the numbers in any band but even so it was possible for some bands to have as many as 70 members as late as 1935. From that time they were firmly established, with the Army at last taking on the financial responsibility of pay, rations, etc., but not the supply of instruments and music, this still being the responsibility of Regiments and Corps to this day. It is in this context that British bands differ so greatly from most other countries' Service Bands inasmuch as they have to earn as much as possible from paid engagements to offset the officers' contributions to their Corps or Regimental Fund.

Just after the 1939–45 War, Bands were classified on a new establishment so that Staff Bands had a commissioned officer as Director of Music and Regimental Bands retained their Warrant Officer Class 1 Bandmaster. The position today is that all Staff Bands – that is Corps, Guards and Household Cavalry Bands – have commissioned Directors of

Music as does the Royal Military School of Music, whilst Regimental Bands of the various Regiments of Infantry and Cavalry have Warrant Officers Class 1 Bandmasters. Now musicians have a career structure and those suitably qualified can rise from Musician to Lieutenant Colonel.

Apart from the primary function of providing musical support for RCT units, at home and overseas, many other engagements are undertaken. These include Massed Band Displays, concerts given for KAPE (Keeping the Army in the Public Eye), recruiting and charity purposes and commercial engagements. The latter include playing in the London Parks and seaside resorts such as Eastbourne and Bournemouth, playing at major association football matches at Wembley Stadium and at the famous Horse of the Year Show at which the Corps Band in 1982 played for the thirty-second consecutive year.

Apart from a marching and platform band, the RCT musicians also form an orchestra and a number of small dance groups, the latter being very much in demand. As an operational requirement decided entirely by ourselves, all Corps musicians are trained HGV drivers.

For many years there had been a wish throughout the Corps to improve the dress of the band by replacing the Number 1 Dress Hat. There is no freedom of choice in such matters. Army Dress Regulations demand that band uniforms and embellishments must be based on tradition and any change can only be effected by establishing that the item was once worn by the Corps or one of its predecessors. Fortunately, we were able to produce evidence that the design of the blue Shako with red and white pompom which we required was worn by the Military Train 1856–1869. The Shako replaced the Number 1 Dress Hat in time for Corps Week 1974.

Left: *The RCT Staff Band and Corps of Drums on the Buller Barracks parade ground.*

[By courtesy of B J & J R Edwards]

Right: *HRH The Duke of Gloucester unveiling a memorial plaque in the new Buller Barracks on 26 July 1967.*

[By courtesy of C & E Roe Ltd]

In 1945 the RCT Director of Music was Major J F Dean. He died suddenly in 1962 and was replaced by Major D Walker who transferred to the Welsh Guards in 1969. Major W Allen MBE succeeded him until retirement in 1978. Major T A J Kenny then became our Director of Music. The Corps Band currently has an establishment of 36.

As a point of interest, after VJ Day in August 1945, the Corps March was modified. The traditional tune of 'Wait for the Wagon' was felt to be too repetitive and Major Dean incorporated the South african trek song "Vat Jou Goed en trek, Ferreira (Pack your things and trek, Ferreira)" into the present Corps March.

BULLER BARRACKS

The original Buller Barracks were built between 1893 and 1895 on the site of the old R, S, X, Y and W Lines in South Camp which had been occupied at various times by all seven battalions of the Military Train from 1859 to 1869, by the first Army Service Corps from 1869 to 1881, the Commissariat and Transport Corps from 1881 to 1888, and finally by the second Army Service Corps from 1888 to 1895.

Buller Barracks, on completion, were fully occupied by the Army Service Corps in 1895, and it was most fitting that the Barracks should have been named after General Sir Redvers Buller VC whose support and encouragement, whilst Quartermaster General, had led to the formation of the Army Service Corps as an established Corps with its own officers and men.

Apart from the site, the link with the old lines remained in the continued use of 'W' Square which had been used by the Corps and its

[By courtesy of B J & J R Edwards]

Aerial view of Buller Barracks taken during Corps Week.

predecessors for ceremonial parades since 1856. This link continues to the present day in that 'W' Square is now the MT Square of 27 Logistic Support Group Regiment RCT.

The Royal Corps of Transport and its predecessors, the Army Service Corps (1888 to 1918) and the Royal Army Service Corps (1918 to 1965) have occupied the Buller Barracks site for 123 years with only three short breaks, from 1893 to 1895 whilst the original Buller Barracks were being built, from 1940 to 1944 when it was occupied by the Canadian Army and from 1967 to 1969 when the present barracks were being built.

A memorial plaque on the exterior wall of the NAAFI building was unveiled by Field Marshal His Royal Highness the Duke of Gloucester, then our Colonel in Chief, on 26 July 1967 to commemorate the rebuilding and modernization of Buller Barracks. The rebuild was completed in 1969 when the barracks were reoccupied but it was considered to be appropriate for the official reopening to be in Corps Week 1970 and carried out by our Colonel in Chief. Unfortunately His Royal Highness the Duke of Gloucester was not well enough to perform this ceremony and Her Royal Highness the Duchess of Gloucester replaced her husband. Accordingly a memorial plaque on the south side of the Drill Square was unveiled by her on 11 July 1970 to commemorate this occasion.

The Corps War Memorial stands proudly in the centre of the barracks. It is inscribed to the memory of 280 officers and 8,187 Warrant Officers, NCOs and Men of the Royal Army Service Corps who laid down their lives for their country during the Great War 1914–1919 and of 286 Officers and 8,871 Warrant Officers, NCOs and Men who died during 1939–1945. Those who have died on operations since 1945 are commemorated in the Church of St. Michael and St. George, Aldershot.

CORPS WEEK

After a wartime lapse of six years, Corps Week was held from Thursday June 27th to Sunday June 30th 1946. The theme adopted in an austerity year was the reunion of the Corps family and was designed to cover all theatres in the world where the Corps was serving or had operated. A War Exhibition to illustrate all wartime activities was held on 'W' Square and there were the usual dances, church parade and luncheon. Except for a Past versus Present cricket match, there was no other sport. The programme followed similar restricted lines in 1947 and 1948 but returned to a six to seven day programme from 1949 onwards; it was always arranged to cover the last week of June. There is no reference in any Corps document to this post-war choice of date but according to the book *Military Customs* by Major T J Edwards MBE F.R.Hist.S., published in 1961, the last week of June was chosen by the RASC for its annual Corps Week in order to fit in with the Bisley Rifle Meeting. It was also the first week of Wimbledon which normally guaranteed good weather!

From 1953 to 1965 the programme became even longer, usually covering ten days because the rifle meeting began on a Thursday in the preceding week; the events also included tennis, cricket, swimming, athletics, golf, the 'At Home', officers, cadets, sergeants and junior ranks dances and balls, church parade, stables and Sunday luncheons. 1965 was the last RASC Corps Week and from 1966 to the present day the programme has become a RCT Corps Weekend, albeit a long one. In 1967, 1968 and 1969 it was held at Crookham during the rebuild of Buller Barracks.

To mark the anniversary of the formation of the RCT on 15 July 1965, the policy was laid down that Corps Sunday would always be the Sunday which is nearest to 15 July and Corps Weekend is celebrated annually during that weekend.

THE CORPS CHURCHES

The rebuilding of churches after the Second World War occupied the minds of many members of the Corps who, by the circumstance of their position, were able to be influential in many practical ways.

The building of the church of St. Christopher at Grobbendonck is a measure of this influence where it was not acceptable in any way that Christmas Communion should continue to be celebrated in the office of the unit commander and other services held in the quartermaster's store, as indeed they were, in the early days of the Advanced Base in Belgium. When the RASC took over their part of the base at Grobbendonck in 1953 they were given a small Nissen hut and £100 for a works service to provide a concrete foundation for a new church. In the months which followed, common interest and the creative achievements of National Servicemen, inspired by the dedication of the late Colonel James Burgess, fashioned a church which would have graced any English village.

Earlier, in 1949, the Chaplain of Neumunster said that the garrison chapel was unworthy and requested that the Commander RASC obtain authority to rebuild it. By April 1950 with the congregation filling a new chapel to capacity, the dedication ceremony took place.

The church of St. Martin at Longmoor was the centre of worship for generations of Royal Engineers of the Transportation Branch. In July 1965 Longmoor became the School of Transport on the formation of the Royal Corps of Transport and St. Martin's continued to be the scene of memorable services giving strength and inspiration to the faithful.

The School of Transport, by then the Army School of Transport, moved from Longmoor in 1977 and in the reorganization of teaching establishments a driver training unit newly designated the Army School of Mechanical Transport settled in Leconfield, North Humberside, and a garrison church was installed under the inspired guidance of the Commandant, Brigadier H R Dray.

During a visit by the Colonel-in-Chief, Princess Alice, Duchess of Gloucester to the Army School of Mechanical Transport on 31st May 1978, the new church was dedicated. It contains many of the fittings and memorials of the old Longmoor church including the beautiful stained glass windows which will continue to enlighten those who worship at the Church of St. Martin, Leconfield.

These examples are typical of the timely intercession and influence of many members of the Corps who similarly devote their time to the honour and glory of God.

At the home of the British Army in Aldershot, and indeed in the spiritual home of the Corps, there were two churches which have held their place in the affection of many generations of serving soldiers.

St. George's Garrison Church stood in Queen's Avenue originally at the Western end of Stanhope Lines. It has for many years represented to the Royal Army Service Corps and the Royal Corps of Transport the traditions that the Guards Chapel bears to the Brigade of Guards. It was consecrated in 1893 and through the years following, it was adorned with Corps memorials; it became known affectionately as the Corps Cathedral.

The Roman Catholic church of St. Michael and St. Sebastian was also in Stanhope Lines and in more recent years was referred to as their Mother Church by the many thousands of Corps Catholics who worshipped there. Much of the redecoration in the church had been completed after the war as a memorial to the officers and men of the Royal Army Service Corps and when the title was changed to the Royal Corps of Transport a memorial chapel was installed in St. Michael's to mark that historic change.

As logistic corps, the Royal Army Service Corps and the Royal Corps of Transport are not strangers to the effects of budgetary cuts in funds granted for the defence of the realm. Such economic necessity had a profound effect on the future of the Aldershot churches. It was decided that the needs of the serving Christian communities of the Aldershot

Major General Sir Cecil Smith
KBE CB MC leading the parade of
Old Comrades at Corps Week.

[By courtesy of RCT Museum]

Military town could more economically be served by the closure of St. Michael's and the adoption of St. George's as the garrison Roman Catholic church, whilst the Church of All Saints would continue as the garrison church for the Church of England faithful.

Whilst the phases of the 'Corps Cathedral' and the 'Catholic Mother Church' are now but a memory, the hearts and minds of those celebrating Corps Week in Aldershot are brought together in the ecumenical act of worship on Corps Sunday at the Church of St. Michael and St. George, the name by which St. George's is now known, and the memorials remain as a testimony to generations of Corps soldiers past, present and to come.

THE ASSOCIATION OF THE ROYAL CORPS OF TRANSPORT WITH THE WORSHIPFUL COMPANY OF CARMEN OF LONDON

On 23 July 1975 at a meeting of the Court of Assistants of the Worshipful Company of Carmen of London, held at Grocers Hall, Princess Street, London EC2, Articles of Association were exchanged between the Worshipful Company of Carmen and senior representatives of the Royal Corps of Transport.

The Articles of Association were signed on behalf of the Royal Corps of Transport by Major General W Bate, CB, OBE, FCIT, the Representative Colonel Commandant, and Major General P Blunt, MBE, GM FCIT, Transport Officer-in-Chief (Army), and on behalf of the Worshipful Company of Carmen by the Master, Mr. Charles W Lloyd and the Clerk, Mr. J Murray Donald.

Also present at the ceremony were Major General V H J Carpenter, CB, MBE, FCIT, Major General P F Claxton, CB, OBE, FCIT and Brigadier N I B Speller, MBE, MCIT.

The signing ceremony was followed by the election of Major General Blunt as an Honorary Liveryman of the Worshipful Company of Carmen and as an Honorary Member of the Court of Assistants of the Company.

At a dinner held later, the Worshipful Company of Carmen presented to the Royal Corps of Transport a silver loving cup and the Royal Corps of Transport presented to the Worshipful Company of Carmen a silver statuette of a soldier of the Army Service Corps of the Boer War period. The loving cup is inscribed:

> 'This Loving Cup was presented by the Worshipful Company of Carmen to the Royal Corps of Transport as a token of esteem and affection and commemorates the association between these two ancient and revered bodies, formally ratified in the Grocers' Hall in the City of London on 23rd July 1975.
>
> C W Lloyd
Master MCMLXXV'

In his speech the Master referred to the historical importance of the association between the Worshipful Company and the Corps and the gracious approval by Her Royal Highness Princess Alice, Duchess of Gloucester the Colonel in Chief. In his reply the Representative Colonel Commandant referred to the roles of the Corps and the extreme importance of the Territorial Army in fulfilling this role.

Since 1975 the Association between the Worshipful Company of Carmen and the RCT has been well maintained. The Master of the Company, together with his representative who serves on the Corps' Professional Activities Advisory Committee, have been entertained on a number of occasions each year. These include visits to major RCT units, attendance as guests of the Corps at the 'At Home' in Buller Barracks, attendance at DGTM's Dinner Nights and also to the Annual Dinner of the Institution of the RCT. In return, the Worshipful Company has invited many Corps Senior Officers to a number of their functions. The Worshipful Company now holds a 'RCT Night' each year and it was on such an occasion in 1979 that the Worshipful Company first presented a sword to an officer of the Royal Corps of Transport. The Worshipful Company in 1978 decided that it would present annually a sword to the highest placed RCT officer in order of merit at the Royal Military Academy, Sandhurst. Recipients of swords to date are:

1979 – Second Lieutenant A P Taplin RCT
1980 – Lieutenant P S Reehal RCT
1981 – Second Lieutenant J McD Ferrier RCT
1982 – Second Lieutenant M R Little RCT

ALLIANCES

Most Commonwealth countries have evolved a system of supply and transport which has benefited from an alliance with the Royal Army Service Corps and the Royal Corps of Transport.

These alliances, which in some cases involve an exchange of personnel, produce not only an efficient liaison but also a bond of lasting friendship.

Alliances have been formally approved between the Royal Corps of Transport and the following:

> The Royal Australian Corps of Transport
> The Royal New Zealand Corps of Transport
> The Army Service Corps of India
> The Army Service Corps of Pakistan
> The Sri Lanka Army Service Corps
> The Malaysian Service Corps

AFFILIATION

In a similar manner, the Gurkha Transport Regiment is an approved affiliated regiment and officers from the Royal Corps of Transport are provided to command the regiment and squadrons of the regiment which is currently based in Hong Kong.

ADDITIONAL REGIMENTAL CLUB ACTIVITIES

In addition to the activities of the Institution, there are several privately organized and funded clubs that are recognized family activities. These are:

> The Nil Sine Labore Masonic Lodge
> The Waggon Club
> The Luncheon Club
> The Central Mediterranean Forces/Middle East Forces Dinner Club

Other luncheon/dinner reunions are held periodically. These include:

> The Airborne Officers
> The Air Despatch Officers
> The Gurkha Officers
> The Corps Quartermasters

The Corps is also closely associated with the Movement Control Officers' Club. This club, founded by Royal Engineer Movement Officers serving in Dover and Calais in 1946 and called the Dover/Calais Dining Club, has as its President the Director of Movements (Army) and its membership is drawn from serving and retired officers of all three Services. Many of its members are well known public figures.

[By courtesy of Depot & Trg Rgt RCT]

A selection of contemporary RCT dress taken outside Buller Mess 1982.

This flourishing club normally meets in London on the second Tuesday evening of each month throughout the year and dines twice a year. Recently members, recognizing the problems of attending in London, have started gatherings, usually quarterly, in other regions of the United Kingdom. Exeter in the South-West, Salisbury in the South and York in the North East are three examples of these centres. It is heartening to note that there are many young members of this club whose current world-wide membership stands at 990, each member receiving a monthly news sheet.

DRESS

Dress has been the subject of considerable change over the years between 1945–1982 not only as a result of Army orders but also because of the whims and ideas of some local commanders around the World who have issued their own orders on the subject. This, coupled with the many variations in dress throughout the Army worldwide makes it impossible to deal exhaustively with dress within the confines of one chapter. In any case, the majority of our dress regulations apply to the whole Army, only a few are distinctive to the Corps. It is not intended therefore to cover the subject in detail but to highlight items which are either traditional to the Corps or which were introduced in the post war years.

Some items of dress such as the officers Mess Dress and Service Dress remain substantially the same as those worn pre-war. The main differences are in the Combat Dress now worn by both officers and soldiers, the Barrack Dress consisting of shirt and green trousers, also worn by all ranks, and the Number 2 Service Dress worn by the soldiers.

During the period between 1945 and the present day the various forms of dress have slowly evolved from the battle dress which was worn

736

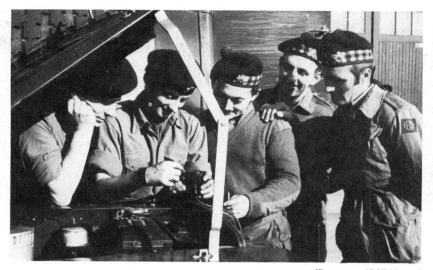

[By courtesy of RCT Museum]

Soldiers of 239 Sqn, 153 (Highland) Regt RCT (V) wearing their distinctive Atholl bonnets.

throughout the Army during the 1939–45 war and well into the post-war period.

Although the basic uniform is now standardized throughout the Army, many Regiments and Corps still retain some elements of their traditional pre-war dress which gives them a regimental identity. The Corps is no exception, the most obvious traditional dress being Mess Dress which has remained unchanged since the first ASC, also certain items of ceremonial accoutrements, the Corps sword, sword knot and slings have a design unique to the RASC which was adopted by the RCT. The uniform worn by our bandsmen also retains many features of pre-war dress, the cross belt and shako headdress being particularly distinctive.

However, not all dress details worn by members of the Corps have pre-war origins. Officers and men who have been trained in air despatch wear a winged brevet on the left uniform sleeve and on the breast of their flying overalls the yellow Dakota flash awarded in 1944 for their service at Arnhem.

Because of a number of reorganizations that have taken place in the Territorial Army, many units with long regimental traditions have found themselves re-badged into the Corps rather than face complete disbandment. These units are now totally integrated into and proved themselves an invaluable asset to the RCT. So as to preserve their individual regimental distinction in dress, the Corps dress regulations allow the following authorized exceptions.

Officers of 225 (Queen's Own Lowland Yeomanry) Squadron RCT (V) are authorized to wear the collar badge of the Queens Own

Lowland Yeomanry in place of the RCT collar badge. Officers of 239 (Highland Yeomanry) Squadron RCT (V) wear the collar badge of the Fife and Forfar Yeomanry/Scottish Horse and their headdress is the Atholl bonnet. Officers of the (Pembroke Yeomanry) Troop of 224 (West Wales) Squadron RCT (V) are authorized to wear the collar badge of the Pembroke Yeomanry. Soldiers of 153 (Highland) Transport Regiment RCT (V) and 154 (Lowland) Transport Regiment RCT (V) are authorised to wear a square of Red McDuff Tartan behind the cap badge worn on the beret. The Pipes and Drums of both Regiments wear kilts and plaids in Red McDuff Tartan.

In the Port and Maritime world there has been a long tradition of specialized forms of dress suitable for wear aboard vessels and for working in a port area. Until 1960 the old cap SD was worn by all other ranks at sea, despite its patent unsuitability. It continued to be worn aboard fast launches until 1966 when it was superseded by the beret.

All Maritime personnel have been permitted to wear Naval white roll-neck sweaters, whilst at sea, since 1957. Other ranks have worn Naval number 8 clothing since 1958. Ocean watch keepers and watch keeping engineers wear a skill-at-arms badge of a gold crown and anchor on a blue or purple background on their left sleeve on all uniforms. Naval foul weather gear is worn by all ranks.

Port operators were initially issued with donkey jackets against foul weather until 1971 when they first received full Naval foul-weather gear and blue waterproof anoraks. While working they must wear industrial pattern white safety helmets and at all times wear the RCT fleet ensign as badges upon each upper arm.

The RCT civilian fleet has its own form of dress based on a modified form of Naval dress but without the White Naval collar.

The normal working dress in barracks for all ranks is now a woollen pullover worn with badge of rank, green trousers and black shoes, the headdress being the Cap Service Dress for officers and blue woollen beret for soldiers.

The Combat Dress has been developed for field service in extremes of climate, the accent being on rugged practicability rather than smartness. However, when the occasion demands, it is still possible to turn out on parade, dressed in Number 2 Service Dress, white belt and gloves and blue forage caps; well up to the traditional standards of the British Army.

The Army, like society generally, changes with the times. In matters of dress the trend has been towards practicality, comfort and ease of maintenance coupled with a more relaxed smartness compared to that which prevailed pre-war.

THE ROYAL CORPS OF TRANSPORT CENTRAL MEDAL COLLECTION

Many visitors to the Royal Corps of Transport Central Medal Collection, housed in Buller Barracks, Aldershot, have extolled the present display which, in recent years, has resulted almost entirely from the interest and generosity of members of the Corps and their relatives who have entrusted medals to it.

The collection began in Aldershot, in a small way, about 1920. While it was always mainly based there, some of the medals were displayed at other Corps locations in the United Kingdom, and this is still the case. In 1963, it was decided to centralize the majority of these modest resources in the Headquarters' Mess at Aldershot and to develop them systematically to portray some of the history and achievements of the Corps, thus originating the Corps 'Central Medal Collection'.

The layout of the present collection falls naturally into three parts: personal displays, breast-mounted groups and the campaign medal type series.

The category known as Personal Displays comprises the replica Victoria and George Cross groups and those accessions which include breast stars and neck badges. The latter are exhibited in the centre and upper cases to add lustre to the collection, mainly by commemorating the eminent services of senior officers of the Corps. Among many distinguished accessions in this section are the medals of a nephew of Her Majesty Queen Mary, the second Marquess of Cambridge, who served as a major in the Corps in the Second World War; those of Commissary-General Sir John Bissett, whom the Duke of Wellington held in such high esteem during the Peninsula War of 1808 to 1814; and a splendid group to a lady member of the Corps, Miss A M Meadows, of the 1914–18 period.

The display of Breast-Mounted Groups, and the Campaign Medal Type Series, which are partially inter-related, is organized thematically on strict numismatic and historical principles, the criterion in every case being the needs of the collection. The aim, here, is to provide a visual spectrum of Corps history from 1794 onwards, through the medium of the honours and awards gained by members of the Royal Corps of Transport and its accepted predecessors in the British service, without regard to rank, and by those who served in the supply and transport organization of India, and of certain colonial forces, prior to the independence of their respective country.

As its name implies, a breast-mounted group consists of two or more medals designed to be worn exclusively on the breast, which were gained by a recipient who served in the Corps or other organization defined earlier. Each of these groups is exhibited for the purpose of featuring one of its constituent medals, or bar or emblem of that medal; the featured item not only determining the relative position of the group in the display, but actually providing the reason for its inclusion, by illustrating some facet of Corps history or achievement which has to be represented. In this way, too, the featured item can be seen in the context of a contemporaneous group, which not only exemplifies the award, but also serves to heighten the interest of related biographical and anecdotal references concerning the recipient, in the collection catalogue. The featured medal is never duplicated.

The bulk of the collection is composed of breast-mounted groups, which include so many fascinating and diverse items that it is difficult to particularize one or two examples. Among these groups is the pair, including the Distinguished Conduct Medal, awarded to Lance-Corporal F Attwood, ASC, for his part in the Defence of Rorke's Drift in 1879; the extraordinary group of Private G R Harratt, Commissariat and Transport Corps, which embodies the British Empire Medal (Civil Division), the Egypt Medal with bar 'The Nile 1884–85', for the expedition to relieve General Gordon in Khartoum, and the Defence Medal 1939–45; and the remarkable group of Driver C Fenwick, RASC, a Buckingham Palace footman, whose last five medals were all personally bestowed by crowned heads whom he had served on state visits before the First World War.

Medals break down naturally into series, according to the purpose for which they are awarded. Classification is necessarily arbitrary, but in a military collection the various series would follow the normal order of precedence in wear and include orders and decorations, campaign medals, commemorative medals, service medals, and Commonwealth and foreign awards. The purpose of a medal type series is to illustrate, in chronological sequence of issue, all the attributable medals of that series as single items, from the point of view of the medals themselves.

At present, only the Campaign Medal Type Series can be displayed in this way, but this, in any case, is arguably the most important series of a military collection from an historical standpoint. For the Corps, this type series commemorates as many as possible of the operations and battles in which its personnel took part throughout its long and distinguished history, spanning almost two centuries, and for which a campaign medal or bar was awarded. The Campaign Medal Type Series also aims to provide a numismatic portrayal of the issues, varieties, bars and authorized emblems of each type of campaign medal attributable to the Corps and its predecessors, by displaying a minimum of two examples of such medals to show the obverse and reverse design of each type. Further examples of the type are included, as necessary, to provide adequate representation of the different die varieties, bars or emblems. It is interesting to note that attributions to the Corps have so far been found for all except two types of British campaign medal, although not all of these are depicted in the collection at present. Among the many treasures in this type series are the Military General Service Medal, 1793 to 1814, with thirteen bars, to Driver William Twigg, Royal Waggon Train, and the Waterloo Medal to Lieutenant Colonel Thomas Aird, who commanded the Royal Waggon Train at the Battle of Waterloo.

This comprehensive coverage of events and awards, over the long period of the Corps' existence, necessarily implies a wide basis of admissibility in permitted attributions and is a major advantage in terms of the scope and appeal of the current display. Not only were members of the Corps and its predecessors present at almost every operation for which a British campaign medal was awarded, albeit perhaps only a handful strong, but their courage, dedication and high professional skill has been widely recognized by the large number of orders and decorations for gallantry and meritorious service, long service medals, foreign awards and other distinctions which are proudly shown in the collection.

The continued support of the collection by members of the Corps, their relatives and others, in making Corps medals available to it, is vital. Happily, this support is much in evidence at present, but, without it, the long-term development of the collection would inevitably be retarded, if not made impossible.

No chapter concerning the medal collection would be complete without reference to the Corps Numismatist, Lieutenant Colonel G T Pearce MBE who, as a serving officer of the Corps and now as a retired officer, has been responsible for the collection since 1963. The authority, expertise and skill, with which he carried out this labour of love, marks the collection indelibly with a hallmark of excellence and makes it one of the finest of any Corps or Regiment in the British Army.

36 · SPORT

THE ARMY HAS ALWAYS encouraged sporting activity as a means of providing mental and physical training.

Although lists at Annex A at the end of this Chapter show only the outstanding achievements by individuals in the field of sport, it would be remiss in this history of the Corps not to acknowledge the thousands of Corps sportsmen who have played and enjoyed their sport at every standard. Without this support, those who achieved high representative honours may never have done so.

The criterion for inclusion at Annex A is representation at National, County, Combined Services and Army level. War emergency and National Service members of the Corps are shown with an asterisk. The ranks recorded are those held at the time of the achievement.

ASSOCIATION FOOTBALL

With National Service continuing after the war, the quality of most sports played in the Army was raised to unprecedented levels. Soccer, the most widely played team game, was no exception and unit teams were filled with professional and high-grade amateur players who were normally able to return home at weekends to play for their civilian clubs.

The summit of Army Association Football is the Army Cup and to be the cupwinners is an achievement that is both cherished and hard-won. The Corps have been cup-winners twice since 1945 and on each occasion that success has been preceded by years of near-misses. The closest near-miss was in the final of 1960 when it appeared that our team had only to turn up to gain the trophy. The champagne was on ice, parties had been arranged in every corner of Aldershot that sported a Corps favour – alas, we lost 1–0! Rules prescribed that an Army Cup team can include only three professionals and on that day Ron Yeats of Dundee United, Chris Crowe of Blackburn Rovers and Alex Young of Hearts all missed the opportunity of gaining Army Cup-winners' medals.

The solution for a Corps team not stumbling again at the final hurdle was found in the following year, when two Corps teams got to the final where 2 Training Battalion RASC from Aldershot made their second consecutive visit and handsomely defeated 6 Training Battalion RASC from Yeovil by 4 goals to 1. Ron Yeats and Alex Young at last gained their winners' medals, alongside George Muir, the other professional from Hibernian.

With National Service at an end the Corps continued to produce successful Corps and unit sides but it was not until 1973 that another Corps team reached the final when the RCT Training Centre won by 2 goals to 1.

This victory had again been preceded by a number of failures, this time at the semi-final stages, and the period around the late sixties and early seventies was also marked by many Corps players being selected to play for the Army and Combined Services. Among them were two players who probably have more Army and Combined Services colours than any other service player.

Corporal Kenny Heath and Corporal Dave Blanche represented their Corps for many years in a sport which almost everyone plays and competition was accordingly the more intense.

Success in this team sport has eluded the Corps in recent years; such success is relative to the amount of time spent at finding the ingredients of near perfection. Time available limits that search and supporters of the game must wait for another day when the Corps can invest some of its effort in pursuit of the Army Cup.

ATHLETICS

There can be few soldiers who at some time have not taken part in unit athletics and from whom Army and representative teams are drawn. At any time therefore, there will be many who recall the achievements of their fellow athletes in representative competition. Annex A gives some of the more notable names.

BASKETBALL

Basketball was introduced as an official Corps sport in 1978 due to the enthusiasm and hard work of 17 Port and Maritime Regiment RCT. It is most commendable therefore that it is possible to record that Lance Corporal S Phillips was selected for the Army in 1979 and there will be other achievements to follow as interest is promoted throughout the Corps.

BOXING

The strength of Corps boxing during 1945–1982 has centred on two main periods, the late 1950s and the 1970s, though it would be unfair not to note the wealth of individual boxing strength that we have enjoyed throughout the whole period. It was in the middle/late 1950s that 15 Training Battalion RASC mustered together a team which won for the Corps, for the first time, the King's Trophy, the prize shield for the Army Team Boxing Champions. Subsequently, some of the boxers of that period went to 6 Training Battalion RASC but as far as team boxing was

[By courtesy of 10 Regt RCT]

10 Transport Regiment RCT Boxing Team. Army Boxing Champions 1973, 1974, 1975, 1977.

concerned, the 1960s were a quiescent period. In 1971, with the help of a small handful of boxers who had boxed for 6 Training Battalion RASC, 10 Regiment RCT formed a team under the training hand of Staff Sergeant G Fuller BEM APTC. With his encouragement and hard work, in its first season the team won the BAOR Championships and subsequently became the Army Boxing Team Champions winning the King's Trophy on four occasions during the period 1973–1977. Individual and Team achievements are recorded at Annex A.

CANOEING

This sport, popular with young men, notably in the Junior Leaders Regiment, has provided the Corps with some meritorious success in international competitions as Annexe A shows.

CRICKET

Since its earliest days in 1908, Corps Cricket has always flourished and is still strong at the very end of this period of Corps history. Through the years the fixture list has been the best of any Regimental or Corps club, featuring not only our military counterparts but also many of the better-known wandering sides such as the Free Foresters, Incognito and Eton Ramblers. After 1945, the Club was soon re-established at the same standard, helped by the continuance of National Service until 1962, which meant that many talented young professional cricketers played at Buller. However, the Regulars more than held their own. The highest score in a Corps match is still 183 by Lance Corporal (later Major) L A Sadler in

1938. No-one has yet taken all ten wickets in an innings; the best bowling figures are 9 for 48 by W M E White in 1947, 9 for 30 by A S Furnival in 1967 and 9 for 44 by W G Dover in 1968. Major F Marrison's career record of 646 wickets is unlikely to be overtaken.

FENCING

Few are gifted with the art of Fencing but since 1945 the Corps has produced two of the highest class:

Major R M Mortimer	Combined Services & Army 1967
Lieutenant R Craig	Great Britain 1968 (Olympics), 1969, 1970 Army Champion 1971

FREE FALL PARACHUTING

The Silver Stars is the name given to the Corps Parachute Display Team. The team is made up of the experienced elite who have all qualified and been officially licenced to give displays to the general public. Free fall parachuting is exclusive to the enthusiast who is prepared to give generously both of his time and money to the sport.

Free fall parachuting first came to notice in this country in the late 1950s, although parachuting at displays goes back to the barnstorming days of the 1930s. In the early 1960s display teams were formed to jump at local town shows, as well as the already fashionable airshows and not unnaturally most of them were Army teams based on military parachutists. The Royal Corps of Transport Free Fall Club was no exception; it was begun appropriately enough during 1963 in 63 Parachute Company RASC by Major Ridgway and Sergeant Ackerman. The first display was given in the following year. There are now a dozen Army display teams that perform at carnivals, shows and fetes in this country and abroad all the year round. The name Silver Stars was adopted in 1975 and is taken from the eight pointed star depicted in the Corps cap badge.

Members of the Silver Stars get together at weekends to perform their displays and are drawn from the most experienced Corps sport parachutists serving in the UK at the time. The team members are drawn from all ranks and a host of different units within the Corps. RCT parachutists from the club have jumped in the USA, Germany, Cyprus, Belgium, Holland, Norway, Singapore, Malaysia, Hong Kong, Jamaica, Ghana, Kenya and Northern Ireland.

The team has grown over the years and achieved its highest results at the major army competitions in 1978/79/80. Our own independent training started in 1976 with the first group jumping at South Cerney in Gloucestershire. In 1980 all student training was moved from South Cerney to the Junior Leaders Regiment RCT at Colerne under the leadership of Captain Abbott and Sergeant Chandler. In 1980 the team trained more students and participated in more displays than ever before and achieved more than any other part or full time team with the exception of the Red Devils. 90% of the students are Junior Leaders and Permanent Staff from Colerne and the Junior Leaders are encouraged to continue parachuting when they join their first units. They will hopefully provide the future representatives at Army level which has been achieved by those listed at Annex A.

GOLF

Until recently Golf had been generally considered to be an 'officer sport'. In the last decade there has been a marked increase in the number of senior and junior ranks playing, many with distinction and success. It may be expected in the next few years that some of these will gain recognition at Army and National level. The Corps sides have, since the early 1950s, won Army Competitions at regular intervals. Several officers have achieved national status, but generations may pass before British golf produces an amateur golfer of Michael Bonallack's stature. He served as a National Service officer in the RASC from 1954–56. For ten years he had no peer as a competitor and his tally of achievements may never be surpassed. Between 1961 and 1970 he won the Amateur and English Championships five times each and won or tied for the English strokeplay on four occasions.

Bonallack was a member of the 1965 Walker Cup team which held the Americans to a sensational tie at Baltimore. In 1971 he triumphantly captained the British Walker Cup team to a historic victory at St. Andrews – only the second home success ever.

When he retired from international team contests in 1974, Michael Bonallack had been a member of nine Walker Cup and six Eisenhower Trophy teams and had played 131 times for England, 45 more than anyone else. He is one of the few overseas golfers to have received the United States Golf Association's Bobby Jones Award for distinguished sportsmanship.

HOCKEY

Though still not as popular as other major sports and consequently not played to a great extent in units, hockey has always flourished at Corps level. Its revival in the Corps after the 1939–45 war may largely be attributed to Colonel Joe Mullington. The Corps has been well represented throughout the period at all levels.

LAWN TENNIS

Ever since Lawn Tennis became an official Army game, the Corps has been well represented at Army level. Since 1945, the Corps has maintained its tradition in the game, the most successful players being Second Lieutenant M F Hayes, who was a worthy Army Champion in 1967 and Captain (now Lieutenant Colonel) B B Trinkwon, who has played regularly for the Army during the last twenty years. Major General P G Turpin CB OBE is the doyen of Corps tennis and has been the winner of the Corps Singles Championship both as a subaltern and major general!

MODERN PENTATHLON

In the years 1949–1966 the Corps had strong teams in this exacting sport, Lance Corporal B Morris winning the British Junior Championship and in one year Lieutenant Colonel (later Major General) E H G Lonsdale, Major P Poole and Captain P Weeks represented the Corps in the British Championships. Corporal I Lillywhite was a magnificent athlete and represented Great Britain in the 1968 Olympics, the Army in 1967, 1968 and 1969, the Combined Services in 1976 and in the World Pentathlon Championships in 1966 and 1967. Major R M Mortimer RCT represented the Army in 1964, 1965 and 1966.

MOTORING AND MOTOR CYCLING

It is perhaps not surprising that the Army's Transport Corps maintains a close interest in competitive motoring and motor cycling, from the safe driving competitions under the auspices of the British Army Motoring Association (BAMA), which the Corps now officially manages, through rallying to racing, and the motor cycle trials held under the rules of the Army Motor Cycling Association (AMCA). During the 1960s the Corps sponsored a rally team of modified Austin 1800 staff cars, with some small success in their class, but motor sport at national and international level is an immensely expensive business, beyond the facilities of a regimental team.

The few listed at the Annexe to this chapter have achieved special success but are representative of a vast number of young men from all ranks who have also motored competitively with enjoyment and success in club and Army events. Sergeants G Webb and M A Soames were Army champion motor cyclists in 1968 and 1969 respectively and currently, Major Burrell's cars are raced in Corps colours.

RIDING

The Corps equestrian tradition stems directly from its early connections with horse transport and apart from one or two individuals with privately owned horses, most of its success in the equestrian field has been achieved by members of its mounted unit, the Animal Transport Training Company RASC which became 'H' Squadron RCT. This squadron was

[By courtesy of Maj J W Aggleton]

BAMA team for 1961 Monte Carlo Rally – Maj Ian Baillie, Life Guards; Maj John Aggleton RASC; Capt Mike Barham RAOC.

disbanded in Aldershot in March 1970 but 414 Pack Transport Troop RCT equipped with mules survived in Hong Kong until November 1975 when it too was disbanded.

The Corps retained its tradition of driving horse drawn transport when Major General Sir Reginald Kerr formed the RASC Coaching Club in 1923. The RASC, later RCT, coach appeared with success at major horse shows throughout the UK; it also supported meets of the Coaching Club of Great Britain and drove members of the Corps on sporting and social activities. It annually drove officers and their ladies to Royal Ascot. The RCT Coaching Club was disbanded in 1973 when qualified drivers were posted from Aldershot and its stabling in Beaumont Barracks was demolished. Both coaches are now on loan in the Royal Mews under the care of Lieutenant Colonel Sir John Miller, the Crown Equerry and President of the Coaching Club of Great Britain. They are maintained in good condition and are used from time to time by members of the Coaching Club. The Corps' four-in-hand harness, footmen's liveries and all other accoutrements were sold in 1976.

RUGBY FOOTBALL

After the Second World War the Royal Army Service Corps recommenced playing Inter-Corps rugby football on that delightfully situated sports

[By courtesy of RCT Museum]

The RASC Coaching Club Maj George Boon driving HM The Queen 1959.

field in front of the old Buller Officers Mess. It says much for the planners that when Buller Barracks was rebuilt in the 1960's they allowed this playing field to remain and even added a sports pavilion. Captain P R B Mitchell emerged as the outstanding Corps player. Representing the Army and Combined Services in 1948 and 1949, he was a pillar of strength in the Corps Team after the War until 1950, when he was posted to Malaya.

The RASC side of the 1950's benefited as did the rest of the Services from the influx of National Servicemen; one of the most promising recruits in 1951 was Private J D Currie who had not then developed in stature or to his full rugby potential. He did not play for the Army although he had a trial but was later to go on and win 25 caps for England and form a memorable second row with R W D Marques who played for the Royal Engineers and the Army in 1954. In this decade six Corps players represented the Army. A notable performer who came on to the Corps scene in the mid-fifties was Major Frank Fenner who, before he was transferred to the RASC, had played full back for the Royal Navy in the Inter-Service matches of 1951 and 1952 and was an England trialist. Frank's stocky figure was to become a permanent fixture as full back for the Corps, continuing right up to his retirement in the early 1970's.

It was during the 1960's that the Corps produced two outstanding players, John Macdonald, a fine prop and useful goal kicker who played eight times for Scotland as well as representing the Army and the

Capt D O'Hare receiving Army Rugby Cup from General Sir Dudley Ward after Corps Troops Column RASC victory in 1959.

[By courtesy of PR HQ NORTHAG]

Barbarians. The second was Graham Lilley, a fast and fearless back row forward who won twelve Army caps in addition to playing for the Combined Services and the Barbarians.

1965 saw the formation of the new Corps – The Royal Corps of Transport and the 1965/6 season was a good one. After losing to REME in the first outing of the season, victories were recorded against the RAMC, RAOC, RAEC and RE. The side was built around 63 Parachute Squadron RCT and against the RAOC there were eleven from that minor unit in the side. There were two old heads to steer this youthful enthusiasm, Terry Barrett, a former Gloucestershire hooker leading the pack, and as always Frank Fenner captaining the side from full back. That season was a good start for the new Corps.

Throughout the early seventies good rugby was still played and between 1965 and 1981 seven Corps players won Army caps in the Inter-Service matches. Mike Bowles, a stalwart second row forward played for the Army from 1973 to 1982 and had the honour of captaining both the Army and Combined Services including their match against the Austra-lian touring side.

In the overseas theatres the Corps colours have been carried on many a foreign field. There has always been an RASC/RCT BAOR side and there were representative sides in Singapore and Malaya.

The Army Cup has seen two Corps teams in the final, the first in 1958 when 1 (BR) Corps Troops Column RASC met 1 DWR. The Corps side which was known affectionately as the Corps Sports Column owed much to the drive and enthusiasm of the Commanding Officer Lieutenant Colonel Peter Taylor, who transformed the regiment into a very good sporting unit, insisting upon peak physical fitness and complete dedication to the game of rugby football. He welded together a team which had no 'stars' but possessed a determination to reach the final. The 'Dukes' just had too much rugby know-how and won 23–5.

The real giant killers in the Army Cup competition were 63 Parachute Squadron RCT who, as very much a minor unit, took on the big boys and were eventually beaten in the final of 1966, again by 1 DWR. 63 Squadron were led by John MacDonald and were super fit, nothing was impossible, they ran everywhere and tackled everything. It says much for the schooling and attitude of mind that they were able to hold 1 DWR to 8–5 because with the exception of their captain they had no 'stars' but they were a mighty fine team.

No report on RASC/RCT rugby football would be complete without mention of the Eassie 7's named after Major General W J F Eassie CB CBE DSO who was IRASC from 1951 to 1954. This event takes place at Buller at the end of every season and a feature of it until 1973 was the appearance of Major General Eassie every year up to his 73rd birthday. He was a great supporter and loved Corps rugby. He died on 13 May 1974 aged 74.

SAILING

The Royal Corps of Transport Yacht Club has been in existence for a long time but competitive sailing in the Army and inter-service competition was the preserve of other Corps and Arms until 1957 when Lieutenant Chris Barnard was selected to represent the Army. Since that time, the Corps has regularly provided Army team members, mainly in dinghy and offshore events. For some reason, keelboats have not attracted much success.

It is in offshore sailing that the Corps has made its mark. Army and Joint Services competitive offshore racing only began in 1975 with the first Army Sailing Association and Joint Service Offshore Regattas. Since 1976, the Corps has been placed 1st or 2nd each year in the Army Championships and Corps boats have been selected to represent the Army in the Joint Services Offshore Race in 1980 and 1981. In addition, since 1977, based on 20 Maritime Regiment, the Corps has been responsible for running all Army offshore regattas and also for running the Joint Services and Royal Ocean Racing Club races to the Channel Islands in 1979 on behalf of the Army.

In a short period the Corps has made an outstanding contribution to Army sailing and many members have participated in national, county and Army events. Lieutenant J A Chinn won the Inter-Services Gold Cup in 1948.

Recruit Driver G Williams winner of 'Green Jacket Cup' 1967 Aldershot District Rifle Meeting.

[By courtesy of RCT Museum]

SKIING

2 Armoured Division Transport Regiment RCT has for many years been the focus of our skiing activity and as such has represented the Corps annually in the Army Ski Championships. Despite its glamorous impression, this is a physically demanding sport with two entirely different disciplines, Nordic (Langlauf and Biathlon) and Alpine (Downhill). In a very competitive sport only a professional approach and hard work will achieve success and the notable achievements of both the regimental team and individuals are testimony to the efforts and dedication of members of the Corps over the years. The regimental team has won the Army Championships (The Princess Marina Cup) three times and various individuals have represented Army, Combined Services and national teams over the years. Although very much a team effort, two individuals deserve specific mention. Both Staff Sergeant Keith Oliver and Staff Sergeant 'Chalkie' White started skiing as Junior Leaders and subsequently went on to achieve considerable success in their own discipline. Staff Sergeant White represented the Army and Combined Services in the downhill events over a number of years culminating with his selection in 1981 as the Army Team Captain, the first time that an NCO had ever been awarded this distinction. Staff Sergeant Oliver was the 'stalwart' of Army and national langlauf and biathlon skiing for many years and represented Great Britain in three consecutive Olympic Games and nine World Championships.

SKILL AT ARMS

The Corps has always prided itself in its skill at arms. It is therefore not unexpected that the list of successes in Army and national competition should be long and distinguished as can be seen in the Annex.

SQUASH RACKETS

Not many regular Corps players of distinction appeared until the 1970s, although P W Le Gros was a war-time officer in the Corps and was still serving in 1945 when this history begins; he was an English International and became President of the Squash Rackets Association. P C Fuente, a National Service officer, played for the Army and England during 1946–48. With the increasing popularity of the game, RASC and RCT representation at Army level has increased in recent years.

SWIMMING

International and national honours have eluded Corps swimmers in post-war years, which is perhaps not surprising in view of the low standard of facilities and the time required to train. Nevertheless, as the list shows, the Corps has been regularly represented in Army teams.

TUG OF WAR

The Tug of War must be one of the older trials of strength for opposing teams. The pre-war successes of RASC Feltham were continued as shown in the list of achievements. It is an unusual honour that 63 Parachute Squadron represented Hampshire in the 1967 inter-counties national championships. However, perhaps the most distinguished success must go to the MELF Field Butchery Section (with a total strength of 10 men only), who in 1951 in the Canal Zone not only won the Army Championships but represented the Army against the RAF, winning in two straight pulls.

Association Football

Individual Achievements

Dvr R Johnstone	Army 1948–49
Pte J Bonthrone	Army 1948–49
Pte M Clews	Army 1949–50
Cpl Jones	Army 1950–51
Dvr Kevan	Army 1953–54
Pte G Meek	Army 1954–55
Dvr Briggs	Army 1954–55
*Pte J Little	Scotland and Army 1954–56
Cpl J G Buchanan	Army 1955–56
Dvr M Costello	Army 1955–56
Pte Ashfield	Army 1955–56
Pte Valentine	Army 1955–56
LCpl K Killworth	Army 1955–56
Dvr A Kay	Army 1955–56
Pte J Shanks	Army 1956–57
Pte Costello	Army 1956–57
Pte B Harris	Army 1957–58
LCpl B Hughes	Army 1957–58
Cpl R Fogg	Army 1957–59
Pte McPhail	Army 1958–59
Pte B Massey	Army 1958–60
Pte R Syddall	Army 1958–59
Pte Tait	Army 1959–60
*Pte C Crowe	England and Army 1960–62
*Pte R Yeats	Scotland and Army 1960–62
*LCpl A Gilzean	Scotland 1959–61
*Pte A Young	Scotland and Army 1960–62
*LCpl K Cains	England Amateur XI and Army 1959–61
*LCpl D Emerson	England Amateur XI and Army 1959–61
*Cpl R R Ardery	England Amateur XI and Army 1959–61
Pte K G Flint	Army 1960–62
Cpl S Davis	Army 1960–61
Cpl M Davies	Army 1960–61
Pte A Reid	Army 1960–61
Pte F Ryecraft	Army 1960–62
Cpl R Barrett	Army 1961–65
Sgt P Barlow	Army 1962–65
Pte B Butterworth	Army 1962–63
Cpl D R Green	Army 1962–63
Cpl J Knight	Army 1962–63
Dvr R Welch	Army 1963–64
Pte Smailes	Army 1965–66
Cpl I Packer	Army 1965–66
Dvr J Rutter	Army 1966–68
Pte W Simms	Army 1966–67
Dvr J A Rankin	Army 1967–68
2Lt W G Dover	Army 1967–68
LCpl M Phipp	Army 1968–69
LCpl K Heath	Combined Services 1968–70
	Army 1965–70
LCpl Blanche	Army 1968–70
LCpl J Robson	Combined Services and Army 1970–75
Dvr G Lockhart	Army 1970–73
Dvr Hughes	Army 1971–72
Cpl Gibbons	Army 1972–73
LCpl Heard	Army 1969–72
Cpl R O Stephens	Army 1978–79

Team Achievements

2 Training Battalion RASC	Army Cup Winners 1961–62
RCT Training Centre	Army Cup Winners 1971–72

Athletics

Individual Achievements

*Lt P A Hethbridge	Army	Long Jump
*LCpl W G Nankeville	Great Britain and Army 1947	880 yards & 1 mile
*Dvr A James	Wales and Army 1948	880 yards
*2Lt P H Valle	Great Britain and Army 1948	100 & 200 yards
*LCpl Sandow	Great Britain and Army 1948	Cross Country
Pte N Farrow	Army 1951–1953	440 yards
Dvr J Prestall	Midland Counties and Army 1952	Javelin
Dvr A Jones	Wales and Army 1960–61	880 yards
Cpl E Byam	Army 1963–68	Shot Putt
Dvr R R Hood	Army 1966	440 yards
2Lt G G Davies	Army 1972	Triple Jump
Cpl J L Dixon	Army 1976–77	100 metres
Cpl J L Young	Army 1976–77	1500 metres
Cpl Morris	Army 1977	100 & 200 metres
Cpl A Mims	Army 1979–80	Javelin
2Lt S P J Burke	Army 1978–80	110 Metres Hurdles
Dvr E Dixon	Army 1980	100 metres
LCpl C J Hamill	Army 1980	Steeplechase
LCpl R Straker	Army 1980	Long Jump

Team Achievements

63 Para Sqn RCT	Army Minor Units 1966–67	Athletics and Cross-Country Champions

BOXING

Individual Achievements
2Lt F Collinson   Great Britain 1971

Hemming Belt Winners: (Awarded annually for the most meritorious boxing achievement
                      in the Corps)

Pte Harper	15 Trg Bn RASC 1956
Dvr Hardy	15 Trg Bn RASC 1957
Dvr Foot	15 Trg Bn RASC 19589
LCpl Elderfield	15 Trg Bn RASC 1959
Dvr Mallon	6 Trg Bn RASC 1960
Dvr Warwick	TA 1961
Not presented	1962–63
Dvr McHugh	52 (Lowland) Column RASC (TA) 1964
LCpl Booth	6 Trg Bn RASC 1965
LCpl Bruce	6 Trg Regt RCT 1966
Cpl Booth	62 (Berlin) Sqn RCT 1967
Cpl Booth	6 Trg Regt RCT 1968
Cpl Booth	12 Trg Regt RCT 1969
Cpl Baker	12 Trg Regt RCT 1970
Lt F Collinson	1 Para Log Regt 1971
Lt F Collinson	1 Para Log Regt 1972
LCpl Dublin	10 Regt RCT 1973
LCpl Dublin	10 Regt RCT 1974
LCpl Rene	10 Regt RCT 1975
LCpl Johnson	10 Regt RCT 1976
LCpl Cannon	10 Regt RCT 1977
LCpl Johnson	10 Regt RCT 1978
Dvr Stephens	10 Regt RCT 1979
LCpl Johnson	10 Regt RCT 1980

Team Achievements
15 Trg Bn RASC   Army Champions 1957, 1958, 1959, 1960
10 Regt RCT   Army Champions 1973, 1974, 1975, 1977

CANOEING

Individual Achievements

LCpl Cook	Army 1966
Dvr Stimpson	Great Britain, 1968
	Army 1965, 1966
LCpl B Jupp	Great Britain 1966, 1968
	Army 1966
LCpl S Warren	Great Britain 1966, 1968
	Army 1966
LCpl Gregory	Great Britain 1966, 1968
	Army 1966
LCpl R Evans	Army 1969
Dvr F Pagnanetti	Army 1969

Team Achievements
63 Para Sqn RCT   Army Long Distance
                         Champions (Senior) 1965, 1966, 1968, 1969
                         Army Sprint Champions
                         (Senior) 1965, 1966

CRICKET

Individual Achievements

*Sgt M J K Smith	England, Warwickshire 1953–54
Major W M E White	Army 1947, 1948, 1956
Lt J S Ryder	Staffordshire & Army 1948–52
Major F N Fenner	Cornwall & Royal Navy 1950–52
Sgt K Allsopp	Army 1955
Lt D G Beckett	Combined Services & Army 1959, 1963–65
Lt A P de B Thorold	Army 1962
Cpl Griffith	Army 1962, 1977
Capt T E G Way	Combined Services & Army 1966
2Lt W G Dover	Combined Services 1965–68
	Army 1971–76
Sgt A Hoyland	Combined Services & Army 1967–70
WO1 F Waller	Army 1967
Capt A S Furnival	Army 1970–72
Capt R J J Fahey	Combined Services 1973–74
	Army 1968–74
Maj I M Vaughan-Arbuckle	Combined Services 1974
	Army 1972–74
Dvr L M Sanderson	Combined Services & Army 1972–77
Dvr R J Davies	Combined Services & Army 1973–77
LCpl S W Dove-Dixon	Army 1977
LCpl J Masterson	Army 1979, 1980

Team Achievements

27 Regt RCT	Army Cup Winners 1972

FREE FALL PARACHUTING

Individual Achievements

Sgt R S Ackerman	Army 1964–68, 1971–72
Capt R Card	Army 1968–74
	Army Accuracy Champion 1972
WO2 (SSM) M Togher	Army 1974–78
WO2 G Raine	Army 1971–72

GOLF

Individual Achievements

Major M R Gardner	Dorset 1946–65
	Army 1946, 1952
Maj T F B Law	Army 1946
Maj H B Booth-Mason	Surrey 1958
	Army 1946–63
Major H B C Davies	Army Champion 1951
	Wiltshire 1968–69
	Army 1951–55, 1959–61, 1965–74
Capt P H Benson	Hampshire 1951–52
	Army 1950–52
*2Lt M F Bonnallack	Army Champion 1955
*2Lt M J Collinge	Hampshire 1956–58
	Army 1956
	Army Champion 1958
Lt Col G G Hill	Wiltshire 1971

GOLF (continued)

Team Achievements

The Army Golf Challenge Cup

Lt Col M R Gardner
Major T F B Law
Capt P H Benson
2Lt P W P Cochrane
} Winners 1952

Lt Col H B C Davies
Capt R D S Marston
Brig H B Booth-Mason
Lt Col G G Hill
Lt Col R A Worth
} Winners 1969

Major H B C Davies
Major R A Worth
*Lt M J Collinge
*Lt M F Bonallack
*Lt S Fletcher
} Winners 1955

Brig P H Benson
Lt Col H B C Davies
Capt R D S Marston
Brig H B Booth-Mason
Capt S W Davies
} Winners 1971

The Ordnance Challenge Cup

Major H B C Davies
Major R A Worth
*Lt M J Collinge
*2Lt M F Bonallack
*2Lt S Fletcher
} Winners 1955

HOCKEY

Individual Achievements

Maj D Ball	Army 1947–48
Lt Col A MacDonald	Army 1948–49
Maj J A Lambie	Army 1948–49
Capt T A Podesta	Army 1948–49
*2Lt A J Dann	England & Army 1949–50
SSM Bischoff	Army 1950–51
Pte T F Rollings	Army 1952–53
Lt D M Winter	Devon 1955–56
Lt G M Cutter	Great Britain, Wales, Combined Services & Army 1956–57
Sgt S D Cook	Lancashire, Combined Services & Army 1956–57
Lt D G Beckett	Combined Services & Army 1956–57
Sgt B Watson	Army 1959–60
Lt G W Cohen	Army 1961–62
Lt T F Rawlings	Army 1962–63
Capt P Mears	Western Counties & Somerset 1963–64
	Army 1962–64
WO11 Petters	Army 1962–63
LCpl V K Nayer	Army 1964–65
Capt P W D Cochrane	Army 1965–66
SSgt V P Hunt	Army 1972–74
Capt J J Treasure	Army 1977–78
Cpl R Virdee	Army 1977–78
2Lt R Bradley	Army 1979–80
2Lt P Wyse	Army 1979–80
Dvr K Boot	Army 1979–80

Lawn Tennis

Individual Achievements

Maj S H A Scroope	Army 1947–49, 1952
Capt M F Turner-Cook	Army 1948–50
Lt Col P G Turpin	Somerset & Army 1945–54
*2Lt C A S Wyse	Hampshire & Army 1960–61
	Army Regimental Doubles Champion 1961
*Pte J Beresford	Army Regimental Doubles Champion 1961
Lt B B Trinkwon	Army 1961–63, 1966–69, 1972–74, 1979
	Army Regimental Doubles Champion 1968
*LCpl R W L Lawie	Army 1964
*2Lt M F Hayes	Army 1966–68
	Army Singles Champion 1967
	Army Regimental Doubles Champion 1968

Motoring and Motor Cycling

Individual Achievements (Motor Cycling)

Sgt G Webb	Army (Individual) Trials Champion 1968
Sgt M A Soames	Army (Individual) Trials Champion 1969

Team Achievements (Motor Cycling)

1 Trg Bn RASC	Army Champions 1961
1 Div Regt RCT	Army Champions 1967
10 Regt RCT	Army Champions 1968, 1970

Riding

Individual Achievements

Brigadier J R Allen	Great Britain 1951
Capt G G R Boon	Great Britain 1959–62
	The King Goerge V Cup 1948
	Sword, Lance & Revolver Championship 1952–53
*Cpl A Oliver	Great Britain 1955–56
	The King George V Cup 1956
Major T J Brown	The King Goerge V Cup 1962
	Sword, Lance & Revolver Championship 1963
Major J Lynch	Edward Prince of Wales Cup 1948–49
Sgt R Graham	Edward Prince of Wales Cup 1965
Cpl D Devereux	Edward Prince of Wales Cup 1969
Major P J Marzetti	Edward Prince of Wales Cup 1974
Capt R A Hill	Sword, Lance & Revolver Championship 1966–68, 1974, 1975
	Edward Prince of Wales Cup 1973

Team Achievements

RASC	Queen Elizabeth II Challenge Cup (Inter-Services Show-jumping) 1960–62, 1965
RCT	Queen Elizabeth II Challenge Cup (Inter-Services Show-jumping) 1967

Rugby Football

Individual Achievements

*2Lt D Bateson	Eastern Counties 1948
*2Lt M Dillon	Oxford University 1946–48
Capt J A W Lerwill	London Counties, Surrey & Army 1946–48, 1952
*2Lt P M Young	Army 1949
Lt F N Fenner	Combined Services, South-West Counties, Berkshire & RN 1947–56
Capt P R B Mitchell	Army 1948–49
2Lt T K G S Barrett	Gloucester & Army 1951
*OCdt A Gibson	Surrey 1953
*Pte Lomax	Cumberland & Army 1953
*Pte J D Currie	England, Barbarians, Oxford University & Gloucestershire 1953
*Sgt M J K Smith	England & Oxford University 1954 Army 1953
*2Lt S R Smith	England & Hampshire 1954
Lt R Hopkins	Army 1955
Pt G Brown	Surrey 1955
*2Lt M L Bellows	Army 1956
*Cpl A Thomas	Dorset, and Wiltshire & Army 1958–59
*LCpl P Lightfoot	Lancashire & Army 1958–59
Capt R Brookes	Hampshire 1958–59
*Dvr E C Thomas	Dorset and Wiltshire & Army 1958–59
Sgt A Hutchins	Army 1961
*Capt R M Taylor	Army 1962
Capt J D MacDonald	Scotland 1966–68 Barbarians, London SE and Southern Counties, Hampshire, Dorset and Wiltshire 1963–68 Combined Services & Army 1964–70
Capt G Lilley	Army, Combined Services and Barbarians
Lt A E Gordon	Hampshire & Army 1964–65
Lt D Lapidus	Army 1966
Capt R Bullock	Hampshire & Army 1967
Capt J E Knowles	Combined Services & Army 1970–74
Capt R P P Ince	Army 1974
Lt G G Davies	Combined Services & Army 1974–75
Capt R G C Campbell	Army 1974–76
Capt J M Bowles	Hampshire 1969–77 Combined Services 1972–80 Army 1969–80
Cpl S Goody	Army 1974–76
Capt A S Furnival	Army 1973
Capt M Winarick	Army 1974
Dvr D MacFarlane	Army 1982

Skiing

Individual Achievements

Capt M Sutton-Pratt	Army 1954, 1955
Capt R T S Daniell	Army 1955, 1956
Pte R G W Pitchford	Army 1957, 1958
LCpl K A Oliver	Great Britain 1969, 1970, 1971, 1972 (Olympics), 1976 (Olympics), 1980 (Olympics)
	British & Army 15km Cross-country Champion 1969, 1971, 1973, 1974, 1978
	British & Army 20 km Biathlon Champion 1971, 1973, 1977, 1978
	International Lowlanders 15 km Cross-country Champion 1970, 1972, 1973, 1976, 1978
	British & Army 10 km Biathlon Champion 1974, 1977
	French National & International 20 km Biathlon Champion 1975
	British & Army 30 km Cross-country Champion 1977
LCpl I M White	Army Downhill Champion 1972, 1974, 1976
	Army Slalom Champion 1972, 1975, 1976, 1978, 1979, 1980
	Army Alpine Champion 1972, 1975, 1976
	Combined Services Downhill Champion 1972, 1974, 1979

Team Achievements

2 Div Regt RCT	Army Ski Champions 1973, 1975, 1981

Skill at Arms

Individual Achievements

Pte K Finlay	Champion Young Soldier of the Year 1948
Capt E W H Brooks	King's Prize, Bisley 1949
Sgt J E White	Queen's Medal and TA Champion, Bisley 1953
Capt C G F Platfoot	Army Rifle VIII, 1956, 1957, 1958
	Army Revolver VIII, 1956, 1958, 1960
	Inter-Services Rifle Champion and Queen Mary Medal 1958
Major H A Aldred	Army SMG VIII, 1958, 1959, 1960, 1961, 1962, 1963, 1964, 1965, 1966, 1967
	SMG Individual Champion, Bisley, 1962, 1964, Inter-Services XX Champion 1954
Lt Col M G M Crosby	Captain, Army VIII, 1957, 1958, 1959, 1960, 1961
LCpl I Hardine	Roupell Cup, Bisley, 1961
WO2 Simms	Army SMG VIII, 1962
Capt D W Cooper	Tyro Individual Pistol, Bisley 1964
	Army Revolver VIII 1965
Maj J M Riches	Army Long & Short Range Match Champion 1966, 1974
	NRA Silver Medal & Bisley Cup 1975
RSM Pearce	Army SMG VIII 1966
Lt P R Cox	The Young Officers Cup, Bisley 1967
WO1 G W Pierce	The Regular & TAVR Challenge Cup, Bisley 1968

SKILL AT ARMS (continued)

Lt J E C Lewis	NRA Silver Medal & Bisley Cup 1968
	Army Long & Short Range Match Champion 1969
Dvr M E Daffy	Rifle Brigade Cup for Young Soldiers, Bisley 1969
Sgt J Downing	Winner of the 'Bisley Bullet' 1971
Cpl Kirkham	Tyro Award (Target Rifle) Bisley 1974
2Lt M Rees	Young Officers Cup & ARA Spoon, Bisley 1978

Team Achievements

6 Trg Regt RCT	The Parachute Regiment, Cup, Bisley 1967
34 Sqn GTR	Squadron Shield (All Arms) Bisley 1968
Gurkha Tpt Regt	King Edward VII Cup, 1st Army Cup, Duke of Connaught Cup, Bisley, 1968
12 Trg Regt RCT	SMG Team Tile Cup, Bisley 1970
90 Sqn RCT	Squadron Shield (All Arms) Bisley 1970
RCT Trg Centre	Parachute Regt Cup, Bisley 1971
55 AD Sqn RCT	Minor Units Rifle Match, Minor Units SMG Match, Bisley 1971, 1972
Gurkha Tpt Regt	ARA Unit Rifle Match, Bisley, 1972
31 Regt RCT	ARA Unit Rifle Match, Bisley 1973
20 Sqn RCT	ARA Long Range Target Rifle Team Match, Bisley 1974
35 Sqn RCT	ARA Long Range Rifle Match Series A(ETR)All-Arms, Bisley 1974
Jnr Ldrs Regt RCT	Junior Soldiers Unit Championship, Other Arms & Services Championship, Bisley 1976
31 Sqn GTR	Young Soldiers Small-bore Match, Bisley 1977
26 Sqn RCT	Other Arms & Services Minor Unit Championship, Series B, Bisley 1978 Other Arms & Services Minor Units Championship, Series A, Royal Signals Cup, Bisley 1979, 1980
26 Sqn RCT	Other Arms & Services Small Bore Match (Malta Command Cup), Bisley 1980
28 Sqn GTR	Malta Command Cup, Bisley 1978
24 Tpt & Mov Regt RCT	Malta Command Cup, Bisley 1979
23 Tpt & Mov Regt RCT	Other Arms & Services SMG Match, Bisley 1980
7 Sqn RCT	Other Arms & Services SMG Match, Bisley 1981

SQUASH RACKETS

Individual Achievements

*Lt P W Le Gros	England 1945
*Lt P C Fuente	England 1946–48
Lt Col P G Turpin	Army 1952
	Buckinghamshire 1952–55
LCpl Costigan	Army 1974–78
Lt I Mosedale	Army 1975–77, 1981
Capt D J Le Cheminant	Army 1975–81
	Wiltshire 1981
Capt R Broad	Army 1977–81

SWIMMING

Individual Achievements

*LCpl E Elvey	Army 1948	J/Cpl B Lillywhite	Army 1962–64
*2Lt M Joseph	Army 1948	Sgt E W Boileau	Army 1962–67
Cpl C M Cackett	Army 1955	Sgt R C Burns	Army 1962
Cpl J Bowman	Army 1955	Pte Clay	Army 1964
*LCpl J Connoly	Army 1956–57	Sgt D Dilly	Army 1964
*Pte E Moston	Army 1957	J/CSM Morris	Army 1966–68
Cpl D Heslop	Army 1958	Sgt R Johnstone	Army 1967

TUG OF WAR

Team Achievements

CSD Aldershot	Army Champions (110 stone) 1947
2 Trg Bn RASC	Army Champions (88 stone) 1956
5 Trg Bn RASC	Army Champions (88 stone) 1959
Depot Bn RASC	Army Champions (100 stone) 1961
63 Para Sqn RCT	British National Champions (88 stone) 1968
	Army Champions (88 stone) 1966, 1968.

Part III
APPENDICES

ROLL OF HONOUR
(Killed by enemy or terrorist action)
14 August 1945 to 31 December 1982

Name	*Rank*	*Unit*	*Theatre*
ADCOCK M	LCpl	8 Coy	Hong Kong
ARNOLD J	Dvr	8 Coy	Japan
BALDWIN R	Dvr	27 Coy	FARELF
BATTRICK C J	Dvr	73 Coy	MELF
BEGLEY W J	Cpl	att SAS	Falkland Islands
BENNETT J	Cpl	1 Coy	Palestine
BLACKMORE N A	Pte	285 Coy	MELF
BOARDMAN M F	Dvr	55 Coy	Malaya
BOLDEN T E	Dvr	55 Coy	Malaya
BOOTMAN W	Dvr	65 Coy	Cyprus
BRATTON H	Dvr	BD & TC	MELF
BRISCOE R W	Lt	att AAC	W Europe
BRITNELL A	LCpl	EFI	MELF
BROWN H	Pte	GHQ 2nd Ech	Malaya
BROWN T E	Pte	80(Z) Coy	Malaya
BRUCE M D	LCpl	3 Sqn	Northern Ireland
BRYANT P	Cpl	799 Coy	Malaya
BULMAN P K	Dvr	17 Sqn	Northern Ireland
BUTLER E	SSgt	60 Sqn	Aden
CARR J A	Capt	EFI	Jerusalem
CLARKSON W H	LCpl	EFI	MELF
COLE G F	Cpl	421 Sup Pl	SEAC
COLLIER F L	Lt Col	HQ MELF	Cyprus
COOPER S P	Dvr	att 1 WG	Northern Ireland
COULTER D	Pte	GHQ	Cyprus
COVINGTON A E	WO2(CSM)	Civil Affairs	East Africa
CRIPPS G	SSgt	Sup Pl Nicosia	Cyprus
DAGG B T	Dvr	55 Coy	Malaya
DAY E W	Sgt	6 Trg Bn	At sea
DEAN L	Cpl	HQ Middle East	Aden
DIXON C J W	Dvr	7 Coy	MELF
DRIVER A A	Dvr	55 Coy	Malaya
DRURY G	Dvr	656 Coy	France
EVANS L	Dvr	Y List	CMF
FLEMING J F	SSgt	152 (Ulster) Regt(TA)	Northern Ireland
FRANKLIN W R	Capt	att 55 Coy	Malaya
FRASER N G	Dvr	60 Sqn	Aden
GARMSTON W J	Dvr	843 Coy	MELF
GARTH R	Sgt	60 Sqn	Aden
GAY M J	Dvr	18/26 Sqn	Northern Ireland
GEALL M A	Dvr	60 Sqn	Aden
GODWIN R F V	Dvr	HQ 1 Comwel Div	Korea

Name	*Rank*	*Unit*	*Theatre*
GOLDSWORTHY R M	Dvr	60 Sqn	Aden
GOODWIN T	SSgt	SIME	MELF
GREENWOOD W C	Dvr	26 Fd Amb	Korea
HAMILTON-WEBB G	Sgt	23 BSD	CMF
HAND F	Cpl	3 Coy	FARELF
HAND J F	Cpl	6 Airborne Div	MELF
HARROP L	Dvr	2 Fd Amb	MELF
HARPER K N	Dvr	3 Fd Amb	Palestine
HENDERSON R	Major	att 2 Bn Malay Regt	Malaya
HEPPENSTALL P	Dvr	att 1 RRW	Northern Ireland
HICKMAN A H G	Dvr	55 Coy	Malaya
HOOPER T F J	Dvr	3 Coy	Malaya
HOGGETT N	LCpl	3 Coy	FARELF
IRONS R	Sgt	258 Coy	MELF
JEEVES A	Dvr	55 Coy	Malaya
JENKINS P G	Pte	Mil Interp Pool	Cyprus
JONES D A	Dvr	55 Coy	Malaya
JONES H R	Pte	HQ Palestine	MELF
JONES J C	Dvr	55 Coy	Malaya
JONES R H	Dvr	3 Coy	FARELF
JONES T R	Pte	HQ ALFSEA	India
JONES W	Dvr	55 Coy	Malaya
JUBB L	Dvr	1 Sqn	Northern Ireland
KELLY G A M	Maj	Aden Protectorate Levies	Aden
KENNEDY D W	LCpl	40 Coy	Cyprus
KITCHEN R M	Dvr	att LI	Northern Ireland
LANE W H	Cpl	55 Coy	Malaya
LAVENTURE D H	Pte	GHQ Camp Main	Cyprus
Le BIHAN E A	LCpl	59 GT Coy	W Europe
LEGGE G	LCpl	24 Coy	FARELF
MABBETT O	Dvr	BLU	Greece
MACHIN F D	Sgt	Tech Eqpt Depot	Suez
MALSON R J	LCpl	7 Ground Liaison Section	Malaya
MATTHEWS B R	Sgt	55 Coy	Malaya
McCORMICK R E	Dvr	800 Coy	MELF
McKAY L M	Cpl	55 Coy	Malaya
McKENZIE N W	Dvr	54 Sqn	Northern Ireland
McMULLIN J	Dvr	55 Coy	Malaya
McSHANE F	Dvr	55 Coy	Malaya
MELTON E V	Cpl	668 Coy	MELF
MERRITT F J	Dvr	55 Coy	Malaya
MOORE D	Dvr	163 Fd Amb	W Europe
MORLEY J T	Dvr	53 Coy	UK
MULLER E H	Dvr	55 Coy	Malaya

Name	*Rank*	*Unit*	*Theatre*
NEILSON G	Dvr	286 Coy	UK
OTTLEY R C	Sgt	HQ SACSEA	FARELF
PARKIN K H W	Pte	2 CRU	India
PENROSE T W	Sgt	HQ NI	Northern Ireland
PLATT L	Dvr	65 Coy	Cyprus
POTTER A A	Pte	HQ SACSEA	India
POUTON F	Dvr	60 Sqn	Aden
PROUD C A	Dvr	61 Coy	Malaya
RANDLE T H	LCpl	55 Coy	Malaya
RICHARDS W J	2Lt	3 Coy	Malaya
RITTER C R	Sgt	3 Coy	FARELF
ROBERTS E	Dvr	55 Coy	Malaya
ROBSON N	Dvr	57 Coy	Korea
SMITH J	Dvr	83 Coy	UK
SMITH J A L	Capt	52 Coy	Malaya
STAPLES A P	Sgt	DSO Palestine	MELF
STEEL A D	Sgt	42 Coy	Cyprus
STOCK H	Cpl	6 Airborne Div	MELF
STONE L	Dvr	X 4a List	CMF
STUDD P	Dvr	55 Coy	Malaya
TAYLOR A W	LCpl	DSO Palestine	MELF
TAYLOR P E	Dvr	799 Coy	Malaya
TEVENDALE J	Dvr	60 Sqn	Aden
THUNDERCLIFFE W	Pte	HQ Palestine	MELF
THOMAS G E	Pte	B Sect Cold Storage Unit	MELF
TIMERICK P	Dvr	8 Coy	FARELF
TOVEY C T	LCpl	B Sect Cold Storage Unit	MELF
TRANTHEM D M J	Pte	EFI	KOREA
UNWIN W S	Pte	HQ ALFSEA	India
VOCE G W	Cpl	195 Fd Amb	Palestine
WAKEFIELD M	Dvr	55 Coy	Malaya
WALTERS M S	Cpl	55 Coy	Malaya
WATERHOUSE B	Dvr	16 Fd Amb	FARELF
WELMAN J	Cpl	55 Coy	Malaya
WEST M N	Dvr	60 Sqn	Aden
WHARTON R H	Major	HQ RASC Moascar	MELF
WHITFIELD S E	Capt	att Palestine Supernumerary Police Dept	MELF
WHITTY A	Dvr	55 Coy	FARELF
WILSON R T	Dvr	799 Coy	Malaya
WRIGHT J	Cpl	1 Coy	MELF

HONOURS AND AWARDS
RECEIVED BY MEMBERS OF
ROYAL ARMY SERVICE CORPS
AND ROYAL CORPS OF TRANSPORT
1 JANUARY 1946 to 31 DECEMBER 1982

To have published the complete list of Honours and Awards received by members of the Royal Army Service Corps and Royal Corps of Transport in all theatres would have taken more space than could be spared for the purpose. It was therefore decided to give only the total numbers in each grade of The Most Honourable Order of The Bath, The Royal Victorian Order, The Most Excellent Order of The British Empire and Foreign Awards, but to publish the names of those who were awarded the Military Cross, the Distinguished Flying Cross, the Medal for Distinguished Conduct in the Field, the Military Medal, the Distinguished Flying Medal, the Air Force Medal and the George Medal.

GEORGE CROSS
Dvr J Hughes GC   1947

THE MOST HONOURABLE ORDER OF THE BATH
Knight Commander	1
Companion	22

THE ROYAL VICTORIAN ORDER
5th Class	4
Silver Medal	2

THE MOST EXCELLENT ORDER OF THE BRITISH EMPIRE
Knight Commander	5
Commander	38
Officer	134
Member	490
Medal	651

MILITARY CROSS
Capt G H Boorman, MC	1946	Lt F L Knight, MC	1946
Maj E W Childs, MC	1946	Capt (EFI) T Shannon, MC	1946
Maj C P Crane, MC	1946	2Lt H N C Paterson, MC	1951
Lt A D Fraser, MC	1946		

DISTINGUISHED FLYING CROSS
Capt D J Ralls, DFC	1968	Capt J G Greenhalgh, DFC	1982

AIR FORCE CROSS
Maj P R Ralph, AFC   1968

DISTINGUISHED CONDUCT IN THE FIELD
WO1 G B Van der Werff, DCM   1946

MILITARY MEDAL

Dvr S P Aggett, MM	1946	LCpl W D Lewis, MM	1946
LCpl E J Chad, MM	1946	Cpl J V Lynch, MM	1946
Sgt B Clarke, MM	1946	LCpl L J Morris, MM	1946
Dvr N K Crouchley, MM	1946	Dvr R H Philpot, MM	1946
Dvr E J Ellson, MM	1946	Sgt H G Simpson, MM	1946
Dvr T Farrell, MM	1946	LCpl J H Tomlin, MM	1946
Dvr J M Fouracres, MM	1946	Sgt J P Turnbull, MM	1946
Dvr E A Francis, MM	1946	Cpl J Webber, MM	1946
Dvr A Fulton, MM	1946	Dvr W Wills, MM	1946
Cpl H Greatorix, MM	1946	WO2 T W Winter, MM	1946
LCpl F Groves, MM	1946	Dvr E Lewis, MM	1947
•LCpl R N Hedley, MM	1946	Pte H V Sprawls, MM	1947
Cpl L Hook, MM	1946	Cpl S G Miles, MM	1954
Cpl J Horlock, MM	1946	Dvr Ismail Bin Musa, MM	1954
SSgt A C Keast, MM	1946	Sgt D S Boultby, MM	1982
Dvr R Killey, MM	1946		

DISTINGUISHED FLYING MEDAL

Cpl A Abbott, DFM	1955	Cpl T E Westbrooke, DFM	1957
Cpl D Wade, DFM	1956	CPL S Liaster, DFM	1958
Sgt D H Rose, BEM, DFM	1957		

AIR FORCE MEDAL
Cpl A G Gilbert, AFM   1954

GEORGE MEDAL

Sgt T Newman, GM	1947	Maj P Blunt, GM	1959
Sgt R Warwick, GM	1949	LCpl J Crossland, GM	1962

MENTIONED IN DESPATCHES
3,464 awards

KING'S COMMENDATION FOR BRAVE CONDUCT
3 awards

QUEEN'S COMMENDATION FOR BRAVE CONDUCT
11 awards

QUEEN'S COMMENDATION FOR VALUABLE SERVICES IN THE AIR
1 award

The following awards were conferred during the period 1 January 1969 to 31 December 1982.

EFFICIENCY DECORATION
Territorial Army Volunteer Reserve   602 awards

ARMY EMERGENCY RESERVE DECORATION
Army Emergency Reserve   180 awards

FOREIGN DECORATIONS CONFERRED BY:

HIS ROYAL HIGHNESS THE PRINCE REGENT OF BELGIUM
ORDER OF LEOPOLD II

| Commander | 1 | Officer | 4 | Chevalier | 12 |

ORDER OF THE CROWN

| Officer | | 2 | Decoration Militaire 1st Class | 2 |
| Croix Militaire 1st Class | | 4 | Decoration Militaire 2nd Class | 9 |

Croix de Guerre with Palm 42

THE PRESIDENT OF THE CZECHOSLOVAKIAN REPUBLIC
MILITARY CROSS

Meritorious Service Medal Class 1   1   Meritorious Service Medal Class 2   5

BRAVERY MEDAL

Meritorious Service Medal Class 1   1

HIS MAJESTY THE KING OF DENMARK

King Christian X Liberty Medal   3

HIS MAJESTY THE KING OF THE HELLENES
ROYAL ORDER OF GEORGE 1, WITH SWORDS   Knight   1
ROYAL ORDER OF THE PHOENIX

| Officer | | 1 | Distinguished Service Medal | 9 |

HER ROYAL HIGHNESS THE GRAND DUCHESS OF LUXEMBOURG
ORDER OF COURONNE DE CHENE

Commander   1   Medaille en Vermeil and Croix de Guerre   1   Medaille en Bronze   3

HER MAJESTY THE QUEEN OF THE NETHERLANDS
ORDER OF ORANGE NASSAU WITH SWORDS

| Commander | 2 | Knight | 5 | Silver Medal | 5 |
| Officer | 12 | Gold Medal | 1 | Bronze Medal | 3 |

BRONZE LION DECORATION

The Bronze Cross   6

HIS MAJESTY THE KING OF NORWAY

King Haakon VII Liberty Cross   2   King Haakon VII Liberty Medal   33

HIS MAJESTY THE KING OF TRANSJORDAN

Order of Istiqlal, 4th Class   1

THE PRESIDENT OF THE UNITED STATES OF AMERICA

Distinguished Service Medal   1

LEGION OF MERIT

Commander	5	Silver Star	1	Medal of Freedom with	
Officer	13	Bronze Star Medal	75	Bronze Palm	5
Legionnaire	1			Medal of Freedom	6

770

LIST OF SENIOR APPOINTMENTS 1945–1982

Director of Supplies and Transport

1943 Maj-Gen Sir Reginald Kerr, KBE, CB, MC	1951 Maj-Gen H C Goodfellow, CB, CBE
	1954 Maj-Gen W H D Ritchie, CB, CBE
1946 Maj-Gen F S Clover, CB, CBE	1957 Maj-Gen Sir William Roe, KBE, CB
1948 Maj-Gen Sir Cecil Smith, KBE, CB, MC	1960 Maj-Gen P G Turpin, CB, OBE
	1962 Maj-Gen Sir John Potter, KBE, CB

Transport Officer in Chief (Army)

1965 Maj-Gen Sir John Potter, KBE, CB	1971 Maj-Gen V H J Carpenter, CB, MBE
1966 Maj-Gen E H G Lonsdale, CB, MBE	1973 Maj-Gen P Blunt, CB, MBE, GM
1969 Maj-Gen P F Claxton, CB, OBE	1976 Maj-Gen P H Benson, CBE

Director-General of Transportation

1977 Maj-Gen P H Benson, CBE

Director-General of Transport and Movements

1978 Maj-Gen P H Benson, CBE	1981 Maj-Gen W M Allen, CB
1978 Maj-Gen F J Plaskett, CB, MBE	

Inspector RASC

1946 Maj-Gen T W Richardson, OBE	1954 Maj-Gen G A Bond, CB, CBE
1946 Maj-Gen W d'A Collings, CB, CBE	1957 Maj-Gen A F J Elmslie, CB, CBE
1949 Maj-Gen W M Whitty, CB, OBE	1960 Brig E R Goode, CBE
1951 Maj-Gen W J F Eassie, CB, CBE, DSO	1962 Brig T H Phillips
	1964 Brig E H G Lonsdale, MBE

Inspector RCT

1965 Brig E H G Lonsdale, MBE	1972 Brig P Blunt, MBE, GM
1966 Brig E W T Darlow, OBE	1973 Brig J D Lofts, MBE
1967 Brig V H J Carpenter, MBE	1975 Brig N I B Speller, MBE
1969 Brig D W E Hancox	1978 Brig B G E Courtis
1971 Brig J Heptinstall	1981 Brig A F R Evans, MBE

Director of Movements (Army)

1963 Maj-Gen P G Turpin, CB, OBE	1971 Maj-Gen W Bate, CB, OBE, DL
1966 Maj-Gen Sir John Potter, KBE, CB	1973 Maj-Gen V H J Carpenter, CB, MBE
1968 Maj-Gen J R Reynolds, CB, OBE, ERD	1975 Maj-Gen F J Plaskett, CB, MBE

GENERAL OFFICERS OF THE RASC AND RCT OTHER THAN DIRECTORS OR INSPECTORS

LT-GEN SIR PAUL TRAVERS, KCB
Chief of Staff Logistic Executive (Army) – 1978–79
Vice Quartermaster General 1979–81
General Officer Commanding South East District 1981–82
Quartermaster General 1982–83

MAJ-GEN D H V BUCKLE, CB, CBE
Director of Supplies and Transport Middle East Land Forces 1953–56
Maj-Gen Administration General Headquarters Middle East Land Forces 1956–57

MAJ-GEN C H STAINFORTH, CB, OBE
General Officer Commanding South East District 1966–69

MAJOR GENERAL SIR WILLIAM ROE, KBE, CB
Major General Administration British Army of the Rhine 1954–57

MAJOR GENERAL SIR CECIL M SMITH, KBE, CB, MC
Major General Administration Northern Command 1945–47
Chief of Staff Northern Command 1947–48

MAJOR GENERAL SIR REGINALD KERR, KBE, CB, MC
Major General Administration
Far East Land Forces 1946–48

AIDES de CAMP TO THE SOVEREIGN

1946	Brig F S Clover, CBE	1959	Brig C E L S Dawson, OBE
1947	Brig W N Craig-McFeely		Brig F K Barnes, OBE
1948	Brig H M Hinde	1960	Brig E R Goode, CBE
	Col W N Craig-McFeely	1962	Brig H H Bruton, OBE
1949	Brig H M Hinde, CBE	1963	Brig R C Crowdy, OBE
	Col W N Craig-McFeely		Brig T H Phillips
1950	Brig J E Witt, CBE, MC		Brig C H Stainforth, OBE
1951	Brig H C Goodfellow, CBE	1964	Brig W M E White, OBE
1952	Brig W J F Eassie, CBE, DSO	1965	Brig E H G Lonsdale, MBE
1953	Brig D H V Buckle, CBE	1966	Brig P F Claxton, OBE
	Brig W G Roe, CBE	1970	Brig W Bate, OBE
1955	Brig H A Potter, CBE	1972	Brig D N Locke
1956	Brig E Dynes, OBE	1976	Brig J K Lomax
1957	Brig F L Saunders, OBE	1978	Brig J D Lofts, MBE
1958	Brig A R Purches, CBE	1981	Brig B G E Courtis
		1982	Brig R E L Jenkins, CBE

AIDES de CAMP TO THE QUEEN (RESERVE ARMY)

1973	Col J Pollard ERD TD	1979/82	Col P D Baldry, TD
1974/76	Col B G Jones, ERD	1979/80	Col W P Howells, OBE, TD, DL
1974/76	Col P D Williams OBE TD	1980/82	Col C G Dickie, TD
		1980/82	Col G T Spate, TD

COLONELS COMMANDANT		REPRESENTATIVE COLONELS COMMANDANT
1933–47	Maj Gen Sir Evan Gibb GB CMG CBE DSO	
1942–48	Maj Gen M S Brander CB OBE	1947
1944–54	Lt Gen Sir Humfrey Gale KBE CB CVO MC	1946, 1949, 1953
1947–50	Maj Gen E H Fitzherbert CBE DSO MC	1948
1949–59	Maj Gen Sir Reginald Kerr KBE CB MC	1950, 1954, 1956
1950–59	Maj Gen Sir Cecil Smith KBE CB MC	1952, 1957, 1959
1950–55	Maj Gen F S Clover CB CBE	1951
1954–63	Maj Gen H C Goodfellow CB OBE	1955, 1958
1955–59	Maj Gen H M Whitty CB OBE	
1959–64	Maj Gen W H D Ritchie CB CBE	1960, 1964
1959–64	Maj Gen D H V Buckle CB CBE	1961
1960–65	Maj Gen G A Bond CB CBE	1962
1963–67	Maj Gen Sir William Roe KBE CB	1963
1964–69	Maj Gen A F J Elmslie CB CBE	1965
1964–70	Maj Gen A T de Rhe-Philipe CB OBE (late RE)	1966
1965–75	Maj Gen P G Turpin CB OBE	1967, 1969
	Maj Gen Sir John Potter KBE CB	1968
1969–74	Maj Gen E H G Lonsdale CB MBE	1970
1969–72	Maj Gen C H Stainforth CB OBE	1971
1971–75	Brig R A J Eggar CBE	1972
1971–78	Maj Gen J R Reynolds CB OBE ERD	1973
1973–80	Maj Gen P F Claxton CB OBE	1974
1974–	Maj Gen W Bate CB OBE DL	1975, 1977, 1982
1975–	Maj Gen V H J Carpenter CB MBE	1976, 1978
1976–	Maj Gen P Blunt CB MBE GM	1979, 1981
1979–	Maj Gen P H Benson CBE	1980
1981–	Maj Gen F J Plaskett CB MBE	

HONORARY COLONEL COMMANDANT
1974–78   Col R N Levitt OBE TD

SENIOR APPOINTMENTS TA OFFICERS

Deputy Inspector Reserve Army Units RASC (TA)
Colonel W H Slack, ERD	6 December 1961 – 6 December 1964
Colonel L T Knights, ERD O St J	7 December 1964 – 14 July 1965

Colonel of Volunteers
Colonel L T Knights, ERD, O St J	15 July 1965 – 31 March 1967
Colonel D Quinn TD	1 April 1967 – 31 July 1968
Colonel J Pollard ERD TD	1 August 1968 – 31 July 1971
Colonel B G Jones ERD	1 August 1971 – 31 July 1975
Colonel P D Williams, OBE TD	1 August 1975 – 26 July 1977
Colonel C Brice, ERD TD	27 July 1977 – 26 July 1980
Colonel J R B Smith, TD	27 July 1980 – 26 July 1982
Colonel D W Heslop, TD	27 July 1982 –

Colonels TAVR/TA

Colonel P D Williams, OBE TD, Wales	1 April 1972
Colonel W P Howells OBE TD DL, Wales	4 October 1976
Colonel P Baldry TD ADC West	1 October 1978
Colonel C G Dickie, TD, North West	19 July 1979
Colonel G T Spate, TD, London District	20 September 1979
Colonel G T Spate, TD ADC, South East	1 October 1982

Sponsored Units Representative on Territorial and Auxiliary Forces Association Council

Colonel B G Jones, ERD TD	1 August 1975
Colonel C Brice, TD	15 July 1980

LIST OF CONTRIBUTORS

MAJOR R N ABLETT

MAJOR W K ADRIAN

LIEUTENANT COLONEL C ADWICK OBE

MAJOR J W AGGLETON MBE

COLONEL K ANDREW OBE

LIEUTENANT COLONEL R P ARLIDGE

LIEUTENANT COLONEL R W ARMSTRONG

BRIGADIER P I ATTACK MBE

LIEUTENANT COLONEL P de L
    BAINBRIGGE

LIEUTENANT COLONEL J A BAILLIE

MR H BAGULEY late RASC

MAJOR D G BALCOMBE

COLONEL T K G S BARRETT

LIEUTENANT COLONEL D S BARKER-
    SIMPSON

MAJOR GENERAL W BATE CB OBE DL

MR B W P BATEMAN MBE

LIEUTENANT COLONEL B B BATESON

MR J BEASLEY late RASC

LIEUTENANT COLONEL G BEDFORD

LIEUTENANT COLONEL I H W BENNETT

MAJOR GENERAL P H BENSON CBE

LIEUTENANT COLONEL M W BETTS

COLONEL J D BIDMEAD CBE

MAJOR D R BIRRELL

MAJOR A W BLACKMORE

BRIGADIER G G BLAKEY

MAJOR GENERAL P BLUNT CB MBE GM

BRIGADIER H B BOOTH-MASON MBE

MAJOR D M BOND

BRIGADIER P C BOWSER CBE

COLONEL R J BOYLES

COLONEL B H BRADBROOK OBE

MAJOR GENERAL D H BRAGGINS

SERGEANT M BRENNAN

MAJOR M B BRETT

COLONEL C BRICE ERD TD

MAJOR C A BROTHWELL

LIEUTENANT COLONEL H P BROWN

MAJOR GENERAL D H V BUCKLE CB CBE

BRIGADIER A P CAMPBELL OBE

LIEUTENANT COLONEL K CAPEL-CURE AFC

BRIGADIER D CARDLE

COLONEL L A CARDY MBE

MAJOR J R CAWTHORNE

MAJOR GENERAL V H J CARPENTER CB
    MBE

LIEUTENANT COLONEL V R CETTI

MAJOR B G CHADWICK MBE ERD

LIEUTENANT COLONEL H I CHARKHAM
    OBE

LIEUTENANT COLONEL M H CHARTERIS-
    BLACK

OFFICER CADET R R H CLARKE

MAJOR GENERAL P F CLAXTON CB OBE BA

MAJOR C W P COAN

LIEUTENANT COLONEL H COLE OBE DL

MAJOR J A COLLAR

MAJOR GENERAL W d'A COLLINGS CB CBE

MAJOR W S COMPTON

MAJOR L R H CONEY

COLONEL H B COX MA

MAJOR P R COX

LIEUTENANT COLONEL G C E CREW BA

MAJOR A K CRISP-JONES OBE TD

LIEUTENANT COLONEL M G M CROSBY OBE
    MC

BRIGADIER R C CROWDY OBE

MAJOR M F I CUBITT MBE

CAPTAIN P B G CUMMINGS

BRIGADIER B G E COURTIS

LIEUTENANT COLONEL T A DANTON-REES

MAJOR C H DARK

LIEUTENANT COLONEL L D DARLING MBE

MAJOR J S DAVIES

BRIGADIER K C DAVIS MBE

MAJOR G T E DAWE MBE

LIEUTENANT COLONEL H M M DEIGHTON

COLONEL R F DISCOMBE OBE

COLONEL T H DOWNES OBE

COLONEL M N V DUDDERIDGE OBE

775

MAJOR P C DURBIN TD RCT

BRIGADIER R A J EGGAR CBE MA
MAJOR GENERAL A F J ELMSLIE CB CBE
BRIGADIER A F R EVANS MBE BA
LIEUTENANT COLONEL J R EVANS
LIEUTENANT COLONEL H M S EVERY

MR E FAUGHMAN late RASC
LIEUTENANT COLONEL P FEAR
LIEUTENANT COLONEL A D FITZGERALD
    MBE
LIEUTENANT COLONEL J A A R FROST

MAJOR M D GALLAGHER
MAJOR J A GARDNER
MR K W S GOODSON
LIEUTENANT S GOVAN
COLONEL J M GRANT OBE
BRIGADIER J S GREEN MBE
COLONEL A G GREVATT
BRIGADIER W C GRIERSON MBE MM
MAJOR A R GRIMSHAW

BRIGADIER D W E HANCOX
LIEUTENANT COLONEL D J HARDING
BRIGADIER R G HARMER
COLONEL R N HARRIS MBE
LIEUTENANT COLONEL W J HEAPS
MAJOR F J HEATHCOTE
COLONEL S M W HICKEY late AAC
MAJOR R A HILL BEM
LIEUTENANT COLONEL C HOLMES ERD TD
BRIGADIER W HORSFALL OBE
MAJOR M F HORTON
LIEUTENANT COLONEL F C W HOWARD

MAJOR J H INNES TD RCT
LIEUTENANT COLONEL D M IVISON

LIEUTENANT COLONEL A C JAMES MC
BRIGADIER R E L JENKINS CBE
COLONEL B G JONES ERD TD
LIEUTENANT COLONEL H L JONES MBE
COLONEL I R JONES OBE

MR S H JONES late RASC
LIEUTENANT COLONEL H A J JORDAN MBE
LIEUTENANT COLONEL E P KELLY OBE
    ERD
STAFF SERGEANT I A N KIDD

LIEUTENANT COLONEL J A W LERWILL
BRIGADIER D N LOCKE OBE
BRIGADIER J K LOMAX
MAJOR GENERAL G H G LONSDALE CB MBE
    MA
MR R J LOVEJOY late RASC
LIEUTENANT COLONEL J C LUCAS
MAJOR W A LYONS BEM

LIEUTENANT COLONEL J D MACDONALD
    OBE
MAJOR O G MALINS MBE MC
MAJOR D J MASON AAC
MAJOR R C A MCALLISTER
LIEUTENANT COLONEL M R U McCARTNEY
CAPTAIN T C M MEYS
MR G F K MITCHELL late RASC
MAJOR S MITTON
LIEUTENANT COLONEL J B MOCKRIDGE
BRIGADIER E V MOLYNEUX OBE MC
LIEUTENANT P S MONGAR
MAJOR R M MORTIMER
WARRANT OFFICER CLASS 2 M V MOSS
MAJOR R MORGAN MBE
MR R MULLARD late RASC

MR D NEALE late RASC
LIEUTENANT COLONEL D NEIGHBOUR
COLONEL C F NEVE OBE
MAJOR F L NEWBERRY-COBBETT MBE
BRIGADIER R A NIGHTINGALE MBE
MAJOR A N NOTLEY TD WRAC
MAJOR A L J NOTMAN
CAPTAIN R L NICHOLSON

COLONEL J O'BRIEN OBE

COLONEL R K M PARRY MBE

776

LIEUTENANT COLONEL E R PATERSON MBE MA

LIEUTENANT COLONEL G T PEARCE MBE

LIEUTENANT COLONEL C E PENN

MAJOR J M PERRY WRAC

COLONEL J K PITT OBE

MAJOR GENERAL F J PLASKETT CB MBE

MAJOR GENERAL SIR JOHN POTTER KBE CB

COLONEL N J PRICE

MAJOR W C REES

LIEUTENANT COLONEL I RENWICK OBE

MAJOR A T RICHARDSON

BRIGADIER B C RIDLEY

COLONEL J S RIGGALL MBE

MAJOR GENERAL W H D RITCHIE CB CBE

COLONEL R J H RIVERS

LIEUTENANT COLONEL E ROBINSON WRAC

LIEUTENANT COLONEL R J ROYLE

LIEUTENANT COLONEL J F RUSH

MR A J SANSON late RASC

BRIGADIER T A K SAVAGE MBE

LIEUTENANT COLONEL W J SCOGING OBE

MAJOR W J B SEAGER

BRIGADIER J C C SHAPLAND OBE MA

LIEUTENANT COLONEL P SHIELD MBE

MAJOR G SHOTTER

MAJOR GENERAL SIR CECIL M SMITH KBE CB MC

MR H J SMITH late RASC

COLONEL J R B SMITH TD

LIEUTENANT COLONEL R C SMITH

COLONEL T M SIMMONS

CAPTAIN G W SOMMERVILLE

BRIGADIER N I B SPELLER MBE

MAJOR C STEWARD

MAJOR T E L STRANGE

LIEUTENANT COLONEL T C STREET

MAJOR A P STRINGER TD

BRIGADIER D J SUTTON OBE

MAJOR C D TAYLOR

LIEUTENANT COLONEL I G THOMAS

MAJOR T C THORNTON

BRIGADIER R C THORPE OBE

CAPTAIN N F TOWNSEND

LIEUTENANT GENERAL SIR PAUL TRAVERS KCB

MAJOR H C TRUEMAN

MAJOR GENERAL P G TURPIN CB OBE MA

LIEUTENANT COLONEL B C VAUGHAN

COLONEL J S M WALKER

LIEUTENANT COLONEL M J WELLINGS

LIEUTENANT COLONEL C J WETHERALL

BRIGADIER W M E WHITE CBE BA

MR E WHITEHEAD late RASC

LIEUTENANT COLONEL M WILCOX

MAJOR GENERAL J E WITT CB CBE MC

LIEUTENANT COLONEL G C C WOOD OBE

BRIGADIER A K WOODS OBE

FLIGHT LIEUTENANT A WOODWARD TD RAAF

MAJOR B V WYNN-WERNINCK MNI

LIEUTENANT COLONEL M H G YOUNG

COLONEL E J YOUNGHUSBAND

The following units, establishments and organizations have assisted in the production of this story by their unstinted research, advice and help.

Logistic Executive (Army)
The Ministry of Defence Library
The Army Historical Branch
The Public Record Office
Council of Territorial, Auxiliary and Volunteer Reserve Associations
Territorial, Auxiliary and Volunteer Reserve Associations
The Army Cadet Force Association
The Combined Cadet Force Association
National Defence College Library
Royal Armoured Corps Library
The Institution of the Royal Corps of Transport Library
Royal Electrical and Mechanical Engineers Corps Secretariat
Army Air Corps Headquarters and Museum
RCT Territorial Army Depot and Training Centre
150, 151, 152, 153, 154, 155, 156 and 157 Transport Regiments (Volunteer)
Headquarters Training Group RCT
School of Transportation RCT
17 Port Regiment RCT
20 Maritime Regiment RCT
29 Movements Regiment RCT
30 Regiment RCT
The Gurkha Transport Regiment
Logistic Support Battalion Allied Command Europe (Land)

There is also a host of contributors to the *Waggoner* and the RASC/RCT *Review* whose articles have been used in compiling this story. Individual acknowledgement is clearly impossible but their efforts have added considerably to the text. To them all — we are most grateful.

EDITORIAL COMMITTEE

BRIGADIER D J SUTTON OBE	Chairman and Editor in Chief
COLONEL J S M WALKER	Deputy Editor
LIEUTENANT COLONEL T A DANTON-REES	Executive Editor
BRIGADIER R A NIGHTINGALE MBE	Reviewer
BRIGADIER D W E HANCOX	Secretaries
BRIGADIER B G E COURTIS	
COLONEL P J MARZETTI	Publicity and Marketing
COLONEL I R JONES OBE	
LIEUTENANT COLONEL HOWARD N COLE OBE TD DL	Historian
LIEUTENANT COLONEL R E WILLS RCT	Reviewer
LIEUTENANT COLONEL M J WELLINGS RCT	Researcher
LIEUTENANT COLONEL D M IVISON RCT	Researcher
MAJOR C W P COAN	Archivist
MAJOR M D ISHERWOOD	Co-opted Financial Advisor

GLOSSARY

AA	Anti Aircraft
AA & QMG	Assistant Adjutant and Quarter Master General – a staff officer usually of Lieutenant Colonel rank.
A Branch	the branch of the Army staff controlled by the Adjutant General and dealing with largely administrative matters.
ACI	Army Council Instruction.
AD	Air Despatch
ADST	Assistant Director of Supplies and Transport – usually a RASC staff officer of Colonel rank.
AQMG	Assistant Quarter Master General – a staff officer usually of Lieutenant Colonel rank.
'Arms'	a common, if somewhat imprecise, term referring to the branches of the Army more usually involved in the actual fighting of a battle e.g. armour, artillery, engineers, infantry.
A vehicles	tracked or wheeled armoured vehicles.
BAOR	British Army of the Rhine.
BLR	damaged equipment beyond local repair.
BMH	British Military Hospital
BRASCO	a RASC officer on a Brigade headquarters staff, usually a Captain.
'Brick' system	the building up of a unit with standard, self-contained sub-units.
B vehicles	unarmoured road vehicles of all types and load carrying trailers.
CAD	Command Ammunition Depot
CASC	Ceylon Army Service Corps
C in C	Commander in Chief
CO	Commanding Officer
Combat Supplies	food, ammunition, POL and defence stores.
Compo	military packed rations
CQMS	Company Quarter Master Sergeant (a Staff Sergeant)
CRASC	Commander Royal Army Service Corps, an officer usually of Lieutenant Colonel rank.
CRCT	Commander Royal Corps of Transport, usually a Lieutenant Colonel.
CSD	Command Supply Depot
CSM	Company Sergeant Major (a Warrant Officer Class 2)
CTMO	Chief Transport & Movements Officer
C vehicles	mobile items of earth moving equipment; cranes; mechanical handling equipment.
C5A	an American cargo aircraft
C130	a Hercules transport aircraft
CVR(T)	Combat Vehicle Reconnaissance (Tracked)
DAAG	Deputy Assistant Adjutant General – a staff officer usually of Major rank

DAA & QMG	Deputy Assistant Adjutant & Quarter Master General – a staff officer usually of Major rank.
DADST	Deputy Assistant Director of Supplies & Transport – a RASC officer usually of Colonel rank.
DAQMG	Deputy Assistant Quarter Master General – a staff officer usually of Major rank.
DCI	Defence Council Instruction.
DGTM	Director General of Transport & Movements, – a Major General, head of the RCT
D Mov (A)	Director of Movements (Army)
DQMG	Deputy Quarter Master General
DST	Director of Supplies and Transport – the senior RASC officer at Ministry or Theatre level. Head of the RASC, Major General or Brigadier rank at Theatre level.
DUKW	a World War II amphibious vehicle capable of operating as a load carrier both afloat and on the land.
DZ	Dropping Zone – a marked area designated to receive parachute troops or supplies.
EAASC	East Africa Army Service Corps
EFI	Expeditionary Forces Institute – NAAFI embodied and mobilized in wartime to provide a canteen service for the troops.
EO	Executive – a Civil Service grade
FFR	Fitted for Radio – a vehicle modified to accept the fitting of a radio transmitter.
'field force'	an imprecise generic term referring to units and formations primarily organized and equipped to carry out combat.
First Line transport	transport organic to a unit.
Fourth line transport	all RCT transport not included in second or third line.
G Branch	the branch of the Army staff primarily concerned with operational matters.
GD	General Duties
GHQ	General Headquarters
GOC	General Officer Commanding – the senior officer commanding a Theatre or District
'Green Goddess'	Home Office fire engines formerly for Civil Defence but now retained for emergency use.
GT	General Transport
G 1098	an abbreviation of Army Form G 1098 which itemized a unit's entitlement to equipment.
G1	abbreviation for Grade 1 staff officer (Lieutenant Colonel)
G2	,, ,, ,, 2 ,, ,, (Major)
G3	,, ,, ,, 3 ,, ,, (Captain)
HGV	Heavy Goods Vehicle
HMAV	Her Majesty's Army Vessel
HMT	Her Majesty's Troopship
HT	Horse transport

IS	Internal security – any military role that involves primarily the maintenance and restoration of law and order and essential services in the face of civil disturbances and disobedience, using minimum force.
KAR	King's African Rifles
LAD	Light Aid Detachment – a small sub-unit of REME mechanics supporting a larger unit.
L of C or LOC	Lines of Communication – all the land, water and air routes that connect an operating military force with one or more bases of operations, and along which supplies and reinforcements move.
Logistics	the science of planning and carrying out the movement and maintenance of forces.
LSL	Landing Ship Logistic
LCL	Landing Craft Logistic
LCM	Landing Craft Mechanized
LCT	Landing Craft Tank
LST	Landing Ship Tank
LCU	Landing Craft Utility
Maintenance area	a field location containing transport, supply, repair and support units to keep a force in condition to carry out its mission.
MASC	Malayan Army Service Corps
MFO	Military Forwarding Organization – an organization primarily concerned with the movement of a serviceman's personal baggage and belongings.
Mk	Mark – a series of equipment e.g. Mk 1, Mk 2 etc.
MK	a model of Bedford 4 ton truck.
MOD	Ministry of Defence
Mogas	Motor gasoline
MOR	Malayan Other Rank
MT	Mechanical transport
NATO	North Atlantic Treaty Organization
NCO	Non Commissioned Officer
O i/c	Officer in Charge
OC	Officer commanding a unit
OCTU	Officer Cadet Training Unit
Order of battle	the identification, strength, command structure, and disposition of the personnel, units, and equipment of any military force.
Other Rank (OR)	a term previously used to designate soldiers without military rank
Pax	a military abbreviation used for 'passengers'
Pig	a wheeled armoured personnel carrier.
POL	Petroleum, Oil and Lubricants.
POW	Prisoner of War

Q Branch	a branch of the Army staff controlled by the Quarter Master General (QMG)
QGO	Queens Gurkha Officer
QL	a model of Bedford 3 ton truck
QM	Quartermaster
Q (Mov)	a Q Branch concerned with Movements
QTO	Qualified Testing Officer – an officer or senior NCO qualified to test learner drivers.

RAAF	Royal Australian Air Force
RAASC	,, ,, Army Service Corps
RACT	,, ,, Corps of Transport
RPL	Ramp Powered Lighter
RCL	Ramp Craft Logistic

Ranks	Full title	Abbreviation
	Field Marshal	FM
	General	Gen
	Lieutenant General	Lt Gen
	Major General	Maj Gen
	Brigadier	Brig .
	Colonel	Col
	Lieutenant Colonel	Lt Col
	Major	Maj
	Captain	Capt
	Lieutenant	Lt
	Second Lieutenant	2 Lt
	Warrant Officer Class 1	WO 1
	Warrant Officer Class 2	WO 2
	Staff Sergeant	S Sgt
	Sergeant	Sgt
	Corporal	Cpl
	Lance Corporal	L Cpl
	Driver (Private)	Dvr (Pte)

Rations	food supplies
RCASC	Royal Canadian Army Service Corps
RCTV	Royal Corps of Transport Vessel
Replenishment	the replacement of equipment and supplies and used in operations.
RHQ	Regimental Headquarters
RIASC	Royal Indian Army Service Corps
RL	a model of Bedford 4 ton truck
RMAF	Royal Malaysian Air Force
RO/RO	Roll on/Roll off ship
RNZAF	Royal New Zealand Air Force
RNZASC	Royal New Zealand Army Service Corps
RSM	Regimental Sergeant Major (a Warrant Officer Class 1)

SAA	Small arms ammunition
Saracen	a six wheeled armoured personnel carrier (APC)

Second line transport	RASC or RCT transport organic to a formation (e.g. a division or brigade)
Spearhead	code name used for units in UK designated for early deployment in an emergency.
SQMS	Squadron Quarter Master Sergeant (a Staff Sergeant)
SRD	Supply Reserve Depot
SSM	Squadron Sergeant Major (a Warrant Officer Class 2)
S & T	Supplies and Transport
Stalwart	a high mobility load carrying vehicle
Supplies	a generic term encompassing those items required to sustain the Army both in barracks or in the field.
'tail'	an imprecise term usually referring to that part of the Army supporting the 'teeth arms' (see below)
TCV	Troop carrying vehicle
'teeth arms'	front line fighting troops, particularly infantry, artillery, engineer and armoured units.
Third line transport	Corps RASC or RCT transport allotted for the support of formations under command
TO-in-C(A)	Transport Officer in Chief (Army) – the one time title for the head of the RCT – a Major General post.
Tpt & Mov	Transport and Movement.
UKLF	United Kingdom Land Forces
UKMF	United Kingdom Mobile Force
VC 10	a transport aircraft
WAASC	West Africa Army Service Corps
WD	War Department
WO	Warrant Officer
Work ticket	an Army form for the authorization of a journey by a military vehicle.

INDEX